HUMAN RESOURCE MANAGEMENT

HUMAN RESOURCE MANAGEMENT

By

Colonel (Dr) Narendar Singh

Former Professor of Human Resource

Vidya Business School, Meerut (U.P.)

&

Invertis Institute of Management Studies, Bareilly (U.P.)

UNIVERSITY SCIENCE PRESS

(An Imprint of Laxmi Publications Pvt. Ltd.)

BANGALORE • CHENNAI • COCHIN • GUWAHATI • HYDERABAD
JALANDHAR • KOLKATA • LUCKNOW • MUMBAI • RANCHI

NEW DELHI

Published by :
UNIVERSITY SCIENCE PRESS
(An Imprint of Laxmi Publications Pvt. Ltd.)
113, Golden House, Daryaganj,
New Delhi-110002

Phone : 011-43 53 25 00
Fax : 011-43 53 25 28

www.laxmipublications.com
info@laxmipublications.com

First Edition : 2011

OFFICES

✆ **Bangalore**	080-26 61 15 61	✆ **Chennai**	044-24 34 47 26
✆ **Cochin**	0484-237 70 04, 405 13 03	✆ **Guwahati**	0361-254 36 69, 251 38 81
✆ **Hyderabad**	040-24 65 23 33	✆ **Jalandhar**	0181-222 12 72
✆ **Kolkata**	033-22 27 43 84	✆ **Lucknow**	0522-220 95 78
✆ **Mumbai**	022-24 91 54 15, 24 92 78 69	✆ **Ranchi**	0651-221 47 64

UHR–9552–350–HUMAN RESOURCE MANAG-SIN **C—**

Typeset at : ABRO Enterprises, Delhi. Printed at : Repro Knowledgecast Limited, Thane

Contents

Preface

People have been regarded as the most important in managing organizations. Their centrality became sharper in today's changing world. There is a widespread realization that while other resources can be acquired and bought, humans cannot be brought into an organization. Human processes are critical in each functional area of management.

While there are several books on Human Resource Management available mainly from the West, especially from the US, they do not address the relevant problems from developing countries. The goal of this book is to fill void in the human resource management literature. The importance of topic is evident from the alignment models that all indicate that organizational effectiveness is dependent upon the alignment of organizational sub systems with one and another. Lawler (1996) presents a model and evidence showing importance of aligning the organizational sub systems to include strategy, processes, people and rewards. Human resources systems primarily reside in the people and reward subsystems so this means that HR systems should be aligned to strategy, process and structure of the organization.

The human resource of an organization constitutes its entire workforce. Human resource management is responsible for attracting, selecting, inducting, training, facilitating in their career, motivating them to perform at high level of efficiency, providing mechanism to ensure that they maintain their affiliations with the organization. It is also an art to develop people. Growth helps individuals to meet their aspirations as also enable them to operate at the optimum efficiency and effectiveness.

About the Book

The book has been designed specifically for students of management. It is an attempt to respond to the need of students from India and third world countries. Managers as well as would be managers of these countries would also find this book useful as it would help in preparing them to meet the challenges faced by organizations.

There has been a shift in employee behaviour and also in employer and employee relationship in globally competitive economy. The field of business has been undergoing a fundamental change. In the 1960s, business expertise was by-the numbers, focused on sharpening strategy, analyzing alternatives, and maximizing the bottom line. By mid 1970's, this numbers-driven model was losing its appeal. The professors at business schools believed that it was no longer useful for a leader to set strategy by knowing the right thing to do, through expertise and in-depth analysis; that approach had led to some well-publicized failures. So business schools developed a new approach, which held that no manager could know everything—that expertise was based in the knowledge an organization's employees developed, and that a smart leader built a strong team that could marshal that knowledge.

The cases students studied taught them to look and listen carefully, to learn from past mistakes, and to build a business plan for action. Students learned to be leaders by talking with—and listening to—their team members, by making tough strategic decisions, by writing a business plan for action, and then by relying on the team to carry out the plan. Most of all, the business school's case method and the Socratic question-and-answer teaching style hammered home the lesson that there is no right answer for most hard problems. Managers had to be adept at analyzing problems carefully, understanding the issues at the core, and then coming to judgments about how best to solve them.

The central lesson of this book is the role of teamwork. This book is also of relationship and love. Love and warmth" the consistent expression of love seems to be able to melt almost anything/any negative emotions if it comes in contact with. All communications are either a loving response or a cry for help. Managers must exhibit love to get best from human resources.

Contents and Structure

The book is organized into 24 chapters. The first chapter and opening chapters provides an introduction to human resource management, its growth and development and prime functions. These form the basis of understanding the Human Resource Management. Chapter 2 deals with Strategic Human Resource Management while Chapter 3 discusses Human Resource Planning. A chapter each covers the process of Recruitment, Job design and analysis, selection, induction and socialization, staffing, training etc. There are chapters on compensation and reward system, career and management development. Emphasis is given to employee unions.

Pedagogy

In order to help the students, they are required to complete some instruments and participate in project works. Each chapter has *review questions* to help student to recollect the main concepts discussed. Questions and case studies have been included to stimulate creativity in students.

Students would be able to internalize the concepts by applying them in practice. The chapter-end class room and field projects to be performed through activities, preferably as a team, provide opportunity for such practice. The topics covered are *action oriented*, so that students can apply the concepts; are embedded in known, established theories, concepts and best practices. The topics also include the latest trends and new developments.

There is a separate *glossary of the main terms* used for quick reference.

Although the book meets the needs of the current syllabi of various institutions and universities, the book includes many other important aspects of Human Resource Management. Our hope is that the book will help people in the human resource field in many different ways. Firstly, we would like to see the book on the shelves of academicians conducting research on human resource management both in traditional and non traditional areas. Secondly, we would like to see the book on the shelves of human resource management practitioner's charges with designing, implementing, and administering human resource management programme's. Lastly, to my fellow colleagues and students to use this book as a textbook to illuminate the path in organizations that human resource professionals are increasingly being asked to deal with.

—Author

Acknowledgement

This is a book about friendship, about loyalty, about believing in one and another. It was because of that friendship, and that belief, we set out on the journey to explore the ideas in this book. I have met many in class rooms—one the professor, the other the student. We have worked together ever since, often seeing ourselves along the journey. This book is not the victory of an idea but of friendship that we have found more meaningful than any idea in the world. It has made our lives rich and ours world more beautiful.

No journey is easy; no friendship is filled only with laughter. But we are excited every day of that journey because we are on a mission to learn and improve. I can name Preeti Sharma, Aditya, Arihant Dilpreet, Styabhama and many more here who joined the journey. They believed passionately in the ideas in this book. These ideas are not for those whose ambition in life is to get by or merely to survive. That was never an interest of ours. If you can be satisfied with that, do not read this book. But if you want to make a difference, to create a company that builds a future where customers, employees, shareholders, and society win, read on. We are not saying it is easy, but it is worthwhile. I acknowledge the contributions made by my students where I shared ideas with them and included in this book. The learning was two way process.

I must thank my parents Lt Col Shyam Singh (Retd) and Late Smt Parkashwati Devi who have been a constant source of inspiration and support. I thank my wife Beena who have been a constant source of inspiration and a silent listener to my chatter. I thank my sons Major Ravi Raja and Dr. Tarun Singh for their singular and unstinting support in helping me to complete the task. I thank our daughter in law Mrs. Tapasaya who is always there to correct manuscripts and give her candid comments. Lastly, I must thank our grandson Sankalp without whom this would not have been possible and makes me realize how little we know of people.

Chapter 1 NATURE, SCOPE AND CONCEPT OF HRM

★ LEARNING OBJECTIVES ★

After reading this chapter, you will be able to understand :

- Nature and scope of human resource management;
- Importance of human resource management;
- The various facets of human resource management;
- Models of HRM
- Essentials for human resource manager
- Genesis and Growth of human resource in India.

INTRODUCTION

Central to all activities that are undertaken on planet earth from time immemorial has been man, and is central to all modern organizations. The advent of free economy, globalization and the advancements in information technology (IT) has transformed the world around us but it has further highlighted centrality of effective and efficient management of human resource. The purpose of all human resource management (HRM) is to enable appropriate utilization of all human resource.

All activities of an organization are initiated and completed by the persons who make up the organizations. The effective utilization of human resources has assumed greater importance in the modern competitive environment where there is cost cutting, down sizing and induction of new technology to have that cutting edge to survive in the competitive world. The primary task thus is to attract, identify, induct, train, provide career to competent human resource in their organization for improving productivity and functional efficiency. Manger manages four M's-money, marketing, machines and men. It is needles to highlight that management of men is fundamental and central as all other sub systems are controlled and managed by men.

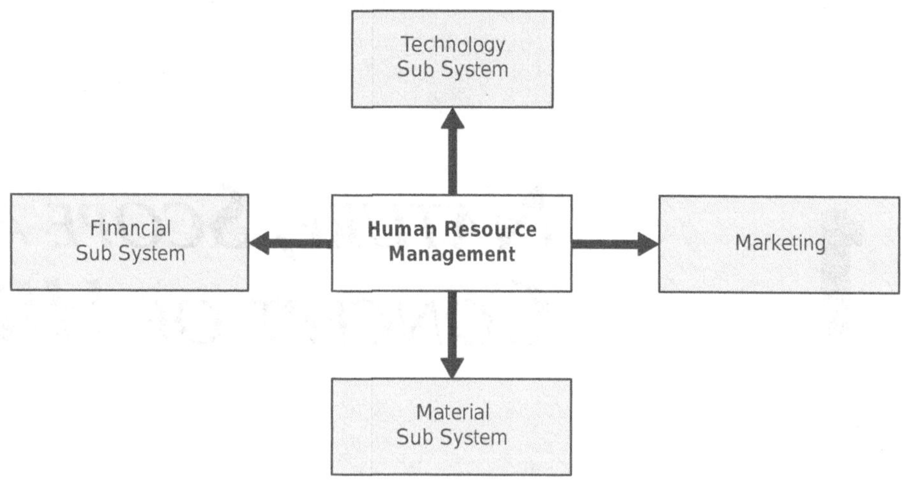

Fig. 1.1. *Centrality of Human Resource.*

Management practice is characterized by power, the ability to influence other's behaviour. By virtue of power that managers hold, the variations in organizational design, relations between managers and employees, and the Human Resource management would be largely shaped by senior managers.

HUMAN RESOURCE MEANING AND DEFINITION

The term 'Human Resource Management' has been subject to considerable debate. Controversy in the area of meaning turns on the imprecision, variability, ambiguity and even contradictions which have been seen to imbue the construct. Noon (1992) asks whether HRM is 'a map, a model or a theory ?' Keenoy (1990) refers to its ambiguity. Legge (1989) exposes its contradictions—as do Blyton and Turnbull (1992). The concept is shrouded in managerial hype and its underlying philosophy and character, because it lacks precise formulation and agreement to its significance. The big ideas can lose something when translated into detail. None the less, it is necessary to attempt a description and analysis of the phenomenon.

Human resources are an increasingly prominent field that is taking shape throughout industries and workplaces world wide. Recognizing the fact that people are a company's greatest asset, business leaders across the globe are coming to rely more and more upon an effective management policy that applies specifically to the area of human resources. Several authors have tried to understand the meaning of human resource. Leon C. Megginson described human resource as, *"the sum total of knowledge, skills, creative abilities, and aptitudes of an organization's workforce, as well as value, attitudes and belief's of an individual."* From national point of view, human resource can be defined as the knowledge, skills, creative abilities, talents and aptitude of the population. Jucius defines human resource or human factors as,

"a whole consisting of inter-related, inter-dependent and interacting physiological, psychological, sociological and ethical components."

Human resource thus can be stated to characterize :

(*a*) As a product of sum total of their inheritance (biological) and interactions with environment.

(*b*) Human resources compromises of large number of personnel with varying and unique qualities, needs and attitudes.

(*c*) Humans are dynamic in that same person behaves differently under different conditions and no two human being react to a common situation in a similar manner.

(*d*) Human provide the greatest growth potential and are the main contributors for development of any organization.

Meaning and Usage of Terms

Mary Parker Follet defined management as, *"the art of getting things done through people."* However, management is much more and can be stated as, *"a field in which managers' plan, organize, staff, direct and control human behaviour."* Pick any advertisement on human resource, what will the advertisement tell you ? Human resource is essentially about training ? Not so. Advertisement refers to three things viz. *planning, design* and *delivery*. It also refers to human resource personnel for *'learning solutions'*, and the professional it seeks to attract are not described as trainers but as a learning and development strategist. Human resource is not a narrow field. Human resource personnel who are required to perform such functions clearly require sophisticated behavioural and functional skills.

The terms we use to describe things matter. Terms matter as we chose to describe things. It bestows identity and influences people's perception. In the past three terms have been extensively used.

(*a*) **Training and Development.** This term is extensively used in government publications', instructions and official correspondence. It is made to appear that training is the only way of achieving development and is highlighted in a way to give it prominence. This approach can be a dangerous as it implies all that counts is a planned learning activity.

(*b*) **Employee Development.** This term found favour, however, it soon lost it efficacy due political pressure. To many it smacked too much of old 'master-servant' relationship. It is no accident that it is falling out of use when many organizations are referring to their employees as partners.

(*c*) **Human Resource Development.** Human resource Development first acquired specific organizational meaning in the United States in early 1970's. It has a short term training objectives and was primarily to acquire skills and some behavioural change. It is defined by its most influential commentator Nadler (1970) as :

'a series of organized activities conducted within a specified time and designed to produce behavioural change'.

1980's saw some commentators moving towards a more strategic perspective. Hall (1984) a well known American author said,

"Strategic Human Resource development is the identification of needed skills and active management of learning for the long range future in relation to explicit corporate and business strategies."

By early 1990's the globalization and internet expanded bringing in need to manage workers with knowledge and information. Human resource development in the United States thus developed into recognizable profession with many members emphasizing their role as agents of organizational change. Human resource development was now to do with the generalized task of renewal (Burrade, 1991).

"Human resource development people have changed to blueprint and lead the way the organizational and individual renewal."

Renewal brought in the concept of Human Resource Management. It encompassed a broader field of management that focuses on managing employees/paid staff well, declining importance of trade unions and importance of individual workers, a large shift from industrial to service sectors. It consists of a framework of activities and practices that support and develop a motivated workforce while at the same time complying with legislation and regulations that govern the employer/employee relationship. It functions within an organization that focuses on recruitment of, management of, and providing direction for the people who work in the organization. Human Resource Management is the organizational function that deals with issues related to people such as compensation, hiring, performance management, organization development, safety, wellness, benefits, employee motivation, communication, administration, and training. Human Resource Management can also be performed by line managers.

However, there was still no universally accepted definition in United States (Nadler, 1992); situation was no clearer in United Kingdom and Europe. In *Managing Human Resources : Personnel Management in Transition*, Stephen Bach (2005 :3) argues that, compared to a decade ago, much of the controversy about the definition of human resources management has dissipated. He considers that, in part, this may be due to the use of a broader and more encompassing definition of human resources management. However, Bach (p.4) shows that the debate has not vanished by disagreeing with Boxall and Purcell's (2003 :1) statement that human resources management refers to :

"... all those activities associated with the management of the employment relationship in the firm. The term 'employee relations' will be used as an equivalent terms as will the term 'labour management'."

Bach argues that this definition is 'a little too broad', stating that such a broad definition makes it difficult to :

- Highlight any distinctive features or values that underpin human resources management.
- Chart changes in the practice of human resources management.
- Understand the controversy surrounding human resources management.

In Bach's opinion, human resources management differs from employee relations in its focus on management practices and tendency to ignore the interests of employees. In fact, he holds quite 'hard' views on the nature of human resources management :

- Human resources management is unitarist (employer and employee interests should coincide) with an emphasis on organizational effectiveness.
- The interests of other stakeholders such as employees are marginalized.
- There is a predominant interest on the individual firm - specifically, within the firm - focused on individual employee motivation and aspiration.
- There is a consequent playing down of external and collective (unionization) issues.

Personnel management implies only the personnel employed.	It involves management of employees skills, knowledge, abilities, talents etc.
In personnel management an individual is treated as an economic identity. His services are exchanged for a wage or salary.	Employee treated as a social being in addition to an economic.
Employee is viewed as commodity and hence, cost to be regulated.	Employee treated as a resource and it is expected that he would contribute to its growth and well being.
An employee is treated as a cost center and hence, management controls the cost of labour.	Human being is used for multiple mutual benefit so an organization.
Personnel function is treated as only an auxiliary function. Usually performed by managers as an additional function.	As personnel used for mutual benefit, it becomes the strategic function of management.

Fig. 1.2. *Personnel Management Versus Human Resource Management.*

Definition

Human Resource Management is defined as a strategic and coherent approach to the management of an organization's most valued assets—the people working there who individually and collectively contribute to the achievement of its objectives.

Large numbers of authors have attempted to define human resources management.

Fisher et al. defines :

"Human resources management involves all management decisions and practices that affect or influence people or human resource, who works for the organization.."

CIPD defines human resources management :

"As the design, implementation and maintenance of strategies to manage people for optimum business performance including the development of policies and processes to support these strategies."

G.T. Milkovich and **Johri W. Bdudreau** define it as :

"A series of integrated decisions that form the employment relationship; their quality contributes to the ability of the organizations and the employees to achieve their objectives."

Cherrington (1995, p. 5) defines :

"Human resource management is responsible for how people are treated in organizations. It is responsible for bringing people into the organization, helping them perform their work, compensating them for their labors, and solving problems that arise."

David A. Decenzo and **Stepehen P Robins** define :

"Human resource management is a process consisting of four functions—acquisition, development, motivation and maintenance of human resources."

Edward Flippo defines :

"Personnel management is the planning, organizing, directing, and controlling of the procurement, development, compensation, integration, maintenance and separation of human resources to the end that individual, organizational and societal objectives are accomplished."

Storey (1989) believes that Human Resource Management can be regarded as a 'set of interrelated policies with an ideological and philosophical underpinning'. He suggests four aspects that constitute the meaningful version of Human Resource Management. :

(*a*) a particular constellation of beliefs and assumptions;

(*b*) a strategic thrust informing decisions about people and management;

(*c*) the central involvement of line managers; and

(*d*) reliance upon a set of 'levers' to shape the employment relationship.

John Storey in HRM A Critical Text defines Human Resource Management as :

"Human Resource Management is a distinctive approach to employment management which seeks to achieve competitive advantage through the strategic deployment of highly committed and capable workforce, using an integrated array of cultural, structural and personal techniques."

The key elements of HRM are summarized below. As seen HRM is an amalgam of description, prescription, and logical deduction. It describes the beliefs and assumptions of certain leading-edge practitioners. Human Resource Management is the organizational function that deals with issues related to people such as compensation, hiring, performance management, organization development, safety, wellness, benefits, employee motivation, communication, administration, and training. Human resource management is strategic and deliberate approaches to the management as human are central to the system.

The HRM Model

1. ***Beliefs and Assumptions***

   (*a*) That it is the human resource which gives competitive edge.

   (*b*) That the aim should not merely be compliance with rules, but employee commitment.

   (*c*) That therefore employees should be carefully selected and developed.

2. ***Strategic Qualities***

   (*a*) Because of the above factors, HR decisions are of strategic importance.

   (*b*) Top management involvement is necessary.

   (*c*) HR practices should be integrated into the business strategy-stemming from it and even contributing it.

3. ***Critical Role of Managers***

   (*a*) Because HR practice is critical to the core activities of the business, it is too important to be left to personnel specialists alone.

   (*b*) Line managers need to be closely involved both as deliverers and drivers of the HR policies.

   (*c*) Much greater attention is paid to the management of managers themselves.

4. ***Key Levers***

   (*a*) Managing culture is more important than managing procedures and systems.

   (*b*) Integrated action on selection, communication, training, reward and development.

   (*c*) Restructuring and job redesign to allow devolved responsibility and empowerment.

Source *: Storey (1989)*

'Storey (1989) has distinguished between hard and soft forms of Human Resource Management, typified by the Michigan and Harvard models respectively. 'Hard' Human Resource Management focuses on the resource side of human resources. It emphasizes costs in the form of 'headcounts' and places control firmly in the hands of management. Their role is to manage numbers effectively, keeping the workforce closely matched with requirements in terms of both bodies and behaviour.

'Soft' Human Resource Management, on the other hand, stresses the 'human' aspects of HRM. Its concerns are with communication and motivation. People are led rather than managed. They are involved in determining and realizing strategic objectives.'

In this book we will define Human Resource Management as :

'The part of management process that specializes in the management of people (human resource) in an organization, practices to integrate them with corporate strategy to meet both efficiency and equity objectives.'

ORIGINS AND EARLY DEVELOPMENT OF HRM

Viewed as a generic activity involving the management of other people's labour in production, human resource management goes back to the dawn of human history. Reference has been found of how to manage labour has been found in Vedas, Ramayana, Mahabharata and Arthshastera by Kautilya. The first visible root of the human resource management as practiced today in modern business organizations appeared in the late nineteenth century more or less contemporaneously in England, France, Germany and the United States. Japan experienced the same development a decade later and India is experiencing the same today.

The modern human resource management department grew out of two earlier developments. The first was the emergence of Industrial welfare work. Starting 1890s, a number of companies started to provide a variety of work place amenities for workers and their families. A new staff position was created to administer these activities, called a 'welfare secretary,' and women or social workers were often appointed. German companies were the pioneers in welfare work and the impetus behind such welfare work was the amalgam of good business practices as envisaged then, humanitarian concerns and religious principles.

The second antecedent was the creation of some type of separate employment office. These offices, often staffed by lower level clerks and supervisors were created to centralize and standardize certain employment related functions, such as hiring, payroll and record keeping. Farnham (1921) reports, that the German steel company Krupp has a long- established Personnelburo to handle staff administration. The movement to create separate employment department in American firms started in 1912 with the formation of the Boston Employment Mangers Association. Quickly the term 'employment management' became the accepted descriptor for this new management function and in 1916 it had spread widely enough to support the creation of an Employment managers Association in US.

The emergence of the employment management function is tightly linked the mergence of the doctrine and practice of scientific management. The new approach found it's most influential and strategic formulations in the writings of FW Taylor, particularly his book *"Principles of Scientific Management"* (1911). In US the employers' interest in applying scientific management to labour management was substantially heightened by two new and much publicized empirical findings reported in the early to mid-1910s. The first was the huge cost of employee turnover often over 100 percent annually; the second was the cost saving from the recently inaugurated industrial safety movement (Jacoby 1985).

The First World War had a great impact on the development of human resource management function throughout the industrial world (Kaufman 2004). The major adversaries sought to harness their economies to maximum war production, greatly stimulating the pressures to rationalize management and achieve higher productivity. Governments in several countries especially England

and Germany sponsored research on industrial fatigue and instituted screening tests for new recruits into the Armed Forces. War production led to economic boom and dramatically higher employee turnover rates, wage pressures and problems with discipline. This period also saw the Bolshevik Revolution in Russia. The revolution caused widespread concern with 'labour problem'. Out of this fear was born a new movement for *'industrial democracy'* (Lichtenstein and Harris, 1993). The companies expanded welfare activities, shop committees and employee representation plans.

In United States two new terms emerged. The first was personnel management (or personal administration). The American companies combined the two functions of welfare and employment management and combined them into a new department called personnel management. The second term was industrial relations. This term found widespread usage in US and Canada. The term was however, not widely accepted in other countries.

During recession of 1920-21 many companies disbanded their newly formed personnel departments as cost cutting measures. The setback was temporary. By 1929 half the firms with over 5000 employees had formalized the human resource management functions. In the vanguard leading the movement were corporate giants like AT&T, DuPont, General Electric etc. These firms abandoned the pre-war market model of human resource management, in which labour was traded and used more like any other commodity and moved to what labour economist John Commons (1919) described as the combination of 'machine', 'good will' (high commitment) and 'industrial citizenship' (democratic governance) model. Also noteworthy Commons (1919 : 129) used the term 'human resource' to connote the idea that investment inhuman skills and education makes labour more productive and counseled employer to take strategic advantage, observing that '[employee] goodwill is a competitive advantage' (1919 : 74).

1920's saw the growth in infrastructure to support human resource management grow; journals, associations, consulting firms and universities teaching and research. After the Industrial Relations Association of America folded, a new association called the National Personnel Association was founded. It later became the American Management Association. Personal Research Foundation was founded in 1922 which promoted academic and industrial research. The Foundation also published the research in 'Journal of Personnel Research.' Other countries lagged behind during the period. Mary Fledderus, a Dutch welfare manager (quoted in Journal of Personnel Research, 1/1 :175) who stated in 1922, 'Broadly speaking, welfare work in Holland seems to me, as in other countries, to have arrived to a transition state. I have the impression that it chiefly looks to America for the lines on which it will go on working.' Japan perhaps was the only exception and it saw most significant advances in human resource management practices. It adopted the Taylor's scientific management. In 1920's large number of individual employers and government sponsored groups from Japan visited United Sates to observe industrial practices being adopted. They took back and adopted number of concepts and techniques especially from Welfare Capitalism project. Kyochokai (Society for Harmonious Cooperation) was formed to promote improved industrial relations practices. Japanese firms began to create personnel/ Industrial Relations departments, and started numerous human resource management practices such as recruiting, hiring tests, incentive wage plans, job evaluation programs and shop committees.

A notable incident in the history of human resource management is the first international conference held in Flushing, (Netherlands) in 1925 titled, Industrial Welfare (Personnel) Congress. The conference lasted seven days and featured first hand reports on the status of the welfare / personnel movement in twenty countries.

From its birth till end 1920s human resource management made considerable progress and was quite favourable, however, the Great Depression which set in 1929 which brought with it drop in gross domestic product and large unemployment, saw fall in the influence of human resource management. Roosevelt administration launched a new deal in 1933, to stimulate economy. This brought about a change from unilateral employer determination of wages, conditions and employment procedures through human resource management was replaced by minimum wages acts, joint determination through collective bargaining. The extent of change was greater in Germany and Japan. Fascist government took overpower in Germany, banished opposition political parties and trade unions and extended state control over Industry, and mobilized their economies for war.

These events helped human resource management in that as unions pushed for wage standardization, job classification systems, formal grievances systems and written employment rules all of which required personnel/labour relations staff and administrators.

The Second World War saw the expansion of collective bargaining and expansion of government regulations on employment. This further limited human resource management independent room for manoeuver. The War also led to some positive developments; the hiring boom created a need for hiring and section staff, growth in war related production plants created a huge demand for training programs and trainers. In order to comply with government regulations and prevent strikes the companies also had to implement new job evaluation procedures and systemize the compensation procedures. The net result was considerable expansion personnel programs and growth in their departments.

In many respects two decades post Second World War saw further advance in US human resource management concepts, practices and procedures. Application of industrial psychology, industrial sociology and 'human relations' to employment problems also emerged in the 1940s, as a hot topic and created new opportunities for human resource management (Wren 2005). The 1950s saw high density mark in union density and collective bargaining. The most popular title for corporate human resource management function was 'industrial relations, which was further sub divided into labour relations section and personnel section.

The Unions density started receding by early sixties and collective bargaining became a routine, resource and programs started moving toward personnel part of the human resource management function (Jacoby 1985). The personnel department typically had little contact with strategic business and employment policy and instead focused on tactical administration of various personnel activities. The personnel function was usually regarded as one of the lowest rungs in the management hierarchy and a place for low level administrator and clerks.

A similar pattern emerged in Japan. The primary sector firms developed distinctive employment system, developed and formalized lifetime employment, seniority wages, extensive job rotations, and enterprise unions. Powerful personnel departments were created to administer. According to Hirano (1969) the Japanese personnel departments had more power than American counterparts. A productivity miracle was experienced by Japan and large number of American and European managers was now visiting Japan to learn about their management techniques. Largely lost from sight was that large number of concepts, procedures had been imported from America ?

Europe by contrast was different it slowly recovered from devastations of the Second World War Malm (1960) wrote a survey of personnel management in Europe and observed that, 'personnel administration does not have the professional status in Europe it enjoys in United States, except for the United Kingdom.'

Outside United States human resource management received little attention in either research or teaching. The main reason for this was that in Europe the labour relations were heavily regulated by the labour law, making legal education more important than management education for Directors.

Contemporary Human Resource Management

The term 'human resource management' first appeared in textbook literature in mid 1960s. The appears to come from a published lecture given several years earlier by economist E. W Bakke titles, 'The Human Resource Function". Bakke (1958, 5-6) states, 'The general type of activity in any function of management... is to use resources effectively for an organizational objective... The function which is related to the understanding, maintenance, development, effective employment, and integration of the potential in the resource 'people' I shall call simply *the human resources functions.*' He further states that, 'the first thing that we ought to be clear on is that there is nothing new about the managerial functions of dealing with people..... Like other sub functions of management..... it has been *carved out of* the *general* managerial function, not put into it.'

For next approximately twenty years the two terms 'personnel management' and 'human resource management' coexisted. But from 1980s two separate line of thoughts appeared. The first said both personnel management and human resource management were different nomenclatures for the same subject while the second, line of thought stated human resource management represented a new model and philosophy of people management that was fundamentally different from the traditional approach to Personnel Management\and Industrial Relations.

The second conception took its form from Beer's and Spector's article entitle 'Human Resource Management : The Integration of Industrial Relations and Organizational Development.' It was further reinforced by the development and popularization of the strategic management concept (Boxall and Purcell 2000). These two were followed by plethora of writings on strategic aspect of human resource management, resulting in the creation of new field called the 'strategic human resource management'.

During this period human resource management was also promoted by large scale regulations of employment, including legislation regulating discrimination and equal opportunity, pensions, treatment of the disabled employees, and family medical leave. Companies assigned the compliance and administration of the new regulations to human resource management departments, thus leading to new staff positions and responsibilities. There was simultaneous decline of the union sector.

Japanese firms had their impact on human resource management. Their model built on high performance practices, participative management, extensive investment in employees, and a mutual gain philosophy.

NATURE

The emergence of personnel management can be attributed to the work of the various authors who dealt the subject of organization and attached great significance to the human factor. Management as stated above is concerned with both human and non-human resources. The nature of human resource management can brought out by the under mentioned :

(*a*) **Centrality of Human Resource.** Human resource management is inherent in the management process. This function is performed by all managers in the organization.

However, if a manager wants to get the best for the company, he should select, train and motivate the employees. It is the personnel who have to produce and give their best to ensure success of any enterprise.

(*b*) **Pervasive Function.** Human resource management is all pervasive and is performed by all, managers, peers, colleagues and staff. In other words all employees from the top of the hierarchical pyramid to the lowest have to perform this function.

(*c*) **People Centered.** Human resource management is personnel centered and is present in all organizations. It has assumed greater importance due globalization, workers moving from industry to services and the necessity to attract and retain the best knowledge worker.

(*d*) **Continuous Process.** Human resource management is a continuous function. The human functions can't be turned off and on like water from any faucet (tap). It requires constant awareness and its importance in everyday functions if an individual has to perform at his optimum.

Storey (1989) has described divided human resource management in 'hard' and 'soft' versions. The hard focuses on the quantitative and the strategic aspects of managing humans and treats humans as any other economic factor. It emphasizes the need for managing personnel to ensure that they contribute towards economic gains of the organization. The soft approach treats the employees as a means of realizing organization objectives through their commitment and by winning them over.

OBJECTIVE

The objective of all business is to earn wealth. It can deduce from it that the objective of human resource management is the proper utilization of all personnel of the organization in a manner that the production is maintained at its optimum. This is best achieved by having good working relationships among the individuals and the employees are able to attain their respective goals and development in the organization.

Human Resource Management at Infosys

Employees are vital to the company. We have created a favourable work environment that encourages innovation and meritocracy. We have also set up a scalable recruitment and human resource management process, which enables us to attract and retain high caliber employees.

Infosys, Annual Report 2007-08, p.26

Aims of Human Resource Management could be :

- **Organizational Effectiveness**. Floukes (March–April, 1975) in his article 'The Expanding Role of the Personal Function,' *Harvard Business Review* quotes, "For many years it has been said that capital is the bottleneck for a developing industry. I don't think this any longer holds true. I think it is the work force and the company's inability to recruit and maintain a good workforce that does constitute the bottleneck for production. I don't know of any major project backed by good ideas, vigour, and enthusiasm that has been stopped by shortage of cash. I do know of industries whose growth has been partly stopped or hampered because they can't maintain an efficient and enthusiastic labour force, and I think this will hold true even more in future."

- **Human Capital Management.** Human capital of an organization consists of people who work there and on whom the success of the business depends. Human capital has been defined by Bontis *et al*[1]. as :

  "Human Capital represents the human factor in the organization; the combined intelligence, skills and expertise that gave the organization its distinctive character. The human elements of the organization are those that are capable of learning, changing, innovating and providing the creative thrust which if properly motivated can ensure the long-term survival of the organization."

- **Knowledge Management.** Knowledge management is 'any process or practice of creating, acquiring, capturing, sharing, and using knowledge, wherever it resides, to enhance learning and performance in organizations (Scarborough *et al.* 1999).
- **Employee Relation.** TATA steel has had an uninterrupted record of 75 years where there has been strike at its plant. This has been possible due to the company's philosophy of ***'inclusive growth'*** which has meant several initiatives that help employees directly—as well as communities that are impacted either directly or indirectly by Tata Steel. This has in turn brought about making it one of the favourite companies for young man seeking employment and for the workforce to give their optimum.
- **Meeting Diverse Needs.** The globalization has brought in diverse workforce, as also in past few years a very large numbers of women have joined the workforce especially in service sectors such as banking, insurance, BPOs etc. This has resulted in challenges for Human Resource Mangers to meet the diverse needs. HR Managers need to evolve good diversity and inclusion strategies. Good Diversity and Inclusion strategies and tactics must be job-relevant, skills-specific, and assist team members in understanding current workforce and marketplace realities. Organizations which tie diversity and inclusion to their business strategy increase performance, productivity and customer satisfaction.

Diversity and Inclusion

"Valuing diversity, endeavouring to provide an interesting and inclusive environment and treating people as we would like to be treated ourselves," these are not just words, they represent a tangible commitment TCS has made to its people, its clients and the communities in which it works and lives. TCS believes that to be a truly innovative organization, it needs to promote an environment that is rich in diversity—acknowledging each person's uniqueness, promoting and recognizing personal achievements

- **Bridging the Gap between Rhetoric and Reality.** The research conducted by Gratton et al. (1999) found that there was generally a wide gap between the sort of rhetoric expressed above and reality. Management may start with good intentions to do some or all of these things but the realization of them 'theory in use' is often very difficult. This arises because of contextual and process problem; other business priorities, short-term, limited support from line managers, an inadequate infrastructure of supporting processes, lack of resources, resistance to change and lack of trust. Purcell et al. (2003) state that *it is the front line managers who bring human resource policies to life, and act accordingly.*

The specific objectives of human resource management could be stated to be to determine the requirement of personnel, attract and recruit the best talent, assist in the growth of an individual so that he contributes towards the organizational goals, retain an employee, ensure a career for an employee and develop policies so that employee and the company achieves their vision. The broad scope could be stated as :

- Advise management on human resource policies.
- Ensure organization has highly motivated and highly performing workforce
- Implementing and maintaining all necessary human resource policies and procedures to enable the organizations to achieve its objectives.
- Providing the support and conditions that will help line managers achieve their objectives.
- Handling crises and difficult human relations situations to ensure that they do not get in the way of the organization achieving its objectives.
- Acting as custodian of organization standards and values in the management of human resources.

Policy Goals of Human Resource Management

Caldwell (2004) has put down 12 policy goals of Human Resource Management :

(*a*) Managing people as assets that are fundamental to the competitive advantage of the organization.

(*b*) Aligning Human Resource Policy with business policies and corporate strategies.

(*c*) Developing a close fit for Human Resource policies, procedures and systems with one and another.

(*d*) Creating a flatter and more flexible organization capable of responding more quickly to change.

(*e*) Encouraging team working and cooperation across internal organizational boundaries.

(*f*) Creating a strong customer-first philosophy through out the organization.

(*g*) Empowering the employees to manage their own self-development and learning.

(*h*) Developing the reward strategies designed to support a performance-driven culture;

(*i*) Improving employee involvement through better internal communication.

(*j*) Building greater employee commitment to the organization.

(*k*) Increasing line management responsibility for Human Resource policies.

(*l*) Developing the facilitating role of mangers as enablers.

Characteristics of HRM

Thus from above it can be deduced that major characteristics of HRM are :

- Diverse;
- Strategic with emphasis on integration;
- Commitment oriented;
- Based on belief that people should be treated as assets (human capital);
- Unitarist rather than pluralist, individualistic rather than collective in its approach to employee relations;
- A management driven activity- the delivery of Human Resource Management is a line management responsibility;
- Focused on business.

AIMS OF HUMAN RESOURCE MANAGEMENT

Ulrich and Lake (1990) remarked that 'Human Resource Management System can be the source of organizational capabilities that allow firms learn and capitalize on new opportunities.' HRM is specifically concerned with achieving objectives in the under mentioned.

Organizational Effectiveness

Cappelli and Cocker Hefter (1996) 'Distinctive human resources practices shape the core competencies that determine how firms compete.' HRM strategies aim at supporting programmes for improving organizational effectiveness by developing policies in such areas as knowledge management, talent management and generally creating 'a great place to work'. This is the 'big idea' as described by Purcell *et al.* (2003), which consists of a 'clear vision and a set of integrated values'.

Human Capital Management

The human capital in an organization consists of the people who work there and on whom the success of the business depends. Human capital has been defined by Bontis *et al.* (1999) as follows :

'Human capital represents the human factor in the organization; the combined intelligence, skills and expertise that give the organization its distinctive character. The human elements of the organization are those that are capable of learning, changing, innovating and providing the creative thrust which if properly motivated can ensure the long term survival of the organization.'

Human capital can be regarded as prime asset of an organization and businesses need to invest in this asset to ensure survival and maintain strategic advantage over it competitors. HRM aims at ensuring the organization obtains and retains the skilled, committed and well-motivated workforce it needs.

Knowledge Management

Knowledge management is ' any process or practice of creating, acquiring, capturing, sharing and using knowledge, wherever it resides, to enhance learning and performance in organizations. '(Scarborough *et al.* 1999). HRM aims to support and development of firm-specific knowledge and skills that are the result of organizational learning processes.

Reward Management

HRM aims to enhance motivation, job engagement and commitment by introducing policies and processes that ensure that people are valued and rewarded for what they do and achieve and for the levels of skills and competency they reach.

Employee Relation

This aims at creating a climate in which productivity and harmonious relations can be maintained through partnerships between management and employees and their trade unions. Credibility of the manager is the essence in this relationship

Credibility

Credibility is the most important predictor of an HR professional's effectiveness, according to the 2007 Human Resource Competency Study (HRCS) by The RBL Group leadership firm. The study looked at the most important roles served by HR people, including change steward, talent manager, strategy architect, operational executor, business ally and credible activist. What's No. 1 ? Credible activist.

"HR professionals who are credible but not activists are admired, but do not have much impact. Those who are activists, but not credible, may have ideas but will not be listened to," the study concludes.

According to advisors at The HR Specialist.com, here are eight key ways to diminish or destroy your credibility :

1. Align yourself too closely with one person or group. For example, having lunch with the same manager every day can generate distrust.
2. Answer questions without the facts. It plays into preconceived notions about HR's lack of business acumen. It's better to say "Let me get back to you on that" than to fake it.
3. Make decisions based on others' emotions. Say a manager and his boss are angry over an employee's behavior and demand immediate discipline.

   "It can be a mistake to let their emotions influence your action," says Tracy Koll, VP of HR for Simmons Bedding Co. Instead, investigate thoroughly and be fair, or you lose credibility with staff.
4. Remain silent at critical times. "HR should be active participants," says Dani Johnson, project manager of the HRCS. "Speak out when you have opinions and don't be a silent note taker at meetings with managers and executives."
5. Fail to initiate any big-picture HR projects. Don't be afraid to take calculated risks that can impress management, such as projects that directly benefit the bottom line.
6. Show a lack of business knowledge. If the financial side isn't your strong suit, take a course so you can discuss balance sheets and budgets.
7. Show a lack of legal knowledge. Your boss—not to mention a jury—will expect you to know state and federal employment laws inside and out.
8. Share confidential and personal information. "It's one of the fastest ways you can lose credibility," says Koll.

Meeting Diverse Needs

HRM aims to develop and implement policies that balance and adapt to the needs of its stakeholders and provide for the management of a diverse workforce, taking into account individual and group differences in employment, personal needs, work style and aspirations and the provision of equal opportunities for all.

Bridging the Gap between Rhetoric and Reality

Research conducted by Gratton *et al.* (1999) found that there was generally a wide gap between the sort of rhetoric expressed above and reality. Managements often start schemes with good intentions however, realization of the same are often very difficult. This arises primarily due lack of commitment, lack of infrastructure and inadequate support from line managers. It is the HRM that must ensure that aspirations are translated into sustained and effective action. To do this HR functionaries must come up with new and innovatory policies and practices. The HR functionaries must appreciate in the words of Purcell *et al.* (2003) that it is the front line managers who bring HR policies to life and set accordingly. The ranking of various human resource management activities carried out by General managers and Human Resource Specialists are given in Table 1.1.

Table 1.1. Ranking of HRM Activities of General Managers and HR Specialist

	All Managers %	*Designated HR Managers %*	*Other Managers which utilize more than 30 percent of their time on HR activities %*
Staffing HR planning	52	30	46
Recruitment	37	60	40
Training	25	30	45
Negotiating Contract	27	44	24
Job Evaluation	12	10	16
Reward Management	11	9	9
Maintenance of Peace and Harmony	8	18	12
Discipline Issues	2	12	4
Retention of Employees	25	30	4

SCOPE

It is more than twenty years that India embarked on economic reforms. It is these reforms that led to change in activities that HR Managers undertake. The activities undertaken vary depending upon such factors as the size and structure of the organization and its holding patterns. Clearly there have been changes in the profile of the hr manager and his functions. Hr managers today spend less time with Trade Unions and more with the needs of each individual employee. There is growing evidence of HR specialists taking over hr functions. Today, approximately eighty percent (80%) of HR Managers reported having responsibility of training and employee development; and retention of work force. Large work places are more likely to employ at least one HR personnel specialist. Large organization may divide HR activities amongst several managers : one specialist for recruitment and selection; one for training and development and another for negotiating and administering the collective agreement.

In order to achieve the objectives of human resource management certain activities are to be performed. The field of human resource management is very wide. It is for this reason that during last hundred years it has been referred by different terms such as 'labour management', 'industrial relations', personnel management etc. The Indian Institute of Personnel Management has laid down the scope of personnel management as :

(*a*) The welfare aspect. This primarily concerns with working conditions of an employee.

(*b*) The Labour or personnel aspect. Mainly deals with the aspect of compensation, promotion, retirement etc.

(*c*) The Industrial Relations aspect.

All human resource activities are generated only after an enterprise has established its business goal and vision. After business goals and vision have been established the firm then formulates its human resource goals and strategy to accomplish that. Based on these the human resource management plan is involved.

There are seven management functions of a human resources (HR) department that are specifically addressed : staffing, performance appraisals, compensation and benefits, training and development, employee and labor relations, safety and health, and human resource research. The wheel of Human Resource Management and Business is given in Figure 1.3.

As companies reorganize to gain competitive edge, human resources plays a key role in helping companies deal with a fast-changing competitive environment and the greater demand for quality employees. Research conducted by The Conference Board has found six key people-related activities that human resources completes to add value to a company :

1. Effectively managing and utilizing people.
2. Trying performance appraisal and compensation to competencies.

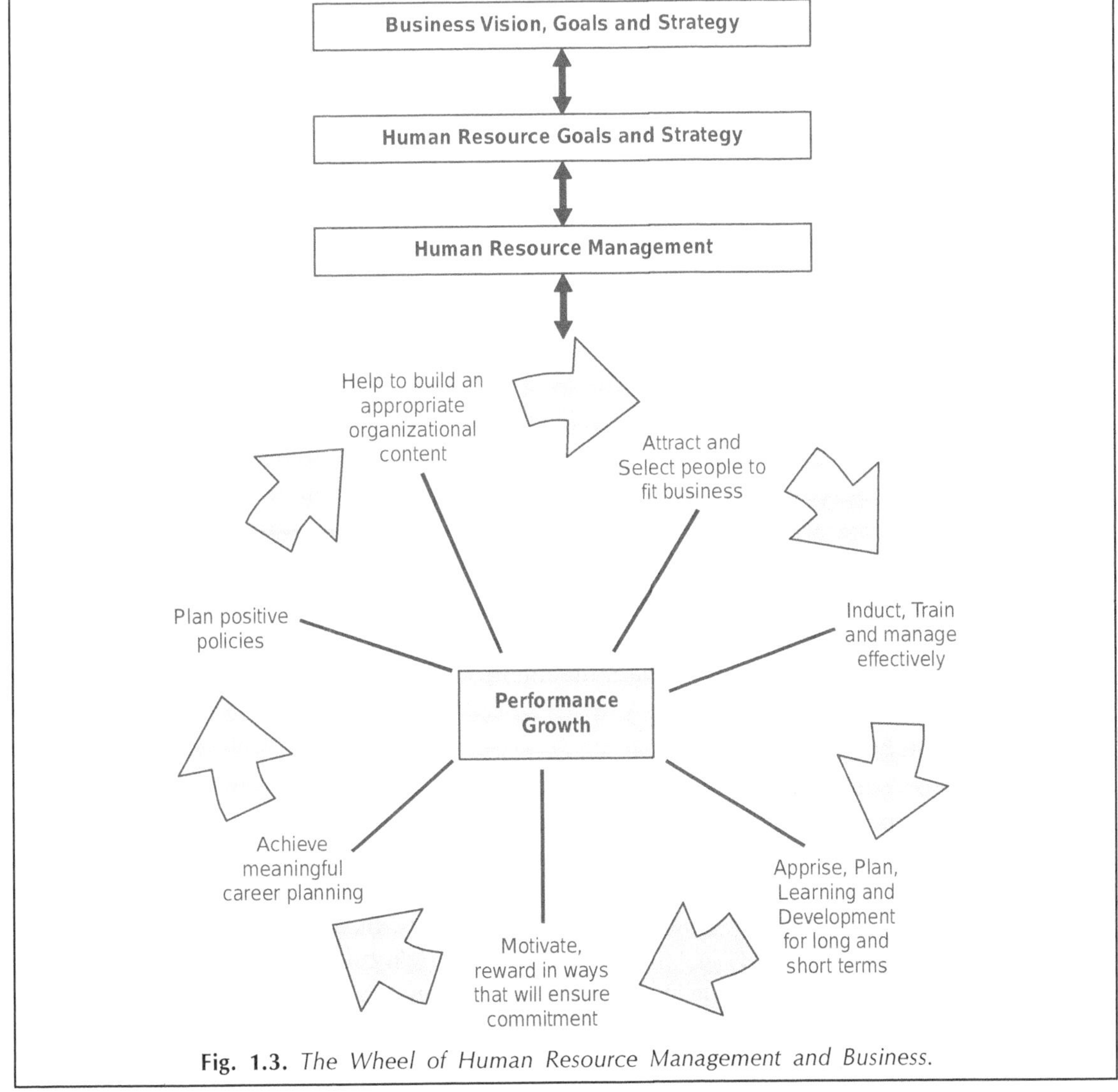

Fig. 1.3. *The Wheel of Human Resource Management and Business.*

3. Developing competencies that enhance individual and organizational performance.
4. Increasing the innovation, creativity and flexibility necessary to enhance competitiveness.
5. Applying new approaches to work process design, succession planning, career development and inter-organizational mobility.
6. Managing the implementation and integration of technology through improved staffing, training and communication with employees.

Lately human resource management has taken a new turn in that due globalization, shift from industry to service sector, the role of information technology is playing in business; there is a shift in the manner the employees are behaving. The life-long careers and loyalty to the firms by employees are things of the part. The concerns or organizations have to make effort to first *attract* and then *retain* the employee. The scope thus has slightly shifted from the seven functions stated above to those given in Figure 1.4 viz. attract, induct, apprise and plan learning and development, motivate, achieve meaningful career planning, plan positive policies, and help to build an appropriate organizational context.

The scope could be listed as :

(*a*) *Planning.* It involves determining the number and kind of human resource.

(*b*) *Attract and recruit* the best talent in the market.

(*c*) *Apprise the individual* to determine the training requirements or for taking corrective steps in placement of an employee if not found suitable or lacking a particular skill.

(*d*) *Motivation and rewards* to earn their willing commitment and for retention of an employee.

(*e*) *Career Planning.* To ensure that individual meets his social and individual aspirations and goals.

(*f*) *Policy.* A positive and welfare oriented policies help in development and retention of an employee. It also brings in the willing cooperation and support of the employee for achieving corporate or organizational goals.

FUNCTIONS OF HUMAN RESOURCE MANAGEMENT

To carry out human resource management functions usually the organizations establishes human resource department headed by Human Resource or Personnel Manager. The department plays a prominent role in maintaining the best organizational culture and provides assistance to all other departments on personnel matters. The main functions of human resource management could be classified as

(*a*) Resource Acquisition.

(*b*) Resource Management

(*c*) Resource Disposal.

Re-Examining "Why HR is Hated"

When it comes to a critique of human resources departments, the best article I have ever read on the matter remains Fast Company's 2005 piece *"Why We Hate HR."*

Keith H. Hammonds outlines in telling and hilarious fashion why HR folk are often ineffective, prevent talented employees from progressing and become slaves to form and legal box-checking.

HR people see themselves as protectors of management from lawsuits and embarrassment rather than nurturers of up-and-coming employees and champions of their companies.

Here's one example. HR relies on the special and often insidious processes to prevent lawsuits and gather dirt on workers. I was a manager at a company where if a problem employee came up, the "PIP" (performance improvement program) kicked in. But PIP was truly Orwellian since it meant anything but improving the employee. Once in PIP, the worker was as good as fired. PIP was designed to gather incriminating information about the employee to be used to intimidate that person when they were dismissed so they wouldn't file a lawsuit.

Keith comes up with a number of perceptive reasons why HR departments end up doing these things. Here's a brief list :

- HR people are often the dregs of the corporate world. Not the "sharpest tacks in the box," HR bureaucrats get to those positions because they often can't handle jobs requiring more talent or imagination.
- HR pursues efficiency in lieu of value. Efficiency is a lot easier to justify numerically and doesn't require a true understanding of what a corporation does.
- HR tries to get executives sucked into their system. These include pro forma, annual personnel appraisals. Raises and advancement depend upon them, but who's to say that annual is the right time frame or you even need them ?
- The corner office doesn't get HR. There's often little communication between the C-Suite and HR, but given the state of many HR departments, may be that's just as well.

To be sure, there are some firms that do HR well, such as Cardinal Health, Yahoo, Procter & Gamble and General Electric. But Keith's scathing magazine piece still rings true.

HUMAN RESOURCE SYSTEM

Human Resource Management operates through human resource systems that bring together in a coherent way (Figure 1.4) :

- **Human Resource Philosophies**. Describing the overreaching values and guiding principles adopted in managing people.
- **Human Resource Strategies**. Defining the direction in which Human Resource Management intends to go.
- **Human Resource Policies**. Which are the guidelines defining how these values, principles and strategies should be applied and implemented in specific areas of Human Resource Management.
- **Human Resource Processes**. Consisting of formal procedures and methods used to put Human Resource strategic plans and policies into effect.
- **Human Resource Practices**. Comprising of informal approaches used in managing people.
- **Human Resource Programmes**. Which enable Human Resource strategies, policies and practices to be implemented according to plan ?

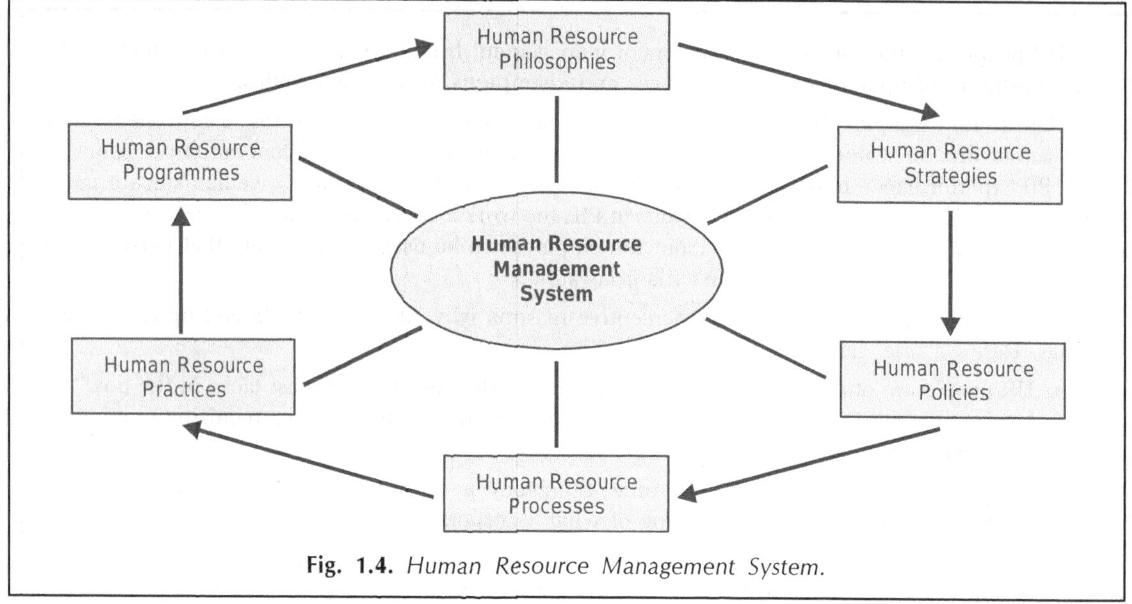

Fig. 1.4. *Human Resource Management System.*

Becker and Gerhart (1996) have classified these components into three levels :

(*a*) the system architecture(guiding principles);

(*b*) policy alternatives and processes;

(*c*) practices.

The human resource management activities can also be said to be managing the human capital in that there are five functions performed the details is in Figure 1.5. The broad five functions are :

(*a*) Organization

(*b*) Resourcing

(*c*) Human Resource Development

(*d*) Reward management

(*e*) Employee Realationship

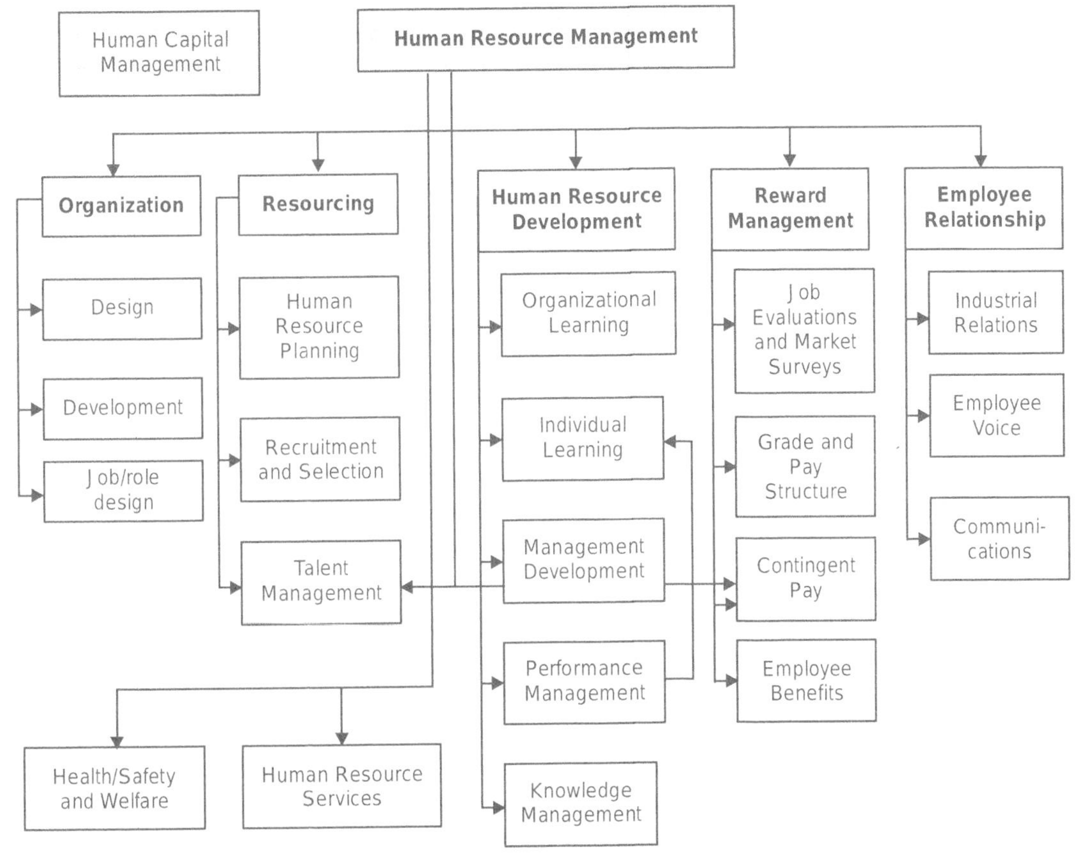

Fig. 1.5. *Human Resource Management Activities.*

MODELS OF HUMAN RESOURCE MANAGEMENT

The conceptual debate on human resource management it is evident that the theoretical significance of subject is debatable between 'hard' and 'soft' versions. The 'soft' version of human resource management emphasizes the importance of high commitment, workplace learning and enlightened leadership. The human resource models whether US or British assert that the organization's 'human resource's' are valued assets and emphasize the commitment of employees as a source of competitive advantage (Legge, 1989). The 'hard' version of human resource management emphasize the calculative, quantitative and strategic management aspect of managing the workforce in 'rational' way (Storey, 1989).

The Fomburn, Tichy and Devanna Model of HRM

One of the explicit statements of HRM concept was made by Michigan School (Fomburn *et al.* 1984) The Michigan School suggested that the Human Resource System and the organization should be managed in a way that is congruent with organizational strategy. They further explained that there is a human resource cycle which consists of four generic processes or functions that are performed in all organizations. (Figure 1.6). These are :

(*a*) Selection – matching available human resources to jobs;

(*b*) Appraisal – performance management.

(*c*) Rewards – management must reward both short and long term achievements, bearing in mind the 'business must perform in the present to succeed in future'.

(*d*) Development – developing high quality employees.

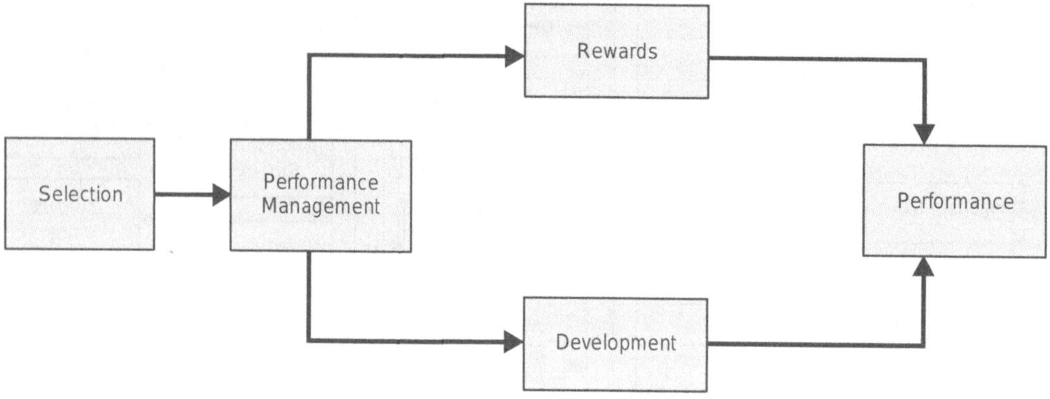

***Source** : Adapted From Fomburn et al. 1984.*

Fig. 1.6. *The Human Resource Cycle.*

The Harvard Framework

The other school of HRM is the Harvard School of Beer *et al.* (1984) who developed what Boxall calls the 'Harvard Framework'. Beer and his colleagues that 'Today, many pressures are demanding a broader, more comprehensive and more strategic perspective with regard to organization's Human Resources'. These pressure need a 'longer tem perspective in managing people and consideration of people as potential assets rather than merely a variable cost.' They were that first to underline the HRM tenet that it belongs to line managers. They also stated that : 'Human resource management involves all management decisions and action that affect the nature of the relationship between the organization and its employees – its human resources' (Figure 1.7.).

The Harvard school suggested that HRM had two characteristics features :

(*a*) Line managers accept more responsibilities for ensuring the alignment of competitive strategy and personnel policies;

(*b*) Personnel has the mission of setting policies that govern how personnel activities are developed and implemented in ways that make them more mutually reinforcing.

According to Boxall (1992) the advantages of this model are that it :

(*a*) incorporates recognition of a range of stake holder interests;

(*b*) recognizes the importance of 'trade offs', either explicitly or implicitly, between the interests of owners and those of employees as well as between various interest groups;

(*c*) widens the context of Human Resource Management to include 'employee influence', the organization of work and the associated question of supervisory style;

(*d*) acknowledges a broad range of contextual influences on management's choice of strategy, suggesting a meshing of both product market and socio cultural logics;

(*e*) Emphasizes strategic choice- it is not driven by situational and environmental determinism.

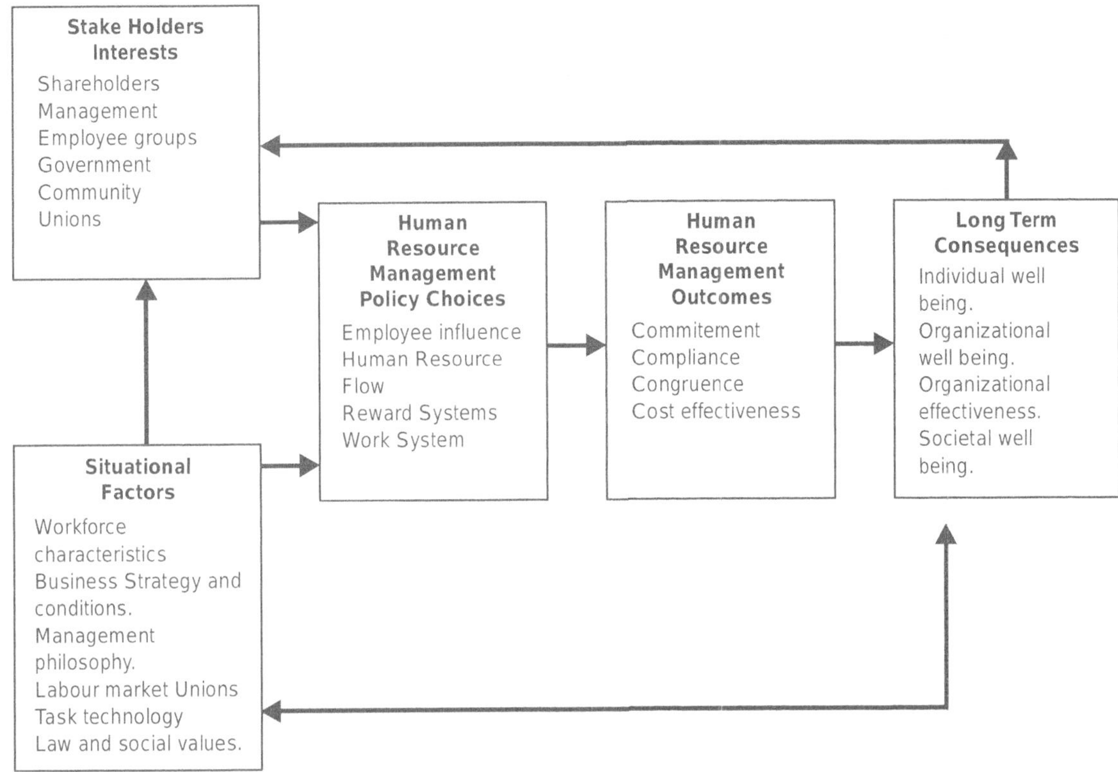

Source : *Beers et al. (1984)*

Fig. 1.7. *Harvard Analytical Framework for Human Resource Management.*

The Harvard Model has exerted considerable influence over the theory and practice of Human resource Management, particularly in its emphasis on the fact that Human Resource Management is the concern of management in general rather than the personnel function in particular.

Guests Model of Human Resource Management

Guest HRM differs from orthodox personnel management and to identify the major assumptions or stereotypes underpinning personnel and HRM

The central hypothesis of Guest's model is that if an integrated set of HRM practices is applied in coherent fashion, with a view to achieving the normative goals of high commitment, high quality, and task flexibility, then superior individual performance will result. It also assumes that this will result in superior organizational performance. The 'Guest Model' has six components :

1. an HRM strategy
2. a set of HRM policies
3. a set of HRM outcomes
4. behavioural outcomes
5. a number of performance outcomes
6. financial outcomes

The model is shown below. The model acknowledges the close links between HRM strategy and general business strategies, differentiation, focus and cost. The 'core' hypothesis, however, is that HRM practices should be designed to lead to a set of HRM outcomes of high employee commitment, high-quality employees, and highly flexible employees (Table 1.2).

Table 1.2. The Guest Model of HRM

HRM Strategy	*HRM practices*	*HRM outcomes*	*Behaviour outcome*	*Performance outcomes*	*Financial outcomes*
Differantiation (Innovation)	Selection		Effort Motivation	High Productivity Quality Innovation	Profits
	Training	Commitment			
Focus	Appraisal		Cooperation		
	Rewards	Quality		Low Absence	ROI
	Job Design		Involvement	Labour Turnover	
Cost (Cost (reduction)				Conflict	
	Involvement	Flexibility	Organizational citizenship	Customer complaints Labour Turnover	
	Status and Security				

Source : *Guest, 1997*

Guest sees high employee commitment as a vital HRM outcome, concerned with the goals of binding employees to the organization and obtaining behaviour outcomes of increased effort, cooperation, involvement and organizational citizenship. High-quality employees refer to issues of workplace learning and the need for the organization to have a capable, qualified and skilful workforce to produce high-quality services and products. Flexibility is concerned with ensuring that workers are receptive to innovation and change and, using Atkinson's (1984) terminology, have functional flexibility. According to model only when all three HRM outcomes – commitment, quality, flexibility—are achieved can we expect behaviour change and superior performance outcomes ? Guest emphasizes, these HRM goals are a 'package' and each is necessary to ensure superior performance and financial outcomes depicted on the right hand side of the model. He argues 'Only when a coherent strategy, directed towards these four policy goals, fully integrated into business strategy and fully sponsored by line management at all levels is applied will the high productivity and related outcomes sought by industry be achieved' (1990 p.378). According to Guest, HRM policies are concerned with more than 'good' selection or training : 'they are intended to achieve the human resource management policy goals' (1989, p.49). A key issue here is the distinctiveness of HRM practices : 'It is not the presence of selection or training but a distinctive approach to selection or training that matters. It is the use of high performance or high commitment HRM practices' (1997, p.273).

The model is prescriptive in the sense that it is based on the assumption that HRM is distinctively different from traditional personnel management (rooted in strategic management, etc.). It is idealistic, implicitly embodying the belief that fundamental elements of the HRM approach (essentially those of the Harvard map) such as commitment have a direct relationship with valued business consequences.

However, Guest has acknowledged that the concept of commitment is 'messy' and that the relationship between commitment and high performance is (or, perhaps, was—given the age of this material) difficult to establish. It also employs a 'flow' approach, seeing strategy underpinning practice, leading to a variety of desired outcomes.

Like its American predecessors, this UK model is unitarist (tying employee behaviour and commitment into the goals of strategic management) and lukewarm on the value of trade unions. The employee relationship is viewed as one between the individual and the organization (Figure 1.8).

	Personnel Management	***Human Resource Management***
Time and Planning Perspectives	Short-term reactive *ad hoc* marginal.	Long-term proactive strategy integrated
Psychological contract	Compliance	Commitment
Control System	External	Self Control
Employee Relations Perspective	Pluralist collective low trust	Unitarist individual and high trust
Preferred structures/systems	Bureaucratic/mechanistic centralized formal defined roles	Organic devolved flexible roles
Roles	Specialist/ professional	Largely integrated into line management
Evaluation criteria	Cost-minimization	Maximum utilization (Human assets accounting).

***Source** : Guest (1987, p. 507).*

Fig. 1.8. *Guests Stereotypes of Personnel Management and Human Resource Management.*

Warwick Model of Human Resource Management

This model emanates from the Centre for Corporate Strategy and Change at the University of Warwick and with two particular researchers, Hendry and Pettigrew (1990). The Warwick Model (Figure 1.11) draws heavily from Harvard Framework to extend the analysis of HRM and has five elements :

1. outer context
2. inner context
3. business strategy content
4. HRM Context
5. HRM Content

The model takes cognizance of HRM business strategy and HRM practices, the external and internal context in which these activities take place, and the processes by which such change take place, including interactions between changes in both context and content. The strength of model is that it identifies and classifies important environmental influences on HRM. Hendry and Pettigrew's research focused on mapping the context, identifying an inner (organizational) context and an external (wider environment) context and exploring how HRM adapted to changes in context.

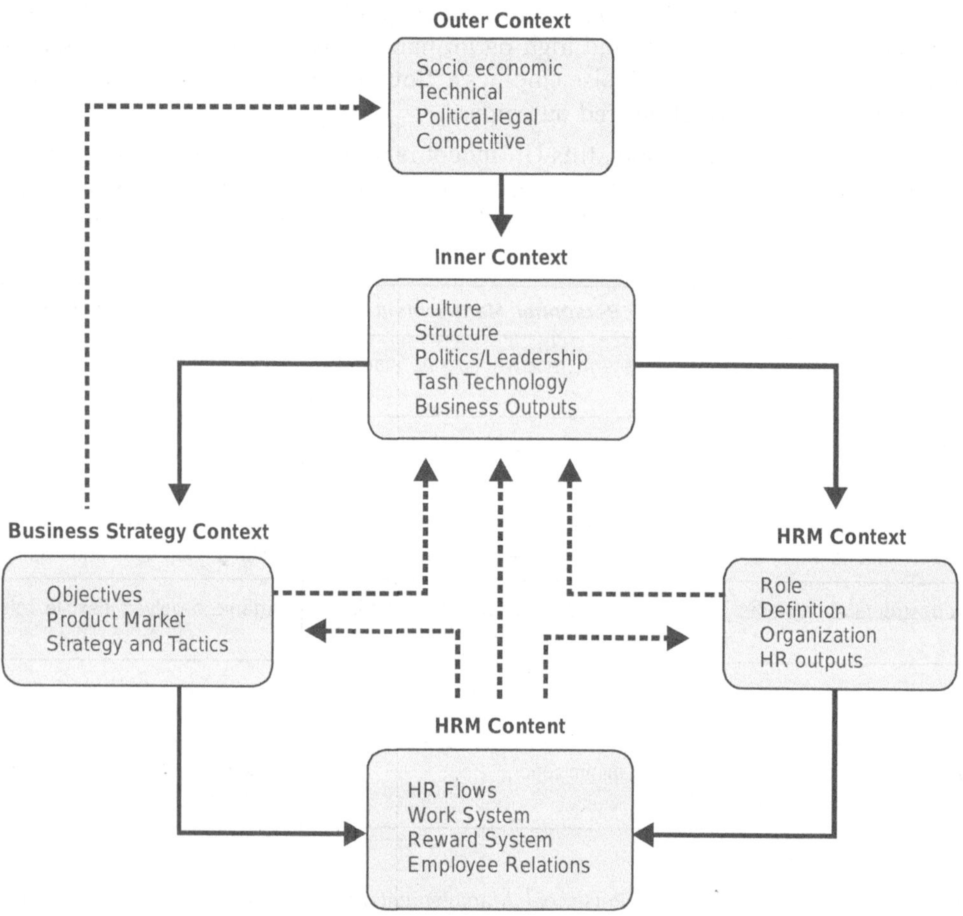

***Source** : Hendry and Pettigrew, 1990*

Fig. 1.9. *The Warwick Model of HRM.*

The model argue Hendry and Pettigrew, provides 'better descriptions of structures and strategy-making in complex organizations and of frameworks for understanding them {which} are an essential underpinning for analyzing HRM (1990, p. 35). While the implication is that those organizations achieving an alignment between the external and internal contexts will experience superior performance, a weakness of the model is that the process whereby internal HRM practices are linked to business output or performance is not developed.

Storey Model of Human Resource Management

Storey's Model stresses the 'Hard' HRM. It stresses the "resource" aspect. The hard model stresses HRM's focus on the crucial importance of the close integration of human resource policies, systems and activities with business strategy. From this perspective human resources are largely a factor of production, an expense of doing business rather than the only resource capable of turning inanimate factors of production into wealth. Human Resources are viewed as passive, to be provided and deployed as numbers and skills at the right price, rather than the source of creative energy (Legge, 1995, p.66-67).

Hard HRM is as calculative and tough minded as any other branch of management, communicating through the tough language of business and economics. This emphasis on the quantitative, calculative and business-strategic aspects of managing the "headcount" has been termed human asset accounting (Storey, 1987). The hard HRM approach has some kinship with scientific management as people are reduced to passive objects that are not cherished as a whole people but assessed on whether they posses the skills/attributes the organisation requires (Legge, 1995; Vaughan, 1994; Storey, 1987; Drucker et al, 1996; Keenoy, 1990).

Beliefs and Assumptions		
Contract	Careful delineation of written contracts	Aim to go 'beyond contract'.
Rules	Importance of devising clear rules/ mutuality	'Can do' outlook; impatience with 'rules'.
Guide to Management Action	Procedure consistency control	'Business need'/flexibility/ commitment
Behaviour referent	Norms/custom and practice	Values/mission
Managerial Task *vis-à-vis* labour	Monitoring	Nurturing
Nature of Relations	Pluralist	Unitarist
Conflict	Institutionalized	De-emphasized
Standardisation	High (for example 'parity' an issue)	Low (for example 'parity' not seen as relevant)
Strategic Aspects		
Key relations	Labour Management	Business Customer
Initiatives	Piecemeal	Integrated
Corporate Plan	Marginal to	Central to
Speed of decision	slow	fast
Line Management		
Management Role	Transactional	Transformational
Key Managers	Personnel/IR specialists	General/business/line managers
Prized management skills	Negotiations	facilitation
Key Levers		
Foci of attention for interventions	Personnel Procedures	Wide ranging cultural structural and personnel strategies.

Selection	Separate, Marginal task	Integrated key task
Pay	Job evaluation, multiple fixed grades	Performance related few if any grades
Conditions	Separately negotiated	Harmonization
Labour Management	Collective Bargaining contracts	Towards individual contracts
Thrust of relations with stewards	Regularized through facilities and training	Marginalized (with exception of some bargaining for change models)
Communication	Restricted flow/indirect	Increased flow/direct
Job design	Division of labour	Team work
Conflict Handling	Reach temporary truces	Manage climate and culture
Training and development	Controlled access to courses	Learning companies

Source *: Storey, 1992.*

Fig. 1.10. *The Storey Model of HRM.*

Storey's model resembles Guest's as a particular set of policies now identified with 'high commitment management' or 'high performance work systems'. Storey defines human resource management 'as a distinctive approach to employment management which seeks to achieve competitive advantage through strategic deployment of highly committed and capable workforce, using an integrated array of cultural, structural and personnel techniques (Storey, 1995, p. 5).

THE CHANGING ENVIRONMENT OF HUMAN RESOURCE MANAGEMENT

The field of Human Resource Management has gradually become broader and more strategic since the days when business people began including "personal departments" in their organization charts. Today, the globalization of the world economy and several other trends are again triggering changes in how companies organize, manage, and use their personnel/ Human Resource departments.

Globalization. Refers to tendency of firms to extend their sales, ownership, and/or manufacturing to new markets abroad. The checker board pattern of production today enables company to secure items from different countries and also from different parts and produce a finished good in different parts of the world to meet the requirements. IBM produces computers in China and sells the same in China, India and others parts of Asia and USA. Globalization also means more competition, and more competition means more pressure to be 'world class' *i.e.,* to do things better and less expensively. The bottom line is that the growing integration of the world economy into a single, huge marketplace is increasing the intensity of competition in wide range of manufacturing and service industries. The challenge is to help companies like TATA cut global human relations costs, formulate selection, training, and compensation policies for expatriate employees, managing globalization in world-class firms in a major Human Resource challenge.

Technological Advances. Many of the improvements that make firms world class involve the technology.

Exporting Jobs. Competitive pressures and the search for greater efficiencies are also prompting more employers to export jobs abroad. Technology facilitates the shifts.

Nature of Jobs. The technology is also changing the nature of work. Even factory jobs are more technologically more demanding. Knowledge intensive high technological manufacturing are replacing factory jobs. Technology is not only trend driving the change from 'brawn to brain' but also the workforce is shifting from producing to delivering services, not products.

Type of Workforce. To keep the costs down, there has been shift to using non-traditional workforce. Non–traditional workforce include those who hold multiple jobs, or who are 'contingent' or part time workers, contract workers, or people working in alternative work arrangements. Workers are also not seeking permanent employment they are freelancers and offer their services for a particular project only. They organize and reorganize teams aimed at just attaining an objective and upon accomplishment these are disintegrated.

Workforce Demographics. The workforce is becoming more diverse as women, minority-group members, and older workers enter the workforce.

This means growing emphasis on knowledge workers and human capital. Human capital refers to the knowledge, education, training, skills, and expertise of a firm's workers. The centre of gravity of employment is fast moving from manual to knowledge based workers, who resist the command and control model that business took from the military 100 years ago.

MANAGERS HUMAN RESOURCE MANAGEMENT JOBS

Most writers agree that all managers perform certain basic functions. These are planning, organizing, staffing, leading and controlling.

- **Planning**, with the help of which the management ensures directing employee efforts towards group and organizational goals attainment. It is necessary to set immediate and long- term goals, and to choose strategies of their achievement. At this stage one should concern himself with the following questions : Where are we now ? What do we want to accomplish ? How are we going to do it ? Planning allows managers to evaluate the future, to grasp the trends, the probable circumstances of the influential factors that shall act (in a positive or negative sense) upon the organization. Based on the extent of the forecast, three types of predictive activities can be identified : prognosis, planning and scheduling.
  - ★ Prognosis is a long term forecast, spreading over a period over 10 years and concretized in prognosis studies and/or scripts based on which strategic decision are made at the superior hierarchic level.
  - ★ Planning is a medium and short-term predictive activity, covering from a few years down to a semester or even less, a month. This activity results into a plan.
  - ★ Scheduling covers short periods of time (10 days, a week, a shift), is very detailed with regard to actions, means and resources used to fulfill a certain plan. The elements included in scheduling need to have a high degree of accuracy and also involve sophisticated methods, such as the Delphi method (Will be discussed later in details).
- **Organizing.**, which consists in translating the planned steps into reality. At this stage it is necessary to assign tasks, to set deadlines, allocate resources, to decide what structures are yet to be created and to whom additional responsibilities should be delegated, etc. It

rationally combines all the elements necessary for the correct functioning : material resources, labor resources, financial means etc. As a management function, organization refers to two distinct aspects :

★ One regarding the structure of the organization.

★ The second regarding the structure of the personnel and of the material and financial resources necessary in order to develop the activity in optimum conditions.

- **Staffing.** It consists of job analysis, recruiting, allocating, training if required to accomplish company's mission,
- **Leading/motivating.** Leading implies managerial activities with the aim of causing proper performance from the employee. Satisfactory fulfillment of this function involves finding out employee needs and creating reward systems for quality and timely work. Motivation should be based on harmonizing the staff's interest with the objectives of the organization through a diversified system of motivational methods and techniques, according to each particular situation. This motivational process is going to be a lot easier if, upon hiring the staff, their abilities and expectations are thoroughly considered. ***Executing*** is one of the most important functions of the manager. The manager is responsible for the accomplishment of the mission. Hence, he should be able to execute the plan which has been prepared. He should have the able to intervene at critical juncture or incase the execution is not satisfactory and give it necessary impetus.
- **Controlling**, consists of supervising the development of the respective system and comparing the results with the expectations. It consists of tools for assessing how close the organization is to the attainment of its goals. The most important issues which have to be addressed here are precise monitoring (diagnosis) of current results and their comparison with what has been planned. Effective managerial control must always be followed by feedback for correcting initial plans. This can be a preventive activity (in order to avoid any possible and predictable errors) or corrective (when it brings the system to the normal functioning parameters). It is a process that, generally, goes through the following steps :

★ Setting the objectives.

★ Selecting the measurement criteria and standards necessary in order to assess the results.

★ Obtaining information with regard to these results (activities).

★ Comparing these results with the objectives of the controlled activity.

- **Assessment** is a process through which information is obtained with regard to the analyzed activity, the results are compared to various objectives or standards and decisions are made with regard to the improvement of the assessed activity. Most of the plans fail as there is no follow up. *Follow up* basically involves resetting the objectives including giving new vision to the company.

IMPORTANCE OF HUMAN RESOURCE MANAGEMENT

Human resource management is important because no manager would like to :

(*a*) Hire a wrong person ?

(*b*) Experience high turnover.

(*c*) People not motivated enough to work at their optimum.

(*d*) Company taken to court for discriminatory actions.

(*e*) Employees think they are being discriminated and are not compensated adequately.

(*f*) Allow lack of training undermine department's effectiveness.

(*g*) Commit an unfair labour practice.

LINE AND STAFF ASPECTS OF HUMAN RESOURCE MANAGEMENT

Line Versus Staff Authority

In an organization the authority is differentiated between line and staff. *Authority* can be defined *as the right to make decisions, to direct the work of others, and to give orders.*

Line Managers are authorized to direct the work of subordinates – line mangers are always someone's superior. It is the line manager who is directly responsible for meting the targets and accomplishes the organizational goals and objectives.

Staff Managers. Staff managers advise and assist the line managers in accomplishing the goals and objectives. Human Resource Managers in most organizations operate as staff and assist the line managers in functions like recruiting, hiring, retaining, compensating etc.

Line Managers Human Resource Management

Line managers have exercised control over all subordinates working under their supervision. It has always been the responsibility of line managers to get the objectives of the organizations achieved. The major responsibilities of line managers towards human resource could be listed as :

(*a*) Placing the right person on the right job.

(*b*) Orienting and absorbing the new employee in the organization.

(*c*) Training and upgrading the employee on the skills required to perform in the organization and at the position employed for.

(*d*) Training employees to meet the future requirements of the organization.

(*e*) Improving performance.

(*f*) Controlling costs of labour.

(*g*) Developing abilities of each employee.

(*h*) Maintaining high morale.

(*i*) Protecting employee's health and physical condition.

In small enterprises employing few people the line manager may perform all the functions of a human resource manager. But as the organization grows there is a need to have specialized people with knowledge and skills to perform the human resource management functions and a separate staff is appointed to carry out this function. The Human Resource Manage performs three functions :

(*a*) **Line Function.** The Human Resource manger performs the line function in his department by exerting the line authority. Human Resource manger does not usually exercise the line authority outside his department but exerts an *implied authority*.

(*b*) **A Coordinative Function.** The human resource manager's also carryout coordination of all personnel activities. This is also referred to as functional control. In this the Human Resource managers implement the organizations personnel policies.

(c) **Staff (Assist and Advice) Functions.** The main function of an Human Resource manager is that of a staff. In this the Human Resource Manager assists in strategy design and execution by helping Chief Executive Officers to better understand the personnel aspects of the company's strategic options. Human Resource assists in recruiting, orienting, training, evaluating, counseling etc. of the employees. It administers the benefits programmes. It plays as **employee advocacy** role—It defines how management should be treating employees, make sure employees can contest unfair practices, and represents the employees' interests within the framework of its main obligation to senior management. "Employee Advocacy Remain HR Priority," *BNA Bulletin to management,* September 26, 1996, p. 312.

The size of Human Resource Department and the number of Human Resource specialists employed reflects the size of the company. See Figure 1.11 for large companies; and Figure 1.12 for small manufacturing unit.

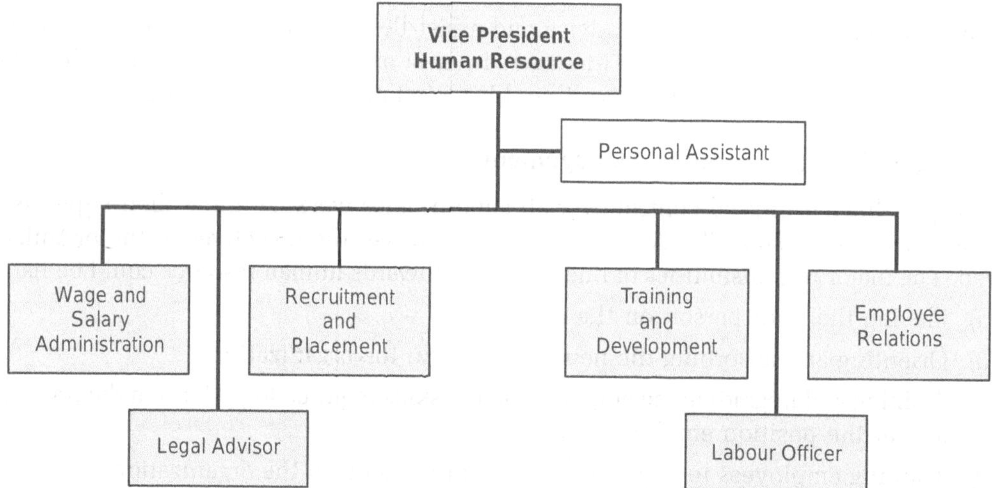

Fig. 1.11. *Human Resource Department Organizational Charg Large Company.*

Note :
- Each of the department could be manned by many oficers depending upon the quantum of work load.
- There could be sub departments in each.

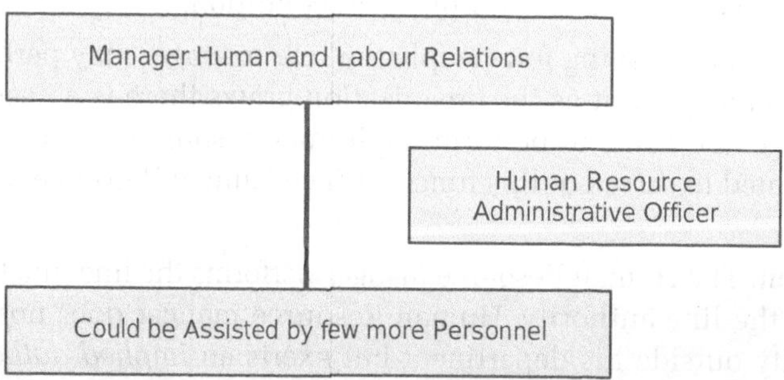

Fig. 1.12. *Human Resource Department Organizational Chart Small Company.*

In summary, HR management is an integral part of every manager's job. Whether you're a first line supervisor, middle manager, or president; or whether you're a production manager, hospital administrator or a retail manager, getting results through committed people is HR manager's major function. To achieve the objective, it is imperative that every manager has a good working knowledge of human resource management concepts and techniques in this book.

HUMAN RESOURCE MANAGEMENT IN RELATION TO OTHER ACTIVITIES

The heart of human resource management is the idea that it should serve the business strategy of an organization. As Fomburn, Tichy and Devanna (1984) put it, "The critical managerial task is to align the formal structure and the HR systems so that they drive the strategic objectives of the organization" (p. 37). This relationship of persons with strategy is not simple derivative. The sound strategy and its effective implementation depend upon 'organizational capability' (Ulrich and Lake, 1990); which in turn depends upon the organizational culture, and what is possible within external and internal constraints. This organizational capability infuses drives and governs the development and implementation of business strategy.

Toady the business strategy has become the output or 'derivative' and organizational capability has become an input. Thus there is shift of viewing an employee from being a cost centre to viewing him as a resource, which in essence is the human resource idea.

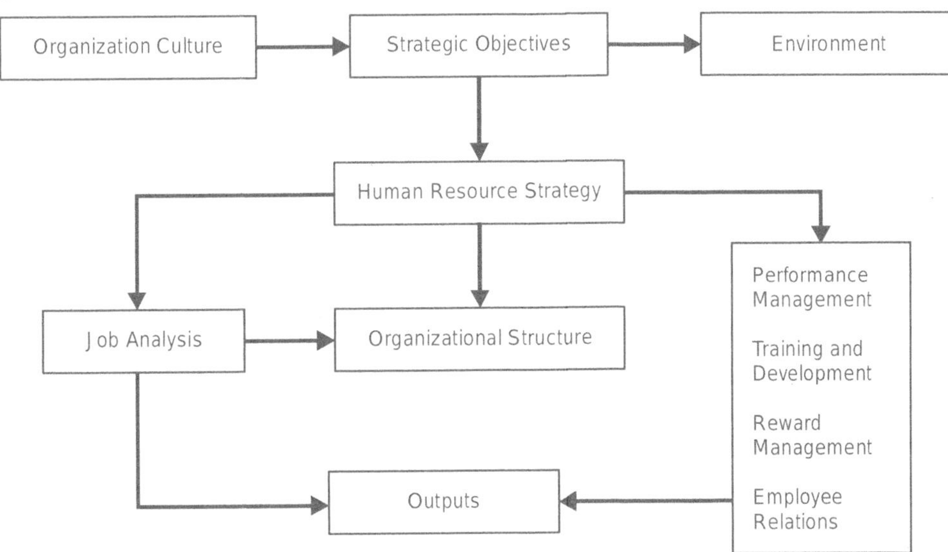

Fig. 1.13. *Human Resource Management in Relation to other Activities.*

Human resource management also contributes to the functioning of an organization over long and short periods of time. Values and culture embody an ingrained way of perceiving the world. These are established over long periods and are slow and difficult to change.

Strategy in company also emphasizes on productivity by minimizing output cost per person. This means downward pressure on numbers of employees and on wages. Human Resource Management is therefore concentrated on

(*a*) Writing explicit job descriptions that leave little room for ambiguity.

(*b*) Narrowly designing jobs to encourage specialization;

(*c*) Administering results oriented appraisal

(*d*) Focused on providing minimal level of training and development.

Human Resource Management also tries to retain tight control on Industrial Relations to control pay and discipline.

RESERVATIONS ABOUT HRM

HRM has been a controversial topic, especially in academic circles. The main reservations have been that HRM promises more than it can deliver. Although all agree that human resource are the most important asset of an organization, yet very few employers are able to harness the full potential of their employees. Lado and Wildon (1994) define human resource system Lado and Wilson (1994) define a human resource system as a set of distinct but interrelated activities, functions and processes that are directed at attracting, developing, and maintaining a firm's human resources. Traditionally, management of this system has gained more attention from service organisations than from manufacturing organisations. However, to enhance operational performance, effectively managing this system is equally important in both types of organisations. Needless to say, sophisticated technologies and innovative manufacturing practices alone can do very little to enhance operational performance unless the required human resource management (HRM) practices are in place to form a consistent socio-technical system (Ahmad & Schroeder, 2003).

HUMAN RESOURCE MANAGEMENT IN INDIA

General

India always had a large population, and it lured invaders due its prosperity and avenues available. In fact Columbus discovered America in his drive to reach India. India from very ancient times had the concept of welfare of its workers. Evidence is available that minimum wages were implemented in this country since ages. Kautitlya's in Arthasasthra has stated that there exists a sound system of management of resources. Most experts however, list Human Resource Management development in India to 1920's. It was due difficult labour situation post World War I, emergence of Soviet Union and increase in Trade Union activities world over. Workers of a textile factory in Ahmedabad under influence of Mahatma Gandhi agreed to settle dispute in 1920 by mutual discussion.

Labour Legislations

The origin of HRM in India can be traced to the concern of the welfare factory workers during the 1920's. Royal Commission (1931) recommended the appointment of labour welfare officers to deal with evils of *'jobbery'*; *'selection'* of workers, settle their 'grievances'; to act as the spokes person of the workers and to help in amicable solution / settlements between workers and the management. These welfare officers were mainly concerned with the recruitment and welfare of workers.

Factory Act of 1948 made appointment of Welfare Officers compulsory in industrial establishments employing 500 or more workers. The Act also prescribes the qualifications and duties of welfare officers. It has been observed that the welfare officers mainly play policing role assisting the management to maintain discipline and industrial peace.

The spirit of 'Labour Welfare' is enshrined in Constitution of India. Article 43- A of the Constitution directs the state "to take steps by suitable legislation or in any other way, to secure the participation of workers in the management of undertakings, establishments and other organizations engaged in any industry."

Two professional bodies were established-

1. Indian Institute of Personnel Management at Kolkota.
2. National Institute of Labour management at Mumbai.

In 1957 Mr Vishnu Sahai Committee recommended establishment of Joint Management Council in Public Sector Undertakings on a voluntary basis with a view to improve working conditions. The 60's saw Personnel Function expand beyond welfare it started encompassing Labour Welfare, IR and personnel administration. Three major areas emerged as complimentary part of HR practice :

1. Labour Welfare
2. Industrial Relations
3. Human Resource Administration

The rapid industrialization of the country changes the perception of HRM the focus shifted to management getting professional. 70's saw shift in professional values from welfare of workers to – efficiency. During this period 20 point programme was launched by Mrs Indira Gandhi. The rapid industrialization saw a change in professional values of human resource. Workers participation at the floor and plant level was made mandatory where 500 or more workers were employed.

1980's rapid induction of new technologies and Indian economic and industrial scene changed. Human Resource Development became major issue to induct the technology and new practices. Professional bodies IIPM and NILM merged to form National Institute of Personnel Management. Government in 1983 passed a comprehensive enactment for workers participation in Central Public Sector Undertakings. It also ensures adequate representations for women if they constitute more than 10% of the total labour force.

The growing awareness of the human resource in industry saw the emergence of Human Resource Management as a separate and distinct discipline.

Impediments to the Development of HRM in India

The major impediments in development and growth of HRM in India are listed below :

1. The legal provision limits the operational functioning of Labour Officers within the preview of welfare, day to day HR functions and Industrial relations. They have both line and staff functions.
2. The attitude of workers and executives is not favourable towards HR executives. Executives especially at line perceive that HR Executives inhibits their functioning, and prevent from doing their jobs.
3. Plethora of labour laws limits the effectiveness of HR functionaries as they spend a large portion of their time and energy attending to disputes and grievances. This inhibits long term planning.
4. HR does not attract talented persons. This is primarily due low priority given to them in industry. Their work cannot be measured in monetary terms.
5. The educational institutions have failed to bring forward new techniques methodology, research for improving HR practices in the country.

Defence Against Discrimination Allegations

Discrimination law distinguishes between disparate *treatment* and disparate *impact. Disparate treatment* means intentional discrimination. It requires no more than a finding that women were intentionally treated differently because of their gender according to the courts.

Review Questions

1. Define human resource management and discuss its nature and scope ?
2. Explain what HR management is and how it relates to the management process.
3. Storey gave the idea of hard and soft human resource management, explain and contrast between hard and soft approaches to human resource management ?
4. Personnel management is a basic management function ? How is it carried out in modern establishments ?
5. Describe the scope of human resource management ?
6. Give examples of how HR management concepts and techniques can be used by all managers.
7. Discuss the 'soft' and 'hard' models of Human Resource Management ?
8. "A manager should pay adequate attention towards human relations". Explain.

Case Study

Sankalp Communications Limited

Sankalp Communication Limited is one of the top IT companies in the country. It has been operating from large number of centers located in various parts of the in the country. The average age of the employees is around 25 years and has a high attrition rate of 20 percent. The company's organization culture is on traditional values and practices. The organization is hierarchical, with well formulated rules and regulations, and a rigid structure. The Vice President, Human Resource in a review meeting identified the following issues :

- Attracting and recruiting a talented young employee.
- Retaining the employees by making the job content challenging.
- Building and sustaining the motivation level of employees.
- Providing learning opportunities
- Providing opportunities for employees excelling in their assignments.

To tackle the above issues, Vice President gave out a plan to accomplish certain actions during a period of one year. He outlined his plan as under :

(*a*) Identify the competencies required and available in the company.

(*b*) Recruitment plan to meet the competencies gap.

(*c*) Redeployment plan of present employees.

(*d*) Framing and implementing new compensation plan.

Questions :

1. *Discuss and analyze the plan of action.*
2. *Discuss the outcomes if any.*

Satyam Computers

Satyam computers is a well established and a known company. It has reputation of following a good organizational culture, follows a proactive human resource policies. The vision and mission statement of the company also categorically enunciate the corporate social responsibility of undertaking environment friendly manufacturing activities. Some of the innovative HR practices of the company are;

1. Cultural building exercises that support self-initiation, openness, honesty, improving skills and team work.
2. Performance management for ensuring deserving cases are not overlooked
3. Development of individuals and grooming them so that they take over leadership assignments.
4. Sharing of knowledge, and use of modern tools for information management.

One day the CEO of the company announced that the company was not having the funds. The issue as well publicized in the print as well as electronic media, and the company's image was tainted. The PR managers carried out extensive campaigns clarifying company's concern. The employees of the company were perplexed with the external information and started doubting the company's holy vision and mission statements and also credibility of the top management

The Government stepped in to take over the company to ensure its continuity and keep the image of the country.

Questions :

1. *Do you think that the company believes in practicing what it preaches ?*
2. *Is the HR department pro active and does it display leadership capabilities in the crisis situation ?*
3. *Do you suggest any additional steps by the HR Department to address the challenges ?*
4. *What steps should the HR department now take to reinforce 'the values based management' ?*

❑❑❑

Chapter 2

STRATEGIC HUMAN RESOURCE MANAGEMENT

★ LEARNING OBJECTIVES ★

After reading this chapter, you will be able to understand :

- Identify the advantages of integrating human resource planning and strategic planning.
- Understand how an organizations competitive environment influences strategic planning.
- Recognize the importance of internal resource analysis.
- Describe the basic tools for human resource forecasting.
- Explain the linkages between competitive strategies and human resource.
- Understand the requirements of strategy implementation.
- Recognize the methods for assessing and measuring the effectiveness of strategy.

INTRODUCTION

In the first chapter, we examined the nature and scope of human resource management; in this chapter, we shall explore an approach to human resource management labeled as *strategic human resource management*. In today's competitive and globalized business environment, it has become imperative for a company to be a leader in its field in the market or as it is popularly known as *'best in the class'*, the company requires a highly competent and dedicated workforce. The competitive advantage lies not only in product or costs differentiation but also in the organizations ability to exploit the core competencies and to rapidly respond to customer's needs and competitors' moves. It is the human resource that provides edge over its competitors and provides stability and growth by exploiting the technology by up-gradation, market feed back and research and development.

The strategic human resource management field links managerial process requiring human resource policies with strategic objectives. Strategic planning has always been there but its importance has increased due increased competition and globalization of economic forces.

Meaning

The word strategy, is derived from the Greek word 'strategus', meaning Commander-in-Chief, was first used in English language in 1656. The development and usage of word suggests that it is composed of 'stratos' meaning *'army'* and *'agein'* meaning 'to lead'. Strategy has been adopted from war by business and reflects broad overall objectives and policies of an enterprise. Strategy is the process *'to achieve an end'* or it can be said strategy is nothing but a *'course of action'* Narendar, (2007)

Glueck and **Jauch** have defined strategy in business as;

"A strategy is unified, comprehensive and integrated plan designed to ensure that the basic objectives of the enterprise and achieved."

In management context 'strategy' has now found being used for 'long term planning', to denote specific pattern of decisions and actions undertaken by the top management or the upper echelons of the organization in order to accomplish performance goals. Strategic management is a continuous process that requires constant adjustment of three major independent variables viz. values of the top/senior management, the environment and the resources available. (Figure 2.1)

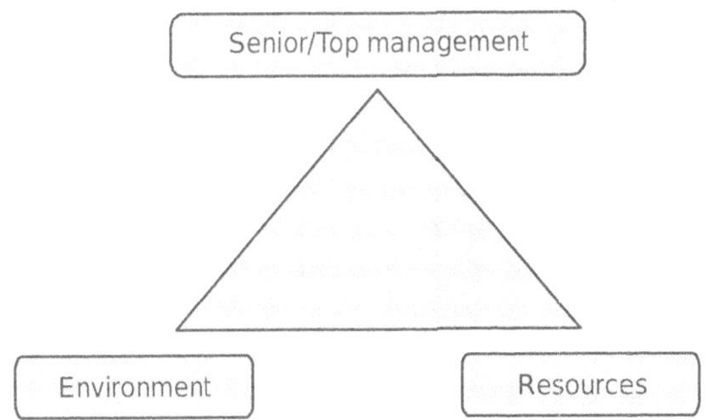

Source : *Adopted from Aktouf (1996)*

Fig. 2.1. *Poles of Strategic Plan.*

A strategic plan of an organization matches its internal strengths and weaknesses with external opportunities and threats in order to maintain a competitive advantage. The managers human resource plan must; firstly, *support corporate productivity and performance improvement effort*; secondly, *employee plays an expanded role in employers performance improvement effort*; and thirdly, *must be more involved in designing—not just executing-the company's strategic plan.*

In modern economies the emphasis is to gain competitive advantage through people, the management while formulating strategy needs input of the managers charged with hiring, training, and compensating the firm's employees. Human Resource personnel therefore must have a clear understanding of the basics of strategic planning.

The term strategic human resource management thus can be stated to mean 'formulating and executing human resource systems, methods, tools and techniques that produce the competencies and behaviour in an employee that an organization requires or may require in a future to achieve the strategic objectives. (Mathis, Robert L. and Jackson, John H.; 2003, p.29)

STRATEGY FORMULATION

The strategy is usually formulated in by carrying out environmental analysis, so as to identify opportunities and threats that are crucial for company's survival. Robert L. Mathis and John H Jackson (2003) defines Strategic Management as

That set of managerial decisions and actions that determine the long term performance of a corporation. It includes environmental scanning, strategy formulation, strategy implementation and evaluation and control. The study of strategic management, therefore, emphasizes monitoring and evaluating environmental opportunities and threats in the light of corporation's strengths and weaknesses.[1]

Strategic planning is part of the company's strategic management process. Figure 2.2 shows, strategic planning includes broad five steps. It includes determining the vision and purpose of an organization, evaluating the firm's internal and external situation, defining the business and developing a mission, translating the mission into strategic goals and crafting the strategy or a course of action.

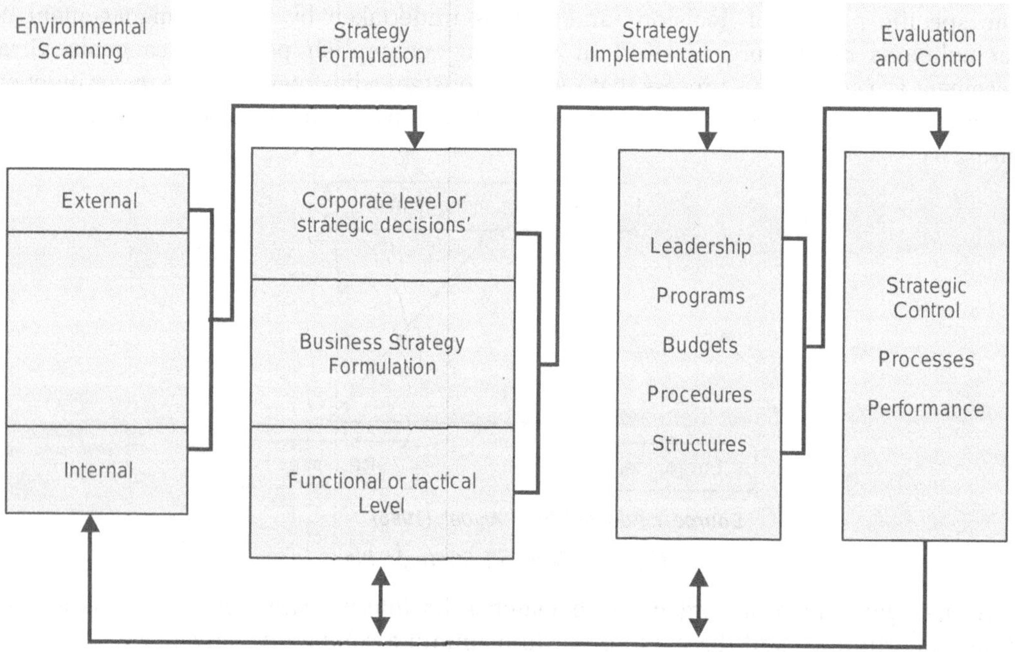

Fig. 2.2. *Strategic Management Process.*

(*a*) Determination of Vision or Purpose

The first step in strategy formulation begins with top management evaluating their positions in relation the organizations current mission and goals. The mission or purpose is the very reason for the existence of an organization. If there is no mission to be achieved, then there is no need for an organization. The vision is the binding force and serves as the motivating force for the organization. The vision or purpose is usually stated in a broad terms. A pharmaceuticals company may have a vision as to provide dependable, standard drugs to the public at a low price. Vision is a *'general statement of the intended direction that evokes emotional feelings in organization members.'* To choose a direction, a leader must first have developed a mental image of a possible and desirable future state for the organization. This image may be vague as a dream or as precise as a goal or mission statement. The vision articulates a view of realistic, credible, attractive future for the organization, a condition that is better is some important ways than what now exists. It has been observed that there are many more terms being used such as goals, objectives etc. However, it should be clearly understood that goals desired ends or objectives that are scheduled to be achieved within a particular time frame say one year and are sought through actual operating procedures of the organization and typically describe short term measurable outcomes (Daft, 2001); while mission are desired states or outcomes. Mission are stated in broad terms

(*b*) Environment Scanning

The second step in formulation of strategy is to carry out the environment analysis. It looks at the internal organizational strengths and weakness and external environment for opportunities and threats. The firm's external environment is dynamic and uncertain. The management has to systematically analyze and determine opportunities and threats to the firm in future. Through environmental analysis, the management develops an *environmental threat and opportunity profile*. The factors that are most important to the organizations future are referred to as strategic factors and can be summarized by the acronym SWOT—Strengths, Weaknesses, Opportunities and Threats. There are five factors that influence environmental scanning :

- *Social* consisting of social values, roles, trends, etc.
- *Political* including political forces, changes. The present UPA government's policy of enrolling larger number of minorities in government jobs.
- *Legal.* Rules and regulation, law of the land, court decisions, regulatory rules all influence the strategy.
- *Economic,* product, labor, capital, factor markets.
- *Technological* changes taking place and the new products which are likely to be popular.

(*c*) Organizational Analysis

In the third step the organization goes into an internal audit organizational strengths and weaknesses analyses or SWOT analysis. This involves using the SWOT chart (Figure 2.3) to compile and organize the process of identifying company's Strengths, Weaknesses, Opportunities and Threats.

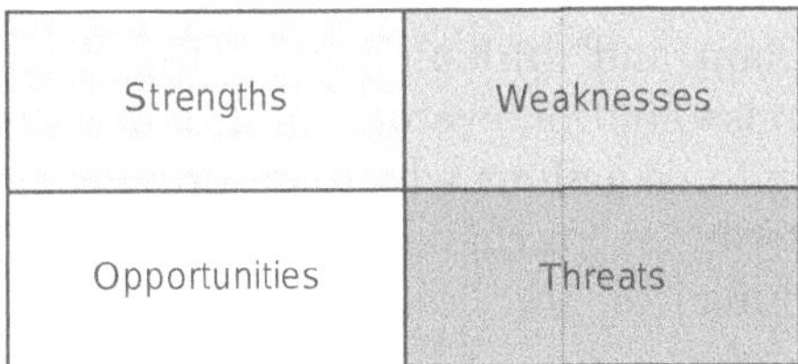

Fig. 2.3. *SWOT Chart.*

While carrying out the analysis the main factors analyzed are :

(*i*) The products of the company its spectrum.

(*ii*) The geographical extent of influence and coverage.

(*iii*) Financial strength of the company.

(*iv*) Differential advantage *i.e.,* special competitive strengths.

(*v*) Human resource strengths, talents, skills available and jobs. Bell Company in USA patents a product at the rate of two to three per three weeks. In last eight years its employees have won ten Noble Prizes.

(d) Developing Strategy

After having carried out the analysis of both external (environmental) and internal (organizational) the top management then develops the strategy to be adopted based on the varied choices or options evolved. Some strategies are formulated at the corporate, business and specific functional levels. The organizations strategy is a bridge connecting where the company is today with where it wants to be tomorrow. The question is, 'How do we get from here to there ?' A knowledge of and commitment to strategy helps employees make decisions consistent with the company's needs.

(e) Choice of Strategy

The last step in the formulation of the strategy formulation is the choice of the strategy to be adopted which suits best to the company. This term raises the question that makes the decision and why they are made (McLoughlin and Clark, 1988). This notion of choice draws the attention that this is a 'political process' where decisions are taken by a power dominant group within the organization. Child (1972, quoted in McLoughlin and Clark, 1988, p.410 affirms this interpretation :

...When incorporating strategic choice in a theory of organizations, one is recognizing the operation of an essentially political process, in which constraints and opportunities are functions of the power exercised by decision makers in the light of ideological values.

In analyzing how decision is made it is important to consider the distribution of power in an organization. Purcell and Ahlstrand (1994, p.45) state that one must consider 'where power lies, how it comes to be there, and how the outcome of competing power plays and coalitions within senior management are linked to employee relations.'

The strategic process is still not complete there are still two more steps to be taken the first is strategy implementation which involves leadership styles, the structure of the organization, allocation of resources, organizing and developing programs, the information and control systems and other business actions to implement the formulated strategy. It should be noted that leadership is the most important and difficult part of the strategic implementation process. Finally there is a need to exercise control, evaluate and redirect the strategic actions in case of any weaknesses noticed or reinforce actions which are proving successful. It is also referred to as strategy evaluation and determines to what extent the actual change and performance match the desired change and performance.

Strategic human resource management here implies aligning the management decisions about the results the management is trying to achieve with decisions about the employees or the people in the organization. It comes down to demonstrating the value of human resource management to the organization.

Managing strategy is an ongoing process. Competitors will introduce new products, innovate, and develop new processes. The customer preferences will change reducing the demands of few products while boosting the demand of few others. Strategic control keeps the company's strategy up to date. Strategic Control is *the process of assessing progress towards strategic goals and taking corrective action as needed.* Management constantly scans the strategic environment (competitors, technological breakthroughs, customer preferences, demographic preferences etc.)

LEVELS OF STRATEGY

The levels of implementation are of strategy is similar to the one followed for war. The three levels of implementation of strategy in an enterprise or an organization are the corporate, business and functional, which correspond to the three levels used in defence forces viz. strategic, operational and tactical levels (Figure 2.4).

There are three levels of strategy :
- Corporate
- Business
- Functional/tactical

Fig. 2.4. *Levels of Strategy.*

Corporate Strategy

This level describes a corporation's overall direction in terms of its overall philosophy for growth and the management of its various units it is the broad vision in outlines the company or an organization wants to achieve. It relates to organization wide policies that are used to diversify, acquire or redesign the company to maintain an edge in the market. Corporate strategy is usually based on :

- A critical factor that affects Firm Performance.
- A factor that contributes to Competitive Advantage in markets.
- Having a long-term focus.
- Plans involve the top executives and/or board of directors of the firm.
- A general framework that provides a perspective for selecting specific policies and procedures.

This level strategy addresses the question, 'What business are we in ?' While devising the strategy for multidivisional company like the Reliance, Tata's or Larson and Turbo involves at least four types of initiatives :

- Establish investment priorities and steer resources into the most promising and attractive business.
- Initiate actions to improve the combined performance.
- Improve performance by synergy between related business units.
- Make decisions dealing with restructuring, diversification, downsizing etc.

A company's corporate level strategy identifies the portfolio of businesses that, in total comprise the company and the ways in which these businesses relate to each other. A *diversification corporate strategy* implies that firm will expand by adding new product lines. A *vertical integration* strategy means the firm expands by, perhaps, producing its own raw materials, or selling its product direct. *Consolidation* is reducing the company's size and *geographic expansion* implies taking the business abroad.

The Business Level Strategy

It is the first functional step taken to achieve the over all corporate strategy. It deals with decisions and actions pertaining to each business unit, the objective being to make unit more competitive. Companies try to achieve competitive advantages for each of its business. Competitive advantage can be defined as 'any factor that allows an organization to differentiate its products or service from those of its competitors to increase their market share. It is here that the issues pertaining to product its marketing and other aspects such as coordination are done. It is at this level that decisions are made to as to how the organization will compete in a given business environment and position itself. In multi-product/diversified companies this level is also called the strategic business unit. It is allowed to make independent decisions within the overall frame work of the corporate strategy.

Porter (1980, 1985) formulated three competitive strategies; ***cost leadership***, differentiation and focus for success of business strategy (Figure 2.5). The *cost leadership strategy* attempts to increase the organizations market share by having the lowest unit cost and price compared to its competitors or aims to be a low cost leader in an industry. The second strategy advocated by Porter is the *differentiation strategy*. This strategy involves provisioning of distinctive levels of service, products quality such that customer is prepared to pay the price. In differentiation strategy the firm seeks to be unique in its industry along dimensions that are widely valued by customers/buyers. The third strategy from Porter is *focus*. In this the organization and its leadership focuses on specific group of customers or a geographic area. In this the market can be narrow or broad, as in the case of niche markets being narrow and focused.

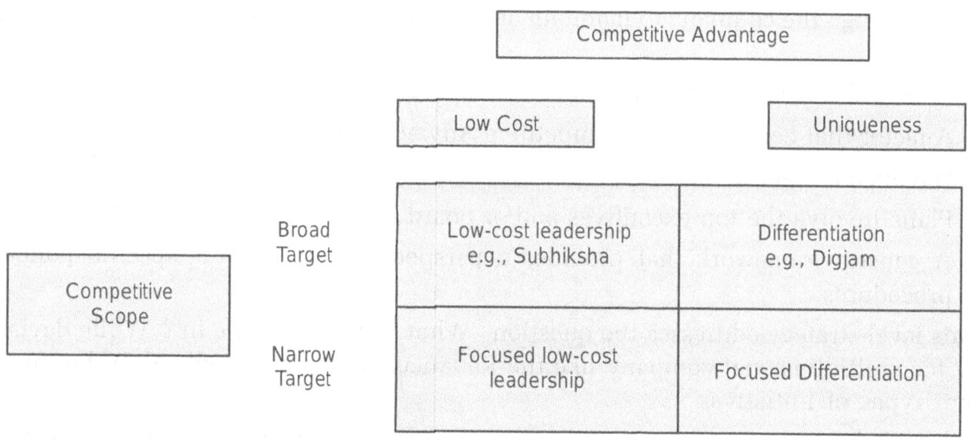

***Source** : Adapted from Porter (1985)*

Fig. 2.5. *Porters Competitive Business Strategies.*

Some of the organizations also adopt *functional strategies*. Functional strategies identify the basic courses of action that each department will pursue in order to help the business attain its competitive advantage. The firm's functional strategies should make sense in terms of its business/ competitive strategy. The "When You're on Your Own", feature illustrates a system you can use to facilitate your planning efforts.

When You're On Your Own

Using Computerized Business planning

There are several business planning software packages available to assist the small business owner in writing top-notch strategic and business plans. Business Plan Pro, from Plan Alto software contains all information and planning aids you need to create a business plan. It contains 30 sample plans, step-by-step instructions for creating each part of your plan (executive summary, market analysis and so on), financial planning spread sheets, and easy to use tables.

Business Plan Pro's wizard helps the manager of small businesses owners develop a business plan, step-by-step. The result is an integrated plan, complete with overall strategic plan, and charts, tables, and professional formatting.

Miles and Snow (1984) have identified four modes of strategic orientation viz. defenders, prospectors, analyzers and reactors. In this the *defenders* are business units or companies with limited products and the management constantly focus on improving the quality of the product and improving the efficiency of their existing operations. The prospectors are the firms with relatively broad product line and focus on product innovation and market opportunities. Reliance and Tata are two such companies. The focus of such companies emphasizes 'creativity over efficiency'. *Analyzers* are companies that operate in at least two different product areas. These have been referred as stable and variable. Here the managers emphasize efficiency in the stable areas and innovation in the variable areas. The fourth type of business strategy is referred to as *reactors*. The reactors are companies that do not have a consistent strategy –structure – culture relationship. In this the senior management does not have any coherent policy but reacts to environmental changes and pressures and thus tend to be piecemeal strategic adjustments. These different competitive strategies influence the 'downstream' functional strategies.

The Functional or Tactical Level

Functional or tactical level strategy pertains to the major functional operations within the business unit. It is the level at which daily decisions are taken and implemented and the organizational representative comes in contact with the customers. The reaction and ability of

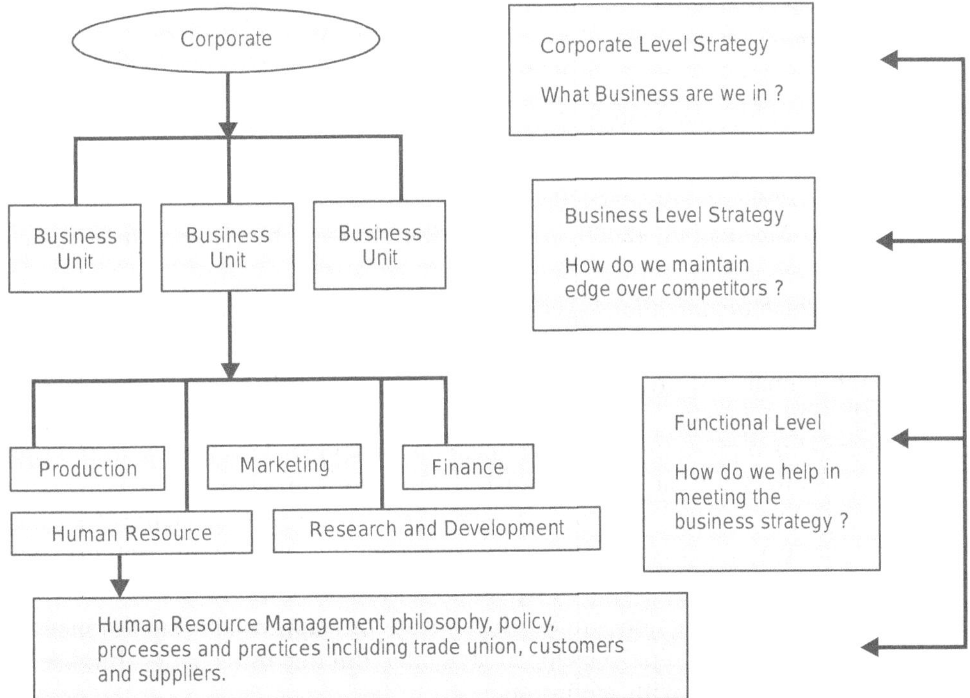

Fig. 2.6. *Hierarchy of Strategic Decision Making.*

the company's representative in meeting the customer's needs goes a long way in meeting the business strategic goals. The tactical or functional level strategy is guided by the business strategy.

These three levels of strategy form a hierarchy of strategy within large multidivisional corporations. In different firms the application of the strategy may vary between 'top-down' and 'bottom up' strategic planning. In top down approach the down stream strategic decisions are based on higher strategic decisions. In the 'bottom up approach' individuals down the hierarchy contributes to strategic planning. Mintzberg (1978) has incorporated this in his model of emergent strategies. To have the optimum results there is a need to integrate the three levels discussed above.

CONCEPTS

The strategic human resource management is rooted in 'manpower' planning, but it was the work of management gurus affirmed the importance of human employees of the organization as a source of strategic advantage. There is logic in this approach of focusing on the skills of the employees and people in the environment and treating them as intellectual assets as the technological advantage would erode quickly, but knowledge base would exist. However, some authors have also argued that by attaching strategic before human resource management the human resource departments and its practitioners are attempting to enhance their status in an organization (Bamberger and Meshoulam, 2000; Whipp, 1999).

There is no clear definition of Strategic Human Resource Management. For Snell et al., (1996, p.1996) strategic human resource management is an outcome :

"As organizational systems designed to achieve sustainable competitive advantage through people."

However, Ulrich (1997, p.89) viewed strategic human resource management as a process and stated :

'the process of linking human resource practices to business strategy'.

Bamberger and Meshoulam (2000, p.6) describe strategic human resource management as :

'A process by which organizations seek to link the human, social, and intellectual capital of their members of the strategic needs of the firm'.

Business and human resource links have also been classified on 'proactive' and 'reactive' continuum (Kydd and Oppenheim, 1990). In a proactive orientation of the firm the human resource professional is represented in all strategic formulations. The arrows on the right hand side of Figure 2.5 show the proactive type of influence both upward and downward. On the other hand the 'reactive' is depicted by one way downward arrow in Figure 2.5. In this the human resource strategy is concerned with the marching the philosophy, policies, programs, practices and processes—the 'five P's'.

Environment and its impact on strategy have been long appreciated by the managers and the firms. Bamberger and Phillips developed a model linking three poles human resource strategy and business strategy with environment.

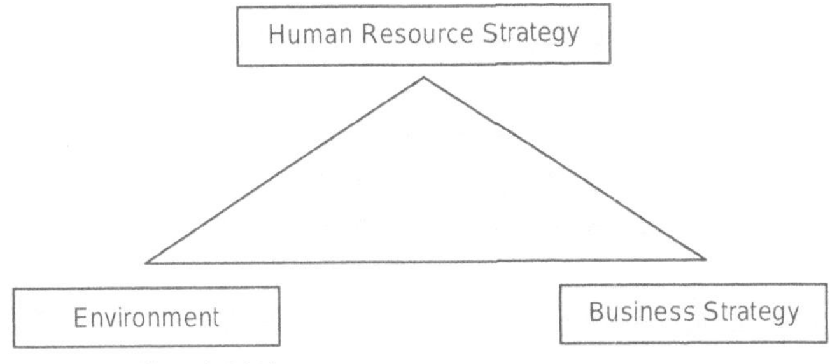

Source: *Bamberger and Philips (1991)*

Fig. 2.7. *Environment as a Mediating Influence for Human Resource Strategies.*

Purcell (1989) using the hierarchy of decisions model in firms identified what he termed as 'upstream' and 'downstream' types of strategic decisions. The 'upstream' or 'first order decisions are concerned with long term direction of the firm while the 'downstream' or the second order decisions are concerned with operational aspects. Purcell (1989, p.71) wrote :

'Strategy in human resource management is determined in the context of first order, long-run decisions on the direction and scope of the firm's activities and purpose .... And the second order decisions on the structure of the firm.'

Another part of the strategic human resource debate is focused on integration. Beer et. al.'s (1984, p.25) states that :

'Organizations' human resource policies and practices must fit with its strategy in its competitive environment and with immediate business conditions that it faces.'

This concept has three aspects :

(*a*) Linking – Human resource policy with strategic management process.

(*b*) Internally making the line managers realize the importance of human resource.

(*c*) Integrating the workforce into the organization to foster commitment with strategic goals.

Devanna et al. 's (1984) evolved a matching model. He stated that *'human resource systems and organizational structure should be managed in a way that is congruent with organizational strategy.'* In Devanna et al. model, the human resource, strategy and structure follow one and another and are influenced environment (Figure 2.8). The authors emphasize the analysis of the linkages between the two strategies and how each provides goals and constraints for other. There is a requirement of integration between competitive strategies and human resource strategy being adopted by the company. The relationship is reactive if human resource strategy is subservient to corporate strategy and marketing. Strategically speaking human resource management must flow from and be dependent upon the organization's corporate strategy. Thus for each of the Porter's competitive strategy there is a requirement of a unique set of responses from workers, or 'expected role behaviour' for which there is a need for generating specific human resource strategy.

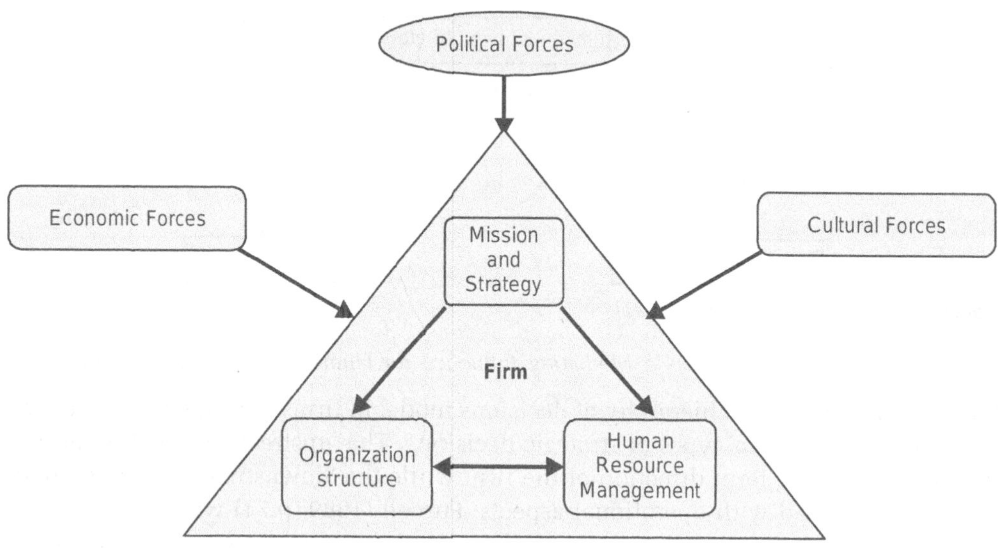

***Source** : Devanna et al. (1984)*

Fig. 2.8. *Devanna Et Al.'s Strategic Human Resource Management 'Matching' Model.*

HUMAN RESOURCE STRATEGY MODEL'S

In today's environment there are three models to differentiate the human resource strategies.

(*a*) Control based model

(*b*) Resource based model.

(*c*) Integrative Model.

Control Based Model

The first approach is based on the nature of control exercised by managers at the workplace. In this approach the human resource strategies along with organizational structure are used to control all aspects of work to secure a high level of productivity and a corresponding level of profitability. The focus is on controlling employee behaviour.

The early managers exercised direct control over the employees. However as the conditions of work changed the individual control was replaced by *bureaucratic control* and *technical control*. Bureaucratic control is exercised by using rules and procedures, while technical control is exercised through utilization of machinery's or systems. These two actions set the pace of work and behaviour at workplace.

In this approach human resource strategy will be consistent with organization's competitive strategy. Thus Porter's cost leadership strategy is unlikely to be adopted if the human resource strategy adopted by the firm is based on outcome. Here the managers would tend to adopt process based controls when means- ends relations are certain; outcome based approach when means and ends are uncertain. The management results in different organizational design and variations in human resource strategy, and results in tensions between management and employees.

The Resource Based Model

The second approach is based on reward—effort exchange. In this approach the managers view their human resources as an asset. Superior performance through workers is underscored when advanced technology and other resources are readily available to competing firms. The skills, employee's knowledge and expertise combined with social relationship provide capabilities to the firm that serve as a source of competitive advantage. In this approach distinctive competencies of workforce are exploited.

Four characteristics of resource capabilities—value, rarity, inimitability and non-substitutability are important in sustaining competitive advantage.

This approach has lately become very popular due emphasis on knowledge and work place learning (learning organizations). It is important today for managers to coordinate workers diverse knowledge and skills and integrate diverse information technology. These are strategic assets which are difficult to replicate. Hence, leadership skills become critical to harness firm's human assets (Figure 2.9).

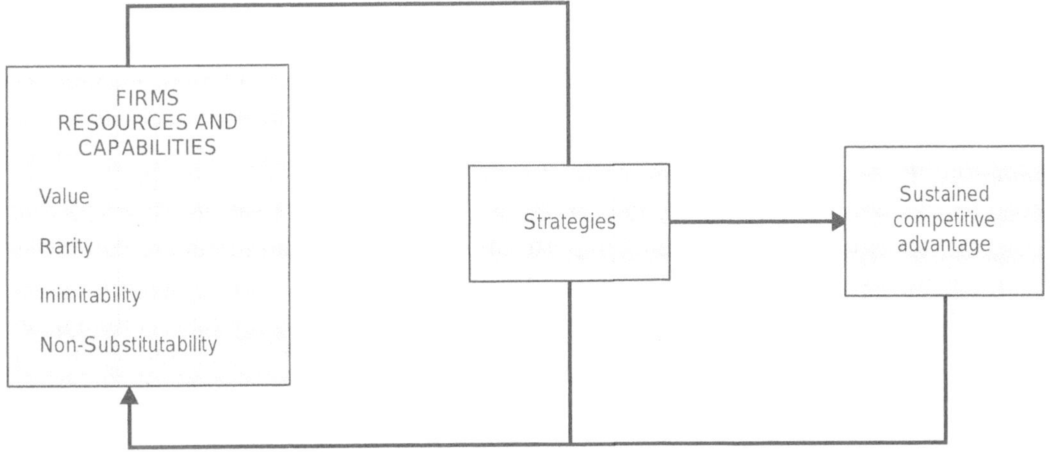

***Source** : Based on Barney (1991) and Hill and Jones (2001)*

Fig. 2.9. *Relationship between Resource, Strategies and Competitive Advantage.*

The Integrative Model

Bamberger and Meshoulam (2000) integrate the two main models of strategy, one focusing on based on managerial control and other focusing on the reward-effort exchange. They developed a model that characterized the strategy as 'acquisition and development' and the 'locus of control'.

Acquisition and development is concerned with developing internal human resources. This can be achieved by high investment in training of the employees. The locus of control deals with monitoring the employee's compliance with process based standards. This thinking results four different dominant human resource strategies :

- Commitment
- Collaborative
- Paternalistic
- Traditional

An effective organization includes a senior leadership team committed to developing more effective ways of doing business, accomplishing results, and investing in human resources. The most important element of successful management is the committed management.

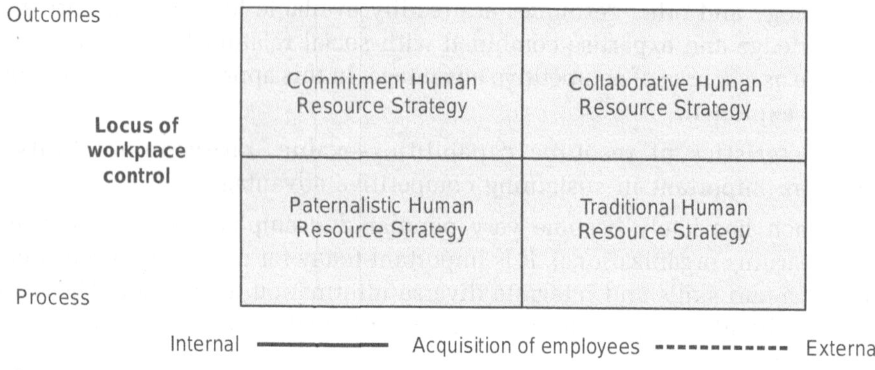

Source : *Bamberger and Meshoulam (2000)*

Fig. 2.10. *Human Resource Management Strategies.*

The *Commitment Strategy* is characterized as focusing on the internal development of employee's skills and competencies and outcome control. *Traditional human resource strategy* focuses on external recruitment of competencies and behavioural or process control. The *collaborative human resource strategy* involves subcontracting and utilization of external independent experts, and evaluates the performance based on end results. The *paternalistic human resource strategy* offers learning opportunities and internal promotion to employees for their compliance with process based control mechanism.

In most of the industry in India especially in small and medium the right bottom quadrant of traditional human resource strategy is adopted. In this managers use technology to control the uncertainty inherent in labour process and insist the workers perform the specified actions to ensure uninterrupted production. The author's experience has shown that traditional human resource strategy is also used in Business Processing Organization's and calls centers, where technical and bureaucratic control is exercised to closely monitor and evaluate their workers.

The commitment human resource strategy (top left quadrant) is utilized in work places where management is unable to monitor the worker closely (*e.g.*, service sector) or evaluate the behaviours required for executing the work. This is typical to 'knowledge workers' involved in research and development, high quality production health care etc. In this strategy the managers have to rely on workers to cope with uncertainties inherent in the process. This strategy is associated with human resource practices that aim to develop highly committed people, participative leadership style that forges a commonality of interest and mobilizes consent to the organizations goals.

DIMENSION OF STRATEGIC HUMAN MANAGEMENT

Human Resource Management and Practices

A number of studies in last decade Baker (1999), Pfeffer (1998), Hutchinson et al. (2000) have found that, in spite of the methodological challenges, human resource practices are positively associated with improved organizational performance.

Reengineering and Strategic Human Resource Management

All models of strategic human resource emphasize the importance of an organization. As stated in Chapter 1 the 'soft' human resource management is concerned with job design. The redesigning of work systems have labeled as 'high performing work system', 'business process reengineering', and 'high commitment management'. The core feature of this is the organizational design that has flattened hierarchy, decentralized decision making, use of work teams and quality circles, 'enabling' information technology, 'strong and committed' leadership and human resource practices that make workers behaviour congruent with organizations goals and culture.

Leadership and Strategic Human Resource

Leadership has been defined as a process by which an individual influences another to perform a particular task or work. Senge (1990) makes an explicit link between learning, leadership and organizational change. The key aspect for developing resource based strategic human resource model is leadership. Hammer and Champy (1993, p. 107) have in their work stated that most of the failures stem from breakdowns of leadership and the force that drives the organizational change is leadership. It should be remembered that leadership shifts the action from process control and advocates power relationship and psychological contract for accomplishment of the organizational control.

Workplace Learning and Strategic Human Resource Management

Formal and informal learning have become the key levers for managers to achieve their human resource goals of commitment, flexibility and quality. The formal and informal learning strengthens an organization's 'core competencies' and thus act to sustain competitive advantage. The ability to learn faster than one's competitors is of essence. The workplace learning also strengthens 'cultural control'; strengthen the power of those at the 'apex of the organization'. Hindustan Lever Limited utilizes this technique in its operations.

Trade Unions and Strategic Human Resource Management

High performance—high commitment model are indeed necessary for high performance work strategy has to succeed. There is a school which argues that human resource strategies which involve high commitment are designed to provide workers with a false sense of job security. There is a conflict inherent in this strategy in that the modern environment of discarding the concept of lifelong careers and job hopping by workers does not entail commitment for long with any firm.

International and Comparative Strategic Human Resource Management

The strategic human resource management process points to its international character and potentialities. The employment relationship is influenced by the local legislations and culture in which it operates. Hence, as business gets globalized variations in national systems and culture would inhibit any convergence in human resource management strategies. Hence, there is need to differentiate between international and comparative strategy.

International human resource management strategy has been defined as :

'Human resource management issues, functions and policies and practices that result from the strategic activities of multinational enterprises and that impact the international concerns and goals of those enterprises. ' (**Scullion,** 1995, p. 356)

International strategic human resource management tends to emphasize the subordination of national culture and employment practices to corporate culture and human resource management practices.

Comparative Human resource management has found place due globalization of business. It involves using of human resource management practices and cultures that have proved effective in one country can be transplanted into another. It has been revealed there is a significant difference between Indian, Asian, European, North American cultures which impact human resource strategies of these countries. It is important to appreciate those 'best' human resources practices do not have universal application since human resource practices vary based on the national culture and legislations.

CRITICAL SUCCESS FACTORS

The from above it can be deduced that there are some critical factors for success of strategic human resource management. These factors are discussed in succeeding paragraphs. These critical factors results in an approach to human resource management which fact based focused on results and mission accomplishment (Figure 2.11). It would be seen that all critical success factors reflect two principles central to the strategic human resource management :

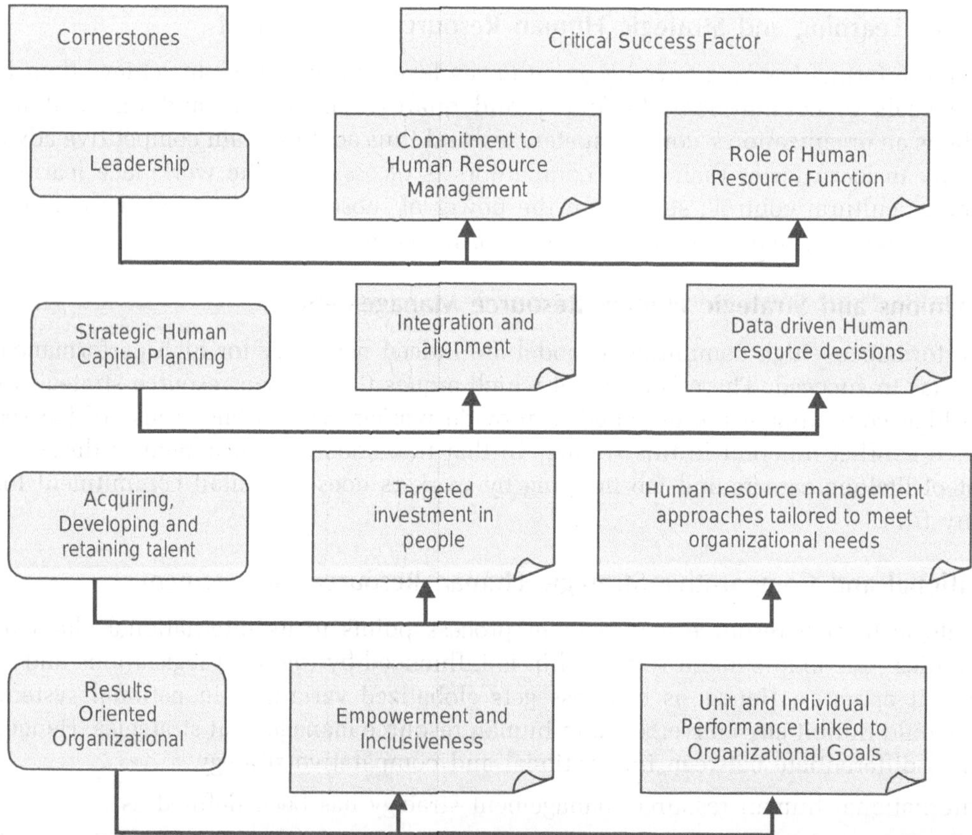

Fig. 2.11. *Critical Success Factors for Strategic Human Resource Management.*

People are assets whose value can be enhanced through investing in them. As with any investments, the goal is to maximize value while managing risks.

An organizations human capital approach should be designed, implemented, and assessed by the standard of how well they help the organization achieve results and pursue its mission.

In the modern knowledge based organizations strategic planning is quite clearly strategic human resource planning. Pfeffer (1998) asserts that there are seven human resource practices which successful organizations should employ. These are the provision of employment security, the selective hiring of new personnel, decentralized decision making, high compensation contingent on organizational performance, extensive training, minimal status distinctions and barriers, and the extensive sharing of financial and performance information throughout the firm. Several authors have expressed views of what the best practices should be in order to link them to high productivity. These are summarized in Figure 2.12.

Authors	***Focus***	***Human resource Practices***	
Arthur (1992, 1994)	American Steel Mills (1992) Manufacturing Sector (1994)	All authors contend that system needs to be combined with a commitment strategy	• Employee participation. • High wages and bonuses or incentives. • Decentralized decision making. • Comprehensive training.
Inchniowski *et al.* (1997)	Manufacturing Sector		• Careful section. • Extensive training. • Team problem solving. • Multi attribute gain sharing. • Skill based pay
Macduffie (1995)	Automotive assembly plants		• Tight hiring standards. • Intensive training. • Participation encouragement, • Information share systems, • Considerable job rotation and • Contingent compensation.
Guest (2001)	Practices should be combined to constitute high performance human resource management and how to measure them.		• Core practices for high performance—selection, training, communications and reward. • Practices reinforce staff retention and regulation of the work—life balance of employees *e.g.,* family-friendly practices.
Guest *et al.* (2004)			• Practices that discriminate between high and low employee performance : team work and training and development. • Practices related to innovation : performance appraisal is the most important, followed by job design and team working. • Employee relations : performance appraisal, keeping employees well-informed and job design.

		• Labour turnover that is affected by the two most important practices, job design and employee involvement. • Teamwork.
Guthrie *et al.* (2002)	A survey of firms using high involvement work practices in alignment with Porter's (1980) frame work	• Differentiating broad skill sets to employees in order to respond to greater levels of external change, uncertainty and employee discretion. • High involvement work practices are particularly beneficial to firms pursuing a differentiation strategy rather than to cost reducers.
Hunter (2000)	A survey to investigate the differences between manufacturing plants and retail stores.	• Total quality management • Self managed teams • Job rotation. • Job sharing. • Flexitime. Flexitime and job sharing are more likely to be adopted in the service sector.

Fig. 2.12. *Views of Authors on What Best Practices should be for Better Productivity.*

There are several practices adopted for strategic human resource management.

(*a*) *Internal career ladders.* A career system is necessary to focus individual attention on the strategic issues facing an organization over the long term. Objectives and reward system tied to short term lead to dysfunctional behaviour and goal displacement.

(*b*) *Formal training systems.* It can no longer be guaranteed that employees will arrive when selected with the requisite skills. Too much of what goes in modern organizations require specific skills. To ensure proper functioning; the employee may be required to undergo training to obtain those specific skills.

(c) Result oriented performance appraisal

(d) Employment security

(e) Employee voice or participation.

(f) Broadly defined jobs

(g) Performance based compensation.

Achieving Strategic Fit

The industrial or organizational leadership is always in a dilemma, should they simply 'fit' the capabilities to the opportunities and threats that they visualize or, should they stretch well beyond their capabilities to take advantage of an opportunity ? Michael Porter emphasizes the 'fit' point of view. He states that all of the firms must be tailored to or fit its strategy, by ensuring that firms' functional strategy supports its corporate and competitive strategies : "It's this 'fit' that breathes life into a firms strategy.

For example Deccan Airlines pursues a low cost leader strategy, and then tailors its activities to deliver low cost, convenient services on its short haul routes. It gets fast, half an hour turn around at the gates, so it can keep its planes flying longer hours than rivals, and have more departures with fewer planes. It also shuns frills like meals, assigned sets, and premium classes of service on which other full service airlines build their competitive strategies. See Figure 2.13.

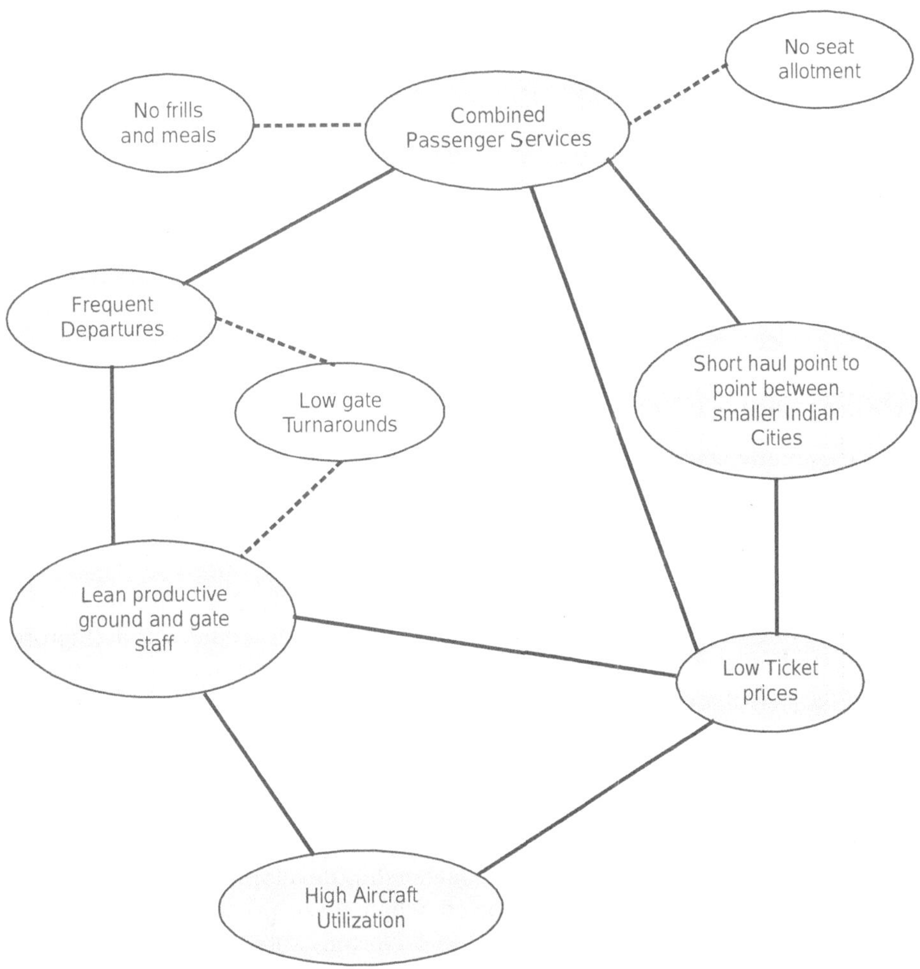

Fig. 2.13. *Deccan Airlines Activity System.*

Human Resource and Competitive Advantage

In order to be effective the company must develop competitive strategy to gain more advantages. Competitive advantage can take many forms, but it is the people and the management that makes the difference (Figure 2.14).

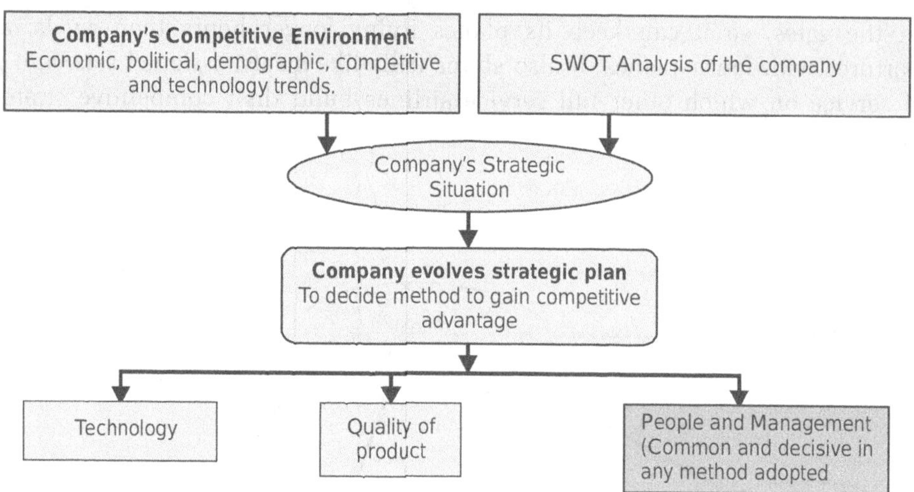

***Source** : Adapted from Gary Desseler, Human Resource Management, 10th ed. p.80*

Fig. 2.14. *Linking Corporate and Human Resource Strategies.*

Human Resource Strategic Role

The Human Resource Executive has two primary strategic roles (Figure 2.15) :

(*a*) **Advisory or Strategy Formulation Role.** The advisory or strategy formulation role of Human Resource professional is to identify the problems that are crucial to their company's strategy and forecast potential obstacles to success. These professional identify the human issues that are vital to business strategy and help establish and execute strategy. A study from University of Michigan concluded that 'high-performing companies' should have their Human Resource professional on the firms' strategic planning executive team. They conceptualize and execute organizational change.

(*b*) **Execution Function.** Strategy formulation and strategy execution are inextricably linked in closed loop process. The human resource strategy and plan to execute has to be in consonance of the company's strategic objectives. Human resource professional guides the firms in goal setting, compensation, wage structure, recruitment and placement, retraining, down sizing, personal and leadership development. Experience has shown that human capital is greatly enhanced when these processes align employees and their development to strategy (Kaplan and Norton, 2004, pp.52-63). Human resource professional also executes the function of internal strategic learning.

Strategy Formulation	***Execution***	
	Strategy Execution	***Strategic Learning***
Environmental Assessment	Communication	Benchmarking
Strategic Planning	Initiative management	Best practice sharing
Assist in Budgeting	Personal scorecards, training etc	Internal coaching and change management

Fig. 2.15. *Primary Strategic Role of Human Resource Management.*

HUMAN RESOURCE STRATEGY ORIENTED SYSTEM

Brain Becker et al. in their work *The HR Scorecard : Linking People, Strategy and Performance* has stated the Human Resource Strategy oriented process consists of three basic components viz. the Human Resource Professionals, Human Resource System to include policies and activities and the Employee Behaviour and competencies.

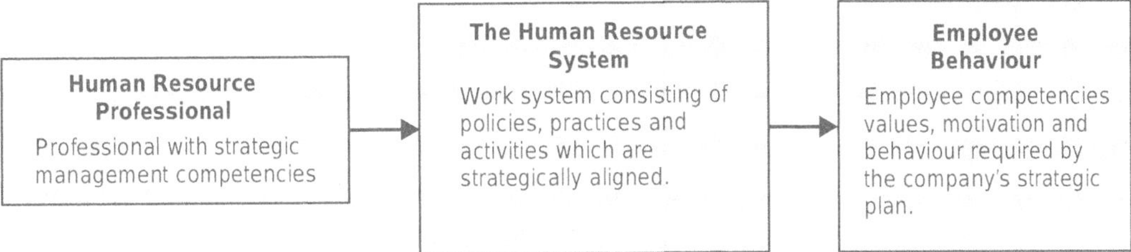

Fig. 2.16. *Human Resource Strategy Oriented System.*

The Human Resource System

In today's competitive environment the Chief Executive Officers of the company do not leave the Human Resource policies and practices to chance. The Chief Executive officers and other managers in the organization try to create high-performance work systems to maximize the competencies, commitment and abilities of the organizations employees.

Translating Strategy into Human Resource Policy and Practice

The Human Resource manager needs a way to translate the firm's new strategy into specific, actionable Human resource policies and practices. The basic process is out lined in Figure 2.17. The management formulates the *strategic plan*. The meet the objectives of the strategic plan there is a *requirement of workforce* with specific competencies, behaviours and inter personal and other skills. Thereafter the Human Resource Manager formulates the Human Resource strategy, policies and practices aimed at achieving the desired workforce. On achieving.

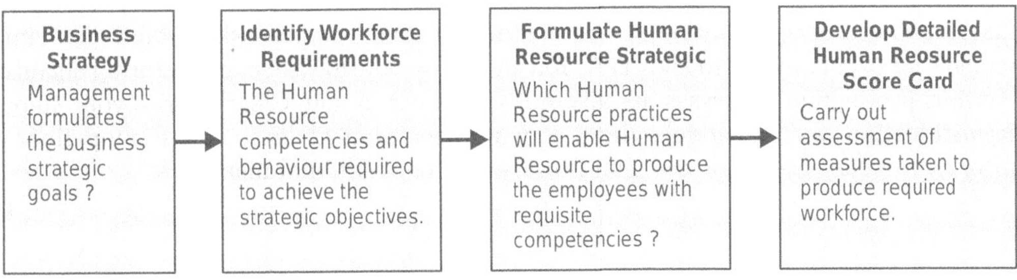

Fig. 2.17. *The Basic Human Resource Structure.*

Review Questions

1. What is meant by 'strategy' ? Explain the meaning of 'first order' and 'second- order' strategies ?

2. Explain the Purcell's statement that 'trends in corporate strategy have the potential to render the ideals of human resource management unobtainable.'
3. Business level strategies may be constrained by human resource issues but rarely seemed to be designed to influence them.' Discuss ?
4. What does a 'resource-based' strategic human resource management model of competitive advantage mean ? What are the implications of human resource management of this competitive strategy ?
5. Why is it important for a company to make its human resource into a competitive advantage ? How can HR professionals contribute to doing this ?

PROJECT WORK

Visit the nearest plant in your city. Find out its vision and goals? Deleimine has this vision is being implemented in human resource planning? Present it in the class.

Case Study

MANAGEMENT PLANNING IN A PLANT

Human resources of an organization are among the most challenging inputs to manage because people are much more complex than machines. Organization's must recognize this aspect and carryout an analysis of its futuristic needs. Work goals should be clear.

A well thought out futuristic needs of skills help in job design, as also meet the social needs of individuals, and their technical capabilities.

Purcell (1989), hierarchy model, Beer et. al's (1984) integrative approach emphasize the need of integration. Every manager understands the importance of integration for future sustenance, hence, he must endeavour to project the technical needs, for production, which incorporates much of the psychological knowledge into a working system that blends both social and technical components.

Assume that your organization, a manufacturer of steel bars, has asked you to do manpower requirements for expanding its 10 lakh TPA. You are totally new to steel manufacturing organization. Even various production processes are also not very clear to you. Clearly write your steps with proper justification and tentatively draw a manpower plan at least at the shop floor level, assuming unit makes use of convenional furnace and conventional machines.

❑❑❑

Chapter 3

HUMAN RESOURCE PLANNING

★ LEARNING OBJECTIVES ★

After reading this chapter, you will be able to understand :

- Understand the Nature and Importance of HR Planning.
- Objectives of human resource planning
- Purpose and scope of human resource planning
- Identify and describe the factors affecting personnel planning.
- Identify the employee planning process, delineate different stages in the process and describe each step.
- Identify prerequisites for successful planning and list the various barriers which render planning ineffective.

INTRODUCTION

Human resource strategy has been defined in Chapter 2 and states that it is the pattern of planned human resource *deployments* and activities intended to enable the organization to achieve its goals. Human Resource Planning is the first component of human resource management strategy and is all about the deployment of the human resources (capital) where it is called for in the organization. All other functional human resource activities are derived from and flow out of the human resource planning process. It has its basics in consideration of future human resource requirements in light of present human resources capabilities and capacities. Human resource plan is a systematic process of matching the interests, skills and talents of individual community members or employees of an organization with long term goals and economic / business opportunities in the community and organization. Human resource planning is proactive and anticipates and prepares flexible response to changing human resources requirements. Matching the requirements of the job with the individual is important at all stages, including the recruitment procedures, in this endeavour. Human resource plan facilitates the realization; it has both an internal and external focus.

WHAT IS HUMAN RESOURCE PLANNING ?

E.W. Vetter viewed human resource planning as 'a process by which an organization should move from its current manpower position to its desired manpower position. Through planning management strives to have the right number and the right trend kind of people at the right place at the right time, doing things which result in both the organization and the individual receiving maximum long term benefit.'

Manpower or human resource planning aims at ascertaining the manpower needs of the organization both in right number and kind. Human resource planning is a futuristic form of assessment. In human resource planning assessment is made of future requirements, organizational objectives, production schedules and demand fluctuations. The human resource planning is an integral part of the overall corporate strategy.

Wickstorm has stated that human resource planning consists of series of activities :

(*a*) Forecasting future human resource requirements.

(*b*) Making an inventory of present human resource and assessing the extent to which these resource have been optimally employed.

(*c*) Anticipate human resource problems by comparing the present resource with the future requirements; and determine it adequacy both qualitatively and quantitatively.

(*d*) Planning the necessary program for selection, training and development, utilization, transfer, promotion, motivation and compensation.

FACTORS UNDERLYING INCREASED INTEREST IN HUMAN RESOURCE PLANNING

There are many factors that account for the increased attention directed to human resource planning, but environmental forces-globalization, new technologies, economic conditions, and changing work force seem particularly potent. These factors are creating uncertainty for organization. Formal planning is one of the most common used tactics by organizations to reduce uncertainty especially environmental.

The changing characteristic of the work force is one environmental characteristic that make planning important. The booming economy of India has resulted in extensive new employment. The proportion of younger people in the work force is on the increase. There is a rapid rise of both husband's and wives working. The mix of labour force is also changing. There is changing demographics and need for increased number of highly skilled labour. These changes will mean fewer quality new entrants, thus increasing competition among employers. The changing demographics bring with it the changes in skills, abilities, interests and values of tomorrow's work force. Shortages of many types of skilled workers are imminent. Figure 3.1 depicts the major factors both external and internal affecting human resource planning.

The values of work force are changing. There is already evidence of job hopping, no loyalty, and no desire for life long careers and even resistance to relocation. Reduction in loyalty and dedication to employers makes it more difficult for organizations to assume they can move employees around anywhere and anytime. At the same time the employees are feeling insecure about their employment.

External Factors	Internal Factors
Government Policies Level of Economics Development Business Environment Levels of Technology Natural Factors International Factors Internal Factors	Policies and Strategies of Company Human Resource Planning of Company Formal and Informal Groups Job Analysis Type and Quality of Information Trade Unions

Fig. 3.1. *Factors Affecting Human Resource Planning.*

The above can be summarized as under :

(*a*) **Employment situation.** There is abundance of educated manpower available in the market but they lack adequate skills and knowledge.

(*b*) **Technological change.** The wide changes in production technology, marketing methods and management techniques are having a profound impact on the context and content of the jobs. These changes are have a direct impact on redundancy, retraining and redeployment of the workforce.

(*c*) **Demographic changes.** The profile of workforce in India has totally changed in terms of the age group the gender, education and skills.

(*d*) **Legislative controls.** There has been large number of laws enacted for the working class. The International Labour Organization and other agencies are watchdogs on the working conditions of the employees. This has resulted in greater awareness of the employees of their rights. These enactments also do not allow employing easily as also firing them. Managers have to look ahead and foresee manpower problems.

(*e*) **Pressure groups.** Trade Unions and other pressure groups put pressure on management for recruitment, promotion, etc.

DEFINITION

Human resource planning is a process by which the management of an organization determines its future human resource requirements and how the existing human resources can be effectively utilized to fulfill these requirements. In the process of human resource planning, the management strives to have the appropriate number and appropriate kind of people at the appropriate place. It involves matching the appropriate kind of people at appropriate place and at appropriate time. It is a system of matching the supply of existing people with openings or opportunities the organizational expectation over given period of time. T.L. Leap and Michael D. Crino (1990) have defined human resource planning as :

'... Includes the estimation of how many qualified people are necessary to carry out the assigned activities, how many people will be available, and what, if anything, must be done to ensure that personnel supply equals personnel demand at the appropriate point in the future.'

David A. Decenzo and **Stephen P Robbins** (1989) states :

"Specifically, human resource planning is the process by which an organization ensures that it has right number and kind of people, at the right place, at the right time, capable of effectively and efficiently completing those tasks that will help the organization achieve its overall objectives. Human resource planning translates the organization's objectives and plans into the number of workers needed to meet those objectives. Without a clear-cut planning, estimation of an organization's human resource need is reduced to mere guess work."

Coleman defined human resource planning as :

"the process of determining human resource requirements and the means of meeting those requirements in order to carry out the integrated plan of the organization."

PURPOSE AND SCOPE OF HUMAN RESOURCE PLANNING

Effective planning enables management to craft its own future, at least to some degree, rather than merely reacting to external events without a coherent motivating force for corporate actions. Management sets objectives and charts a course of action so as to be proactive rather than reactive to the dynamics of the business environment. The assumption, of course, is that through its continuous guidance management can enhance the future state of the business. The basic purpose of human resource plan is to have accurate information of the number of employees required with the matching skills to meet the organizational goals.

The objectives of human resource planning could be summarized as :

(*a*) Ensure optimum utilization of existing human resources.

(*b*) Forecasting human resource requirements including assessing or forecasting future skill requirements for the accomplishment of the organizations overall objective.

(*c*) Effective management of change to cope with changes in market condition, technology products and government regulations in an effective way.

(*d*) To provide control measure to ensure availability of necessary human resources when required.

(*e*) Human resource planning is required for realizing organizational goals.

(*f*) To control cost of human resource.

(*g*) To formulate transfer and promotion policy.

The scope of human resource planning can be deduced from Leon C. Megginson statement in which he states that :

'Human resource planning is an integrated approach to performing the planning aspect of the personnel function in order to have sufficient supply of adequately developed and motivated people to perform the duties and tasks required to meet organizational objectives and satisfy the individual needs and goals of organizational members.'

The scope thus could be :

(*a*) Analyzing the current human resource with the organization.

(*b*) Assessing the utilization of current manpower.

(*c*) Reduction/ downsizing of manpower.

(*d*) Analyzing the requirement of manpower in view of expansion, retirement and skill up-gradation in the light of company strategy and technological changes.

(*e*) Making plans to attract and procure manpower.

(*f*) Designing training programme.

(*g*) Evolving policies to retain manpower.

NEED AND IMPORTANCE OF HUMAN RESOURCE PLANNING

The benefits of human resource planning two fold.

(*a*) To participate in the decision process by providing information and opinion on each option. This forms part of the information collated from the organization as a whole including :

- redundancy of recruitment costs;
- Consequences on morale.
- Redeployment/ outplacement of opportunities.
- Availability of skilled staff in the organization.
- Availability of suitable people in the market.
- Time constraints.
- Development and training schedule needs,
- Management requirements.

(*b*) To support the managers dealing with the people consequences of implementing the decision. Information gathered forms the basis of human resource plan.

The systematic manpower planning is an important tool of human resource management and provides the benefits such as :

- It helps in reduced labour costs as it helps in anticipating the requirement of manpower and the types of skills required by each employee.
- It helps in anticipating imbalances in manpower by the way of shortages and surpluses.
- It is a better basis for planning training and development by identifying skill gaps. The training programmes can be made more effective.
- Leads to improvement in business planning process.
- Helps in formulating managerial succession plan.
- It serves as a tool to evaluate the effect of alternative manpower actions and policies.

KEY ASPECTS OF HUMAN RESOURCE PLANNING

A human resource plan is a systematic and part of conscious planned process rather than something that happens almost by accident. It is a continuing process and does not stop as the environment and personnel behaviour constantly change; so does technology and market demands.

It is both short term and long term with emphasis on the need to plan for longer term for survival and growth of the enterprise. For optimum benefit the human resource plan should be fully integrated with corporate planning process. Resource requirement need to be assessed in both qualitative and quantitative terms. The level of resources will depend on what can be afforded but the quantum should be at the level required for organizational effectiveness.

Stainer recommends nine strategies for human resource planners :

1. Collect, maintain and interpret information. The information must be relevant and one that impinges on the ability of the enterprise to employ human resource strategies.
2. Should report periodically human resource objectives and requirements. Analyze the skills with existing employees.
3. Should develop techniques and procedures to determine the different types human skills and abilities required over a period of time to meet organizational goals.
4. Develop measures for utilization of human resources available as component of forecasts of human resources requirements along with validation.
5. Adopt techniques leading to more effective utilization of human resource by effective allocation of work.
6. Conduct research to determine factors hampering effective contribution of individual and groups to the organization with a view to modifying or removing these handicaps.
7. Develop and employ methods of economic assessment of human resources to reflect its features as income generators. Costs the human resource accordingly to improve decision process and decisions affecting it.
8. Should periodically evaluate the procurement, promotion and retention of employees.
9. Analyze the dynamic process of recruitment, promotion, and loss to the organization of human resources. Thereafter, take action to control the attrition with a view to maximizing the individual and group performance without involving high costs.

Human resource planning is carried out at all levels commencing from government which looks after the national level planning to home, society and an individual. The human resource planning in a business system is shown in Figure 3.2.

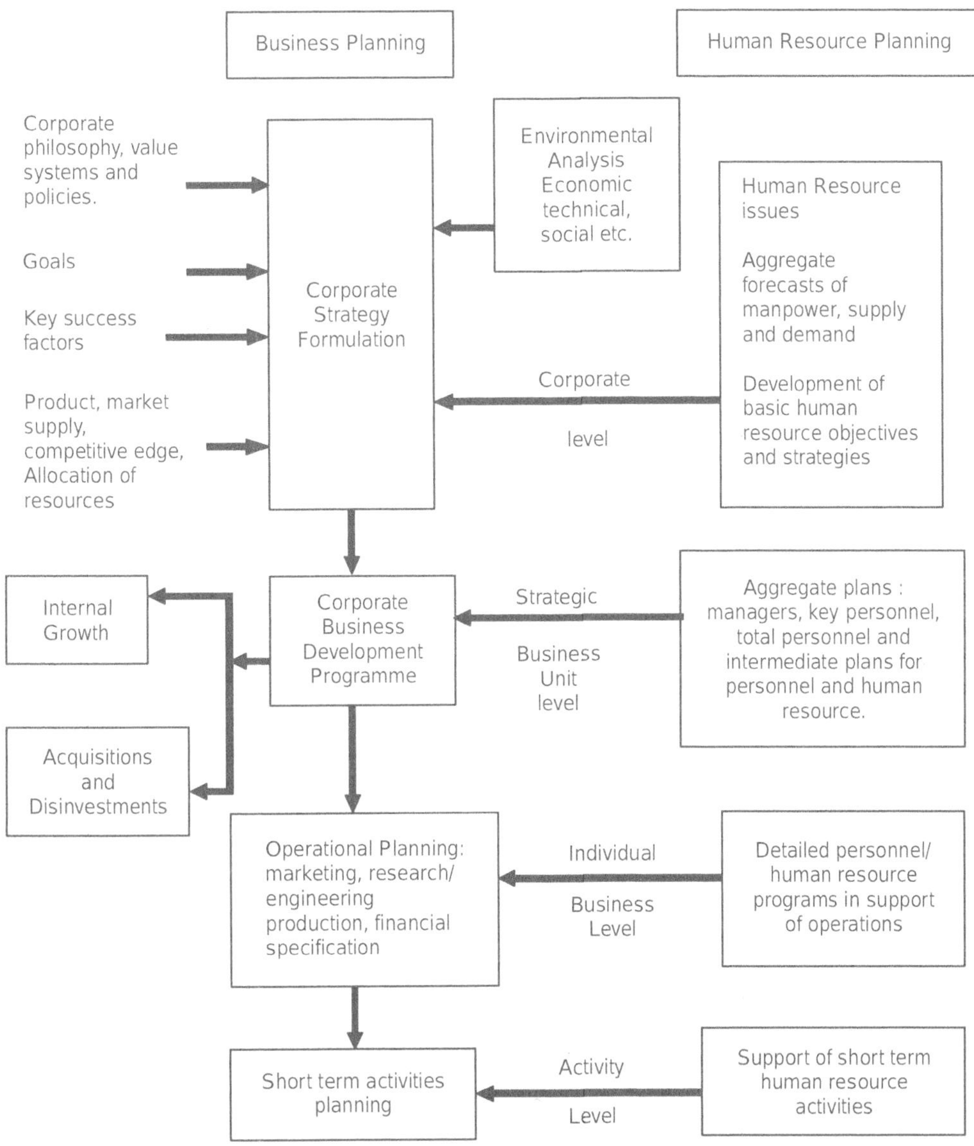

Fig. 3.2. *Human Resource Planning in Business System.*

PHASES OF HUMAN RESOURCE PLANNING

There are four phases of human resource planning :

(*a*) Gathering and analyzing data to forecast expected human resource demand, given plans of the future and to forecast future human resource supply.

(*b*) Establishing human resource objectives

(*c*) Designing and implementing programs that will enable the organization to achieve its human resource objectives;

(*d*) Monitoring and evaluating these programs.

The activities of human resource planning are conducted in three time horizons :

(*a*) Short term—a time horizon of up to one year. It is usually divided into two :
- Operational Planning—Usually cover a period up to a year.
- Activities Planning—Day to day and week to week plans

(*b*) Intermediate term—time horizon of one to three years

(*c*) Long term—a time horizon of more than three to five years. Also popularly known as the strategic plan.

These time plan correspond to typical time horizons for business planning. For success of planning all the activities associated with different time horizons are integrated and carried out simultaneously. The business plan as envisaged is linked to human resource planning process. (Figure 3.3).

Planning Level and Horizon	Business Planning Process	Link	Human Resource Planning Process
Long Term/ Strategic Plan (5 years or more)	Involves corporate philosophy, value systems, policies, goals and objectives. It takes into consideration the key success factors such as product mix, market scope etc. Endeavour's to retain competitive edge. Allocates resources.	Issue Analysis	Analyzes the issue raised by external factors and environment. Raises employment demand projection. Carries out analysis of existing human resources and projects the demands.
Intermediate Range (3–5 years)	Evolves programmes to implement strategic plan. Carries out organizational evaluation and evolves a organizational structure. Deploys the resources for optimum utilization. Acquisitions, divestments and internal development of product line.	Programming Requirmeents	Forecasting total level of staff and their skills requirements. Forecasting total number of managers and other key personnel. Forecasting changes in managers and other key personnel.
Short Range (*a*) Operational Planning (up to a year)	Detail programs specifying actions, responsibilities and costs, time schedules and other organizational aspects including profitability.	Integrated control requirements	Detailing of personnel. Human resource activities that are required to fulfill one year business plan.
Short Range (*b*) Activities Planning	Day to day and week to work schedule plans. These are decentralized and are carried out at floor or department levels.	Implementation actions	Personnel assigned specific tasks in support of the objective and plans for Personnel/human resource departments.

Source *: Adapted from Klatt, Murdick, and Schuster.*

Fig. 3.3. *Linking Business Planning and Human Resource Planning*

STEPS IN THE PLANNING PROCESS

The planning process is directly related to organizational considerations, management style, maturity of the organization, and employee professionalism. These factors vary among industries and even among similar companies. Yet all management, when applying a scientific method to planning, perform similar steps. The time spent on each step will vary by company. Completion of each step, however, is prerequisite to successful planning. The main steps are :

- Conducting a self-audit to determine capabilities and unique qualities
- Evaluating the business environment for possible risks and rewards
- Setting objectives that give direction
- Establishing goals that quantify objectives and time-frames
- Forecasting market conditions that affect goals and objectives
- Stating actions and resources needed to accomplish goals
- Evaluating proposed actions and selecting the most appropriate
- Instituting procedures to control the implementation and execution of the plan

The human resource process follows the strategic plan mentioned above. The process commences when a firm or an organization carries out self assessment/ audit. There is a need for solid understanding of the organizational priorities and the business planning cycle. Then the human resource plan is aligned with business goals. This carried out by asking the question :

- What are the key commitment and priorities of the concern ? Including any new commitment made ?
- What are the departments' current and long term business priorities ?

Manpower planning is a continuous process as shown in Figure 3.4. The manager responsible for human resource planning essentially involves forecasting personnel needs, assessing personnel supply and matching demand-supply factors through personnel-related programmes. *Demand* refers to the number and characteristics (*e.g.*, skills, capabilities, abilities, pay levels, experience etc.) of people needed for a particular job at a given point of time and at a particular place. *Supply* in human resource refers to both the numbers and characteristics of people available for those particular jobs.

Environmental scanning is the phase which is carried out immediately after the business plan is made. Manager's carryout out assessment of several factors but essentially analysis is done of economic factors, regional conditions impinging on the employment scenario, legal, technological, demographic, political and social conditions. After carrying out environmental scanning the planner establishes the objectives based on business strategy. A.F. Sikula states that 'the ultimate purpose of manpower planning is to relate future human resources to future enterprise need so as to maximize the future return on investment in human resources.' The planner thereafter carries out analysis of current manpower inventory. Analysis involves determining the function, occupation, levels of skills or qualifications required to fill each positions. Projection for manpower requirements of managers and supervisors is complex because required talent is not available at short notice.

The planner thereafter carries out demand forecasting. The demand forecasting techniques are discussed subsequently in this chapter. The major factors considered in demand forecasting are the employment trends (determined by analyzing the past trends of each group and departments); replacement needs (based on trends in retirement, sickness etc), productivity, growth needs, absenteeism etc. The planner thereafter carries out the analysis of availability of personnel to fill the vacancies anticipated. This is carried out by tapping both internal and external sources. The internal source of supply is determined carrying out internal human resource audit. This facilitates redeployment and redundancy of employees to optimize performance.

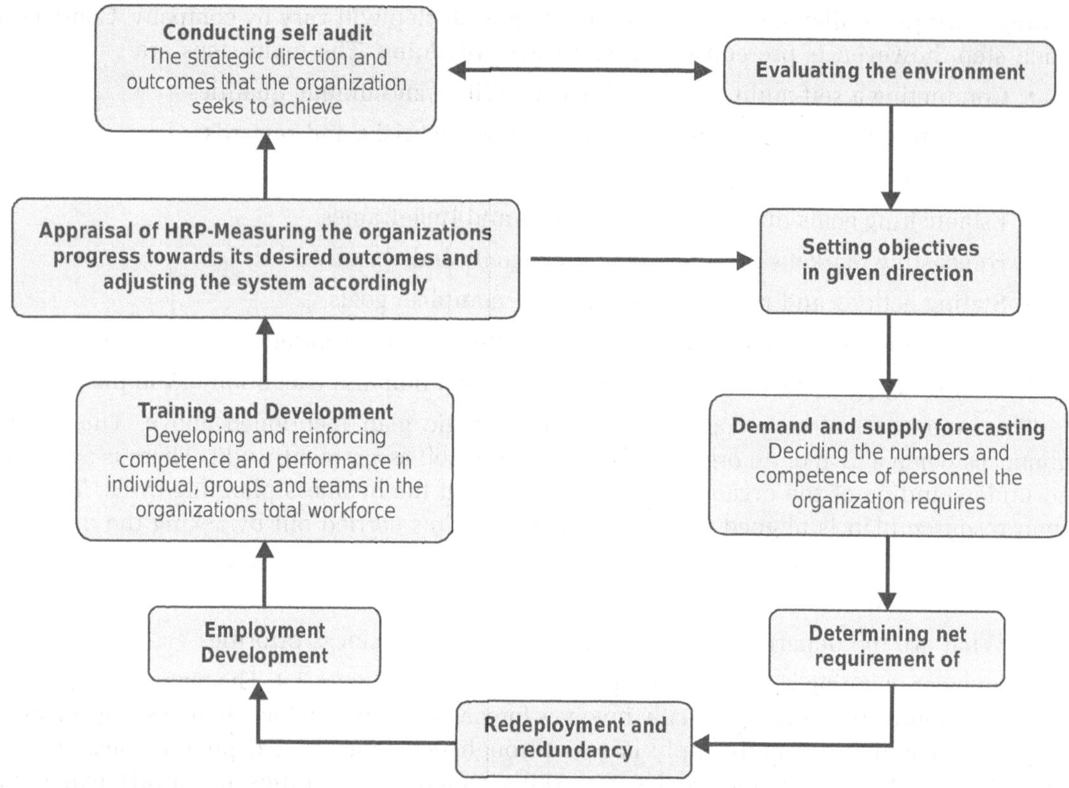

Fig. 3.4. *Human Resource Process.*

The planner then determines the total requirements and creates an employment programme to attract and recruit personnel from external environment. At the same time the planner also carries out planning for training of personnel employed to improve their skills to ensure availability of personnel from within the organization.

Time Horizon

Personnel planning are affected by time horizon. Burack and Mathis (1987) have stated that time span of plans depends upon the uncertainty prevailing in the organization. Plans for companies operating in unstable conditions like the Information Technology are for short period. Plans for stable environmental conditions are usually term plan. It can safely be deduced that greater the uncertainty, shorter is the plan's time horizon and vice versa. Figure 3.5 summarizes the degree of uncertainty and length of the plan period.

Short Planning Period-Uncertainty/ Instability	***Long Planning Period - Certainty/ Stability***
Many new competitors Rapid changes in social and economic conditions	Strong competitive position Evolutionary rather than rapid social, political and technological change.
Unstable product/ service demand patterns Small organizational size, poor management practices (crisis management)	Stable demand patterns Strong management practices.

Source : *Elmer H. Burack and Nicholas J. Mathis, (1987). Human Resource Planning- A Pragmatic Approach to manpower Staffing and Development, Illinois : Brace -Park Press, p. 129.*

Fig. 3.5. *Degree of Uncertainty and Length of Plan Period.*

Type and Quality of Information

The information used in carrying out analysis and forecast personnel needs is received from multitude of sources. The planner decides on the quality and type of information that must be used by him for making his decision and forecasts. Table 3.6 illustrates the type of information useful to personnel planners.

Strategic Information	General Organizational Information	Specific Information Necessary for Human Resource Planning
Product Mix Customer Mix Competitive emphasis Geographic limits of market	Organizational Structure Informal flows Operational and Capital Budgets Functional area Objectives Production schedules Distribution Channels Sales territories Production Processes Level of technology Planning Horizons.	J ob Analysis Skills Inventories Management Inventories Available training and development programmes. Recruitment Sources Labour market Analysis Compensation programme Constitutional provisions and labour laws Retirement Plans Turnvoer Data

Fig. 3.6. *Degree of Uncertainty and the Length of Planning Period.*

APPROACHES TO HUMAN RESOURCE PLANNING

The Two Approaches of human resource planning are quantitative and qualitative.

The Quantitative Approach

Quantitative approach is concerned with determining the number of employees required in a future period of time. The quantitative approach sees employees as numerical entities and groups them according to age, sex, experience, skills, qualification, job level, pay, performance rating or some other means of classification. The focus is on forecasting human resource shortages, surpluses and career blockages; its aim is to reconcile the supply and demand for human resources given the organization's objectives.

The quantitative aspects of human resource planning involve demand forecasting and supply forecasting. The approach uses statistical and mathematical techniques. Quantitative forecasting includes trend projection, econometric modeling and multiple predictive techniques.

Demand Forecasting

Demand forecasting involves predicting the number and types of people the organization will need at some future point of time. There are two general approaches to demand forecasting judgmental and statistical. Using a statistical approach, an organization predicts its needed workforce size on the basis of certain business factors. A business factor is an attribute of the business, such as sales volume or market share, which closely relates to the size of the needed workforce. For example, a hospital could use the business factor of projected patient load to predict the number of nurses it would need at some point in time. Techniques of human resource demand forecasting are given in Figure 3.7.

A statistical approach to demand forecasting typically is used when an organization operates in a stable environment, where an appropriate business factor can be predicted with some degree of certainty. For example, a statistical approach may be appropriate for a hospital located in an area with little population growth. Organizations operating in less stable environments (*e.g.*, a hospital in an area experiencing explosive growth and change) are more likely to rely on a judgmental approach.

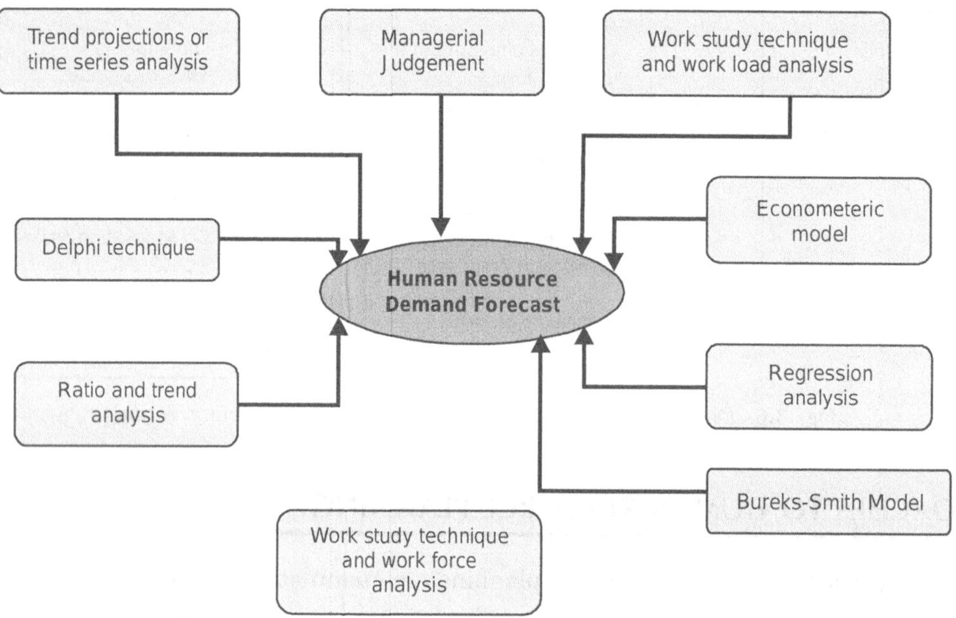

Fig. 3.7. *Techniques of Human Resource Demand Forecasting.*

Trend Projections or Time Series Analysis

Trend analysis is based on the assumption that the future can be extrapolated from the past. Trend projection or time series analysis predictions work by projecting trends of the past and present into the future. This technique is based on the assumption that the future will be a continuation of the past.Trend analysis incorporates certain business factors that include units produced, revenues etc. In a manufacturing company, the sales budget would be translated into a manufacturing plan giving the number and types of products to be made in each period.

In the labour demand, changes can be forecasted by forecasting changes in the business plan and productivity ratio. This trend includes :

(*a*) Determine the appropriate business factor that relates to the size of the workforce.

(*b*) Identify the historical record in relation to the size of the workforce.

(*c*) Calculate productivity ratio (average output per worker per year).

(*d*) Determine the trend.

(*e*) Make necessary adjustments in the trend, past and future.

(*f*) Project to the target year.

If the trend analysis is to be successful, there must be critical use of the appropriate business factor.

Managerial Judgment

The most typical method of forecasting used in smaller companies or those who do not have access to work study data, is managerial judgment. In this process mangers think about the future workloads and decide how many people they need. The process may be 'bottom up' with line managers submitting proposals for approval by the top management.

The 'top down' approach can be used in which forecasts are prepared by top management possibly acting on advice from personnel and organization and methods departments. These forecasts are then analysed and agreed with departmental heads.

The best way to use managerial judgment is to adopt both 'top down' and bottom up' approaches, guidelines are issued to all about future activity levels. The targets are established. Then departments and managers prepare their forecasts and then these are reconciled and final report prepared. This approach is sometimes also referred to as 'right angled method'.

Work Study Technique or Work Load Analysis

Work study technique can be used when it is possible to apply work measurement to know how long operations should take and the amount of labour required. Under this process the total workload of each department is estimated on the basis of sales forecasts, work schedules, growth rates, expansion plans, etc. Then these are translated into work performance for the various departments of the enterprise. The departmental workloads are converted into man-hours in terms of different skills required. Work load analysis is used to determine how many employees of various types are required to achieve total production targets.

Illustration

A factory manufacturing toys manufactures plans to manufacture 1,00, 000 units during the year 2007-08. The standard man-hours required to complete a unit of the product is 10 hours. The past experience reveals on an average a worker contributes 2,500 hours per year. The total work load may be calculated as under :

(*a*) Production budget for the year	- 100000
(*b*) Standard man-hours required per unit	- 10 hours
(*c*) Planned man-hours for the year ($a \times b$)	- $100000 \times 10 = 10{,}00{,}000$
(*d*) Man-hours contributed by one worker	- 2500
(*e*) Total number of worker required (c/d)	- $1000000/2500 = 400$

Thus 400 workers are required to manufacture 1,00,000 toys. But this figure cannot be relied upon fully as the actual production is influenced by many others factors such as availability of inputs, power, breakdown of machinery, lock out etc.

Work Force Analysis

All the existing workers are not likely to be available for work throughout the year, due to absenteeism and turnover. It is therefore, necessary to make provision for loss of current manpower due to these factors. Both these factors operate to reduce the numbers of workers available. Therefore, it is essential to do work force analysis in the light of these major problems. Aon the basis of past experience factory may estimate that there are 5 percent of employees absent themselves everyday, and on an average another 5% may be lost during the year due resignations, retirements and other causes. Thus the actual numbers of workers required are :

$$400 + 400 \times 5/100 + 420 \times 5/100 = 441$$

Such analysis will require detailed study of the past trends, behaviour, performance pattern.

Statistical Technique

The earlier techniques provide only a rough approximation of the number of employees required and are suitable only for short range demand forecasting. Long range personnel forecasting is more amenable to statistical or mathematical techniques. The most commonly used statistical methods of demand forecasting are trend, ratio, and regression analysis. Byars and Rue give time series on staffing levels, personal ratios and productivity ratios. In trend analysis, the future demand for human resources is projected on the basis of past business trends regarding a business factor.

Ratio and Trend Analysis

Ratio analysis is the process of determining future human resource demand by computing an exact ratio between the specific business factor and the number of employees needed. The main emphasis is on the ratios which are calculated for the past data relating to number of employees for each category, of production, sales, and activity levels. It thus provides a more precise estimate than trend analysis. For instance, the demand for professors at a university could be forecast on the basis of the student-faculty ratio. Suppose that a university has 10,000 students and 500 professors; the student-faculty ratio is thus 10,000 : 500 or 20 : 1. This ratio means that for every 20 students, the university needs 1 professor. If the university anticipates a student enrollment increase of 1,000 for next year, it would need to hire 50 new professors. This is in addition to any hiring needed to fill vacancies from existing faculty who might leave in the meantime.

Econometric Modeling

Econometric modeling and multiple predictive techniques involve building complex computer models to simulate future events based on probabilities and multiple assumptions. In order to build an econometric model, it is necessary to analyse past statistical data and to describe the relationship between a numbers of variables in a mathematical formula. The independent variables affecting human resource requirements are the investment, production, sales etc. and the dependent variable would then be the number of employees. The formula could then be applied to forecast movements in these variables to determine and produce a manpower forecast.

Regression Analysis

Regression analysis is similar to both trend and ratio analyses in that forecasts are based on the relationship between a business factor and workforce size. However, this method is more statistically sophisticated. Using statistical software, the analyst first creates a scatter diagram depicting the relationship between the business factor and workforce size. The software can then calculate a regression line, which cuts right through the center of the points on the scatter diagram. (The regression line is mathematically determined using a formula found in most statistical texts.) By inspecting values along the regression line, one can see how many employees are needed at each value of the business factor. Both ratio analysis and regression analysis are aspects of human resource management systems packages, and therefore provide the business with the capabilities to calculate more accurate and timely forecasts.

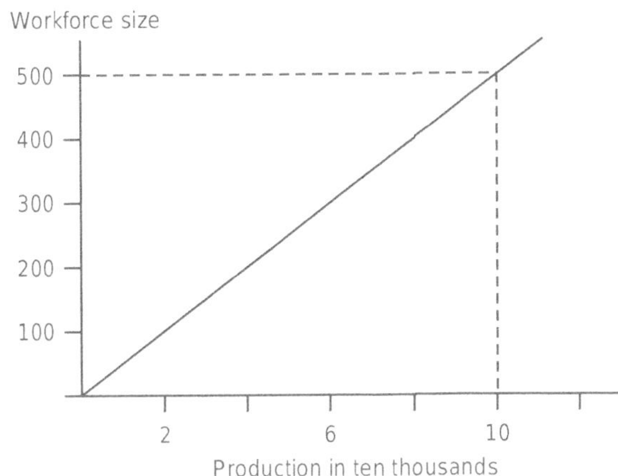

Fig. 3.8. *Regression Line Depicting Relationship between Production Volume and Workforce Size.*

Productivity Ratios

In this historical data is used to examine past levels of a productivity index (P). A systematic relationship is determined between productivity and number of personnel employed. Human resource requirements are then computed by deriving a predicted work load.

$$\textbf{Productivity Index P} = \frac{\textbf{Work Load}}{\textbf{Number of People}}$$

Bureks-Smith Model

Elmer H Burkes and Robert D Smith (1977, p.128), evolved a mathematical model for personnel forecasting based on selected key variables that affect the organizations overall human resources.

$$E_n = \frac{(\text{Lagg} + G)\ 1/X}{Y}$$

Where E_n is the estimated level of demand of personnel, in a planning period of '*n*' years.

Lagg is the variable *e.g.*, current level of production, aggregate level of current business, overall turnover etc.

G is the anticipated growth in business activity anticipated through the period of n years.

X is the productivity improvement anticipated from today through planning period of *n* years. (*e.g.*, if X = 1.91 it means the average productivity improvement of 91 percent).

Y is conversion figure relating today's overall activity to personnel required.

The main purpose of this model is to predict En, the level of personnel necessary in n period. Prior to applying this model, estimates of *G*, *x* and *y* must be made. Such estimates may be based on the previous experiences of management, as well as on future strategic choices to which the organization decision makers are committed (Terry l. Leap and Michael D. Crino, 1990, p.166).

QUALITATIVE APPROACH

The qualitative approach to human resource planning uses expert opinion (usually a line manager) to predict the future (for example, the marketing manager will be asked to estimate the future personnel requirements for the marketing department). The focus is on evaluations of employee performance and capacity for promotion as well as management and career development. The phenomenon of determining the nature of job together with minimum acceptable qualities on the part of personnel required for adequate performance of job is caked the job analysis. Edward B. Flippo (1984, p.113) states that *'job analysis is the process of studying and collecting information relating to the operation and responsibilities of a specific job.'* With the help of the facts and information obtained two statements are prepared viz. job description and job specification. These would be discussed in detail in Chapter 4 of this book.

Qualitative forecasting includes Delphi Technique and Nominal Group technique.

Delphi Technique

A refinement on this basic approach is the Delphi technique : a panel of experts such as key line managers makes independent anonymous predictions in answer to questions relating to human resource planning. A panel of 'experts' each make their own judgments of what staffing demand will be in the applicable areas, along with the reasons for their judgments. Then each member of the panel is shown usually in a presentation what the other experts guessed, and why. The responses are analysed by the human resource department and the confidential results are fed back to the experts along with another series of questions. The managers revise their original estimates in light of this new information. This process is repeated until a consensus forecast is obtained.

They are then allowed to revise their own judgments based on the others. This continues until most experts roughly agree on the estimates. The technique can be standardized by using network computers to give their preference and opinions. Its main advantage is that it is quite futuristic and includes future plans. It has however some major disadvantages viz. it is very time consuming and it is subjective and sometimes may not include past data (Figure 3.9).

Nominal Group Technique

Nominal group technique is similar to Delphi technique. The main difference lies in that the experts join in a conference and have face-to-face interactions, discussions and share their opinions. All the opinions of the members are presented either on a big screen or boards so that these can be freely and immediately be ranked so as to arrive at a consensus. The advantages are that it facilitates group thinking and exchange of ideas. This technique has on major disadvantage that it is also prone to subjectivity.

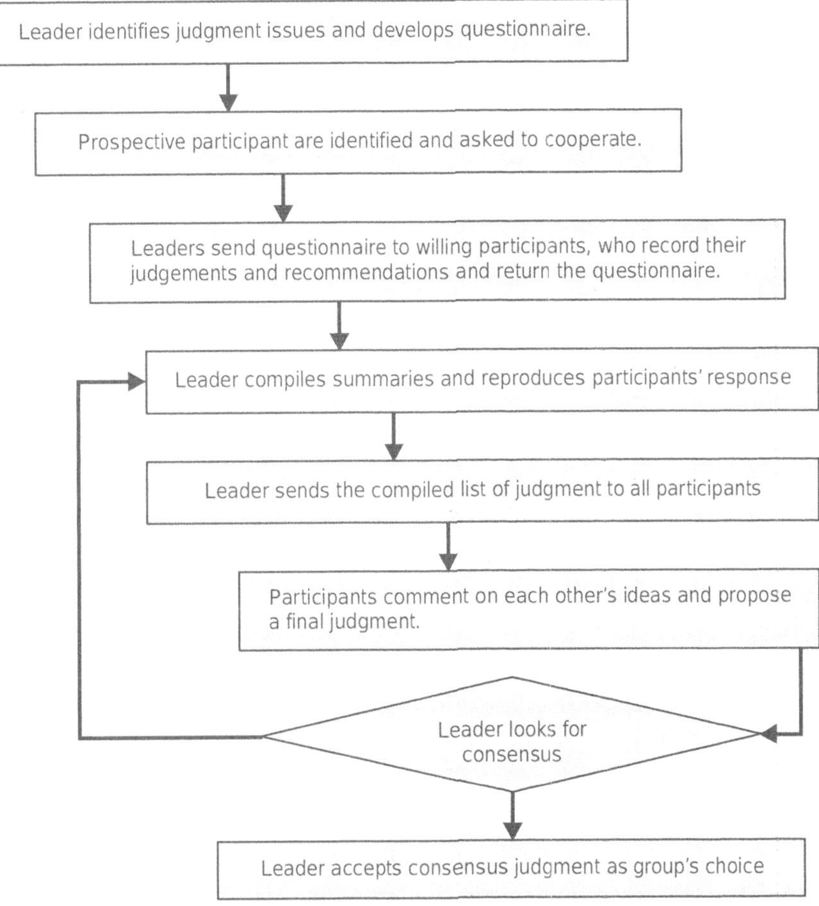

Fig. 3.9. *The Delphi Technique.*

HUMAN RESOURCE SUPPLY FORECASTING

The demand analysis has given the quantum of and type of personnel required over a period of time. The next step for the management is to determine whether it will be able to procure the required number of personnel and the sources for such procurement. Supply forecasting is concerned with the estimate of supply of manpower given the analysis of current resources and future availability. Supply forecasting measure the number of people likely to be available from within and outside the organization, after making allowance for absenteeism, internal movements, wastage and other conditions of work (Michael Armstrong, *A Handbook of Personnel Management Practice*, 3rd ed. Kogan Page. p.210)

- The supply forecasting benefits the organization by :
- Determining number of people and positions expected to be available in future to help the organization realize its plans and meet its objectives.
- Determine staff mixes that will exist in future.
- Assess and evaluate existing staff levels in different parts of the organization.

- Helps in ensuring there is no shortage of people where and when they are most needed.
- Ensure legal compliance.

Here the personnel planner must consider both external and internal supply. External supply of personnel is important because :

(*a*) The normal separation due retirement, death and discharge.

(*b*) Meet the organizational growth and requirements.

The internal supply is influenced due :

(*a*) Potential changes due promotion transfer etc.

(*b*) Effect of changing conditions of work.

(*c*) Potential losses due wastage and loss.

(*d*) Availability of skills.

There are three steps in assessing supply capability, viz. :

- Assess what human capabilities currently exist in the organization to fulfill needs.
- In light of this, assess how adequately the current workforce supplies needs (is there a shortage or surplus of the right kind of staff based on forecasted demand ?)
- Therefore, assess what changes need to be made to perfect the HR supply (strategic staffing goals and plans—do we hire/downsize/relocate/etc.)

The step looks at current people and skills. There are several readily available information sources within the organization that make it possible to do this. These include :

- *Skills inventory*. It is a register of current human resources capabilities, incorporating information on each employees' skills, demographics, test scores etc.
- *Management inventory*. It is similar to skills inventory, but tailored to management, often including subjective assessments of ability etc.

Markov Analysis. Markov analysis is concerned with analyzing current behaviour of some variables so that the future behaviour of the variable can be predicted. The analysis is widely used to for solving operational research problems under uncertainty. The importance of this technique lies because most of the real life systems or actual systems have randomness and uncertainty as inherent in them, though it may vary in extent. The physical systems like an enterprise, an industry or an organization there is randomness. A Markov analysis uses historical flow rates of workforce to predict future rates. Data are collected and reviewed for number of years in order to estimate the likelihood that persons in a particular job will remain in that job or be transferred, promoted, retired etc. Remember that we are looking at the current internal supply, not external labour market supply. Thus, the organization uses its own internal workforce movements as a proxy for future movements.

Transitional Matrices. Are historical flows of personnel transitions through the organization are represented by probabilities ? The probabilities are arranged in a 'transition matrix' and future personnel flows are estimated on the basis of the matrix.

Replacement Planning. Replacement plans are short term replacement schedules that plot who can replace whom within the organizational hierarchy. This is mostly utilized if the replacement is needed quickly. This method is useful in predicting internal supply, especially as regards managerial positions.

Succession Planning. Succession plans take a long term career development approach. They effectively 'earmark' employees for development through the hierarchy. Thus, they show something of the more long-term internal supply situation. Succession planning is the process that is used by planners to convert personnel information about current employees into decisions about future internal job placements. Succession planning is usually limited to key employees and top executive positions. A firm by carrying out succession planning ensures that key jobs are not left unattended and important vacancies are filled as these arise. Succession planning has a direct impact on the morale and performance of the employees. It assists an individual to have a career in the organization. It also helps in identifying skills deficiencies before the vacancies arise. A proper succession planning ensures greater continuity, better qualified individuals and more unified and dynamic organizational culture (Figure 3.10).

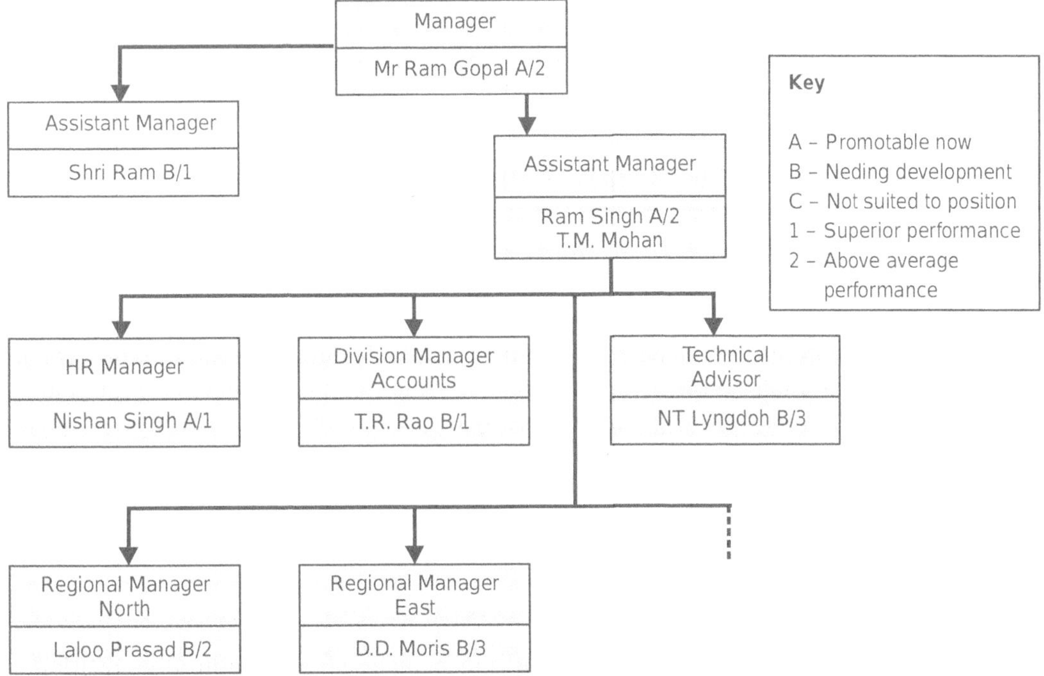

Fig. 3.10. *Succession Planning.*

Vacancy Analysis. Vacancy analysis is essentially Markov analysis based on judgment instead of history.

Benchmarking. Benchmarking is a very different approach. It involves proactively comparing human resource in your organisation to those of your competitors. In this way, one can ascertain especially the quality of your internal supply as opposed to the quantity.

Best Practices Benchmarking. Similar to the plain benchmarking, but in this case the comparison is with successful human resource practices in any organization. In other words, the organization seeks out excellence in the staffing of other organizations, and thus assesses its own internal supply. For example, you may assess an organisation known for its extreme efficiency in production lines. You note that they have combined man and machinery to require half the workers that you need for the same job. You may then make plans to follow suit.

Simulation. This technique is based on Markov analysis, the simulation technique considers alternative flows which are examined for effects on future manpower supplies. Alternative flows reflect the anticipated results of policy or programme changes concerning voluntary an involuntary turnover, retirement, promotion etc. Mathematical models are used in computer and simultaneously used in extrapolation, indexation and survey results, to compute future human resource demands.

Goal Programming. This concept is relatively new in that it was developed in late 1960's by Charnes Cooper and Lee. This technique is useful when multiple goals of an organization are conflicting, goal programming is extremely useful. In this technique the planner tends to optimize goals employing operational research techniques. The goals to be optimized are the desired staffing level. In this technique all goals of the management are considered as the objective function and only business environment constraints are treated as constraints. Goals are set to be satisfied to the best fit solution 'as close as possible' level and not for optimal or best fit solution. It must be noted that goal programming aims at satisfaction of the goals set by the management or decision makers. Exact achievement of the objective is not aimed. The technique attempts to so in order of priority of the objectives again decided by the management.

This first step in assessing supply thus gives us only an indication on internal capabilities. These then need to be compared to need, which is discussed next.

ASSESSING ADEQUACY OF CURRENT STAFF

Once the current or future workforce capabilities and demands have been assessed then these are matched to determine the requirement. The planner responsible for ensure availability of personnel should classify the employees by function, occupation, level of skills and status to optimize goals. Effort should be made to review the current resources available cutting across organizational and occupational boundaries to provide inventories of skills and potential. It is important to have the analysis of the present employees. This can be done by frequent human resource audit summarizing each employee's skills and abilities. The audits of non managers are called 'inventories' and those of managerial staff is called the 'management inventory'. The summary gives the planner a comprehensive understanding of the capabilities found in the organizations workforce (William B. Werther and Keith Davis, (1993), p.176).

Skills Inventory

Skills inventories consolidate information about non managerial staff in an organization. This information is used as an input for internal movement within an organization. Normally the information available in such inventories includes :

(*a*) Personal data.

(*b*) Education and Skills

(*c*) Special qualifications and abilities

(*d*) Job History

(*e*) Individual preferences and goals.

Skills inventories have become popular with the introduction of computers for maintaining personnel data. This is popularly called the human resource information service and would be discussed later in the book. A popularly designed and updated skills inventory system permits management to readily identify employees with particular skills in order to satisfy the changing needs of the company.

Management Inventories

Management inventories consolidate information about managerial staff in an organization. This information is used as an input for internal movement within an organization. Normally the information available in such inventories includes :

(*a*) Work history
(*b*) Strengths and weaknesses
(*c*) Potential
(*d*) Career Goals
(*e*) Personal Data
(*f*) Budget managed and experience
(*g*) Previous management duties.

Internal Supply

After the human resource planner has conducted a internal audit of human resource he proceeds to carry out analysis of internal supply. The techniques used are (*i*) labour wastage; (*ii*) labour stability index; (*iii*) length of service analysis; (*iv*) conditions of service analysis; (*v*) productivity level; (*vi*) internal movement.

Labour Wastage

Labour wastage should be analyzed in order to forecast future losses and to identify the reasons for people leaving the organization. Efforts should be made to determine unnecessary losses and remedial actions should be undertaken to minimize the losses.

Labour turnover index. It is the traditional method of determining the losses of manpower.

$$\frac{\text{Number of personnel who left the company in specified period}}{\text{Average number of employee during the same period}} \times 100$$

This method is in common use because it is easy to calculate and to understand. This formula has one limitation in that the figure of turnover can get inflated due high turnover of relatively small proportion of labour force. A company employing 1000 workers may have an annual turnover index of 20 meaning that 200 jobs become vacant during the year. It could mean that 200 employees leave the company. These 200 could be spread throughout the company or it could also be that one of the department is losing 20 employees at a time and this process was repeated ten times during the year. These are different situations and need to be analysed and appreciated or else wrong deductions could be made.

Labour Stability Index

This determines the tendency for longer service employees remaining with the company, and therefore, shows the degree to which continuity of employment. It is considered as an improvement on the labour turnover index.

$$\frac{\text{Number of employees with one year's service or more}}{\text{Number of employees one year ago}} \times 100$$

The disadvantage of the labour stability index may be partly overcome if an analysis is also made of the average length of service of people who leave. This index also gives the index of labour turnover. In this process each service category can be compared with the numbers leaving with numbers employed. If, for example, the total number employed with less than six months service was 100 and the total more than three years was 100, the proportion of leavers in each category would be respectively 50 percent and 10 percent. Figures which are better for analysis and can reveal many trends.

Conditions of Work and Absenteeism

Changes of conditions of work such as normal weekly working hours, overtime policies, the length and timing of holidays, retirement policy, the policy for employing part-timers, shift system need to be analyzed.

Absenteeism is understood as unauthorized absence from work. Absenteeism is calculated thus :

$$\frac{\text{Number of persons} - \text{days lost}}{\text{Average number of persons} \times \text{number of working days}} \times 100$$

Absenteeism obviously reduces the number of employees available for work. If the absenteeism is 5 percent then only 95 employee out of 100 are available. The effect of absenteeism on production and inurn on future supply of labour should be allowed for, and trends in absenteeism should be analysed to trace causes and remedial actions taken.

ESTIMATING FUTURE HUMAN RESOURCE NEEDS

Combining the results of the supply and demand forecasts within each job group derives specific staffing needs. For example, consider a firm that currently employs twenty-five secretaries. As the result of its supply forecast, the firm predicts that five of these secretarial positions will become vacant by the end of the planning period because of retirements, promotions, and so forth. Its demand forecast predicts that three new secretarial positions will be needed during the coming period because of an increased demand for the company's product. By combining these two estimates, the firm now realizes that it must hire eight new secretaries (five to replace those expected to vacate their positions, plus three to fill the newly created positions).

OUTCOMES OF THE HUMAN RESOURCE PLANNING PROCESS

When the human resource planning process is completed, a firm must establish and implement human resource management practices in order to meet its human resource needs. Following is a brief overview of how human resource management practices can help organizations to deal with anticipated oversupplies and undersupplies of personnel.

The trend toward organizational restructuring usually results in a smaller workforce. Therefore, when an organization's strategic plan calls for restructuring, the human resource management response usually is one of downsizing. Downsizing usually results in layoffs. Because of the negative outcomes that are often associated with layoffs, employers are encouraged to seek alternatives, such as hiring freezes, early retirements, restricted overtime, job sharing, and pay reductions.

If the results of demand and supply forecasting project an undersupply of personnel at some future point in time, the organization must decide how to resolve this problem. The solution may involve hiring additional staff, but there are other options. When human resource plans indicate an undersupply of employees, firms can recruit personnel to staff jobs with anticipated vacancies. Human resource management systems packages provide employers with capabilities to carry out recruitment in all of its steps. The first step is to conduct a job analysis to determine the qualifications needed for each vacant job.

The next step is to determine where and how to recruit the needed individuals. For instance, a company must decide whether to fill its vacancies externally (*i.e.*, from the external labor market) or internally (*i.e.*, from its own current workforce). When recruiting externally, an organization should first assess its attractiveness in the eyes of potential applicants; unattractive employers may have trouble generating a sufficiently large applicant pool. Such employers should attempt to increase the number of people who are attracted to the organization and thus interested in applying for a job there. This may be accomplished by increasing starting pay levels and/or improving benefit packages. Another option is to target certain protected groups whose members may be underemployed in the local labor market, such as older, disabled, or foreign-born individuals.

Internal recruitment efforts can be improved through the use of career development programs. When designing such a program, the organization should collect work history and skill level information on each of its employees. Such information would include age, education level, training, special skills (*e.g.*, foreign language spoken), and promotion record, and should be stored on a computer. This employee information allows the organization to identify current employees who are qualified to assume jobs with greater responsibility levels. For instance, in departments where skilled managers are in short supply, a management replacement chart can be prepared that lists present managers, proposes likely replacements, and gives an estimate of when the replacement candidate will be trained and available to fill an open position.

Instead of hiring new workers to meet increasing demands, an organization may decide to improve the productivity of the existing workforce through additional training. Other options include the use of overtime, additional shifts, job reassignments, and temporary workers. Another option is to improve retention rates. When this aim is met, firms will have fewer job vacancies to fill.

Retention rates can be improved at the outset of the employer/employee relationship, when applicants are first recruited. Retention rates are likely to improve when applicants are given a realistic preview of what their jobs would actually be like (warts and all), rather than an overly glowing one.

Workers want to feel valued and needed by their organization. In a climate characterized by mergers, acquisitions, and layoffs, many workers feel very insecure about their jobs. Employees with such feelings often begin shopping around for other jobs. These fears can be eased by implementing HR plans for training and cross-training. Such plans allow workers to perform a variety of functions, thus ensuring that they have the necessary skills to continue making contributions to the firm. Management training also is crucial in this regard. Organizations must train managers to be good supervisors. Poor "people management" is a primary cause of voluntary turnover. Managers at all levels should know what is expected of them, in terms of managing people instead of just managing budgets.

Companies also can improve retention rates by creating a work environment that encourages employees to participate actively in the company's total welfare. Workers want recognition for their contributions to organizational progress, but this recognition must be tailored to the workers' individual needs. While some workers may be motivated by monetary rewards, others seek recognition by peers and managers, feelings of accomplishment, or job satisfaction.

Workers now demand more flexible schedules to best fit their lifestyles. Organizations can improve retention rates by implementing programs to accommodate these needs, such as job sharing, shortened workweeks, and telecommuting via computer and modem.

Finally, companies also can improve retention rates by offering attractive benefit packages, such as generous retirement plans, stock ownership, health and dental insurance, and employee discount programs. Many firms are now offering "cafeteria plan" benefit packages, which are tailored to the specific needs of each of their employees.

Outsourcing is another method the company may employ to meet its personnel needs. Several organizations outsource part of their work to outside parties. The outsourcing could be either in the form of sub-contracting or even ancillarisation. Outsourcing is being done by both the private and public sector.

BENEFITS OF HUMAN RESOURCE PLANNING

Manpower planning is an important tool in the hand of management to accomplish the organizational goals and objectives. Human resource planning assists the management;

(*a*) It checks the corporate plan as it carries out assessment of the environment for the availability of the personnel with necessary skills to implement the plan.

(*b*) The human resource plan offsets any uncertainty that may be lurking in the mind of the management as to the efficacy of the business plan and strategy.

(*c*) Human resource planning assists in employee development that is designed to make optimum use of workers skills within the organization.

(*d*) It helps management to foresee changes in values, aptitude and attitude of the workforce.

(*e*) Assists in identifying gaps in the existing workforce and evolves measure to overcome the same.

(*f*) Maintain the costs of workforce by anticipating salaries and other benefits.

(*g*) Ensure law of the land is enforced and no legal issues are raised.

Limitations of Human Resource Planning

The human resource planning like all planning has its own limitations.

(*a*) Problem of accuracy. The workforce behaviour is linked to many factors and it is next to impossible to predict it in future terms. Changing trends as being observed today have brought in a revolutionary shift in work plans.

(*b*) Lack of Understanding of the rationale of Planning. It has been observed that mangers and planners do not fully understand the rationale or purpose of human resource planning especially in India where there is a large labour force available in the market although may not posses the necessary skills.

(*c*) Insufficient Support from the Hierarchy. Usually the human resourced planners are not given the type of support required for implementing the human resource plan. It is mandatory for the success of the plan that the top management directly gets involved to ensure success of planning. In the long run the human resource are the key for success of the company and are its key capital which needs to properly harnessed and maintained.

HUMAN RESOURCE UTILIZATION

Last phase of human resource planning involves efficient utilization of organizations' existing human resources. Effective utilization of human resources is determined by :

(*a*) Human resources in an organization are placed in a manner that to ensure optimum allocation.

(*b*) Human resource utilization involves achieving optimum and efficient utilization to optimize productivity.

There are two methods for assessing human resource utilization.

(*a*) *Manning Ratio*. It is based on the relationship between the number of people employed in an organization and a specified amount/number of productivity. The manning ratio helps in identifying the extent of problem in production due manpower problems; however, it does not pinpoint the cause of underutilization or poor productivity.

(*b*) *Work Study Method*. By this method the planners carryout detailed observation and collect data on the method of operations/functioning to ascertain how the employees spend their time during work hours.

The study of manpower utilization helps in optimum utilization as three vital questions are answered.

(*a*) Is the organization structure suitable and most efficient ?

(*b*) Have the job requirements being met ?

(*c*) What are the numbers of personnel required to carryout the functions.

All the three factors stated above are within the preview of the management and can be fulfilled to get the best from the 4 employees.

Human Resource Planning Model

Having studied the human resource planning process a model can now be evolved. (Figure 3.11).

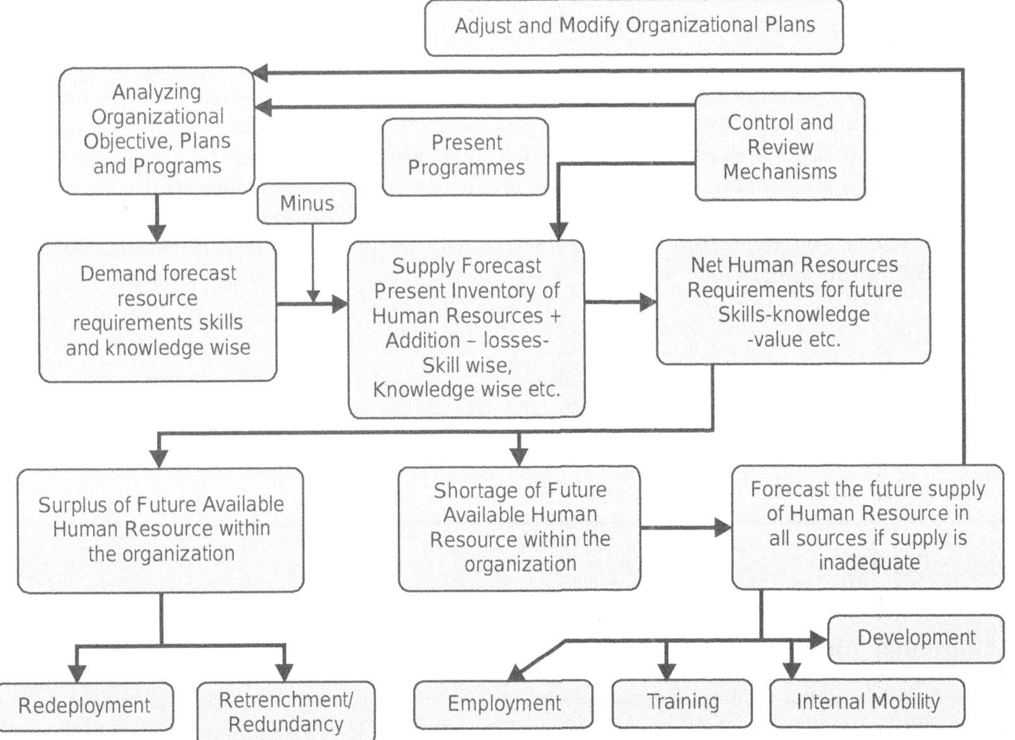

Fig. 3.11. *Human Resource Planning Model.*

Review Questions

1. What do you understand by human resource planning ? Discuss its benefits and limitations.
2. 'Human resource planning is a pre-requisite for effective for effective management of human resources.' In the light of the statement analyse the significance of human resource planning.
3. Explain the concept of manpower planning. How is manpower planning carried at various levels in the enterprise ?
4. Write notes on :

   (*a*) Human resource inventory

   (*b*) Human resource flows

   (*c*) Levels of Human Resource Planning

   (*d*) Techniques of Human Resource Planning.
5. 'The logical approach to staffing begins with a careful assessment and planning of current and prospective requirements.' Comment ?
6. How are the requirements of manpower determined in large organizations ? Discuss the sources of obtaining manpower ?
7. Briefly discuss the quantitative and qualitative aspects of human resource planning ?
8. What is human resource audit ? Briefly discuss how human resource audit in an organization can be undertaken ?
9. What is human resource accounting ? Briefly discuss the various methods of human resource accounting. Explain the benefits of human resource accounting/
10. Explain the steps in human resource planning process ?
11. Discuss the problems in human resource planning. How can you plan for human resource requirements in an effective manner ?
12. Sankalp Tech India is a manufacturing and a marketing company. The manufacturing unit of the company is located in the State of Uttranchal and has its manufacturing offices in all major cities of India. During past five years the company has been growing at a reasonable rate has been able to establish its product in the market. It has currently a market share of ten percent. In a recent meeting the Board of Directors of the company took a decision to diversify its products and expand its market network. Suggest the kind of human resource planning the company should undertake and discuss the steps and techniques which will be useful for human resource plaknning of Sankalp Tech India.

Project Work

Study the human resource and employment planning in a retail company. Prepare a case study on employment planning based on the data collected. Prepare a brief write up on the efficacy of employee planning and its relation to the organizations business roles.

Case Study

Anil Dhirubhai Ambani Energy Limited.

Careers in Anil Dhirubhai Ambani Energy Limited are based on the basis of team operations. The teams are responsible for achievement of specific goals, from concept to development and implementation of plans. Anil Dhirubhai Ambani Energy Limited provides it employees a seamless merging of functional roles to provide a sharper business focus and groom employees for larger responsibilities. The company believes that working smarter would mean not just doing the job well, but also stretching it into profit making. This has led to a much broader role for human resource personnel, leaving a greater impact on the company performance.

Career Development

There is a wide scope for employees to grow and improve their skills by :

(*a*) Having a greater exposure to latest technology.

(*b*) Able to implement and learn latest and best of kind managerial practices.

(*c*) Multifunctional skills.

(*d*) Customer relationship management

(*e*) Fast growth.

Recruitment

The company does not go in for short term recruitment. The company is translating corporate strategy into a manpower plan and developing a long term program accordingly. Anil Dhirubhai Ambani Energy Limited tracks down people with knowledge, skills, experience and behaviour best suited for achieving the company's objectives. The focus of recruitment programme is on :

(*a*) Attracting people with multidimensional experience and skills.

(*b*) Induct new talent with perspective to lead the company and make it a profit centre.

(*c*) Develop an organizational culture that attracts people with talents to the company.

(*d*) Locate individuals whose behaviour and personalities fit the company's values.

(*e*) Devise methodologies for assessing psychological traits.

(*f*) Design entry compensation that competes on quality as well as quantum.

(*g*) Anticipate and find people for positions proactively.

Induction

A formal induction programme is conducted for the new inductee to the company. Induction programme is carried out for :

- Lateral Inducts
  - o Provides overview of the organization to the new recruits and familiarizes employees with various business processes, culture and business practices of the company.
  - o It covers soft skills modules like team building, change management, communication etc.
- Graduate Engineer Trainees.
  - o Provides technical training
    - ■ On the job
    - ■ Class room
  - o Functional training
  - o Managerial skill development.

Performance Management

To ensure the company attracts the best talent that can help achieve its goals, company creates an appropriate working condition by :

(*a*) Evaluating all jobs so as to assign them to the individuals best suited for them.

(*b*) Designing customized jobs, if necessary employing behavioural science and industrial psychology.

(*c*) Creating environment and manpower configuration to boost the ability to the individuals.

(*d*) Balancing the interests of individual and the corporate by designing individual career paths.

Objective of the Company's Performance System

- Create culture of excellence that inspires every employee.
- Match organizational objectives to individual aspirations.
- Equip people with skills to perform their duties.
- Clear growth paths for talented individuals.
- Provide challenges to rejuvenate stagnant careers.
- Forge partnership with employees for managing their careers.
- Empower employees to take decisions without fear of failing.
- Imbibe teamwork in all operational processes.

Performance Appraisal System

The performance appraisal system provides for :

- Recognition of individual's performance.
- Continual learning and development.
- Better skills and employability.
- Monetary and other rewards'.
- Contribution to the achievement of company's goals.
- Increased productivity and profitability.

Training and Development

With the business environment becoming more and more dynamic, a need on a continual basis for improved domain expertise is the need of the hour. The core function of the company's training department is to bridge the gap between the changing requirements of the job and the abilities that individuals need to perform these tasks such as self directed leadership, self motivated teams and self generated creativity to excel in their respective areas of performance.

Objectives of Training and Development

- Make learning the fundamental of the company.
- Use training to bridge gap with the external work.
- Link organizational and individual training needs.
- Install training systems that substitute work experience.
- Use training for constant upgrading of employees skills.

Questions :

1. *Critically analyse the human resource practices of the Anil Dhirubhai Ambani Energy Limited.*
2. *Evaluate the linkage between the career plan and recruitment practices.*
3. *Analyse the performance management system and suggest changes to optimize performance.*
4. *Analyse the approach of the company towards the training and development.*

❑❑❑

Chapter **4**

JOB ANALYSIS AND JOB DESIGN

★ LEARNING OBJECTIVES ★

After reading this chapter, you will be able to understand :

- Concept, nature and purpose of job analysis.
- Definition
- Objectives of job analysis.
- Uses of job analysis.
- Process and methods of job analysis
- Job description
- Job specification
- Job design approaches.
- Role analysis
- Methods of job designing

INTRODUCTION

The human resource planning process is followed by the next logical step of work analysis and design. Job analysis is apart of overall planning known as 'work design'. It is the analysis, measurement, control and redesign of set of activities. Job designing is a prelude to job analysis. Job analysis is performed after the job has been designed and an employee is functioning on it. Job analysis is a systematic process of gathering information about work, jobs, and relationship between jobs. Job analysis is a scientific and systematic analysis of job with a view to obtain pertinent details on performing it. Job analysis is performed upon ongoing jobs. Jobs and process for performing it are always subject to change; job analysis may become obsolete within a short span of time. Job analysis and work design are tools of motivation used by management.

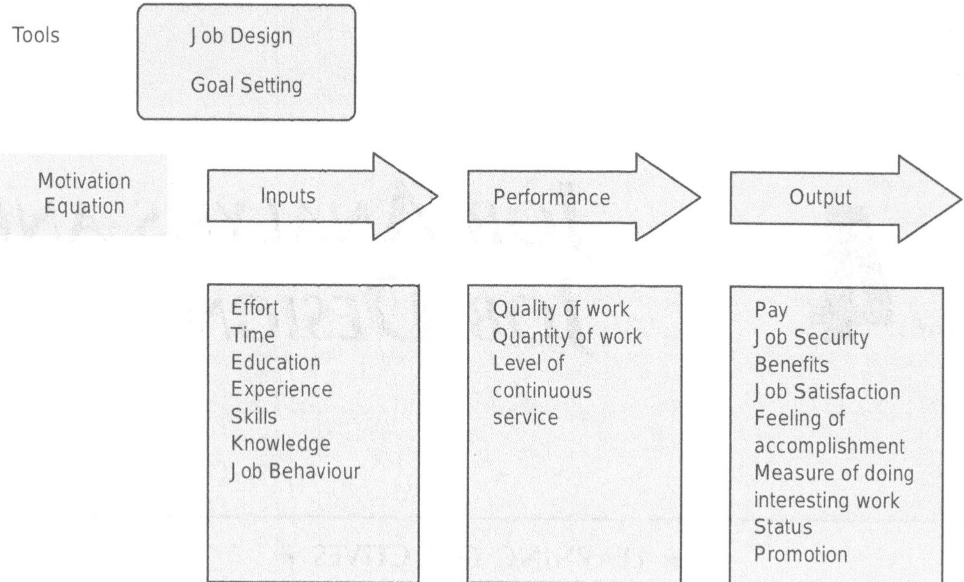

Fig. 4.1. *Motivating Tools.*

The business owners and organizations including government agencies like defence etc. base their personnel policies on explicit well proven principles. The organizations or enterprises that follow these principles have higher performance and better growth rates then those that do not follow them. The most important of these are :

(*a*) Positions in organization should be filled with people who are willing, devouted and have the requisite qualification.

(*b*) The more accurate and realistic are the specification of the skill requirements for each job, more likely it is that the employee selected would match the job requirement and hence, be able to perform better and in a competent manner.

(*c*) Proper and specific job description and definitions is the key to communicating the organizational expectation.

(*d*) This helps in choosing the best person and hence, the performance is high and image of the organization is built.

The process of selecting a competent person for each position is best accomplished through a systematic definition of the requirements for each job, including the skills, knowledge and other qualifications that employees must possess to perform each task. Performance appraisal has to be carried out of each employee so the enumeration that are designed for him are right and he deserves it, based on skills, education, abilities, experience etc.

THE CONCEPT OF JOB, POSITION AND OCCUPATION

There are large number of terms used when an employee enters any organization the three most common are, "I have got a *job* ?", 'They have yet to decide what *position* they would be giving me ?", and thirdly "I have an *occupation* now. ?" What do these terms means must be clear before any individual seeks an employment in an organization.

In the latter half of the 20th Century E.J. McCormick approached the description of work in a systematic taxonomic vein which has been widely recognized for its utility. Firstly, *Job*, may be defined *as an assignment of work to be performed by an employee calling for a set of duties, responsibilities, knowledge, skills and conditions that are different from those of other work assignment.* It can also be defined as a position or a group of positions that are similar as to kind and level of work. It is the smallest unit into which work can be divided. Job involves group of positions involving same duties. A duty relates to number of tasks. For example, two gardeners who are performing similar duties and who require similar training, knowledge, skills, experience and qualities are said to hold same kind of job although they may be working in different locations.

Position is the location assigned to an individual in an organization for accomplishment of tasks assigned. There are as many positions in an organization as the number of persons. It relates to duties and responsibilities. A position refers to one or more duties performed by an individual in an organization.

The term 'occupation' is used in a wider sense. An occupation refers to a group of jobs that are similar as to kind of work or that possess common characteristics. There is similarity in the kind of work and possess certain characteristics.

Another term popular but does not affect job analysis is 'career'. A relates to all jobs, positions or occupations held by an individual during one's working life.

DEFINITION

Job analysis is the systematic investigation that collects all information pertinent to each task performed by an employee. From the analysis, one is able to identify the skills, knowledge, ability required of that employee, and determine the duties, responsibilities and requirements of each job.

Process of defining a job in terms of its component tasks or duties and the knowledge or skills required to perform them.

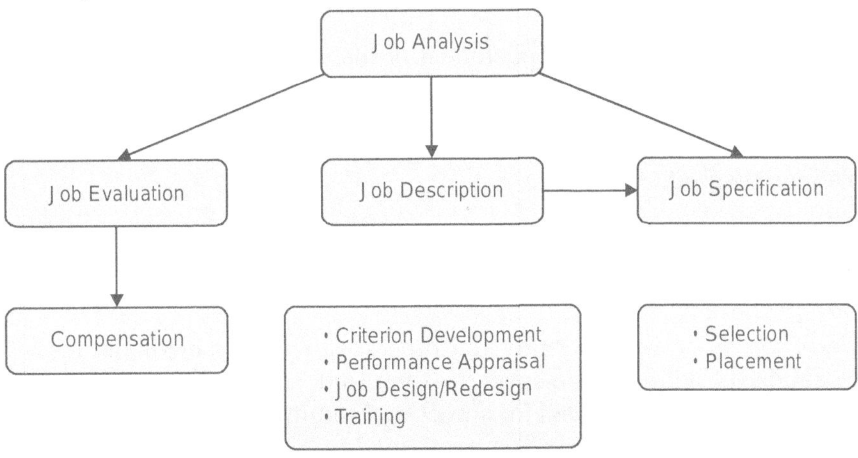

Fig. 4.2. *Job Analysis.*

Edwin B Flippo (1984, p. 114) has defined by stating

'Job analysis is the process of studying and collecting information relating to the operations and responsibilities of a specific job. The immediate products of this analysis are job descriptions and job specifications.'

David A DeCenzo and **S.P. Robbins** (1989, p.111) define

'Job analysis is a systematic exploration of the activities within a job. It is a basic technical procedure, one that is used to define the duties, responsibilities and accountability of a job.'

US Department of Labour defined :

Job analysis as *'the process of determining, by observation and study, and reporting pertinent information relating to the nature of specific job. It is the determination of the tasks which comprise the job and of the skills, knowledge, abilities and responsibilities required of the worker of a successful performance and which differentiate one job from all others.'*

Gael captures the essence of by stating :

Job analysis is *'a major support activity for the primary functional activities of organizational staffing, employee training and development, employee compensation, labour relations, and job design. Jobs are analyzed in order to identify the ability requirements necessary for an employee to complete successfully a job's tasks, and to identify rewards associated with the job and how these rewards can be used to motivate employee work behaviour and satisfy important employee needs.'*

From definitions it can be deduced that job analysis is:

(*a*) A systematic study of jobs;

(*b*) It identifies the nature of job;

(*c*) Provides inputs for selecting an appropriate person;

(*d*) With right skills, experience, knowledge, abilities and behaviour.

The process of job analysis is essentially one of data collection and then analyzing that data. The data can be classified as :

(*a*) Job identification.

(*b*) Nature of job.

(*c*) Operation involved in accomplishment of the job.

(*d*) Material and equipment used for doing the job.

(*e*) Personal attributes and behavioural skills required.

(*f*) Relations with other jobs.

OBJECTIVES OF JOB ANALYSIS

The objective of job analysis is to study the processes, simplify methods, measure work for establishing standards both with respect to time and standards, provide information for compensation, and improve all process for attracting, recruitment, retention of employees. These can be classified as :

(*a*) Job redesign – for simplification of work process/procedure.

(*b*) Appraisal, retention and compensation – by establishing work standards.

(*c*) Support other personnel activities as promotion, training and development etc.

JOB ANALYSIS AND COMPETITIVE ADVANTAGE

The job analysis has a direct bearing on all aspects of human resource management and is an important component of it.. Job analysis enhances the effectiveness of human resource activities as it helps in identifying the right person; employ him on the right job to have optimum results. It helps in selection, training and development, performance appraisal and enumeration fixation.

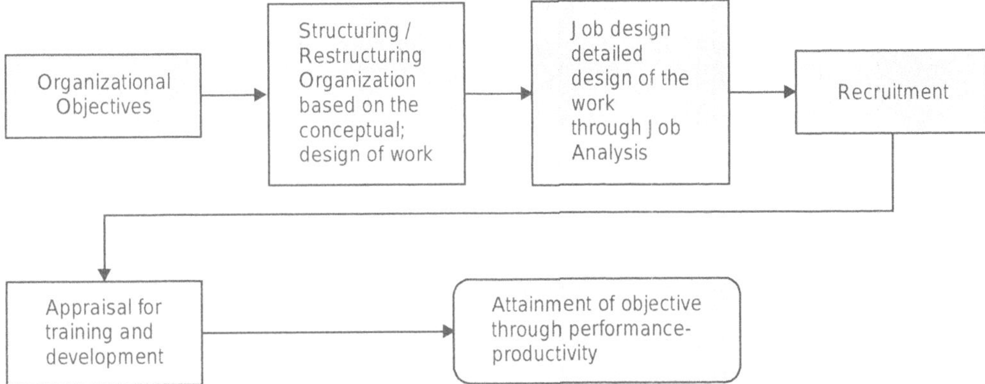

Fig. 4.3. *Uses of Job Analysis.*

(*a*) *Human Resource Planning.* By carrying out job analysis it is possible to determine the qualitative requirements of a job. It helps in determining the job demands in terms of responsibilities and duties and helps in translating these in to requirements of skills, qualities etc. It also helps in determining the number of positions in an organization.

(*b*) *Attracting and Recruiting.* Job analysis helps in making clear statements of job, which in turn helps employers to fill the positions. This in turn facilitates the in making employment program successful as it matches the job requirements with workers aptitudes, abilities and interests.

(*c*) *Placement.* Job analysis facilitates the matching of job requirement with the knowledge, skills and abilities of the individual thus helping him be allotted appropriate position. Thus each person is allotted a job meeting his interest and best suited to him.

(*d*) *Appraisal.* Job analysis facilitate appraisal of an employee against a set standard. The appraisal facilitates in evaluating performance, planning training and development based on performance, as also in determining the employee's suitability for promotion or other positions of responsibility.

(*e*) *Job Design.* Job analysis helps in designing / redesigning of jobs by industrial engineers.

Ash and Levin have pointed out the major organizational purpose for which job analysis can/ have been used. These are

(*a*) *Job Description.* It involves job information, job summary, duties, responsibilities, specification and standards.

(*b*) *Job Classification.* Arrangement of job into classes, groups, families according to classification schemes.

(*c*) *Job Evaluation.* Establishing the relative worth of jobs using internal and external reference to set enumeration.

(*d*) *Personnel Requirements/ Specifications*. For attracting, acquiring, and deploying personnel. Setting forth the knowledge, skills and abilities required for successful performance of the job.

(*e*) *Performance Appraisal*. Factors or dimensions forming the basis for the performance appraisal should be relevant *i.e.,* job related.

(*f*) *Worker Training*. Providing for the performance oriented task basis, and or 'worker characteristics' required for accomplishment of the job.

(*g*) *Worker Mobility*. Career development, career lattices, necessary to progress individuals into and out of positions, jobs and occupation.

(*h*) *Efficiency and Safety*. Designing the most efficient and safe work procedures, layouts and standards.

(*i*) *Manpower and Workforce Planning*. Ensuring the organization has the right kinds and number of people in the right places at the right time doing the right work / job. Also ensuring the self actualization and growth of people and the utilization of their skills and talents.

(*j*) *Legal, Quasi-Legal Requirements*. Framing work in conformity with legal requirements or obligations imposed by legislative bodies or courts. Framing work to comply by government, industries, union's regulations or guidelines.

A Human resource specialist or a supervisor collects one or more of the following types of information :

(*a*) *Work activities*. Collects information about the job's actual work activities.

(*b*) *Human behaviour*. Information regarding human characteristic required to perform the job are collected.

(*c*) Details about machines tools and equipment required to perform the job.

(*d*) Job context involves information about job conditions, work schedules etc are also made available.

(e) Human requirements to perform the job are also collected.

THE PROCESS OF JOB ANALYSIS

Strategic Choices

Figure 4.4 illustrates the process of job analysis.

The organization makes specific choices with regard to job analysis. The company has to determine who will be in-charge, what will be the extent of involvement of employees, the level and depth of analysis to be carried out, past oriented versus future oriented job analysis, schedule and frequency, and sources of job data. The analyst here must answer how the analysis is expected to be employed / used ? In an organization which has rapid changes due technological change, a more future-oriented approach to job analysis may be desired. Here future orientation to job analysis is given and predictions made as to how the job will be done. This enables the organization to select employees and train them so that they are ready to occupy positions when need arises.

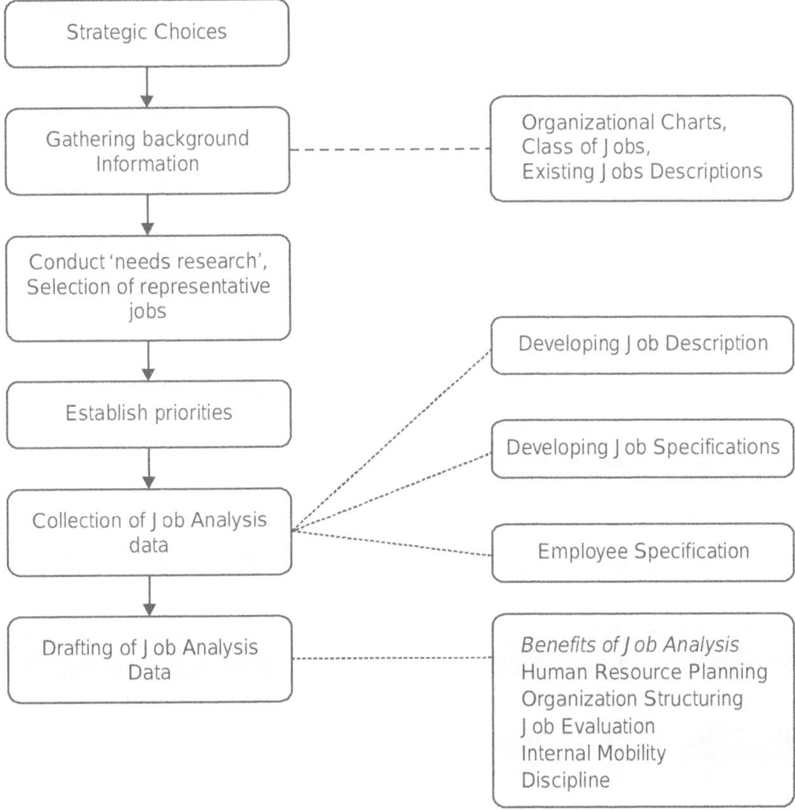

Fig. 4.4. *Process of Job Analysis.*

Gathering Background Information

The job analyst after getting direction looks at the organizational chart to determine number of positions, current position descriptions, job specifications, systems and flow charts. The organizations usually have an organizational chart with positions marked depicting the organization of division of work and the process charts providing more detailed picture of flow of work in its simplest form.

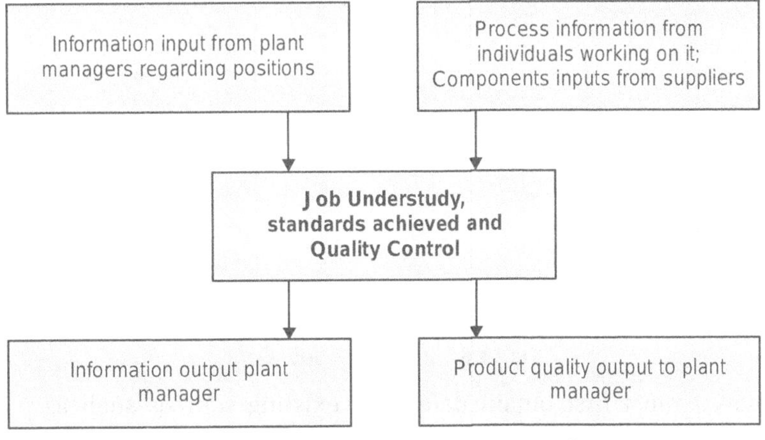

Fig. 4.5. *Organizational and Process Charts.*

'Needs' Research

In the next step the analyst carries out 'need' determination. He identifies the requirement and where the information and analysis carried out would be utilized, then selects a representative position to collect data.

Establish Priorities

After having determined the need then the analyst must determine the priority in which he must conduct an analysis.

Collection of Job Analysis Data

The analyst thereafter collects data about the selected jobs as these are being currently performed. The analyst employs one the established techniques for carrying out analysis. Thereafter, the analyst develops job specification, job descriptions and employee specification. Usually the job descriptions are written statements.

Drafting Job Analysis Data

The analyst thereafter develops a job analysis data, which is utilized for various activities in the organization involving the recruitment at one end to training and development, to internal mobility and promotion, evaluation of performance on the other end of the spectrum. It is here that the analyst actually interacts with the worker performing the job. Then develop job specifications and job descriptions.

SOURCES OF JOB DATA

The analysis of job requires collection of data about the jobs. There are two sources from this data can be collected viz. human sources and non-human sources. See Figure 4.6.

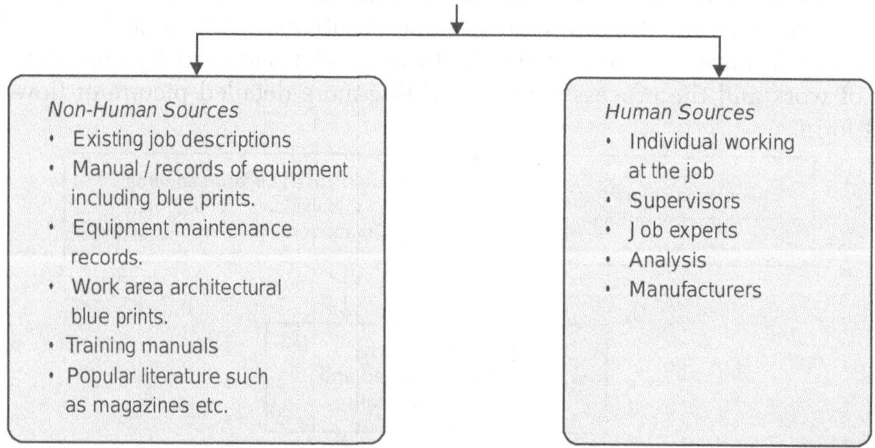

Source: *Adapted from Cynthia D. Fisher et. al. Human Resource Management, p. 140*

Fig. 4.6. *Sources of Job Data*

The job analyst must first obtain data from existing sources such as product manuals, training manuals, job cards etc. In addition the job analyst must interact with persons performing on the job. This would provide him with an opportunity to see how the job is being performed. Endeavour should be made to collect data from as wide a spectrum of persons as time permits. This is because the duties performed by more experienced persons tend to vary substantially from those having lesser experience.

The data collected has multifarious functions. The data especially stands handy when the firm defends its human resource practices in courts of law. The courts are particularly interested in the adequacy of the job analysis information.

The relevance of job analysis is becoming vague due flattening organizations, use of empowered teams, which make firms highly responsive, flexible and competitive. This has replaced job descriptions with a metrics of skills and skills levels required to perform the function. Thus shifting focus from listing specific job and duties to developing the skills needed for the employees' broader, empowered and undefined responsibilities.

The firms are also getting *de-jobbed* – implying jobs are getting more amorphous and difficult to define. De-jobbing is the result of rapid changes taking place in the business environment today.

METHODS OF COLLECTING JOB ANALYSIS INFORMATION

Job analysis is a systematic exposition of activities within a job. It is a scientific method employed to define duties, responsibilities and accountability of a job. Hence, it involves the identification and description of what is happening on the job. There are several methods of collecting information. Some of the most prominent ones are—(*i*) Interview, (*ii*) observation, (*iii*) diary or logbook of job incumbent, (*iv*) checklist method, (*v*) technical conference etc.

Interview

Personal interview of job incumbent, his supervisor is the most commonly used method of job analysis. The job analyst employs two methods while conducting an interview. Un-structured questionnaires or job analysis worksheets are employed when the analyst wants to draw out job description information from the job incumbent as he sees it. This method is especially utilized when the analyst wants to develop the task lists. Here the job analyst must have considerable skills and knowledge about interviewing techniques, the objective being to obtain complete unbiased information from the respondents.

The interviewer can conduct interview individually, in a group with employees with same jobs or supervisor interview. The group interviews are best used for managerial and supervisory positions or in conjunction with desk audit when there are several positions and the analyst wants to make sure that nothing is missed out. It tends to generate very good selection information (criteria for choosing new employees).

The process is quite time consuming. The interviewer would have to undertake a deliberate exercise by way of an initial interview to gather maximum information of the process. Thereafter, the analyst would have to carry out initial analysis and finding gaps would conduct a follow up interview for clarity and correctness and may then have a final interview to polish his findings.

The success of an interview is dependent upon the preparation made for the interview. It is important for an analyst to prepare for an interview by intimating to all concerned the objective of the interview, preparing a questionnaire, draft task lists etc. In addition all administrative aspects should be tied up like location time etc. The next step that an analyst has to take is to build rapport with the workers. An effort must be made to dispel the fears and any apprehension they may have. It is important or else there would be no information forthcoming resulting in poor analysis. Lastly all information obtained by the analyst should be verified. This is easily accomplished by having a group of employees performing the same job interviewed. Interview is a costly and a time consuming method.

Observation Method

In this method the analyst directly observes the worker or a group engaged in doing the job. He thereafter takes notes to describe that tasks and duties performed. If a particular job is simple and repetitive, observation may be the only technique required for carrying out job analysis. Draughtsman's, weavers, mechanic are the examples of such jobs. It is an excellent method for understanding and appreciating the conditions under which work is performed. It enables analyst to experience aspects of job that worker may not be aware of.

Use of this technique is limited because there are many jobs involving mental processes and circumstances which cannot be directly observed or jobs that do not have complete observable cycle. Observation method can be effective only when the analyst is skilled enough to know what to observe and how to analyze what is observed. It is preferable to combine observation method with interview technique to get better results.

Questionnaire

Use of this approach when there are several positions and it is not feasible to bring large number of employees together for interview. In this method the analyst prepares a questionnaire or uses the standard questionnaire readily available of the shelf to conduct job analysis. The questionnaire consists of basic information and some questions relate to his or her responsibilities. Analyst prepares the questionnaire or selects the test after a brainstorming session or by conducting one or more desk audit. Questionnaires can also be designed to clarify information gathered during brainstorming, desk audits etc.

Quantitative Techniques

In this method the standard actions are quantified. Each action is represented by a figure giving degree of difficulty or repetitive nature or criticality of action. This facilitates easy comparison.

Position Analysis Questionnaire

There is a standard Position Analysis Questionnaire for analyzing jobs in quantitative form. It was developed by McCormick in 1972 because of the criticism that job analysis relied on observation and is not quantifiable. It has 194 questions to which the respondent has to answer. These are grouped in six groups as under :

(*a*) Information input- Basically dealing with how information is obtained by an employee.

(*b*) Mental Processes dealing with reasoning, planning, organizing and decision making.

(*c*) Work Output. What physical activity is undertaken and tools and machines used.

(*d*) Relationships. What contact is developed and maintained while carrying out the job both internally within the organization and externally.

(*e*) Job Context. What is the physical and social context in which job is performed ?

(*f*) Other Job Characteristics. Any other specific characteristics of the job that is not covered in question above.

This questionnaire determines the extent to which each task is applicable to performance of the job. There is a provision of rating each job. A specific rating scale is designated to be used with each job element, in particular the scale considered most appropriate to the content of the element. All but the 'A' (applicability) scale are six (6) point scales, with '0' (which is coded an 'N') being used as does not apply.

There are six types of rating scales used.

Letter Identification	*Type of Rating Scale*
U	Extent of Use
I	Importance to the Job
T	Amount of Time
P	Possibility of Occurrence
A	Applicability
S	Special Code

A specific rating scale is designed to be used with each job element. All but 'A' (applicability) scale are 6-point scales with '0' which is 'N' (being used for does not apply).

Rating	*Importance to the Job*
N	Does not apply
1	Very minor
2	Low
3	Average
4	High
5	Extreme

Source : *William P. Anthony, et.al. (1993). Strategic Human Resource Management, Dryden Press, p. 223.*

Fig. 4.7. *Rating Scale to be used with Position Analysis Questionnaire.*

Management Position Description Questionnaire

Another prepared questionnaire frequently used is the Management Position Description Questionnaire. Management Position Description Questionnaire is highly structure questionnaire and contains 208 items relating to managerial responsibilities, restrictions, demands and miscellaneous position characteristics. These 208 items are grouped under thirteen (13) categories.

The Positional Analysis Questionnaire and Management Position Description Questionnaire yield standardized information about the worker.

Categories	Elements
1	Product, marketing and financial strategy planning.
2	Co-ordination of other organizational units and personnel.
3	Internal business control.
4	Products and services responsibility
5	Public and Customer relations
6	Advanced Consulting
7	Autonomy of Actions
8	Approval and financial commitments
9	Staff services
10	Supervision
11	Complexity and stress
12	Advanced financial responsibility
13	Broad personnel responsibility

Source : *Lloyd L.Byars and Leasile W. Rue. (1997). Human Resource Management, Irwin*

Fig. 4.8. *Categories of Management Position Description Questionnaire.*

Functional Job Analysis

Functional job analysis is a worker-oriented job analytical approach which attempts to describe the whole person on the job.

Functional job analysis is a worker-oriented job analytical approach which attempts to describe the whole person on the job. The functional job analysis helps to differentiate what is being done and what an employee must do to get things done. The employees utilize interpersonal skills, mental and physical resources and correlate the same to accomplish the task. The levels of difficulty in performing the tasks are hierarchical and can be represented on an ordinal scale. Figure 4.9 defines the levels of difficulty for various jobs with regard to data, people and things. The lower the number associated with the function, the more difficult the function is. Example Compiling data (3) is more difficult than tending things (5) and tending things (5) is more difficult than handling people (7).

This method has two advantages. It rates the job not only on data, people and things but four other factors. The factors on which rating is done are :

(*a*) The extent to which specific instructions are required to perform the job.

(*b*) The extent to which reasoning and judgment are required to perform the task.

(*c*) The mathematical ability required to perform the task

Data	People	Things
0- Synthesizing	0- Mentoring	0 - Setting Up
1- Coordinating	1- Negotiating	1- Precision Working
2- Analysing	2- Instructing	2- Operating -controlling
3- Compiling	3- Supervising	3- Driving- operating
4- Computing	4- Diverting	4- Manipulating
5- Copying	5- Persuading	5- Tending
6- Comparing	6- Speaking -signaling	6- Feeding- off bearing
7- Serving	7- Handling	
	8- taking instructions and helping	

Source : *Lloyd L Byars and Leslie W. Rue (1997), p. 93.*

Fig. 4.9. *Levels of Dificulty for Worker Functions in Functional Job Analysis.*

This data can then be compared with the job elements reported in the Dictionary of Occupational Titles, which is a standardized data-source describing a wide range of jobs. Once the closest job on the Dictionary of Occupational Titles is located then the accompanying job description can be modified to fit the specific job being analyzed. Functional Job Analysis is easy to learn as it uses a standardized format.

Diary or Log of Job Incumbent

This method involves recording by job incumbent of job duties, noting the frequency of a task performed after the duties have been accomplished. The diaries can be good source of information if these have been kept up to date. It can be used as a source of comparison in carrying out duties. By careful analysis of the diaries the analyst is able to determine the routineness and non-routineness of a particular function. It facilitated analysis of jobs which are difficult to observe.

Critical Incident Technique

In this method incumbents brainstorm about critical incidents that happen routinely and infrequently while working. The method was evolved by Flanagan in 1949. It identifies behaviours that indicate success or failure on the job (effective and ineffective behaviours are determined). The incidents are analyzed and classified according to the job areas these describe. A fairly clear picture of actual job requirements can be obtained by distinguishing between effective and ineffective behaviour. The critical incidents include context I which the incident occurred, behaviour exactly what the individual did that was effective or ineffective and consequences of the behaviour and whether or not the consequences were in employee's control. This method helps the analyst to generate two lists of incidents one which indicates good performance and other which indicates poor performance. The technique is excellent for determining training and development needs and selection strategies. For selection process success the analyst would have to extrapolate the list of critical duties from incidents that helped an employee carry out the job successfully.

Checklist

The check list method is similar to a questionnaire method. In this method the respondents usually answer in yes or no. The checklist may contain variety of activities but the incumbent or the respondent only ticks the function performed by him. However, the preparation of checklist is a daunting task. It requires knowledge and skill of the job under consideration. This can be accomplished by gaining information first from job performer and then after the check list has been prepared it be circulated to good workers to check. The major advantage of this technique is that large number of personnel can give their opinion at the same time.

Technical Conference Method

In this the services of the talented people and the supervisors are utilized. They are called for a conference and there the analyst initiated the discussion which provides details about jobs. The actions are discussed and report prepared. May not be very accurate as the main person who actually carries out the function may not be present or some details may be missed out.

Once the information has been collected and analyzed it is used to prepare job descriptions and job specification. Any of the techniques could be used by the analyst. However, job analyst normally uses a more specific widely used technique that incorporates various features of these general techniques.

JOB DESCRIPTIONS

A job description is a written statement of the duties, responsibilities, required qualifications and reporting relationships of a particular job

A job description is a written statement of the duties, responsibilities, required qualifications and reporting relationships of a particular job. Job description is based on objective information obtained through job analysis. Job description being a factual statement discloses what, how and why of a job.

It clearly spells out the responsibilities of a specific job. It also includes information about the tools, resources, relationships with other positions and skills needed for accomplishment of the job. It also helps in clarifying all legal bases. It ensures that candidates are fully conversant and aware of what an organization is looking for in them. It also helps the present incumbents to understand the extent and limits of new incumbent's responsibilities.

The major contents of a job description include :

(*a*) Job Title

(*b*) Location

(*c*) Job Summary

(*d*) Duties to be performed

(*e*) Machines, tools and materials.

(*f*) Relation to other jobs.

(*g*) Nature of supervision.

(*h*) Working environment.

Job Title : Benefits Manager **Occupational Code** : 166.167.019

Reports to : **Job No. 1100**

Functionally - Director, Human Resource

Administratively - Vice President, Operations

Supervises - Staff of four

Environmental Conditions - Not Applicable

Objectives of the Job - Maintain best staff at all times.

Functions - Manage the employee compensation and benefits.

Principal Duties and Responsibilities :

- Plan and direct compensation program.
- Plan and distribute written statements about benefits programs.

Job Characteristics :

(a) Incumbent should have sufficient knowledge of policies and practices involved in human resource management.

(b) Excellent written and verbal communication.

Authority Limits : xxxxxxxx.

Fig. 4.10. *Example of Job Description.*

Preparation of Job Descriptions

Job descriptions provide the data of the job itself in terms of duties and responsibilities. Detailed information has to be collected before the document can be prepared. The information can be collected by one of the many methods available.

(*a*) Observation.

(*b*) Discussion with supervisors.

(*c*) Questionnaire.

(*d*) Technical conference.

All these methods have been elaborated above. Under mentioned guidelines should be observed while preparing a job description.

(*a*) *Clarity*. Job descriptions should be clear and have no reference to any other job descriptions.

(*b*) *Scope of Authority*. When position is being defined, the scope of authority should be indicated. Sometimes, it is essential to add some additional duties it give it a wider perspective.

(*c*) *Specific*. Although details are required in job descriptions but these should be inserted with specific words, known as 'action words' such as assemble, deliver, gather etc.

(*d*) *Brevity*. Brevity is the essence of job descriptions. Use of short accurate terms help in accomplishing brevity.

(*e*) *Re-check*. Once the job description has been compiled it is essential it is observed and looked into from a newcomer's perspective. Help of a employee can be taken to check its accuracy and validity.

Responsibility of Preparation and Validity. The responsibility and accountability for preparation of job description is of both the line manager where the position is located and the human resource manager. The validity of the job description is dependent upon how accurately it reflects job contents. The validity becomes clear when it is used for employment and evaluation purposes. Job description also has an impact on compensation. A poorly prepared job description may result in good job getting poor compensation.

JOB SPECIFICATION

A job specification is a document which states the minimum acceptable qualifications and human qualities required by an individual to perform the task efficiently.

A job specification is a document which states the minimum acceptable qualifications and human qualities required by an individual to perform the task efficiently. Job specification identifies the qualifications, appropriate skills, knowledge, abilities, experience and personality qualities required to perform the job. Job specification translates the job description into a human qualification and levels of performance required for successful performance on the job at a particular position. As far as possible the specification should be quantified.

Job specification lately is not very popular with the firms as these firms have experienced that it is very difficult to present an accurate standard of personnel. Instead these firms deliver job descriptions. This enables the recruiters to have a wide variety of persons to select from as job description gives aspect of performance and not qualities. Job specification is the measuring tool for measuring personnel as it lists qualities required for successful performance of job.

Job specification provides two distinct advantages over job description as it includes;

(*a*) Job identification

(*b*) Human requirements.

The major information included in a job specification are the

(*a*) Physical specification

(*b*) Mental specification

(*c*) Emotional and social specification.

(*d*) Behavioural specification.

Position Title	:	Manager Human Relation (Wage administration)
Deapartment	:	Human resource
Education	:	MBA with specialization in Human Resource / Social work A degree or diploma in labour law desirable. Proficiency in accounting preferred.
Experience	:	5 years is similar position.
Age	:	Between 30-40 years.
Other Attributes	:	Good health, Pleasing personality etc
Any other requirements	:	xxx

Fig. 4.11. *Specimen Job Specification.*

Preparation and Accountability of Job Specification

The job specification should define the minimum acceptable standards for employment and performance on the job. Exceptional functions, which are of non-routine nature, should not be allowed to influence the overall job description. Job specifications are developed with help of supervisors by human resource department personnel. It is the responsibility of the personnel manager to ensure the correctness, accuracy and validity of the job specification although he takes helps of supervisors who have greater knowledge of the process of the job.

Cognitive Work Analysis

Traditional approaches tend to emphasis centralized work organization; where as turbulent, dynamic environments tend to require more distributed work organizations. Cognitive Engineering Laboratory has adopted Rasmussen's (1986) frame work for cognitive work analysis as a basis for supporting worker adaptation. The focus of the cognitive work analysis is on identifying the constraints that shape behaviour rather than on trying to predict behaviour itself. Rasmussen's frame work provides separate descriptions of different classes of constraints.

Work Domain. It is the functional structure of the work domain in which behaviour takes place.

Control Tasks. These are generic tasks that are to be accomplished.

Strategies. The set of strategies that can be used to carry out these tasks.

Social Organizational. The structure of the organization.

Worker Competencies. The competencies required by operators to deal with these demands.

Cognitive work analysis can be viewed as a complement to traditional task analysis in that it not only retains the benefits of these methods but also adds the capability for designing for unanticipated by describing the constraints on behaviour rather that behaviour per se.

Cognitive work analysis has been used extensively by Cognitive Engineering Laboratory to design interfaces, experiments and training; as well as to analyze data and categorize performance measures and knowledge elicitation techniques. It has proven to be an invaluable research and design tool.

JOB ANALYSIS AND TOTAL QUALITY MANAGEMENT AND STRATEGIC HUMAN RESOURCE MANAGEMENT

Job analysis appears to be inconsistent with total quality management. The total quality management would be discussed later in the book. However, it is important to note that job analysis which endeavours to distinguish one job from another seems to be inconsistent with total quality management. Total quality management expects employee to be involved and do everything so as to improve the overall quality.

PROBLEMS/DIFFICULTIES IN JOB ANALYSIS

There exist some major problems while carrying out job analysis.

(*a*) *Support of management*. The management normally does not get involved and thus the quality of information gathered suffers as the desired support from the organization is not forthcoming.

(*b*) *Means and Source*. The quality of analysis depends upon the tools used in preparing the job analysis. However, the analyst normally employs the easiest and simple tool and compiles the data. Thus the quality of analysis suffers.

(c) *Training and Motivation*. Job analysis helps in identifying the skill gaps and facilitates in developing training and development programs to fill the skill gaps.

(d) *Industrial Relations*. Job analysis facilitates recruitment, compensation and development thus making better and cordial relations as the employee is selected, enumerated and promoted against a definite standard.

RECENT DEVELOPMENTS

There have been large numbers of studies and models developed to assist selection, retention, compensation and other benefits of an employee. Some of these are discussed here.

Role Analysis

Job analysis is based on a premise that jobs in an organization are relatively static and it is possible to predict critical job related behaviour which makes an employee perform effectively. There are many intangible that play a role in successful accomplishment of a job. Hence, there are many situations under which it is not possible to predict job related behaviour or the behaviour may not be consistent. The behaviour changes with the situation and the environment under which the employee operates. Therefore, it is necessary to undertake role analysis to obtain a realistic picture of the job as also the attributes required for performing the job effectively. Role analysis is helpful in writing the duties and responsibilities of managers which involve many intangibles. It helps in determining the behaviour pattern expected from an individual occupying that position as also work out interpersonal problems effectively. The role analysis is carried out in two steps :

(a) The manager describes the job consisting of both tangible and intangible contents. He also describes the prescribed and the discriminatory elements. This followed by manager being questioned by others (superiors or managers performing the same role) to seek clarification and fill in the gaps that may be evident.

(b) Thereafter a list of expectations from ach of the role is prepared through discussion and mutual agreement. The analyst thereafter writes the details of role. He includes all aspects of the job both tangible and intangible.

Cognitive Work Analysis

Cognitive Work Analysis (Vicente, 1999) is a work centered conceptual frame work developed by Rasmussen, Pejtersen & Goldstein (1994) to analyse cognitive work. The purpose of Cognitive Work Analysis is to guide the design of technology for use in the work place. By this method it is possible to analyse real life phenomenon while retaining the complexity inherent in them. Cognitive Work Analysis considers people who interact with information 'actors' in their work related actions, rather than 'users' of systems. Focusing on information behaviour of the job, Cognitive Work Analysis views human information interaction in the context of human work activities. It assumes that in order to be able to design systems that work harmoniously with humans, one has to understand :

- The work the actors do
- Their information behaviour
- The context in which they work
- The reasons for their actions.

The Cognitive Work Analysis focuses simultaneously on the task actors perform, the environment in which it is carried out, and the perceptual, cognitive and ergonomics attributes of the people who do the job. A graphic presentation of the framework is given in Figure 4.12. In this each set of attributes is represented by a circle and is considered a dimension for analysis. Each dimension has host of attributes, factors, or variables—depending on the purpose of study as also the methodology being used. Cognitive Work Analysis provides large number of templates for both analysis and modeling.

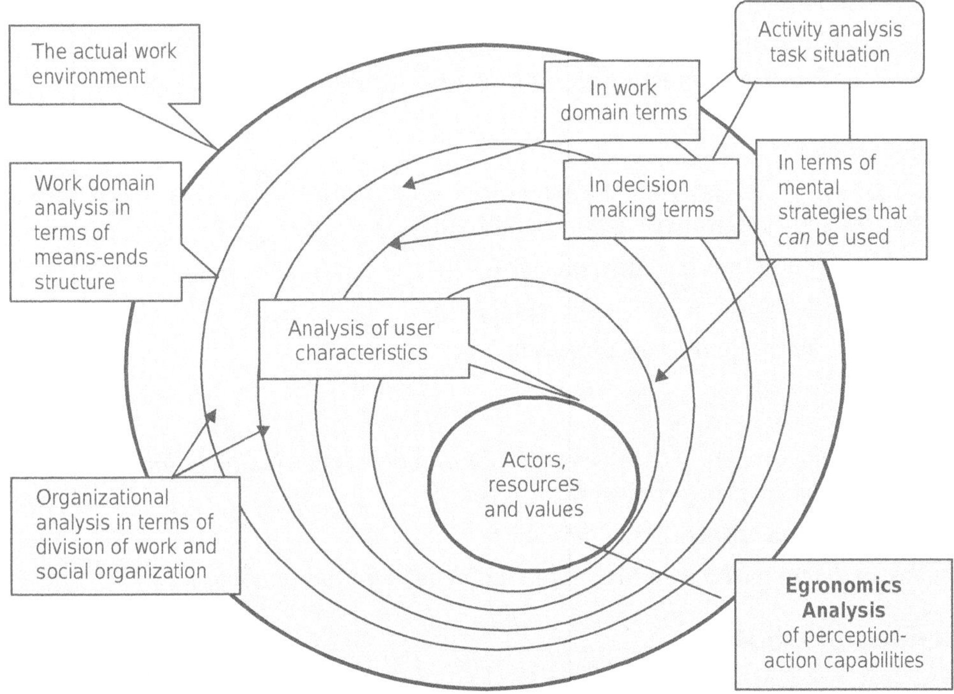

Fig. 4.12. *The Dimensions for Analysis in Cognitive Work Analysis.*

Each dimension has host of content. Figure 4.13 illustrates few of them.

Dimension	***Illustration***
Environment	What external elements affect the organization ?
Work Domain	What are the goals ? The constraints ? Priorities ? Functions ? Physical processes ?
Organizational Analysis	How is the work divided ? What are the criteria's used for division of work ? What are the organizational values ?
Task Analysis in work domain	What are the tasks/ What information is required ?
Task Analysis in decision making terms	What decisions are made ? What information is required ? Which all sources are useful ?
Task Analysis in terms of strategies	What strategies are possible ? What strategies are preferred ? What type of information is needed ?
Actors resources and values	What is the formal training of the actor ? Area of expertise ? Experience ? Personal priorities ? Personal values ?

Fig. 4.13. *Contents OPF Dimension.*

JOB DESIGN

Introduction

Job design has lately emerged as an important tool of work analysis. Job design has a direct impact on turnover, motivation, levels of job satisfaction and industrial relations. Many of the negative consequences of the work place can be avoided if job designing is accomplished with care so that both employee and organizational objectives are fulfilled.

Job design is the structuring of jobs to improve efficiency of the business and improve employee satisfaction. Un-interesting and boring jobs would create problems.

What is Job Design ?

Job design is the way the tasks are combined to form a complete job. It specifies the tasks that make up the job. Job design involves determining :

(*a*) What is to be done (*i.e.*, responses) ?

(*b*) How it is to be done (*i.e.*, tools etc.) ?

(*c*) Why it is to be done (*i.e.*, purpose) ?

Definition

The process of linking specific tasks to specific jobs and deciding what techniques, equipment, and procedures should be used to perform those tasks.

Robbins and **Stuart-Kotze** have defined :

'Job design refers to the way tasks are combined to form complete jobs.'

Characteristics of Job Design

Jobs where employees experience a high level of satisfaction generally have the following characteristics.

(*a*) *Task variety.* The ability to vary the tasks performed. This ability to vary the tasks provides a change in mental activity as well as physical well being through movement and changes in body posture. Variety involves a different process than challenge in the task.

(*b*) *Task Identity.* Where possible the task should fit together to make a complete job. This provides the employee a sense of satisfaction in seeing that the job has been done by him from beginning to the end. People feel

(*c*) *Task Significance.* Employee wants to have a sense of achievement. It is important for them to be recognized and that they have contributed towards accomplishment of the organizational goals.

(*d*) *Autonomy.* The employees should be provided with inputs as to how their jobs are done. They should be involved in decision making process especially where it affects their performance.

(*e*) *Feedback.* Supervisor should provide constructive feedback regarding employee's performance.

Principles of Job Design

It is rarely possible for jobs to be designed to incorporate all the characteristics listed. Ideally however the job should :

(*a*) Form a coherent whole, either independently or with other related jobs. Performance on the job should make a significant contribution to the completion of the product or service, a contribution that is visible to job holder.

(*b*) Provide some variety of pace, method, location and skill.

(*c*) Provide feedback of performance, both directly and through other people.

(*d*) Allow some discretion and control in the timing, sequence and pace of work.

(*e*) Include some responsibility of outcome.

(*f*) Be seen as leading towards some sort of desirable future.

(*g*) Provide opportunity for development in the ways that the individual find relevant.

How to Design a Job ?

Job design determines the manner in which way the set of tasks or an entire position is organized. Job design helps to determine :

(*a*) What tasks are to be done ?

(*b*) When and how the tasks have to be done ?

(*c*) How many tasks have to be done ?

(*d*) In what order the tasks have to be done ?

(*e*) Factors that affect the performance at the job.

(*f*) Organization and the content of the task.

A good job design incorporates the relationship with organizational goals and human efficiency and comfort. The job design should allow :

(*a*) Allow for employee inputs.

(*b*) Give employees a sense of accomplishment.

(*c*) Include training and development requirements.

(*d*) Provide good work and rest schedules.

(*e*) Provide feedback.

Process of Job Designing

Jobs should not be designed in isolation from other jobs within the work area. The organization structures and objectives of the work area should be taken into account while preparing a job design.

(*a*) The first step in job design is data gathering. In this stage the analyst ask the under mentioned questions :

(*b*) What are the future directions and objectives of the organization ?

(*c*) What are the tasks to be performed ?

(*d*) Why these tasks need to be done ?

(*e*) How will these be done ?

(*f*) How will these jobs impact other positions in the area ?
(*g*) Where will the work be performed ?
(*h*) Who will the position report to ?

APPROACHES TO JOB DESIGNING

There are various approaches to job designing. In today's context job designing assumes greater significance for human resource managers. Job design assists in reduction of stress, enhances motivation and provides greater satisfaction to employees. This facilitates improvement of performance of employees enabling organizations to effectively compete in the global market. (Figure 4.14).

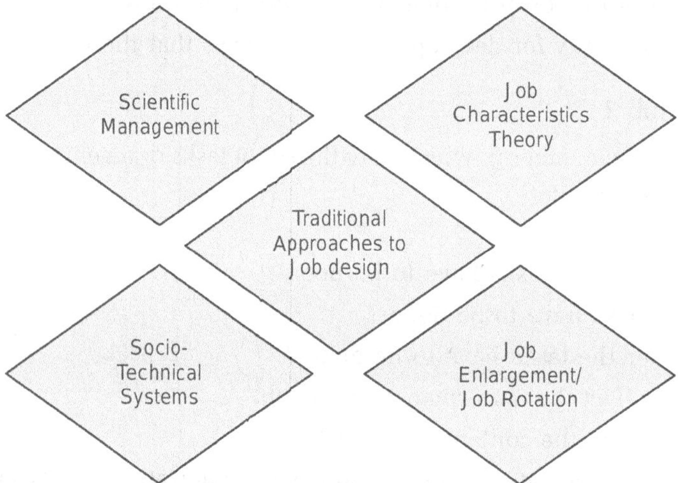

Fig. 4.14. *Approaches to Job Designing.*

Traditional Approach

Under this approach, the company allocates duties and responsibilities consistent with the common practices of tradition. This method has many advantages. Firstly, it simplifies the recruitment, selection and determination of compensation. Secondly it is consistent with the employees' expectation and formal training. Thirdly, it is easier to implement since traditional organization of work has developed over many years and it has been acceptable to many organizations.

Scientific Management or Job Specialization

The approach has its origin in the scientific management movement which popularized time and motion studies. F.W. Taylor popularized the concept of management to be scientifically and analytically based as the practice of engineering. It emphasizes the analysis of jobs, and the simplification and standardization of the tasks performed. The process involves breaking jobs into small component parts and utilization of set of principles and practices designed to increase the performance of individual workers by stressing job simplification and job specialization. Each job was then assigned to a specialist. This would result in greater productivity. It would reduce the need for elaborate procedures for selection and training. It would also help in greater dexterity and faster learning by an employee. As the individual will constantly work in same position there, would less or no time lost in internal mobility or up-gradation of machine and tools.

Specialization also helps company to pay for only needed skills. Thus, it would result in simplification of jobs for economic benefit. Pay is the principal outcome used to motivate workers to contribute their inputs. The employee is paid on piece-rate pay system *i.e.*, he is paid depending upon his performance. Scientific management focuses exclusively on extrinsic motivation and ignores the important role of intrinsic motivation.

The major disadvantages of scientific management are :

- Workers may feel that they have lost control over their work behaviors.
- Workers may feel as if they are part of a machine and are treated as such.
- Workers have no opportunity to develop and acquire new skills.

Job Characteristics Theory

This approach focuses on job redesign, work structuring, job enrichment etc. here the job design aims at identifying characteristics that make job intrinsically motivating and to specify the consequences of those characteristics. Heckman and Oldham Job Characteristic Model is in Figure 4.15. It has four key components :

(*a*) *Core Job Dimensions.* Heckman and Oldham have stated that the employee performs better when certain job characteristics or dimensions are generated. The important core characteristics having a direct impact on performance are :

- **Skill Variety** : The extent to which a job requires a worker to use different skills, abilities, or talents.
- **Task Identity** : The extent to which a job involves performing a whole piece of work from its beginning to its end.
- **Task Significance** : The extent to which a job has an impact on the lives or work of other people in or out of the organization.
- **Autonomy** : The degree to which a job allows a worker the freedom and independence to schedule work and decide how to carry it out.
- **Feedback** : The extent to which performing a job provides a worker with clear information about his or her effectiveness.

A measure of the overall potential of a job to foster intrinsic motivation or Motivational Potential Score can be calculated. The score is a computational combination of the measure of skills variety, task identity, task significance, autonomy and feedback.

$$\text{Motivational Potential Score} = \frac{(SV + TI + TS)}{3} \times A \times F$$

Where : SV – for Skill Variety

TI – for Task Identity

TS – for Task significance

A – for autonomy

F – for feedback

The formula reveals that out of all the job dimensions, autonomy and feedback are most critical. If score on either of them is zero (0) then Motivational Potential Score will also be zero which means the job has no motivating potential. Motivational potential score can range from 1 to 343. The average score is usually around 110 to 150. Motivational Potential Score implies that the job has high motivating potential and *vice versa*.

(*a*) Critical Psychological States. The three psychological states that determine his motivation, satisfaction and performance are :

- Experiencing Meaningfulness of the work. It is the degree to which workers feel their jobs are important, worthwhile and meaningful.. This is mainly achieved by incorporating skill variety, task identity and task significance in the work.
- Experiencing Responsibility. It is the extent to which an employee or job holder feels personally responsible and accountable for the result of the work performed. Autonomy in performing the job is the core job characteristics or dimension which results in experiencing responsibility.
- Knowledge of Results. The degree to which workers know how well they perform their jobs on a continuous basis. A regular feed back on performance is the core job dimension for knowledge of results.

Critical psychological states results in four key outcomes for workers and their organizations :

- High intrinsic motivation.
- High job performance.
- High job satisfaction.
- Low absenteeism and turnover.

(*b*) **Consequences.** The critical psychological states have a direct impact on outcomes or consequences for both the job and the job holder. The positive outcomes are given at Figure 4.

(*c*) **Individual Differences.** The psychological states provide intrinsic motivation only for those people who have a high need for learning and growth on the job. This desire for personal feeling of accomplishment and growth is called growth need which serves as a motivator.

The job characteristics model has important implications for job design. It suggests that only those employees will respond positively to the five core job dimensions who have strong growth needs and who are satisfied with the company's internal environment. Therefore, individual's personal traits and need patterns of a job holder must be considered in redesigning jobs. The positive outcomes will occur only when there is a fit between job and the job holder.

Hackman and Oldham suggested guidelines for job redesign so as to develop the five core dimensions in a job.

(*a*) *Combining Tasks*. By combining tasks a longer work module can be formed.

(*b*) *Forming Natural Work Units*. It involves identifying basic work items and grouping them into natural categories.

(*c*) *Establishing Client Relationships*. It involves identifying the client, developing the most direct contact and specifying criteria by which client can evaluate the quality of product or service.

(*d*) *Vertical Loading of Job.* Reducing the gap between planning, implementing and controlling the work.

(*e*) *Opening Feedback Channels.* Achieved by establishing client channels, providing performance feedback to worker and allowing him to control quality of the product.

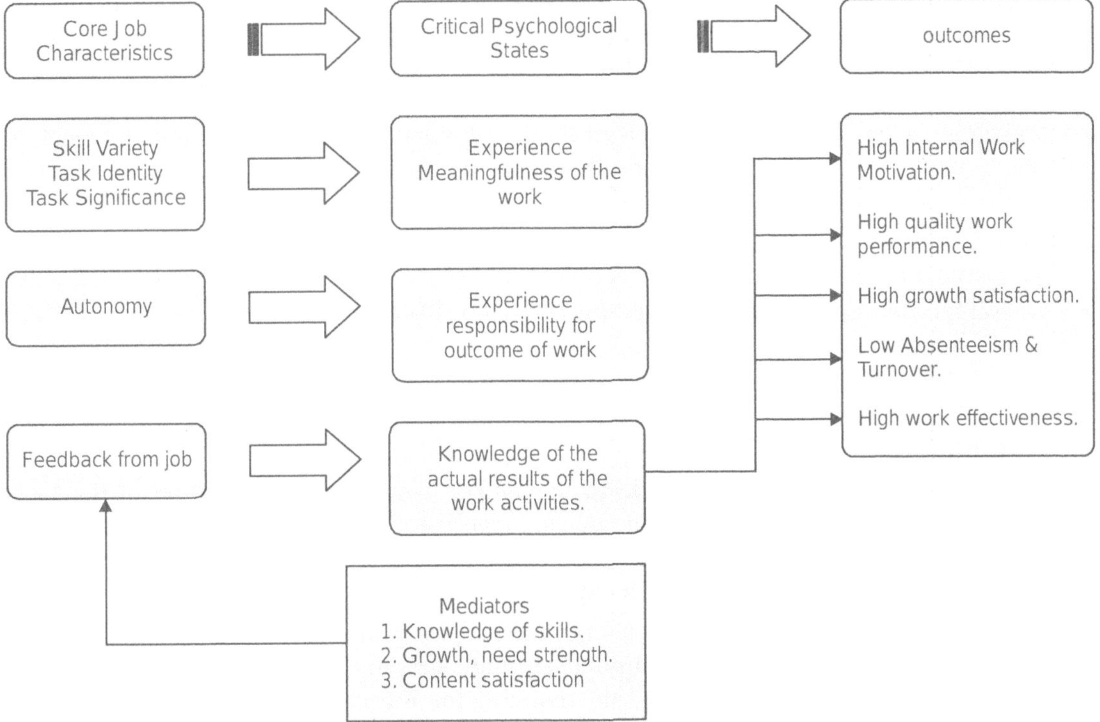

Fig. 4.15. *Heckman and Oldham Job Characteristics Model.*

Socio-Technical Systems Approach

The system involves meshing up of the technical and social aspects of the job. In order to create jobs that are supportive relationships. In modern organizations each employees plays an assigned role in accomplishing group objectives. Redesigning work through socio technical system involves the combined effort of employees, supervisors, unions etc. Works are not designed to make it intrinsically motivating; rather these are designed to get the work accomplished. Hence, jobs should be designed by taking a holistic or systems view of the entire job situation, including the physical and social environment. The essential elements in socio –technical system are;

(*a*) The job should be challenging for the individual and yet provide variety. The challenging should not only be based on endurance.

(*b*) Employees need to constant keep on improving skill and add knowledge and abilities (a constant learning process should be there).

(*c*) Employees must participate in decision making and should have some autonomy in working.

(*d*) Employees need some social support and recognition in society.

(e) The employees should be able to relate to the job being performed by them.

Ergonomics

Taking into account the human factors in designing the employee's workstation is often termed as *ergonomics*. Ergonomics is an approach for job design. The relationship between the employees and their workstations is considered to include the machines, lighting, noise, chairs and so on. An ergonomically designed workstation will allow a worker to work in neutral, relaxed and ideal conditions that will minimize the effects of fatigue and boredom. Ergonomics is the study of the man-machine system intended to design the machine for its users fitting it to their physiological requirements to minimize fatigue and maximize output (Broom). Ergonomics has assumed greater significance as the workforce stays at workstations longer and jobs are altered to meet the challenging physical needs. The *Ergonomics Handbook* of the IBM Corporation in the USA stresses the need to design the job to fit the person in several respects (Tinarelli, 2000, p. 17), including the following :

- Posture. Incorporate enough movement in design of the job to prevent prolonged immobility in the same position, which causes fatigue and discomfort.
- **The Back**. Many employees suffer from back pain. The best way to prevent back injuries is to design lifting tasks carefully. Often a simple change in the layout of common lifting tasks can eliminate the twisting of the torso when lifting, the most common cause of back injuries.
- **The Hand**. Excessive back-and forth movement can cause inflammation of the hand. Women are three times more susceptible to repetitive-motion injury than man. An effective means of eliminating such injuries is to avoid the use of hand tools that cause constant compression of the palm of the hand.
- **The Environment.** Noise can be distracting and harmful when it is higher than routine background noise. The use of sound absorbing material and machine covers reduce the noise levels. Higher light levels are required for intricate work. Position of work in relation to light source is critical. Eye strain and general fatigue can easily affect job performance.

Work Flexibility

In recent years there has been expansion of business, globalization and thereby increasing the working force. There has now been a trend in that the working class is not looking for a lifelong career with the same company. Hence, the employer has to consider the behavioral change in the work force. There has been a trend to design jobs in a manner in that employees have flexible working hours, job sharing, working at home, work module etc.

TECHNIQUES OF JOB DESIGN

The techniques for job design and redesign include work simplification, job rotation, job enlargement and job enrichment as shown in Figure 4.16.

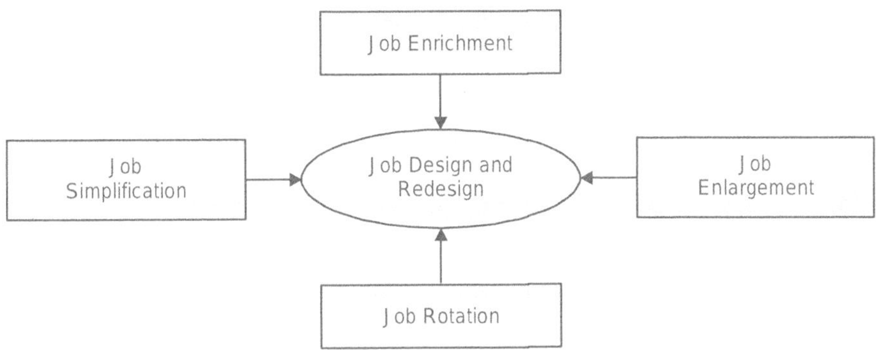

Fig. 4.16. *Techniques of Job Design.*

Job Simplification

In job simplification, the complete job is broken down into small subparts, usually consisting of few operations. This is done so that employees can do these jobs without much specialized training, many small jobs can also be performed simultaneously so that the complete operation can be done more speedily.

Job Rotation

Job rotation is an alternative to boredom at work place. It involves internal mobility *i.e.*, shifting people from one position to another within a working group or an organization so that there is some relief and variety without fundamentally changing the nature of the job. The broad objectives of job rotation are reduced boredom, broadening of employee's skills and knowledge, and making them more competent. Although there are significant advantages but job rotation also suffers from few drawbacks. Frequent shifting of people from one job to another causes interruptions and drop in productivity and alienation in a new job. The job rotation also does not provide any challenge to the employee. Herzberg has characterized this approaches merely substituting 'one zero for another zero.'

Job Enlargement

Job enlargement involves adding more tasks to a job. It is a horizontal expansion and increases jobs scope and give variety of tasks to the job holders, lengthens the work cycle time, provide wholeness and identity with the task and increases the knowledge necessary to perform it. Job enlargement is essentially adding more tasks to a single job. Job enlargement definitely reduced boredom at job but there is no evidence that it helps in motivating the individual in the desired direction.

Job Enrichment

Job enrichment was first coined by Herzberg. It implies increasing the contents of a job or the deliberate upgrading of responsibility, scope and challenge in work. 'Job enrichment is a motivational technique which emphasizes the need for challenging and interesting work (Herzberg, 1966).' It simply implies adding few more motivators to a job to make it more rewarding, challenging and offer autonomy and pride to the employee (Beatty and Schneider, 1975). The job holder is given discretion in making operational decisions and contribute his or her ideas to the to the organization's success. Job enrichment increases the job depth that refers to the degree of control employees have over their work. It just provides while retaining accountability.

Jobs can be enriched (Figure 4.17) by :

(*a*) Providing autonomy and freedom to employees in deciding about work methods, pace etc.

(*b*) Increase responsibility and accountability.

(*c*) Checking own performance related to quality.

(*d*) Provide feedback to employees.

(*e*) Training guiding and encouraging new learning amongst employees.

(*f*) Have authority to communicate directly with people who use his or her output.

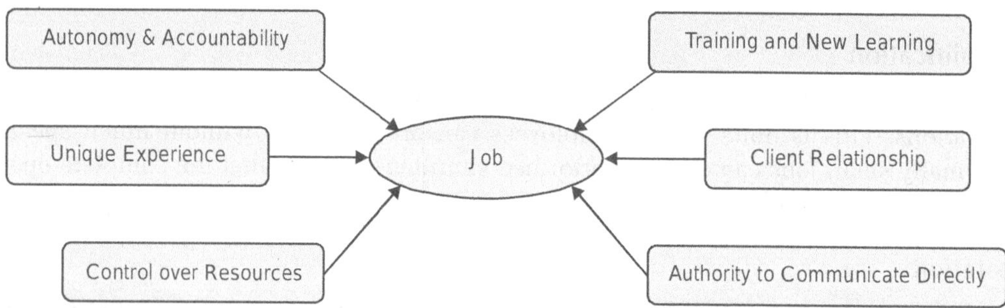

Fig. 4.17. *Techniques for Job Enrichment.*

Like other techniques Job Enrichment has both advantages and disadvantages. On the advantages side, it may be stated that the job enrichment benefits employees and organizations by making work more interesting, helps in motivating, enhanced performance, knowledge, skills, abilities (Figure 4.15). Limitations are also there in job enrichment. Technological changes and development does not permit enrichment of all jobs. It has also been observed that job enrichment cannot replace good management. Also any changes in the process or work profile is always met by resistance from employees.

Job Analysis in a 'Jobless' World

Job is generally defined as 'a set of closely related activities carried out for pay,' but over last few years concept of a job has been changing quite dramatically. As one observer put it :

'The modern world is on the verge of another huge leap in creativity and productivity, but the job is not going to be part of tomorrow's economic reality. There still is and will always be enormous amounts of work to do, but it is not going to be contained in the familiar envelope we call jobs. In fact, many organizations are today well along the path toward being *'de jobbed'* (William Bridges, 1998).

"De-jobbing" is a global phenomenon. De-jobbing involves broadening the responsibilities of the company's jobs, and encouraging employees not to limit themselves to what's on their job descriptions. The organizations today have to accept the rapid changes in the technology, products, deregulation, global competition, political instability, demographic changes and a shift to service economy. This calls for the firms to be flexible, responsive and more competitive. This has led the firms to have jobs not very clearly defined and delineated.

Flatter Organizations. Instead of traditional, pyramid shaped structure, organizations are getting flatter with few hierarchical layers. Because of flatter organizations the managers end up supervising larger number of subordinates. This has led to less direct supervision and enhanced responsibilities and breadth of work for subordinates.

Work Teams. Managers are today resorting to organizing work around teams and processes rather than around specialized functions. In such organizations the responsibilities and work changes daily and the worker stops viewing their work in narrow set of responsibilities.

Boundary less Organizations. In a boundary-less organization the wide spread use of teams and cross functional task forces reduces and makes more permeable boundaries that typically separate departments and hierarchical levels (Larry Hirschhorn and Thomas Gilmore, 1992).

PRODUCTIVITY ISSUES

Productivity is a popular term. Not a day goes by without the media depicting the Indian manufacturing and service sectors' problems and successes. Inevitably, the numbers used to reflect something nebulously called productivity, which generally refers to the quantity or volume being produced.

For businesses the primary objective of productivity measurement is to gain competitive advantage. The idea is to establish the prevailing productivity levels and then to improve these ratings by systematic organizational or technological steps so that the business performs better than their competitors. As illustrated in Figure 4.18 productivity has, among other things three main components :

(*a*) Utilization.

(*b*) Efficiency

(*c*) Effectiveness.

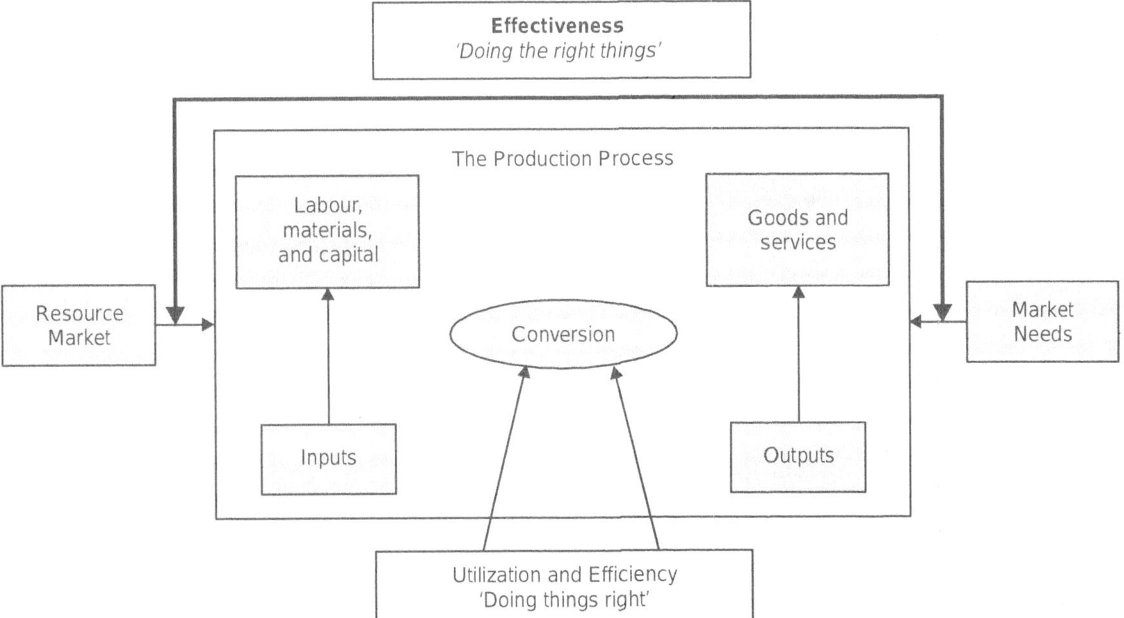

Source : *Adapted from Du Plosy, E. and Jackson, D. (1995) Productivity Measurement, Productivity SA 21(2), 16.*

Fig. 4.18. *Three Major Components of Productivity : Effectiveness, Efficiency and Utilization.*

Many Indian Managers suffer from misguided notion that productivity is measured solely in terms of output per man hour. Labour productivity only constitutes one aspect, albeit the important one, of the may constituents of productivity.

Efficiency is the rate of conversion while resources are being used. Efficiency is measured in terms of maintaining a satisfactory relationship between cost and benefits. The more efficiently the company controls its raw material the better the benefits.

Effectiveness is measured in terms of 'doing the right things'.

It would be observed that better a system is at acquiring and converting selected resources into marketing goods or services, the more productive it becomes.

CONCLUSION

It can be stated that Job Analysis is an important Human Resource Management Tool. It can be used to determine used for determining and implementing all functions of human resource management (Figure 4.19).

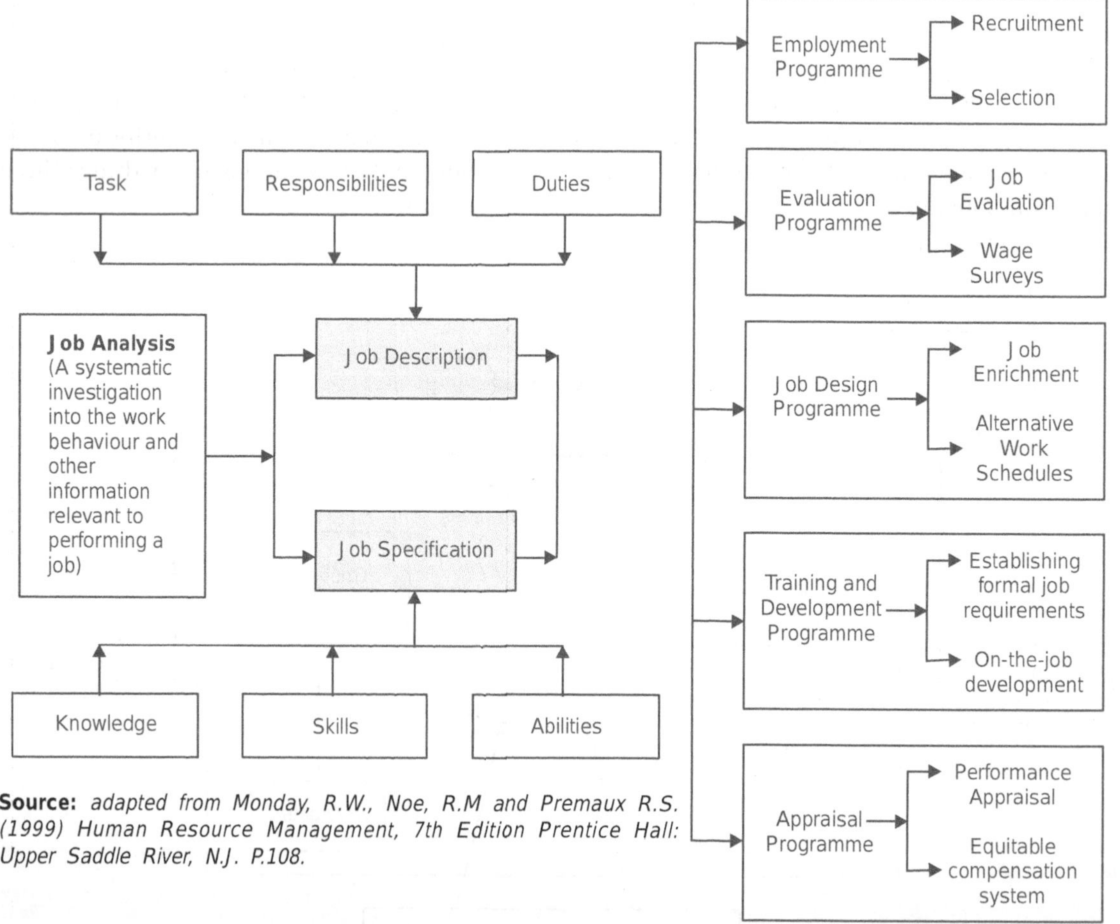

Source: *adapted from Monday, R.W., Noe, R.M and Premaux R.S. (1999) Human Resource Management, 7th Edition Prentice Hall: Upper Saddle River, N.J. P.108.*

Fig. 4.19. *Job Analysis Human Resource Management Tool.*

Review Questions

1. What do you understand by Job Analysis ? What is its importance in the management of human resources ?
2. Define Job Analysis. Discuss the importance of Job Analysis in recent time, its uses and application.
3. Describe in brief the necessity work analysis and design in an organization.
4. Explain the following :
   - Socio-technical approach in job design.
   - Scientific management approach to job design.
   - Job rotation.
   - Sources of job enrichment.
   - Ergonomics.
5. Do you think work analysis and design would lead the present job match ? Justify ?
6. Define work measurement and discuss in brief the techniques of work measurement.

PROJECT WORK

Prepare a brief report of emerging trends of work analysis in present Indian context. Based on the field work, suggest for better implementation of results of work analysis.

Case Study

Consultants and Human Resource Solution Inc. a consultant company was enlisted by Godwin's a retail and real estate management company to identify the critical knowledge, skills and abilities required for successful job performance for their entire salaried, non- union classifications. The project demanded the creation of custom competencies for more than 2,000 individual positions. These competencies were integrated into the company's hiring processes to align its staffing strategies including on internet with corporate mission and goals.

Challenges

- Defining best practices competency development that conformed to legal and professional standards.
- Training staff on ongoing work methodologies.
- Incorporating work into downstream processes, such as attracting, selecting, retaining and appraisal.

Methodology

- Group positions based on similarity of work behaviour to minimize the number of employees.
- Integrate company's values and vision in competency development programme.
- Defined a list of competencies applicable across positions in a company. This list served as the foundation for building competency development programme.
- Equipped employees with requisite knowledge and skills to facilitate the competency development programme.

- Leverage computer network to facilitate sharing of information throughout the competency development programme.
- Listened out issues and short comings related to the process.

Results

The firm defined an efficient, job related approach to identify critical knowledge, abilities and skills. These were done by training the employees.

The identified the critical knowledge, skills and abilities required for successful job performance.

The firm integrated the competencies with hiring process including internet based

The firm defined more than 2700 work behaviours describing the activities performed by 2000 positions.

Assignment

1. Examine the work practices of Consultants and Human Resource Solution Inc.
2. Do you think competency development approach would help job analysis and design ?
3. Examine the methodology followed by the company.

Chapter 5

RECRUITMENT AND RETENTION

★ LEARNING OBJECTIVES ★

After reading this chapter, you will be able to understand :

- The process of recruitment.
- Nature, objectives and importance of recruitment.
- Factors affecting recruitment.
- Methods of recruitment.
- Significance of recruitment process for retaining people.

INTRODUCTION

Having determined the number and the kind of person required to fill the position the company starts the process to attract a suitable candidate and fill the position commences. Recruitment involves identification of sources from where employees can be recruited and finding candidates with suitable knowledge, skills and abilities for employment Recruitment forms the first stage in the process, which continues with selection and ends with placement. Recruitment makes it possible to acquire the number and type of people required to ensure continued operation of an organization.

Recruitment is a constant process in the organizations life. Employees leave, retire or die in the saddle creating vacancies. The organizations also expand and grow all these require additional and new persons to occupy positions so created. Recruitment only ceases when organization ceases to exist.

Recruitment scenario in the nation has gone a complete change in last few years in the wake of rapid growth, globalization and opening up the economy. Recruitment from being a staff function has today become a strategic priority for an organization to attract and retain the best talent in the company from the market. In this chapter, we shall discuss the process, nature, constraints and challenges facing recruitment.

PURPOSE OF RECRUITMENT

The main purpose of Recruitment is to provide equitable and effective means for bringing competent employees into the company. To effectively accomplish this the organization undertakes :

(*a*) Announcement of vacancies so that all who are interested make an application.

(*b*) Creation of tests and testing procedures in order to determine the ability of applicants to perform the work in satisfactory manner.

(*c*) The certification of qualified applicants to fill vacancies.

NATURE AND OBJECTIVES OF RECRUITMENT

Meaning and Definition

The process of identification and procuring of applicants for actual or anticipated vacancies in an organization is recruitment. It is the process of searching the candidates for employment and stimulating them to apply for jobs in the organization (Edwin B. Flippo, 1984).

In the words of **Yoder et.al.** (1972) *'Recruitment is a process to discover the source of manpower to meet the requirements of the staffing schedule and to employ effective measures for attracting that manpower in adequate numbers to facilitate effective selection of an efficient working force.'*

Werther and **Davis** (1993) define recruitment *'It is the process of finding and attracting capable applicants for employment. The process begins when new recruits are sought and ends when their applications are submitted. The result is a pool of applicants from which new employees are selected.'*

Recruitment thus is an attempt to draw attention of applicants in market, get interested applicants and generate a pool of perspective employees so that management can select the right person for the right job. Recruitment precedes the selection process. Recruitment needs are of three types—planned, anticipated and unexpected. Planned need arise from changes in the organization and retirement policy etc.

Challenges for Recruitment

All organizations, large or small, have to engage in recruitment. Some organizations continuously indulge in recruitment while others do it infrequently. It has been observed that firms having a large work force tend to recruit continuously. Here the size may be of importance. This practice is more prevalent in multinational corporations and service organizations. However, an ideal situation for an organization would be if there are large numbers of applicants for every vacancy occurring in the organization. However, this is not the case. There are occasions when there are large numbers of applicants but these do not necessarily have the requisite qualifications, skills, knowledge and abilities. Hence, recruitment of best talent is a challenge. The major constraints are discussed below.

The first major constraint in attracting applicants is the image of the company.[1] It is a known fact that candidates are attracted to a reputed organization. This is especially so with college

[1] Kampani, Nimesh, 'Norms a Must for Holding Cos', *The Economic Times*, 26 Feb 2008, New Delhi, p.7.

leaving students. In India there was a tendency for lifelong careers as there was large supply of manpower compared to demand. People were interested in securing jobs in government or public sector undertakings. This was the scenario existing since independence till mid eighties. However, with the opening of Indian economy and new economic policy the people preference for employment has shifted to multi national corporations and companies with reputation like the Hindustan Lever Limited, Infosys, TATA, ANZ Bank, Microsoft, IBM etc. However, all companies don't have such reputation and are not sought after by employees. The main reason is the lack of enthusiasms among the people to seek employment with such companies is the perceived low reputation due organizational culture prevalent, location of the firm, inadequate working conditions etc.

The next major constraints are the organizational policies. Each individual seeks two things growth and environment in an organization. It is important that a firm provides opportunity for growth as also a conducive working environment to enable the employee to utilize his talents and have a feeling of satisfaction. Corporate culture is a key factor in attracting employees. Corporate employees are no longer considering just remuneration at work as the sole criteria for taking up new jobs or continuing in their present assignments.

The next challenge is to weigh the pros and cons of internal and external recruiting. The internal and external recruiting would be discussed subsequently. Needless to say that both the sources have advantages and disadvantages. Internal recruiting helps in motivation, while external motivation brings in new skills and processes.

The recruiter also has to distinguish among the major selection methods and use the most legally defensible of them. He should clearly understand the legal constraints on the hiring process. The recruitment process should abide by the law of the land.

The recruitment process also faces challenge of selecting the right person for the job. The process involves making staffing decisions that minimize the hiring and promotion of the wrong people.

In modern market conditions, due globalization, cost cutting, efficiency and knowledge based work there is are reasonable job expectations. The modern worker looks for quality of life and a reasonable remuneration. His loyalty is fickle and would shift and hence there should be reasonable package to attract the talent. Compensation and benefit package offered by an organization.

It is also important to know that a recruitment process is an expensive proposition. Hence the firm or an organization may like to employ methods to cut cost in recruiting process.

Keeping the above challenges and constraints in view it is imperative for an organization to have an elaborate policies framed. Such a policy always enables the firm to assert it is objectives for recruitment and provides a framework of procedures for implementation of the recruitment program in the form of procedures. Yoder (1972) has listed some of the features for framing a recruitment policy.

(*a*) Carefully observing the letter and spirit of the relevant public policy on hiring and on the whole employment relationship.

(*b*) Providing individual employee with maximum job security;

(*c*) Providing each employee an opportunity to grow and develop his skills and talents.

(*d*) Assuring each employee of the organizations interest in his personal goals and employment objectives.

(*e*) Assuring all about fairness in all relationships, including promotions and transfer.

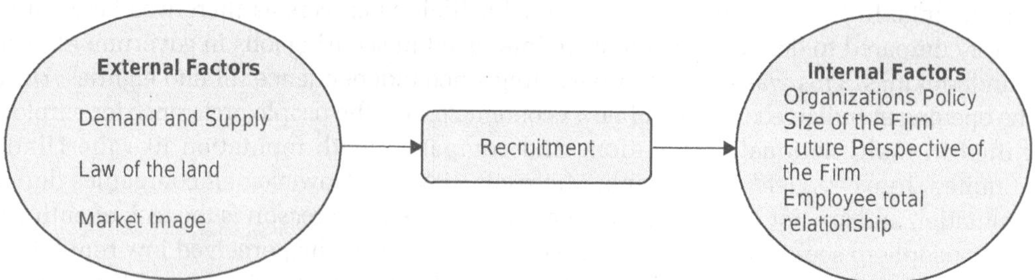

Fig. 5.1. *Challenges for Recruitment.*

Objective or Purpose of Recruitment

The main purpose or an objective of any recruitment is to :

(*a*) Determine the present and future requirements

(*b*) Attract a sufficient number of applicants to allow an optimal selection ratio.

(*c*) Aid in meeting organizational goals by ensuring requisite number of employees with knowledge, skills and abilities are available.

(*d*) Increase the pool of job candidates at minimum costs.

(*e*) Help increase the success rate of the selection process.

(*f*) Help reduce the probability of selected candidate leaving.

(*g*) Meet the organizations legal and social obligations.

(*h*) Increase the organizational and individual effectiveness.

(*i*) Evaluate the effectiveness of various recruiting techniques.

(*j*) Maintain goodwill and positive image of the company in the market.

Where does Recruitment Fit in HRM

Figure 5.2 depicts the relationship between activities of HRM and Recruitment.

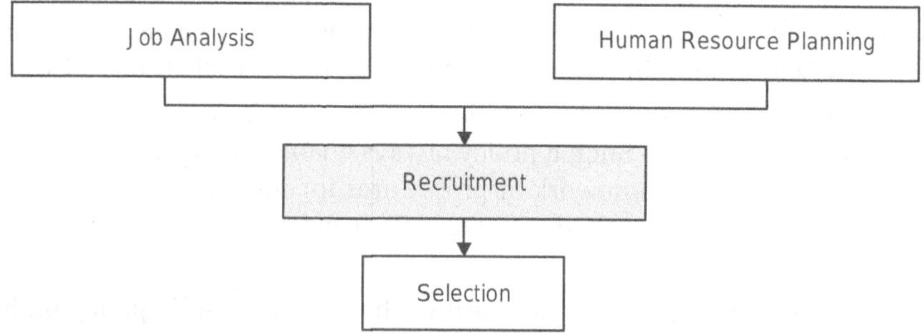

Fig. 5.2. *Recruitment in Relation to HRM.*

SOURCES OF RECRUITMENT

The source of recruitment may be many but these for ease can be grouped into two.

(*a*) Internal Sources including Employee referrals.

(*b*) External Sources.

Internal Sources

Internal recruitment seeks candidates from among the ranks of those currently employed. Organizations attempt to develop their own employees for higher positions in the organizations. There are two important internal sources of recruitment, namely, transfer and promotion. Transfer involves movement of an employee from one position to another in an organization without substantial change in job content. Promotion on other hand involves movement to a position with larger span of control, pay, status and responsibilities. Jack Stack (1998)has listed the advantages of internal recruitment.

(*a*) Internal recruitment leads good public relations.

(*b*) Builds employees morale and helps in productivity.

(*c*) Helps talented and good employees to rise up the hierarchy.

(*d*) Helps in making positive decision on selection as greater information is available.

(*e*) Involves less cost.

(*f*) Easy for the employee selected to adjust as he is fully conversant with ethos, organizational culture and values.

The above variables are co related with turnover, absenteeism, and productivity rates. Like in all methodologies internal recruitment also suffers from certain demerits.

(*a*) Limits induction of fresh talents, and in turn fresh ideas and processes are inhibited.

(*b*) The employees tend to rake things for granted and become lethargic as they are confident of being picked up for promotion when vacancies occur.

(*c*) Limits growth of talented employees as competition is hampered or not encouraged.

(*d*) The existing employees do not act as change masters in spite of the fact that change is a necessity.

(*e*) Limits creativity and environment does not foster conditions for it.

In high performance work systems companied practicing internal recruitment are more likely to be successful than companies that rely on external recruitment financially. Bank of America has a policy in which newly hired employees are briefed of the career progression with typical timetable for progression within the organization for their best employees.

The companies with a clear plan for internal recruitment, there is a deliberate succession planning carried out. In some companies especially small there may not be succession planning in the case 'job posting' is carried out. Job posting is a process where announcement of positions available/ vacancies anticipated are posted on a board or circulated through a news letter, intranet, etc. All employees are then free to apply for the vacancy.

Employee Referrals

Employee referrals are an excellent means of locating potential employee for vacancies for which are difficult to fill. These are usually of highly skilled in nature or of managerial appointments. A recommendation of current employee regarding the job applicant as a best source, as the reputation of the employee recommending is at stake.

This method with its advantage has pitfalls also as some of the employees recommend their friends. This may lead to unhealthy groups and nepotism.

External Recruitment Process

External source of recruitment is a larger process of recruitment than internal replacements. Vacancies are created as employees are always leaving the organization, retiring, dying in saddle etc. Hence, there will always new people that have to enrolled or brought into the organization. There is evidence that external sources of recruitment brings in new processes and ideas in the organization.

External recruitment is a process the recruits from outside the organization. The major methods of external recruitment are given in succeeding paragraphs.

Direct Recruitment, Walk in/Write In. Direct recruitment is an important method and source of recruitment. Vacancies are advertised and recruitment done at the factory gate. This practice is generally followed for vacancies requiring low skills or for unskilled workers.

Casual Callers or Unsolicited Applications. The organization which have a reputation in market and are considered good employers attract a steady flow of unsolicited applicants. This serves as a valuable source of manpower. The major advantage of this source is that it limits the expenditure towards cost of recruitment.

Advertisement in Media other than Telecasting. Advertisements in newspapers, trade and professional journals are generally used to attract potential skilled employee or an employee with special abilities. The higher the position in the organization and more specialized the skills sought, the more widely dispersed the advertisement is likely to be. A good advertisement will visualize the type of applicant one is trying to recruit; advantages and benefits an employee is likely accure. An advertisement including those over the internet should include the under mentioned :

(*a*) The job content.

(*b*) Realistic description of working conditions.

(*c*) Location of the job.

(*d*) Compensation including benefits.

(*e*) Skills and abilities required.

(*f*) To whom should the application be submitted ?

Telecasting. Lately there has been boon in telecasting extending its reach and coverage. The number of channels that are available has resulted in competition. Telecasting is an important medium for attracting attention of the viewers. Telecasting also is an important source for building reputation of the company. It can give visual display of the conditions prevalent. However, it is not very popular with companies for recruiting purposes due its high cost, advertisement may be missed out by candidates etc.

Employment Agencies and Head Hunters. Government run employment exchanges as a source of recruitment. In some cases government has made it mandatory for notification of vacancies to the employment exchange. Today, there are large number of agencies in private sector that specialize in placement services. These agencies charge either the employer or the employee for their services. These are most effective when an organization has difficulty in finding or searching for a potential candidate or when the particular skill is scarce. These concerns also maintain a data bank of persons with different skills and abilities. ABC Concultants, AF Ferguson, Mantec Consultants are few of the concerns specializing in placements.

Campus Recruitment. Today due complexity of job large number of companies maintain close liaison with universities, colleges, technical institutes to meet their recruitment needs.

Campus recruitment offers excellent source of technical and managerial talents. This method has gained popularity in recent times. The philosophy being to catch them young.. In this method the process begins much before academic session ends. Normally a presentation by the company is made giving out the background of the company and what they are seeking. Thereafter the placement officer of the institute coordinates with recruiter and pre-placement talks are initiated. Thereafter the candidate is encouraged to apply for selection. This method has proved its effectiveness. It enables companies to build a pool of applicants to choose from. This also helps companies to subsequently mould the applicants selected as they are young.

Voluntary Organizations. Some of the voluntary organization also helps in placement. They are basically dealing with handicapped, widows, retired personnel etc.

Professional Organizations or Guilds. Professional organizations are also a source of recruitment. However, these are restricted to people belonging to a particular profession. A perspective employer can approach the organization if it is seeking a person with a specific requirement.

Professional Teams. These are temporary groups which come together for accomplishment of specific job or assignment. Normally these are professional free lances. This scheme has not yet picked up in India but is gaining popularity lately.

Advantages of External Recruitment

An external source of recruitment has its own advantages.

(*a*) It helps in procuring the best talent from the market.

(*b*) External recruitment provides a wide canvas and larger number of applicants to select from.

(*c*) Over a period of time there comes stagnation in the organization and it needs rejuvenation. In such a situation it is best infuse talents from outside. Induction of fresh talent would infuse new ideas and skills thus enabling the organizational culture to improve.

(*d*) The policy of external induction enables company to generate competitive spirit. Current employees would work hard and show better performance.

Disadvantages of External Recruitment

There are demerits in external recruitment.

(*a*) External sources of recruitment impact the motivation level of the employees. This dissatisfaction of frustration amongst employees leads to rapid turnover and exit.

(*b*) External recruitment process is timer consuming and expensive.

(*c*) The firms are also cautious on external recruitment as they are uncertain

Some Current Trends in Recruitment

Outsourcing. Large number of concerns is drawing the manpower requirements from an outsourced concern. This is also referred to as leasing of human resource functions. The outsourced firm in turn develops their pool of human resource personnel by employing people for the parent concern and make same available to them. This process has some major advantages.

(*a*) Companies need not plan their human resource requirements in advance. Personnel with knowledge, skill and ability can be drawn from out sourced firm.

(*b*) The parent company is not responsible for maintenance of human relations.

(*c*) Parent companies can dispense with services of an employee moment their services are no longer required.

WIPRO EXPANDS ROLE OF CONSULTANTS FOR HIRING

Hiring has become a ever-growing challenge for the Indian IT Industry with companies evolving their own strategies for meeting the growing demand for quality talent. Wipro Technologies is expanding the scope of its partners for recruiting software professionals.

Partners or manpower consultants are important constituents for IT companies in sourcing the required talent. Wipro General Manager for Strategic Resourcing said the company is broad basing the role of its partners. The partners would be providing IT professionals for a particular business vertical.

Poaching /Raiding. Oxford dictionary gives poaching meaning as—capture by illicit or unsportsman like methods. Poaching in recruitment envisages recruiting a person already employed with another reputed company which may be rival in the industry. Preventing poaching and raiding is a challenge for modern human resource personnel.

Ex-Serviceman. India has one of the largest standing armies in the world. These personnel retire early from service. A very large proportion of these men have varied specializations. Large number of concerns is today re-employing these people. The companies are able to exploit their talents as also get a dedicated and disciplined work force.

E-Recruitment. Internet's popularity has increased so has it usage. Large number of organization today advertises their vacancies through World Wide Web. Alternatively the job seekers put their Curriculum Vitae on World Wide Web. The major advantage of e-recruitment is low cost of recruitment, time savings etc. There are large numbers of Indian firms that have taken e route for recruiting. Cognizant has an exclusive blogs and networking forums for potential hires. Wipro is hosting training material on its site for recruitment. These steps are basically taken to facilitate students to be prepared for industry. (Ranganathan, Chandra and Sivakumar, Nandini, 'IT firms take e-route to lure students', *The Economic Times,* 26 Feb 2008, New Delhi, p.6.)

Employee Leasing. The companies are today resorting to lease employees for temporary shortfall. In this the leasing company temporarily leases employees on its pay rolls for assignments to other companies.

Employee Leasing Catching on in India

Hindustan Times in its report dated Dec 01, 2003 that companies like Delhi based Team Lease and Chennai based Mafoi have become front runners in temporarily leasing out employees on their payrolls to fill up the temporary positions in other companies.

Ashok Reddy the Managing Director of TeamLease Services states that employee leasing accounts for 2.5 percent of the total labour work force in developed economies and globally it is a 140 billion dollar business. However, in India it is a new phenomenon.

The main advantage for the clients is that all they have to do is to identify their requirements and finally cut a pay cheque at the end of the month. The search, hiring, documentation and legal processes are all handled by the leasing company at a very nominal servicing charge.

Global Dimension in Recruitment. Large number of multi nationals has opened their factories in India at the same time there has been a shift in Indian Companies perspective in that these have globalized their operations. The recruitment practices in these companies readjustment to look at global perspective. The globalization has been a boon and a doom story. The talented personnel are attracted to better perspectives and hence, there may be a brain drain. However, there has recently been a shift in trends and that large number of people from developed economies has returned to their home country for growth and development. Dowling (1989) carried out a study and identified critical issues for global recruitment. The major aspects that need attention during global recruitment are :

(*a*) Political and legal issues of host country.

(*b*) Human resource functions are more difficult due differential methods in different places.

(*c*) Motivation of employees to take oversea assignment may be difficult especially if the appointment is in one of the least developed economies.

(*d*) Difficulties in establishing criteria's for oversea assignments.

(*e*) There is a greater need of collaboration and connection between strategic and human resource plan of the enterprise.

(*f*) Commitment of the employ from another company need to develop. It also involves relocation which may not be appreciated by many employees.

(*g*) Use of virtual interviews in that people are interview by video conferencing or telephones,

RECRUITMENT PROCEDURE

Responsibility

In a small company with few employs the recruitment is more informal process. The manager or owner meets informally with candidates and appoints him based on his abilities, knowledge and skills. In this the selection is normally done by one man.

In large companies the responsibility is subdivided, firstly the human resource department develops source of applicants. Secondly, the recruitment team carries out the initial selection of the candidate. Thirdly a professional team carries out final selection. It is important to understand that in large organization the recruitment function should be the responsibility of one specific department in order to develop a good and perennial source of recruits/ new employees.

Stages of Recruitment

The stages of recruitment process include identifying the need to recruit which is arrived at after receipt of requisition from the department. The human resource department or department nominated to recruit then identifies the job requirement, by going over job description and person specification. In the next stage the recruiter decides from where the employee can be recruited and decides the selection method. Thereafter, the candidates are short listed after selection process and notified (Figure 5.3).

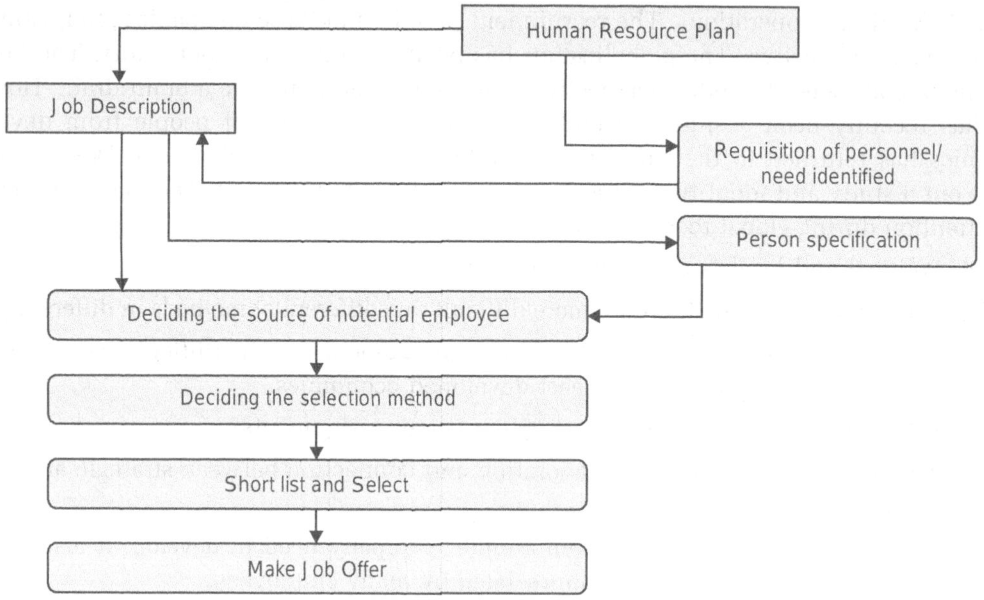

Fig. 5.3. *Stages of Recruitment.*

Requisition for Recruitment

Recruitment is an on-going it never ceases. However, the process of recruitment commences when a vacancy occurs or is anticipated to occur then a requisition is made by the department. This is normally done on a personnel requisition form or other document as required by firms standing orders or policy. The requisition form normally includes details of the position to be filled, qualifications, skills and abilities required, any particular behavioural pattern desired.

Process

Process of recruitment generally begins with requisition. The department responsible for recruitment in an organization (usually the Human Resource Department) thereafter starts by projecting the need. This is done by advertisements so that the information is made available to the potential candidates. The department then starts locating the sources of required number and type of employees. Thereafter the department starts locating prospective employees with requisite qualification and communicating to them information of the organization. The department then attempts to motivate and encourage the target prospective employees to apply for jobs. Thereafter the department carries out evaluation of the recruiting process. The success of the process depends if large number of persons with requisite qualifications, skills, abilities and experience compete for each vacancy.

According to Famulrao, recruitment process consists of five elements namely; recruitment policy, organization, developing sources of recruitment, techniques used to tap the sources and methods of assessing the recruitment program. Figure 5.4.

Recruitment Organization

The recruitment practice of different organization is different. The government departments, public sector, large private units' etc. follow a centralized recruitment, while private sector and small and medium enterprises follow a decentralized system. Both centralized and decentralized have their merits and demerits. Under centralized system a separate organization exist to carry out human resource functions. The human resource department is responsible for all actions of recruitment elucidated above.

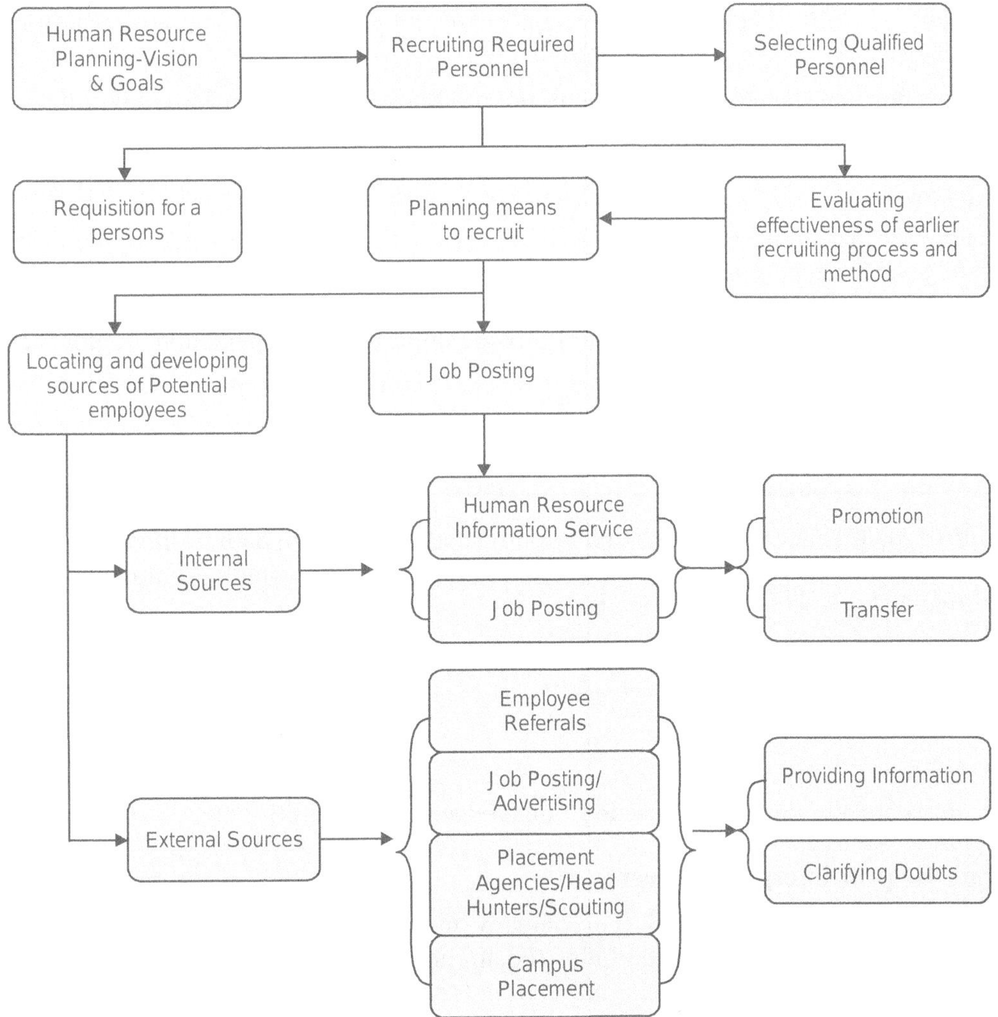

Fig. 5.4. *The Recruitment Process*

RETENTION OF EMPLOYEES

The major challenge facing the management is retaining the talent. Even if the selection of a prospective employee is complete there is a possibility he may not turn up for the job. Job hopping has become a common phenomenon especially with new entrants. Several factors are enticing the employees to job hopping especially if he has specialized skills or rare talents.

Companies and organizations should focus not only on recruitment but on retention of the employees. This could be achieved by firstly, planning ahead and anticipating the possible move of the employees. The human resource manager and management have to be sensitive to such moves and proactive action should be taken in the form of counseling the employee. However, effort to find suitable candidate should commence.

The next step in retention is making sure that there is perennial source available to replace a candidate. Job clarity, design and work analysis would go a long way in ensuring satisfaction of the employee.

Lastly the management should focus on compensation and working environment. The compensation should be competitive in the existing labour conditions. Good support system, infrastructure, inter personal relationship and working environment all contribute to the retention of an employee.

Lately the personnel have started looking for a challenging and satisfying job. They are willing to work if the job meets their goals and aspiration, hence, the organization must always try to create an environment where there is challenge as also recognition of the efforts of the employee. To this end management should provide opportunity for personnel to grow and have promotional avenues available for them.

THE REALISTIC JOB PREVIEW

The realistic job preview provides complete job-related information, both positive and negative to the candidate. A realistic job review provides an applicant or potential employee with clear information on :

- Expectations
- Norms
- Roles
- Values
- Assistance in developing needed Knowledge, Skills, Abilities etc.

Accurate Help in Interpreting Events

A realistic job preview also helps the company in vaccinating potential employees against unrealistically high expectations and helps the applicant to carry out :

- Self-Selection
- Does it meet individual and job needs ?
- Coping Effect
- Develops coping strategies
- Personal Commitment
- Based on personal choice

When to Use Realistic Job Previews (RJPs)

The realistic job previews can be used :

- When candidates can be selective about jobs
- When there are more applicants than jobs

- When recruits lack necessary information
- When replacement costs are high

Issues in RJP Content

Major realistic job previews must have :

- Descriptive or Judgmental Content
- Facts or feelings ?
- Extensive or Intensive Content
- All information stressed, or pertinent only ?
- Degree of Content Negativity
- Positive or negative approach ?
- Message Source
- Actors or company members ?

Review Questions

1. What do you understand by recruitment ? Explain the process of recruitment.
2. Identify the emerging trends in recruitment. Do you agree with the statement that recruitment is no longer a staff but a strategic function ? Justify.
3. Discuss the role of recruitment in an integrative human resource strategy.
4. Describe the nature and importance of employee recruitment ?
5. What sources would you recommend for the appointment of the management personnel ? Why ?
6. Campus recruitment is popular mode of recruitment. Would you as a personnel manager of a corporation like to send old and tried hand or a alumni of the institute serving with the company to carry out further recruitment ? Justify your choice of with reasons.

PROJECT WORK

Study the recruitment pattern of a medium sized company carrying out production and a retail store. Compare the strategies and methods adopted by the two. What are the unique features of the two concerns. Prepare a critical report.

Case Study

Harsh Dalal, Personal Manager in a bank was worried of the quality of personnel being recruited. Typically the divisional heads were responsible for recruiting. Mr. Harsh responsibility lay in providing assistance to divisional heads in their recruitment process when sought. From records it was observed such assistance was normally confined to routine work like checking / verifying applicant's previous employment. Occasionally the staff of Mr. Harsh may visit some campuses to interview few candidates.

Mr. Harsh's concern about the recruitment process was the inability of the bank to attract high caliber personnel. This was especially in sales department of the bank where personnel were routinely terminated.

On careful analysis of the personnel whose jobs were terminated Mr. Harsh found that these person were those who routinely shifted jobs. Mr. Harsh went over the training and development program, compensation package etc, but found no apparent weakness in these areas. He then decided to talk to the managers and division heads to determine the source. He found that most of the employees recruited were from unsolicited applications and no other means was adopted.

Question

Analyze the study and recommend how can the recruitment process be modified to ensure high caliber personnel are attracted to apply ?

❑❑❑

Chapter 6

SELECTION

★ LEARNING OBJECTIVES ★

After reading this chapter, you will be able to understand :

- Nature and Purpose of Selection
- Steps in Selection process
- Methods of selection
- Selection testing
- Issues involved in selection

INTRODUCTION

After the organization has identified the vacancies to be filled, the process of recruitment begins and pool of applicants is created and then commences the process of selection from amongst this pool of applicants. Selection is matching of qualifications, skills and abilities with the individual with the job requirement.

NATURE AND PURPOSE OF SELECTION

Selection is a process of choosing the most suitable candidate amongst the pool of applicants. It is a process of weeding out unsuitable candidates and finally identifies the most suitable candidate. The process of selection leads to employment of persons whose posses the ability and qualifications to perform the job which has fallen vacant in the organization. Selection process divides the candidates in two categories, namely, 'those who will be offered the job and those who will not be.' Wendell (1974) has called selection as a negative process in contrast to recruitment which is positive in nature. Therefore, selection is the process of making a "hire" or "no hire" decision regarding each applicant for a job from a pool of applicants. The process typically involves determining the characteristics required for effective job performance and then measuring applicants on those characteristics which are based on job analysis.

Selection can be defined as *'series of steps by which a candidate are screened to identify and select the most suitable person, based on abilities, skills, knowledge to fill a vacant post.'*

Thomas S Stone (1989, p.173) defined selections *'as the process of differentiating between applicants in order to identify (and hire) those with greater likelihood of success in a job.'*

Steps in Selection Process

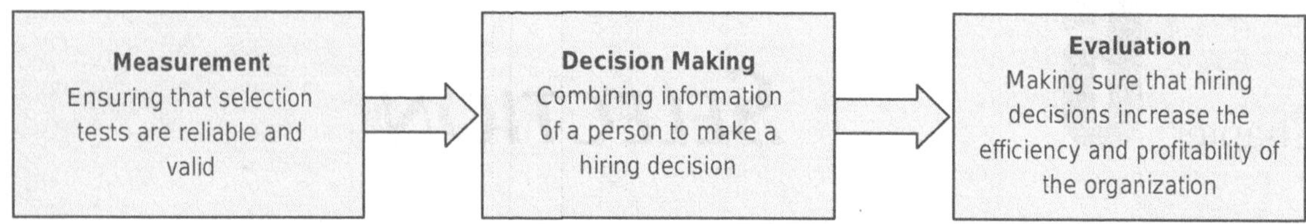

***Source** : Fisher, Schoenfeldt, & Shaw (2003), Figure 7.1*

Fig. 6.1. *Selection Process.*

Selection process basically involves three steps.

(*a*) **Measurement**. Measuring the applicant's qualifications, knowledge, skills and abilities of the applicants by using standardized tests which are reliable and valid.

(*b*) **Decision Making**. Make a decision to hire an applicant based on his performance on the test.

(*c*) **Evaluation**. Evaluation of the process to determine its efficiency in selecting the right candidate for the job.

The selection methods measure the applicant's qualification for the job. The selection of candidates typically follows a standardized procedure (Figure 6.2).

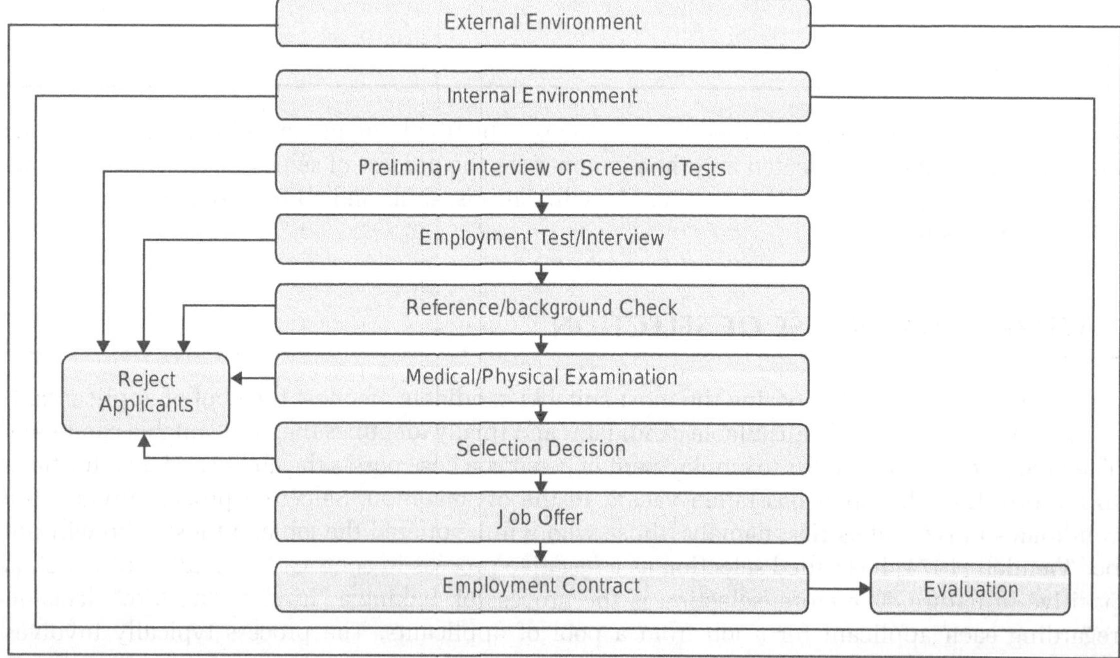

Fig. 6.2. *The Selection Process.*

***Source** : Adapted from R.W. Mondy and R.M. Neo III, Personnel- The Management of Human Resources, p.156*

The purpose of selection process is to select the most suitable candidate who would meet the requirements of the job. The most suitable person is selected after following a process. The process has set of tests or hurdles an applicant must cross before he is finally offered the job. According to Dale Yoder an applicant has to go through 'go' and 'no go' gauges. This technique is called the successive hurdles technique. The process is discussed with reference to steps identified.

Step 1 : Analysis of the Environment

The first step in selection process is to study and analyze the external and internal environment. No process can be successful if proper analysis of the environment is not carried out. It is also important to make sure that the procedure is legally correct and is defensible.

Step 2 : Preliminary Interview/Screening Tests

Preliminary Interview or screening teats are carried out to weed out the unqualified or non serious candidates. Normally a large number of applications are received by the organization at the end of recruitment process. The larger the pool of applicants, the wider will be the choice of organization. During preliminary interview information is elicited from the candidates about their education, skills, experience, salary expected etc. If the candidates meet the organizational requirements he is selected for further screening. It is not necessary to invite all the candidates for preliminary interview or testing. The criteria for selection vary from company to company. Reliance Communication only calls first class graduates for interview other companies may not so strict.

Companies carrying out campus placements usually carryout a presentation and then interview the candidates. A short list is then prepared from amongst the candidates interviewed and called for further interview.

Step 3 : Application Blank or Form

Application form is traditional way of collecting information. To ensure that the companies obtain information critical to them an application blank is filled. Application blank is an outline format on which the candidate's information is solicited. Some of the formats may be too detailed or descriptive, while some others may be brief and comprehensive. An application blank is usually a brief history sheet of an employee's background. This enables the company to focus on their requirements and predict the candidate's chance of success in the job. Information sought should be relevant to the organization objective of selection. The major information is usually collected on the under mentioned :

(*a*) *Biographical data*. These are like name, fathers' name, age etc.

(*b*) *Educational Details*.

(*c*) *Experience*. Previous work experience.

(*d*) *Reference checks*.

(*e*) *Any other detail*.

Application blanks have one great advantage of weeding out applicants who do not meet the basic requirements. Validity of application blank is poor (Typically $r > 0.20$).

Weighted Application Blanks. Certain companies prepare special application blanks to generate weighted scores. It has been observed some of the skills or characteristics are important for successful performance of the job. In these applications or resumes specific keywords are utilized and then these are rated numerically These are identified and candidates having experience in those or who exhibit those characteristics are given extra points during screening. This process facilitates in speeding up the process as also screening the number of candidates for further selection process. Validity of weighted application blank is good (typically $r \approx 0.50$)

Application blanks help the selection process by :

(*a*) To weed out candidates who do not poses requisite qualifications, or other eligibility criteria's.

(*b*) Helps in formulating questions to be asked in the interview.

(*c*) Data contained in the application form forms the basis of future records with human resource department.

Step 4 : Employment Test

The organizations are getting complex and require different skills, abilities and knowledge to perform successfully at different positions. To choose the right candidate for the job from the pool of candidates it is essential to use some form of tests, which are objective. Tests are based on the assumption that no two individuals have similar traits, and these traits can be measured. Test help reduce bias in selection by serving as supplementary screening device. Tests help in better matching of candidate and the job. It should however, remember no tests are foolproof, tests just reveals that the candidate who have scored above predetermined cut off points are likely to be more successful that those scoring below the cut off point.

There are large number of standardized in the market Parekh has collected series of test in his works which can be used for most of the requirements. Standardized tests are reliable and have validity. Standardization implies uniformity of procedure in administering the tests. It provides instructions as to how to administer the tests as also 'norms'. Norms in standardized tests implies the average or normal performance. The obtained raw data from the candidates can be interpreted against the backdrop of norms and candidate can be assessed. The second criterion is 'reliability'. Reliability refers to consistency of scores irrespective when the test is administered. Reliability is usually stated in the form of index in the manual. Reliability index is an indication of how many times the test can be repeated to the same candidate.

Employment test are used today to determine the suitability of the candidate for the job. These tests bring out the qualities and weaknesses of individuals which can then be analyzed before offering a job.

Step 5 : Employment Interview

Interview is one of the most popular methods of selection. Sometimes it is used along with employment tests to determine the suitability of he candidate. Some of the concerns only carry out interview to select a candidate. The scope of interview normally is quite comprehensive and in that it integrates all the relevant characteristics of he candidate. Interview is used to find out more information from the candidate; determine suitability and also give the candidate an opportunity to know about the company, its organization and policies. Hence, an interview is exchange of information between an interviewer and an interviewee. To make an interview a success both the interviewer and interviewee should do their homework and prepare properly. Interview may be conducted by a single person or a panel of interviewers.

A proper physical arrangement is a must for interviews. Proper arrangements enhance the reputation of the organization in the eyes of the candidate. The environment for interview should be free from disturbances and interruptions. Conducive atmosphere enables the interviewer to build rapport with the candidate. This brings out the best from the interview.

Step 6 : Checking References

Some of the concerns call for references. A referee is potentially an important source of information about a candidate's ability and personality. This is an important source of information on past performance of a prospective candidate. It is very important step especially in identifying people at top management positions. Sometimes however, it is difficult to obtain frank opinion from the referee.

Stage 7 : Medical Examination

A pre-employment physical examination or medical test of a candidate is an important step in selection process. There are large numbers of jobs requiring physical stamina, endurance, clear vision etc. A proper medical examination ensures high standard of physical fitness, and in turn it reduces absenteeism, accidents, labour turnover etc. physical examination also limits unwarranted claims under workers compensation laws or against law suits for damages. It also prevents any communicable disease spreading in the existing work force.

Step 8 : Hiring Decision

After the candidate has gone through all the steps enumerated above, the now has to make a decision whether to hire the candidate or not. A wrong decision would cost the organization dearly as it may lead to loss of confidence in the selection process. There are four possibilities when the management decides to appoint a particular person (Figure 6.3).

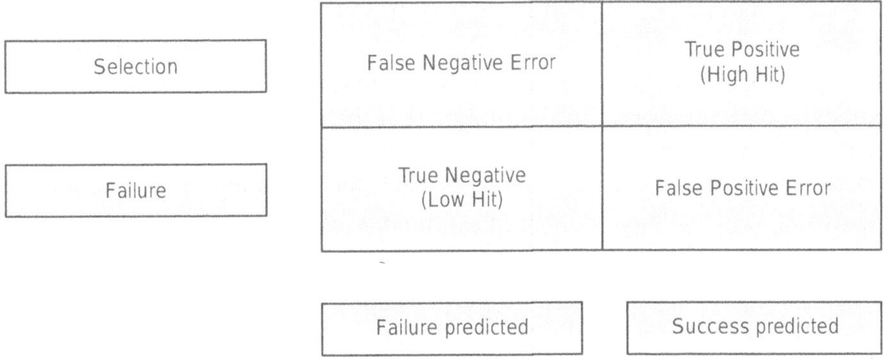

Fig. 6.3. *Outcomes of Selection Decision.*

Source : *Stone, Thomas S. (1989). Understanding Personnel Management, CBS College Publishing, p.175.*

The four possible outcomes are :

(*a*) False Negative Error.

(*b*) False Positive Error.

(*c*) True Positive (High hit).

(*d*) True Negative (Low hit).

Of the above decision in selection True Positive and True Negative are the right decisions, while other two decisions are selection errors. True positive implies that the candidate selected was right and has performed and succeeded on the job as expected. True negative involves rejection of the candidate based on the premise that he would not succeed. False negative error is rejection of the candidate who could possibly have succeeded based on predictions of failures. While false positive error occurs when a candidate is selected on a premise that he would succeed. However, he does not come up to the expectations. It is false positive error which results in costs incurred for the organization. The costs incurred include :

(*a*) Costs incurred in hiring the individual.

(*b*) Costs incurred in training, transfer of the individual to overcome the deficiencies.

(*c*) Costs incurred in discharging/termination of services of the individual and costs incurred in finding replacement, hiring and training him.

Selection process involves mutual decision making between the candidate and the organization (company). The candidate decides whether the job fits his or her needs, abilities, skills and aspirations. The organization on the other hand decides whether the candidate has the requisite abilities, skills, knowledge to fit the job. However, the organization would have to decide fast especially if there are shortage good candidates in the market.

SELECTION TESTS

The use of selection test is perhaps the most controversial of all personnel procedures. Attitudes range from reliance on these tests to totally ignore the results of these tests. The employment tests have been accepted world over. Defence forces have elaborate test to determine the suitability of an individual as an officer in defence forces. These tests have stood the test and proved their worth. These tests should be considered as a step and not a replacement of other stages of selection process.

The existence of individual differences is the basis of the selection tests. The tests are administered to the individuals on the assumption that there is a direct and important relationship between the possession of one or more of these qualities and the individual's ability to do certain jobs. The relationship enables the recruiter to predict the candidate's eventual job performance.

Tests reduce the cost as large number of candidates can be administered the tests at the same time. If the employer wants to retain the competitive edge then the costs of hiring and training of an employee must be kept at the minimum. Psychological tests can help in predicting the success of an employee by measuring their attitude.

Tests can also help the management to uncover the dormant trait and characteristics which otherwise would have been over looked. This could help the organization in better utilization of the talent.

Types of Tests

Intelligence Tests. Intelligence tests are basic mental ability tests. Intelligence tests reveal the application of knowledge capacity of an individual to a given situation for efficient resolution of the problem. Intelligence tests measure the ability to understand instructions and make decisions. Intelligence tests do not refer to any single trait, the tests also comprises variety of aspects, such as vocabulary, numerical ability, reasoning etc. Intelligence tests are classified in two categories viz. those which intelligence quotient (I.Q) or mental age normally referred to as General Intelligence Tests and Those hat give indication of persons standing in various constituents or elements or factors of intelligence—called as test of mental ability. Some of the popular intelligence tests are Weschler Adult Intelligence Scale, Stanford Binet Test. Otis Self Administering Test of Menatal Ability. etc. These tests are useful for selecting employees in wide variety of jobs. The tests are useful for initial screening of candidates. In India these tests are criticized as being discriminatory against weaker section of society.

Aptitude Tests. Aptitude tests are specifically designed to measure job specific skills. The aptitude may vary but the tests are most promising indices in predicting workers' success. There are two basic types of aptitude tests viz. Cognitive ability tests which measure mental and intellectual aptitude; and Motor test which measures physical dimensions such as manual dexterity, perceptual speed, visual insights etc. These tests are useful for selecting personnel entrusted with the job of operating machines. These tests have high reliability of 0.90–0.96 and validity of 0.40–0.60.

Personality. Personality tests probe the personality of the individual as a whole. Personality is interpreted as a combination of traits, most of the tests try to identify the various dimensions that are included in personality. Some of the popular personality tests are the California Psychological Inventory test, Minnesota Multiphasic Personality Inventory (MMPI) test. These tests are exhaustive and lengthy.

Psychological Tests. A psychological test is essentially an objective and standard measure of a sample of behaviour. Psychological tests are used for counseling, diagnostic purposes to assess personality; and selection of candidates.

Projective Tests. Projective tests are part of the personality determination tests. These tests try to understand an individuals personality and its various characteristics by seeing it through his projections. Projection is employed in psychology to indicate an unconscious process whereby an individual ascribes his or her thoughts, attitudes, feelings, motives, needs to other persons or objects or situations in his environment and thus draws incorrect or unwarranted inferences from his experience. Main features of these tests are is that these allow subjects a relatively ambiguous or unstructured task which allows him an opportunity to impose upon it his personality interpretations, which may be freely revealed through his responses. In this a series of picture are shown and the candidate asked to write a story on it. It has been seen when the individual interprets, his motives, attitudes and aspirations get projected on the theme. By this method individual's aspiration, frustrations and underlying motives can be known. These tests measures both intellectual and non intellectual personality traits. These tests tells about general intelligence level, methods of tackling problems and facing problems, creativity etc. Some of the popular projective test are Thematic Appreciation Test, Rorschach Ink Bolt test etc.

Interest Tests. Interest inventories are not instruments of measuring traits. These tests determine person's values, attitudes and interest. These tests are inventories of candidates like and dislikes in relation to work. These tests are used to discover person's area of interest and to identify the kind of work that will satisfy him. The basic idea behind the use interest test is that people are likely to succeed and perform better in the jobs that they enjoy. This helps individual to determine their interest. The popular tests of interest are the Strong Vocational Interest Blank; Strong Complete Interest Inventory, The Kuder Preference Record. etc.

Achievement Tests. These tests measure the effects of learning. The emphasis is on what the individual can do at a given time. Some of the tests are Tests of Achievement and Proficiency, Test of Academic Skills, California Achievement Test etc.

Development of Tests

The development and design of tests for selection requires careful planning, analysis, experiment and technical knowledge. The tests are carefully developed instruments, following certain highly standardized and often intricate procedures. The tests must meet certain criteria of validity, reliability, and objective, easily interpretable and standardized.

A criterion's for Selection Tests (Figure 6.4).

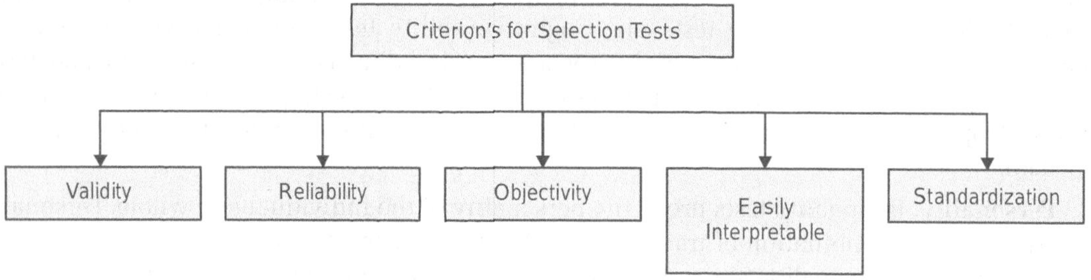

Fig. 6.4. *Criterion's for Selection Tests.*

(*a*) **Validity.** Validity of a test is expressed in *coefficient of correlation*. In which the test score is correlated with some performance criterion. It should be remembered that validity of a particular test is for a specific purpose i.e. a good testing instrument is valid for a specific purpose only. Validity depends upon the proof that a selection method assesses the particular knowledge, skill and ability that it purports to measure. There are three types of validity evidence viz. construct, content and criterion (i.e. empirical). Construct validity evidence is recorded through theoretical and empirical evidence that a particular psychological or physical trait exist apart from other known traits and can be accurately measured. Content Validity Evidence of a test is demonstrated when a particular selection method measures certain knowledge, skills and abilities that have been identified through job analysis. This is judgmental evidence and is accepted for validating direct measures of job knowledge or skills—but not abilities which are considered psychological constructs. Content Validity ration index determination is given in Figure 6.5. Criterion Validity Evidence requires an employer to conduct an empirical study to demonstrate a statistical correlation between applicant's scores on the selection method and subsequent scores during job performance.

There are three types of Criterion Validity Studies viz. Concurrent, Predictive and Validity Generalization. Concurrent uses a sample of current employees. It suffers from one disadvantage as it tends to underestimate the true validity because the employees have completed training and have job experience which may cause them to test differently. The result for selection may be different. The Predictive validity is evolved by hiring a set of people, training them and then evaluating them over a period of time. The tests are reasonable but expensive as the people have to be hired and have to be paid for a period of time. The third criterion validity study is the validity generalization in which the employer uses criterion evidence from published studies as evidence of the general validity of a given selection method for certain specific jobs. There is one limitation which has been recorded in that research has determined that low selection validity for ability tests was mainly due; small sample sizes, restriction in the range of performance score and unreliability of performance ratings.

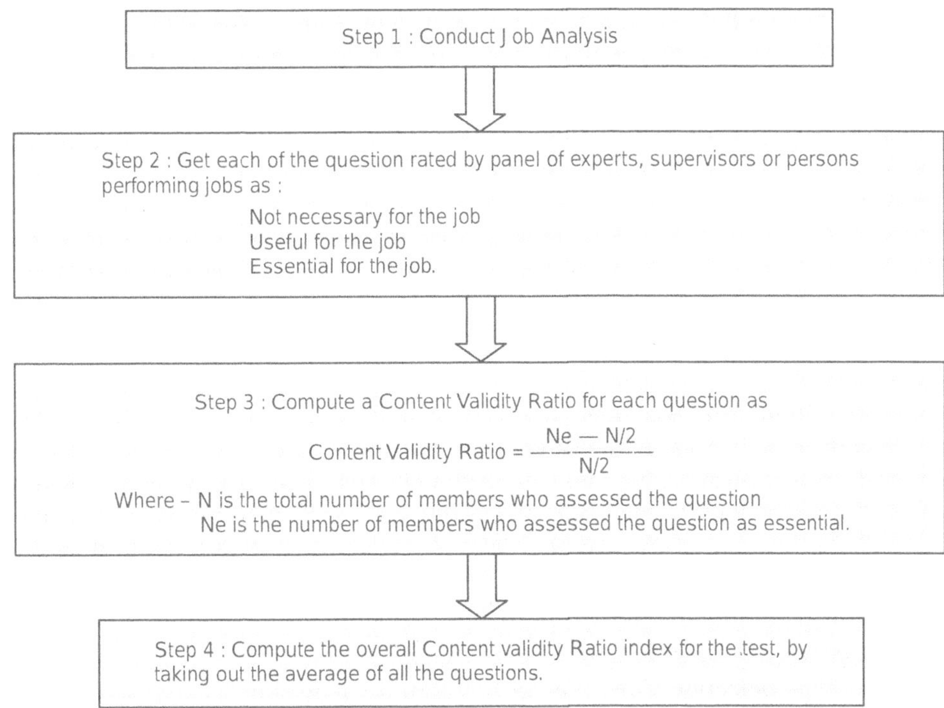

Fig. 6.5. *Content Validity Ratio Index.*

(*b*) **Reliability**. Is the degree to which people earn the same score each time they are administered the test ? Reliability is expressed as coefficient of reliability and usually determined by repeating the test to group of subjects more than once and then correlating the scores. If the subjects show same/ similar results the coefficient of reliability is high. A test with a coefficient of reliability of less than 0.80 is regarded not satisfactory.

(*c*) **Objectivity**. The test should be objective and person should be able to answer it. Tests should not consist of items which are assessed in subjective manner.

(*d*) **Easily Interpretable**. The test should be so constructed that it can be easily understood by the subject being administered. At the same time the assessor should easily be able to interpret and have no doubts or ambiguity in interpreting the responses..

(*e*) **Standardization**. The test should be standardized, and have the ability to be administered to large number of people at the same time. The test should deliver norms or standards so that comparison can easily be done. The test should be truly representative of the people in that it can be understood and given by people in general.

Steps in Selection Test Development

Selection test can be developed to meet the requirements of an organization by going through specific steps.

(*a*) **Step 1 : Planning**. Planning is the first step in the development of the test. In this the test constructor must ask, "Am I going to measure any specific ability, aptitude, personality trait or proficiency.

(*b*) **Step 2 : Listing Behaviours**. The test constructor then analyses the job to identify the behaviours required. Then the test constructor how the listed characteristics would manifest.

(*c*) **Step 3 : Test Item Construction**. Writing test item is only exploratory stage of test construction. Guidelines must be made so that the item evokes the kind of response desired.

(*d*) **Step 4 : Try Out**. In this step the tests are tried on group of subjects who are representative of the population for which the tests are being constructed. For administration of tests the group and tests should be prepared in a formal manner that is as close to the final finished form Number of items to be tested in this sample form should be three to four times greater than the final form.

(*e*) **Step 5 : Item Analysis**. Item analysis is one of the most important steps in test standardization because of the validity and reliability upon which depends the soundness of the test, is always dependent upon the characteristics of the items making up the tests. Items analysis follows only when the test has been administered to the analysis or standardization group and the data collected and treating it by utilizing various statistical procedures. The test constructor has two objectives during analysis viz. to determine the difficulty of each individual item and discriminating value of each items *i.e.*, whether the item is really measuring the function for which it was constructed.

(*f*) **Step 6 : Item Selection**. After having analyzed the items the constructor then selects the items to be included in the selection test based on its difficulty and discriminating value.

(*g*) **Step 7 : Organizing the Test**. The next obvious step is to organize the selected items into a reasonably administrable format and to develop an appropriate and fool proof system of the test. Factors to be considered before finalizing :

- Directions to test administrators about methodology.
- Determining the length of the tests.
- Dividing the tests in sub parts for ease of administration.
- Clear Instructions for scoring procedure.
- Difficulty level of each item.

(*h*) **Step 8 : Final Form**. It is the shape in which the test is available for administration to subjects.

Advantages of Selection Tests

The employment tests offer advantages as under :

(*a*) Employment tests are standardized and objective. It eliminates biases in the selection process.

(*b*) Tests can identify talents of individuals which might otherwise be overlooked.

(*c*) Tests reduce the costs of selection and placement because large number of applicants can be evaluated within the least possible time.

(*d*) Psychological tests can help in measuring the aptitude of candidates and predict their success.

Limitations of Selection Tests

Employment tests are often criticized for :

(*a*) Tests measures only part of the total information needed to make an accurate selection.

(*b*) No test can measure with guarantee the complex combination of characteristics required in numerous positions.

INTERVIEW

Interview is the most widely used tool in personnel selection and has considerably longer history then employment tests. Interview is the most complex selection technique because its scope includes measuring all the relevant characteristics, integrating and classifying all other information about the applicant. An interview is an attempt to secure maximum information from the candidate concerning his suitability for the job under consideration.

According to Jucius Michael (1971), 'An interview is a face to face, oral, observational and personal appraisal method.' Interview is more than a means of gaining information, it is a give and take process in which interviewer and interviewee exchange information and make up mind. It is to get the feel of the candidate, observe his appearance, mannerism, confidence, typical ways of reacting to questions of various sorts and to exchange information that company thinks is useful to the organizations.

Types of Selection Interview

There are various forms of interview, these are discussed below.

(*a*) **Structured Interview.** The structured interview is based directly on a thorough job analysis. It applies a series of job-related questions with predetermined answers consistently across all interviews for a particular job. The replies / answers by the applicants are compared with critical scores and used in determining who is selected. The interviewer prepares standard questions and same are usually asked to all applicants. In this interviewer actively participates by asking questions and interviewee is expected to answer only. The emphasis is on the applicant's response to the questions. Structured interview has a reliability factor of 0.80–0.85 and the validity factor of 0.40–0.60.

(*b*) **Unstructured Interview**. An unstructured interview is largely unplanned and the interviewee does most of the talking. It applies a series of questions which are more related to personal preferences and desires of an interviewee. Interviewer tries to create an atmosphere in which interviewee feels free to express his opinion. Different questions are asked to different candidates. These lack uniformity and miss out on certain critical applicant's skills and background. Emphases are laid on personal characteristics rather than information exchanged.

(*c*) **Preliminary Interview**. It is shortest interview and is intended to determine if more extensive, testing and review of complete application blank or resume is worthwhile. It is primarily screening devices which aims at scrutinizing the applicants and select the best amongst tem for further selection process. Preliminary interview results in saving time and money.

(*d*) **Background Information Interview**. Primarily consists of questions to determine the history of the applicant. This type of interview requires detailed preparations in advance regarding the questions to be asked. Background Information Interview method demands more matured understanding of human behaviour and development.

(*e*) **Stress Interview**. The term stress interview is usually applied when an applicant is interviewed under deliberately created induced conditions resulting in stress on the interviewee. It requires that the interviewer must be tactful and skilful. It is used for selection of higher posts.

(*f*) **Telephone Interview/ Video Conferencing**. In view of the global nature of the companies and the workforce being employed in various parts of the country telephone interview has become popular means of selection. These types of interviews could be unannounced, prearranged, sales interview and research interviews. With improvement of technology video conferencing is also gaining popularity. In this the interviewer is able to see the reaction of the interviewee on a screen.

Other types of interview are face to face in which the interviewer and interviewee are alone and one to one; panel interview in which a panel usually consisting of subject experts interview and ask question pertaining to their respective subjects; sequential interview as the name suggests the interviewee is interviewed in sequential order by different interviewer, this is done to remove biases; peer group interview undertaken by perspective co-workers of a candidate etc.

Significance of Interview in Selection

The major advantage in interview is that the candidate is physically present; the interviewers get an opportunity to evaluate various aspects of his personality. Interview enables the interviewer to know the attitude, ability, linking capability etc of the candidate. The mental makeup of the candidate is manifested in an interview. Interview being an audio visual technique and seeing and hearing can provide an opportunity to an interviewer to observe number of personality traits of the applicants, such as sense of humor, mannerism, quickness of reaction, mastery of language, ability to organize thoughts, physical vigour, cultural level, sophistication etc. It has been observed that most of the concerns do not go through elaborate selection procedure but rely only on interview to select a candidate for a job.

Errors in Interviewing

There are certain common errors /pitfalls in an interview against which the interviewer must guard against.

(*a*) **Personal Biases/ Similarity Effect**. Interviewers are humans and over of period of time develop biases. Their likes and dislikes of particular visual or expressed traits with candidate affect their judgment. The interviewer gives more favourable assessment to those who share beliefs and personality.

(*b*) **The Halo Effect**. Halo effect is to be influenced by the reputation of the person or to single predominant characteristics of the candidate. Example, the candidate may belong to a reputed business institute and this may affect the judgment of the interviewer. Interviewer may grade the candidate higher than others.

(*c*) **Leniency**. A single assessor may be at times too lenient in rating the candidate. This may be due to attitude of playing safe, lack of confidence or many other reasons. The single interviewer may also be very strict due very high expectations, lack of understanding, and rigidity of personality of the interviewer.

(*d*) **Contrast Error**. The interviewer assesses the candidates on the basis of comparison with other interviewees rather than set an absolute criterion. A qualified candidate may be rejected just because the previous candidate was brilliant.

(*e*) **First Impression**. The interviewers have a tendency to make up their minds in first 2-4 minutes of the interview. Hence, the initial interaction of first few minutes between interviewer and interviewees influences the subsequent information and interaction.

(*f*) **Negative Weighting**. In this the interviewer gives larger or greater emphasis to a negative quality or trait observed that to positive qualities and a suitable candidate is rejected.

(*g*) **Caste / Sex / Age Biases**. Demographics characteristics play a very important effect on the selection of the candidate especially in India. Candidates are selected or rejected just because they belong to a particular caste, sex or age.

(*h*) **Non-Verbal Communication Style**. Communication style, animation, body language, clothing, and other visual characteristics influence the interviewer.

(*i*) **Listening and Memory**. Interviewer may not be able to recall up to seventy per cent 70% of the interview, particularly in the absence of format and recording procedure.

Interview Procedure

Interview procedures and techniques vary considerably from organization to organization. The interview should be planned and conducted in a manner that the candidates take positive feel of the organization. The first aspect of planning should be that both the interviewer and interviewee have sufficient time to prepare and plan for the interview. This is followed by checking all the relevant facts and information of the interviewee. The interviewer then plans the interview in the light of information supplied / available. The interviewer must match the facts supplied by the candidate with the job requirements as available from job analysis. There is lot of literature on interviewing. Richard W. Beatty and C.E. Schneir (1981) have listed guidelines for interviewer and interviewee. The guidelines for Interviewer are in Figure 6.6

Planning - Plan for interview, get information of candidate, arrange good environment and match job requirements with information available.

Structuring Interview. The interviewer should then structure the interview.

Personal Impact. The interviewee's first impression is given by personal demeanor of the interviewer and the impression is carried throughout.

Responding to the Applicants. Concern of the applicant's feeling while maintaining control over the interview.

Recording. The interviewer must record salient points and not leave it on memory.

Fig. 6.6. *Guidelines for Interviewer.*

Guidelines for Interviewee are given in Figure 6.7.

Carry out research of the company it values, ethos and beliefs where you have to go for interview.
Be punctual, dress appropriately
Find out about interviewer
Be attentive, responsive and communicate your interest.

Be responsive to every part of the question.
Make notes of the interview on its completion for subsequent follow up.
Be certain of the responses filled by you in application blanks.
Thank the interviewer in the end.

Fig. 6.7. *Guidelines for Interviewee.*

GROUP DISCUSSIONS

Group discussion is a widely used method for selection of candidates. Group discussion assists in analyzing the social behaviour, social framework, personality, interests and various social traits of some candidates simultaneously. In situations where leadership ability is an important factor like defence forces group discussions are held as a part of selection process. In group discussion or situational tests, judgment can be made on the basis of actual behaviour of each individual in the group. It has also an advantage that the personality can be more accurately judged as the individual traits manifest in a broader social situation.

Other Selection Methods

Work Simulation. A typical work simulation exercise involves simulation of conditions under which the candidate would have to work under actual conditions. The ability of the candidate to handle typical situations involved with particular job are assessed in work simulation. The basic procedure involves choosing tasks that are crucial to performing the job for which a candidate is being recruited.

Assessment Centers. An assessment centre has been described as a selection procedure that uses multiple methods of selection. An assessment centre usually puts the candidate through a program of tests which include exercise, interviews, group discussions, psychological tests and assess wide range of abilities, skills, knowledge and behavioural characteristics and potential required for effective performance of skills. Usually the assessment centres are outsourced agencies with specialized personnel for conduct of tests and assessment.

Customer Situation. These are usually conducted for persons manning the sales and service department. In this the situation are painted where a customer behaviour and a product problem is posed to be resolved by the candidate. The candidates would then meet to decide the strategy to meet the complaint.

Hiring for Team Work

The modern industry/organizations are now more relying on teams to carryout functions. There are some specific talent and behavioral characteristics that are peculiar to team operations. An effective team member should be able to recognize a possible conflict and reduce or eliminate it, participate and collaborate in problem solving, communicate openly and supportively and coordinate and synchronize activities. Hence, there is a necessity to identify these behavioral characteristics. The team member should show distinct personality characteristics of conscientiousness' and 'agreeableness.' Group discussion is a simple technique used for determining the team work of the candidate.

Social Media Searches

"Google him!" "Let's look at his/ her profile. "Did you see those photos of him/ her drinking beer ?" These are the common things that can be heard in any office when a potential new hire comes in for an interview. According to MSNBC, 23% of recruiters already research social networks as part of their hiring process. Sometimes it seems like a contest, with all the current employees seeing who can find the most information about the new hire on the internet. The problem is that it is not a game. Traditional background checks are a serious business and have rules clearly defined. However, social media searches are unchartered territory. Consequently, there are no best practices established when using them to make hiring decisions. These are some suggestions for a framework of standards that your organization can use when searching social media for employment purposes.

Employers should absolutely use social media searches when qualifying candidates. Employers don't necessarily care about "drunken spring break photos" on a candidate's Orkut or Facebook page. However, they do care about their company's credibility and public image. A corporate reputation that took generations to build could be ruined in seconds because a single employee has chosen to mismanage their online profiles. On the Internet, once an association is made between a person's online identity and an organization, the damage lasts forever.

Social Media Searches should act as a supplement to traditional background checking services, NOT as a replacement. These two functions need to work in tandem in order to make responsible hiring decisions. First of all, nothing can replace a criminal background check, which is imperative for avoiding potential fraud and danger in the workplace. Furthermore, as it becomes easier and easier for anyone to upload ANY information to an online profile it becomes even more necessary to confirm what is found through your social searches. Education and work experience verifications are still necessary.

As is the case with traditional background checks, employers should get permission/ inform candidates when running social media searches. Currently, the law is unclear on the legal obligations pertaining to running unauthorized social media searches and there have been no high profile issues to date. If an employer uses Google to run the searches, there is a high probability they will pick up "false positives." Therefore, there is no way to know that the information they are looking at pertains to the actual candidate in question. The idea of the search is not to spy, but to ensure that the organization and the candidate are in fact a good fit for each other. For example, our company recently made a hiring decision based on the enthusiasm and insight a candidate displayed through his twitter profile. Social media searches do not have to be just about digging up skeletons in someone's closet, they could actually help you learn more about who someone is and what they aspire to be.

Selection in India

Conditions in India are different from what has been observed world over. India is a strange phenomenon with large scale unemployment juxtaposed with shortage of skilled labour. Unemployment prevails among people who are unemployable but do not possess requisite skills.

India also has problems of corruption, favouritism, and influence in selection process. Selection is at times not systematic and at times takes unique and unorthodox methods.

The Junior Leaders Academy, Bareilly had to appoint a chowkidar. As per orders Government on the subject the names were sought from employment exchange and also notified in the press. The employment exchange forwarded a list of more than one hundered and fifty to select from. In addition there were more than two thousand direct applications. The test of selection became a test for elimination in that all were made to run a distance of one kilo-meter and the first few in each group were retained. Then the selected group was again made to do few physical activities and some more eliminated; till a reasonable group was left for testing.

However, for selections of personnel in senior cadres have been refined and proper procedures are used. There are specialists' agencies available for carrying out selection.

Selection Methods Used in Other Countries

Every nation in the world has its own selection methods based on culture, education level and regulations of the government. European countries have more control on the use of tests for selection, but there is considerable variability in usage. Unions have great influence in European Countries and they inhibit the use of tests in selection process. Italy forbids use of selection tests by law. United States has been using employment tests. It has of late been observed that China makes extensive use of test for selection. In fact China is one of the pioneers in use of tests.

Review Questions

1. Discuss in brief what you understand by selection. What is the significance of selection in an organization ?
2. What are the steps in selection process ? Explain them briefly.
3. Discuss the various methods of employment tests ? How can you ensure subjectivity during tests ?
4. Discuss the potential problems of selection in a growing economy.
5. Give the merits and demerits of employment tests. Briefly explain the various kinds of tests used.
6. Answer the following in brief :
   - What is the purpose of selection ?
   - What is poaching ? What are your views on it ?
   - What do understand by validity ? Explain ?
   - What do you understand by reliability ?
   - What is outsourcing of recruitment ?
   - Write a note on e-recruiting ?

PROJECT WORK

Study the selection process being followed by an organization of your choice. Critically analyze the selection process vis-á-vis the human resource strategy. Does the selection process assist in achieving the goals of the organization ? Present the study in the class.

Case Study

Dr Ramesh was appointed as the Director at one of the leading institute of management. Dr Ramesh had been referred to by Prof Gopal a close associate of Academic Advisor. Dr. Gopal and Dr. Ramesh were childhood friends. Being an internal referral the management called Dr. Ramesh for an interview. He was a MBA and had Ph.D. from a foreign university and had worked with many leading colleges of management. After a number of interviews the management found him to be an impressive candidate and found him to be an exact fit for what they were looking for. The offer was generous that gave him 100 per cent hike over an above of what he was getting, plus a relocation bonus.

Dr Ramesh family shifted to the area of institute location. Dr Ramesh came up with number of ideas and earned a reputation of being an achiever and someone who could get things done. Dr Ramesh joined the institute and soon became the blue eyed boy of the management.

Over the period that Dr Anand was with institute the Human Resource Department carried out the routine reference and document check that is required for Director and Senior Professors through a third party hiring company Consultant & Solutions. During the check the firm Consultants and Solution found that the information regarding Dr. Ramesh's, Ph D was false and that he was not enrolled with the University which he claimed to have studied in United States.

The management was now in dilemma. On previous occasions the management had terminated the services of junior lecturers who provided false information in his application. However, Dr Ramesh was a top performer and was liked by the rest.

Questions

1. *Critically analyze the selection process of the institute.*
2. *Analyze the technique used by the institute to establish credibility.*
3. *If you are head of the management of the institute, what would you do and why ?*
4. *Suggest a selection process which such organizations should adopt.*

Chapter 7

INDUCTION AND SOCIALIZATION

★ LEARNING OBJECTIVES ★

After reading this chapter, you will be able to understand :

- Concept of placement and induction
- Objectives of Induction
- Process of formal induction
- Advantages of formal induction
- Making induction effective
- Socialisation.

INTRODUCTION

After accepting a job offer, most new employees are very keen to learn more about the job and the organization. Induction, which is also known as orientation or socialization, is the process of integrating new employees into the organization and acquainting him or her with the details and requirements of the job. It can thus be regarded as a process of transforming a complete outsider to participating and effective members of an organization. This process may take place either by means of a formal programme or it may be an informal introduction.

Starting a new job is considered to be one of the most stressful life experiences and a proper induction process that is sensitive to the anxieties and uncertainties ass the needs of a new employee. Induction is closely related to recruitment and selection that precede it and training and development that succeeded it.

The next step in induction is 'placement'. Placement is the process of assigning a specific job to the selected candidates. Placement involves assigning a specific position to an individual in an organization. Placement, in simple words, means sending the newly employed person to some department for work. Pigors and Myers (1987) states; "Placement is the determination of the job to which an accepted candidate is to be assigned, and his assignment to that job. It is matching of what he imposes in strain, working conditions, and what he offers in the form of payroll, companionship with others, promotional possibilities, etc." It is the responsibility of the organization to ensure optimum utilization of human resource and that is best achieved when the person is located at a position that he is best suited.

There are many challenges confronting the new employee upon entering the organization (Barkhuizen, 2002; Cawyer *et al.*, 2002). In addition to the new inductee acclimatizing to organizational culture and learning the 'ropes', the organization assumes that the new inductee or the novice is ready to take over a position and perform.

ORIENTATION AND INDUCTION

Orientation and induction are two terms constantly used in relation to welcoming a new employee to an organization. Orientation is derived from Orient as per Oxford dictionary means to determine how one stands in relation to ones surrounding; while orientation is a process to getting oriented to relative position, information etc. Induction as per oxford dictionary means preamble, prologue or introduction. It has been observed that when a person goes to new place, he finds himself as a complete stranger to the people and the environment. This leads to a feeling of insecurity and nervousness. This feeling of insecurity and nervousness can be reduced or overcome by familiarizing the newcomer with the job and the organization. This process of welcoming and absorbing a newcomer within its folds is called induction or orientation.

DEFINITION

There are as many definitions of induction as authors. **Robert L Mathis** and **J H Jackson** have defined induction as (1982, p.225)

'Planned introduction of employees to their jobs, their co-workers and the organization'

Edwin B. Flippo (1989) has defined induction or orientation as the

'welcoming process to make the new employee feel at home and generate in him a feeling of belongingness to the organization.'

Michael Armstrong (1976) defines orientation or induction as

'a process of receiving and welcoming an employee when he first joins a company and giving him the basic information he needs to settle down quickly and happily and start work.'

Werner and **DeSimone** (2006, p. 288) defines organizational socialization as :

"The process by which an individual acquires the social knowledge and skills necessary to assume an organizational role"

Warnich, Pieter and **Surette** (p.206) have defined it as

'Induction can be more precisely defined as the process of introducing new employees to the goals of the organization, its policies and procedures, its values and the co-workers, as well as the activities of the tasks to be performed and the equipment to be used.'

SOCIALIZATION

Socialization is the process by which newly-hired employees learn about, adapt to, and come to identify with the organization (Van Maanen and Schein, 1979). Socialization refers to the communication process involving a new employee negotiation into the organization (Albrecht and Bach, 1997). Socialization concerns with the new member learning organizational ways, as well as communication process that mutually influence both the new staff member and the organization (Bullis 1993; Miller and Jablin, 1991).Studies on new staff members (Bullis 1993; Louis, 1980) highlight that socialization during entry can be particularly challenging. There are three common issues arise for newcomers; negotiating differences between their expectations and the realities of the organizational life (Albrecht and Bach 1997) and the sense of isolation that a new employee often experiences. How employee adjusts to new organization affects his commitment and performance; work group satisfaction; start up costs; retention and if the employee leaves the replacement costs. Socialization takes some time it is not a discrete event.

Improving the socialization processes enhances the quality of role performance. Socialization is a learning process and it is basically an individual's responsibility to fit in the organization (Bauer, et al., 1998). If socialization is left mainly to the newcomer, the organization risks the new employee not full reaching his or her potential as a contributing colleague. Socialization process is series of steps that a new inductee goes through as they learn to fit in the organization. Socialization in induction of employee concept is typically a time limited cycle of initiation or indoctrination into an organization. We extend the process of socialization to a dynamic organizational context wherein processes and values are created and led by strategic change. The definition of Louis (1980) holds in this context : 'A process by which an individual comes to appreciate the values, abilities, expected behaviours, and social knowledge essential for assuming an organizational role and for participating as an organization member" (p.29). Wanous (1992) has described socialization as four stage process :

1. **Confront the reality**. New inductees learn and negotiate their own expectations with the requirements of their role in the organization.
2. **Achieve role clarity**. In this the new inductees learn and negotiate the expectations and the requirements of their role in an organization.
3. **Locate oneself in the organization**. New inductee learns how their work contributes to the work of the organization.
4. **Assess success**. New inductee assesses the value of their contribution to the overall achievement of the organizational goals.

The premise that it is the responsibility of the individual to learn and fit into the organization has its limitations in that it overlooks or underestimates the effect of the group on the socialization process; and it leaves the outcomes of socialization process to the individual, who because of his or her status as a new comer are not in best position to acquire much of the information helpful toward successful socialization in the organization.

The four stages stated above are unidirectional, however, the socialization process it appears is a reciprocal process comprised of interactions between the new inductee and the existing workers and the primacy is in relationship building. Hence, the socialization process involves :

1. Develop co-worker relationship and social network.
2. Develop role and task enterprise.

3. Achieve membership in a group.
4. Develop career opportunities.

It should be appreciated that the organizations are made of people. Hence, the priority of any socialization process is relationship building between workers. Organizations have recognized the importance of socialization experiences of new inductees to the organization in terms of productivity and performance, attitudes, organizational commitment and turnover (Bauer, Morrison and Callister, 1998; Cooper-Thomas and Anderson, 2006). Departments and institutions need to find effective ways to share information and tacit knowledge with new staff members and allow the new employee to self observe and work through 'expectations—realities' differences. It is the organizations responsibility to ensure that an employee inducted depicts set of behaviour expected of individuals who hold a given position in a group or organization.

Socialization would have a great impact on the induction of an employee. The outcomes of this interaction between an individual and co workers can be depicted by a matrix (Figure 7.1).

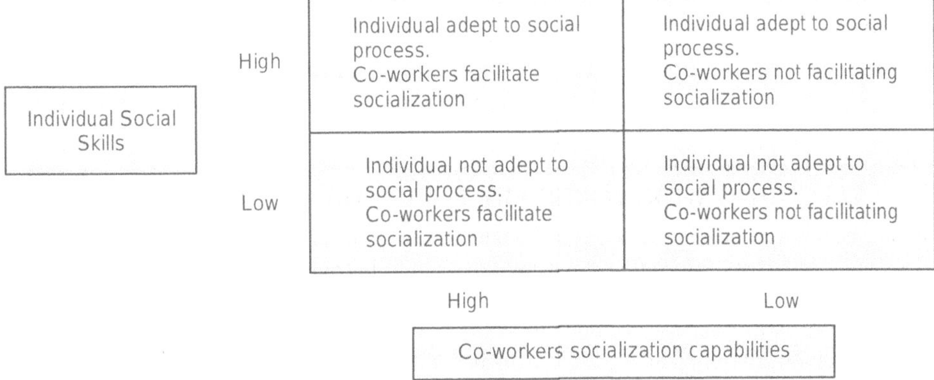

Fig. 7.1. *New Inductee or Individuals and Co-workers Socialization Capabilities.*

It would be observed that the best socialization process is when both the individual and co-workers collaborate and have necessary skills. In addition, quadrant two and three state that some sort of collaboration will be there if either the individual or the co-workers are adept in social networking. Here the organizational responsibility increases. A new inductee is apprehensive of the environment but if the co-workers assist his induction into the organization would be much smoother. Therefore, the socialization can be stated as a three stage process *i.e.*, pre-arrival, encounter and metamorphosis. The pre-arrival stage recognized that all new recruits arrive in the organization with a pre-conceived views and set of values, norms and expectations. The encounter stage involves interaction with the colleagues and co-workers. During this phase the employee encounters the actualities that exist on the ground. It is at this time the maximum turmoil takes place in the minds of new inductees. If the realities and the inductee's expectations coincide then he adopts to the situation rapidly and if there is wide gap he quits the organization.

From above it has been observed that organization plays a dominant role in socialization process. The major methods that an organization employs to induct an employee are :

- Inclusionary. The firs function is to include an individual into its fold.
- Functional. The second is assigning a functional role to a new inductee in an organization.
- Hierarchical. Appoint him to occupy a position in an organization (*e.g.*, line employee, supervisor, management, officer).

OBJECTIVES OF INDUCTION

Organizations are known to spend considerable time to welcome and orient an employee. The objectives achieved are :

1. To assist an individual to overcome his natural shyness fear and nervousness while operating in a new environment.
2. To provide an inductee information about the organization, it rules and regulations and work ethos and culture.
3. Assist in developing a close and cordial relationship between the new inductee and the existing employees.
4. Assist new inductee to develop trust and confidence.
5. Assist the new inductee to understand the organizational goals and values.
6. Ensure that a new inductee does not form a negative impression as also limit/ reduce the gap between expectations of new employee and actual ground reality.

It is important to ensure smooth induction of an employee. The manner in which the employee is integrated would go a long way in ensuring that an employee puts in his best for the concerns.

MANAGING WORKFORCE KEY FOCUS AREA FOR COMPANIES

With business environment in constant state of flux, human resource function is gaining in complexity. Host of factors internal and extraneous factors perpetuate the need in the way induction is organized and conducted. Deependra L. Chumble, Chief People Officer states that performance and talent management is the hottest segment today. The human resource function has been pressured to respond to changes in legislation, shifts in business models, market uncertainties and demanding and diversified workforce. The need to streamline human resource processes, improve employee experiences and to quantify human resource contribution to business has never been so acute.

The companies are increasingly hiring from tier II and tier III cities. These students are more focused. However, they have to be worked on their personality and communication skills. Hexaware has started Early Intervention Program for fresh recruit even when they are in campuses. The program helps a non IT students to acquire sufficient fundamental knowledge of Computer Science before they join Hexaware.

TYPES OF ORIENTATION PROGRAMS

The organizations have their own methodologies for organizing Orientation. : J. Van Maanen (1978) has classified the strategies (Figure 7.2) for conduct of induction as :

Formal versus Informal

Individual versus Collective

Sequential versus Non-sequential

Fixed versus Variable

Tournament versus Contest

Serial versus Disjunctive

Investiture versus Divestiture

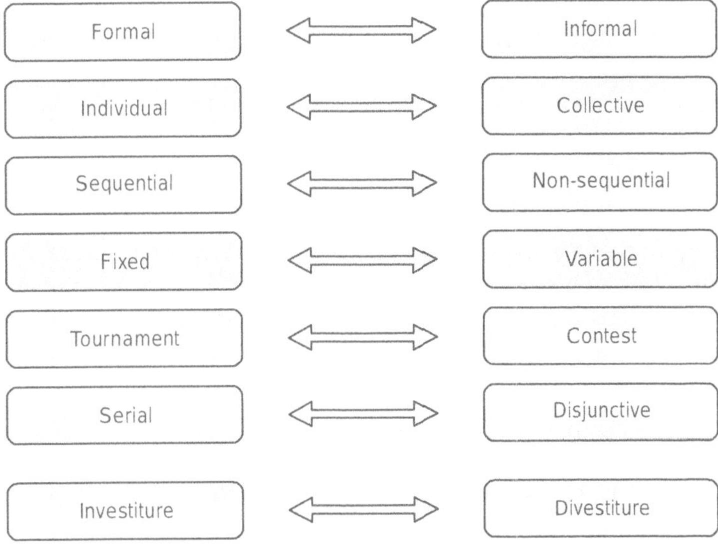

Fig. 7.2. *Employee Orientation Program Strategic Choices.*

Formal Versus Informal

Formal induction of an employee is carried out outside the daily routine and the management has a structured program. In informal orientation, new inductees are directly put on jobs and expected to learn and imbibe the organizational culture as a self learning process. In informal orientation the new inductee is oriented while he operates in a regular work environment. The choice of formal or informal orientation depends upon the firms policy.

Individual Versus Collective

The next strategic choice available for induction involves carrying out the new employee's orientation individually or as a group. Normally individual orientation is carried out of senior management group or if only one odd employee is recruited or the establishment is small. In large organizations where large number of employees are inducted a group orientation is carried out. Both processes have advantages however, it should be remembered for socialization and smooth induction group orientation is better as group camaraderie formed, versus feeling of isolation. Collective orientation is also cost effective.

Sequential Versus Non-Sequential

In a sequential orientation individual progresses through a series of established stages to achieve a position *e.g.*, mail clerk, mailroom supervisor, information manager. In non-sequential orientation individual achieves position immediately and then learns as the days in position progresses. *e.g.*, six-month training program to become a bank branch manager.

Fixed Versus Variable

Fixed Orientation has a set routine and fixed number of days. Employee knows when transition period will end, however, in variable the length of transition period varies from individual to individual depending upon the feed back from peers and superiors.

Tournament Versus Contest

Tournament orientation in which as time passes, candidates are sorted according to potential, ambition, background, etc., and then assigned to various tracks. Contrast to this is contest in which all individuals pass through all stages according to observed abilities and interests.

Serial Versus Disjunctive

Orientation becomes serial when an experienced employee becomes a mentor of a new employee. The experienced employee acts as a tutor and a guide of the new employee. Tends to perpetuate the status quo as the old employee becomes a model for the new employee, hence, customs, traditions are maintained. This strategy brings in dogmatisms with little desire for change. Disjunctive uses outsiders to provide mentoring, encourages innovation and helps employees to be creative because the new employees are not burdened by traditions.

Investiture Versus Divestiture

Investiture orientation seeks to preserves newcomer's identity. It then tries to utilize the talents and skills brought for the benefit of the organization. Most of the senior levels appointments orientations follow this approach. Divestiture orientation seeks to make minor modifications or suppress certain characteristics (*e.g.*, basic military training) in the new employee. This is done to seek better fir between a new member and the organization.

EMPLOYEE ORIENTATION PROGRAMS

There are large numbers of issues that need to be covered while carrying out orientation viz. personal, company information, norms and values etc. First and foremost the function of organization's towards new inductee is to reduce stress, apprehensions, fear and other psychological stress that occurs when an individual enters into unfamiliar surroundings and reassure him that he has joined an organization that would meet his desires. The second aspect that should be included is about job. How it is to be performed in order to reduce start-up costs. The third aspect that should be included is to make an individual conversant how his career can progress and what he has to do to achieve it. Once the goals of the individual are coinciding with organizational satisfaction level will rise as also turnover would reduce.

The induction program must expedite proficiency. The individuals who join have large number of skills, but may find the process which he has learnt varies in its application, hence, endeavour should be made to hone the skill required to attain proficiency in the job.

The new inductee is not known to any individual with whom he has to perform. The induction program must assist in newcomer assimilation within the group or subgroup of the organization. This would require understanding and adjusting to work group and norms. Lastly in a group dynamics the inductee should be encouraged to have positive attitude.

The inductee should be oriented with the information about company as a whole. The major issues to be covered are :

1. Overview of company. General overview, background, history, layout etc.
2. Key policies and procedures. It should include all relevant policies or procedures of importance especially those related to personal issues.
3. Mission statement.

4. Company goals and strategy
5. Compensation, benefits, safety, discipline procedure
6. Employee relations.
7. product services offered
8. Company facilities. Facilities made available to companies.

The orientation program must include job-specific information :

1. Department functions
2. Introduction to supervisors
3. Job duties and responsibilities
4. Polices, rules, and procedures
5. Tour of department
6. Introduction to departmental employees
7. Introduction to work group

The formal orientation programs are usually conducted as given above. There may be variations but these are mainly of the nature of emphasis being placed by companies.

Designing and Implementing an Orientation Program

The orientation program covers a wide canvas, however, it should be remembered that socialization and assimilation within a work group is going to be a slow and steady process. The person earmarked for conduct of induction n must cover the salient aspects and then follow it up be taking measures of feedback and counseling or meeting with new inductee. It should be ensured that a deliberately designed orientation program goes a long way in ensuring a smooth and satisfactory induction. The designer must :

1. Set objectives. The objectives of the program must be clearly defined. It should not be too ambitious.
2. Research orientation as a concept. Before conducting or developing the program the person responsible for induction must go over all relevant material, meet people who conducted and see the merits of issues to be covered.
3. Interview recent new hires. Check from recently inducted persons what benefited them most to settle in the organization. Include issues which assisted settlement.
4. Survey other company practices. The other company induction practices should be seen, good and relevant points should be included.
5. Review existing practices. Carryout assessment of the practices being followed in the organization.
6. Select content and delivery method.
7. Pilot and revise materials. Al relevant material to be handed over to the new inductee should be current. The tendency to provide old existing material reflects poorly on the inductee and he thinks it is a routine. The interest level thus goes down.
8. Produce and package the printed and audiovisual materials. Audio visuals are better for presenting data. It also helps in maintaining interest.
9. Train supervisors and install program.
10. Evaluate program effectiveness.
11. Improve and update program.

Problems with Orientation

The orientation has some severe limitations that need to be overcome for its effectiveness. The first major hurdle is that when a new inductee arrives he is handed over a bunch of papers. These papers need large number of details to be filled. The individual at times find it frustrating to fill same details at three or four places. The induction is carried out in short span of time. There is information overload. Large amount of information doled out during induction at times is irrelevant. The individual is unable to assimilate or associate with the information and soon loses interest.

It has been observed that large amount of emphasizes is placed on performance and its related issues. This over drive sometimes results in 'scare'. The scare tactics is not appreciated by new inductee may quit even before he starts. Lastly there is too much "selling" of the organization in such programs. 'Over sell' should be avoided as the inductee has chosen the firms after careful analysis. He is quite conversant with the merits and demerits.

PLACEMENT

Placement is a process of assigning a specific job to each one of the selected candidates. It is assignment and reassignment of an employee to a new or different job. Here we shall confine just to placement of a new inductee. Placement has assumed greater importance in view of the changes in work ethics. The employees are today career oriented and are seeking specific job. Hence, the individual abilities, skills and knowledge have to exploit to the maximum. This has been compounded by regulations of the government regarding employing certain categories of people. This requires profiling each individual so that jobs can be matched optimally within the constraints set by available jobs.

The jobs are carried out in three manners, independently, sequentially or pooled. However, in recent times independent jobs are on the decline and most of the functions are carried out as team. Hence, there is a need to carryout group profiling especially in health, mutual fund, banking sectors. It has been observed that when the head leaves he carries his team with him. Apollo Hospitals learnt it when Dr. Trehan an accomplished cardiologist left them to establish his own set up. With his departure his team left the Apollo. The individual characteristics must match the sub group characteristics. This was followed to great extent in defence forces where the senior officers usually could pick their staff. Thereafter the characteristics must be matched with work profile to obtain optimum results.

Global Placements

Global placements are carried out in the companies which have a global footprint. The last few years saw large number of companies establishing themselves in India and abroad as a deliberate strategic plan to maximize benefits or profits. This globalization results in certain placement problems such as managing relocation, providing variety of services for relocation and building relationships in countries where company is operating. The placement involves identification of job related skills, leadership skills, willingness to relocate and most important cultural openness and adaptation.

ORGANIZATION CULTURE

Basically, an organization is a group of people intentionally organized to accomplish an overall, common goal or set of goals. Business organizations can range in size from two people to tens of thousands. Environmental influences such as social pressure and personal factors such as personality and behaviour are reciprocally determined. This has been identified as a 'triadic reciprocally' by Bandura (1977, 1982). Organizational culture is one type of environmental influence which impacts the way people (employees) think, perform task and communicate/interact with one and another. Schein (1985), culture is "a pattern of basic assumptions—invented, discovered, or developed by a given group as it learns to cope with its problems of external adaptation and internal integration—that have worked well enough to be considered valid and, therefore, to be taught to new members as the correct way to perceive, think and feel in relation to those problems." Hofstede (1984) describes organizational culture as *"the way things are done in the business."* More specifically, organizational culture is the *"shared perceptions, patterns of belief, symbols, rites and rituals and myths that evolve over time and function as the glue that holds the organization together"* (Zamanou and Glaser, 1994). Campbell et al. (1970, p. 393) states, *"Organizational Culture is concerned with how employees perceive the basic organizational characteristics like individual autonomy, structure, reward, conflict and consideration."* Edgar Schein, goes on to define Organizational Culture as *The set of shared, taken-for-granted implicit assumptions that group holds and that determines hoe it perceives, thinks about, and reacts to it environment."*

Based on the above, it is easy to see that organizational culture existing in provides a corporate framework that provides guidance on issues like how work is done, the use of technology, how people think and standards for interaction and communication.

The shared perceptions and beliefs that make up an organization's culture are fostered and cultivated by communications and interactions among people inside and outside the organization. These perceptions and beliefs then effect and can be influenced by people's behaviours on things like how to solve problems, how to conduct a job and how to communicate. These, in turn, affect an individual's job performance and satisfaction, and then affect an individual's job performance and satisfaction, and in turn the organizations performance. Organization culture has a direct impact on firm's performance, increased productivity and competitive advantage. On an individuals level organizational culture directly impacts employee participation and involvement.

Functions of Organizational Culture

Organizational culture is a deep rooted phenomenon, and cannot be easily changed. Organizational culture is a pattern of basic assumptions that a given group has invented, discovered or developed to cope with its problems of external adaptation and integral integration. There are four primary functions of 'Organizational Culture' (Figure 7.3); firstly, Organizational Culture provides the members with the sense of *'organizational identity'*. It gives the employees the status and feeling of pride to belong to a particular organization. Secondly, "organizational Culture generates a sense of commitment in the employees towards organizational goals, beliefs and values that are larger than their personal goals, beliefs and values. Thirdly, 'Organizational Culture' promotes stability in the system by permitting sub systems to flourish, Ideas can be generated from any part within the organization, and then the system articulates and implements particular ideas and values as a vision. These ideas give shape to success and thus allow stability in the system. The organization culture allows promotion of sub cultures in the overall gambit of a dominant culture of an organization. Fourthly, it is a sense making devise in that it interprets why an individual behaves/functions/operate in a particular manner. The behaviour or functioning in an organization is due culture that is prevalent in the organization.

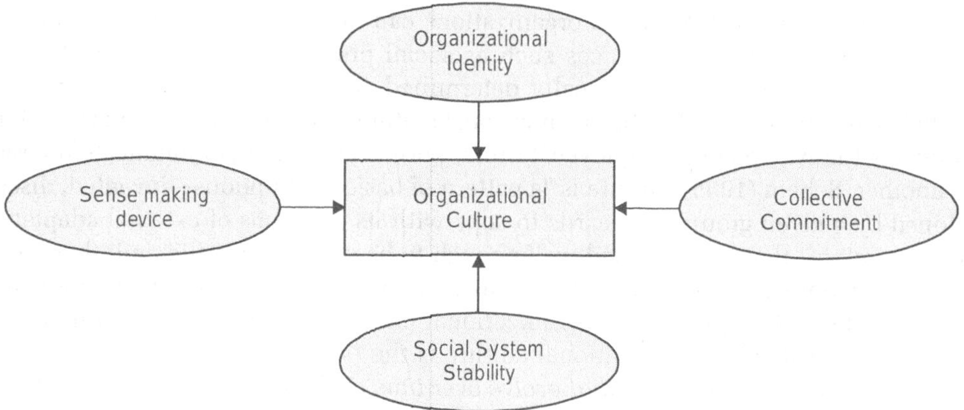

Fig. 7.3. *Functions of Organizational Culture.*

Types of Organizational Culture

From organizational perspective, the collective values and beliefs of the individual members of that organization represent 'organizational culture'. It constitutes a pattern of basic assumptions held by the people in the organization that it uses to address its problem of adaptation and integration (Schein and Edgar, 1990, pp. 109–119) identified a number of factors related to organizational culture. Four of these factors can be seen as type of organizational culture.

(*a*) **Openness to Change/Innovation Culture**. This type of organizational culture has humanistic orientation, affiliation, achievement, self actualization, task support, task innovation, and hands on management; in this type of culture the managers should not just plan, but participate (Xenikoy et al. 1996, pp. 349–371). An organization scoring high on this factor might be considered 'friendly' and 'open to change'.

(*b*) **Task Oriented Organizational Culture**. In this group the concept of being together, being the best, innovation, attention to detail, quality orientation, profit orientation, and shared philosophy ((Xenikoy et al. 1996, pp. 349–371). The authors compare this to the 'Kaizen' philosophy espoused by successful Japanese companies that stress caution, incremental improvement. An organization scoring high in this factor might be considered 'task oriented' versus 'people oriented'.

(*c*) **Bureaucratic Organizational Culture**. This type of culture has the concept of approval conventionality, dependence, avoidance and personal freedom ((Xenikoy et al. 1996, pp. 349–371). The authors describe this culture as formal, with centralized decision-making. An organization scoring high on this factor might be considered 'constructive' or 'prudent'.

(*d*) **Competition/ Confrontation Organizational Culture**. In this type of culture it is observed there is competition, oppositional orientation, power, competition and perfectionism (Xenikoy et al. 1996, pp. 349-371). In this type of culture perfection is the goal, and where individuals might tend to react negatively towards the ideas of others and/or resist new ideas. An organization scoring high on this factor might be considered as 'perfectionist' organization, negatively, one might call it resistant to change.

An organizational culture that is open to change, innovation and achievement appears to be one in which there are likely to be more relational channels, because it is likely to support and nurture the human-to-human communications. It is also likely to exhibit partner similarity, leading to reduced friction. Such organization is also likely to exhibit organizational self-knowledge, which will support the seeking out and identification of those with knowledge to share. Such organizations are also likely to have low divergence of interest, as the openness and communication is likely to foster the type of communication that leads to shared understanding and therefore shared goals.

The advantages of a sound organizational culture are reflected in employee performance and satisfaction. The image of an organization is increased and people are satisfied with the performance of the organization. A strong culture ensures better performance.

Dominant and Sub Cultures

Organizational culture is not a monolithic phenomenon. Sub cultures often exist within organizations. In a large organization each sub division develops its own culture representing the sub culture of the system. An organizational culture emerges when there is an integration of all the departments into unified whole. Within any given unit, the tendency for integration and consistency will be assumed to be present, but it is perfectly possible for co-existing units of a larger.

Schein (1990) differentiated between three different types of culture in one organization—executive culture, engineer culture, and operator culture. Executives and engineers are focused more on task and specialty than on people. Their reference groups are outside the organization. Singh, Narendar (2008) found that organizational cultures in India are hierarchical and based on castes. The structuring principles are 'reproduced non-identically' in India's modern industrial network in two core aspects. First, the principle of heredity specialization is socially functional in that there is strong correlation between certain caste backgrounds, educational choices and professions. Secondly, and more significantly, the principle of the opposition of the pure and impure remains strong. It finds expression in a marked social distance between different employee's categories and in a strong preference of mental over physical work.

Creation of Organizational Culture

Edgar Schein (1992, 1996, 1999) in his works states that creation of an organizational culture is a very lengthy and complicated process. Evolution of common assumptions of the organizational members is the starting stage of creation of culture. These assumptions act as the basis of creation of shared values. Both assumptions and values are non-observable elements of the culture. It is after assumptions and values have been ingrained then the organization members start seeking observable items or artifacts. These actions can be also observed taking place simultaneously. Thus according to Edgar Schein the Organizational Culture exist at three levels : on the surface are the artifacts, underneath lies the values and behavioural norms; and at the deepest level lies a core of beliefs and assumptions (Figure 7.4).

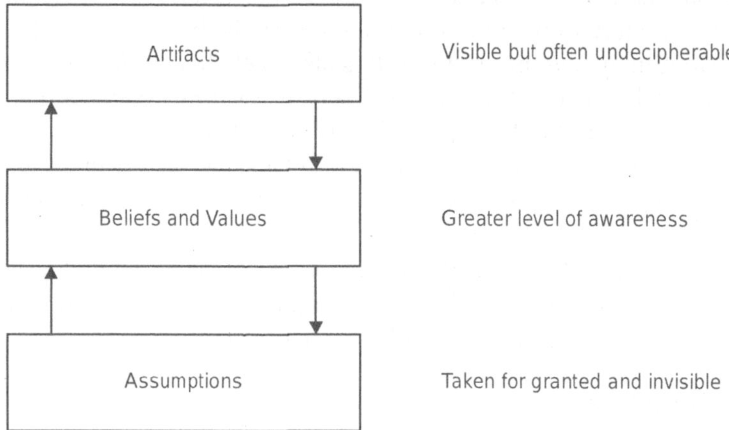

Fig. 7.4. *Edgar Schein three Levels of Organizational Culture.*

Observable Artifacts

These are symbols of culture in the physical and social work environment and are most visible and accessible such as organizational heroes; ceremonies and rites; stories and cultural symbols.

Shared Values and Beliefs

Values and beliefs are reflected in the manner the employees or members of the organization actually behave. Values reflect an organization's underlying beliefs as to what should be and what should not be. Values are those principals and qualities that shape the thinking and behaviour of the organizational members. Values are emotionally charged priorities. These are learned during the process of socialization.

Values can be classified into two; *"instrumental values"*, and *"terminal values"*. Instrumental values define such enduring beliefs that certain behaviours are appropriate, at all times irrespective of the objectives or outcomes. Terminal values are beliefs that certain more tangible objectives are worth striving for and the objectives become more important than the appropriateness of the behaviour in achieving such objectives.

Common Assumption

Assumptions are at the deepest and most fundamental level of an organizations culture. These are the core or deeply held beliefs, and manifest themselves in the behaviour of the people so strongly that any violation of such beliefs would be unthinkable.

Review Questions

1. What is orientation ? How is formal orientation program conducted ?
2. What is socialization ? How does socialization affect performance ? What measures can be taken to improve interaction during induction ?
3. What do you understand by three stages of organizational socialization ?
4. Illustrate with example the difference between socialization and formal orientation of an employee.
5. Identify the importance of orientation and how would you orient a new management trainee.
6. What do you understand by placement ? How does it impact an organization ?

PROJECT WORK

Prepare a write up on placement process in a telecommunication company. Critically evaluate the induction process and suggest improvements if any.

Case Study

Case Study Number 1

A global company with offices all over the world is people oriented and is keen to implement as many global processes as possible, with customization to meet country- and business-specific needs. The company's induction practices are going to change, partly due to feedback from staff about induction and partly through a need to communicate coherently at the organizational level. The company has launched a web based induction program consisting of four elements; company strategies, values, structures and processes. At the country level in India a new induction program was to commence. Although new inductees understood their roles and place in the local organization, they were however, less clear about how the different Indian businesses fitted together and contributed to the world wide business of the company.

The managers have a check list which they are required to use as soon as a new appointment is made. The recruitment and induction program is linked. The checklist contains actions to be taken by the new inductee before he arrives, on arrival and later on. The responsibility of induction is that of managers. There is no central check. Managers will set objectives for new inductee for six months period. Any issues arising from an ineffective induction should be highlighted.

Questions

1. Critically examine the induction process and its role in placement.
2. Do you think the three tier induction would be sufficient for successful placement of employees ?
3. Examine in detail the individual orientation vis-à-vis-centralized orientation.

Case Study Number 2

Google's Organizational Culture

Google Inc (Google) has been hailed as the one of the most successful Internet start up companies. Today, it is the most preferred search engine the world over due to its precision and speed of delivering search results. Apart from technological edge it had over its competitors Google's success was attributed to its ability to attract the best talent and retain these employees. This has been made possible by Google's organizational culture. During the dotcom boom in the late 1990's Google was the only company that did not experience any employee turnover, while all other technological companies experience employee turnover rates of around 20–25 percent. Google's work culture became legendary. However, not everyone was impressed with Google's organizational culture. Some felt that Google would not be able to sustain its growth with its present culture.

Background

Google was founded by Larry Page and Sergey Brin. They extended their summer project (at Stanford University) workon search engine "Blacvk Rub'. By 1997, it gained popularity due to its unique approach to solving search problems on the Internet. Soon they set up a Corporation Google Inc. It soon gained popularity amongst internet browsers. In 2000, Google introduced wireless search technology for WAP phones and hand held devices. It also launched 10-non English Language versions for its search capabilities. Google emerged as the largest search engine in the world with its index reaching I billion URLs and Yahoo also selected Google as its search engine. Over the years Google added new features such as Google Number Search (GNS), Google Toolbar, Country specific domain etc.

Google's Organizational Culture

Google had an informal culture at Googleplex (its headquarters). The founders wanted Google to be a fun place to work in. Refelcting their belief, the headquarter was decorated with Lava Lamps and painted in bright colours of the Google Logo. Googlers were allowed to bring their pets in workplace and were provided free snacks, lunch and dinner prepared by celebrity Chef Charlie Ayers. In addition Google provided sports and recreational facilities.

Both Sergey and larry believed in open communication across their organization. Googlers were free to approach top management without any restrictions. The top management kept their doors open so that any employee could walk in to talk. Googlers were encouraged to communicate across the departments.

Google did not have management structure. Wayne Rosing, Vice President engineering said, "We had management in engineering. And the structure was tending to tell people, 'No, you don't do that.' So Google got rid of the managers. Now most engineers work in teams of three, with project leadership rotating among team members. If something isn't right, even if it is product that has already gone public, teams fix it without asking anyone (Hammonds, 2003).

Recruitment

Sergey and Larry also focused on recruiting people with right frame of mind. They were themselves personally involved in the recruitment process. In order to attract high performing candidates, Google posted the top ten reasons to work for Google on its web sites.

TOP TEN REASONS TO WORK FOR GOOGLE

1. Hot award winning technology.
2. Intelligent, fun, high energy teammates.
3. great culture and amazing perks such as massage therapy and all the snacks you can eat.
4. Backed by two premier VCs.
5. Free gourmet lunches served daily.
6. Start up environment with excellent benefits.
7. Stock options.
8. Spacious, colourful, fun work environment.
9. Located in the heart of Silicon Valley.
10. Millions use Google- your ideas will make a difference.

Source : *www.google.com*

Google recruited people with diverse skills and qualities. While recruiting, Google attached a lot of importance to academic excellence. Google also laid emphasis on recruiting people who gave preference to term goals rather than their personal goals.

QUALITIES SOUGHT BY GOOGLE

1. **People with broad knowledge and expertise in many different areas of Computer Science and mathematics (such as distributed systems, operating systems, data mining, information retrieval etc.).**
2. **People with world class programming skills.**
3. **People with excellent communication and organization skills.**
4. **People who are passionate about their work and are great colleagues.**
5. **People who enjoy working in a high-energy, unstructured environment on very small project teams to build amazing products used by millions of people everyday.**
6. **People with diverse interest and skills.**

Source : *www.google.com*

Google encouraged Googlers to refer their friends and realtives to work.

Innovation at Google

Management focused on encouraging innovation and creativity at work place. It realized that to maintain growth, the company had to come oput with new products/ features. However, the company faced problems on how to tap ideas that could be turned into successful products. Said Silverstton, "We always had great ideas, but we didn't have a good way of expressing them or capturing them." To overcome the problem, Google set up and internal web page for tracking new ideas through a programme called 'Sparrow'.

After ideas were selected, every Friday, Googlers had an hour long session discussing the feasibility of new ideas. Every engineer whose idea was selected was given 10 minutes to defend his/her idea. If he /she was successful in defending the idea, then it would be turned into a product/ feature, with project being headed by Googler who proposed it. Commenting o innovation at Google, Jonathan Rosenberg, Vice President, product management said, "We never say, 'This group should innovate, and the rest just do their jobs'. Everyone spends a fraction of their day on RandD.

A Critique of Google's Culture

Many analyst feel the Google's zero percent employee turnover rate during the dotcom boom, was a testament to its salubrious organizational culture. But not everyone was convinced that Google had got it right in terms of its work culture. They felt that company's culture was not set to manage its growth.

A 12 hours working day had become a norm at the company. Googles recruitment process was also criticized by analyst. It was pointed out that Google had become too narrow in its recruitment by focusing only on the academic records and graduate ranks of the applicants rather than on. The management defended the recruitment process saying that valued intelligence and brainpower more than experience.

Google was also criticized for the treatment meted out to its contract workers. It was reported 30 per cent of Googles total employees were recruited on contract basis. These workers were not given any employee benefits or stock options, nor did they get access to company's intranet, meetings, or social events. Analyst's feel this may lead to unrest in the company over a period of time.

Business partners of the company wee critical about organizational culture. It was pointed out that the lack of hierarchy resulted in confusion about control and decision making power. Google had recruited many Engineers with the same job title. Further it was pointed out that Googlers had become arrogant. It was alleged Googlers never kept their appointments and always turned up late for their clients presentations. Refuting the charges of being arrogant the founders defended their engineers by stating that in Google culture, priority was not placed on attended meetings. Sergey said, "If people aren't prepared in meetings, it is not because they think they're too good for them, but because they're working around the clock."

Analysts feel that Google needs to rethink its organizational to be able to withstand the competition and also increase its profitability and revenue.

Questions

1. *Analyst feels that Google was a perfect blend of technology and culture. Analyze organizational culture at Google and how it contributed to the success of the company.*
2. *Analyse the recruitment process at Google ?*
3. *Analyse the negative aspects of Google work culture ?*

Chapter **8**

TRAINING

★ LEARNING OBJECTIVES ★

After reading this chapter, you will be able to understand :

- Nature and Concept of training
- Need and Importance of training
- Objectives
- Designing training
- Methods of training
- Evaluation of training.

INTRODUCTION

In the present competitive, high-tech, global and dynamic environment it is imperative that company keeps improving its product and services, build and sustain competencies that would provide them with the sustained competitive advantage. The need for advanced skills and tools is a critical issue facing both employer and employee. Dynamic and growth oriented organizations adopt a strategic and planned approach towards the maintenance of human resources. In this knowledge era, where human assets are the biggest assets it is imperative that their skills, knowledge is constantly developed and hence, training has assumed added importance.

Satyam Computers

Satyam Computers earned the first place in American Society for Training and Development prestigious list of the World's Top Organizations in workplace issues and performance areas. Ed Cohen who runs the Satyam School of Leadership states :

- **Every senior executive participates in leadership coaching and mentors at least three less experience colleagues, or 'Full Life Cycle leaders'.**
- **Satyam features a 'flat', Full Life Cycle Business organizations structure that enables associates to recognize opportunities and act upon them quickly—the way leaders do.**

Training is a part of human resource development, along with other human resource activities such as recruitment, selection and compensation. The role of training is to improve the organization's effectiveness by providing employees with knowledge, skills and attitudes that will improve their current or future job performance.

On joining the organization the new inductee is assessed after certain duration for his performance. His abilities are determined and his suitability is then re-identified. If the new employee matches with the skills he continues in the same position for some time to gain experience; but if he is found wanting then he is either put through a training package or relocated. Training helps to develop skills, personality, increase motivation and retention of employees.

Training is also required to sustain growth and development of an individual and the company. Training is viewed as an organizational investment; hence, getting a satisfactory return on investment means linking the training function and activities with the company's overall business activity. If organizations wants highly motivated, up to date, creative and productive workforce, they need to start and build strategy for the future. This strategy has to recognize that corporate performance is totally dependent upon the performance of the people employed in an organization. This leads to clear commitment fro the management to invest in their people through training.

Traditionally, identification of the training needs has been the responsibility of the Human Resource Departments in an organization. To keep pace with the needs of the organization, the Human Resource Department usually identifies the training needs and prepares a calendar of the training events/ modules and circulates the same to the departments. However, lately due specialization and requirements of varieties of skills and to optimally utilize the knowledge available, the identification of training needs is now left with the respective departmental heads, who due to their proximity with their employees can suggest training and development needs.

NEED AND RATIONALE OF TRAINING

Training is an important facet of the organizational function to sustain competitiveness, maintain its quality and uniqueness. A skill acquired by an employee is retained within an organization till either the employee leaves or there is change in technology calling for fresh skills. The need for training can be broadly divided into two viz. organizational requirements and individual needs (Figure 8.1).

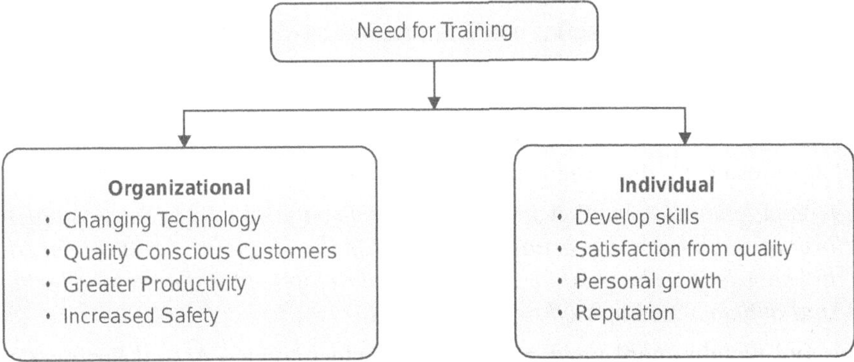

Fig. 8.1. *Need for Training.*

Training is an 'opportunity' for learning and it is accomplished by providing employees with opportunities to learn, hence, training focuses on the acquisition of knowledge, skills and attitudes needed to perform more effectively on one's current job and prepare them for changes in their jobs.

Organizational Requirements

The organizational needs arise from its desire to retain competitive edge. Modern organizations are well aware that their real value is in the quality of its workforce. Organizations endeavours to upgrade skills of its workforce to maintain competitive edge. An organization also keeps on adding and upgrading technology and this requires upgrading of the skills of the employees who have to make the optimum user of it. In addition the organization must keep upgrading processes by training personnel in new methods and procedures. Second, the customers have become quality conscious, this requires constant efforts on part of the organization to maintain and improve quality to retain existing customers and secure some more from others. Thirdly, it should be remembered a trained and skilled employee is more efficient and hence, is able to produce quantity with quality. Fourth, training enhances safety reduces accidents. This in turn raises the reputation of the company in the market as also limits costs in terms of litigations, damages to injured worker and costs of replacement of man and machine.

Individual Needs

Every individual when he joins and organization seeks career, growth and reputation. In order to ensure that he does not become redundant and maintains an edge over peers and other fellow workers he needs constantly upgrade skills to utilize the technology, produce quality product and at a competitive price. He therefore, has to constantly learn, relearn and upgrade his skills to maintain edge in his performance. The rate at which technology changes has resulted in individuals finding themselves not suitable for the job and hence, to maintain a job individual has to upgrade. Training becomes an essential for individual and one of the mandatory need along with food, sleep etc. *This is an era of constant learning and relearning, and an individual can only ignore training at his own risk.*

MEANING AND NATURE OF TRAINING

The verb 'to train' is derived from the old French word *'trainer'*, meaning 'to drag' hence, English meanings may be found as to draw along; to cause; to grow in the desired manner; to prepare for performance by instructions, practice etc. Training can be described as 'providing the conditions in which people can learn effectively.' To learn is to gain knowledge, skills and ability (King, 1968, p.125). Training is a process through which an individual enhances his efficiency, capacity and effectiveness at work. There are many definitions of training as many authors.

Randall L Schuler, *et. al.,* (1989, p. 385) defines

It is an attempt to improve current or future employee performance by increasing an employee's ability to perform through learning, usually by changing the employee's attitude or increasing his or hers skills and knowledge. The need for training and development is determined by the employee's performance and deficiency computed as follows.

Training and development need = Standard Performance – Actual Performance

Edwin B Flippo (1989, p.209) defines training as

'Training is an act of increasing the knowledge and skills of an employee for doing a particular job.'

Michael J. Jucious defines training as :

'Training is any process by which the aptitude, skills and abilities of employees to perform specific jobs are increased.'

From the above it would be observed that training brings about a change in skill, knowledge and attitudes of the workers. Training thus can be said as an organized human resource development activity to increase knowledge, hone skills, a systematic procedure of transferring technical know-how to the employees and improve their problem solving abilities. Hence, the training can be defined as :

Training and development refers to the imparting of specific skills, abilities and knowledge and bring about attitudinal change in an employee.

We shall be using this definition for balance of our discussion.

Concept of Training

The entire philosophy of training rests on the principle of ***learning and relearning***. Training is the process of increasing knowledge, abilities and skills for doing specific job. It is an organized and a deliberate effort. The aims at improving skills an attitude, however, it is often used loosely for development Human Resource Development. Training takes time and effort and hence, it should be such that it serves goals, needs and requirements of both the organizational and individuals. A successful training programme will begin with identification of training needs and creation of right kind of environment for both conducting training and learning by trainee. The trainers should have the requisite skills knowledge and expertise and also relate the value of training to an enterprise. Training is an organized activity and should follow learning oriented guidelines viz. increase knowledge; hone skills; systematic procedure of transferring technical know-how to the employees; improve problem solving ability; developing potential; reinforcement and education.

The training can be successfully accomplished by maintaining similarity between training and work situation, providing adequate experience with tasks during training, providing for a variety of examples when teaching concepts and skills, identifying important features of the task, and making sure that the trainee understands general principles.

Formal systematic training involves the following steps (Figure 8.2) :

- Assessing the requirements, skills and abilities needed by learners.
- Designing the training, including identifying learning goals.
- Developing training methods and materials.
- Implementing the training.
- Evaluating whether the objectives set have been achieved.

Step 1
Assessing the requirement
Step 2
Designing the training program
Step 3
Developing training methods
Step 4
Implementing the training
Step 5
Evaluating whether the objectives set have been achieved.

Fig. 8.2. *Steps for Formal Training.*

A systematic approach is goal oriented. It produces result at each step for both the organization and the trainee.

Objectives of Training

From the definitions it is clear that training is to enhance effectiveness and attitude of an individual. The objective of training may be seen as 'ensuring that the organization has the people with the correct mix of attributes, through providing appropriate learning opportunities and motivating people to learn, and thus enabling them to perform at the highest levels of quality and service' (Bentley, 1990, p. 25). Training must therefore be managed as frontline business activity. Training activities and businesses objectives are related each other as links. With the effective training program, organization easily catches their objectives. The basic purpose is to bridge the gap between standard performance expected and actual performance, the objectives thus could be listed as :

(*a*) Enhance knowledge of the worker in doing specific jobs.
(*b*) Enhance the skills required to perform a specific job efficiently.
(*c*) Improve overall performance of an employee by bringing about attitudinal change.
(*d*) Improve efficiency by reducing wastage of material and accidents.
(*e*) Develop employee to takeover positions of greater authority and responsibility.
(*f*) Orienting new employee to the organization and their job.
(*g*) Helping employees perform their current jobs well.
(*h*) Helping employees qualify for the future jobs.
(*i*) Keeping employees informed.
(*j*) Providing opportunities for personal development.

IMPORTANCE OF TRAINING

Effective training produces many benefits for both employees and organization overall.

Benefits for the Employees

Training provides greater job satisfaction and enhances morale among employees. Employees take more satisfaction in a job when they know how to do it well. If they are not sure what to do or how to do it properly, they can become frustrated and dissatisfied with their work. The combination of job satisfaction and peer acceptance leads to improved self-esteem. Training provides opportunity to advance in the organization; employees who demonstrate excellent performance at one level in an organization often have the opportunity to advance to other levels of responsibility. Training assists in increased employee motivation.

Benefits for the Organization

Training helps in increased productivity. The employees who know how to perform their jobs are more effective and more productive than those who learn through error and trial are. Training provides higher levels of customer satisfaction. Employees are able to take care of customers properly and have better skills for solving customer-related problems. The products are of high quality and standards are met when people know what the organization expects from them. Training helps organizations to retain competitive edge by increased innovation in strategies and products. It helps in reduced employee turnover and enhances company's image. A study of fifteen countries of the Organization for Economic Cooperation and Development (OECD) found training benefits organization by :

1. Improved productivity
2. Greater workforce flexibility
3. Savings on materials and capital costs
4. A more motivated workforce.
5. Improved quality of product and services.

TRAINING METHODS

Training methodologies and techniques are evolved everyday to meet changes in the environment. The method employed depends upon the type of training intended, the trainees selected, the objectives of the training. It should be clearly understood that training is a situational process that is why no single method is right for every situation.

Training methods can be broadly classified as cognitive and behavioural approaches. Cognitive approach provides written and verbal information demonstrating relationships among concepts and providing rules how to do something. These methods are usually carried out off the job. Cognitive methods are best for knowledge development and behavourial methods for skills (Blanchard and Thacker, 1998, p. 277). The other method is on the job training. This method allows employee or trainee to practice behaviour in real or simulated conditions (Figure 8.3).

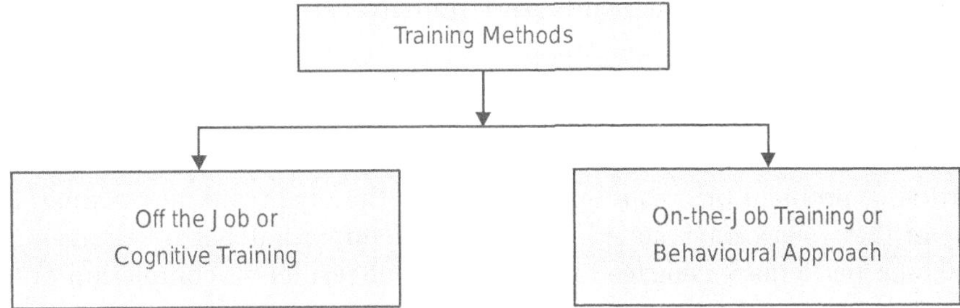

Fig. 8.3. *Training Methods.*

Cognitive or Off the Job Training

It is the training which is conducted off the actual work place. Cognitive training methods provide verbal or written information, demonstrate relationships among concepts, or provide the rules for how to do something. These stimulate learning through their impact on cognitive processes and are associated most closely with changes in knowledge and attitudes. This training is usually organized when there are large numbers of employees who have to be trained in common or shared matter rather than an individual need. Lectures, computer-based training (popularly known as CBT packages), games, simulations, sending employees to training institutes all form part of this type of training. This type of training is also called off-the-job training methods.

Lecture Method. The lecture is best used to create a general understanding of a topic or to influence attitudes through education about a topic. The most common form off-the-job training is the oral presentation of information to an audience (Blanchard and Thacker, 1999, p. 278). In lectures large amount of information can be delivered in a relatively short span of time to a large number of people. Lectures suffer from one major drawback in that no allowance is made during the lectures for analyzing the level of understanding by the students. The trainees do not actively involve in training process, hence, have a tendency to forget things. If too much information is conveyed it becomes an information overload. If the training objective is to convey specific factual information it is better to put material in text form (Drummond, 1999).

Computer Based Training. Computer based training can be defined as that any training that occurs through the use of computer. Computer based training has become popular due easy accessibility and time flexibility. The trainee can choose the place and time for learning. The training is carried out on computers as name suggests. Large number of companies are shifting to computer based training as it is cost effective, reduces trainee time, trainee studies only what he needs, increases access to training, allows trainee to master learning, there is instructional consistency, and has been found the best way to maintain interest and motivation high (Jerris, 1999, p.330). Kearsly (1984), states that the most important advantage of computer based learning is the control over the content of the material, method of presentation, and movement of the trainee through sequentially structured learning episodes based on previous trainee responses. There is one major drawback in this type of learning in that the predictions of ones behaviour and reactions are impossible. E-Learning is a new way of delivering training programs are constantly being developed in the attempts to match the high speed at which businesses are moving. One of the new methods of delivering training programs is with online. It is recommended that E-learning should try to reinforce other methods and should not be the only method. Lee (2000) states that the important dimension of human behaviour cannot be conveyed through computer based learning.

Games and Simulations. There are large numbers of games and simulation developed and designed to introduce or reinforce important concepts. Trainees experience processes, events and circumstances that occur in the job in a controlled setting area. Simulation exercises place the trainee in an artificial environment that closely imitates actual working conditions where the trainer demonstrates on the same kind of machine and using the same procedures that trainees will use on the job. This enables the trainee to develop their skills or discover concepts that will improve their performance. Games often involve group participation, so that the team members working in harmony are required to make decisions or formulate a course of action that will help resolve a particular problem or create opportunity for the organization. Newman and Hodgets (1998, p.195) in their work have stated that the most important part of the games is not the activities in which participants engage but processing of results on completion of the game.

Vestibule Training. It involves the virtual duplication of work environment in an off-the-site setting. In this the trainee/employee is placed in an artificial environment that closely imitates actual working conditions. The trainer/instructor demonstrate on the same kind of machine and using the same procedures that trainees use on the job. The theory is that if managers or employees have faced with similar situations, even if these are simulated, they will be more likely to make right decisions (Woods, 1995; p.180).

Business Games. As the name suggests business games are simulations in which participants learn how to deal with variety of issues in a simulated business environment. Business games attempt to indicate the way in an industry, company, or subunit of company functions. Generally, they are based on a set of relationships, rules, and principles derived from the theory or research. The trainees are provided with a situation are expected to analyze and make decisions based on the information available. The trainer/system then provide feedback on the impact of their decision and are then asked to make further decisions. This process continues till predefined state of organization exists or specified number of trials has been completed (Blanchard and Thacker, 1998, p.295). Business games usually involve an element of competition, either against other player or against the system. The purpose of business games is usually to strengthen executive and upper management skills, improving decision making skills at all levels, demonstrating principles and concepts, integrating separate components of training into an integrated whole, exploring and solving complex problems, developing leadership skills.

Case Study. This method has become very popular lately. In case study, details of series of events, either real or hypothetical, takes place in a business environment. In case study the participants are asked to go through data provided in the case to identity the principal issues and then propose solutions to these issues (Woods, 1995 : p.183). The objectives are primarily to have the trainees apply known concepts and principles and discover new one. A variation of case study is the incident process, in which trainees are given only a brief description of the problem and m trainee must gather additional information from the trainer by asking specific questions (Pigor and Pigor, 1987, p.414)

In-Basket Exercise. These are a form of simulation in which participants are asked to prioritize problems, messages, reports and other items that might be found in managers' in-basket (in-tray) (Jerris, 1999, p.330). In basket exercises are used to clarify, how to identify which issues require the most immediate response, to teach participants how to delegate those problems which do not require personal attention and instruct employees how to work on several problems simultaneously (Woods, 1995, p.183). The in basket primarily focuses on decision making and allows an opportunity for both assessing and developing decision making knowledge, skills and attitudes. In-basket is best at developing procedural and strategic knowledge (Blanchard and Thacker, 1998, p.297).

Role Playing. The role playing gives participants an opportunity to perform a role of a particular position and experience situations in a controlled setting. The trainees are provided with a description of the context usually a topic, the general description of the situation, a description of the role and the problem they face. The trainees then act their role by interacting with one and another. Role play is used to develop interpersonal skills such as communication, conflict resolution and group decision making. Structured role plays provide trainees with more detailed description of the situation and the character's attitude, needs and opinions. Spontaneous role plays are loosely constructed interactions in which one of the participants plays him/ her self while the others play people with whom the first trainee has interacted in the past (Goldstein, 1993).

Behavioural Modeling. It gives the participants a chance actually see how a model would act in a certain situation, rather than simply be told how to act. Behavioural modeling uses natural tendency for people to observe to learn how to do something. The techniques generally used in combination with other techniques (Woods, 1995; p. 185). Behaviour modeling differs from both role plays and simulations by first providing the trainee with an understanding of what the desired skill level looks like (Goldstein, 1993). Behavioural modeling gives emphasis on doing rather than telling. Managers can be shown how to delegate, communicate, conduct meeting, interview an applicant or discipline an employee. It is useful for almost any type of skill training. It has been used for training in interpersonal skills, sales, interviewer, safety, interviewee training and many other areas (Decker and Naten, 1985). Behavioural model is an excellent technique of training managers and supervisors.

Sensitivity Training. It is also called as laboratory training and is often used to develop interpersonal skills. It helps make participants more aware of their own behaviours as well as their behaviour towards others. This type of training can supplement and provide cost effective alternative to portions of the classroom and on-the-job training programs. Sensitivity training allows participants to see how others see them in constructive way. The principal disadvantage is that the process can sometimes become dangerously personal for the employee.

Behavioural or On-the-Job Training

Behavioural training methods places employees in actual work situation and make them immediately productive. This method allows trainee to practice behaviour in real or simulated fashion. On-the-job training involve learning by doing, relies on demonstration and coaching. These methods stimulate learning through behaviour and are best for skill development and attitude change. These methods provide an employee with task specific knowledge and skills in work area. The knowledge and skills presented during on-the-job are directly related to job requirements. This form helps particularly to develop the occupational skills necessary to manage an organization, to fully understand the organization's products and services and how they are developed and carried out. Job instruction technique, job rotation, coaching and apprentice training are common forms of on-the-job training methods. The success of learning in on-the-job training depends upon the four steps of *prepare, present, tryout and follow-up.*

Job Instructions Training. It is a structured approach to training. It involves trainees going through a series of sequential steps. The technique uses behavioural strategy with the objective of skill development. While the training is in progress the trainee also gains some factual and procedural knowledge. This type of training is good for task oriented duties such as operating a machine etc. Job instruction technique consists of four steps viz. preparation, present, try out and follow up (Blandchard and Thacker, 1999, p. 306).

Induction training is also part of Job instructions training and it is important as it enables a new recruit to become productive as quickly as possible. It can avoid costly mistakes by recruits not knowing the procedures or techniques of their new jobs. The length of induction training will vary from job to job and will depend on the complexity of the job, the size of the business and the level or position of the job within the business.

The following areas may be included in induction training :

- Learning about the duties of the job
- Meeting new colleagues
- Seeing the layout the premises

- Learning the values and aims of the business
- Learning about the internal workings and policies of the business.

Job Rotation. It is a systematic movement of employees from job to job or project to project within an organization, as a way to achieve different human resource objectives such as; orienting new employees, exposing employees to diverse environment (Woods, 1995, p.188). A well orchestrated job rotation program can decrease the training costs while increasing the impact of training, because job rotation provides a trainee a hand on experience. Job rotation makes individuals more self-motivated, flexible, adaptable, innovative, and eager to learn and communicate effectively. The major difficulties with job rotation are that it increases the workload and decreases the productivity as employee takes time to settle down in new assignments, also it increase the time required to be spent by management with lower level employees. Job rotation may be especially valuable for organizations that require firm-specific skills because it provides an incentive to organizations to promote from within (Jerris, 1999, p.329).

Coaching. It is the process of one-to-one guidance and instruction to improve knowledge, skills and work performance. Coaching is becoming popular means of development, and often includes one-to-one with the trainee to conduct need assessment, set major goals to accomplish, develop an action plan and support the trainee to complete the training plan. The trainee drives the activities and the coach provides continuous feedback. Coaching is directed to employees with performance deficiencies, but also as a motivational tool; for those performing well. Coaching helps in solving precise problems such as communication, time management and social skills. Executive coaching may continue for several years. Coach is inducted when an organization structure is changed, when a team is not performing well, where new skills are to be imparted. Coaching assumes that you are fine but could be even better.

Apprentice Training. This is the oldest forms of training and very popular in India where people take up heredity jobs. Apprenticeship was the major approach to learning craft. In this method planned, practical instructions are imparted over a period of time. The apprentice works with a recognized master craftsman.

Internship. Internship are opportunities for students to get real world experience, often during summer vacations as a part of fulfilling requirements for degree programs. Internship are offered usually by organization to college students wanting to find work experience. The internship offer precious, real life job experience and the organization often get skilled, highly dedicated service. Some of the professions have mandatory period for internship after completing their degree programs.

On-the-job training is clearly useful method for skill development, since trainees implementing their knowledge in the actual job conditions. Transfer of training naturally occurs. Because employees getting on-the-job training are actually working, not being trained in classroom, it has clear cost advantages, if it is done effectively. Productivity will be lower during the training, because neither the trainee nor the trainer will be producing full capacity. But it is real that on-the-job training method is really cost effective method over simulations, games and computer based training modules.

Training for Special Purposes

Globalization of economies has increased the need for specific training to meet the international needs. Global business training samples include :

- Executive etiquette for global transactions.

- Cross-cultural technology transfer.
- International protocol and presentation.
- Business basics for the foreign executive.
- Language training.
- Diversity training.
- Cross-cultural sensitivity.
- Results examples :
  - o Improving technical skills.
  - o Socialization.

This would be covered in detail later in the book.

Blanchard and Thacker (1999, p. 304) have depicted the various methods and their comparative efficacy to address various training objectives. Table 8.4 depicts a broad guide to determine the effectiveness of various training techniques.

Table 8.1. Training Methods Effectiveness at Meeting Knowledge, Skills and Objectives

Training Methods	*GOAL OF TRAINING*					
	Knowledge			*Skills*		*Attitudes*
	Declarative	*Procedural*	*Strategic*	*Technical*	*Interpersonal*	
Off-the-Job Training						
Lecture	3	2	1	1	1	3
Computer Based Training	5	4	3	2a	2	3
Case Study	1	3	2	5	1	2
Business Game	2	3	5	2	2b	2
In-Basket	1	3	4	1	2c	2
Role Play	1	2	2	2	4	5d
Behaviour Modeling	1					
On-the-Job Training						
Job Instructions Training	3	5	4	4	2	5
Apprentice	5	5	4	5	2	5
Coaching	3	5	4	4	4	5
Scale : Not Effective-1 Mildly Effective-2	Moderately Effective-3 Effective-4 Very Effective-5					

Notes :

(*a*) This rating is for general technical skills. For some specific skills the rating would be 5.

(*b*) If the business game is designed for interpersonal skills, this rating would be 4.

(*c*) If multiple baskets were used in this rating would be 3.

(*d*) Specifically role reversal.

Source *: Adapted from Blanchard and Thacker (1999, p.304).*

Thus either behavioural or cognitive learning methods can effectively be used to change attitudes, though they do so through different means. Cognitive methods are best for knowledge development and behavioural methods for skill development. The decision about what approach to take to training depend on several factors that include :

- The amount of funding available for training,
- Specificity and complexity of the knowledge and skills needed,
- Timeliness of training needed, and the capacity and
- Motivation of the learner.

DESIGNING TRAINING

A main guideline in the design of a training program or session is to set aside everything and put one's thoughts towards the trainee or audience; to think in terms of what the trainee(s) will be able to do, demonstrate, or explain by the end of the training.

The only exception to this rule is in the preliminary stage while designing, and the subsequent actions taken :

1. "What is expected of the trainee(s) *i.e.,* he is able to do, demonstrate, or explain by the end of the training ?"
2. "What training resources and activities will facilitate learning ?"
3. "How will the desired change in behaviour measured ?"
4. "What tools and process will be used evaluate method of instruction and the training content ?"
5. "What is the best way to reinforce learning ?"

At this preliminary stage of designing the training program the designer is the central figure as the planner, decision-maker, trainer, and facilitator. The training however, cannot be planned until needs analysis has been carried out and training needs identified. Training needs are the perceived gaps between a desired and an actual situation (the measurable or observable performance and behaviour of the trainee/s).

Training Needs Analysis

There is an axiom which states that all training provision should be based on the accurate identification of learning needs. However, all too often the actual process of identifying training needs is done quickly or omitted altogether. Training provides an essential component in the implementation of the strategic plan of the company. It determines where the company is and where it wants to move. Thus, training need analysis increases the chances that the time and money spent on training would be spent wisely as. It helps in determining the benchmark for evaluation of training and increases the motivation of participants.

What is Training Needs Analysis ?

Training need analysis is the systematic gathering of data to find out where there are gaps in the existing skills, knowledge and attitudes of employees. It involves the gathering of data about existing employees' capabilities and organisational demands for skills, and the analysis of the implications of new and changed roles for changes in capability. It often flows from the business strategy, as the aim of identifying needs is to be able to build a plan to offer appropriate learning opportunities to fill the gaps identified and ensure that there is sufficient capability for the organisation to meet its objectives.

Strictly speaking, the analysis of gaps in knowledge and skills identifies what employees will need to learn in order to be fully competent in the jobs they will be doing now and in the future. How these gaps are filled may involve formal or informal training provision, or other opportunities for the necessary learning to be carried out. However, training and learning professionals have been using the acronym 'TNA' for the process of identifying these gaps for many years.

Training need analysis allows trainer to present logical explanation, at the start of training about what is not happening now (but should be) on the job, and how the training will be useful. For most types of training, need analysis will increase the relevance effectiveness of training.

Importance of Training Need Analysis

Careful analysis of training needs is important because :

- Unless the right quality of human capital is present, organisations may struggle to implement strategies and achieve targets. Analysing the areas where cpabilities are to be enhanced allows organisations to create a human capital investment strategy to support business objectives.
- Providing learning opportunities to staff enables them to develop and achieve personal and career goals.
- Well-planned training is an effective retention strategy, particularly for ambitious and externally mobile employees.
- All training provision should be designed to meet previously identified learning needs in order to be cost-effective. If an initial assessment using the correct assumptions is made about who needs to learn what, then it is likely that effective training or learning provision will result.
- Having a clear idea of what needs to be learned and the outcomes expected provides a foundation for training and learning professionals to evaluate the effectiveness of implementation of the learning strategy.

Levels of Training Need Analysis

Training need analysis is carried out at three levels :

(*a*) Organizational

(*b*) Specific department or project

(*c*) Individual

Organizational Training Need Analysis

It is usually undertaken to determine the types of learning that will be needed to ensure that all employees have the right knowledge, skills and attitudes to perform the jobs they do or would be needed in future to meet the organizations strategic objectives.

There are six issues types of training need analysis to collect data. This would contribute the best value to decision making process. It should be clearly understood that the breadth of training need analysis information collected is directly proportional to number of training needs analysis methods used. The six methods are :

(*a*) Competency Studies.

(*b*) Context training needs analysis. While carrying out context needs analysis data is collected to answer questions such as : 'Who are the decision makers ?'; 'Is the management committed to the proposed training initiative ?'; 'What are the preferred methods of conduct of training and criteria's to judge the success of learning programme ?'

(*c*) Content training needs analysis. While determining the content of training needs data is collected by answering the questions.

(*d*) User training needs analysis. Information for user training needs is determined by answering questions such as : 'What level of subject matter knowledge do the learners and trainers possess ?'; 'How do they prefer to learn ?'; What is the availability of trainees and trainers ?'; What are the expectations.

(*e*) Suitability of training.

(*f*) Results on investments.

Sources of Conducting Need Analysis

There are many sources by which the need analysis could be carried out. Surveys have revealed that the training needs of an organization are primarily determined by the top management. Certain organizations (especially government and public sector units) have a specific committee to advice management on the training needs of the organization. These advisory committees carryout detailed analysis and link the company strategy with training. Advisory committees are good in anticipating impending and future problems like expansion of business, introduction new products and services etc. advisory committees also assess the organizational changes concerned with manpower inventory for the present and future needs may also necessitate a training programme.

The second method is by comparing the job description and job specification (Job Analysis) with the individuals' profile of knowledge, abilities, skills and behaviour. Some firms carryout work sampling to determine the training needs. Job evaluation, performance appraisals are a good method of determining the training needs. Training need analysis can also be carried out by conducting a survey by providing a questionnaire to the employees or conducting a skill test. See Exhibit 8.1.

EXHIBIT 8.1 : SURVEY QUESTIONNAIRE

For Trainees.
(Please fill the following details.)

1. Name
2. Numbers of Years in Service
3. Job Title Code
4. Grade
5. Number of years in present Grade
6. Number of people directly reporting to you.
7. Training programmes attended during last one year (Give name of the programme if attended)
8. Give brief Career History
9. Skill Requirements
10. Strategic Awareness
    Application to risk management
    Working with cross functional teams
11. General Skill Requirements
    A. Markets (Market Knowledge, Product Knowledge, Commercial Knowledge)
    B. Processes
12. Any other issues

for Answering Question Number 9, use under mentioned scale

Level of Importance	Degree of Difficulty
A. Crucial	1. A great deal
B. Very Important	2. Quite a lot
C. Fairly Important	3. A little
D. Minor	4. None

One of the best methods of determining the needs is by conducting an exit interview.

There are other methods which are often used such as observations, group discussions, conferences, analysis of various reports, and recommendation of supervisory staff (Figure 8.4).

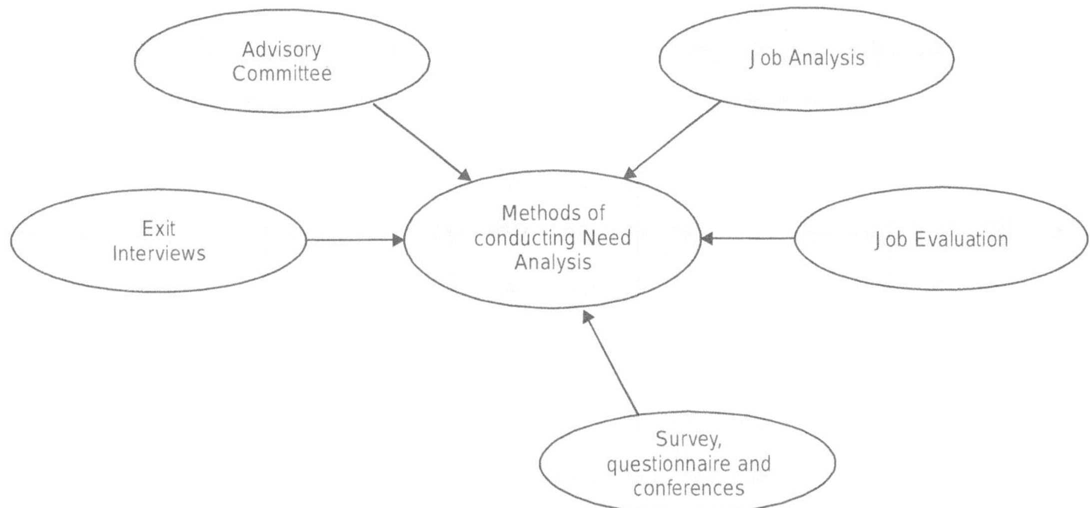

Fig. 8.4. *Method of Conducting Need Analysis.*

In addition to above the other methods in use are discussed below.

Training Suitability Analysis. The first step is to determine whether training is the desired solution to the problem. Training is one of the many methods available to the management to solve a particular problem. Training may not be the ideal solution always, and hence, it is important to carryout training suitability analysis.

Context Analysis. It is an analysis of the business needs for the desired training. The important question that are sought to be answered by this analysis are

1. Who decided the training should be conducted ?
2. Why is the training program seen as the best alternative to overcome the problem ?
3. History of the organization on training ? Etc.

User Analysis. This analysis deals with potential participants and instructors involved in the training process. It involves answering questions such as; who will receive the training ? What is their present level of proficiency ? What is their learning style ? Who are the instructors ? Etc.

Content Analysis. This pertains to the analysis of documents, laws, and procedures used on the job. It answers question about knowledge and information used on the job. Content of training should not conflict or contradict the documented job requirements. It is best performed by leveraging the experience of a worker who performs the job and also domain knowledge of the subject matter.

Cost Benefit Analysis. Cost benefit analysis is carried out by analyzing the return on investment on training. Effective training results in a return of value to the organization that is greater than the initial investment to produce or administer the training.

DESIGNING A TRAINING PROGRAME

Training requires more than just providing information—giving or skills development. It requires the trainer to have a thorough knowledge and understanding of the training process, role of planning and evaluation of the program. Proper designing of the training programmes is an essential prerequisite for success of training programmes.

Programme has to designed at the planning phase and depends upon the training intends to achieve and how best it can be achieved. The important steps are in Figure 8.5.

Step 1. Assessment of Training Needs.
Step 2. Specifying Training Objectives.
Step 3. Prepare a Work Plan.
Step 4. Organize training Content.
Step 5. Select Training Methods and Techniques.
Step 6. Identify the Training Resource.
Step 7. Assemble and package Lessons Plan.
Step 8. Develop Media for Training.
Step 9. Pre-test Training Programme.
Step 10. Implement and Manage Training.
Step 11. Evaluate the Training.

Fig. 8.5. *Steps in Designing Training Programme.*

Assessment of Training Needs. This is the first step in designing the training programme. It is the need analysis which provides the base line information upon which the training programme is designed and developed. The assessment can be carried out by answering the question who, what and whom ? *Who* answers the question about the categories of people who have training needs ? *What* unearths the kind of needs of participants in the training programme ? *Whom* helps in identifying proper trainers (in house or external) ? It is important that a discussion is held with potential trainees and possibly their supervisors.

Formulating and Specifying Training Objectives. Once the training needs have been identified, it is important to translate those needs as realistic objectives. Training objectives are the changes, which an organization seeks to accomplish through the training. The objective should be precise, it must help in designing the conduct of training and provide the trainees with a clear understanding of knowledge and skills they require.

Prepare a Work Plan. A work plan is a plan of operations. It helps to establish what is needed.

- Training – who require it, when, where, how long ?
- Media Communications – what is required, where will it be obtained ?
- Equipment – what we need and where ?
- Transport required – where and when ?
- Finance – requirement, who controls it ? Are adequate funds available ?

Organize Training Content. The content should be derived from the training objectives. Trainers must develop a framework that draws out the content of training.

Select Training Methods and Techniques. Content should have learning activities that help the trainees to accomplish the training objectives. To help them understand the training material, it is necessary to use training methods that allow reviewing the key points communicated, use relevant and realistic examples, and restate new ideas in different ways using familiar words and analogies. It is especially important when communicating that there is consistency in the definitions and unit of analysis used. Different trainees can be exposed to different methods of training to ensure they derive the maximum benefit and get optimum results.

Identify Training Resources Required. The trainer must identify all the relevant training material that may be required to conduct the training including facilities, equipment, materials required, administrative and personnel support.

Assemble and Package Lesson Plans. At this point the training objectives, content, training methods and the training resources needed to conduct the training are collected and lesson plans prepared for conducting training. The plan should serve as a written record on how the training is conducted.

Develop Media for Training. The material needed for training is then prepared in packets for day to day work for the trainees. It is expected that the material included in the packets would meet the dual needs of organization and individual.

Implement and Manage the Training. Implementation of the training also follows a number of steps;

1. **Preparation** . Involves the knowledge of the objectives of the training and being clear on the strategy to apply and content of the training.
2. **Setting**. Ensuring a cheerful and relaxed environment for the conduct of the training.
3. **Breaking the ice and openers**. Introducing means for each participants to know each other.
4. **The Learning Experience**. This is the main aspect of the training and could be said its core. It should be ensured that participants or trainees should be actively involved; they should encouraged to express their ideas and question the material being provided.

EVALUATING EFFECTIVENESS OF TRAINING

Training evaluation determines the value of training through systematic process. This is ensured through assessment of effectiveness of training, learning, application of new knowledge and skill in work practices. A model of training evaluation design recommended by Jackson (1989) is in Figure 8.6.

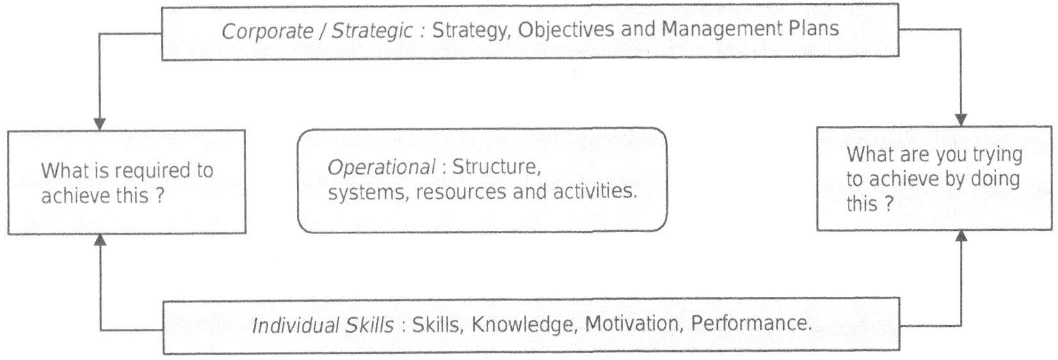

Fig. 8.6. *Training Evaluation Design Model.*

Need for Evaluation

It is necessary to evaluate the extent to which training program have achieved the aims for which these are designed. Such an evaluation would provide useful information about the effectiveness of training as well as about the design of future training program. Evaluation enables an organization to monitor the training program as also update and modify in future programs. There are some criteria for measuring the success of training; direct cost, efficiency, performance to schedule, reactions, learning, behaviour change etc. (Sheppard, 1999). One of the studies has depicted that only ten per cent of the companies carry out evaluation of training. While another study states that training is only moderately effective.

Concept of Training Effectiveness

Training effectiveness can be stated as the degree to which the trainees are able to learn and apply the knowledge and skills acquired in the training program. The effectiveness depends upon the attitude, interest, values and expectations of the trainees and the training environment. The training would be effective only when the trainees want to learn, are involved in their jobs and have career strategies. Contents of a training program, and the ability and motivation of trainers also determine training effectiveness.

To be effective, training method should :

- Motivate the trainee to improve performance.
- Provide for active participation by the trainee.
- Encourage positive transfer from training to job.
- Provide timely feedback on the trainee's performance.
- Be structured from simple to specific problems.

Designing the Training Programme

The content of the training programme depends upon who we are involving and how much time has been allocated. However, the training should be so designed that there are mix of approaches even if the training session is short.

The steps involved in designing training programme are discussed below.

1. Selecting Strategies. First step in designing is to determine the strategy of training. Strategy enables the trainers to prioritize training objectives and also help in selecting the training areas, which could include skiis, developing conceptual understanding, etc.
2. Breaking Objectives. The second step is to break the objectives into different parts like knowledge, understanding and skills. Each sub part of the training objective is matched by an appropriate training event.
3. Choosing Methods. After having determined the objectives and what the events are the trainer then determines and selects the best method by which training can be imparted.
4. Deciding on Training Package and the Programme. Once the methods have been selected then the trainer identifies the package to be imparted and then schedules the training event.

Sample training programme is shown in Figure 8.7.

Day	Activity	Purpose (for participants)	Purpose (for organization)
Day 1	Understanding the change imperative	To understand the degree of change in individual way of doing day to day activities.	To have positive attitudinal change, thus enabling employees to be competitive.
	WTO, ILO, and economic reforms and their impact on Trade Unions.	To understand the impact of economic reforms on trade union practices globally.	To create supportive role of Trade Unions.
	Collective Bargaining scenario.	To understand changed collective bargaining scenario.	To get the advantage of excellent practices of trade unions and convert them as partners in organizational growth.
	Case Studies	To put learned lesson into action.	To measure training effectiveness.
Day 2	Creativity and innovations in managing customers	To develop creative and lateral thinking	To get benefit of creativity and translate creative thinking into action.
	Conflict management	To manage conflict and translate the same into better performance.	To reduce dysfunctional conflict.
	Trade Unions under disinvestment scenario.	To understand the degree of change in Trade Unions way of doing day to day activities.	To reap the benefit of positive attitudinal change of trade unions and remain competitive with active support and cooperation.
	Quizzes and case studies	To practice learned lessons and measure.	To measure effectiveness in training and put into use learned lesson.

Fig. 8.7. *Training Programme for Trade Union.*

Programme Content and Schedule

The above designed programme is then converted into a schedule. This usually contains the date, time, event, location and name of the instructor conducting it. All have been seeing training programmes since they joined school. See Figure 8.8.

Day and Date	Time	Type	Subject	Name of Instruction	Reference	Location	Remarks
23 Feb Monday	0900–1000h	T/D	Understanding Change	Mr. Tarun Singh	ILO Chapter 1	Room No 203	
	1000–1100	T/D	Six Sigma as Change Management	Mr. Sankalp Singh	Six Sigma	Room No 203	

Fig. 8.8. *Training Programme for Trade Union.*

Evaluation Criteria

The evaluation of training involves seeking information of the effects of training and assessing the value of training in the light of that information. Hamblin in his work 'Evaluation and Control of Training', effectiveness of training can be measured in terms of the reactions of trainee to the objectives, contents, and methods of training; to the extent trainees have acquired the desired knowledge; has helped trainee to improve behaviour and ultimately the improvement in productivity or performance. Evaluation is done on two criteria Training and performance level criteria.

Training-Level Criteria involves determining the *reactions* of trainee as to how much does trainee like the program, and how much do they think they learned and *learning* criteria : *i.e.*, What did the person learn ? Which is analyzed by conducting examinations ?

Performance Level Criteria involves determining the behavioural change and results in the form of increased efficiency at work place. Behaviour Criteria concerns the trainee's behaviours on the job that might have been due to training; 'Do they do what they were taught ?' and results criteria : did the training increase efficiency ?

Calculation of Cost Benefits of Training

Most of the training decisions taken by organizations are incremental. Business heads calculate and evaluate the cost effectiveness of training courses by assessing cost and effect within their own business domain. The incremental approach however is no longer adequate to determine the return on investments. Particularly, when things go off-scale, managers need to look beyond return on investments. Hence, return on investments measurement techniques vary at different levels of the organization. Figure 8.9 illustrates how measurement areas change with the change in levels.

Function	***Goal***	***Measurement***	***Scope***
Manager - Human Resource	Reduce Skill gaps	Individual performance	Business Unit specific training
Sub Unit Heads	Achieve Business goals	Project Goals, business metrics.	
Corporate level Managers	Identify the best alternative	Financial metrics, business case	Whole organization wide learning through knowledge management, e-learning infrastructure.
Top Management	Gain competitive advantage, organizational transformation	Business case, share holder value.	

Fig. 8.9. *Measuring Return on Investments at Different Levels.*

In very simple financial terms, return on investments is calculated with following formula;

$$\text{Return on Investments} = \frac{\text{Gains} - \text{Investment Costs}}{\text{Investments Cost}}$$

Simple return on investment is the most frequently used form and is most easily understood. With simple ROI, incremental gains from the investment are divided by investment costs.

Return on Investment is only factor in making investment decisions. In training, other factors include available financing and operating factors such as available labour and facilities. Return on Investment could also be measured through one simple abbreviated formula as under :

LE + WE = BR = ROI

Where

LE is Learning Experience;

WE is Work Environment

BR is Business Results

It is, therefore, evident that training based return of investment is quantifiable increase in market share, financial gain and employees' behavioural shifts. Whether return of investments is positive is based can be understood with the measurement of the following items :

1. Incremental financial gains
2. Market share growth
3. Employee loyalty and growth
4. Customer loyalty
5. Strategic and tactical gains

TRAINING EFFECTIVENESS MEASURING MODELS

Beginning with World War II, evaluation research in training and evaluation activities has developed as a result of substantial support from United States Federal Government. It basically provides an answer to the question 'do we implement or repeat a program or not ?' and 'if so, what modifications should be made ?' (Stone and Watson, 1999). Europe also was not lagging. It also carried out its own research and developed models for evaluating training different from United States.

The Kirkpatrick's Four Levels Approach

First model for evaluation is Kirkpatrick's Four Levels of Evaluation. It was created in 1959 by Donald Kirkpatrick, then Professor of marketing at the University of Wisconsin. It is still one of the most widely used methods. It involves measuring : *reactions* – a measure of satisfaction; *learning*- a measure of learning; *behaviour*- a measure of behaviour change and *results*- a measure of results (Philips, J., 1997, p. 39). The conceptual framework answers four very important questions (Table 8.2).

Table 8.2. Kirkpatrick Four Levels of Evaluation

Level 1 – Reaction	Were the participants pleased ? What do they plan to do with what they learned ?
Level 2 – Learning	What skills, knowledge, or attitudes have change ? By how much ?
Level 3 - Behaviour	Did the participants change their behaviour based on what was learned in the program ?
Level 4 - Results	Did the change in behaviour positively affect the organization ?

Source : *Stone J. and Watson V., (1999). Evaluation of Training, www.ispi-atlanta.org.*

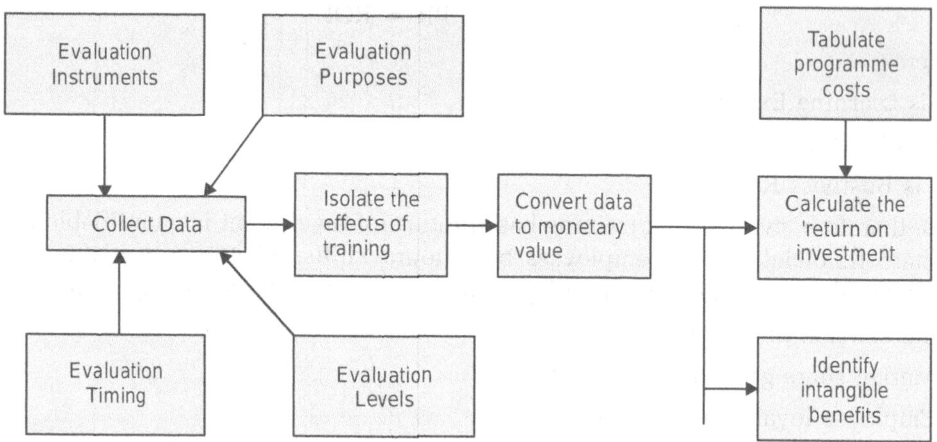

Fig. 8.10. *Kirkpatrick Four Levels of Evaluation.*

Kaufman's Five Level of Evaluation

The shortcomings of Kirkpatrick' four level approach, attempted, modified and added to the basic framework of Kirkpatrick's Model. Kaufman expanded the definition of Level 1 and added a fifth level addressing social issues (Philips, 1997; p.40) (Figure 8.11).

Level	***Evaluation***	***Focus***
5	Societal Outcomes	Societal and client responsiveness, consequences and payoffs.
4	Organizational Output	Organizational contributions and payoffs.
3	Application	Individual and small group (product) utilization within the organization.
2	Acquisition	Individual and small group mastery and competency.
1b	Reaction	Method's, means' and processes' acceptability and efficiency.
1a	Enabling	Availability and quality of human, financial and physical resource input.

Source : *Philips, J. (1997), p.41.*

Fig. 8.11. *Kaufman's Five Levels of Evaluation*

At level 1, enabling addresses the availability of various resource inputs necessary for successful intervention. At level 5, evaluation focus is on societal and client responsiveness and consequences in payoff. This enables evaluation beyond the organization, and examines the extent to which the performance improvement program has its impact on society and environment around organization.

Context, Input, Reaction and Outcome (CIRO) Approach

Warr, Bird and Rackman developed a developed a different way to evaluate training then being researched and conducted in United States. European framework had much broader scope than the traditional use of the term 'evaluation' as perceived in United States. As with other approaches, four general categories of evaluation are described, which form the letter CIRO (Context, Input, Reaction and Outcome) (Philips, 1997, p.39).

Context evaluation includes obtaining and using information about the recent operational conditions or context to determine training needs and objectives. Input evaluation includes gathering and using information about possible training resources to select between alternative inputs to training process. Reaction evaluation includes obtaining and using information about learner's reactions to improve the training process. Outcome evaluation includes gathering and using information about the findings and outcomes of training. Outcome evaluation is considered the most important part of the evaluation. If outcome evaluation is to be successful, it needs careful preparation before training programme begins (Philips, 1997, p.41).

The Five Level Returns on Investment Framework

Returns on Investment (ROI) is a measure of the monetary benefits obtained by an organization over a specified time period in return for a given investment in a training program. A Return on Investment is the extent to which output of training exceeds inputs. Returns on Investments can be used to justify planned investment and to evaluate the extent to which desired returns are achieved. This process has however limitations in that it cannot evaluate all aspects of training such as whether the trainees liked the training; the extent to which the trainees personal goals have been accomplished (Sheppard, 1999) (Figure 8.12).

A return on Investment adds the fifth level. Like all training evaluation models it has its advantages and disadvantages of calculating Returns on Investment of training programme. The costs of training are known and expressed in monetary terms, but benefits are often soft, subjective and difficult to quantify and convert in the monetary terms. Costs are known up front, before training, but benefits may accrue slowly over time. But on the other hand, course objectives and content will become more lean, relevant, and behavioural with focus on monetary results rather than on the acquisition of information (Parry, S., 1996, p.72).

Level	***Evaluation***	***Focus***
1	Reaction and Planned Action	Measure's participant's reaction to the program and outlines specific plans for implementation.
2	Learning	Measures skills, knowledge or attitude changes.
3	Job Applications	Measure change in behaviour on the job and specific application of the training material.
4	Business Results	Measures business impact of the program.
5	Return on Investment	Measures the monetary value of the results and cost for the program, usually expressed as a percentage.

Source : *Philips, J., (1997), p43.*

Fig. 8.12. *Five Level of Returns on Investment Framework.*

Other Related Models

There are some other commonly used models such as Training Validation Model (TVS) Approach (Fitz –Enz 1994); and input, Process, Output/Outcome (IPO) Model (Bushnell, 1990).

A comparison of several system based models (CIPP, IPO, TVS) with Kirkpatrick's Model is presented in Figure 8.13.

Kirkpatrick's	*Systems based Model*		
Goal based Model	***CIPP Model (1987)***	***IPO Model (1990)***	***TVS Model (1994)***
1. Reaction to collect data on participants reaction	Context : to obtain information about the educational needs to establish program objectives.	Input : to evaluate performance indicators like; trainee qualifications, availability of materials, appropriateness of training etc.	Situation : to collect pre-training data on current performance levels and to define a desirable level of future performance.
2. Learning : to evaluate how far the learning objectives have been met.	Input : to identify training strategies to achieve the desired results	Process : to plan, design, develop, and deliver the training programmes.	Intervention : to identify the reason for the gap between the present and desirable performance and assess how training can solve the problem.
3. Behaviour : to assess change in job performance as a result of training.	Process : to assess the implementation of educational programmes.	Output : to gather data from the training interventions.	Impact : to evaluate the difference between the pre- and post- training data.
4. Results : to assess costs vs benefits of training.	Product : to gather information on the results of the training intervention and interpret its worth and merit.	Outcomes; to measure long-term results in profitability, competitiveness etc.	Value : to measure differences in quality, productivity, service or sales.

Fig. 8.13. *Comparison of Kirkpatrick's Goal Based Model and Systems Based Model.*

Benjamin Bloom's Taxonomy

Bloom's Taxonomy was primarily created for academic education; it is relevant to all types of learning. Bloom's model provides an excellent structure for planning designing, assessing and evaluating training and learning effectiveness. The model also serves as a checklist, by which it can be ensured that the training is planned to cover all aspects of training needs of the trainee. This model also provides a template by which validity and coverage of existing training can be assessed. The model has three pars of overlapping domain.

1. *Cognitive Domain* – intellectual capability *i.e.,* knowledge or ability to grasp the intricacies and 'think' through the problem.
2. *Affective Domain* – involves emotions, behaviour or simply 'attitude'.
3. *Psychomotor Domain*- involves manual and physical skills.

Figure 8.14 depicts the Bloom's Taxonomy Model.

Cognitive (Knowledge)	***Affective (Attitude)***	***Psychomotor (Skills)***
Recall data	Receive (awareness)	Imitation (skills)
Understand	Respond	Manipulation
Apply (use)	Value, understand and act	Develop precision
Analyse (structure)	Organize (personal value system)	Articulation
Synthesize (create/ build)	Internalize value system	Naturalization (automate, become expert)
Evaluate (assess, judge in relational terms)		

Fig. 8.14. *Bloom's Taxonomy Model*

Financial Utility model

This model was utilized by Godkewitsch (1987) to calculate the financial utility to a company for implementing a training programme. The model is described by an equation :

$$F = N\,[(E \times M)] - C$$

Where :

F is the financial utility

N is the number of people in the training programme.

E is the effect or outcome of the training programme.

M is the financial value of the effect or outcome.

C is the financial cost per person of implementing the training programme.

TRAINING POLICY

The economic opening of the world has resulted in new opportunities and intensified global competition. This has resulted in business houses adopting new processes and techniques. The corporate world thus has embarked on reviewing and upgrading of the human skills continuously to keep pace with such changes.

> ***Wipro to Retrain staff***
>
> It has been reported that *Wipro* is embarking on a massive training programme to ensure that employees are multi skilled.

The training policy establishes linkages with prevailing organizational human resource such as performance management, career planning, rewards and compensation, promotion and transfer.

A training policy serves the organization by :

1. Provides guidance for allocating departmental resources such as trainers, money and time.
2. It lays down guidelines for training activities.

3. Outlines the responsibilities and authority of various functionaries involved in training.
4. Provides tools for evaluating the success of the department's effort.
5. It helps in ensuring that less time is spent in determining the needs, there are fewer errors and there is a consistent answer.

Need for a Training Policy

To ensure that training policy serves the organization by :

Defining what the organization intends to accomplish through training.

1. Allocates responsibilities for conduct of training.
2. Identifies the type of training to be imparted including on the job, informal and formal training.
3. Spells out duration, time and place of training.
4. Indicates the requirements of outside assistance and institutions where training has to be arranged.
5. Incorporates the laws of the land in respect of training.

Characteristics of Good Training Policy

The overall goal for any policy or procedure document is for the design to be *simple, consistent*, and *easy to use*. In order to ensure a consistent format between documents, templates are used. Good training policy is usually :

- Written in clear, concise, simple language.
- The statements address what is the rule rather than how to implement the rule.
- The statements are readily available to the community and their authority is clear.
- Designated "policy experts" (identified in each document) are readily available to interpret policies and resolve problems.
- As a body, they represent a consistent, logical framework for action.

Writing Style

- Concise, minimum of verbiage.
- Factual—double-check accuracy!
- Don't include information that may be quickly outdated (*e.g.*, names).
- If you use an acronym, spell it out the first time you use it.
- Include step-by-step instructions for completing (paper or electronic) forms (procedures only).
- Not too technical—simple enough to be understood by a new employee.

Structure of Training Policy

The training policy usually should contain the under mentioned :

1. Outline Mission Statement
2. Objectives to b achieved
3. Responsibilities

4. Schedule of events
5. Standards to be achieved
6. Fee plans if any
7. Performance appraisals

Review Questions

1. What are the factors that should be taken into considerations while designing an effective training programme ? Mention the various steps in designing the training programme ?
2. What are the methods through which operatives are provided training ? Differentiate between and Cognitive and Behaviuoral methods of training.
3. Are the training and development practices inconsistent with modern organization theory ? What are the training needs and objectives ? How will you assess training needs ?
4. What do you understand by industrial training ? Discuss its significance to the management and to the employees.
5. How will you evaluate effectiveness of training ? How can such an organization be created ?
6. 'The purpose of training is multi-fold. Training may be required for several purposes'. In the light of this statement discuss the various types of employees training.
7. Critically examine the effectiveness of business game as a tool in training programmes ?
8. Do you think recent economic liberalization programme of the Government of India has made training function more important for an organization ? Elucidate.

PROJECT WORK

Your company is a new start up with their multi-location project sites for developing manufacturing facilities of consumer durables have made a request to you for designing three day intensive training programme for their newly recruited project managers, as a part of their specific induction training.

Discuss this in yourclass.

Case Study

Case Study 1

One morning Rohit Kumar, a recent recruit of a reputed management institute of Delhi walked into the sales office at Gwalior as a new sales trainee. Balkar Singh, the Zonal sales manager for a large computer hardware firm was there to greet him. Balkars job consisted of seeing the work of sales, sales officers, field executives and trainee salesman numbering over 100 in for areas of Raipur, Bhopal, Indore and Gwalior. The sales growth of computer sales was highly satisfactory, especially in recent years.

Balkar collected several reports, catalogues and pamphlets describing in detail the types of office equipment sold by the company. Raghavan after pleasant chat about their respective backgrounds gave Sanjay the material gathered and showed him to his assigned desk. Thereafter, Balkar excused himself and did not return. Sanjay spent whole day scanning the material and left for home at 5 pm.

Questions

1. *What do you think of induction by Balkar ?*
2. *What should have been done by Balkar ?*
3. *What method of training is best under such conditions ?*

Case Study 2

Ramesh had all the answers. He was a legend in his own mind. A very experienced and knowledgeable senior technician, people were constantly drawing on his analytical abilities. There didn't seem to be a technical or system problem he couldn't solve. Although you often got more "war stories" and background than you wanted, Ramesh could connect many current problems to similar ones that were faced in the past. He used his technical know-how like a sword to "cut down the fools" who didn't follow his flawless logic. If he wanted any of your bright ideas, he'd give them to you.

Since changes were hitting the company from many sides at once, various changes and improvement efforts were underway. These included focusing on customer needs and improving service levels, cross-departmental teams, process improvements, leadership development, and an enterprise-wide integration of computer systems. Ramesh dismissed most of this with his usual cynicism. "If we lay low long enough, this too shall pass," he liked to quip. "I've been round and round the mulberry bush on this before. So many of these management fads are like the ties in my closet, if I wait long enough, they'll come back in fashion."

Preeti was a very knowledgeable senior technician who worked along side Hank. They were about the same age and had both started in the company around the same time. She had a lot of respect for Ramesh's towering intellect, had learned a lot from him, and continued to draw from his technical depths. People who went to Preeti often became part of her questioning process rather than getting quick answers. She was constantly asking why and digging deeper to understand the underlying technical, process, or human issues to many of the problems she helped to solve. She seemed to have an unquenchable curiosity for a wide variety of subjects both on and off the job. She was constantly reading, surfing the Internet, taking a course, or networking with colleagues in other companies. Her motto was summed up in a Henry Ford quotation she'd framed and put on her desk, "Anyone who stops learning is old, whether at twenty or eighty. Anyone who keeps learning stays young. The greatest thing in life is to keep your mind young." She supported the company's floundering change and improvement initiatives because she knew how critical they were to the changes hitting their industry.

That Friday, Rahul came back from lunch with his vice president deeply troubled. Both Ramesh and Preeti reported to him. As part of the major organization changes going on, he and his vice president had agreed that the department had to be restructured and reduced in size. There wasn't going to be room for both Ramesh and Preeti "We've struggled with our change programs because they've been just that — programs rather than a way of life," the vice president said. "We've got to go deeper than just more tools and techniques. We have to shift our culture toward continuous learning and constant improvement. We need to build a focused, fast, and flexible department around the remaining senior technician." No discussion was needed; they both agreed that Preeti was the obvious choice. Rahul dreaded the scene he would have with Ramesh. He also felt sorry for him. With his rigid mind set, poor people skills, and traditional view of the world, Hank would have a tough time finding another job.

Preeti demonstrated — and Ramesh discovered too late — that what I am going to be tomorrow is determined by what I am becoming today. If I continue to do what I've always been doing, I will continue to get what I've always been getting. To get somewhere else, I need to grow into someone else.

Questions

1. *What is the difference in approach to training of Ramesh and Preeti ?*
2. *Hoe do you propose to improve his performance ?*
3. *Should the situation have been discussed with Ramesh by the management ?*
4. *Why has such a situation risen ?*

❑❑❑

Chapter **9**

MANAGEMENT DEVELOPMENT

★ LEARNING OBJECTIVES ★

After reading this chapter, you will be able to understand :

- Nature and Concept of management development
- Need and Importance of management development
- Objectives
- Designing management development
- Methods of management development
- Evaluation of management development

INTRODUCTION

Contemporary organizations have realized the importance of the human capital and are increasingly finding it necessary to continuously train and develop human resources. The quality of top management determines the standard of performance of the company, hence, in a fast changing and dynamic environment there is a necessity to carryout management development. Anyone with responsibility for organizing resources or people is a manager and any action to improve his skills, abilities, knowledge and behaviour for the benefit of the employing organization is 'management development'. Usually, this term management development refers to the activities involved in enhancing leaders', managers' and supervisor's abilities to plan, organize, lead and control the organization and its members. Consequently, many view the term "management development" to include executive development (developing executives), leadership development (developing leaders), managerial development (developing managers) and supervisors' development (developing supervisors).

Management development refers to the activities involved in enhancing one's ability to carry out top-level roles in the organization. Some key skills for managers includes understanding the whole system that includes external environment of the organization, leadership, strategic planning, financial forecasting and analysis, organizing, program planning and human resource management, etc.

Today's rapidly changing business landscape demands a new approach to developing managers/ leaders. Research shows that the top executives in large companies and a variety of sectors around the world believe that face peculiar challenges such as :

(*a*) Increased competitive pressure.

(*b*) Rapidly changing market conditions.

(*c*) Failure to innovate.

(*d*) Satisfying customer demands.

Managers are Different

Managers in an organization differ from other employees and are partly defined by having a status which provides benefits (such as advantageous share option schemes or special bonuses) not available to other employees. Managers at board level or just below, have major strategic responsibilities. Managers are likely to respond to many learning and development issues just like any other people in the organization, but there are significant factors about this group of managers that make them genuinely different from the rest of the employees.

- **Status.** Managers wield power, and hence, they are likely to be sensitive to their senior status. Even in relatively egalitarian organizations they are likely to see their development needs as different.
- **Terminology.** Many senior managers see training as an activity for more junior people and are likely to resent the idea that they can be subject generalized training courses. They may even reject the idea that they need to learn. This has resulted in use of the term 'development'—not 'training' or even 'learning'.
- **Numbers.** Mangers are comparatively few in number than the balance of the workforce. Although the organizations are getting flatter but most organizations retain a pyramidal hierarchy (even if the pyramids have been flattened over the years). Such a structure must of necessity have few people at the top. This again points away from standardized solutions.
- **Isolation.** A great deal of the learning that goes on in organizations is when people share problems and talk together about solutions. These can vary from a quick conversation at the coffee machine or water cooler to formal team meetings. Many senior managers lack opportunities especially where they may be burdened with significant problems that they feel unable to talk about to more junior managers. Being in the top of a pyramid structure the managers may find themselves in an isolated role without a peer group. Very senior people, such as Chief Executive Officers, feel the loneliness of the job and the impossibility of others really understanding the pressures on them. This point is crucially important in thinking about development issues. Sometimes people in middle management roles imagine that, as they report into a senior manager, they understand what the role is like but they may well be in for a shock.
- **Political skills.** Senior managers often need highly refined political skills in order to survive. Most organizations would not want to run courses for senior managers on how to be a better corporate politician. Yet there does need to be some legitimate assistance provided for new senior managers in this area.

All the above points justify organizations planning specifically for management development. One major benefit of getting managers tuned into learning and development processes is that it makes it so much easier to get support for development programme at lower levels. There is absolutely no doubt that a major stumbling block to create a learning culture in an organization is when senior managers are not themselves committed to their own development.

WHAT IS MANAGEMENT DEVELOPMENT ?

There are at least as many definitions of management development as there are books on the subject. But for the purpose of this chapter management development has taken to cover the entire structured process by which managers learn and improve their skills for the benefit of their employing organizations and themselves. The word 'structured' is important because, like everyone else, managers learn all the time from experience (on the job)—from doing their jobs. Only if that informal learning is picked up or used in some kind of formal process should it be counted as 'management development.'

According to **Chhabra**, **Ahuja** and **Jain** (1997),

'Management development is the process by which managers acquire not only skills and competencies in their present jobs but also capabilities for future managerial tasks of increasing difficulty and scope.'

Management development includes all activities and programme which have substantial influence on changing the capacity of the individual to perform his present assignments better and in doing so are likely to increase his potential for future management assignment.

So management development includes :

(*a*) Informal learning or on the job training which is an on going process and will take place. Informal training is based on work-based methods.

(*b*) Formal training courses of various kinds are very specific courses on technical aspects of jobs to courses or on wider management skills.

(*c*) Education which might range from courses for (perhaps prospective) junior managers or supervisors to executive training programme's at institutes.

REASONS FOR UNDERTAKING 'MANAGEMENT DEVELOPMENT'

The modern conditions need specific talents to retain edge in the competitive world. The leaders must possess :

(*a*) Business acumen to set and implement strategies.

(*b*) An understanding of how day to day decisions impact the overall performance of the company.

(*c*) People skills required to engage and develop others.

(*d*) Willingness to take values based actions.

Shortages of leadership talent and complexity of leadership skills are driving growth in development activities for executives, managers and high potentials. The management developments are intended to create bench strength of talented managers based on unity and alignment with teams as well as enhanced individual skills and abilities. The dynamic and changing environment of business needs constant up–gradation of skills to maintain competitive edge.

(*a*) To sustain a competitive edge the organization must keep on changing and developing. Hence, up–gradation of skills and competencies at all levels especially at management levels is necessary.

(*b*) The environment in which today managers operate has seen a sea change. The organizations need 'leaders' and not managers.

(*c*) Learning and knowledge development helps managers to gain respect of their subordinates.

(*d*) People management skills, along with technical skills, play a crucial role in the growth and evolution of managers. 'Management development' addresses the need for developing and improving human competencies.

(*e*) Networking between executives.

In the words of **Peter Drucker,** *"an organization that cannot produce its own managers will die. From over all points of view, the ability of an institution to produce managers is more important than its ability to produce goods efficiently and cheaply."*

Objectives of Management Development

The organizations seek that their managers are competitive, strategists, global, technologically up-to-date and flexible. The management development program aims at achieving the objectives of the organization and meets the aspirations of the individual managers.

(*a*) Improve performance.

(*b*) Develop managers to occupy higher positions.

(*c*) Ensure availability of qualified and requisite numbers of managers.

(*d*) Develop the right attitude and have capability to operate as a team.

Principles of Management Development/Learning

Irrespective of the technique employed for development of mangers, a sound training programme must be based on some basic principles :

- Management development must be based on the principles of individual differences. It should be borne in mind that individuals differ in ability and speed to learn, interests and other personal characteristics (Pigors and Myres).
- The depth and nature of development should be worked out.
- Both the trainer and trainee must actively participate. In management development it is essential the Chief Executive Officer should be actively involved.
- All development is self development; learner's participation is essential.
- Feedback on learning process should be provided to the learner.

MANAGEMENT DEVELOPMENT PROCESS

The training and development programme cannot be identified in isolation but has to be viewed in context to individual needs and organizational strategy (Chapter 8). Management development has become part of organizational strategy and one of the key corporate objectives. Given that senior managers will often be moving to the top of the organization, different needs at different stages will need to be identified. Broadly there are three situations around a job change :

- Preparing for the change
- Going through the transition
- Adjusting to the new role.

These issues can be translated into development needs at each stage. Preparation for change calls for manager needs to learn new skills for promotion. Transitional development involves managers seeking specific support, such as coaching or mentoring, while they are making the transition into the new role. The support here often needs to be quite timely and focused. Then there is role development in that the person is new into their role and they may need help in adjusting to new demands. One need is often for senior managers to stop doing things that they did in their previous role—and this can be a major learning issue. (Figure 9.1).

The process must meet the above three situations. Like any other training program development executive development has to go through similar process :

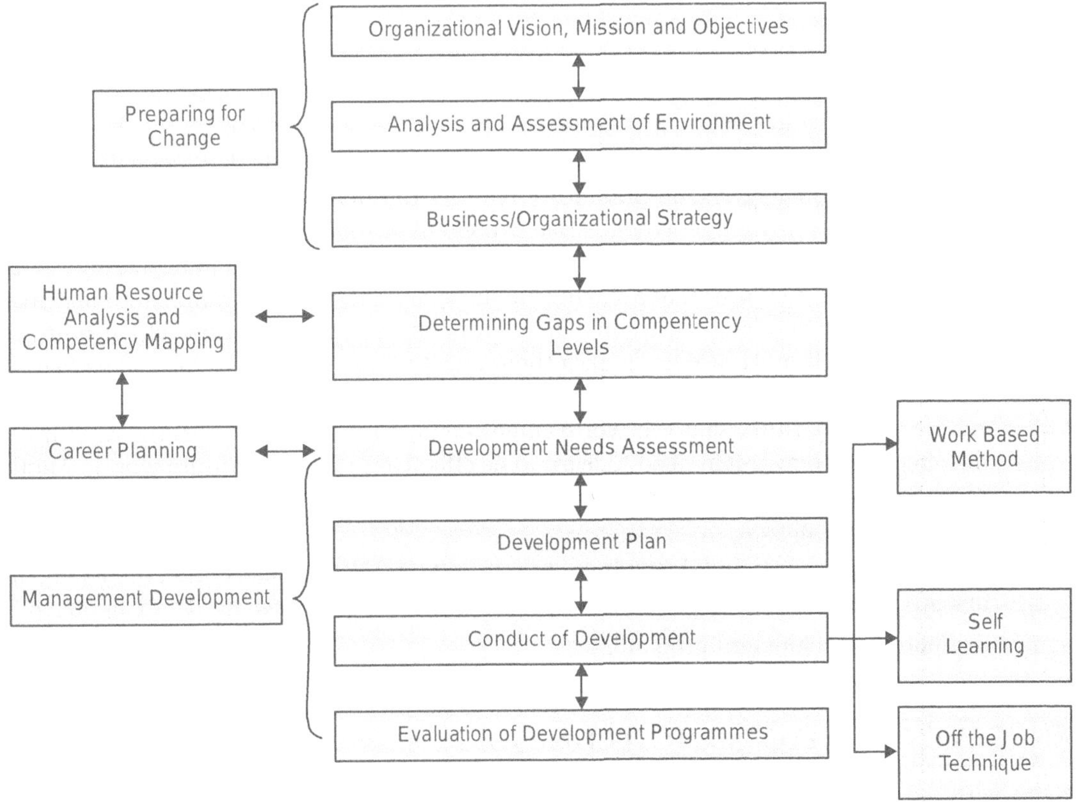

Fig. 9.1. *The Process of Management Development.*

(*a*) **Analysis of the Development Needs.** Often senior managers doubt that trainers and developers, being usually at a more junior level to them, really know what is needed at senior levels. Hence mechanistic training needs analysis may be less than useful.

Senior managers may dress up 'needs' in acceptable language or not admit to real needs. In theory, development needs should be adequately identified in a performance review, but this may not always happen.

(*b*) **Appraisal of the present managerial talent**. Since the 1970s, many organizations have operated appraisals, in which an individual's manager regularly records performance, potential and development needs in a top-down process. Many of these systems have evolved into a more rounded process known as performance and development review meetings, in which the dialogue is more open and two-way, enabling those involved to reflect on past performance as a basis for making development plans. The key difference between the traditional appraisal and the development review is that the former concentrates on performance, with development as something of an after-thought, while in the development review the main focus should be on the development of the individual. Thus a qualitative assessment of the existing managers to determine the type of talent available within the organization.

(*c*) **Inventory of executive manpower**. The inventory of human resource has been discussed earlier chapters. The organization must carryout an inventory check of all managers to determine the skills and abilities with each. Normally this information is readily available with the organization in the form of profile card/ replacement charts. However, for senior executives it would be prudent to get feed back from them as they may have acquired some more skills as self development efforts also most of the managers do not subscribe to the normal skills listed on the forms.

(*d*) **Planning individual development programmes**. The next step is to determine development needs of each manager. One possibility is to let the managers define their own needs and to create a programme which is free of content so that they can do this. Asking them what they are good at doing, what makes them effective senior managers, their skills, capabilities, knowledge? Then asking them where these came from. The most likely answer is that they learned them. This can open up a conversation which builds on the point that if most of what makes them effective has been learned, maybe learning is a key to future progress. If a person says that they are already effective, the challenge can be 'do they think that the world might change in the future'. And if it will, does this mean that they might need to learn to be effective in this new future world? Another route is to use outside consultants, as long as they in turn use the more successful methods listed above.

(*e*) Establishing training and development programmes. Having determined the needs then the programme is developed to conduct training. Already discussed in Chapter 8.

(*f*) Evaluating development programmes.

MANAGEMENT DEVELOPMENT TECHNIQUES

The techniques used for management development are wide and varied. Each of the techniques summarized below is a subject in itself and readers wishing to know more about them should refer to the relevant literature. The list follows the distinction made above between work-based methods and formal training and education, although clearly there are links between them (for example, an individual may need to take a training course before being given additional responsibilities, and most management education courses include projects in which the student draws on experience at work or seeks to solve problems there). Although people skills are a key element of management, formal training interventions are rarely good at producing improvements in inter-personal behaviour. Work-based methods appear to be most effective here and in some other areas (Figure 9.2).

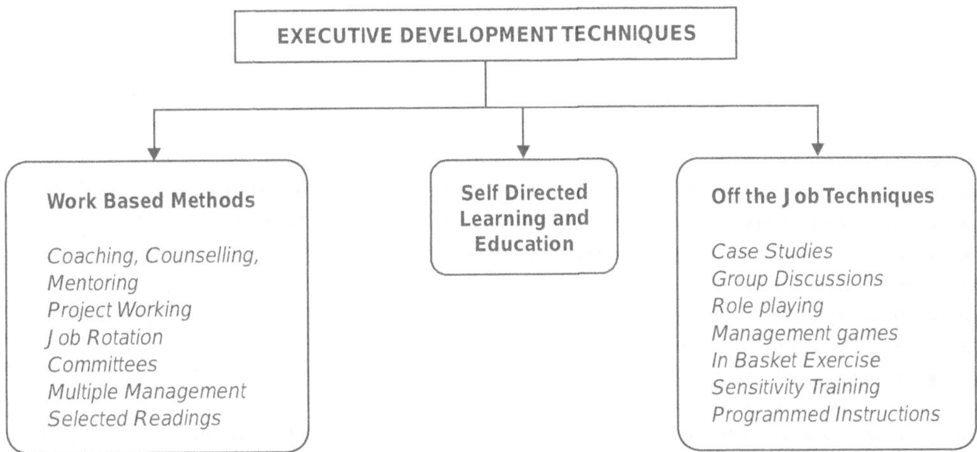

Fig. 9.2. *Executive Development Techniques.*

Work-based Methods

Senior managers are likely to use work–based approaches a great deal and there is specific advice on these (Cunningham, 2004). For open minded and non-defensive senior managers, the whole array of methods that could be used with more junior staff can be appropriate. And it may be important not to lose sight of the fact that obvious approaches, such as reading or going to conferences, can apply to this group.

Coaching, Counselling and Mentoring

Coaching is about improving skills and performance, usually for the current job, but also to support career transitions. In this method the coach guides and instructs the trainee. Coaches seek to bring an objective perspective to a structured dialogue to bring about sustainable solutions. Usually coaches are hired from outside the organization, but increasingly some organizations expect all line managers to operate as coaches, and it is often true that a young manager will learn more from senior colleagues than from any other source or formal learning intervention. Coaching's focus on skills distinguishes it from counselling, which is about helping people with personal concerns such as motivation and self-confidence.

Coaching offers several advantages in that it is learning by doing; every superior or supervisor can coach his subordinates even if there is no management development programme; periodic feedback and review can be carried out; helps new person to orient easily to new position requirements and involves close interaction. Like all process coaching also suffers from limitations in that it perpetuates current management style and practices, requires understanding and coaching ability in superiors and lastly the availability of time.

Recent CIPD learning and development surveys suggest that coaching, counselling and mentoring are growing, with over 80 per cent of organizations using them to develop at least some of their people. These one-to-one methods offer personally–tailored reflection and discussion in confidence between a manager and another individual about that manager's development.

Mentoring as name suggest is taking of responsibility of training a new entrant by a old experienced worker. Mentors usually come from inside the organization. Typically mentors will be experienced managers (but not individuals' line managers, because frankness is needed in exchanges) who regularly meet more junior colleagues to help them perform better and groom them for career advancement. But for more senior managers, outside mentors may sometimes be hired. This blurs the difference between coaching and mentoring, but the differences are perhaps that mentors have relatively long–term relationships with their junior colleagues and their focus is less on events than it is in coaching.

Understudy. Understudy is a person selected and being trained as the heir apparent to assume at a future time the full duties and responsibilities of the position presently held by his superior. In this way, a fully trained person becomes available to replace a manager during his long absence or illness or on his retirement, transfer, promotion etc. Understudy technique provides certain advantages in that the trainee receives constant guidance; gets an opportunity to see the full job; trainee gets the feel of the job as he shares the job; ensures continuity.

Position Rotation

It involves movement or transfer of executives from one position to another or one job to another on some planned basis. The objective of rotation is to build and broaden knowledge, skills and abilities of the executives. Job / position rotation helps to reduce monotony; facilitates departmental coordination and cooperation; provides opportunities to understand the functioning of particular department.

Project Working

Project working involves putting together a group of persons to prepare and develop the project. In modern businesses, managers increasingly work in cross–functional teams, exposing them to different functions and enabling them to learn about different aspects of the organization and ways of doing things. By working on the projects the individuals learn work procedures and techniques. Putting people on such teams is one way of broadening their experience and effectiveness.

Committee Assignments

Executives are made members of permanent committees. Individuals participating gain knowledge of the decision making, alternative methods of problem solving, functioning of other departments, etc.

Action Learning

Most people learn best by doing, *i.e.*, performing on the job or we can say by 'practice makes man perfect'. Action learning utilizes this tendency of learning by structuring the process. Action learning sets help to achieve this by making their members focus on solving live issues in their normal working environments by trying out different approaches, with discussion and support from colleagues to help them reflect on their impact. This technique was developed by Charles P. McCormick of the McCormick Corporation of Baltimore, USA. The junior executives learn decision-making skills and the Board of Directors or top management levels. In this process the junior managers constitute a board or committee is constituted to analyze a problem and make recommendations to Board of Directors. This process helps the junior executives to learn decision-making and analysis of problems. In this way the participants get practical experience and the management is able to identify executive talent. The process is relatively in-expensive.

Performance and Development Reviews

Since the 1970s, many organizations have operated appraisals, in which an individual's manager regularly—usually annually—records performance, potential and development needs in a top–down process. Many of these systems have evolved into a more rounded process known as performance and development review meetings, in which the dialogue is more open and two–way (indeed, the person being reviewed should do most of the talking), enabling those involved to reflect on past performance as a basis for making development plans. The key difference between the traditional appraisal and the development review is that the former concentrates on performance, with development as something of an after–thought, while in the development review the main focus should be on the development of the individual.

Education and Training

Formal Training Courses

In large organizations especially, formal training is given in the shape of courses, particularly at key transition points such as first management jobs and as preludes to promotion. Their content will vary according to the organization and the role the individual is to fill, but in the private sector finance and business strategy is a key component. Change management appears to be increasingly popular.

In the past, such training tended to be delivered as long, single residential courses, but increasingly they are delivered in modules, with work–based projects and may be coaching and mentoring in between. This is not only because it is easier to spare people from work for short periods but because there is growing recognition that people learn best in 'chunks', supporting the theoretical knowledge learned in courses with practical experience. Such training might be delivered by in–house training specialists, by business schools, by large training consultancies, by individual freelance trainers, or by any combination of these.

Self Directed Learning

Self–Directed Learning is Ideal for the Workplace. Self–directed learning programs hold numerous advantages over traditional forms of classroom instruction for employees in the workplace, whether they are leaders, managers, or individual contributors. Bouchard (Self–directed Learning in Organizational Settings (working paper), Concordia University, Montreal, Canada) explains, "Over the years, it has become increasingly clear that traditional approaches to program design and delivery in the workplace and in associative organizations present some important weaknesses. Problem areas include : coping with the short life span of useful knowledge; passing down acquired competencies to succeeding cohorts; accommodating the demands of productivity while providing for a continuity of learning; [and!] enabling learners to pursue activities that correspond to their learning styles and needs"

After many years of reflection about learning, eminent psychologist, Carl Rogers (1961, p.276), founder of self-directed therapy, asserted that "anything that can be taught to another is relatively inconsequential, and has little or no significant influence on behavior" He adds, "The only learning which significantly influences behavior is self-discovered, self-appropriated learning" (p.276).

Self-directed learning programs are more effective in development because learning accommodates employees' learning styles and objectives; saves substantial training costs because learners learn to help themselves and each other with practical and timely materials; and achieve increased employee effectiveness in their jobs as they learn to learn from their own work experiences and actually apply their learning in their places of work.

The supervisor's attitude and knowledge about learning has a tremendous impact on the development of employees. Thomas D. Fisher, in Self–Directedness in the Workplace : A Re–Examination cites numerous suggestions in order to better enable self–directed learning in the workplace. Some of those suggestions are listed below, and are wonderful ways for supervisors and learners to turn the workplace into a classroom. Help the learner identify the starting point for a learning project and discern relevant [ways!] of examination and reporting.

- Encourage adult learners to view knowledge and truth as contextual ... and that they can act on their world individually or collectively to transform it
- Create a partnership with the learner by negotiating a learning contract for goals, strategies and evaluation criteria
- Be a manager of the learning experience rather than an information provider
- Teach inquiry skills, decision-making, personal development, and self–evaluation of work
- Help learners develop positive attitudes and feelings of independence relative to learning
- Recognize learners' personality types and learning styles
- Use techniques such as field experience and problem solving that take advantage of adults' rich experience base
- Encourage critical thinking skills by incorporating ... such activities as seminars
- Create an atmosphere of openness and trust to promote better performance

Fisher adds that "Self–directed learning is more than a form of education; it is a component in human development" (p. 7).

E–learning and Blended Learning

Increasingly, organizations are seeking to supplement traditional courses by e–learning, which is the use of computers to deliver training, often delivered through corporate intranets. It provides large populations with the same material, and access is flexible so that people can learn in their own time. Against this, e–learning does not appeal to everyone, and it works better for 'hard' knowledge than softer skills like communication or leadership. But mixed with other forms of learning (as 'blended learning'), it can be a valuable tool.

Off the Job Training

The Need for External Stimulus

Senior managers often feel the need to get inspiration from outside their own organisation. This may be through external consultants/developers being invited inside the organisation to support development activity. From evaluations of successful programmes, senior managers do typically comment on the value of going outside their own organisation. And they often say how relieved they are to find managers in other organisations facing the same problems. This can be a considerable boost to self confidence. They also say that they glean new ideas and new perspectives from the interaction with those outside their own organisation.

They also feel, with the internal politics that they face, that they will find it easier to talk to people at the same level but from different organisations. Hence many senior managers prefer to go outside the organisation altogether for formal programmes.

Secondment

Secondment involves sending an employee to work outside the organization, taking an assign or occupying a position in another organization through Secondment for a year or two. Sometimes, in the case of senior people, Secondment also involves taking up non–executive directorships in another organization. Recently Government of India decided to second its employee to work in private sector to gain experience and get trained.

The term secondment is used broadly to cover a temporary movement or 'loan' of an employee to another part of an organization or to a completely different organization. Employees can be seconded into organizations ranging from major commercial concerns through public services and schools to small local groups and charities. Organizations benefit from both inward and outward secondment. Typically, paid secondments require formal arrangements, are full time and lasts for certain duration.

Secondment is increasingly being recognised as valuable for development. As organisations adopt ever flatter management structures, opportunities for promotion through a succession of line management positions are limited. Hence, Secondment offers employees career development opportunities and are increasingly being used as part of talent management programmes. They also provide organisations with the chance to develop their skills base.

Secondment is often regarded as a marginal activity that is supported and undertaken in large organisations, however, the increasing flexibility of working patterns means that it may become increasingly important in the future. According to the Chartered Institute of Personnel and Development's Managing employee careers survey, secondment is one of the top ten most commonly used career management practices and 67% of respondents considered them to be 'effective' or 'very effective'. Similarly in the Chartered Institute of Personnel and Development leadership forecast, 63% of respondents identified external assignments as very effective (the highest response rate) for developing leaders. (Chartered Institute of Personnel and Development. 2003a).

Secondment can take place either within an organization; or externally to another organisation (*i.e.*, public sector to private or vice versa, to a voluntary organisation). Secondment within an organization is a valuable way of providing management development opportunities, particularly within flat organisational structures with limited opportunities for promotion. It is also useful for resourcing short–term assignments or projects. The employee benefits by gaining wider experience and acquiring new skills without the disruption of relocation and with the benefit of continuity of employment. The main disadvantage for all parties is that there is not the completely fresh outlook that an external secondment may bring.

External Secondment can benefit all parties by exposing firstly the host organisation and the employee, then subsequently the seconding employer, to different work practices. However it is essential that all three are clear about their responsibilities in this situation. Specific questions that need to be answered prior to a secondment include :

- Duration of Secondment viz. for a fixed term or for an indefinite period that is subject to notice ?
- Arrangements of salary, the seconding employer will generally be responsible for basic salary, however, the arrangements for the same including overtime, bonuses, expenses, training etc should be clearly defined ?
- How will supervisory and disciplinary matters be dealt with ?
- If it is long–term, how will performance appraisal, feedback management and development is to be managed ?
- Who will fill the role in the home organisation ? How will the secondee retain contact ?

- Management of secondment including performance of duty during absence and appointment on return ?

It is essential that all parties are clear about their obligations, expectations, accountabilities and performance objectives before secondment is undertaken.

Secondment benefits all the secondee, secondee's employer and the host organization. Benefits to secondee include providing an opportunity of wider career and personal development than at work; acquiring valuable experience by testing and applying specific skills in a different organizational environment and gain new skills and experiences in challenging areas.

The secondee's employer gains enhanced employee skills, team working and cross functional communications; improves workforce morale and motivation; develops wider networks and contacts and builds a reputation as a good employer and contributor to the community.

The host organization gains assistance with projects and gets an external perspective.

Development Centers

The purpose of development centers (sometimes known as assessment centers) is to focus on opportunities for personal development, and to gauge potential and help make selections for promotion. Although they take place off the job, they include work–related activities and group work, as well as counselling and psychometric assessments, so they can be included under the heading of work-based methods. They are expensive to run, so are mainly for large organizations.

360 Feedback

Appraisals and even performance and development reviews can be perceived as subjective and over-dependent on the views of the person doing the reviewing. The process of 360 feedbacks seeks views from a range of relevant viewpoints – peers, superiors and subordinates, and sometimes even outsiders like customers and suppliers – based on a framework of competencies. The aim is that the process will provide a more accurate assessment than a review from one individual and point to areas where development (or even simply behavioural change) is needed.

Sensitivity Training or T-Group Training

Sensitivity Training or T-Group Training is also known as laboratory training as it is conducted under controlled conditions. It means the *development awareness and sensitivity to behavioural patterns of oneself and others.* 'T' Groups are helpful in unlearning and learning certain things. They help the participants to understand how groups actually work and give them a chance to know how others view them in a group. This type of training also aims at increasing the tolerance power of the individual and his ability to understand others.

Outdoor Development

Outdoor development is sometimes used for team building purposes, while in-house providers or external deliverers can provide 'one–off' training to fill particular gaps which might be identified because of organizational needs or through the review and one-to-one processes mentioned above. An important aspect of getting people together away from the workplace is that they can exchange ideas outside the classroom, while meeting people from elsewhere in the organization helps in corporate networking.

Learning Groups

Getting groups of senior managers to meet together to work on their learning needs is almost like group mentoring. Such groups need to consist of five or six managers that create their own learning agenda and a skilled learning group adviser to make it work. One variant of this model is the action learning set, where individuals might take on projects, either singly or as a team so long as the projects are realistic and the managers focus on the 'learning' and not the 'action'.

COACHING

Although there is a lack of agreement among coaching professionals about precise definitions, these are some generally agreed characteristics of coaching in organisations :

- It is essentially a non-directive form of development.
- It focuses on improving performance and developing individuals' skills.
- Personal issues may be discussed but the emphasis is on performance at work.
- Coaching activities have both organisational and individual goals.
- It assumes that the individual is psychologically well and does not require a clinical intervention.
- It provides people with feedback on both their strengths and their weaknesses.
- It is a skilled activity which should be delivered by trained people.

Developing a Coaching Culture

Clutterbuck and Megginson (2005) describe a coaching culture as one where 'coaching is the predominant style of managing and working together and where commitment to improving the organisation is embedded in a parallel commitment to improving the people'.

Of those respondents to the Chartered Institute of Personnel and Development's Learning and Development survey 2007 who use coaching, the majority (76%) said that they believe that coaching activities are closely linked to business goals to a greater or lesser extent. Three-quarters (75%) identify coaching as integrated into wider human resource learning and development. As coaching becomes more of a long term intervention, it is important that coaches are trained and their skills are updated.

The primary relationship in any coaching activity is between the coach and the individual, but this is not the only important relationship. Other key stakeholders include the person representing the organisation's interests–most frequently an human resource practitioner and the individual's manager. Both of these parties are interested in improving the individual's performance and therefore their contribution to the organisation. The Figure 9.3 below explains how this works in an organisational context. Jarvis (2004) developed the concept of four corned contract which he depicted by the central triangle of relationships.

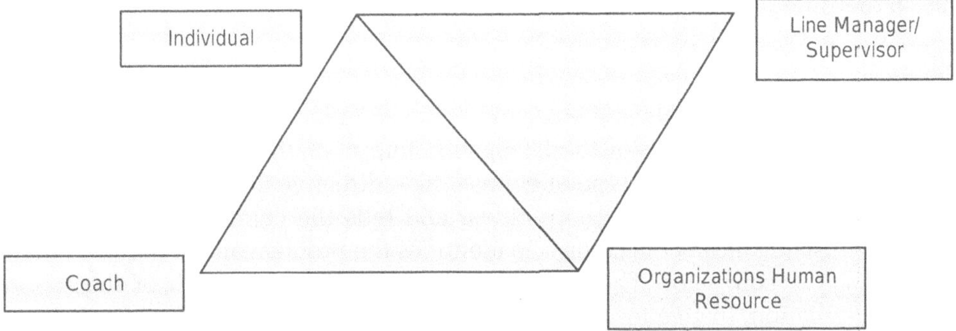

Fig. 9.3. *The Four-cornered Contract Depicting Stake Holders.*

When is coaching the best development intervention ?

Coaching is just one of a range of training and development interventions that organizations can use to meet identified learning and development needs. Its merits should be considered alongside other types of development interventions, such as training courses, mentoring or on–the–job training. Employee preferences should also be borne in mind. It is important that coaching is only used when it is genuinely seen as the best way of helping an individual learn and develop. A Jarvis (2004) developed a useful decision tree tool to determine whether coaching is best intervention method for development. Figure 9.4 has been adapted from Jarvis model.

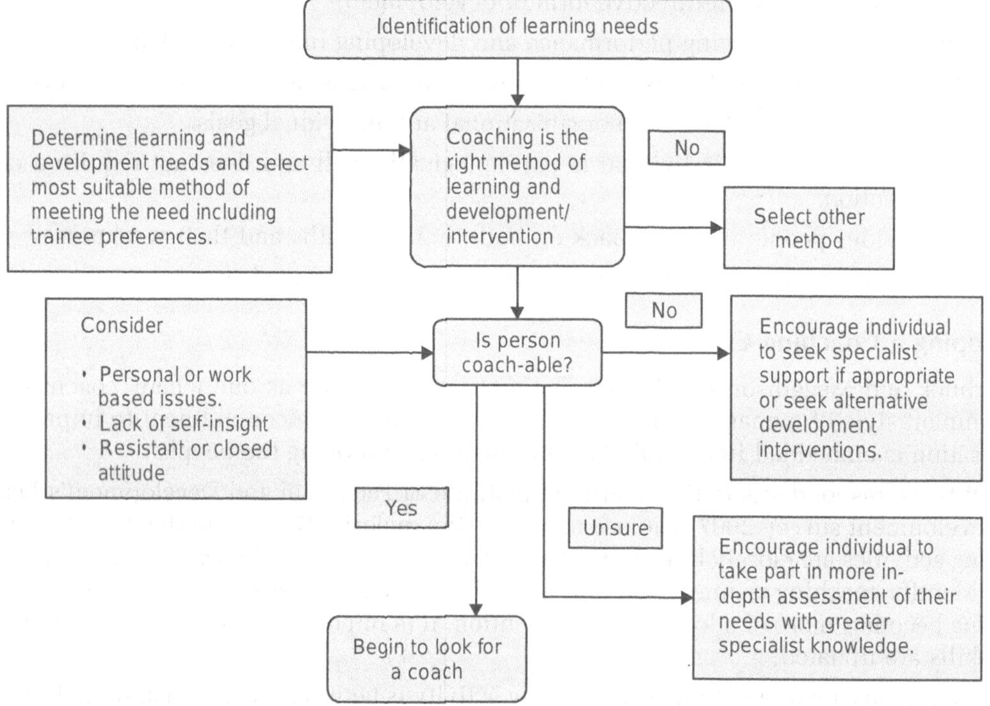

Source : Adapted from Chartered Institute of Personnel and Development's version 2007

Fig. 9.4. *Decision Tree : Is Coaching an Appropriate Intervention.*

Coaching is ideal for helping compotent trechnical experts develop better interpersonal or managerial skills; developing an individual's potential and providing career support; developing a more strategic perspective after a promotion to a more senior role; and handling conflict situations so that these can be resolved effectively.

Counseling

Under this method the immediate superior guide's development needs at different career stages of a subordinate. Counseling has a powerful, long-term impact on the learners and the effectiveness of the organization. There are two type of counseling – directive and nondirective. In directive counseling, the counselor identifies the problem and tells the counselee what to do about it. Nondirective counseling means the counselee identifies the problem and determines the solution with the help of the counselor. The counselor has to determine which of the two or some appropriate combination, to give for each situation.

MENTORING

Mentoring is a long standing form of training, learning and development and an increasingly popular tool for supporting personal development. Mentoring is primarily about developing capability and potential in the role rather than performance and skills. It is a specific learning and development intervention which can be used widely but in a specific context such as development, induction, or sponsorship. It should be delivered and evaluated through appropriately qualified mentors and overseen by the human resource department. It often works together with coaching but should be seen as a distinct activity.

MENTORS MAKE AN ORGANIZATION BETTER

For companies and workers seeking to change direction in their industry, climb to the next level, or adjust too mergers and structural change, management experts say finding a mentor could be their best transitional tool. Where can an ambitious person find a mentor ? Try retirees looking to give back or stay engaged, and business leaders seeking to improve their managerial skills.

Insight you can Get from Reports

Companies looking to promote diverse workforce often encourage their managers to be mentors –the teaching can go both ways. As the mentee is often younger, he or she can help enlighten the mentors about new trends in the industry or give them insight into another generation.

"If you're still active and the company wants to market the younger people, what better opportunity than to sit with younger person ?" asks Scott Allen, a consultant on social networking and building business relationships online, and an active mentor and mentee. "You will get insight sitting there with one-on-one face time that no market research report could ever give you." And if the mentor is lucky he may learn thing or two about technology.

Set Commitment Goals

Successful mentorship can be in any number of forms; on line or in person, in both formal and informal settings, on a temporary or long term basis, and between individuals and in group. What are essential, experts say; are direction, dedication and openness. To be sure that the time spent is fruitful; experts recommend setting specific goals and revisiting them along the way, as well as looking for mentor who has traveled the career path you seek and has skills you need, instead of seeking out a mentor whom you like for personal reasons.

An Aid to Talent Attraction and Retention

Speth an attorney at Jaburg Walk Phoenix says, "Your mentors shouldn't tell you what your goals are, they should just ask you what your goals are." The benefits of mentoring are far reaching. It helps in recruitment and more importantly in retaining talent. More and more people are attracted to organizations that help them grow and learn."

Don't Make Promises you Can't Keep

Mentors and mentees must be dedicated to skill–building for relationships to sustain. Mentees should avoid seeking relationships for political or nebulous reasons. Mentors should avoid making promises they can't keep. One of the worst things that can happen is committing to a mentee and then not being able to be there when they need you.

Source : Adapted from 'Mentors make an organization better by Emily Keller, *The Economic Times*, New Delhi, 25 March 2008, p.5.

Traditionally, mentoring is the long term passing on of support, guidance and advice. In the workplace it has tended to describe a relationship in which a more experienced colleague uses their greater knowledge and understanding of the work or workplace to support the development of a more junior or inexperienced member of staff. Mentoring is a process of communication and interaction between a mentor, usually a senior colleague such as the business owner or a manager and a protégé/ mentee who is usually a junior member of staff or a new joinee. The aim is to help the mentee to change something—improve performance, develop leadership skills, realize vision or provide organizational wisdom.

Mentoring involves listening with empathy, sharing mutual experience, developing professional friendship and supporting development insight through introspection and reflection in an encouraging manner. Mentors assume such role both informally and formally. Eric Parsole of The Oxford School of Coaching and Mentoring states, "Mentoring is to support and encourage people to manage their own learning in order that they may maximize their potential, developing their skills, improve their performance and become the person they want to be."

Mentoring comes from the Greek myth where Odysseus entrusts the education of his son to his friend Mentor. Mentor served as a teacher, advisor, friend, surrogate father and an overseer of Odysseus' son, Telemachus. In Indian mythologies too we have Lord Krishna play a role of mentor to Arjun. In Japanese businesses, a senior executive called *'sempai'* is often paired with a junior executive called *'kohai'* or *'kosai'*. The *'sempai–kohai'* relationship is held together by a bond of trust and loyalty, almost all aspects of the *kohai's* life are carefully scrutinized by the senior 'sempai'.

It's also a form of apprenticeship, whereby an inexperienced learner learns the tricks of the trade from an experienced colleague, backed–up as in modern apprenticeship by offsite training. In the technology driven 21st century, the need for facilitated mentoring is far greater than ever before. Organizations are made of people who require even greater skills for mastering the increasingly complex issues and tasks. A good mentor is one who acts as a source of information, offers insight into the organizations culture and philosophy, is a confidante in times of personal crisis and gives feed back of observed behaviour and performance. Hence, it is important for the mentor to be non judgmental and constructive at all times. A good mentor needs to have good interpersonal skills, have complete knowledge and understanding of business and organization, and is approachable.

Mentoring is used specifically and separately as a form of long term tailored development for the individual which brings benefits to the organization. The characteristics of mentoring are :

- It is essentially a supportive form of development.
- It focuses on helping an individual manage their career and improve skills.
- Personal issues can be discussed more productively unlike in coaching where the emphasis is on performance at work.

Mentoring activities have both organizational and individual goals. The following table, adapted from Alred et al. (1998), highlights the differences between mentoring and coaching. It is separate and distinct from coaching, but coaching and mentoring can often overlap.

Mentoring	*Coaching*
Ongoing relationship that can last for a long time.	Relationship generally has a short duration.
Can be more informal and meetings can take place as and when the mentored individual needs some guidance and or support.	Generally more structured in nature and meetings scheduled on a regular basis.
More long term and takes a broader view of the person.	Short–term (sometimes time bound) and focused on specific development areas/issues.
Mentor usually passes on experience and is normally more senior in organisation.	Not generally performed on basis that coach needs direct experience of clients formal occupational role.
The focus is on career and personal development.	Focus generally on development/issues at work.
Agenda is set by the mentored person with the mentor providing support and guidance to prepare them for future roles.	Agenda focused on achieving specific, immediate goals.
Revolves more around developing the mentee professionally.	Revolves more around specific development areas/ issues.

Fig. 9.5. *Comparison between Mentoring and Coaching.*

Ideal candidate as mentee could be a new employee, someone going through transition, one who is willing to be mentored and takes responsibility for personal development and is receptive to feedback and coaching. For the mentee one of the most valuable assets a career could have is a good mentor.

Mentees wants mentors who are organized, patient, understanding, knowledgeable and realistic. For the mentor it is a fulfilling and a learning experience as well as an opportunity to hone leadership skills.

Developing a Mentoring Approach

Clutterbuck (2004) in 'Everyone needs a mentor' describes how mentoring works and organization benefits from it. Benefits that accrue to the organization can be stated as :

- Mentoring has significant impact upon recruitment and retention.
- Effective succession planning.
- Makes organisations adapt to change.
- Increased productivity through better engagement and job satisfaction.

Benefits to the mentored person are :

- Development outcomes which may include, knowledge, technical and behavioural improvements.
- Better management of career goals and developing wider network of influence.
- Increased confidence and self awareness which helps build performance and contribution.

Mentoring helps in fostering strong careers, transfer wisdom to next generations and fortify industry with the best talent. Mentoring can be an effective tool for organizations to develop and retain talent. As someone has aptly said, "A lot of people have gone further than they thought they could because someone else thought they could."

INTERNATIONAL MANAGEMENT DEVELOPMENT

Dennis Cottrell, Institute of Personnel Development's, Vice President said, "with markets becoming increasingly internationalized and more and more companies globalizing their activities across many cultures.... Companies must focus their attention on international management development, and the personal professional must be aware of this (Dickman, 1997).' Globalization has resulted in increased realization on the parts of organizations to create a truly diverse employee and to ensure that their leaders reflect the diversity of the organizations global scope.

International management development remains a priority, the trends includes :

(*a*) The pivotal role of the Chief executive and senior board members in nurturing talent.

(*b*) Acknowledgement that the leadership development and diversity are inseparable intertwined. There are three styles of leadership which has universal acceptance charismatic, team–oriented and participative. House et al (2002) states that 'charismatic' leadership appears to be universally accepted the interpretations of charisma is different in different societal settings. Similarly 'team oriented' will interpreted differently in individualistic cultures a opposed to family or group oriented cultures.

NESTLE

Nestle is one the companies with international footprint and takes keen interest in leadership development. In an interview for a magazine, Peter Braheck–Lemathe, Nestle CEO, said continuing success of the company hinged on the talent the company nurtures. He acknowledged the importance of leveraging cultural diversity while instilling a sense of corporate identity and principles : "We want to make sure that the employees at all our regional companies maintain their original cultures, but follow the same Nestlé principles .... We don't want to transform a Chinese into a Chilean or an American into Australian. All we're asking for is that he or she embraces the common values that we have.

(*c*) Adopting a dual–dialogue approach to international career planning. It has been observed that there is reluctance on parts of high potential employees to take up international assignments due to dual career, family and other issues. It has also been observed that many high performing employees move to other organizations, either during the assignment or on return (Suutari and Brewster, 203). For global organizations it needs to align its career development. Therefore, it is preferable for organizations to be careful or in selecting and it is preferable to have a dual–dialogue while carrying selection and organizing international management development.

(*d*) Adopting decentralized approach to succession planning, with only the top two or three tiers of jobs being managed centrally.

(*e*) Linking international management development interventions to the strategic needs of the organizations.

(*f*) Employing a variety of international management development techniques aimed at self directed, work based and learning rather than training for example use mentors, coaches, learning sets and project based learning.

(*g*) Managing international mobility for international management development purposes. In multinational organizations, international assignments play an important role in building both organizations human capital and individual career capital.

(*h*) Determining methods of evaluating the effectiveness of international management development techniques.

Having determined the needs it is important to determine the process of international management development which should include agreeing an international management development strategy, defining global leadership competencies, ensuring diversity in top management positions, career management, identifying potentials, designing and evaluating development interventions and managing international mobility of international management development.

In globalized companies executive development is seen as an intrinsic part of developing an organization's strategy as well as potential source of competitive advantage. It results in both knowledge and capability gain for employees and organizations. The companies are expect partnership in delivery, modular and multi–site programmes, with inter–modular projects and designated facilitators to integrate learning in the organization. The companies want learning as well as elements of distance learning ranging from internet chat rooms to more sophisticated virtual learning projects.

Cross–cultural frameworks, such as Hofstede's (1980) and Trompennars' (1993), provide evidence of distinct national differences in working values and behaviours, hence, it is important that international management development includes the training in understanding national sensitivities also the leadership is cultural sensitive. While there are clear cultural differences in perceptions but organizations must develop leaders who can manage the increasing complexity of running global organizations. The core competencies required are :

(*a*) Increased intercultural skills.

(*b*) Greater flexibility and adaptability.

(*c*) Broader understanding of global business.

(*d*) Expanded social networks.

The Role of HRD Professionals

One problem is that often in–house HRD professionals are not seen as credible in assisting the development of senior managers. It is useful to distinguish between the following roles for HRD staff :

- The brokerage role—advising on development opportunities, and fixing it so that senior managers can avail themselves of such opportunities.
- The direct delivery role.

HRD professionals may have a key role in relation to brokerage. However, it may be that internal HRD staff is not able to play a role in delivery, whether through course provision or coaching or other direct development methods.

THE STRATEGIC ROLE OF EXECUTIVE DEVELOPMENT

Organizations are increasingly sending their top management personnel to business schools for customized programs tailored specifically to meet individual and organizational needs. Such course place less emphasis on conventional learning such as accounting, finance etc but focuses on helping organizations meet high–level strategic challenges. While writing the objectives for the executive development programme that author stated to his team that objective of the programme is to help organizations through some of their most pressing strategic issues; to work closely with the senior or top managers and help them devise plans to execute their strategy. If required help the organizations with frameworks to refine their strategies.

Executives Development's Role in Strategic Planning and Execution

The strategic planning process–formulating the organization's high level goals and execution plans—is an especially compelling area of focus for executive development and education. Why ? Strategy formulation is the process of choosing the best path for the organization—based on the customer's needs, competitive realities and internal capabilities. Organizations that can integrate all three effectively are likely have more robust and lasting strategy.

What is Typical ?

Many Chief Learning Officers argue that executive development can have a direct role in contributing to both the execution and creation strategy for organizations. However, in practice it has been observed that organizations when crafting strategies for organization do not consider or even link management development to the business strategy.

Why the Disconnect ?

The organizations need individuals who understand the development processes and have expertise in management evaluation and development, balanced with long term–term strategic planning and insight into the operational realities of the organization. Most often, these developmental professionals are not "at the table" for the executive management meetings (since they are likely the Vice President of Human Resource), nor are they involved with corporate planning.

Three Types of Integration

Integration might categorize organizations into three types : those that treat executive development as a discreet process, others that partially integrate it with strategic planning and a third set that has fully integrated it as a driver of strategic planning. (Figure 9.6)

For those organizations that already understand the role the executive development plays in driving change and improving corporate performance, as well as those who are new to this concept, there are some key principles the Chief Learning Officer can adopt.

The first principle is that the Chief Learning Officer must acquaint with the current strategy formulation process. Transformations are sought by the board, Chief-level executives and these people don not interface with training and human resource. David Sachs, Harvard's Business School's, Executive Director of Executive Education agreed, "We often are hired by and work hand–in–hand with Chief Executive Officers." Executive management acknowledges the importance of executive development, but turns neither to the Chief Learning Officer nor to the Vice President of Human Resource to manage the interface with the outside specialists.

	Discrete process	*Partial Integration*	*Integrated and Divine Strategy*
Goal of Executive Development process	Build general skills for key managers so they can handle 'typical' management situation.	Help management execute strategy once it is completed.	Help management craft and implement corporate strategy.
Number of Organization	50% or more.	35–45%.	5–10%.
Common Characteristics	• Developmental plans do not take current business imperatives into account. • Training executive likely not at table of senior management.	• Development plans are formed as a result of current business imperatives. • Training executive likely to be present at table of senior management.	• Developmental plans result from current business imperatives into account, provide input into strategic direction. • Training executive proactive in strategic planning
View toward executive developmental activities.	Often cynician of developmental 'spending'.	Worthwhile activity.	Critical investment
Source : 'Transforming Corporate Leadership : Best Practices of Executive Education,' ExecSite, 2004			

Fig. 9.6. *Level of Integration.*

The second principle is the senior level management involvement should be insisted. Chief Learning Officers need to ensure that top management is not only aware of the development program, but he is also involved in the process.

How Should the Strategic Role be Integrated ?

What should be done ? To ensure good implementation of the process the Chief Learning Officer should insist on;

(*a*) Insist on his inclusion in all strategy development meetings.

(*b*) Acquaint with current strategy and its formulation process, time frame etc.

(*c*) Insist on involvement of Top/Senior Management in all training and development activities.

(*d*) Integrate the business strategy and executive development programme.

(*e*) Ensure training does not impact daily work.

(*f*) Assess the development programme.

ORGANIZATIONAL DEVELOPMENT

Significant organizational change occurs when an organization changes its overall strategy for success, adds or removes a major section or practice, and/or wants to change the very nature by which it operates. It also occurs when an organization evolves through various life cycles, just like people must successfully evolve through life cycles. For organizations to develop, they often must undergo significant change at various points in their development. That's why the topic of organizational change and development has become widespread in management development, communications about business, organizations and leadership.

Davis (1981, p. 221) states :

'Organizational development is a long-term strategy which focuses on the whole culture of the organization in order to bring about planned change. It seeks to change beliefs, attitudes, values and structure – in fact, the entire culture of the organization – so that the organization may better adapt to technology and live with the pace of change.'

From above it can be deduced that the organization development is the process of development and bringing about change in the entire aspects of the organization. **Beckhard (1969, p. 9)** in his work states :

"Organizational development is an effort planned organization wide, and managed from the top to increase organizations effectiveness and health through planned interventions in the organization's processes, using behavioural science knowledge."

Leaders and managers continually make efforts to accomplish successful and significant change—it's inherent in their jobs. Some are very good at this effort, while others continually struggle and fail. That's often the difference between people who thrive in their roles and those that get shuttled around from job to job, ultimately settling into a role where they're frustrated and ineffective. There are many schools with educational programs about organizations, business, leadership and management. Unfortunately, there still are not enough schools with programs about how to analyze organizations, identify critically important priorities to address (such as systemic problems or exciting visions for change) and then undertake successful and significant change to address those priorities.

Characteristics of Organizational Development

- Organizational development is an educational strategy for bringing about planned change in the organization.
- Organizational development aims at improving process, and in turn organizational effectiveness.
- Change agents are employed to bring about organizational changes by various intervention techniques.
- There is an intimate working relationship between the change agent and the organizational personnel.
- It is to be managed by the top management personnel from the inception till fructification and its implementation.

Significance of Organizational Development

Organizational Development is dynamic disciplines directed towards using behavioural science knowledge to assist organizations adjust more rapidly to change. The benefits that accrue of organizational development include using of systems approach; provides opportunity to all personnel of the organization to develop to his full potential; seeks to make organization more effective and supports an environment for innovation and creativity.

Like all process organizational development also came under criticism from researches and academicians. One of the major limitations that have been repeatedly highlighted is the heavy dependence on behavioural science. Second major limitation normally expressed is leadership.

Organizational development needs a visionary leadership and should have the drive to change things.

Change Agent

Implementation of any planned change requires change agents. A change agent is a person who implements the needed change to increase organizational effectiveness. The change agent needs to have the vision and the determination to bring about change. Managers of the organizations are the major change agents as they are constantly busy bringing about changes to improve efficiency and reduce costs. Change agents usually act as a consultant, counselor and a facilitator.

Planned, Systemic Change Process

A typical planned, systemic (and systematic) organizational development process often follows an overall action research approach. There are many variations of the action research approach, including by combining its various phases and/or splitting some into more phases. This section provides resources that are organized into one variation of the action research approach. Note that the more collaborative you are in working with members of the organization during the following process, the more likely the success of your overall change effort.

Phase 1 : Clarifying Expectations and Roles for Change Process

This phase is sometimes called the "Contracting" and/or "Entry" phase. This phase is usually where the relationship between the initial change agent and other members or employees starts, whether you are an external or internal consultant. Experts assert that this phase is one of the most—if not the most—important phases in the organizational change process. Activities during this stage form the foundation for successful organizational change. The quality of how this phase is carried out usually is a strong indicator of how the project will go.

Phase 2 : Joint Discovery to Identify Priorities for Change

The more collaborative the change agent is in working with members of the client's organization, the more likely that the change effort will be successful. Your client might not have the resources to fully participate in all aspects of this discovery activity — the more participation they can muster, the better off your project will be.

Whether you are an external or internal change agent, the process will take effect better if all in the organization understand more about the overall priority of the change effort and how all can effectively address it. It might be a major problem in the organization or an exciting vision to achieve. Together, all will collect information, analyze it to identify findings and conclusions, and then make recommendations from that information. Sometimes the data-collection effort is very quick, for example, facilitating a large planning meeting. Other times, the effort is more extensive, for example, evaluating an entire organization and developing a complete plan for change. The nature of discovery also depends on the philosophy of the change agent and client. For example, subscribers to the philosophy of Appreciative Inquiry (referenced above) might conduct discovery, not by digging into the number and causes of problems in the organization, but by conducting interviews to discover the visions and wishes of people in the organization.

Sometimes, people minimize the importance of – or altogether skip – this critical discovery phase, and start change management by articulating an ambitious and comprehensive vision for change. Many would argue that it is unethical to initiate a project for organizational change without fully examining the current situation in the organization. Focusing most of the change efforts on achieving a robust vision, without at least some careful discovery, often can be harmful to organization because the process can end up dealing with symptoms of current issues, rather than the root causes. Also, the process could end up pushing an exciting vision that, while initially inspiring and motivating many, could be completely unrealistic to achieve — especially if the organization already has many current, major issues to address. Therefore, when working to guide change in an organization that already is facing several significant issues, it is better to start from where the organization is at—that usually means conducting an effective discovery to identify priorities for change.

(*a*) Preparation—Establishing a Project Team. One of the most powerful means to cultivate collaboration of personnel in an organization is working with a project team. Besides, no change agent sees all aspects of the situation in the organization — team members help to see more of those various aspects.

(*b*) Joint Planning and Conducting Data Collection.

(*c*) Joint Analysis of Research Results.

(*d*) Joint Generation of Findings and Conclusions.

Phase 3 : Joint Planning of Organizational Development Activities to Address Priorities

In the previous phase about discovery, the change agent and the employees of the organization jointly discovered various priorities that needed attention, generated recommendations to address those priorities, and shared information with each other, through feedback or meetings. Part of meeting includes discussions – and decisions – about the overall mutual recommendations that organizations should follow to in order address the priorities that were identified. This phase is focused on further clarifying those recommendations, along with developing them into various action plans. The plans are sometimes integrated into an overall change management plan. Thus, the early activities in this phase often overlap with, and are a continuation of, the activities near the end of the earlier discovery phase. This is true whether the change agent is external or internal. Action plans together can now provide a clear and realistic vision for change. They provide the "roadmap" for managing the transition from the present state to the desired future state.

Development of the various action plans is often an enlightening experience for members of their organization as they begin to realize a more systematic approach to their planning and day–to–day activities. As with other activities during change management, plans can vary widely in how they are developed. Some plans are very comprehensive and systematic (often the best form used for successful change). Others are comprised of diverse sections that are expected to somehow integrate with each other. Subscribers to the philosophy of 'Appreciative Inquiry' might do planning by building on past positive outcomes and on the strengths of members of the organization. This step involves :

(*a*) Selecting Organizational Development Activities to Address the Findings from Step 2 above.

(*b*) Joint Development of Action Plans.

(*c*) Joint Development of Evaluation Plans.

(*d*) Joint Development of Learning Plans.

Phase 4 : Change Management and Joint Evaluation

During this phase, emphasis is on sustaining and evaluating the change effort, including by addressing resistance that arises from members of the organization — and sometimes in the change agent, as well.

(*a*) Organizations ongoing Communication of Action Plans.

(*b*) Organizations Implementation of Action Plans.

(*c*) Organization and Change Agent Maintain Momentum During Change.

Organizational Development Strategies

Figure 9.7 depicts three basic strategies to achieving successful organizational change. The three strategies are not mutually exclusive and all three could be used concurrently to bring about systemic change. One or the other, however, may be more conducive to the type of change needed in a particular organization. For this purpose, they are shown as being three different strategies.

The **behavioural strategy** takes an employee training and development approach. It posits the employee learning would bring about the organizational change needed. Learning would consist of gaining knowledge, skills and new attitudes, which would lead to new behaviours. The new behaviours would then lead to improved quality.

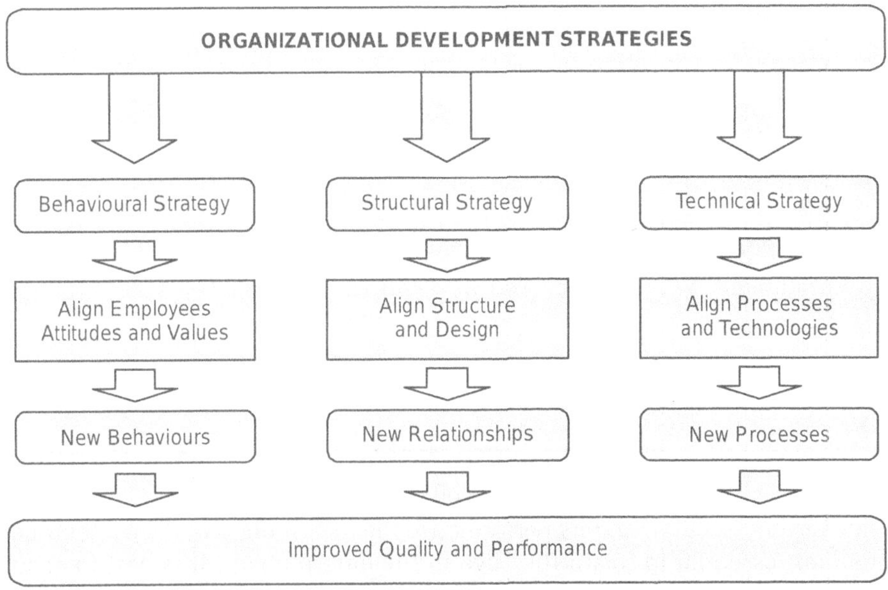

Fig. 9.7. *Organizational Development Strategies.*

The **structural strategy** takes an organizational design approach. It posits that organization structure and design should be aligned (or realigned) consistent with the vision, direction, mission, or goals of the organization. The Structural Strategy would incorporate changes in the organization chart. Employees, units, divisions, and departments could be realigned to optimize resources. For example, hierarchies could be flattened and decision–making could be placed closer to the point of action. Significant work could be done in chartered, self–directed teams. Such realigned relationships would lead to improved quality and performance.

The **technical strategy** takes a continuous improvement approach. It posits that processes in the areas of customer focus, product and service delivery, support, and supplier and partnering could be improved. This strategy also maintains that technology be continuously updated and aligned with the processes of production and service to make work more efficient and effective. Continuous process improvement with aligned technology would lead to improved quality and performance.

Techniques of Organizational Development

The broad techniques that could be employed for organizational development are :

(a) Sensitivity or T-Group Training. Discussed above in this Chapter.

(b) Management by Objectives. It is a dynamic system which integrates the company's need to achieve goals for profit and development. Ordiorne (1965)states that Management by Objectives can be described as a process whereby the superior and the subordinate managers of an organization jointly identify its common goals, define each individual's major areas of responsibility in terms of results expected of him, and use these measures as guides for operating the unit and assessing the contribution of each of units members. Ordiorne also stated that Management by Objectives is not merely a set of rules, a series of procedures or even a set of method of managing, but it is a way of thinking about management.

(c) Grid Development. Grid development is based on Blake and Mouton's (1969) model of leadership called the Managerial Grid. This would be discussed in detail later. Needless to say it depicts two prevailing concerns that is of productivity and personnel. Management by Objectives helps managers evaluate their concerns for personnel and productivity but also stresses te importance of developing team management leadership style.

(d) Organizational redesign. It involves restructuring to have better flow of authority and feedback.

(e) Work Design. Will be discussed in detail in Chapter 11.

(f) Job Enrichment. Will be discussed in detail in Chapter 11

(g) Survey feedback.

SUMMARY

- Executive development is a deliberate well thought out, and executed plan. The executives impact the organization and its performance the maximum and hence, their development is the most essential to retain the edge in the environment. It is best to ensure that the top management is intimately involved in the planning and execution of the executive development.

Review Questions

1. What do you understand by 'management development' ? Discuss briefly the methods of management development ?
2. Differentiate between education and executive development. Why is executive development necessary ?
3. Examine the need for executive development. Explain any three methods for executive development ?
4. What is sensitivity training ? Discuss its importance for 'management development' ?
5. Discuss the nature of Organizational Development ?

6. Discuss role playing and management games. Hoe do these techniques help in management development ?
7. Analyse the process involved in designing the 'management development programmes' ?
8. Write short notes on :
   (*a*) Conference methods
   (*b*) Multiple management
   (*c*) In basket exercises
   (*d*) Position / job rotation.
9. Discuss and debate the interdependency of 'management development' and 'organizational development' ?

PROJECT WORK

Study the 'management development programme' of any company located in vicinity. Analyse the process of management development and recommend an alternative plan. Discuss the same in the class.

Case Study

Strategic Executive Planning Gets a Lift

Deutsche Lufthansa AG, one of the world's largest airlines, has over 92,000 employees worldwide. With such large workforce4, a priority for the development of management is have a transparent overview of the group's human resource potential at all times.

With reported tax results of £453 million and sales of £18.1 billion at the end of 2005, the aviation group has grown rapidly in recent years. Its main focus is on its core competencies in the six business areas : Passenger Airlines; LH Cargo, LH Technik (aircraft maintenance, repair, and overhaul), LSG Skychefs (catering), Thomas Cook AG (travel agency), and LH systems.

To be commercially successful, a service provider must consider its employees as its most important resource.

"For this reason, systematic and targeted management development is absolutely essential," says Dr. Sylvia Branke, Director of Executive Development Strategies at Deutsche Lufthansa AG, when describing the main challenge in terms of human capital facing an aviation group with worldwide operations like Deutsche Lufthansa AG.

"The available leadership qualities, competencies, and technical expertise must be in synch with strategic corporate plans and objectives," said Branke.

"develop executives to support succession and career planning"

In addition to needing a crystal clear overview of the talent within the group so that any vacancies can be filled quickly and immediately with in–house personnel, another ongoing key task is to further develop executives in a talented manner to support succession and career planning. In order to implement the steer–able group–wide executive development system she designed, Branke required an efficient talent management solution. Lufthansa turned to a global software group which offered solutions for wide variety of tasks including career and succession planning, skills and competency management, and performance management.

This totally web based solution was welcomed by both human resource specialists and IT experts. Using a top down approach, software implementation began in 2002 with senior management and then, after close coordination with individual divisions, worked its way down to include other management levels.

"administer and monitor potential and performance–related data"

Within the scope of its Executive Asset management Deutsche Lufthansa is using software to administer and monitor potential and performance related data of its executives and junior managers. It maintains information pertaining to competencies, strengths, special skills and similar characteristics of about 1200 employees at these levels group wise.

In a flexible multifunctional manner, the tools help to compile and generate reports pertaining to human capital, including the capability of carrying out an ad hoc analysis. It is used to determine the up coming shortages as well as potential candidates among current executives and junior managers in the group. By comparing job specifications against individual qualifications, Lufthansa's human resource managers can locate suitable talents that can be prepared as potential candidates for a given position using specific skill and competency acquisition training.

"Essentially, we have created an executive development steering system that gives transparency over management potential in the group and its development. We can analyze the effects of job changes, generate a ranking for suitable candidates, or project excesses or shortages in job groups," explains Branke.

Questions

1. *What do you think is the difficulties in managing a large pool of managers ?*
2. *What do you think should the forward looking managements do to maintain transparency ?*
3. *Do you think the Lufthansa's management development programme needs reassessment ? What are factors that should be taken into consideration ?*

❑❑❑

Chapter **10**

CAREER DEVELOPMENT

★ LEARNING OBJECTIVES ★

After reading this chapter, you will be able to understand :

- Meaning of Career Planning
- Career and Manpower Planning
- Career and Succession Planning
- Objectives of career Planning
- Career Counseling

INTRODUCTION

Webster's dictionary defines term career as 'one's life work or employment pursuing the stated occupation as a lifework.' Career is sequence of positions occupied by a person during the course of his or her life. Each employee has an aspiration to advance and grow in his life and also a desire to realize a sense of fulfillment.

Today's rapidly changing business landscape demands a new approach to career development. Top management of the companies around the world believes that besides shortage of right talent at the top there are new challenges that put their business to risk.

(*a*) Increased competitive pressure.

(*b*) Rapidly changing market conditions.

(*c*) Failure to innovate.

(*d*) Satisfying customer demands.

The shortage of top management comes at a time when leadership is becoming more complex. Top management must have unique abilities :

(*a*) Business acumen to set and implement strategies.

(*b*) An understanding of how day to day decisions impact the overall performance of the company.

(*c*) People skills required to engage and develop others.

(*d*) Willingness to take value based actions.

Shortage of leadership talent represents a significant business risk. It raises the stakes for selecting and preparing people for increased levels of responsibility. The cost of poor hiring decisions is estimated by one global human resource consulting firm, DDI, as nearly $108,000, and Valero Energy recently estimated the cost of unfilled positions with "high impact" on the business to be in the tens of billions of dollars. Complexity of leadership skills are driving growth in development activities for executives, managers, and high potentials personnel's. These investments are intended to create bench strength based on unity and alignment within management teams as well as enhanced individual skills and abilities. Companies are taking action to build skills but at the top rung it is essential that career management is done to ensure no slot falls vacant.

There is a growing concern to career development and management due significant changes of a social, economic or political nature; these factors are now considered classic, whereas we now call attention to other current factors of a demographic, technological or psychological nature (Watts, 1980). Demographic aspects are particularly important, increased life expectancy and additionally, increased number of women involved in the work world. There is growing number of professions which did not exist earlier and working adults are making career choices. Cultural and economic changes can create frustration for large number of workers. Changes in values, needs and expectations lead a large proportion of adults to reformulate their career plans (Lankard, 1993). On account of these organizations are witnessing growing career flexibility leading to the thought that career development is not only vertical but also lateral; needs for ongoing training leading to a requirement for making consistent career decisions; early retirement, alternative activities; resulting in individuals making and remaking career decisions and remake initial career plans. Thus, new competencies and new adjustment formulas are needed.

The workforce appears to be becoming increasingly 'market driven', needing management through 'new deals' based around enhancing employability and marketability rather than job security and career advancement within the company. There is an increasing need for individuals to take charge of the development of their own learning and careers for a variety of reasons; increasing rate of change of our organizations and in the knowledge and skills we need to perform our jobs; shrinking or disappearing career ladders as reorganizations lead to flatter structures; an ever-increasing need for us to keep learning to keep up with the rapid growth in knowledge and the rate of change of our workplace environments; and, involvement in one's own development fosters greater commitment to the process than other-directed activities.

Career planning is important because the consequences of career success or failure are linked closely to each individuals self concept; identity and satisfaction with career and life.

CONCEPT OF CAREER

In everyday parlance the word career is used in number of different ways. The meaning and definition of 'career' is understood differently. This lack of clarity maintains ambiguity and continues to prevent a common ground of thinking in this area. From the time of Parsons (1909), the terms career, vocation, occupation, career planning, career management have often been used. Traditional definitions restricted career to professional work life which included advancement, and several researchers proposed the broadening of this conceptual definition.

According to Wilensky, *"A career denotes a succession of related jobs, arranged in a hierarchy of prestige, through which persons move in an ordered, predicted sequence."* In words of Edwin Flippo (1984, p. 248), *"A career is a sequence of separate but related work activities that provide community, order and meaning to a person's life."*

The US Department of Education and Science (1989, p.2) defined career as :

"The variety of occupational roles which individuals will undertake throughout life. It includes : paid and self-employment; the different occupations which a person may have over the years and periods of unemployment; and unpaid occupations such as that of student, voluntary worker or parent."

The concepts of time and life have been included in the definitions; the concept of career has broadened to include prevocational and post vocational activities. This broadening is reflected in definition by Super (1976, p.20) :

"The sequence of major positions occupied by a person throughout his pre-occupational and post-occupational life; includes work related roles such as those of student, employee, and pensioner, together with complementary vocational, familial and civil roles."

Arthur, Hall and Lawrence (1989, p.8) proposed a more concise definition describing work as :

"The evolving sequence of person's work experiences over time."

DEFINITION

The definition and explanation of career above takes us to the concept of career development which Brown and Brooks described as :

"For most people a lifelong process of getting ready to choose, choosing, the typically continuing to make choices from among the many occupations available in our society".

The concept of 'career development' was first advanced by Ginzberg, Ginsberg, Axelrad and Herma (1951) who proposed the occupational choice is a developmental process which occurs over a number of years. Sears (1982, p. 139) defines as :

"Career development is the total constellation of psychological, sociological, educational, physical, economic and chance factors that combine to shape the career of an individual over the life span."

The other terms used along with career developmen are career planning and career management which have been defined in succeeding paragraphs.

Career planning is a deliberate attempt by an individual to become more aware of his or her skills, interests, values, opportunities, choices and consequences. It involves identifying career related goals and established plans for achieving these (Hall, 1986).

Career management is considered to be an organizational process that implements and monitors career plans undertaken by individuals alone or within the organizations career system.

A number of authors recently have identified the social and cultural shift which has impacted work life (Amudson, 2005; Storey, 2000). As such the notion of career development is also undergoing a significant paradigm shift (Hartung, 2002; Jarvis, 2002) from talking about career development to development through work and other life roles.

The era today is of self career management *i.e.,* individuals managing their own careers. Individuals have to play a larger role in their own career development, Watts (1996, p.46) states "Careers are forged, not foretold". Employees today act as free agents, developing personal enterprises and marketing personal skills. Individuals today need to focus on employability rather than job security, and learn skills which will assist them in taking responsibility for the direction and evolution of own careers.

THEORIES OF CAREER

Career development theory has had a relatively short history and a new field. Isaacson and Brown (1993, p. 20) commented that 'the behavioural sciences', of which career development theory is a part, 'are still in developmental stage'. Parsons (1909) is credited with being the founder of vocational guidance and his work has had a profound influence on career theory and practice. Theories and interventions in the context of Guidance were for many years devoted exclusively to the adolescent. Looking at a typical psychological textbook, any one would be inclined to think that human development is completed at the age of 21 (Hopson and Scally, 1980). However, formulation of models which span the life cycle and which address the specific issues of adult subjects is a quite more recent concern.

The evolution of career development conceptions, and in particular the lifespan developmental models, as well as a set of demographic and technological factors, have awakened in society in general, and in the scientific community in particular, an interest in the study of the adult. This interest is primarily due to the uncertainties of the economic environment and to the technological changes, as well as new attitudes toward work.

Parsons' theorization is uncomplicated. He identified three elements of career selection as being 'self knowledge', 'knowledge of the world of work', and 'true reasoning on the relations of these two groups of facts' (Parsons, 1909, p.5).

Gradually it became recognized that the process of guidance is more complicated than Parsons' descriptions. In the decades of 1930–50, we find evolution of differential psychology and of psychometery. 'Rogers' in his work 'Counseling and Psychotherapy' focused on the individual, as shown by the importance given to motivational and affective aspects, in the focus of self acceptance and self-understanding, in attention to the subjects verbalizations as a source of information. Further more, Rogers work gave stimulus to research and practice regarding the counselor/ client interaction (Crites, 1969, 1981).

During 1950's saw emergence of theories on lifespan career development which brought about a change in theoretical conception of 'Guidance'. The innovative nature of these theories consists in understanding human psychological development based on a life span perspective, highlighting the study of all changes in the context of individual's physical, intellectual, affective, social, personality and vocational development (Jepsen, 1990). Work by Ginsberg constitutes a decisive contribution towards this change.

Out of these beginnings, a number of theories evolved which focused on the content of career choice, such as characteristics of the individual and of the workplace and became known as the trait and factor theories. "Career advising and individual counseling are inextricably related. Career problems have strong emotional components .... it is almost impossible to separate or categorize a problem as being career problem or a personal one" (Krumboltz, 1993, p.143).

Changes in environment and workforce behaviour demands a relook at existing models and construct new concepts. Crites started a new trend by making the distinction between non-psychological (accidental, economical, cultural and sociological) and psychological theories (trait-factor, psychodynamic, developmental and decision-making). Most of the theories thereafter focused on the person. Walsh (1990) underscores the trait factors theories; Osipow (1990) identifies a set of four theories that stand out historically and culturally : trait factor, work adjustment, social learning and developmental. Herr and Cramer (1996) make the distinction between trait factor approaches, decision theories, situational, sociological and contextual approaches, psychodynamic approaches and developmental approaches.

Structure of Career Development Theory

Herr and Cramer (1992) identified eight different groupings which had been offered by a number of authors, including those of Crites (1969), Osipow (1968), Herr and Cramer (1992), Osipow and Fitzgerald (1996), Osipow (1990), Minor (1992) and Patton and McMahon (1999). Categories are given in Figure 10.1. These categories are not mutually exclusive or independent, but they attempt to explain differential career behaviour and choice of some what different critical /vantage points. Historically career developmental theories focused on either content or process. Content refers to the influences on career development, such as interest and values, while processes refers to accounts of change over time and decision-making process.

Authors	***Categories***
Crites (1969)	Non Psychological Theories Psychological Theories
Osipow (1968)	Trait and factor approaches Sociology and career choice Self-concept theory Vocational choice and personality theories
Herr and Cramer (1992)	Trait and factor Actuarial or matching Decision Situational or sociological Psychological and developmental
Osipow and Fitzgerald (1996)	Time-factor Society and Career choice Developmental/ self conceptions Vocational choice and personality Behavioural
Osipow (1990)	Developmental Trait oriented Reinforcement based Personality focused
Minor (1992)	Theories of content Theories of Process
Patton and McMohan (1999)	Theories of content Theories of Process Theories of content and process Wider explanations.

Fig. 10.1. *Categories of Career Theories.*

Theories of content refers to the influences on career development which are intrinsic or emanate from within the context (environment) in which the individual lives. Major theories focusing on 'content' of career development include Parsons and Holland's psychological approaches of trait and factor theory; Bordin's psychodynamic theory; Brown's values-based theory; Dawis and Lofquist's the work adjustment person-environment correspondence theory and McCrae and John's personality based five factor theory.

Process refers to interaction and change over time as a series of stages through which and individual passes through his work life. Ginzberg, Ginsburg, Axelrad, and Herma. Ginzberg and Super theories have attempted to account for the process of career development. Gottfredson attempted to include both content and process variables into her model; by focusing on developmental stages.

The modern research has found the behaviour of career development to be too complex. Career development took place due both content and processes. Hence, need for theory to include both content and process was recognized which led to new models being generated. Theoretical models based on the social learning theory, social cognitive theory, learning theory, Social Cognition Career Theory, social cognitive perspectives and cognitive information processing approach have attempted to integrate both content and process.

Theoretical propositions have emerged that clearly reflect the influence of the constructivist with emphasis on holism. Constructivist views the person as an open system, constantly interacting with the environment, seeking stability through ongoing change Mahoney (2003) presented five basic assumptions which can be derived from theories of constructivism : active agency, order, self, social-symbolic relatedness, and lifespan development. Active agency implies that individuals are actively engaged in constructing their lives. Much of this activity focuses on ordering processes that is patterning one's experiences to create meaning. The third assumption is that this ordering of personal activity is mainly self-reliant, that the focus is on personal identity. The fourth assumption is that the development of self is embedded in the social and symbolic systems or contexts within which the individual lives. A final core assumption is that the activities of the previous assumptions are embedded in an ongoing developmental process that emphasizes meaningful actions by developing self working towards homeostasis. Savickas attributes the influence of constructivism to the change in the structure of work and the emphasis on individuals becoming agents in their own lives and careers; emphasizing self-organizing and self-managing of positions of individuals and actively construct a meaningful position in work context. In this the individual is central in construction of lives and careers.

Theories that Influence

There are other theories that also influence guidance, behaviour and in turn career selection and career development. Due to increased diversity in the work force population, and the fact that many of the established "theories are especially wanting in regard to their appropriateness for explaining development in minorities, gay and lesbian persons, and women" (Creamer, p. 31), there is need to understand theories of identity development associated with race, class, gender, sexuality, and special populations (King, 2005; McKewen, 2003). Such a broad range of theories may prove to be overwhelming, and as Hendey (1999) states, "the fact that there are many different developmental theories only makes a precise common understanding of developmental advising more difficult...It all gets rather complicated and confusing". However, while Hendey cautions advisors "not to get bogged down in specific theories of development, [he does] think it is necessary to have some knowledge of several of the specific theories".

Amongst the multiple theories that provide a foundation for effective development, cognitive development, career development, learning, decision-making, multiculturalism, retention, personality, moral development, and adult development (Creamer, 2000). There are three theory clusters important to the practice of academic advising : psychosocial theories, cognitive development theories, and typological theories (Creamer, 2000). The psychosocial theories of development, which can be applied to the development of identity in students, were proposed by such well-known figures as Erikson, Chickering and Reisser, Levinson, Marcia, and Josselson. These theories "describe how development is shaped by the resolution of developmental tasks that occur in chronological sequence throughout the life cycle" (Creamer and Creamer, 1994, p. 18). All of these theorists established a particular number of stages which individuals pass through in the course of their lifetimes. "People are seen as making systematic progression in a certain order through a series of phases. Step by step they move closer to some form of adult status. This movement can be seen as involving changes in intellectual and physical powers (for example around changes in intelligence, expertise and ability to reason); and the impact of life events and experiences" (Smith, 1999, p.7).

Roe's Theory of Career

According to this theory, it is the childhood orientation that leads to interest development and career choice. Roe's theory hypothesizes that childhood interactions with your parents greatly influence your career decisions. Parent child interactions predict psychological needs later in life and these affect the choice of career. Children from homes that put premium on warm satisfactory relationships within family tended to enter occupations that provided further such warmth and support and vice versa. Children with minimum contact often worked in solitary activities.

She classified all occupations on the dimensions of *'field'* and *'level.'* The field dimension is based on interest, and the level dimensions are defined in terms of responsibility, capacity and skill in occupation. Roe also stated vocational activity is largely the product of genetic differences which result in difference of interests and the way people attempt to manipulate various aspects of environment.

Ginzberg's Theory of Career Choice

There are some ideas to ponder based upon one of the most popular career planning and development theorists, Ginzberg, Ginsburg, Axelrad, and Herma. Ginzberg et al. They were the first group of career theorists to take a holistic approach to career planning. They looked at the whole person and the development of a career decision over the time.

Ginzberg et al. postulated that career decision making is a process. This process happens from puberty through the early 20s. Ginzberg et al. stated that the process of career decision making is usually irreversible, once crystallized. The resolution of the career choice process is a compromise, according to the theorists. According to them the career choices are influenced by :

(*a*) The reality factor.

(*b*) The influence of the educational process.

(*c*) The emotional factor.

(*d*) Individual values.

According to them career choice is a process that extends from 10–21 years, principally through high school and under graduate courses. It passes through developmental path that leads to career choice. Ginzberg et al., state career decision-making occurs in three phases and is determined by series of interlocked decisions, starting from pre-teen and ending in young adulthood. Individuals pass through three clearly marked stages :

1. **Fantasy Period**. Takes place until about the age of eleven. Children role play and imagine themselves in various work situations. During this phase, children begin to think about which careers they might like to do in the future.
2. **Tentative Stage** (11–18 years). Beginning in the pre-teen and continuing through high school children begin to make tentative or preliminary career choices based upon information gathered. Children define their interests in, capacity for values, recognizes the consequences and responsibility of that choice. This is accomplished through sub-phases :
   - *Interests* (Age 11 or 12) : The child makes more concrete decisions about him or her likes, dislikes, and interests.
   - *Capacity* (Age 13 or 14) : The teenager becomes more aware of his or her particular abilities as they relate to potential career.
   - *Values* (Age 15 or 16) : The teenager considers their personal values and priorities in life, as well as his or her occupational lifestyle.
   - *Transition* (Age 17 or 18) : At this point, the individual becomes aware of the decision for making a vocational choice.
3. **Realistic Stage**. Spanning from mid-adolescence through young adulthood adolescents go through exploration and crystallization and start to crystallize and specify occupations of interest. This final phase is made up of the following sub-phases.
   - *Exploration* : After considering options, the individual begins to narrow/ restrict his or her career choices based on personal likes, skills and abilities.
   - *Crystallization*. In this sub-phase an occupational choice is made.
   - *Specification* : The individual selects a job or profession. The individual then pursues the educational training program and experiences as required for achieving career of choice.

Later on in his career, Ginzberg (1984) stressed that "career choice is a lifelong process of decision-making for those who seek major satisfactions from their work." According to Ginzberg, the point of his theory is that people make their career decisions which balance their interests and values with the opportunities and talents available, as well as the cost of pursuing the opportunities.

Supers Theory of Career Development

Donald Super has generated a life span vocational choice theory and stated choosing a career basically means implementing a self concept. It is a continuous process and projects into adulthood, as individuals continuously adjust to a career. He follows traditions of hallo theory of continuous development. It involves two steps :

- Awareness of need to choose a career.
- Specificity of information and planning.

Donald Super stated that there are six life and career development stages.

(*a*) The crystallization stage between ages 14–18.

(*b*) The specification stage between ages of 18–21.

(*c*) Implementation stage between ages of 21–24.

(*d*) The stabilization stage between the ages 24–35.

(*e*) Consolidation stage, around age of 35 years.

(*f*) Readiness for retirement around 55 years of age.

The greatest contribution of this theory to career development has been its emphasis of the role the self concept plays in development. Super recognized that the self-concept changes and develops throughout people's lives as a result of experience. Individuals successively refine their self-concepts over time and application to the world of work creates adaptation in their career choice. Although this theory of career development provides foundation for the professional workforce but its research as omitted special groups, an essential aspect in the changing nature of the work force and nature of work.

Holland's Career Typology

John Holland evolved a concept based on what he states as model personal orientation or a developmental process established through heredity and individuals life history of reacting to environmental demands or 'individuals are attracted to a particular occupation that meets their personal needs and provides them satisfaction.'

Holland's concept rests on four assumptions :

(*a*) Person's are categorized in a culture or society. The broad categorizations are realistic, artistic, social, conventional ort enterprising etc.

(*b*) The environment present six model environments viz., realistic, investigative, artistic, social, enterprising and conventional.

(*c*) People search for environments that will let them exercise their skills and abilities, express their attitudes and values and take on agreeable problems and roles.

(*d*) Behaviour is determined by interaction between personality and environment.

A hexagonal model was developed to illustrate relationship between personality and occupational environment (Figure 10.2).

Much of the subsequent research supports Holland's typology. The strongest criticism is based on gender bias because females tend to score high in three personality types (artistic, social and conventional). Holland attributes this to our society that channels females into female oriented/ dominated occupations.

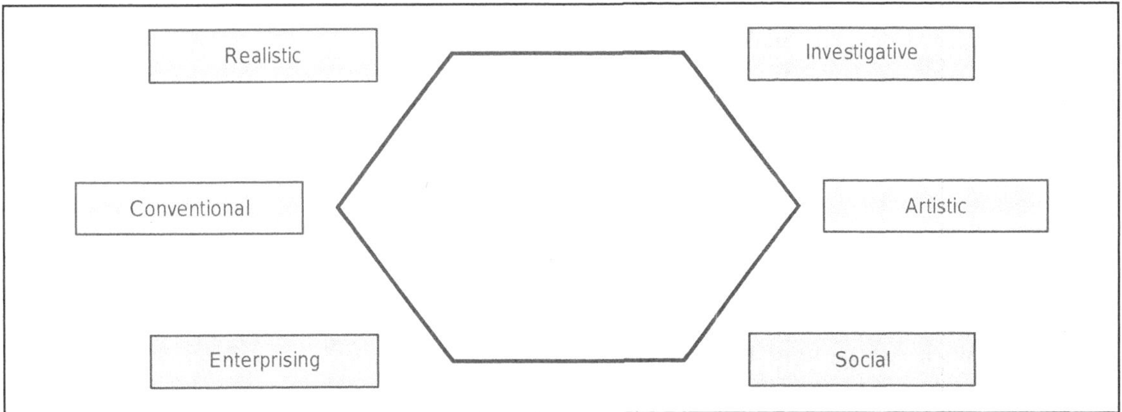

Fig. 10.2. *Model Illustrating Relationship between Personality and Occupational.*

The Social Cognition Career Theory has grown out of Albert Bandura's social cognitive theory and attempts to address issues of culture, gender, genetic endowment, social context and unexpected life events that may interact with and supersede the effects of career related choices. The Social Cognition Career Theory focuses on the connection of self-efficacy, outcome expectations and personal goals that influence an individual's career choice.

Social Cognition Career Theory proposes that career choice is influenced by the beliefs the individual develops and refines through four major sources :

(*a*) Personal performance accomplishments.

(*b*) Vicarious learning.

(*c*) Social persuasion.

(*d*) Psychological states and reactions.

These aspects interact together as a process and an individual develops a particular ability and expertise for an endeavour. This process reinforces one's self-efficacy or belief in future continued success in the use of this ability/expertise. As a result the individual is likely to develop goals that involve continuing involvement in that activity. What is critical to the success of the process is the extent to which one views the endeavour as one which they are successful and offers valued compensation. The contextual factors come into play by influencing the individual's perception of the probability of success. If the person perceives few barriers the likelihood of success reinforces the career choice, but if the barriers are viewed as significant there is a weaker interest and choice actions.

By adolescence, most people have a sense of their competence at a vast array of performance areas, along with convictions about the likely outcomes of a career. Through a process of intervening learning experiences that shape further one's abilities and impacts self-efficacy and outcome beliefs, one's vocational interests, choices and performances are shaped and reshaped.

The Social Cognition Career Theory differs from other theories in its dynamic nature. Through it's focus upon the role of the self-system and the individual's beliefs the inherent influence of the social and economic contexts are addressed.

Crites Model

Formulated a model of career maturity encompassing both content and the process of career decision-making, it combines Ginzberg's focus on ego function in career decisions-making with Super's emphasis on the dimensions of career maturity and adding components from factorial analyses of ability. Crites formulated a model of career maturity that encompasses both the content and the process of decision making.

Common dimensions identified most frequently are

- Security
- Autonomy
- Affiliation
- Respect
- Self expression.

Theory of Work Adjustment (Dawis and Lofquist, 1984)

This approach, which is now referred to as Person-Environment-Correspondence Counseling (Lofquist and Dawis, 1991), reflects the trait-and-factor tradition of the University of Minnesota.

While this approach has gained wide-spread acceptance, it is not considered one of the newer emerging theories.

The Cognitive Information Processing model's perspective on career development is based on 10 basic assumptions. Using these assumptions as a focal point, school counselors provide students with a series of learning events designed to develop their processing skills. In this way, students develop capabilities as career problem solvers. The counselor's function is to identify the students' needs and to develop interventions aimed at helping them to acquire the knowledge and skills necessary to satisfy those needs. Gary Peterson and his colleagues stress that career problem solving is primarily a cognitive process that can be improved through the utilization of a sequential process known as what ?

CAREER ANCHORS

Career anchors are the basic drives or dimensions identified that create the urge in an individual to take up a certain type of careers Figure 10.3. The common dimensions identified as affecting the most include :

(*a*) *Security*. Economic this is one of the prime concerns especially with countries having large populations and serious unemployment problems. In India economic security is prime concern when identifying a career. It is for this reason Government jobs in India are still very popular.

(*b*) *Autonomy*. Freedom to take action. Autonomy ranks high amongst talented.

(*c*) *Affiliation*. Humans are social animals and like to be affiliated with an organization, group, team etc. Better the spoken reputation of an organization greater the desire of an individual to be affiliated with it. Affiliation brings social status which is an important dimension in status conscious Indian society.

(*d*) *Respect*. Along with status there is a desire of men to wield some influence and be respected by his colleagues.

(*e*) *Self-expression*. It is one of an important dimension in choosing a particular career and pursuing it.

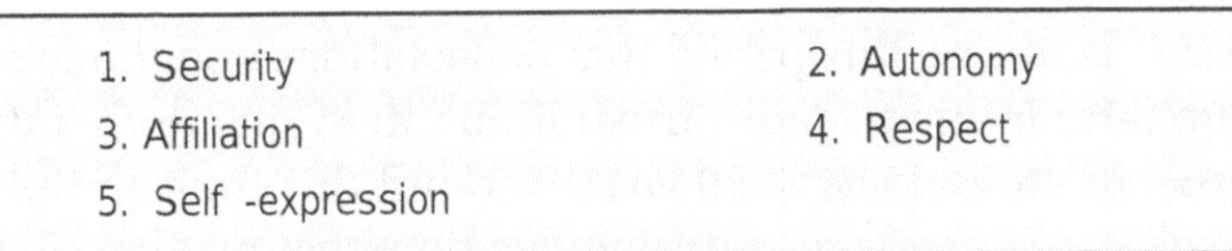

Fig. 10.3. *Career Anchors.*

CAREER STAGES

If one looks around, he would realize that all individuals occupying a position in a hierarchy have gone through number of stages. Evan's (2002) proposed a wide rangoing, non subject specific interpretation, rather than a model, of teacher development. She interpreted development as a process. For an individual at any one point in time this process might be continuing or completed. However she stated that the process was never truly completed as repeated development might occur in the same or different areas. Evans in his work has evolved six stages of career development (Figure 10.4).

(a) Stage I – Exploration.

(b) Stage 2 – Establishment.

(c) Stage 3 – Mid-Career.

(d) Stage 4 – Late Career.

(e) Decline.

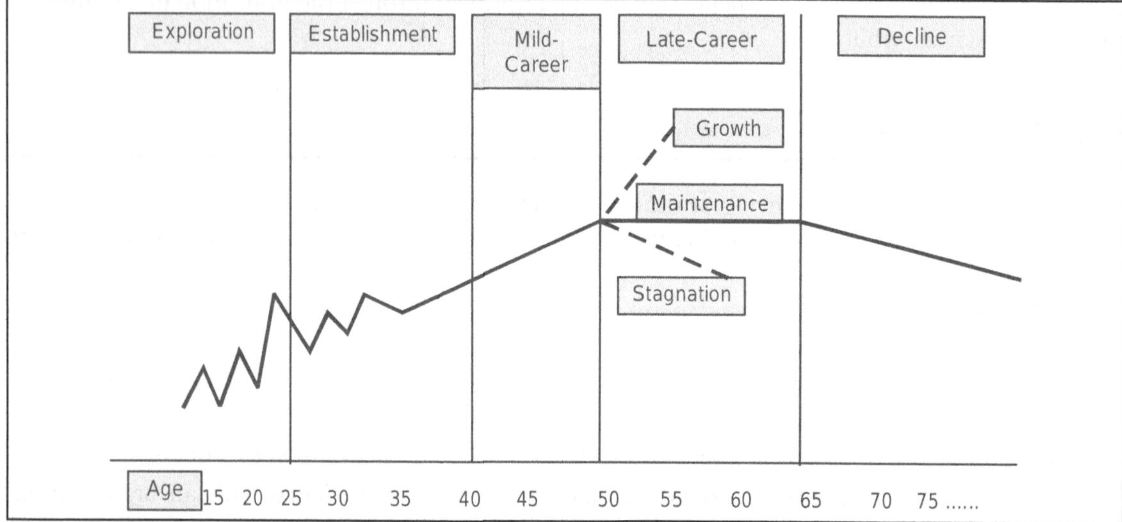

Fig. 10.4. *Evan's Model of the Stages in Career Development.*

Stage 1—Exploration

Exploration represents pre-employment stage. The exploration stage ends moment an individual makes first career decision. The critical decisions of a particular career are made prior to entering the first employment. Individuals very early in their lives start narrowing down their career decisions. Large numbers of environmental factors influence an individual in deciding and identifying their career. It is during this period that expectations about one's career are developed and these may prop up later in life to cause frustration after lying dormant for number of years. A critical period may occur around age of 30 years, around this time an individual may question his decision about the choice of career. It is during this time that maximum movement takes place in the workforce.

Stage 2—Establishment

It covers the period commencing from around age of 25 to 35 years. The individual during this period has a great desire to establish his standing and reputation in the organization. It begins with anxieties and is marked by making mistakes, learning from such mistakes and gradual assumption of greater responsibilities. The individual works for career advancement, and tries to establish a place in the society. These tasks reflect the person's need for independence and for recognition from those who are important in his or her life. During the establishment stage an individual seeks a mentor who can show him how to operate efficiently and profitably. By the end of this stage the nature of career is well set.

Stage 3—Mid-Career

This is the stage usually between the ages of 35 to 45 years. The person is well established in his career, he is no longer viewed as a learner and any mistakes committed are viewed seriously by his superiors. During this period starts reevaluating where he is heading in his career and also life. The mid-career is often considered as stressful and full of tension. Persons making successful transition at this stage, get greater responsibilities, attractive and appreciable rewards.

Stage 4—Late Career

This commences from mid forties and continues for next fifteen to twenty years. The career graph at this period may be characterized by growth or stagnation. For those who continue to grow this period is a pleasant experience. The person starts playing the role of elder statesman. The value to the organization lies in this persons varied experience, sharing and teaching others based on knowledge gained.

Stage 5—Decline

At this stage individual ids forced to sidestep out of limelight and give up major component of his identity. It is probably the toughest time for those who have been high achievers. The main task now is to reorganize your life, make critical choices about the components of life, and build new structures around them. Work which has been an important component of in ones life will no longer hold central place. This would require that individual to make adjustments and get along with people and things to lead a happy retired life.

CAREER DEVELOPMENT

Career development is essential for implementing career plans. It consists of activities undertaken by the individual employees and the organization to meet career aspirations and job requirements. Career development model is shown in Figure 10.5.

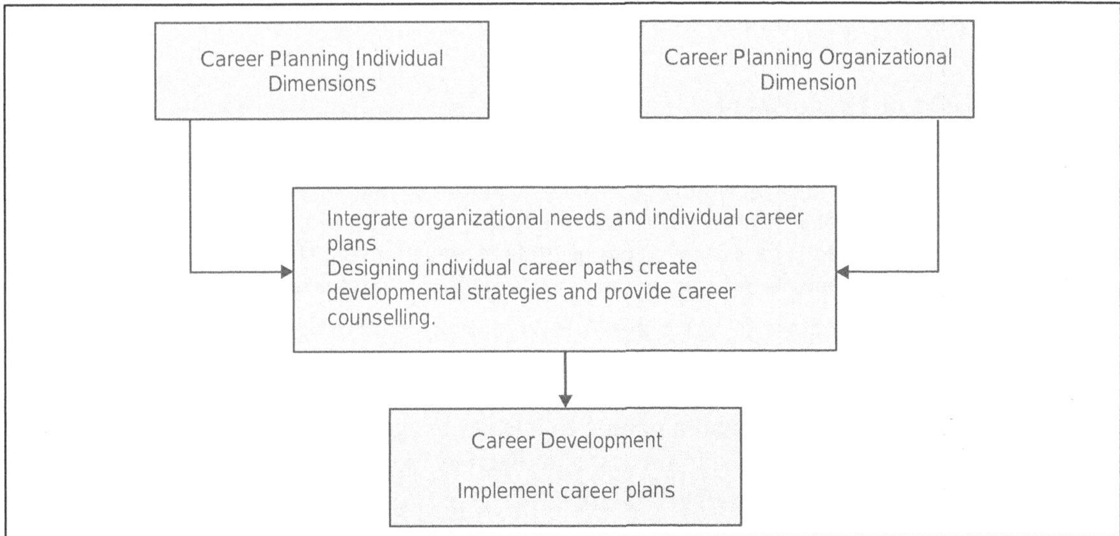

Source : Adapted from Careell, M.R. and Kuzmitts, F.E., (1982, p.408)

Fig. 10.5. *Career Development Model.*

The characteristics of career development are :

(*a*) It is a process of developing human resources.

(*b*) It is means of managing people and obtaining optimum results.

(*c*) Career development is a continuous process. The aim being to integrate organizational and individual needs and meet goals of both.

Career development activities involve :

(*a*) **Career Need Assessment**. Career needs of employees can be judged by evaluating their aptitudes, abilities and potential. Many employees may not be aware of what they are seeking and they should be counseled. The organization can assist an individual in identifying, developing and clarifying their career goals.

(*b*) **Career Opportunities.** Career opportunities coming on way must be identified through job analysis.

(*c*) **Need-Opportunity Alignment**. In this stage an individual should align his needs with career opportunities.

(*d*) **Monitoring Career Moves**. It is necessary to maintain career moves inventories to maintain progress towards predetermined career goals. This will enable the human resource department to identify discrepancies and to adopt corrective measures at the right time as also help an individual to identify his needs including adequate career plans.

Career Planning Individual Dimension

From the individual perspective career planning is the process by individual fixes career goals and lays down the path to achieve these goals. Individual determines the path to provide continuity, order and meaning to his life. Traditionally career planning at individual level has been restricted to occupational advancement which is clear and easy to measure. However, with the trend of downsizing, globalization, technological development, information explosion and emphasis on knowledge worker has compelled the worker to think differently. Multi-skilling, constant up-gradation of knowledge and cross functional experiences has become essential for career development and continued employability.

Choosing a Field of Employment

The old career structure which emphasized commitment to one career for life was based on routine production, economies of scale and structural stability. That structure stressed job security and favored a static long-term commitment to your Right Career. You found your career track and stayed in place. Employees in the early stages of their career lifecycle still seek job security in an environment in which there is no longer any job security for anybody.

The new career structure is one where individuals are active agents in their own career development. The career process is one which insists that we each construct self-images such as vocational identity that influence our response to the environment. This identity or vocational self-understanding is developmental in nature, that is, it changes over time in somewhat regular patterns we all share and it is rooted in intrinsic motives (*e.g.*, nurturance, curiosity, achievement) that help guide our career choice and development.

The biggest challenge for companies today is to retain the employees that have been recruited and placed in an organization. Employees are today more concerned with their jobs than with the organizations. This trend of workers migrating to greener pastures is observed across the entire globe including countries with large unemployed workforce like India.

The First Step

The first step is to think in terms of where one wants to be ultimately in one's work life. Accordingly an individual determines his goals and means to achieve it. The individual then organizes in regards to positions and jobs that have to be occupied that will help him accomplish those goals.

Focus on Career Goals

It is important that an individual focuses constantly on his career goals and regularly updates his skill and knowledge to meet it. To this end in modern society and individual has to constantly update himself or have continuing professional development programme. A continuing professional development programme has been defined as :

"Continuing professional development is the systematic maintenance, improvement and broadening of knowledge and skill and the development of personal qualities necessary for the execution of professional and technical duties throughout practitioner's working life (Construction Industrial Council, 1986, p. 3 as cited in Friedman and Philips, 2004)."

Professional development consists of natural learning experiences and those conscious and planned activities which are intended to be of direct or indirect benefit to the individual, group or an organization and which contribute to better performance on the job. It is the process by which, alone and with others, and individual review, renew and extend their commitment; and by which they acquire and develop critical knowledge, skill and emotional intelligence essential for good professional thinking, planning and practice throughout their work life.

The individual must constantly focus towards achieving his career goals and keep acquiring knowledge and skills towards that end.

Assess Indicative for Job Change

Career excepting for few is not a straight line to the top. It is a series of 'S' curves. Figure 10.6. Trouble starts as an individual approaches the crest of a particular job. The individual gets into anxiety and disorientation. He is not sure whether to continue or change the job. Secretary of Labor Robert B. Reich calls these individuals as "anxiety class." The anxiety class lives of economic and vocational uncertainty and instability created by a highly competitive and rapidly evolving marketplace which depreciates the job security of every worker who is not growing and changing in response to market forces; everyone from the entry level trainee to the occupant of the presidential suite is vulnerable. Inner turmoil can build to the point where it hurts health and family. Disorientation and confusion can lead to leave the fast track and end up drifting from one job to another.

The careers of most persons are hence sequence of curves; the summits keep coming like the waves making way towards the shore, each changing place with the one which goes before.

Having peaked at a particular job the individual and has surmounted all challenges, the less ambitious person is likely to coast at this point, the over achievers bears down even harder to produce even more stellar results. It is at this point that individual's performance starts to slip and he gets into discomfort and unease. He plans change of job.

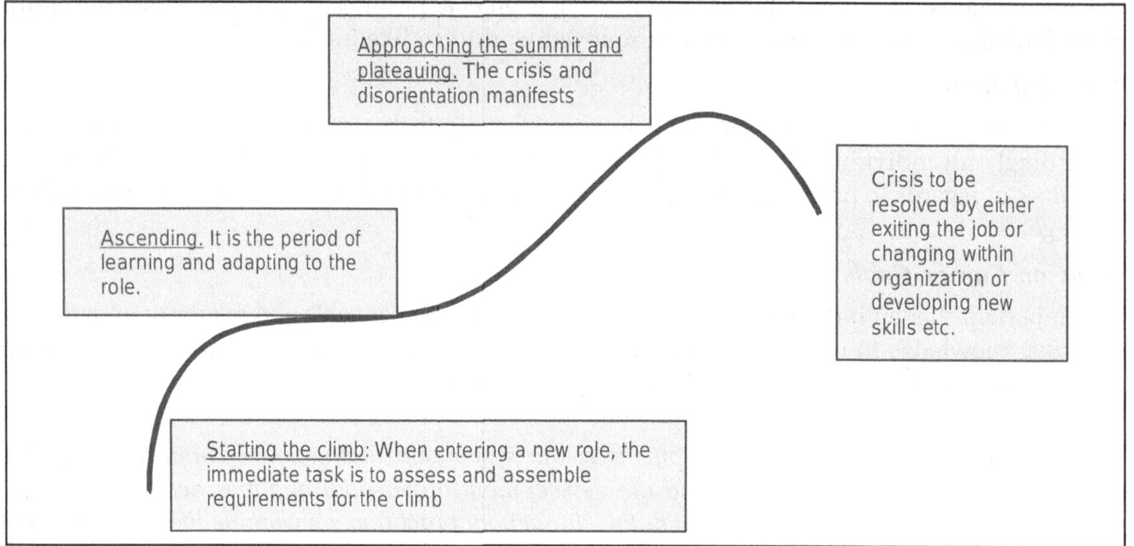

Fig. 10.6. *The Career Curve.*

Plan the Exit Carefully

The necessity to plan exit is equally important as accepting a job or an assignment. An individual should plan his exit so that he does enter into any discomfort or unease. The career loss or change impacts his environment including his family. The individual has to seek another employment and hence, has to ensure that his exit does not impact his standing or spoken reputation.

Career Planning Organizational Perspective

A career development programme provides a long term focus on company's employment needs combined with support for employees so they can prepare for future jobs in the company. For career planning for organizational needs we turn to an examination of organizational career management practices, using labour market segmentation theory and theories of corporate strategy and human resource systems. A particularly useful framework linking career systems and human resource strategies is provided by Miles and Snow (1978), and it is this framework which will be adopted here after a discussion of labour market segmentation.

In the 1980s, labour market segmentation theory was developed to help analyse the ways in which organizations employ different kinds of labour, with consequences for career paths and processes. Employees differ in terms of whether they have flexible skills specific to an organization and the degree to which work contains discretionary elements providing stable earnings. Different approaches to the management of employment relationships, including the management of careers, will be adopted for different groups of employees. Those in the primary internal labour market will typically possess important, scarce skills specific to a particular organization; hence, an organization is likely to retain and develop such employees and expose them to a range of human resource management techniques, including career management techniques. Other employees with specialized but general skills in the primary external market may also be actively recruited and offered career development. Employees in the secondary internal market may be seen as less important, except in terms of availability at peak times. Such employees (*e.g.*, part-time, seasonal or temporary employees) may not be subject to a wide range of human resource management practices, and more specifically, not offered much in the way of career development opportunities.

Proponents of labour market mobility and specifically in the model of the 'flexible firm'; work force is divided into a 'core' group and a variety of peripheral' groups. Workers in the 'core' group, expected to deliver functional flexibility, to include employees with firm-specific skills and high-discretionary elements in their work, to be offered a range of career development opportunities. Such opportunities may be less available to 'peripheral' workers, such as part-time, temporary and casual workers, consultants, and workers on government-financed schemes. The concepts of flexibility and the flexible firm have been subject to considerable critique, as well as praise, but there does seem to have been an increase in certain kinds of flexible working practices in the 1990s, with implications for career management practices in organizations. Responsibility for career development may increasingly be laid on individuals in the 'periphery', whereas employees, especially managers, in the 'core' may still find that organizations take some responsibility for their career development.

Miles and Snow (1978) have demonstrated how human resource systems can support, and even drive, an organization's business strategy. Miles and Snow identify four basic organizational types, termed prospectors, defenders, analysers, and reactors.

Prospectors. These firms seek to locate and exploit new opportunities, develop new products and create new markets. Their HR systems must therefore locate, recruit, develop and retain technical experts who are creative and independent. They particularly emphasise innovation and flexibility. They are likely to recruit extensively in the primary external labour market for employees with specialised skills.

Defenders. These firms tend to have narrow and relatively stable product/market domains, which they seek to protect through efficient production, strong control mechanisms and continuity and reliability. Their human resource systems must therefore seek to recruit, develop and retain long-term, loyal members high in commitment to the organization. They are likely to rely heavily on an internal labour market strategy, seeking to develop employees with flexible but specific skills.

Analysers. These firms fall between the first two groups, taking fewer risks than prospectors but excelling in the delivery of new products and services. Their HR systems need to recruit and develop people who take moderate risks but who also remain loyal to the organisation. They are likely also to rely on an internal labour market strategy, but with some recruitment of external specialists.

Reactors. These are firms which display little ability to adapt to their environment. Their human resource systems often try to dispense with staff through lay-offs, discharges, early retirements and outplacements, whilst at the same time engaging in a limited recruitment of 'turnaround' experts. They may make heavy use of the external labour market for temporary and casual staff, with limited use of the internal labour market.

The four strategic types described, and the shifts between them, affect the kinds of careers offered to people. For example Sonnenfield and Peiperl (1988) describe a four-stage typology of career systems using the two dimensions supply flow (whether jobs are filled internally or externally) and assignment flow (whether people are assigned and promoted to new tasks primarily on their individual contribution or on their group contribution). Once again, labour market segmentation is seen as a crucial factor in analysing organizational career practices.

This model tries to link corporate strategies to the way organizations go about recruiting and promoting people (in particular, managers and executives) and to the assessment criteria used to make placement decisions. Baseball teams emphasise recruitment, on-the-job development and high turnover—career moves tend to be between organizations, with heavy use of the external labour market. They tend to be prospectors, with rapid movement into new markets and grasp of opportunities. They need to attract 'star performers' to keep a competitive edge. Examples might include professional organizations, such as law firms and management consultancies, advertising agencies, or entertainment and public relations firms. A central, prospecting, Indian Premier League cricket team may allocate stars to acquired 'reactor fortresses' to help turn them around.

Academies, on the other hand, emphasise development, and characteristically are analysers, not necessarily at the leading edge of technology but careful in their entry into new markets or products, always attempting to ensure reliable, high-quality delivery. Needing both specialist expertise and wide business knowledge, they tend to recruit young and promote internally, with stars getting rapid promotion. Here we might expect to see the full panoply of sophisticated career development practices in operation. Organizations tend to emphasise retention, internal recruitment and promotion on the basis of group contribution. Valuing loyalty and equity, they are typically defenders who wish to retain a particular market, often through monopolies or regulated competition. They may emphasise community service and develop generalists rather than specialists. However, under the impact of deregulation and international competition in the financial services sector, and privatisation and government legislation in local and central government, many clubs have tried to become more like academies.

Finally, fortresses tend to emphasise retrenchment, recruiting externally and exhibiting high turnover, redundancy and low levels of commitment to their staff. They tend to be reactors, often buying in new top management teams and cheap replacement labour. Many organizations have become reactors when they get into difficulties due to recession and competition, and many club defenders may become reactors on their way to trying to become academies.

Such shifts may place new demands on employees, disrupting the psychological contract between organization and individual. Many people will have joined financial services organizations because they seemed to offer, in return for individual commitment and loyalty, relational contracts: job security, stability and slow but steady promotion. However, such organizations are now attempting to move towards more entrepreneurial, risk-taking commercial cultures, offering transactional contracts. Job security may be threatened, old skills devalued and radical changes in values demanded, entailing a massive disruption of the psychological contract and causing stress and discomfort, a loss of commitment and a need for new human resource policies and systems, including career development systems, to help employees meet these new demands.

Career Development Practices in Organizations

A number of authors have provided lists of career development practices used by organizations (*e.g.*, Bowen and Hall, 1977; London and Stumpf, 1982). These practices range across the career development spectrum from career planning to career management. Baruch and Peiperl (1997) developed a list of 17 career management practices. (Figure 10.7) They omitted processes reaching beyond the organization, such as outplacement counselling or facilitating external networking for later employment, processes held to be characteristic of 'boundaryless' or 'post-corporate' careers (*e.g.*, Peiperl and Baruch, 1997; Arthur, 1994). They also omitted 360° appraisals, developmental job assignments including secondment, and management development generally. The most frequently used practices did not necessarily include apparently effective techniques, such as succession planning, assessment centres, and peer and upward appraisals.

Baruch and Peiperl (1997) also used factor analysis to explore how these various practices cluster together. Five factors emerged, labelled 'basic' (*e.g.*, elementary practices such as job posting, formal education, pre-retirement programmes, lateral moves), 'active planning' (forward-looking, proactive practices such as career-orientated appraisals, supervisor career counselling, career counselling, and succession planning), 'active management' (bi-directional, information gathering practices such as assessment centres, formal mentoring, and career workshops), 'formal' (uni-directional, organizational provision of information through written personal career planning, dual career ladders and books/pamphlets on career issues) and 'multidirectional' (increasing options for feedback and development through peer appraisal and upward appraisal).

Baruch and Peiperl (1997) proposed a two dimensional model involving level of sophistication of the practice and level of involvement by the organization. The basic cluster is seen as the least sophisticated, the multi directional the most, with active management in between. The formal group is seen as requiring least involvement by the organization, the active management a moderate amount, and the active planning the most involvement. (No measure of involvement was used in the study). Baruch and Peiperl (1997) also report on several case study companies whose career development practices focus on different clusters. Building generalist managers through using lateral moves, succession planning and hierarchical performance appraisals were most emphasised. There appeared to be less evidence of the multi dimensional or formal clusters, though an elite cadre may be managed through assessment centers and active management.

Job Postings
Formal education and tuition reimbursement
Personnel Assessment for Career Planning
Counselling by manager
Lateral moves/ Job rotation.
Counselling by HR
Pre-retirement Programmes
Succession Planning
Formal Mentoring
Common Career Paths
Dual Ladder
Career Books/Pamphlets
Written Individual Career Plans
Assessment Centers
Peer Appraisal
Career workshops
Upward Appraisal
Appraisal Committees
Training programmes for managers
Orientation Programme
Special needs (dual career couples)

Fig. 10.7. *Baruch and Peiperl Useful Career Practices.*

Managing International Careers

Of further interest in exploring changing career patterns is how specifically international careers are managed, especially as such careers are growing in frequency and importance. Baruch and Altman (1999) present a typology of international management careers, distinguishing them in terms of their intensity (Figure 10.8). They distinguish the Empire option (international careers as a normal career path), the Colonial option (an overseas posting as a move away from the central power base), the professional option (employing a market-driven 'foreign legion' as perpetual outsiders), the peripheral option (special niche markets offering rare international opportunities) and the expedient option (optional, opportunistic international careers). Figure 10.8 shows the key features of these different careers, as well as the case of fringe careers (making occasional international forays).

Intensity	***Organization Frame***	***Antecedents***	***Values***	***Organising Principles***
Frequent	Empire	Established Multi national Companies, Global Enterprises.	International careers are the standard.	Global trotting is the lead institutional process, reflected in organizational structures.
	Colonial	Established Multi national Companies, centralised decision making.	Loyalty and patriotism; international careers as a mission.	Episodes of service abroad and sojourn at home are common throughout.
	Professional	External hire for assignments abroad.	Professional identity.	Overseas posts (periphery) separated from home-based (core).
Infrequent	Peripheral	Minor Multi national Companies, niche markets.	Overseas posts highly desirable.	Transparent and equitable human resource policies for service abroad.
	Expedient	Little experience of international careers and few resources.	Ambivalence; potentially high failure.	Ad-hoc; learning as one goes.
Occasional	Fringe	Small organizations, first attempts at internationalising.	Necessity driven, possibly curiosity.	Marginal activity visits, trade conferences, etc.

Fig. 10.8. *International Careers—The Key Features.*

Companies with developed international careers tend to have an established human resource function, compared to companies in which international careers are in their infancy. There is a strong association between having human resource represented on the Board and the following :

- Having an expatriate policy.
- Having a stronger overseas presence (ten markets on average compared to only six).
- The likelihood of having an active policy on international careers.
- The likelihood of having dedicated international HR services.

International careers are clearly on the ascent. A sea-change perhaps, if an employee works for a multi national corporation, it is likely that he or she is already 'enlisted' into an international career. If employees follow the Professional or Peripheral model, they are likely to be internationally oriented anyway. If they are Expedient or Fringe fraternity, they may well be experiencing a conversion. This is set against the background of how a company benchmarks itself.

To prevent job turnout and obsolescence and improve quality of workers life Callahan and Greenhouse gave a few recommendations for employers and companies.

- Provide employees with tools and equipment to enhance the skills.
- Create environment for continuous learning.
- Provide opportunities for additional training and orientation.
- Have managers trained as coaches.
- Reward system that supports organized career development.
- Careers program are integrated.

Career development program form company perspectives require the following :

(*a*) Long term plans—companies must determine what jobs will be available in the future, how many people will be needed in each job, the knowledge and skills those employees will require.

(*b*) Career paths. It is progression of related jobs with increasing skill requirements and responsibility. This provides employees the opportunity to advance, make additional contributions, and receive increased satisfaction from their work.

(*c*) Employee Evaluations—involves obtaining and maintaining up to date records on the skills and abilities the employee possesses and the skills and abilities an employer needs in order to make effective career decisions. Employee should be carefully evaluated so that those in need of additional training and development and those ready for further advancement/promotion can be identified.

(*d*) Career Counselling—employees should be made aware of career opportunities so that they can schedule for the plan activities. A common endeavour between the employee, manager and the human resource specialist should be made to evolve a plan.

Career and Human Resource Planning

Career planning is an integral part of human resource planning in an organization. Human resource planning cannot be effective without proper and adequate career planning. The main issues involved are :

(*a*) Human resource planning provides inventory of skills required but career planning determines who can be groomed.

(*b*) Human resource planning provides information about human resource available with organization.

(*c*) Career planning tells who will succeed in case of retirement, death etc.

(*d*) Human resource planning facilitates career planning. Human resource planning facilitates career planning by providing inventories of human resource; manpower needs in an organization; nature and extent of knowledge, skills and behavioural changes required to meet manpower needs.

Benefits

Effective career planning accrues benefits as mentioned :

(*a*) Assist individual to have knowledge of various careers.

(*b*) Help individual to select career.

(*c*) Help organization to identify talented employees.

(*d*) Help in employ retention.

(*e*) Improve employee performance.

(*f*) Increased job satisfaction.

(*g*) Organization gets a better image.

Problems of Career Planning

Major drawbacks of Career planning are :

(*a*) Career planning can be a reality only if opportunities for vertical mobility exist.

(*b*) In family businesses, members of family expect to progress faster.

(*c*) Some careers do not have scope of much progress.

(*d*) Careers often reach a declining stage due to the influence of the technological or economic factors.

The career development in an organization in modern structures may not be a very good option as the organizations are getting horizontal and more and more assignments are team based. In addition the very character of work force is undergoing a rapid and total overhaul in their behaviour.

Challenging initial jobs.	Career development workshop
Dissemination of career option	Periodic job changes.
Information	Sabbaticals (leave granted at
Job postings.	intervals) to attend development
Assessment Centers.	programs and courses
Continuing education and training	

Fig. 10.9. *Steps in Career Development.*

Essential for Success in Careers

Casico, W.F. (1989, p. 517) has listed out four attributes for success in career.

(*a*) **Performance**. Success in career is judged by objective and psychological success. Objective success is assessed by measuring tangibles like pay, position etc. Person drawing higher pay is considered more successful than one drawing lesser pay. Objective success depends upon how well one performs one's job and the extent to which it is valued by others in the firm. The psychological success occurs when a man develops self esteem or the value one places in ones self. Self esteem basically is achieved when one starts developing confidence and competence in one's job, ensured economic security and family commitments are met.

(*b*) **Attitude**. It is individual attitudes related to work. These are evolved over a period of time from the day one commences job till he finally retires.

(*c*) **Identity**. Every individual is unique and wants a clear position for himself in the world, society and environment around him. Career identity is that particular facet that relates to individuals identity related to occupational activities. Employee's performance at work place has direct impact on his identity; as also his status in society and family which in turn impacts psychological behaviour.

(*d*) **Adaptability**. Adaptability is one of the core characteristics or quality for success of an individual especially at top management positions. Adaptability is the individual's capacity to change occupations and/or work setting in order to maintain his or her standards for career progress.

Problems in Career

Like in all other activities there are some inherent difficulties that occur in career development. The first and foremost problem is mobility. Mobility implies moving from one position to another mostly upward and sometimes lateral and to new places. It also involves quick adaptation to new environment and settings. The mobility can be both external and internal and would be discussed in detail separately.

The next important factors are the impact of career on family. Profession takes both time and energy and this has a direct bearing on the well being on family. Professional men tend to focus more on their careers and leave the family issues to their spouses and not face problems at home. This at time causes disturbance/ turbulence in the personal life.

In modern society both partners pursue professional careers. These dual- career families have their typical pressure of role performance. These role pressures compel individuals to develop new strategies to include commitment to both career and families. Both partners make adjustments to his or her plans as required, volunteer to take on responsibilities etc.

Review Questions

1. What is career development and what are its objectives ?
2. Explain career development process with suitable illustrations ?
3. Distinguish between career and manpower planning ?
4. Write short notes on
   (*a*) Career Anchors.
   (*b*) Career Stages.
   (*c*) Career Curve.
   (*d*) Managing international careers.
5. How is career planned and developed in an organization ?
6. Define career development and its importance in the context changed work-force behaviour, short tenures and team operations ?
7. What is the importance of career development from individual's perspective ?
8. Explain the role of organizations in employees career development programme ?
9. Do you agree with thought that the 'career development paradigm will totally shift to individual perspective in future' ?

PROJECT WORK

Identify a company or study your own institution as to their career development practices and policies ? Prepare a career plan for an employee in your institution spanning a period of five years.

Present the write up in the class.

Case Study

Work Culture : HCL Perot Systems

HCL Perot Systems is a joint venture of HCL Technologies and Perot Systems Corporation. The company's emphasis on human resource gets reflected in the infrastructure, work culture and even the method of communication with employees as well as customers. HCL Perot Systems provides IT application services in verticals like finance, travel, telecommunication, healthcare and insurance. The wanted to do away with all those human resource policies that most of the time create conflicts within the organization. This meant transforming into a flat organization, having no titles to define people (everyone being called associates), and working as a team. The company was first to evolve the concept of spouse working in the same organization and at the same location. HCL Perot Systems has evolved over the years as an employee-friendly company.

A Matter of Freedom

At HCL Perot Systems, one mantra that overrules all is 'having fun at the work place'. Firmly believing that a good atmosphere can help increase productivity, HCL Perot Systems has invested a lot in making the workplace a lively and fun place. HCL Perot Systems is very conscious of its employees' preferences and most of the changes within the organization are made keeping their suggestion in mind.

Recruitment Process

Entry into HCL Perot Systems is not an easy task. The basic characteristics required to a placement in the company are individual's technical and behavioural strengths, along with domain knowledge and leadership skills. In addition company emphasizes on the entrepreneurial spirit and an individual's enthusiasm to make thing happen. HCL Perot Systems generally employs graduate engineers, MCA's and MBA's for all technical positions, with domain expertise.

Continuous Training

Training is an ongoing process at HCL Perot Systems. Apart from induction training the company also organizes monthly and quarterly training. The company also has a Competency Development Centers and Centers of Excellence which helping improving their manpower capabilities. The Competency Development Centers take care of the continuous enhancement of organizational and associate level capabilities. They also analyze trends and develop programmes to equip associates with expertise in new technology areas. The Centers of Excellence on the other hand, focus on developing emerging technologies and product competencies.

HCL Perot Systems also has a specialized programme for their top performers. Titled RACE (Renewed Adaptability in Changing Environment) Training, the programme help participants to understand and apply newfound knowledge, skills, and perspective within a single learning initiative. It is a combination of various forms of learning such as class room, psychometric-tool-based, outbound and one-to-one coaching.

Human Resource Policies

The company is very innovative in its human resource policies and has introduced the concept of 3Ts, 3Cs and 3As. The 3Ts stand for 'Triumph through Team Work', 3Cs stand for 'Contact, Connect and Communicate' and 3As stand for 'Access, Assist and Advice'. The company follows project based hierarchy with no designations to differentiate associates from one project to another. HCL Perot Systems firmly believes that employee development activities results in the overall growth of the organization, the company pays a lot of emphasis on career development activities of its employees. There is a wide scope of lateral movement and also emphasis on the rotation plan to utilize the latent potential of professionals

Appraisal System

For appraisal HCL Perot Systems does not follow a formal structure. After end of every project, HCL Perot Systems does project reviews. This helps the company in assessing an individual's true competence, which can later be used for career development, and to identify 'under performers' HCL Perot Systems has a robust management system called "Performance Improvement Plans". There are also schemes to identify star performers.

Questions

1. *Critically examine the work culture at HCL Perot Systems ?*
2. *Does the company support career development plans of organization and individuals ?*
3. *Do you think the human resource policies are adequate ? Suggest changes ?*

Chapter 11

JOB EVALUATION

★ LEARNING OBJECTIVES ★

After reading this chapter, you will be able to understand :

- Nature and concept of Job evaluation.
- Need and importance of job evaluation
- Objectives
- Explain the purpose of wage surveys

INTRODUCTION

A sound wage and salary structure is one of the prerequisite of good employer–employee relations and Industrial peace. In order to ensure pay is related to the nature and worth of job, it is essential to maintain pay differentials. These differentials should be based on sound principles which could be easily understood by all. To arrive at these differentials it is important to evaluate each job scientifically. This is accomplished by job evaluation.

What is Job Evaluation ?

Job evaluation is a systematic process for defining the relative worth or size of jobs or roles within an organization in order to establish internal relativities and provide the basis for designing an equitable grade structure *i.e.,* grading jobs in the structure and managing relativities. It is a process of methodically establishing a structure of jobs within an organization based on a systematic consideration of job content and requirement. Job evaluation basically specifies the relative value of each job in an organization. The purpose of job structure or hierarchy is to provide a basis for the pay structure or serve the purpose of compensation procedures.

Job evaluation developed out of civil service classification practices and has been in existence for over one hundred years. The first point system of evaluation was developed in 1920s. The spread of trade union movement gave impetus to job evaluation as employees gave more attention to wage structures. Job evaluation has received a great deal of attention in recent times as a result of social concerns.

Definition

The International Labour Organization has defined job evaluation as *"an attempt to determine and compare demands which normal performance of a particular job makes on normal workers without taking into account the individual abilities or performance of the workers concerned"* (ILO, New Series No . 56, 1960, p. 8).

The Bureau of Labour Statistics, USA defines job evaluation, *"as the evaluation or rating of the jobs to determine, their position in the job hierarchy. The evaluation may be achieved through the assignment of points or the use of some other systematic rating method for essential job requirements, such as skill, experience, and responsibility. Job evaluation is widely used in the establishment of wage rate structures and in the elimination of wage inequities. It is always applied to jobs rather than the qualities of individuals on the jobs* (Bureau of Labour Statistics, Bulletin 983, p. 11-12).

The British Institute of Management (1951, p. 77) defined it as, *"the process of analysis and assessment of jobs to ascertain reliably their relative worth using the assessment as a basis for a balanced wage structure."*

In the words of Netherlands Committee of Experts on Job Evaluation, *"job evaluation is a method which helps to establish a justified rank order of jobs as a whole being a foundation for the setting of the wages. Job evaluation is the only one of the process for establishing the relative differentiation of base wage rates."*

Kimball and Kimball define job evaluation as *"an effort to determine the relative every job in a plant to determine what the basic wage for such a job should be."*

Wendell French defines job evaluation *"as a process of determining the worth of various jobs within the organization, so that differential wages may be provided to jobs of different worth."*

We may define job evaluation as *"a method of determining the relative worth of a job to an organization"*. It is a process of analyzing and describing positions, determining their relative value by comparing duties of different positions in terms of their different responsibilities and other requirements. It is the quantitative measurement of relative job worth for the purpose of establishing consistent wage rate differentials by objective means. Job evaluation does not fix the price of a job but it merely fixes its relative worth.

When to Use Job Evaluation ?

Organizations often begin the process of designing wage structure by determining their job structure through job evaluation. Hence job evaluation is often used when :

- Determining pay and grading structures.
- Ensuring a fair and equal pay system.
- Deciding on benefits provision—*e.g.*, bonuses and fringe benefits etc.
- Comparing rates against the external market and environment.
- Undergoing organizational development in times of change.
- Undertaking career management and succession planning.

It is essential to have clear, detailed and up-to-date job descriptions on which to base the job evaluation. Most of the organizations utilize job evaluations as a major determinant for job classifications and wage determination. Formal job evaluation or informal comparison of job content is the almost universal base of pay rates. Job evaluation determines the relative position of the job in the organization's hierarchy. It is assumed that as long as job content remains unchanged it may be performed by individuals of varying abilities and proficiency.

Objectives of Job Evaluation

The job evaluation is primarily carried out to help the management to determine wage differentials in a systematic and logical basis; help in equitability of wage structure within the firm and consistency of firm's overall wage structure with that of the industry which the firm operates (Bureau of Labour Statistics, Bulletin 983). The general purpose of job evaluation may include a number of more specific goals :

(*a*) To provide a basis for a simpler, more rational wage structure.

(*b*) To provide an agreed-upon means of classifying new or changed jobs.

(*c*) To provide a base for individual performance measurements.

(*d*) Provide a framework for periodic review of wages and salaries.

(*e*) To provide information for compensation negotiations.

International Labour Organization in its report has clearly stated that the aim of the majority of systems of job evaluation is to establish, on agreed logical basis, the relative values of different jobs in a given plant or machinery, *i.e.*, it aims at determining the relative worth of a job. The principle upon all job evaluation schemes are based on assessing the relative value of jobs in the firms in terms of a number of factors, the relative importance of which varies from job to job. The main guiding principles involve :

(*a*) To secure and maintain complete, accurate and impersonal descriptions of each distinct job or occupation in the entire plant;

(*b*) To provide a standard procedure for determining the relative worth of each job in a plant;

(*c*) To determine the rate of pay for each job which is fair and equitable and is in consonance with other jobs in the plant, community or industry ?

(*d*) To ensure that like wages are paid to all qualified employees for life work.

(*e*) To promote fair and accurate consideration of all employees for advancement and transfer.

(*f*) To provide a factual basis for the consideration of wage rates for similar jobs in community and in an industry.

(*g*) To provide information for 'work organization, employees' selection, placement, training and numerous other similar problems.

TYPES OF JOB EVALUATION

There are two main types of job evaluation : analytical schemes, where jobs are broken down into their core components, and non-analytical schemes, where jobs are viewed as a whole. The use of an analytical scheme offers a better defense if a claim is made to an employment tribunal for equal pay for work of equal value.

Analytical Schemes

These offer greater objectivity in assessment as the jobs are broken down in detail, and are the ones most often used by organizations. Examples of analytical schemes include Points Rating and Factor Comparison.

Points Rating

This is the most commonly used method. Under this method, a quantitative evaluation of different jobs in terms of various factors is made. The key elements of each job, which are known as 'factors', are identified by the organization and then broken down into components. Each factor is assessed separately and points allocated according to the level needed for the job; the more demanding the job, higher the point's value. Maximum points are assigned to job factors required to be considered. Each factor is assessed separately and points allocated according to the level needed for the job. The more demanding the job, the higher the point's value, each job is then awarded points for each of the factors. The wage level appropriate for each job is fixed on the basis of total points scored by it. Factors usually assessed are given in Table 11.1.

Table 11.1. Factors Usually Included in Points Ranking Method

Knowledge and skills • work experience • qualifications • external qualifications • specialist training • length of service	**People management** • human relations skills • ability to deal with work pressure • supervisory responsibility
Communication and networking • social skills • enthusiasm • diplomacy	**Freedom to act** • depth of control • supervision received
Decision-making • Judgement • initiative • analytical ability	**Working environment** • knowledge of special working practices • breadth of management skill required
Impact and influence • efficiency • impact on customers • responsibility • results of errors	**Financial responsibility** • budgeting

The procedure for design of point method involves :

(*a*) **Listing of Jobs**. The jobs in an organization start from top management to floor worker, each requiring different skills and abilities. These jobs have unique characteristics requiring different mental and manual skills. Endeavour should be made to evaluate each of the job separately and distinctly. Jobs requiring dependability, adaptability and other character qualities and less tangible traits make it difficult to write adequate job descriptions and specifications.

(*b*) **Number of Factors.** There is no standard list of factors that may be considered for a job. It should however, be clearly understood that adequate number of factors should be considered to carryout evaluation of the job and its relative standing with other jobs in the organization. The selected jobs are analyzed and factors common to all these jobs are identified. The factors chosen should be measurable, significant, mutually exclusive and acceptable to both management and workers. The selected factors may be sub divided into sub-factors (Figure 11.1).

Factors	Sub-factors
Skill	Education, experience, training
Efforts	Physical and mental
Responsibility	Quality of output, raw materials, machinery etc.

Fig. 11.1. *Subdivisions of Factors into Sub-factors.*

(*c*) **Defining the Factors.** After the factors have been identified then these should be clearly defined to ensure proper evaluation. These definitions should be clearly made available to all evaluators.

(*d*) **Degree.** Having defined the factors then the next step involves determination of degrees for each factor. It is advisable to have even numbers degrees in the development of point method. Same number of degrees should be used for all factors to maintain consistency. The degree of education could be defined as given in Figure 11.2.

Degree	Definition
1	Should be able to do ordinary counting and understand verbal instructions.
2	Should be able to read and write.
3	Should be able to carry out mathematical calculations.

Fig. 11.2. *Defining Degree of a Factor.*

(*e*) **Allocation of points to Degrees.** The relative value of various factors depends upon their significance to the job. For assigning the points to degrees a committee may be appointed. The committee then determines how points should be apportioned among various factors. The percentage so assigned will become the number of points for first degree of that factor. The points to subsequent degrees of same factors should be assigned in arithmetic progression (Figure 11.3).

Factor	***Point Value of Degree***				
	1	***2***	***3***	***4***	***5***
Education	12	24	36	48	60
Experience	10	20	30	40	50
Responsibility	20	40	60	80	100

Fig. 11.3. *Allocation of Points to the Degrees.*

(*f*) **Evaluation of Jobs**. The points so assigned to different factors in a job are added up to find the total points which indicate the relative worth of a job. The information so collected should be studied carefully and compared it with degree definitions.

(*g*) **Assign Money Values**. Once the worth of a job in terms of total points is known these are connected to money values keeping in view the prevailing wage rates. A standard unit is assigned to each unit to convert point scores into monetary values

This scheme has the following advantages :

- Point method provides a rationale why jobs are ranked differently.
- It may be entered as a defence to an equal value claim.
- Assigning of points and money values is consistent thereby minimizing bias and human judgment.
- It will be seen generally as less subjective than non analytical techniques.
- Systematic wage differentials according to content of the job can be determined.

Like all other process there are some disadvantages. It is time consuming to introduce and can be complex and costly to undertake. In addition it can be seen to be an inflexible form of job evaluation in times of rapid change and can imply an arithmetical precision which is not justified.

Factor Comparison

Factor Comparison is similar to Points Rating, being based on an assessment of factors, though no points are allocated. Use of the Factor Comparison method is not as widespread as the Points Rating systems, because the use of points enables a large number of jobs to be ranked at one time.

Thomas E. Hitten was the first to introduce this method for job evaluation. The method determines the relative rank of the jobs to be evaluated in relation to monetary scale. It is mostly used to evaluate the white collar jobs. The method essentially employs the combination of ranking and point method. Like rank order method, it rates jobs by comparing one job with another job.

In this method five factors are generally evaluated for each job. The factors can be more however, the factors customarily evaluates are (*i*) mental requirements; (*ii*) skills; (*iii*) physical requirements; (*iv*) responsibilities; and (*v*) working conditions. The evaluation of job under this method involves :

(*a*) **Select factors and define them clearly**. This similar to process given in point method above.

(*b*) **Select the key job**. The key job so selected becomes a standard against which all other jobs are relatively assessed or compared.

(*c*) **Rank key job by factors.** Job descriptions are carefully analyzed and the key jobs are rated in terms of the selected factors.

(*d*) **Decide rates for key jobs**. A fair and equitable wage rate is determined for each job.

(*e*) **Evaluate the remaining jobs**. Each job is evaluated and compared to each other jobs in terms of each factor.

The factor comparison method provides certain advantages in that :

(*a*) It is relatively objective and more analytical as weights are not selected arbitrarily.

(*b*) It is flexible and has nor upper limit on the rating that a job may receive on a factor.

(*c*) The method utilizes few factors thus eliminating the likelihood of overlap.

(*d*) The procedure of rating new jobs by comparing with other standard or key jobs is logical and not too difficult.

The method suffers from limitations such as the use of present wages for the key jobs may initially build errors into the plan. The method is more complex and difficult to understand. The content and the value of these jobs may change over a period of time and this will lead to future errors. The method is expensive as experts need to be appointed and is time consuming.

Hay Group Method

The Hay approach to job evaluation is based on analyzing and measuring the extent to which each job in an organization requires the three elements of Know-how; problem solving and accountability. The analytical job evaluation scheme breaks jobs down into three factors which are each further sub-divided. Points are awarded for each factor using a predetermined scale which Hay published in the form of guide charts. The total points determine a job's place in the ranking order The scheme offers a framework for assessing jobs of all types and at all levels, although it has been used in practice for managerial jobs more than any other type of job. It reflects the contribution to the organization of jobs whose nature and balance of responsibilities may be quite different and allows for a wide range of information about the job to be taken into account. It is operated through trained job evaluation panels using guide charts to give a numerical score to each job. The guidance in using the guide charts has been modified by the Hay Group over time with the addition of sector-based sets of guidance as used in the NHS and latterly in higher education. The guide charts themselves and therefore the scoring systems are universal.

1. **Know-how**. Is defined as the sum of every kind of knowledge skill and experience to do a job. It consists of three independent but interrelated dimensions of
   - **Depth and breadth of know-how**. This related to the depth and breadth of knowledge and experience of practical procedures, specialized skills and techniques and professional disciplines, and covers the specialized knowledge required to do a given job. Such knowledge may be acquired either through formal education or through experience and exposure to practical issues, or a combination of these.
   - **The degree of planning, organizing, supervising, coordinating and managing**. This looks at the requirement of jobs for planning and organizing and relates to factors such as complexity, time span and scale. It can therefore, relate to activities within an individual role and/ or that are required in managing a network of relationships, line management or advising others to achieve a given end.
   - **Communicating and influencing**. The factor measures the requirement within jobs for working with, and through, others to achieve the results. The extent of human relations skills required. As such it takes into account elements such as the requirement to exchange information, influence, persuade, negotiate and change behaviour.
2. **Problem-solving**. It is defined as the self starting thinking required by the job holder in analyzing and evaluating information to arrive at conclusions, take actions and make recommendations. It consists of two interrelated dimensions :

- **The thinking environment**. Involves the complexity and intensity of problems arising in the job and the nature and scope of the thinking required to solve them. The extent to which job holders has rules, instructions, precedents, policies or parameters to define these issues which should be addressed. The fewer of these that are in place, the greater is the scope for problem solving in the job.
- **The thinking challenge**. The amount of analysis, judgment and innovation involved in analyzing situations by the job holder and making innovative and original recommendations.

  The problem solving factor is related to the know-how factor through the scoring scheme.

3. **Accountability**. Accountability is the answerability for action and for the consequences of that action. It is intended effect of the job on the university, the wider academic community or discipline. All jobs are accountable for producing and achieving some end results. The accountability of a job is analyzed and measured in terms of two independent but inter-related dimensions of
   - The degree of authority and discretion vested in the job and the answerability for the exercise of it or the extent to which the job holder has Freedom to Act, or can make decisions within limits defined by rules, procedures, policies, precedents or directions from superiors.
   - The type of service provided or the scope of roles impact on scale of the areas of activity on which the job is expected to have an impact and the nature of that impact.

     In addition to above the method also evaluates the physical and the environmental factors. These factors assess physical and environmental elements involved in the performance of jobs, over and above those experienced in a normal office environment. It has two dimensions (*i*) the physical effort or strain placed on he job holder in performing the job to the required standard; and (*ii*) the unfavourable working conditions to which the job holder is necessarily exposed in order to carry out the job to the required standard.

360° Performance Evaluation

The 360-degree evaluation is a common tool in human resource management. Simply put, it is a mechanism for evaluating someone's performance based on feedback from everyone with whom the individual comes in contact—supervisors, coworkers, partners, subordinates, the general public. It is a method of collecting input from many sources in an employee's environment.

Non-Analytical Schemes

The defining feature of non-analytical evaluation schemes is that whole jobs are compared with each other without any attempt to break down and analyze jobs under their various demands or components. These types of job evaluation schemes are particularly prone to discrimination because where whole jobs are being compared (rather than scores on components of jobs) judgments made by the evaluators can have little objective basis other than the traditional value of the job.

These are less objective than analytical schemes, but are often simpler and cheaper to introduce. Methods include job ranking, paired comparisons and job classification.

Job Ranking

It is the simplest of all the methods. Ranking is the process of comparing whole jobs with one another and arranging them in order of their perceived value to the organization. No specific factors are used for consideration. Job ranking is a simple process which reflects what people tend to do when comparing jobs, but :

- There are no defined standards for judging relative worth and there is therefore no rationale to defend the rank order—it is simply a matter of opinion.
- Ranking is not acceptable as a method of determining comparable worth in equal value cases.
- It may be hard to justify slotting new jobs into the structure or to decide whether or not there is a case for moving a job up the rank order, *i.e.,* re-grading.

Job ranking is done by putting the jobs in an organization in order of their importance, or the level of difficulty involved in performing them, or their value to the organization. Judgments are made about the roles based on aspects such as the jobs' scope and impact, their level of autonomy, the complexity of their tasks and the knowledge and skills needed. Once this analysis is done, the jobs together form a hierarchy which indicates the different levels, or ranks, within the organization.

Organizations often divide the ranks into grades. The number of grades chosen will depend on the organization's needs. This process is easily understood by employees and is relatively cheap to undertake.

Jobs are usually ranked in each department and then the department rankings are combined to develop an organizational ranking. Table 11.2 is a hypothetical illustration of ranking of jobs.

Table 11.2. Array of Jobs According to the Ranking Method

Rank salaries	*Monthly*
1. Accountant	Rs. 3,000
2. Accounts clerk	Rs. 1,800
3. Purchase assistant	Rs. 1,700
4. Machine-operator	Rs. 1,400
5. Typist	Rs. 900
6. Office boy	Rs. 600

Ranking done by utilizing job descriptions is done by studying and analyzing each job description. The difference between them is noted and key points selected for comparison. The rater then identifies which job requires the least amount of characteristics to perform it satisfactorily. The rater then puts that job at the lowest rank position. The rater then determines which job next requires the next higher amount of characteristics to perform it satisfactorily and places it next to preceding jobs rank and so till all jobs are ranked. When two or more jobs fall in the same rank position, these are assigned the same rank position. Several raters independently rank each job. The average of these ratings is calculated to determine the final ranking Table 11.3.

Table 11.3. Depicting Job Evaluation using Job Description to Rank the Jobs

Job	*Rater X*	*Rater Y*	*Rater Z*	*Average*
A				
B				
C				

Paired Comparisons

This is also a relatively simple technique. Each job is evaluated as a whole with each other job in turn, and points (0, 1 or 2) awarded according to whether its overall importance is judged to be less than, equal to, or more than the other jobs. Points awarded for each job are then totaled and a rank order produced. This method of job evaluation has all the advantages of job ranking and is slightly more systematic. However, it is best limited to organizations with a maximum of 30 jobs in a particular job population and, like job ranking; it does not involve any analysis of jobs nor indicate the extent of difference between them. Paired comparisons are not acceptable as a method of determining comparable worth in equal value cases.

This is a statistical technique used to compare each job with others in an organization. Using a ranking form, points are allocated to the job :

- Two points if it is considered to be of higher value.
- One point if it is regarded as equal worth.
- No points if it is less important.

The scores are added up and then the final overall ranking can be given. Paired comparisons gives greater consistency, but takes longer than job ranking as each job is considered separately Table 11.4.

Table 11.4. Paired Comparison Method of Job Evaluation

Pair	*More Difficult Job*	*Rank*
Refund Clerk – Transfer Clerk	Refund Clerk	1
Refund Clerk – Upper Division Clerk	Upper Division Clerk	2
Upper Division Clerk – Assistant	Assistant	3

Ranking Along a Number Line

This method is an extension of job description and paired comparison method. Here ranks obtained by paired comparison or from job descriptions are spaced along a number line. Job *x*, the highest ranked job is placed at the end of abscissa, as done in Table 11.5. Now another job *y*, is taken and a decision regarding its closeness to the highest ranked job which is *x* in the present case; on the basis of closeness of *y* to *x*, he former is located some selected distance from *x*. Similarly, other jobs can also be spaced by considering the closeness with the highest ranked and preceding the job.

Table 11.5. Ranking Along Number Line

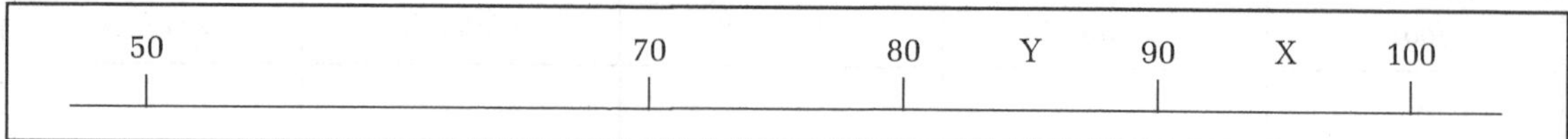

To establish rates of pay for these specific jobs, the rates of pay can be associated with those jobs in the rank order. Presumably the jobs already have wage rates attached to them, the ranking system is used to judge whether these are equitable. Ranking method is suitable for organization of relatively smaller size. Smaller size of organizations permits job raters to grasp job descriptions better. Ranking method has limited usefulness. A lot of subjective judgment is required to determine the relation and position of jobs in the rank order.

Job Classification

This method is also known as job grading. Before classification, an agreed number of grades are determined, usually between four and eight, based on tasks performed, skills, competencies, experience, initiative and responsibility. Clear distinctions are made between grades. The jobs in the organization are then allocated to the determined grades.

Job classification is the process of slotting jobs into grades by comparing the whole job with a scale in the form of a hierarchy of grade definitions. It is based on an initial definition of the number and characteristics of the grades into which jobs will be placed. The grade definitions may refer to such job characteristics as skill, decision making and responsibility. Job classification is the most used form of non-analytical job evaluation because it is simple, easily understood and at least, in contrast to whole-job ranking, it provides some standards for making judgments in the form of the grade definitions. However, it cannot cope with complex jobs which will not fit neatly into one grade; thee grade definitions tend to be so generalized that they may not be much help in evaluating border-line cases; fails to deal with the problem of evaluating and grading jobs in dissimilar occupational or job families where the demands made on job holders are widely different and grade definitions tend to be inflexible and unresponsive to changes affecting roles and job content..

Internal Benchmarking or Job Matching

Internal benchmarking or job matching simply means comparing the job under review with any internal benchmarked job. The benchmarked job is believed to be properly graded and paid for. Thereafter, all other jobs are slotted into the same grade as the benchmark job. The comparison is usually made on a whole job basis without analysing the jobs factor by factor. Internal benchmarking is a simple and quick method of job evaluation, but :

- it relies on judgements which may be entirely subjective and could be hard to justify.
- it is dependent on the identification of suitable benchmarks which are properly graded and such comparisons may only perpetuate existing inequities.
- it is not acceptable as a defence in equal value cases.

DESIGNING JOB EVALUATION SCHEMES

Both analytical and non-analytical schemes can be developed. Organisations can develop a system themselves, use consultants, buy a consultancy's off-the-shelf package, or employ the consultancy to tailor the package to suit the organisation.

The Hay Guide Chart-Profile Method is the most widely used scheme, but there are many other schemes developed by other consultancies. What is chosen will depend on the size of the organisation and the aim of the job evaluation exercise. It is possible to use different schemes for different types of employee.

Implementing a Scheme

When introducing job evaluation for the first time, it's important to communicate with employees. The process is at Figure 11.4. For efficient implementation of a wage scheme it is important that Job evaluation is carried out. Job evaluation will follow the five steps as illustrated in Figure 11.4.

Step 1-Communicate. The management must communicate the idea to the employees. Usually the employees suspect any measure to carryout evaluation of their job. They consider it a ploy to get more work out of them and pay less. Hence the first step is to communicate and bring stake-holders on board to agree to carryout job evaluation

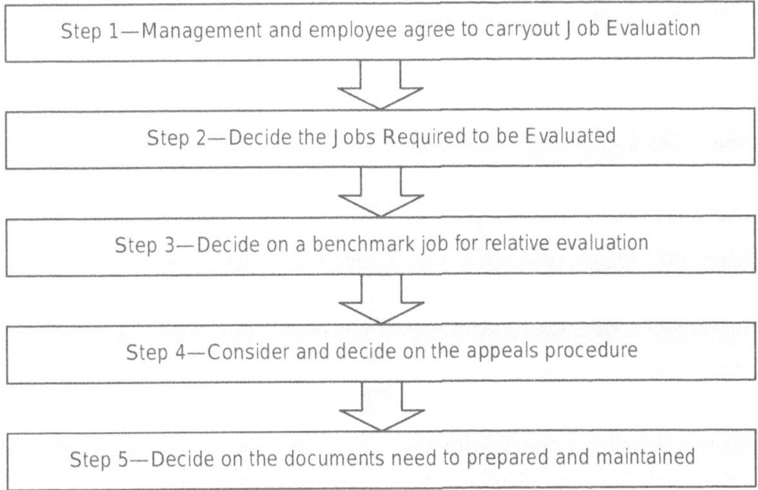

Fig. 11.4. *Process of Job Evaluation.*

Step 2-Determine Jobs to Be Evaluated. The second step is to decide the jobs to be evaluated and ensure that proper job descriptions of the same are available to the evaluators.

Step 3-Decide on Benchmark Job. The next step is for all stakeholders to determine and agree for a job against which the relativity of the other jobs would be compared and compensation decided.

Step 4-Decide on Appeal Procedure. The workers are suspicious of Job Evaluation and hence it is imperative that the stakeholders decide on the method of appeals if they are not satisfied with the outcome of evaluation.

Step 5-Decide on Documentation. Compensation is an emotional issue. It has a wide psychological impact on persons. The documents enable persons to scrutinize and satisfy himself that justice has been done while determining his compensation. For any process to stand legal scrutiny it is imperative that proper documentation should be prepared.

In wage setting it is beneficial to reconcile market information and job evaluation results than to singly rely on either. Unique jobs are more appropriately priced on the basis of job evaluations. Firms can depend more heavily on job market for common jobs. In most cases employees have to satisfy both job evaluation and the market. To state it simply, so long as the supply of workers exceeds the demand for workers, there will be bidding for jobs. This means that unemployed workers will take jobs for a lower wage, thus bidding down wages. On the other hand, when the demand for workers at a certain wage, exceeds the supply of workers who are seeking jobs, then establishments must offer more to secure the workers. This tends to bid up the wage which must be paid.

To summarize wages tend to be fixed by demand and supply at the point where the wage is equal to the marginal product.

Not all workers are equally efficient. Some workers are stronger, or more intelligent, or have been on that particular job much longer (seniority); thus are worth more because they produce more. Why, then, should all workers receive the same wage ? True, in real life workers are not all alike. Workers, who consistently produce more because of one or more of the reasons just noted, generally are aware of this fact and demand a higher wage. Their firms or companies are apt, also, to be aware of their superior efficiency and to pay them higher wages. Otherwise such workers may seek other jobs.

Review Questions

1. What is Job Evaluation ? How is it different from Job Analysis ? Discuss.
2. Define Job Evaluation and discuss its advantages and disadvantages ?
3. Examine the concepts of job evaluation and describe the different schemes of job evaluation.
4. Explain the different techniques of job evaluation. What are the advantages and disadvantages of each technique ?
5. Explain briefly the analytical techniques of job evaluation ?
6. Explain the process of job evaluation ?
7. 'Job Evaluation determines the worth of a job and not a job holder.' Comment.
8. Examine the concept of job evaluation and describe the different schemes for job evaluation.
9. Should job evaluation depend on an appraisal of the job holder's performance ? Why ? Why not ?
10. Briefly discuss the quantitative methods of job evaluation.

PROJECT WORK

Visit the firm adjacent to your location. Ascertain the job evaluation process used and present it in the class.

Case Study

Case Study 1

THE MAHESHWARI SUGAR MILLS

The Maheshwari Sugar Mills is a well established and a reputed company. However, in spite of large number of people applying to find a job with it there are no takers to work in the boiler room. The work is hot, dirty and heavy. It requires physical endurance. The job evaluation of the company has rated the job low in intelligence and physical ability. Most of the jobs in the boiler room are weighted relatively lower at the bottom of the wage scale.

Management is finding it difficult to find people to work in the boiler room. Often management has to employ people who cannot get jobs elsewhere. This has led to breakdowns and lowering of the status of the workers employed in the boiler.

Questions

1. *How the problem should be handled ?*
2. *Is there a need for reevaluation of jobs in the firm ?*
3. *How should management deal with the reactions of other workers and raise the status of boiler workers ?*

Case Study 2

The foundry has always been regarded as one of the worst places to work in Bhushan Steel manufacturing Company. The work is hot, dirty and heavy. Physical endurance, rather than brains and intelligence, is considered as chief requirement to get the job done in the foundry. Yet according to job evaluation plan of the company, 'physical ability' and 'working conditions' are weighted relatively lower than 'responsibility', 'training' and 'skill'. As a result, most of the foundry jobs are rated lower or are at the bottom of the wage scale of the company.

In recent years, it has become increasingly difficult to get men for working in the foundry. Often, management had to employ men who could not get jobs elsewhere due to their personal limitations in terms of ability, intelligence and competence. This has led to further lowering of the already low social status of the foundry in the eyes of other employees in the plant. The matter has reached a level of crisis now. There are vacancies but no person to fill, as no new men are coming forward for the job.

The human resource manager of the company has a difficult task on his hand.

Questions

1. *How this problem should be handled ?*
2. *What should the human resource manager suggest to the management ?*
3. *How should management deal with the reaction of other workers if it decided to increase foundry wages ?*

Chapter 12

COMPENSATION

★ LEARNING OBJECTIVES ★

After reading this chapter, you will be able to understand :

- What is compensation ?
- Objectives of wage and salary administration.
- Explain employer concern of developing a strategic compensation plan.
- Factors Affecting Compensation.
- Methods of compensation evaluation.
- Identify major provisions of Indian Laws affecting compensation.

INTRODUCTION

Compensation is what an employee receives in exchange for the services rendered in an organization. Determination of an equitable compensation structure is one of the most important phases of employee-employer relations. The term 'compensation' refers to all forms of financial returns and tangible benefits that employee receive as part of the employment relationship. For harmonious working environment it is imperative that each employee receives sufficient salary to maintain a dignified life and feel satisfied with the relationship with his wages and wages of other people. The primary objective of compensation administration is that each employee is equitably compensated for the services rendered by him to the enterprise on the basis of (*i*) nature of job; (*ii*) present worth of that type of job; (*iii*) the effectiveness with which the individual performs the job.

The first two are closely related to job evaluation and the thirds to performance appraisal. Generally, compensation within an organization is determined by a flow of events including job analysis, writing of job descriptions and specifications, job evaluation, surveys of wages and salaries etc. This sequence is depicted in Figure 12.1.

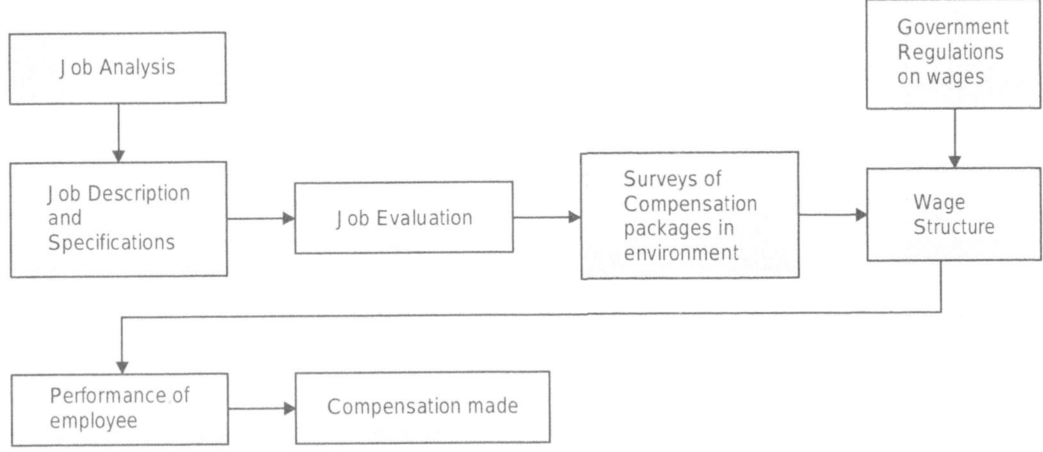

Fig. 12.1. *Sequence of Determination of Compensation Package.*

For the employer too, employee remuneration is significant because of its contribution to the cost of production. It is also the main cause leading to strikes, lockouts and conflict between management and the workers.

Meaning of Compensation

Compensation practices are intended to be effective tools in addressing business needs. In English 'compensation' is something that counters balances, offsets, or makes up for something else, which means entitlement, return and reward. Compensation is what man receives in exchange of his labour or services rendered in an organization. The term 'compensation' refers to all forms of financial, non financial returns and tangible benefits that employees receive as a part of the employment relationship. (Figure 12.2) It can be stated that compensation is a statement of an employee's worth by an employer and is designed to :

(*a*) Attract capable employees.

(*b*) Motivate for better performance.

(*c*) Retain an employee.

Compensation may be defined as money received in the performance of work, plus the many kinds of benefits and services that organizations provide their employees. Money is included under direct compensation; while the benefits come under indirect compensation, and may consist of life, accident and health insurance etc. M. Bloom has defined compensation as;

"Compensation is a return received in exchange for people's efforts and ideas at the workplace. Exchange is key part of relationship. For most people, many of the terms and conditions for their employment exchanges are left unstated, forming an implicit contract."

There is an implicit contract between employers and employees over their reciprocal obligations and returns. Employees contribute towards achieving the goals of the employers in exchange of returns given by the employer and valued by the employee.

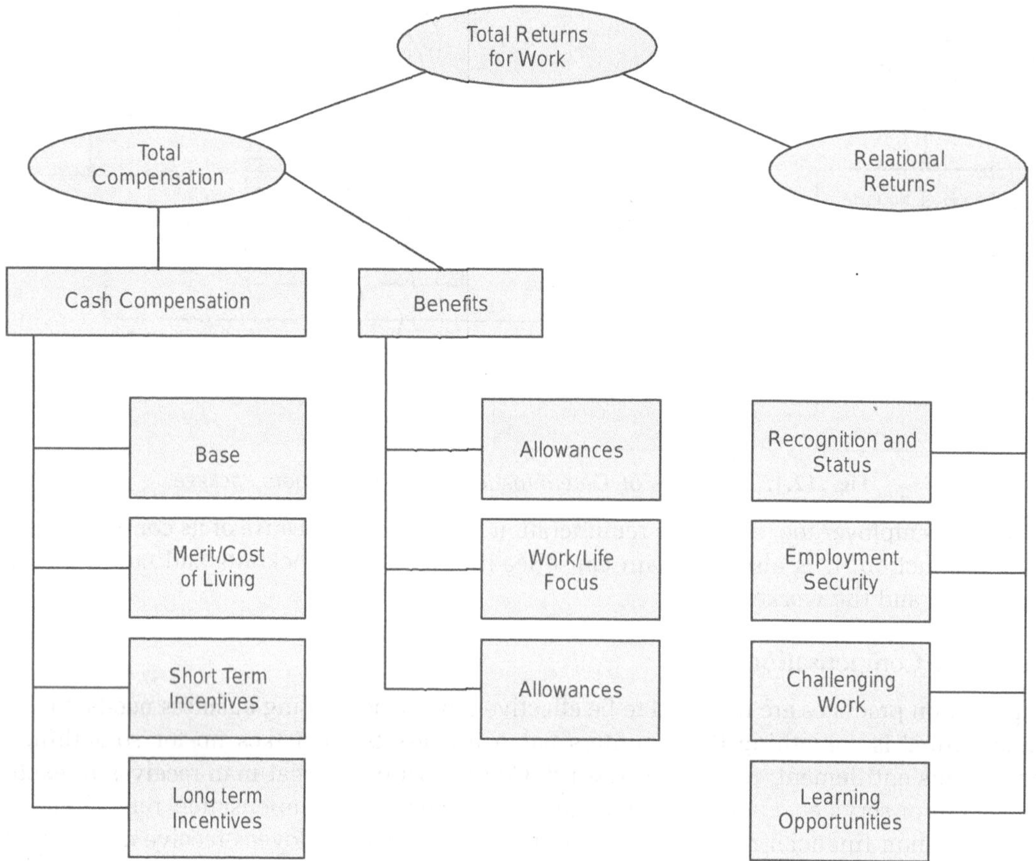

Fig. 12.2. *Total Return for Work.*

Compensation is an important work reward for most people. Employees/workers expect their wages will (*i*) cover their basic living expenses, (*ii*) keep up with inflation, (*iii*) leave some money for savings or recreation; and (*iv*) pay should increase over time.

COMPARABLE WORTH DOCTRINE

We will first distinguish between *comparable worth* and *equal pay for equal work.* Some work in an organization may be filled mostly by men and others by women this is slowly changing. However, it is seen women work is underpaid in comparison with different but comparable 'men's work.'

Earning Gap

Advocates of *comparable worth doctrine* agree some jobs are dominated by women and some by men and some by women and women often earn less than man. The earning gap between man and women has been cited by advocates of comparable worth as clear evidence of discrimination. This analogy can be extended to minorities, handicapped and many more groups.

Advocates of comparable worth feel that market orientation should not be the only criteria but job evaluation should be the basis of determining the wages.

A 'wage' is the remuneration paid, for the service of labour in production, periodically to an employee/worker. In broad sense it means any economic compensation paid by an employer under some contract to an employee for the services rendered by him. "Wages" usually refer to hourly or daily rate paid to such groups as production and maintenance employees (usually the blue color workers).

Salaries' normally refer to the weekly or monthly rates paid to clerical, administrative or professional employees, usually referred to as 'white color employees'. The basic wage is the remuneration by way of basic salary paid to an employee. Allowances are on the other hand paid in addition to the basic wage to maintain the value of the basic wage over a period of time. Such allowances include holiday pay, overtime, bonus and social security. Under Payment of Wages Act, 1936, Section 2 (*vi*), 'any award of settlement and production bonus, if paid, constitutes wages.'

Objectives of Compensation Planning

To be objective any compensation paid should be tied to performance. While incentives can yield the clearest link between performances and pay these are not suitable for all jobs. Compensation motivates the employee for increased work performance. The objectives of compensation are to :

(*a*) Assist in attracting and retaining qualified and competent employees.

(*b*) Motivate for better performance, fosters a feeling of equity, and provides direction to their efforts.

(*c*) It supports, communicates, and reinforces an organization's culture, values and competitive strategies.

(*d*) Retain an employee.

The other important objective of any compensation system is fairness and equity. To establish fair and equitable remuneration, there should be fair internal and external equity in remuneration paid to employees. Internal equity means similar pay for similar work. In other words the differential in wages should be in proportion to the worth of the jobs. External equity implies pay for a job should be equal to pay for similar job in other organizations. Payments based on employee's performance, industry levels, minimizes favouritism and inequities in pay; and lastly *Individual Equity* which ensures equal work for equal pay that is, each individual pay is fair in comparison to that of another person doing the same or a similar job.

Pay is the dominant organizational reward. Organization provides reward to their employees to encourage and motivate them to perform at their optimum level as also retain qualified and competent employee.

THEORIES OF WAGES

Different thinkers and writers have come up with many theories for determination of wages.

Subsistence Theory

The subsistence theory was propounded by David Ricardo. The theory has also been referred to as *'Iron law Wages.'* The theory is based on two assumptions;

(*a*) The law of diminishing return applies to industry.

(*b*) There is rapid increase in population.

The theory states that the 'workers are paid to enable them to subsist and perpetuate the race without increase or diminution.' There is a minimum limit of wages below which labour supply will not be available. This theory also limits labour to minimum standard of living and no chance for improving his condition.

This theory has its limitation :

(*a*) The theory is based on the concept of population increasing if the standards of living improve. In fact it has been observed there is drop in rate of population if the living conditions improve as is observed in developing countries.

(*b*) The theory also limits itself to supply of labour and not to demand. The rate of wage is dependent on the demand and supply. A person with scarce talent is paid higher wages than trades easily available.

(*c*) The theory does not emphasize the working trends or efficiency of the work force.

(*d*) The theory also fails to give reasons for differential in wages due different categories of workers and geographic locations.

Wage Fund Theory

The theory was developed by Adam Smith and further expounded by J.S. Mill. The theory states that the wages are paid out of a predetermined fund which lay surplus with wealthy persons, as a result of their savings. The quantum of wages to be paid is determined by the size of the fund; if the fund is large higher wages could be paid, but if the fund is small the wages could be reduced to subsistence level. J.S. Mill opinioned that the quantum of wages paid is determined by demand and supply of labour; or the proportion between population and capital available. The amount of wage fund being fixed the wages cannot be increased without proportional decrease in labour or vice versa. In this theory it is stated that it is the wage fund that will determine employment and wage or it is wage fund that determine supply of labour.

This theory has its limitation in that it is clear from where the wage fund would come from; the theory is silent on efficiency of workers; also theories base is questionable in that it states that first wage fund be created and then wages paid.

Surplus Value Theory

Karl Marx propounded this theory. According to this theory labour is an article of commerce which could be purchased on payment of *'subsistence price.'* The price of any product is determined by the labour time required for producing it. In actual fact the labourer is not paid in proportion to the time spent in producing the product but much less, and large proportion of surplus goes to meet the demands of other expenses viz. interest, up keep etc.

Residual Claimant Theory

Francis A. Walker propounded this theory; according to him, there are four factors of production viz. land, labour, capital and entrepreneurship. Wages represent the amount of value created in the production which remains after payment has been made for other three factors of production. It can safely be assumed that labour is a *residual claimant.* The wages thus represent :

$$\text{Wages} = \text{Total Production} - (\text{Rent} + \text{Interest} + \text{Profit})$$

This theory takes in to consideration of efficiency and rise in productivity. It states if the productivity of worker rises there would be larger production and in turn greater surplus for distribution as wages. This theory also recognizes the importance of workers stakes in the national income.

Marginal Productivity Theory

This theory is developed by P.H. Wicksteed (England) and J.B. Clark (USA), it states that wages are based upon entrepreneur's estimate of the value that will probably be produced by the last or marginal worker. It assumes that wages are dependent upon demand and supply of labour. Consequently workers are paid what they are economically worth. The result is that the entrepreneurs have larger share of in profit. As long as the worker contributes more to profit the entrepreneur will keep on hiring but if it turns uneconomical the entrepreneurs will stop hiring and seek new technology.

Like all other theories this theory also has its limitations in that in actual practice the workers are paid less than the marginal productivity of labour. The theory places it concepts in idealistic conditions which do not exist in actual practice and lastly it views that larger number of people can be hired, however that is possible only if additional facilities are created. It has also been observed that trade Unions are able to secure greater wages for worker even though the employer should be fair.

Bargaining Theory

John Davidson while writing stated that wages are determined by relative bargaining power. When Trade Unions are involved the wages and other compensation is determined by the relative strengths of employers and trade unions. This is possible in large plants; as the profits earned by the enterprise play an important role in determining the bargained wages.

Behavioural Theory

Many of the behavioural scientist and psychologists have presented their views on wages and salaries on the basis of research studies and action programmes conducted by them. It has been found that wages are determined by factors such as :

(*a*) Size of the Company

(*b*) Reputation of the Company

(*c*) Strength of Unions.

(*d*) Political Climate.

(*e*) Government Policies.

Wage differentials are explained by researchers due norms, traditions, customs prevalent in the organization, psychological pressures on the management, prestige attached to certain jobs and need to maintain internal and external consistency.

PSYCHOLOGICAL CONTRACT

Modern Organizations can't succeed unless the people they employ agree to contribute to their mission and survival. But flatter organizations, dispersed workforce geographically, and ever increasing aspiration levels for service and innovation make it impossible for employers to motivate workers strictly through supervision or monetary incentives. Instead, workers and employers need to agree on contributions that workers will make to the firm and vice versa. Understanding and effectively managing these psychological contracts can help organizations thrive.

Definition

Psychological contracts are beliefs, based upon promises expressed or implied, regarding an exchange agreement between an individual and, in organizations, the 3 employing firms and its agents (Roussearu, 1995).

In essence psychological contracts motivate workers to fulfill commitments made to employers when workers are confident that employers will reciprocate and fulfill their end to the bargain.

Features of Psychological Contract

Scholars have identified six features (Rousseau, 1995).

1. **Voluntary Choice**. Psychological Contract motivate people to fulfill their commitments because they are based on the exchange of promises in which individual has freely participated. Commitments made voluntarily tend to be kept.
2. **Belief in Mutual Agreement**. An individual's psychological contract reflects his or her own understanding of the commitments made with another. Individuals act on that understanding as if it is mutual, regardless of whether that is the case in reality.
3. **Incompleteness**. Psychological contracts tend to incomplete as neither the employer nor the employee can spell out all the details of long term relationship. Hence, psychological contracts tend to become more elaborate over the course of employment.
4. **Multiple Contract Makers**. Contract is influence by multitude of stakeholders providing inputs. These inputs impact the psychological relationship between employer and employee.
5. **Managing Losses when Contracts Fail**. When two parties rely on psychological contract to fulfill obligations then the failure of one party to fulfill anticipated commitments result in 'losses.' Such losses are the main reason for why violation of psychological contract generate strong reaction of anger, disgust etc.
6. **Contract Model of Employment** Relationship. Psychological contract provides a stable understanding of what to expect in the future and guides efficient action without much need of practice.

Types of Psychological Contract

Although the psychological contract can involve a host of relational commitments, there are general pattern that differentiate how workers and employers behave towards each other (Roussearu, 1995).

Relational Psychological Contracts includes such terms as loyalty and stability. Workers with relational contracts tend to be more willing to work overtime whether paid or not, to help co workers on the job and support organizational changes. Workers in relational mode are likely to be more upset when contract is violated. Failure to remedy the situation leads to turnover (Roussearu, 1995).

Transactional Psychological Contracts includes such terms as narrow duties and a limited or short duration. Workers with transactional contracts tend to adhere to its specific terms and to seek employment elsewhere fail to live up to their agreement. Transactional contracts shift the risk associated from employer to the employee.

Balanced Psychological Contracts have emerged recently. These contracts combine the open ended time frame and mutual concern of relational agreements with performance demands and renegotiations of transactional contracts. It combines commitment on the part of the employer to develop worker and anticipating that the worker will be flexible and willing to adjust if economic conditions change. In such contracts renegotiations are anticipated as conditions of work and needs change overtime.

It should be appreciated that agreement between worker and employer on what each owes to other is critical to the employment relationship's success.

From the employers point of view the important aspect is the role that managers play. Managers play an important role in shaping workers psychological contract, supportive managers can serve to amplify or downplay messages sent by firms human resource practices. Mangers also report using psychological contract in the way they use rewards, motivate and inform employees about firm's future plans. Psychological contract for employer covers the aspects of competence, effort, compliance, commitment and loyalty.

Schein in his works has suggested that people who work effectively and are committed shape their psychological contracts in a manner :

(*a*) The degree to which their expectations are met by the organization or their career goals fulfilled.

(*b*) The nature of what is actually to be exchanged. The workers who have negotiated special employment arrangements not available to others are more likely to believe they have relational contracts. These psychological contracts have powerful effects when created among current employees as opposed to during recruiting.

(*c*) Thirdly, personality plays an important role in psychological contracts. Workers who are conscientious and possess high self esteem are more likely to report having relational contract, because they behave in ways that employers value highly. In contrast the transactional workers are likely to be more sensitive to issues like fairness, terms and conditions and formal contract.

Some Points for Implementation of Psychological Contract

In modern global environment where teams operate and organizations are becoming flatter, the need for psychological contracts has assumed greater importance. Consequently the employers should manage the psychological contract.

(*a*) Organization should endeavour to implant psychological contract with its workers throughout by taking responsibility of the messages it sends.

(*b*) Organizations should have clear rules about the rules of contract. It requires open exchange of information between parties to learn about others interests, goals, and constraints.

(*c*) Psychological contract rests on pillars of promises, expectations and obligations. Given the environmental conditions, competitiveness, need to innovate, adapt and evolve rapidly; it is imperative that there should be flexibility in psychological contract must also be flexible enough to allow the company to adapt. The company in turn should be sensitive to losses if any being incurred by employees.

EMPLOYMENT RATIONALE

Having seen the meaning and theories of compensation it is essential to understand the rationale of employer's attitude towards hiring an employee. There are two distinct type of employer attitude that has been observed viz. transactional and relational.

In transactional system the employer usually treats the employee as a commodity and compensates him for his labour. In this there is no commitment towards the growth and development of the employee. In turn there is less commitment of the employee towards the organization. In relational system there is greater commitment of the employee towards the organization.

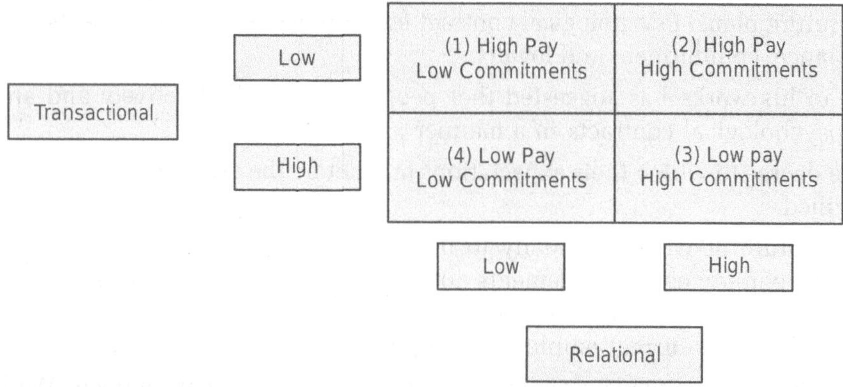

Fig. 12.3. *Model of Employment Rationale.*

If the transactional and relational systems are placed on two dimensional models as depicted in Figure 12.3, it would be observed that at the left lower where the employer has high transactional behaviour and low relational attitude then there would low pay and low commitment (Quadrant 4). It will be observed that if there is high transactional and high relational (Quadrant 3) there would be low pay and high commitment. The best for an organization would be high relational and low transactional behaviour for an employee and employer.

METHODS OF WAGE PAYMENTS

Wages are paid to an employee for his labour. Wage payment is an important function of an employer as it affects the total wage bill and in turn total expenditure. Higher the expenditure without incremental increase in production/ sales reduces the profit margin. It can be safely stated that wage bill has a direct impact on the profitability. International Labour Organization Classifies all incentive scheme in four categories.

(*a*) Schemes where the workers' earnings vary in the same proportion as output.

(*b*) Schemes where earnings vary less proportionately than output.

(*c*) Schemes where earnings vary proportionately more than output.

(*d*) Schemes where earnings differ at different levels of output.

Incomes Varying in Same Proportion as Output

Piece Wage System

In these schemes the gains or losses resulting directly from a workers output accrue to him or her leaving to the employer any gains or losses in overhead costs per unit of output. In piece wage system the worker is paid on the basis of output. The workers are paid on the basis of the number of units produced or amount of work completed.

Wages = Number of Units Produced × Rate per Unit

In this system the rate per unit remains the same irrespective of the number of units produced. This is also referred to as **Straight Piece Rate System.** F.W. Taylor introduced the **Differential Piece Rate System**. Under Differential piece Rate System different wages are prescribed. The higher piece rate is meant to be paid for efficient worker and lower rate is paid to an inefficient worker. Taylor wanted to use the Differential Piece Rate System as an incentive plan. It has been observed the employees/workers prefer Straight Piece Rate System.

Piece rate system is preferred method :

(*a*) When methods of production are standardized and the job is of repetitive nature.

(*b*) When the productivity of the worker is to be improved.

(*c*) When out put is high quality.

(*d*) Where work does not require high skills.

Advantages of Piece Wage System. The major advantages of piece wage system are :

(*a*) **Fairness**. The major advantage of piece wage system is it is very fair. It has direct relationship between wage and productivity of the worker. It provides incentive to worker to increase production.

(*b*) **Costing**. Costing of production becomes easier as wages are a constant factor of each unit of output.

(*c*) **Economy**. The process is economical as the total cost of production comes down with larger output. The fixed overhead burden can be distributed over a greater number of units.

(*d*) **Supervision**. This system is based on individual's effort. Greater the productivity of worker higher the wage and hence, it requires less supervision. However, quality control has to be ensured/ maintained. This system is not very suitable for highly technical, sophisticated and quality products.

Disadvantages. The piece wage system suffers from certain drawbacks like all processes. The piece wage system is suitable for low end products. The workers are constantly under tension in that if they do not produce they will not be paid. The employees are also under threat that employer can cut prices if the workers start producing large quantity of product. There is large administrative work to determine output of each employee as also to ensure quality of product.

Time Wage System

It is the oldest and most common system of wage payment. It is based on the basis of time spent on a job. The period of time may be an hour, a day, a week a fortnight etc. however, the wages are paid after the time fixed for work has been completed. In the standard hour system also called

100 percent gains sharing, standard time in terms of hours is fixed for completion of the job. It is a non variable method of wage payment.

Wages = Number of Hours Worked × Rate Per Hour

Use of Time Wage System. The time wage system could be used in :

(*a*) When it is difficult to fix the standard time for completing the job.

(*b*) When quality of work is of utmost importance.

(*c*) When job relates to office/administration etc.

(*d*) When work requires intellectual activity.

(*e*) Where the technology used is complex and requires greater professional and skill competencies.

Advantages of Time Wage System. The Time Wage System offers advantages as :

(*a*) **Acceptable**. Oldest and easily understood system, Labour Unions prefer this system since this form of payment does not make any discrimination.

(*b*) **Simplicity**. An important advantage is its simplicity in calculating wages which depends upon the time spent on job.

(*c*) **Equality of Wages**. Under this method all workers doing similar work are paid equal wages.

(*d*) **Adaptable**. The system is adaptable as work greater skills and professional knowledge can earn higher wages.

Disadvantages. The major disadvantages of this system is that it breeds in efficiency as all workers are paid similar wages for time spent and there is no linkage of wage with efficiency/ productivity; time wage system does not motivate an employee to perform at greater efficiency; lastly it requires greater supervision as there is human tendency to shirk work (especially in India worker will not produce any good if not supervised).

Table 12.1. Comparison of Time and Piece Wage Systems

Basis	*Time Wage System*	*Piece Wage System*
Basis of payment	Wages determined on the basis of time spent	Wages determined on the basis of pieces produced.
Nature of Wage	Wages guaranteed to every worker present.	Wages directly linked to productivity.
Efficiency	Not an efficient process	Efficient as worker paid on productivity.
Quality	High	Low
Cost of maintenance	Low	High; worker concerned with production only.
Supervision	Need for close supervision.	Low, payment of wages on productivity.
Attitude of Trade Union	Support it.	Trade Union dislikes this system.

Income Varying Proportionately less than Output

Four allied but different schemes come in this group. The common feature in all is that *time* is used as the measure of output and bonus is paid on the time saved, that is, the difference between the standard time set for the job and the time actually taken. These schemes are referred as 'gain sharing schemes' as both the employer and employee share the gains resulting from the saved time. These systems are often applied in cases where it is not possible to set standards or to measure the worker's output accurately.

Halsey System

Under this system, standard time is fixed for the completion of a job and rate hour is then determined. This is combination of time piece and rate piece methods. The worker is guaranteed a time rate with an alternative piece rate. If the worker piece rate wage exceeds the time wage system he is granted credit. If however he piece rate wage is less than time wage, the worker is paid time wage but the deficit is carried forward as debt to be recovered in future (Table 12.2).

Table 12.2. Balance of Debt Method

Worker	*Piece Rate Wages (Rupees)*	*Time Rate Wages (Rupees)*	*Credit (Rupees)*	*Debit (Rupees)*	*Balance (Rupees)*
Ram	150 × 2 = 300	300	Nil	Nil	Nil
Rahim	150 × 1 = 150	300	Nil	150	Nil
John	150 × 3 = 450	300	150	Nil	150

From the Table 12.2 it would be observed that the piece rate wage is Rupees 150/- while the Time rate wage for a duration is Rupees 300/-. In this the worker Ram gets no credit as he is able to produce two pieces of a product during the time stipulated for time rate by employer. However, the worker John produces three he gets the credit of one piece or Rupees 150/- while Rahim produces only and hence he is in debit of Rupees 150/-. It would be observed all are paid the wage of Rupees 300/-. In this method the employees gets a sense of security about his employment at the same time there is an incentive for a worker to work harder and earn more than his guaranteed wage.

Rowan Plan

Incentive bonus here is not calculated at a fixed percentage of time saved. It is the ratio of the actual time taken to the standard time of the job. Under this system standard time and rate hour are fixed. If the time taken to complete the job is equal to or exceeds the standard time, the employee is paid for the time taken at the rate per hour. If the time taken is less than the standard time taken then he is paid bonus. The bonus is usually paid as a percentage of the worker's time rate. Incentive bonus is used by using the formula :

$$\textbf{Bonus} = \frac{T}{S}(S - T) \times R$$

Where,

T = actual time taken by the worker

S = standard time set for the job.

(S – T) = Difference between standard and actual time.

R = Hourly rate of wages.

Rowan system operates as under :

Standard Time : 8 hours.

Rate per hour : 4 Rupees Per Hour

There are three individuals A, B and C. A produces the item in 8 hours, B produces the item in 10 hours, and C produces the item in 6 hours. Then the payments would be as under :

A would receive :

Time taken 8 hours, at the rate of Rupees 4/- per hour or Rupees 32/-.

B would receive :

Time Taken 10 hours, at the rate of Rupees 4/- per hour or Rupees 40/-.

C would receive :

Time taken 6 hours, at the rate of Rupees 4/- per hour or Rupees 24/-. In addition he would receive a bonus in proportion to time saved or Rupees 2/8 × 4= Rupees 1/- or Rupees 25/-.

Barth Variable Sharing System

This system does not guarantee the time rate. The workers pay is ascertained by multiplying the standard hour by the number of hours actually taken to do the job, taking the square root of the product and multiplying it by the workers hourly rate.

Taking the example of the example of Rowan Plan of A, B and C. The payments would be as under :

A would receive $\sqrt{8 \times 8} = 8$ at the rate of Rupees 4/- per hour Rupees 32/-.

B would receive $\sqrt{8 \times 10} = 8.94$ at the rate of Rupees 4/- per hour Rupees 35. 77/-.

C would receive $\sqrt{8 \times 6} = 6.96$ at the rate of Rupees 4/- per hour Rupees 27.71/-.

Bedaux Scheme

Under the Bedaux Scheme, standard time for a job is fixed. Each minute of the standard time is called a point or B. Each job has a standard number of Bs. The worker receives the bonus at the rate of seventy five percent of the number of points earned, in excess of 60 per hour, multiplied by one sixtieth of the workers hourly rate.

Taking the same case as explained in Rowan plan. A and B would receive payments as hourly basis as no bonus is earned. C would be paid as under :

Actual time 6 hours at the rate of Rupees 4/- or Rupees 24/-.

Bonus :

Standard Bs = 8 × 60 = 480.

Actual Bs = 6 × 60 = 360.

Bs Saved = 120.

Bonus = 75% of 120 × 4/60= Rupees 6/-

Total Earnings = 24 + 6 = Rupees 30/-

Priestman Production Plan

This is a popular group incentive plan. In this the employees are paid a guaranteed time wage and incentive bonus for increase in productivity in proportion to the per capita output. Under the scheme, a standard output level is determined on mutual agreement between the employer and employees. Then actual output is compared with the standard output to decide the incentive bonus. Percentage of productivity bonus payable to each employee is determined as per the following formula :

$$\frac{\left(P^1/W^1\right) - (P/W)}{\left(P^1/W^1\right)} \times 100$$

Where

P^1 – Actual production during assessment year

W^1 – Number of workers in employment during the assessment month.

P – Standard production in the base month.

W – Numbers of workers in the employment during the base month.

P^1/W^1 – Actual production per worker during the assessment month.

P/W – Standard production per worker during the base month.

Earnings Vary Proportionately More than Output

This category includes two methods

(*a*) High price rate

(*b*) The high standard hour system

Under high price rate the earnings of the worker are in proportion to his or her output like in straight piece work discussed above. However, the increment in earnings for each unit of output above the standard is greater. The individual may earn three to four times the earnings above the standard. The higher rates start applying after the standards have been reached. Similarly the earnings also three to four times in the high standard hour system, the worker earn more if he saves time from the standard working time.

The employers do not welcome this method primarily due the high labour cost per unit for levels of output above standards; hence, the workers have to share the additional overhead charges which result from additional output.

Earnings Differing at Different Levels of Output

This group has several methods; these can best be explained by describing how earning vary from maximum to minimum at different levels of output. Earnings for one part of the range may vary proportionately less than output and for another part proportionately more, or more usually in the same proportion as out put (International Labour Organization, 1951, p.19).

The Taylor's Differential Piece Rate System, Merrick Differential Piece-Rate System, The Gantt Task System, The Emerson's Efficiency System and Accelerating Premium System fall under the this category where earnings differ at different levels of output.

Taylor's Differential Piece Rate System. This system was developed by F.W. Taylor in 1880. Under this there is low rate for output below the standard and higher piece rate for output above the standard This can be illustrated as under :

Standard Output - 100 units.

Rate per unit - Rupee 1/-

Differential to be applied

110 percent of piece rate for output above the standard.

90 percent of piece rate when below the standard.

Earnings = Number of Units Produced × Differential Ratio × Rate

Earnings

(*a*) If 120 units produced.

Applying the above formula

Earnings = 120 × (110/100) × 1 or Rupees 132/-.

(*b*) If 80 units produced

Earnings = 80 × (110/100) × 1 or Rupees 88/-

The Merrick Differential Piece Rate System. It is similar to Taylor system. In this one large step is broken into two to encourage new and average workers. In this system the worker is paid wages at straight piece rate for up to 83 percent of production. At this the worker is awarded 10 percent bonus of the time rate with a further 10 percent bonus on reaching the standard output.

Merrick System can be illustrated as :

Standard Output - 100 units.

Rate per unit - Rupee 1/-

Earnings would be as under :

(*a*) If only 80 pieces produced then

Output = 80 units

Efficiency = 80/100

Earnings : As the efficiency is less than 83 percent, only the base rate applies *i.e.*, Rupees 1/- per piece or Rupees 80/-

(*b*) If output is 90 pieces then the earnings would be :

Output = 90 units

Efficiency = 90/100 or 90 percent.

Earnings as the efficiency is more than 83 but less than 100 percent, 110 percent of the base piece rate applies

90 × (110/100) × 1= Rupees 99/-

(*c*) Similarly if the number of pieces produced is 110 then the earnings would

Output = 110 pieces.

Efficiency = (110/100) × 110 percent.

As the efficiency is greater than 100 percent 120 percent of base price applies.

110 × (120/100) × 1= Rupees 120/-.

Gantt Task System. In this method the worker is guaranteed his or her time rate for output below the standard. On reaching the standard which is usually set very high the worker is entitled to bonus at the rate of 20 percent of the time wages.

Let us see the example as given above.

No of pieces produced in 8 hours are 80.

Rate per hour be Rupees 10/-.

High piece rate Rupees 2/-.

(*a*) If the output of worker is 70 pieces

As the output is less than the standard, the worker is entitled to time wages only or Rupees 80/-.

(*b*) If the output is 80 pieces

As the output is equal to the standard the worker is entitled to time wage plus 20 percent time wages as bonus.

Time Wages 10 × 8 = Rupees 80/-

Bonus of 20 percent of time wages (20/ 100) X 80 = Rupees 16/-

The total earning s would be Time wages + Bonus or Rupees 80 + 16 = Rupees 96/-.

(*c*) If the output is 100 units the worker would be entitled to high piece rate of Rupees 2/- or he would earn 100 × 2 = Rupees 200/-

Emerson's Plan. Under this system a standard time is set for each job. The efficiency of each worker is determined by dividing the time taken by the standard time. Up to 67 percent efficiency the worker is paid by time rate. Thereafter, a graduated bonus, which amounts to 20 percent bonus is paid at 100 percent efficiency. Thereafter, an additional bonus of 1 percent is paid for each additional 1 percent of efficiency.

Emerson's Efficiency Plan

Efficiency Rate	*Remuneration*
Below 66.7 percent	No incentive bonus only time wages.
Over 66.7 percent up to 100 percent	Time wages + proportionate Bonus for Incremental output percentages, rising up to 20 percent at 100 percent level.
Over 100 percent	Time wages + 20 percent bonus + 1 percent bonus for each 1 (one) percent increase in efficiency beyond 100 percent.

Example 1 : Number of units produced by worker in ten hours is 100 which have been accepted as standard.

Rate per hour Rupees 10/-.

(*a*) Earnings if the worker produces 50 units would be :

As the out put efficiency is 50 percent then which is below 67 percent, hence the worker is entitled to only time wages *i.e.*, Rupees 10 × 10 or Rupees 100/-.

(*b*) If the worker produces 100 units then his earnings would be :

Efficiency 100 percent hence, the worker is entitles to 20 percent bonus *i.e.*,

Time wages + bonus (20% of time wage)

10 × 10 + [(20/100) × 100] = Rupees 120/-. Worker would earn Rupees 120/-.

(c) If the output is 120 units then the earnings would :

Output in 10 hours is 120 units

Efficiency is 120 percent.

The worker earning would be 20 percent of time wage as bonus up to 100% efficiency. Thereafter one percent increase for every one percent increase in efficiency *i.e.,*

The worker is eligible for 40 percent of time wage as bonus or Rupees 140/-.

Example 2 : *Hourly wage of employee is fixed at Rs. 5/- per hour. The worker is assigned different jobs in a day and each job unit with company has fixed a standard time. Based on tabulated information, compute the total earnings for the day.*

Job Code	*Quantity Produced*	*Standard time set per unit (in hours)*	*Time taken (in hours)*
A-1	2	1/2	1.25
B-3	4	1/2	1.75
C-2	20	1/3	5.00

Solution : Bonus for each job has to be computed separately. The calculation could be as under :

Job Code	*Standard time for the job (in hours)—quantity × standard time per unit*	*Time taken in hours*	*Bonus earned, if any (@ 50 percent of time saved) in Rupees*	
A-1	2 × 1/2	1 hour	1.25	Nil
B-3	4 × 1/2	2 hours	1.75	0.625
C-2	20 × 1/3	6.67 hours	5.00	4.175
Total	Rs. 4.8/-			

The total earnings for the day = (8 × 5) + 4.8 = Rs/ 44.8

Accelerated Premium System. Under this system the earnings of the workers increase with output, the rate of increase itself rising progressively with the output. In this system the worker receives strong incentives to improve his productivity and efficiency.

THE PROCESS OF WAGE DETERMINATION

The wage determination is done after great deliberation and each organization uses several methods to formulate a competitive pay rate (Figure 12.4). The first step is to carryout job analysis. The data so generated is used to prepare job descriptions and job specifications. On the basis of these two statements standards of job performance are laid down. (Already discussed in).

The second step is to carryout job evaluation. The relative value of every job is determined and converted into money value so as to fix basic wage for the job.

Wage survey is the third step. Wage surveys are carried out to determine the wage/salary levels prevailing in the region or industry for similar jobs.

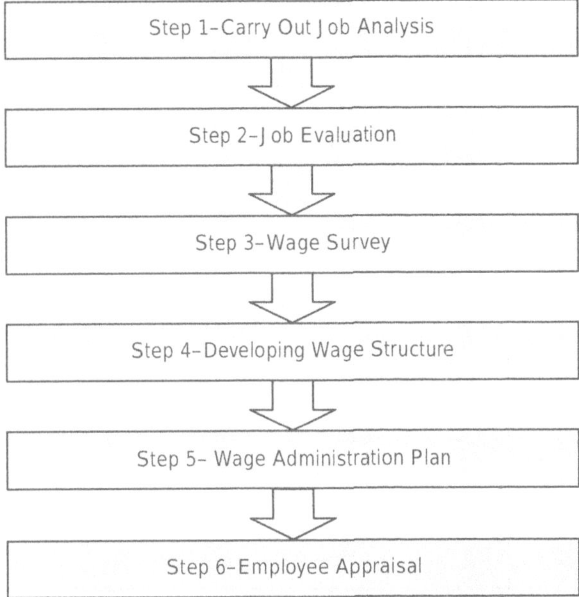

Fig. 12.4. *The Process of Wage Determination.*

After having carried out wage surveys the organization thereafter carries out wage structure development. Wage structure development involves establishment of pay rates that are compatible with the ranks, classifications or points arrived through job evaluations. The wage structure in an organization primarily depends upon its philosophy external forces and environment does have its impact. The organization can choose through several options from several options available to fix the wages. The job evaluation provides the necessary inputs for developing an organizations overall pay structure. While determining wage structure the organization has to consider :

(*a*) Government and local regulations and legislations relating to wages.

(*b*) Conduct of Surveys.

(*c*) Reports of wage boards, reports of Ministry of Labour, pay commissions etc.

(*d*) Provision for merit increase.

(*e*) Differentials between pay plans.

(*f*) Special cases, determining wages for jobs that are not in line.

The wage structure has to be in consonance with the rules as applied or made by the organization. It involves determining rate and amount of increments, promotions and how other benefits have to be paid. The rules once formulated should be extensively propagated and no ambiguity should be left. Thereafter, the similar jobs are grouped into grades for pay purposes. By grouping jobs into grades the organization can focus on ten to twelve grades of pay instead of large number of pay rates. A pay grade usually consists of jobs of equal difficulty requiring similar or equal level of professional competence and skills.

Employee appraisal is the next step in determination of wage structure. This helps in rewarding merit and performance. Some wage differentials are maintained on the basis of employee's performance.

Wage Structures

Wage structures; help illustrate many of the decisions made about the pay. Since abilities and actual performance vary remarkably among individuals, even in the same type of job, individual differences can be acknowledged if each job has a *rate range* (Figure 12.5). Higher rates or 'upper steps' in the range could be given to employees with longer service, seniority, merit or a combination of all three. In Figure 12.4 pay grades with ranges have been depicted. Each pay grade is represented by a rectangle; rate ranges by the height of the rectangle.

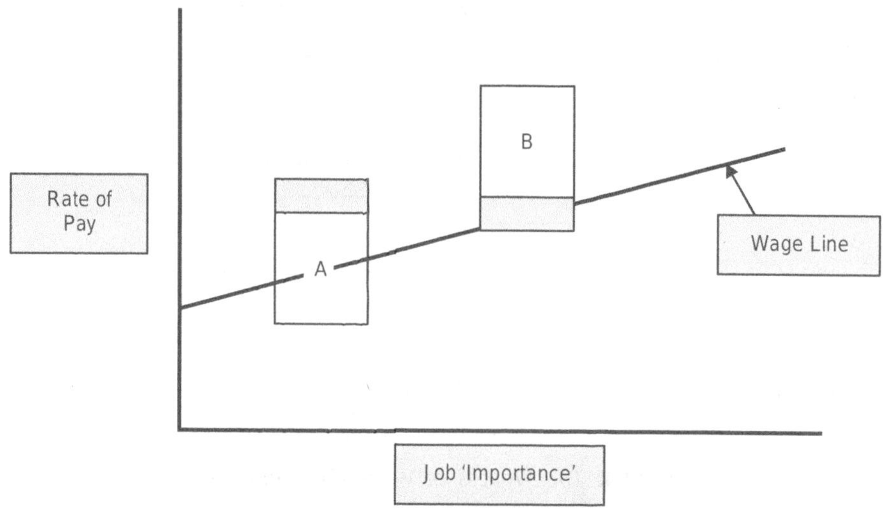

Fig. 12.5. *Rate Ranges of Wages.*

A person in at the top of the step within a pay grade may earn more than a person in higher pay grade, but at a lower step. Wage line reflects *wage differentials* between jobs. The steeper the wage line slope, the greater the differences in pay between jobs. Wage line also reflects the overall pay level of the organization. The number of *pay grades* and the scope of *rate range* are represented by the height of a pay grade (Figure 12.5), that is, the difference between the lowest and highest pay within the grade. For example, the minimum and maximum salaries of a peon could be ₹ 3000/- and ₹ 4000/- per month.

The more the pay grades, the finer the distinction between the jobs. Alternatively, *broad-banding* is used for fewer pay grades but larger rate ranges. Broad-banding allows employees to step out of narrow or rigid job descriptions. Broad-banding may result in significant differences in jobs going unrecognized, and pay equity concerns may arise (Henderson, 1982; pp 284–285). In organization with few pay grades, there may be larger rate ranges in each grade. This allows room for pay increases within the grades. Where many grades exist the employees may get raise by moving from one grade to another.

This is also referred to as 'wage curve'. The minimum and maximum wage lines are drawn on the curve Figure 12.6.

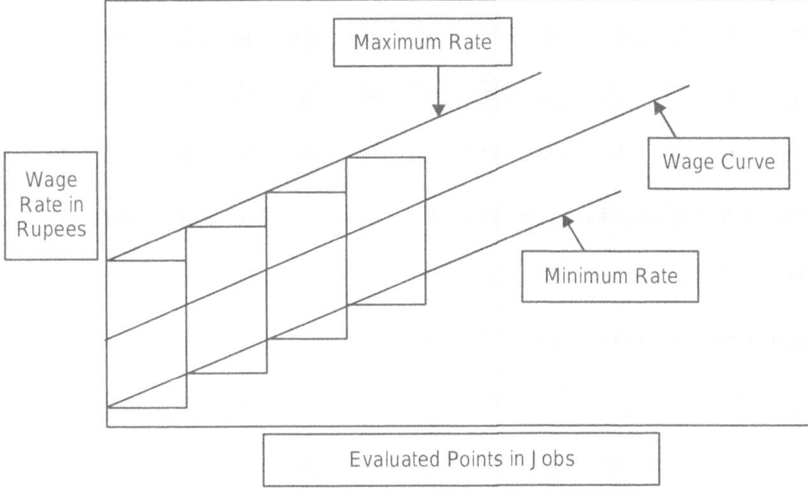

Fig. 12.6. *Wage Curve.*

COMPENSATION AND ORGANIZATIONAL STRATEGY

The compensation to be paid to an employee has to be commensurate with the goals, mission, objectives, philosophies and the culture of an organization. It is also referred in some books by authors as *strategic compensation planning*. It serves to mesh the monetary payments made to an employee with specific function of the Human Resource program in establishing a pay for performance standard, the objective being to motivate employees through compensation.

The organization has to carryout an assessment of compensation plan to see if it advances the needs of employees and goals of the organization. The compensation plan must support plan and actions of the organization.

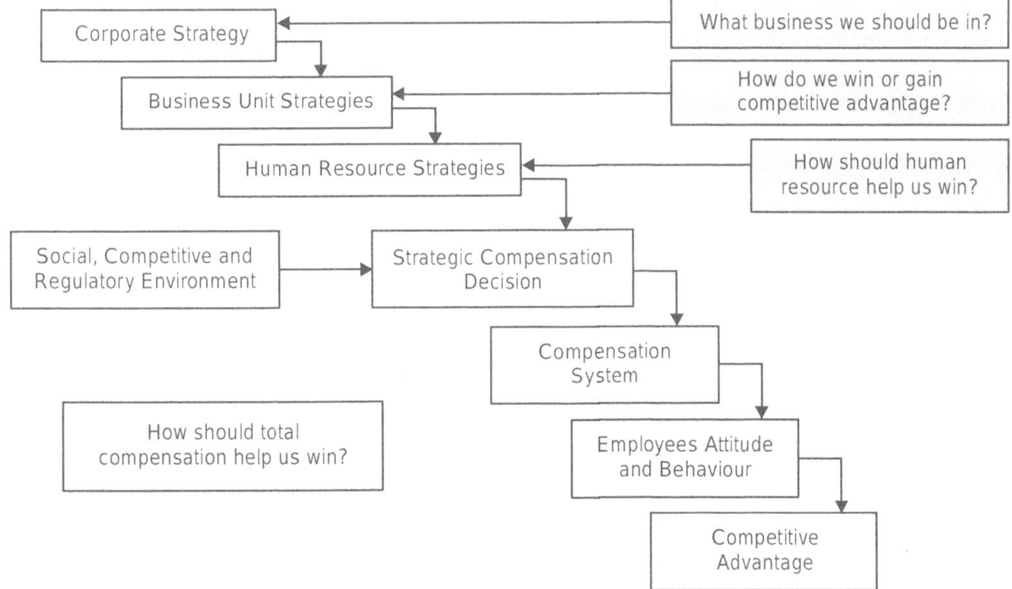

Fig. 12.7. *Strategic Choices.*

Compensation strategy helps an organization in recognizing and grouping compensation components so that they influence employee's motivation in a positive manner and lead to improved organizational performance. Figure 12.7 depicts that compensation is one of the strategic choices that helps company attain competitive advantage and in turn help it to attain its objectives.

The organization also utilizes the reward system as a strategy for better performance. In reward system an organization designs and implements rewards to focus workers attention on the specific behaviours the organization considers necessary to achieve its desired goals and objectives.

The total reward system comprises of two components (Figure 12.8);

(*a*) Compensation Component

(*b*) Non-compensation Component.

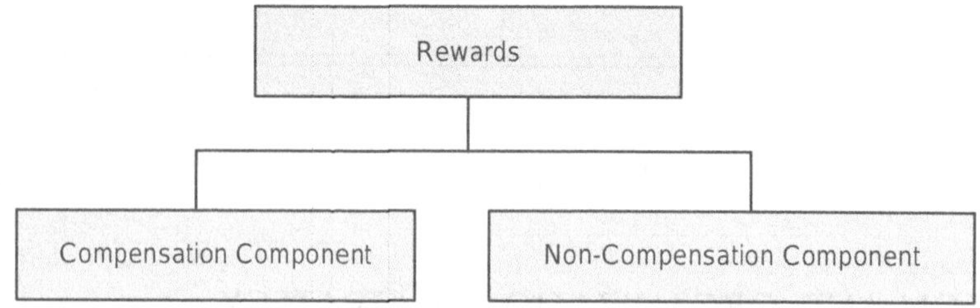

Fig. 12.8. *Total Reward System.*

The compensation component results from allocation, conversion and transfer of a portion of the income of an organization to its employees for their monetary and in kind claims on goods and services (Figure 12.9).

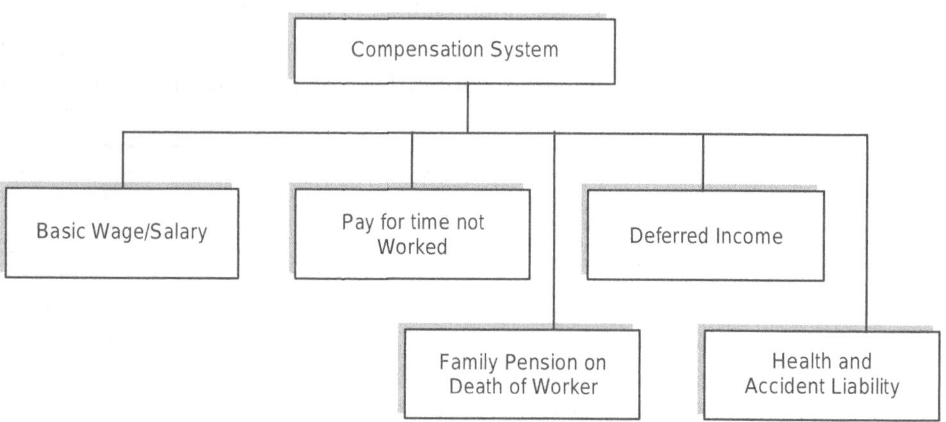

Source : Adapted from Henderson, Richard. I, 2006.*'Compensation Management in Knowledge Based World'*. (New Delhi : Pearson) p.30

Fig. 12.9. *Compensation System.*

Non-compensation systems are all situation related reward not included in compensation package. These include performance related awards, saving in company, product development etc. These are usually one time to motivate the employee to perform better (Figure 12.10).

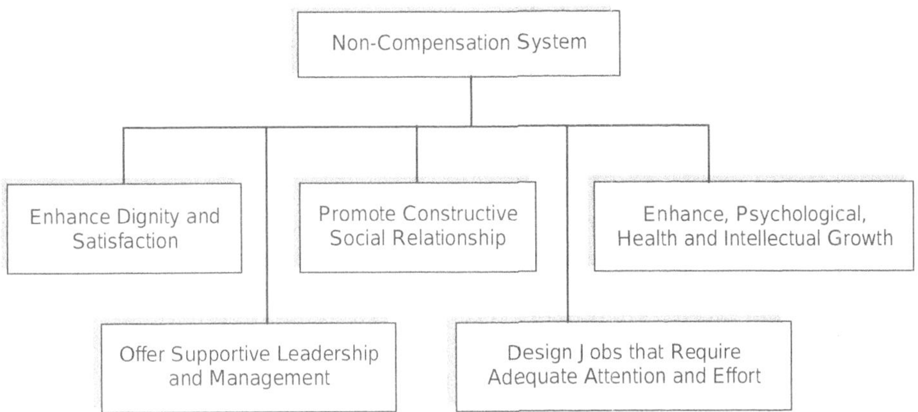

Source : Adapted from Henderson, Richard. I, 2006.'*Compensation Management in Knowledge Based World*'. (New Delhi : Pearson) p.30

Fig. 12.10. *Non-compensation System.*

The components can now be regrouped as a direct component or that part of the compensation which an employee receives ion monetary or in kind allocations. Then there is an indirect component which is primarily relational and may be in the form of monetary claims or non-monetary. To be specific the elements compensation comprises of direct component and indirect component (Figure 12.11).

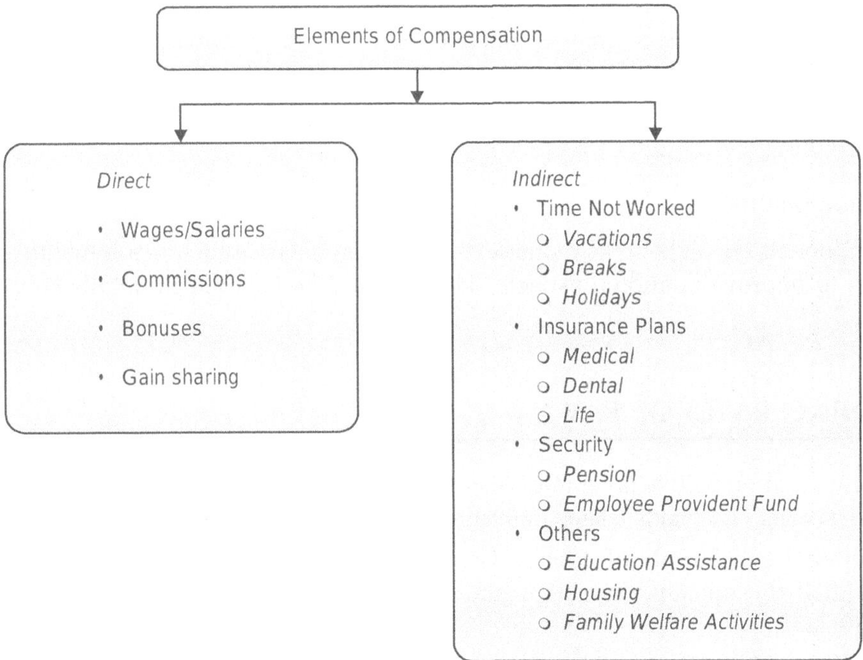

Fig. 12.11. *Elements of Compensation.*

Direct Components

The direct component of wages includes wages, salaries, commissions, bonuses and gain sharing. It results from allocation, conversion and transfer of a portion of the income of an organization to its employees for their monetary and in kind claims on goods and services.

Wages and Salaries

Base Compensation involves monetary benefits to employees in the form of wages and salaries. Wages refer to hourly rates of pay and salary refers to the monthly rates of pay, irrespective of the number of hours put in by an employee. Wages refer to the earnings of employees whose pay is calculated on an hourly basis.

Commissions and Incentives

Commissions and incentives are also referred to as 'payments by results'. Incentives and commissions are paid in addition to wages and salaries to the workers. Incentives depend upon productivity, sales, profit, or cost reduction efforts. These vary greatly from company to company, but are generally based on the Rupee amount of sales made during the payroll period. Commission income is considered same as wages or salaries for withholding and reporting purposes. Commissions/incentives are usually computed on a certain percentage or commission rate.

Bonuses

Bonuses are paid to share the prosperity of the company with its employees. Bonuses are paid for performance. However, this has come under Bonuses Act in India and has become sort of a wage. It has lost its purpose of incentive for better performance and results.

Gain Sharing

This is mainly for senior appointments that get incentives for earning profits, taking innovative steps to improve efficiency etc. Task carrying no rewards and difficult are reluctantly performed. The management thus introduces gain sharing to motivate persons to take action to improve efficiency, relations etc.

Indirect Components

Indirect components are all benefits monetary and non-monetary which re allotted to an employee for his work to improve relational aspects. These would be covered in details subsequently in the chapter.

DETERMINING RATES OF PAY

The total compensation paid to an employee is based the factors that are both internal and external to the organization. The major issues determining the wages/salary are :

(*a*) **Demand and Supply of Labour.** Greater the availability of the skill lesser is the wage paid. If the demands are high and skills available are scare then the wages would increase.

(*b*) **Ability to Pay.** The next important factor inhibiting salary/wages is the ability of the organization to pay.

(*c*) **Cost of Living.** The worker works to meet his/ her needs. If the cost of living is high the wages move upward. Higher the cost of living greater is the wage.

(*d*) **Labour Unions.** Labour/Trade Unions are always striving to get to the workers better and better wages. It has been observed where the Trade Unions are more effective the wages are usually higher.

(*e*) **Government Enactments.** To maintain industrial peace and harmony, government regulates the wages. It enacts laws and lays down minimum wages to be paid. It also appoints inspectors and regulators to ensure that laws are complied with.

(*f*) **Prevailing Rates in the Market.** While determining salary/wages the industry or an organization carries out survey to determine wages being paid in the environment. This would lead to salary being in consonance and there would be no large scale movement as also upheaval in the market. Paying very high wages may result in internal turmoil as other workers and earlier employees may seek more pay to maintain parity and paying too little may result in employees seeking employment elsewhere.

(*g*) **Philosophy of Management.** The wage package also depends upon the philosophy of the managements. Some of the companies lay great emphasis on relational issues like schooling for children of employees, housing, terminal benefits like sick leave, retirement benefits etc.

MAINTAINING PAY STRUCTURE

Maintaining pay equity within a compensation structure it has been developed in an ongoing challenge. Employees traditionally progress within a grade on the basis of merit and/ or seniority. Here we shall look at :

(*a*) Seniority Based Raises.

(*b*) Merit Based Raises.

(*c*) Promotion pay

(*d*) Out of Line Rates

(*e*) Cost of Living Adjustments

Seniority-Based Raises

Systems providing periodic raises regardless of evaluated merit may be based on the assumption that ability grows with time in job or experience. Many organizations use pay increases to reward employees for 'belonging'/'continuity' with the organization. As long as the employees are able to sustain minimum standards of performance their pay increase is assured.

Some employees value the certainty of seniority-based pay, and their needs for increase in pay through time are met. Seniority-based pay promotes continuous service and may reduce turnover. Organizations which give raise on the basis of seniority value the maturity and experience of senior workers, but they sometimes feel relieved when senior workers leave as senior workers cost organizations disproportionately higher wages and benefits.

Organizations to retain employees also give smaller but frequent pay increases early in employees career; while increases later on in the career are given at slower pace. This also limits the speed at which an employee rises to higher grades of pay.

Merit Based Raises

Merit based wage increases are designed to recognize improved employee performance and contribution to the organization. In theory, in a merit system workers earn wage increments proportional to their performance. Pay on performance limits the problem of giving permanent raises based on present or past performance.

Incentives can have a disrupting effect on an internal wage structure. Organizations who use incentive pay systems for some jobs and not others may find workers in some lower 'value' jobs earn more than those in higher level ones (Whyte, 1957). Organizations utilizing pass/fail merit reviews are conducted at specified time-service intervals – and where employees tend to pass, the process may be viewed as a 'seniority system' in another way. In such a system workers would experience the same positive and negative benefits of a seniority system.

Managers may feel unduly constrained when given a choice between recommending an employee for raise or not. To deserve no raise the employee should have performed quite poorly. In this manager also is responsible as he is supposed to counsel and guide his subordinate to improve and bring out their best. No recommendation for raise also reflects on the manager's inability to get best out of his subordinates.

Some workers may rise faster to the top of the pay scale than others. The employees who advance too quickly may not have any further economic increase to look forward to, and experience a feeling of stagnation. The only growth left now being looking forward for promotion or a change of job.

Promotion Pay

A steep wage structure permits room for larger wage increases after raises or promotions. The wage differential on promotion will depend on the height of rate range occupied by the employee within the present pay grade, as compared to the height in the grade promoted to. Greater pay increase will accompany those promotions where the employee moves up more than one pay grade.

Out of Line or Colour Rates

There are instances when employees are paid more or less that their actual worth in the labour market. Different colour rates are commonly used by compensation specialists to indicate particular out-of-line pay relationships (Sibson, 1997; pp. 129-131). Red and Green illustrate either over or under compensated jobs when compared to current market worth.

Although colours imply employee lose money with the first and gains with the latter, but both situations if not corrected speedily will disturb the internal and external equity.

Red rates represent over paid jobs. If rates are allowed to stay out of proportion to the rest of the farm jobs, other workers in the organization may feel mistreated. It also impacts the wage bill as it would be higher for the organization than it actually should be.

Green rates represent the under paid job. Green rates can be brought up into line with internal structure in one or two steps (Belcher, 1974 : pp. 286-287). An organization may cut its wage bill with green rates but the benefits may be short term as it will be difficult to retain valuable workers. Two likely green indicators are the increase in turn over and forced to start inexperienced new workers up near the middle of a pay grade. If however, an organization is forced to start an inexperienced new worker up near the middle of a pay grade then no sound basis for pay differences among workers may remain. It is possible hat an employer does not have a green rate, but the whole wage structure might have failed to keep up with the market.

Cost of Living Adjustments

Inflation can especially have a devastating effect on workers ability to make end meet. We have see employers whose pay falls below market values may have difficulty attracting and retaining personnel. Some corporations (and often union contracts) stipulate a cost of living adjustments based on the consumer price index. The index is supposed to reflect cost-of-living changes. The prices of common commodities purchased by most consumers are observed and compared.

INCENTIVE ADJUSTMENTS

Incentives are monetary benefits paid to workmen in recognition of their good performance. Milton L Rock in *Handbook of Wages and Salary Administration* has defined incentives as 'variable rewards granted according to variations in the achievement of specific results.' The International Labour Office refers to incentives as 'payment by results'. However, Subramaniam (1979) state that it can be called 'incentive systems of payment' emphasizing the point of motivation, that is, the imparting of incentives to workers for higher production and productivity. It is important to understand that unlike wages and salaries which are relatively fixed, incentives generally vary from individual to individual, and from time to time for the same individual.

Advantages of Incentives

Incentives are primary means of motivation and acknowledging workers contribution towards betterment of the organization. Incentives make people work harder and improve productivity thus reducing cost of production. Incentives also bring in additional income to workers; enabling them to improve their standards of living.

Incentives also helps in reduced supervision, better utilization of machinery, tools and equipment, limited or reduced wastage or scrap. Incentives also help to improve the motivation level; thus there is better understanding amongst the members, coordination leading to improved attendance.

Incentives in India are also used by managers because it does not affect employer's contribution to Employees provident Fund and other retirement benefits.

Disadvantages

The major disadvantage of incentive payments especially where actions are related and teams operate identification of individual for incentives lead to heartburning. It may result in relations being snapped due jealousies.

It is important that incentive plan has a base for working or determining the rate. The organization must set either the piece or bonus rates. There is a problem of judgement in setting rates which leads to errors. The management has to be careful in setting rates. If the rates are set too low would not motivate an individual and he would be under pressure to work very hard. However, if the rates are set too high then the workers may slacken so that management does not ask for revision of rates. Workers at times decide how much he wants to earn and is not interested to work beyond that.

Prerequisites for Effective Incentive Schemes

Careful analysis of the industries it has been observed that well designed system of payments shall yield advantages to all concerned.

The first and important prerequisite for effective incentive scheme is the involvement and acceptance of the employees. The employees would otherwise find ingenious ways to defeat it. The incentive to be appropriate should be in consonance with the type of work, attitude and culture of the work force. The rewards in modern time should be clearly indicated for individual and team effort.

Lastly, incentive schemes need deliberate management. There has to be deliberate planning, commitment of management, assessment and implementation of incentive plans.

Scope of Incentives Schemes

The incentive scheme have universal application, however, it is important to identify its true application. Incentive work well in certain important industries, as these is difficult to apply. Incentives are difficult to apply where it is difficult to measure the output or where psychological circumstance may be prejudicial to output; or in industries where quality is of utmost importance or in industries where safety is great concern.

Incentive can be very effectively used where administrative and engineering staff is there to supervise, ensure quality and control production. Incentives can be successfully employed in small concerns/undertakings which may, in case of need, utilize services of experts to design an incentive programme (International Labour Organization, 1951, pp.179–180).

EXECUTIVE COMPENSATION

The growth of executive pay over the past decade has increased the attention given to the subject 'Executive Compensation' especially in India. In addition to its direct role of motivating and retaining executives, executive compensation is often referred to as the acid test of 'corporate governance' (Warren Buffet). There is substantial heterogeneity in pay practices across firms and industries, most executive pay packages contain four basic components; a base salary, an annual bonus tied to accounting performance, stock options and long-term incentive plans (including restricted stock plans and multi-year accounting-based performance plans). In the words of Mr. Kofi Annan, former Secretary General of United nations," You have to listen to not only what is being said, but what is not said—which is often more important than what they say." How apt, Mr. Kofi Anan states it is applicable for Executive compensation.

Executive Compensation

Mr Mukesh Ambani, Chairman and managing Director of Reliance Industries got a total payout of Rupees 44.02 Crores in the financial year 2007–08. This pay cheque comes primarily in the form of commissions that the company pays to select executives as a ratio of its profits. Mr Mukesh Ambani got a salary of Rupees 60 lakhs per annum, and another Rupees 48 lakhs per annum as perquisites and allowances. In addition Mr Ambani was paid Rupees 18.75 lakhs as 'retieral benefits' and Rupees 4,275.44 lakhs toward commission on net profit.

Mr Mukesh Ambani was also the top paid executive in the year 2006–07 also.

Source : PTI, 'Ambani Pay Cheque gets fatter to over 44 crore.' *The Economic Times*, New Delhi, 20 May 08, p.5.

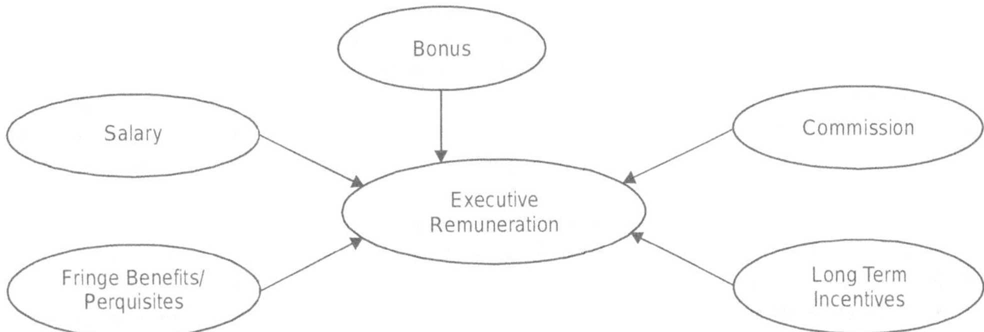

Fig. 12.12. *Components of Executive Compensation*

Salary

Salary is the first and basic component of executive compensation. Normal techniques of job evaluation and other methods may not be suitable for determining executive salary. Executives are paid for their capabilities and experience that they bring with them, hence, norms of salary and wage fixation are generally not applied to them. Executive base salary levels are often more influenced by the opinion of the compensation committee, which is often dependent upon information from salary surveys of similar companies. Base salary of the Executives is set to be competitive with other executive salaries in the market and thus may be very high in comparison to the pay of employees in their own companies.

Bonus

In the basic salary of executives, most receive variable pay, a compensation that fluctuates according to some level of performance. Bonus or use of compensation beyond base salary is intended to motivate executives to reach certain organizational performance goals. Bonuses are usually one time payment tied to some short term performance. Bonus may be based on any number of performance outcomes, ranging from judgments of executive performance by the board of directors, to levels of company profit or market share. Nearly all executives now receive some sort of bonus as a part of their compensation package.

Long Term Incentives

In recent years, incentives have become important for rewarding the Executives for their performance. Bonuses are for short term performance while stock option is a long term benefit. Long term benefits now make up about one half of total executive compensation. The most common long term incentive is the stock option, which either gives the executive free company stock, or allows him or her to purchase company stock at reduced price for a period of time. Stock options are valuable as long as share of price keeps increasing. If the share price crash when the company starts incurring loss the executives also stand to lose.

Stock options are attractive to shareholders too. Firstly, it is not a bonus; hence, executives have to use their own resources to own it. Secondly, the executives have a similar stake in the prosperity of the company as the shareholder. Stock option is an instrument of profit sharing and links financial success of the executive with the success of the company. Finally, stock option enables executives to receive large rewards without embarrassment to the company. Executives can sell these stocks when the value has appreciated, therefore providing compensation beyond the employee's tenure with the organization.

Alternative Pay

It refers to alternative ways of paying people other than for their tie, which is the most common method. Thus alternative pay plans generally include hose listed under Variable Pay Systems. Also included in alternative pay system is skill based pay for knowledge. Under this system, an employee's compensation is based on the number of specified skills or tasks he or she has mastered.

Commission

Some companies pay commission to their executives. Commission constitutes a very major share in executive remuneration. According to Companies Act, an enterprise can pay up to 11 percent of its profit as commission. The actual break up is left at the discretion of the Board of Directors.

Fringe Benefits Perquisites

Perks constitute a major source of income for executives. In addition to the normally allowed perks like provident fund, gratuity etc. corporate executives often receive extraordinary fringe benefits that are not provided to other corporate employees. Perks take care of Any property or service that an executive receives in lieu or in addition to regular taxable wages is a fringe benefit. The fringe benefits are now taxable in India like many other countries. The major fringe benefits provided to executives are :

(*a*) Club membership.

(*b*) Corporate Credit Card. Many companies provide corporate credit cards to executives and other employees. The difference mainly being that executives are generally allowed to use the card at will, with the monthly statement mailed directly to the corporation and the account being paid in full without submitting business expense report.

(*c*) Executive Dinning Room. Meals furnished on the employers business premises for the convenience of the employer.

(*d*) Loans. No cost/ Low cost/Disguised Compensation are provided by many companies to their executives.

(*e*) Transportation.

(*f*) Housing. Company hired or constructed house.

(*g*) Spousal and Dependant Insurance.

(*h*) Transfer of property. Remuneration to an executive may also take the form of property. Property may include real and personal property other than money or an unfunded and unsecured promise to pay money in the future. Property may include beneficial interest in assets. Property may take many form such as real estate, furniture, equipment, phones etc.

(*i*) Relocation expenses.

(*j*) Leave travel and paid vacations.

(*k*) Qualified retirement planning.

Stock Plans

Sock plans are a popular method of compensating employees. Employee Stock Option (ESOP) involves offering specified number of stocks to employees.

WAGE POLICY IN INDIA

Pay structure in any organization or a firm or a company depends upon multitude of actors as discussed above. In India, State has played a predominant role in shaping wages. One of the Directive Principles of State Policy embodied in Article 43 of Indian Constitution narrates :

"It can scarcely be disputed this securing of living wages to labourers which ensure not only bare physical subsistence but also maintenance of health and decency, is conducive to the general interest of the public. In case, it is in the interest of general public the labourers should be secured adequate living wages, the intentions of employer, whether good or bad, are irrelevant."

Pay structure in India generally is composed of the under mentioned components :

(*a*) Basic salary

(*b*) Dearness allowance

(*c*) Bonus and Other incentives

(*d*) Fringe benefits.

Basic Salary

It provides for the foundation of the pay packet. It is a price for services rendered by an employee. The basic wage varies according to professional qualifications and skills required. In India, basic wage has been influenced by statutory minimum wage, wage settlements, and awards of wage boards. According to the Fair Wages Committee any attempt to evolve principles for governing the fixation of wages must be made against the background of general economic conditions of the country and the level of national income. The Fair Wages Committee gave three concepts relating to basic wages.

(*a*) **Minimum Wage**. Minimum wage is that wage which is required to cover bare physical needs of a worker and his family. The committee also recommended the minimum wage should not only cover the bare necessities required but also for meeting some basic other needs as health, education, medical and other needs for human growth and development. Statutory minimum wage is fixed and has to be paid to all workers irrespective of the capacity of the industry to pay it. The Fair Wage Committee defined the components of minimum wage but did not quantify it. The Government of India enacted the Minimum Wages Act, 1948 to ensure minimum wages for the workers. The Indian Labour Conference at its 15th Session held in July 1957 formally quantified the minimum wage. The Conference laid down the under mentioned criterion :

- The standard family should be taken to consist of 3 consumption unit for one earner disregarding the earnings of women, children and adolescent.
- Minimum food requirements should be calculated on the basis of net food intake of 2,700 as recommended by Dr. Aykkroyed for an average Indian adult of moderate activity.
- Each consumption unit is authorized 18 yards per annum.
- Rent to be calculated as per the subsidized Industrial Housing Scheme for low income group.
- Fuel, lighting and other miscellaneous expenditure is to constitute twenty (20) percent of the minimum wage.

The above norms were revised by the 41st Labour Ministers Conference in 1992 as under :

- The standard consumption unit should be taken to comprise 5 consumption units instead of 3 consumption units.
- Minimum food requirements should be calculated on the basis of 2,700 calories per consumption unit in conformity with the food habits of the region.
- Clothing requirements should be calculated at 80 yards per family per year.
- Fuel, lighting etc should comprise 20 percent of the total minimum wage.
- House rent should be the same as under the subsidized industrial housing scheme.
- 25 percent of the total of earlier components should be provided for children education, medical, social needs as per the Supreme Court Judgment in the case of *Workmen vs Management of Raptakos Brett and Co. Ltd.*

(*b*) **Fair Wage**. Fair wage concept involves combining two aspects viz. the minimum wage requirements of a worker and the capacity of the industry to pay. While the minimum wage is set, the upper limit of the wage should depend upon the capacity of industry to pay. The objective is fair enumeration and ensures efficiency of the industry is maintained. Between these two extremes fair wage depends on several factors;

- The productivity of labour.
- The prevailing rates of wages in the same or similar occupations in the same region or neighbouring region
- Level of national income and its distribution.
- The place of industry in the economy of the country.
- The employer's capacity to pay.

(*c*) **Living Wage**. It is the wage that provides amenities in addition to certain necessities of life for the well being of the worker in a particular society. The Fair Wages Committee in its report published by Government of India in 1948 defined living as :

"living wage should enable the male earner to provide for himself and his family not merely the bare essentials of food, clothing and shelter but also health, requirements of essential social needs and measure of insurance against the more important misfortunes including old age."

The concept of living wage is dynamic and is directly related to the level of economic development in the country. The wages improve progressively with improvement in the economic condition of the nation. Living wage is the target that in workers wants to achieve through higher productivity and better economic conditions of the country.

Regulation of Wages in India

In order to realize these objectives of Directive Principles of State Policy, the Government of India enacted various regulations.

- **The Minimum Wage Act, 1948**. The Act lays down the fixation of (*i*) a minimum time rate of wages; (*ii*) a minimum piece rate; (*iii*) a guaranteed time rate; (*iv*) an overtime rate for different occupations, localities or classes of work and for adults, adolescents, children and apprentices. The minimum rate of wages may consist of a basic rate of wages and a cost of living allowance; or a basic rate with or without the cost of living allowance and the cash value of concessions in respect of essential commodities supplied at concessional rate. The Act lays down wage shall be paid in cash.

- **The Payment of Wages Act, 1936.** The object of the act was to regulate the payment of wages to certain class of persons employed in industry. The regulation contemplated is of two kinds; firstly, about the date of payment of wages and; secondly, about deduction of wages whether fine or otherwise.
- **The Equal Remuneration Act, 1976.** The Constitution of India contains several provisions regarding equal treatment of men and women workers in the field of economic activity. Article 39 of the Constitution envisages that the State shall direct its policy, among other things, towards securing that there is equal pay for equal work, the Government promulgated Equal Remuneration Act, 1976.
- **Wage Boards.** Government of India sets up Tripartite Wage Boards on industry wise basis to fix and revise pay. These boards are set up on ad hoc basis on the demand of trade unions and employers as there is no law providing for its establishment. A Wage Board consists of an impartial Chairman, two independent members and 2 to 3 representative of workers and employers each. The recommendations of Wage Boards are first submitted to the government. Once accepted, the parties are requested to enforce the recommendations.
- **Pay Commissions.** Wages and salaries of Central and State Government employees are determined through Pay Commissions. The disputes arising out of pay commission awards and their implementation are decided by commissions of inquiry, adjudication by tribunals and the joint consultative machinery.

Dearness and Other Allowances

This allowance is given to protect the real wages of workers during inflation. Under, Section 3 of Minimum Wages Act it is described as cost of living allowance. Dearness allowance has now become an integral part of the wage system in India. It comprises of :

(*a*) **Flat Rate.** In this method the Dearness Allowance is paid to all workers at a flat rate irrespective of their wage levels and regardless of the of changes in the consumer price index. This method was used in industries in West Bengal in the earlier days of adjudication.

(*b*) **Graduated Scale.** Under this method, the dearness allowance increases/ decreases with each slab (Table 12.3).

Table 12.3. Graduated Scale of Dearness Allowance

Pay Scale	*Amount of Dearness Allowance*	*Dearness Allowance as Percentage of Maximum of the Pay Scale*
3000–5000	600–1000	20
5001–8000	750–1200	15
8000–12000	960–1200	12

(*c*) **Indexed based Dearness Allowance.** In this method a flat rate per point is prescribed so that all workers receive the same amount of Dearness Allowance irrespective of their pay scale. If the rate per point is fixed as Rupees 2/- per point. Hence, if the All India

Consumer Point Index (AICPP) increase by 5 points the all workers would be paid Rupees 10/- irrespective of their pay scale.

(*d*) Dearness Allowance Linked to Index and Pay Scale. This is a very popular method employed by Central and State Government to pay its employees. It involves paying higher rate of Dearness Allowance to employees receiving lower pay scales and lower Dearness Allowance is paid to employee's receiving higher rates of pay.

Bonus

Bonus has a long history. It was initially paid to textile workers in Bombay (Mumbai). It has been stated the bonus is the workers share of enterprises prosperity. Bonus Commission (1961), bonus is *'sharing by the workers in the prosperity of the concern in which they are employed. In the case of low pads workers such sharing in the prosperity augments their earning and helps to bridge the gap between the actual and the need based wage.'*

The bonus paid is now has little direct incentive effect as it is now being paid to all workers at the same rate irrespective of their individual efficiency and long after he closure of the financial year.

The Government of India enacted the payment of Bonus Act, 1965 for payment of bonus to persons employed in specified establishments. This Act imposes a statutory liability upon an employer to pay bonus.

National Wage Policy

The Government of India has been mandated by the Constitution to secure for all workers a living wage and conditions of work which ensure a decent standard of life as well as full employment. The Constitution also lays down equality in pay, *i.e.*, 'equal pay for equal work' irrespective of caste, creed, religion or gender.

India does not have an identified and a clear National Wage Policy, however, various committees have laid down the guidelines for the same.

(*a*) **Committee on Fair Wages (1948).** The first committee to be established post independence to regulate the wages; this committee gave the notion of 'fair wage', 'minimum wage' and 'living wage'. The committee also sated that any principle of fixing of ages should be made against the backdrop of the general economic condition of the country and the level of national income.'

(*b*) **National Commission on Labour (1969).** It is a body mandated by Government of India The commission suggested "The wage policy has to be framed taking into account such factor as the price level which can be sustained, the employment level to be aimed at, requirement of social justice, and capital formation need growth." The commission has found its task difficult and has apprised the Government that national minimum wage is not feasible due to widespread regional differences in the country.

(*c*) **Chakraborty Committee (1974).** The committee stressed the need for uniformity in wage payments across the regions, industries and occupations. It is suggested that National Wage Commission and National Board should be set up. These authorities will evaluate all jobs, workout a grade structure on the basis of skill differential and fix wages for each grade.

(*d*) **Bhootalingam Study Group (1978).** The group recognized widespread disparities and anomalies in the wage structure in the country. The committee suggested that appropriate guidelines should be evolved to reduce such disparities and to raise gradually the areas of unduly depressed wages. The report was implemented as the Trade Unions across the country opposed the report.

(*e*) **National Commission on Labour (2002).** The commission recommended that government should notify the minimum wage. It also stated that every employee must pay each worker his one month's salary as bonus before an appropriate festival. The commission also recommended that the system of two wage ceilings for reckoning entitlement should be suitably enhanced to ₹ 7500/- and ₹ 3500/- for entitlement and calculation respectively.

Despite practical difficulties it is important that a national wage policy is enunciated. It should be based on scientific principles, and should consider various social factors. 'No principle wage policy can be applied in variance and in disregard of the realities of the situation. Wage policy has to be pragmatic as well as scientific.'

Review Questions

1. What is compensation ? Explain the principle of wage and salary administration.
2. What are the different theories of compensation ? How does it differ from bench marking ?
3. What are wage incentive plans ? Discuss the advantages and limitations of wage incentive plans ?
4. What do you understand by profit sharing ? Describe the features of profit sharing ?
5. Explain the working of Time Wage System and Piece Wage System ? Which would you prefer ? Explain.
6. What is meant by employee stock option plan ? What are its features and merits ?
7. Write notes on
   (*i*) Wage incentive in India
   (*ii*) Scanlon plan
   (*iii*) Employee stock option
   (*iv*) Wage Policy of India
8. During the recent years there has been a rapid increase in the compensation packages offered to managerial employees of the private sector especially MNCs. Explain the current phenomenon and examine their implications.
9. Increasing companies are 're-mixing' their compensation to emphasize Variable Performance based components.
10. What is variable pay ? Elucidate the advantages and disadvantages of variable pay.

Project Work

Study the compensation patterns in a manufacturing organization. Study the compensation pattern of a worker and executives. Critically relate the various theories with the compensation structure prevalent in the organization being analyzed. Present it in the class.

Case Study

Ravi Furnitech is a state of art modular furniture manufacturer, started with initial investment of Rs. 200/- crore raising term loan from different financial institutions. The company took the ambitious plan to manufacture and sell worldwide hard wood furniture, as their study indicated that India market for furniture is still unorganized and affluent class uses the imported furniture made out of concentrate waste product.

To achieve this goal, the company recruited the best designers, business heads, and production people, selecting from worldwide. Many designers are even trained abroad. The biggest challenge the company is now facing is in designing the managerial compensation.

Managerial compensation has received attention primarily for validating its performance implication and strategic fit in the company. The HR developed the model of compensation keeping the following guidelines :

- Make incentive pay contingent upon product life cycle, emphasizing on technology.
- Study compensation system, relating to market and organizational strategies.
- Citing Miles and Snow (1978) Typology, in executive compensation design try to be more prospectors (innovative) to explore new market opportunities and grow by taking risk philosophy rather than defenders, analyzers or reactors.

Question

Based on the above guidelines suggest a model for executive compensation, covering all aspects of compensation.

❑❑❑

Chapter **13**

Performance Appraisal

★ LEARNING OBJECTIVES ★

After reading this chapter, you will be able to understand :

- What is Performance Appraisal ?
- Objectives of Performance Appraisal.
- Uses and importance of Performance Appraisal.
- Process of Performance Appraisal.
- Methods of Performance Appraisal
- Performance Management
- Potential Management

INTRODUCTION

Performance appraisal systems are among the most important human resource practices and also a comprehensively discussed topic. Bretz et. al. (1992, pp 312-352) as well as Levy and Williams (2004) for instance provide extensive reviews of the huge literature on appraisals. The history of performance appraisal is quite brief. Its roots in the early 20th century can be traced to Taylor's pioneering Time and Motion studies. But this is not very helpful, for the same may be said about almost everything in the field of modern human resources management. As a distinct and formal management procedure used in the evaluation of work performance, appraisal really dates from the time of the Second World War - not more than 60 years ago. Yet in a broader sense, the practice of appraisal is a very ancient art. In the scale of things historical, it might well lay claim to being the world's second oldest profession!

There is, says Dulewicz (1989), "... a basic human tendency to make judgements about those one is working with, as well as about oneself." Appraisal, it seems, is both inevitable and universal. In the absence of a carefully structured system of appraisal, people will tend to judge the work performance of others, including subordinates, naturally, informally and arbitrarily.

Performance appraisal can be viewed as the process of assessing and recording staff performance for the purpose of making judgments about staff that lead to decisions. Performance appraisal should also be viewed as a system of highly interactive processes which involve personnel at all levels in differing degrees in determining job expectations, writing job descriptions, selecting relevant appraisal criteria, developing assessment tools and procedures, and collecting interpreting, and reporting results.

Definition

Performance appraisal may be defined as a structured formal interaction between a subordinate and supervisor, that usually takes the form of a periodic interview (annual or semi-annual), in which the work performance of the subordinate is examined and discussed, with a view to identifying weaknesses and strengths as well as opportunities for improvement and skills development. In simple terms, performance appraisal may be understood as the assessment of an individual's performance in a systematic way.

In many organizations—but not all—appraisal results are used, either directly or indirectly, to help determine reward outcomes. That is, the appraisal results are used to identify the better performing employees who should get the majority of available merit pay increases, bonuses, and promotions.

By the same token, appraisal results are used to identify the poorer performers who may require some form of counseling, or in extreme cases, demotion, dismissal or decreases in pay. (Organizations need to be aware of laws in their country that might restrict their capacity to dismiss employees or decrease pay.) Whether this is an appropriate use of performance appraisal—the assignment and justification of rewards and penalties—is a very uncertain and contentious matter.

Dale S. Beach (190, p. 290) has defined performance appraisal :

"It is the systematic evaluation of the individual with respect to his or her performance on the job and his or her potential for development."

Randall S. Schuler (1981, p. 281) has defined performance appraisal :

"Performance Appraisal is a formal, structured system of measuring and evaluating an employee's job related behaviours and outcomes to discover how and why the employee is presently performing on the job and how the employee can perform more effectively in the future so that the employee, organization, and society all benefit."

A term which has become popular recently is Performance Management. Performance management is a holistic process, bringing together many elements which go together to make up the successful practice of people management, including in learning and development.

Armstrong and **Baron** (2004) define performance management as;

"Performance management is process which contributes to the effective management of individuals and teams in order to achieve high levels of organizational performance. As such, it establishes shared understanding about what is to be achieved and an approach to leading and developing people which will ensure that it is achieved."

From the definition it is seen that performance management has a broader context than just Performance Appraisal. Performance management relates to every activity of the organization set in the context of human resource policies.

Rational for Policy on Performance Appraisal

Objectives for performance appraisal policy can best be understood in terms of potential benefits. Mohrman, Resnick-West and Lawler (1989) identify the following :

- Increase motivation to perform effectively.
- Increase staff self-esteem.
- Gain new insight into staff and supervisors.
- Better clarify and define job functions and responsibilities.
- Develop valuable communication among appraisal participants.
- Encourage increased self-understanding among staff as well as insight into the kind of development activities that are of value.
- Distribute rewards on a fair and credible basis.
- Clarify organizational goals so they can be more readily accepted.
- Improve institutional/departmental manpower planning, test validation, and development of training programs.

Let us look at a Performa of performance appraisal. Please note that every company designs its own performance appraisal form.

Name		Date of Joining: And Grade: Rs.		
Date of Birth:		Date of Continuous Appointment to present Grade:		
Academic Qualifications:				
(*i*) Present Designations: (*ii*) Grade of Pay: Rs. (*iii*) Present Pay: Rs.		Promotions Date: Grade: Rs. Received		
	Outstanding	***Above Average***	***Average***	***Below Average***
1. **Job Knowledge** Consider how much does he know about the requirements of the job he is working on, in relation to the extent of knowledge required for his job.	Excellent knowledge of all phases of his work. ☐	Thorough knowledge Knows job sufficiently well. ☐	Possesses the minimum knowledge required to do the job. ☐	Knowledge inadequate to retain in job without improvement. Has not gained adequate comprehension of his job requirements. ☐
2. **Quality and Dependability of Work** Consider output of satisfactory work under normal conditions. Please cite actual instances on this trait in comments.	Has excellent knowledge of this own job and related matters. Justifies complete confidence. ☐	Well informed on all phases of the job. Fulfils all demands. ☐	Reasonably well informed about his job. Meets job requirements. ☐	Needs frequent instructions even on routine jobs and often unreliable. ☐

3. **Quantity of Work**	Usually high output ☐	Always turns out good volume. ☐	Turns out fair amount of work. ☐	Output consistently below average. ☐
COMMENTS AND EXPLANATIONS:				
4. **Planning, Organizing and Controlling** Consider effectiveness in anticipating needs, establishing objectives; effectiveness in distributing work—load, granting authority; effectiveness in keeping unit working towards objectives; measuring accountability and performance; interpreting results to take corrective action.	Maintains high degree of effectiveness in planning, organizing and controlling ☐	Is effective in performing the managerial duties described. ☐	Meets the minimum requirement in this respect. ☐	Does not possess the required capability to perform the functions described. ☐
5. **Developing People** Consider effectiveness in the selection, appraisal, training and development of his team.	Highly effective ☐	Fully aware of responsibility and devotes considerable time for this function. ☐	Should devote more effort to this function. ☐	Is incapable of developing other people. ☐
XXXXXXXXXXXX				
11. **Integrity**	ABOVE BOARD ☐		QUESTIONABLE (if so, give comments below). ☐	
COMMENTS AND EXPLANATION				
12. **Evaluation of overall performance**	Extraordinary all round performance ☐	Performance much beyond normal requirements. ☐	Performance satisfactory but requires improvement in certain phases. ☐	Performance inadequate ☐
COMMENTS AND EXPLANATIONS.				

Signature of the counter signing officer **Designation :** **Date**	**Signature of the reviewing officer** **Designation :** **Date**	**Signature of the reporting officer** **Designation :** **Date**

Fig. 13.1. *Performance Appraisal Series—Form 'A'.*

PURPOSE OF PERFORMANCE APPRAISAL

The performance appraisal has two primary purpose viz. evaluations and a feedback. The main aim of the evaluation system is to identify the performance gap (if any). This gap is the shortfall that occurs when performance does not meet the standard set by the organization as acceptable; while the objective of the feedback system is to inform the employee about the quality of his or her performance. (However, the information flow is not exclusively one way. The appraisers also receive feedback from the employee about job problems, etc.)

The introduction of formal performance appraisal systems is often guided by multiple objectives. Cleveland et. al. (1989) gives several uses of performance appraisal : First, appraisal is used to make *between-person decisions*, liker promotion, termination of appointment, salary etc.; second, it is used for making *within person decision,* to determine strength and weakness and develop a competency profile; third, performance appraisal is carried out to meet the *organization objectives,* such as personnel planning, documentation etc. A survey by Cleveland et. al. (1989) shows that appraisal has the greatest impact on salary administration, performance feedback and identification of strength and weaknesses.

In other words the performance should be in two terms viz. first, *strategic* relating to broader issues and longer terms goals; second, *integrated-* which includes and combines aspects of the business, people, individual and teams. One of the best ways to appreciate the purposes of performance appraisal is to look at it from the different viewpoints of the main stakeholders : the employee and the organization.

Employee Viewpoint

From the employee viewpoint, the purpose of performance appraisal is four-fold (Cash, 1993) :

(1) Tell me what you want me to do

(2) Tell me how well I have done it

(3) Help me improve my performance

(4) Reward me for doing well.

Organizational Viewpoint

From the organization's viewpoint, one of the most important reasons for having a system of performance appraisal is to establish and uphold the principle of accountability.

For decades it has been known to researchers that one of the chief causes of organizational failure is "non-alignment of responsibility and accountability." Non-alignment occurs where employees are given responsibilities and duties, but are not held accountable for the way in which those responsibilities and duties are performed. What typically happens is that several individuals or work units appear to have overlapping roles.

The overlap allows—indeed actively encourages - each individual or business unit to "pass the buck" to the others. Ultimately, in the severely non-aligned system, no one is accountable for anything. In this event, the principle of accountability breaks down completely. Organizational failure is the only possible outcome.

In cases where the non-alignment is not so severe, the organization may continue to function, albeit inefficiently. Like a poorly made or badly tuned engine, the non-aligned organization may run, but it will be sluggish, costly and unreliable. One of the principal aims of performance appraisal is to make people accountable. The objective is to align responsibility and accountability at every organizational level. Performance appraisal serves over a dozen different organizational purposes. These are discussed in subsequent paragraphs.

Providing Feedback. Providing feedback is the most common justification for an organization to have a performance appraisal system. Through its performance appraisal process the individual learns exactly how well she did during the previous twelve months and can then use that information to improve her performance in the future. In this regard, performance appraisal serves another important purpose by making sure that the boss's expectations are clearly communicated.

Facilitating Promotion Decisions. Almost everyone in an organization wants to get ahead. How should the company decide who gets the brass rings ? Performance appraisal makes it easier for the organization to make good decisions about making sure that the most important positions are filled by the most capable individuals.

Facilitating Layoff or Downsizing Decisions. If promotions are what everybody wants, layoffs are what everybody wishes to avoid. But when economic realities force an organization to downsize, performance appraisal helps make sure that the most talented individuals are retained and that only the organization's marginal performers are cut loose.

Encouraging Performance Improvement. How can anyone improve if he doesn't know how he's doing right now ? A good performance appraisal points out areas where individuals need to improve their performance.

Motivating Superior Performance. This is another classic reason for having a performance appraisal system. Performance appraisal helps motivate people to deliver superior performance in several ways. First, the appraisal process helps them learn just what it is that the organization considers to be "superior." Second, since most people want to be seen as superior performers, a performance appraisal process provides them with a means to demonstrate that they actually are. Finally, performance appraisal encourages employees to avoid being stigmatized as inferior performers (or, often worse, as merely "average").

Setting and Measuring Goals. Goal setting has consistently been demonstrated as a management process that generates superior performance. The performance appraisal process is commonly used to make sure that every member of the organization sets and achieves effective goals.

Counseling Poor Performers. Not everyone meets the organization's standards. Performance appraisal forces managers to confront those whose performance is not meeting the company's expectations.

Determining Compensation Changes. This is another classic use of performance appraisal. Almost every organization believes in pay for performance. But how can pay decisions be made if there is no measure of performance ? Performance appraisal provides the mechanism to make sure that those who do better work receive more pay.

Encouraging Coaching and Mentoring. Managers are expected to be good coaches to their team members and mentors to their protégé's. Performance appraisal identifies the areas where coaching is necessary and encourages managers to take an active coaching role.

Supporting Manpower Planning. Well-managed organizations regularly assess their bench strength to make sure that they have the talent in their ranks that they will need for the future. Companies need to determine who and where their most talented members are. They need to identify the departments that are rich with talent and the ones that are suffering a talent drought. Performance appraisal gives companies the tool they need to make sure they have the intellectual horsepower required for the future.

Determining Individual Training and Development Needs. If the performance appraisal procedure includes a requirement that individual development plans be determined and discussed, individuals can then make good decisions about the skills and competencies they need to acquire to make a greater contribution to the company. As a result, they increase their chances of promotion and lower their odds of layoff.

Determining Organizational Training and Development Needs. Would the organization be better off sending all of its managers and professionals through a customer service training program or one on effective decision making ? By reviewing the data from performance appraisals, training and development professionals can make good decisions about where the organization should concentrate company-wide training efforts.

Validating Hiring Decisions. Is the company hiring stars, or is it filling itself with trolls ? Only when the performance of newly hired individuals is assessed can the company learn whether it is hiring the right people.

Providing Legal Defensibility for Personnel Decisions. Almost any personnel decision—termination, denial of a promotion, transfer to another department—can be subjected to legal scrutiny. If one of these is challenged, the company must be able to demonstrate that the decision it made was not based on the individual's race or handicap or any other protected aspect. A solid record of performance appraisals greatly facilitates legal defensibility when a complaint about discrimination is made.

Improving Overall Organizational Performance. This is the most important reason for an organization to have a performance appraisal system. A performance appraisal procedure allows the organization to communicate performance expectations to every member of the team and assess exactly how well each person is doing. When everyone is clear on the expectations and knows exactly how he is performing against them, this will result in an overall improvement in organizational success.

PROBLEMS OF RATING

Performance appraisals are subject to a wide variety of inaccuracies and biases referred to as 'rating errors'. These errors occur in the rater's observation; judgment, information procession and can seriously affect assessment results. The most common rating errors are leniency or severity, central tendency, halo effect, rater effect, primacy and regency effects, perceptual set, performance dimension behaviour, spill over effect and status effect.

Leniency or Severity

Leniency or severity on the part of the rater makes the assessment a subjective. Subjective assessment defeats the very purpose of performance appraisal. Ratings are lenient due :

- Rater feeling that anyone under his jurisdiction who is reacted unfavorably will reflect poorly on his or her own worthiness.
- Rater comprehending that anyone who could have been rated unfavorably has already been discharged from the organization.
- Feelings that a derogatory rating will be revealed to the ratee to the detriment of the relations between the rater and the ratee.

- Rater may be projecting someone.
- Rater may be feeling it necessary to always approve of others in order to gain approval for him or herself.
- He or she may be operating on the premise, "whoever associates with me is meritorious, and therefore I am meritorious."
- He or she may rate leniently because there exists, in culture, a response set to approve rather that disapprove.
- In India it is not in culture to rate employees poorly.

Central Tendency :

This occurs when employees are incorrectly rated near the average or middle of the scale. The attitude of the rater is to play safe. This safe-playing attitude stems from certain doubts and anxieties are:

- "Do I know the man sufficiently well to be able to give a fair assessment of him ?"
- If I rate the way I think I should, what will be its influence on his relations with me and on his performance in the future.

Close to the error of central tendency is the problem of range restriction. Range restriction may involve clustering all employees around any point on a scale, often in combination with leniency errors at the very top. What is distinctive in the error of central tendency and the error of range restriction is failure to note real performance differences, either intentionally or due to insufficient attention.

Halo Error

A halo effect takes place when one aspect of an individual's performance influences the evaluation of the entire performance of the individual, just as the assessment of the performance of as student in his or her examination being influenced by the opening paragraph of every answer. If the introductory paragraph is poorly written, the chances of scoring high marks in that answer are diminished, however good the subsequent portion of the essay may be.

In an organization halo error occurs when an employee who works late constantly might be related high on productivity and quality of output as well as on motivation. Similarly, an attractive or popular employee might be given a high overall rating. Rating employees separately on each of a number of performance measures and encouraging raters to guard against the halo effect are two ways to reduce the halo effect.

Rater Effect

This includes favoritism, stereotyping and hostility. Excessively high or low scores are given only to certain individuals or groups based on the rater's attitude towards the rate, not on actual outcomes or behaviours. Sex, age, race and friendship biases are examples of this type of error.

Primacy and Regency Effects

The rater's ratings are heavily influenced either by behaviour exhibited by the rate during the early stages of the review period (primacy) or by outcomes, or behaviors exhibited by the ratee near the end of the review period (recently). For example, if a sales person captures an important contractor/sale just before the completion of the appraisal, the timing of the incident may inflate his or her standing, even though the overall performance of the sales-person may not have been encouraging. Like-wise, a blunder committed just before the appraisal period may diminish chances of securing a favorable rating, even if the overall performance is good.

Perceptual Set

This occurs when the rater's assessment in influenced by previously held beliefs. If the supervisor, for example, has a belief that employees hailing from one particular region are intelligent and hard working, his subsequent rating of an employee hailing from that region tends to be favorably high.

Performance Dimension Order

Two or more dimension on a performance instrument follow or closely follow each other and both describe or rotate to a similar quality. The rater rates the first dimension accurately and then rates the second dimension similar to the first because of their proximity. If the dimensions had been arranged in a significantly different order, the ratings might have been different.

Spillover Effect

This refers to allowing past performance appraisal ratings to unjustifiably influence current ratings. Past ratings, good or bad, result in similar rating for current period although the demonstrated behaviour does not deserve the rating, good, or bad.

Status Effect

It refers to overrating of employees in higher-level job or jobs held in high esteem, and underrating employees in lower-level job or jobs held in low esteem.

It is not the rater's errors alone that are barriers to accurate and valid measurement of employee performance. Barriers lie deep within the genetic and acquired makeup of all people concerned with performance appraisal. A wide variety of emotional, psychological, intellectual and any number of ways during the appraisal process to completely neutralize or nullify any programme designed to measure employee performance.

Solving Rater's Problems

The best way to overcome the problems is to provide training to the raters. At HP, a two-day training course is organized every year to prepare mangers to handle appraisals better. Not that training is a "cute-all" for all the ills of appraisal systems. From a practical point of view, several factors, including the extent to while pay is related to performance ratings, union pressure, turnover rates, time constraints and the need to justify ratings may be more important than training, influencing the ratings they actually give. This means that improving rating systems involves not just training the raters but remedying outside factors; such as union pressure. And it means that a rater training, to be effective, should also address real-life problems such as the fact that union representatives will try to influence supervisors to rate everyone high.

But training can help improve the appraisal system to extent of distortion that occurs due to the rater's errors such as halo, leniency, central tendency and bias. In typical training, raters are shown a videotape of jobs being performed and are asked to rate the worker. Ratings made by each participant are then placed on a flip chart and the various errors are explained. For example, if a trainee is rated on all criteria (such as quantity and quality) about the same, the trainer might explain that halo error had occurred. If, on the other hand, a trainer rated all videotaped workers very high, this might be explained as a leniency error.

What Should be Rated ?

One of the steps in designing an appraisal programme is to determine the evaluation criteria. It is obvious that the criteria should be related to the job. The six criteria for assessing performance are :

- **Quality.** The degree to which the process or result of carrying out an activity approaches perfection in terms of either conforming to some ideal way of performing the activity, or fulfilling the activity's intended purpose.
- **Quantity.** The amount produced, expressed in monetary terms, number of units, or number of competed activity cycles.
- **Timeliness.** The degree to which an activity is completed or a result produced, at the earliest time desirable from the standpoints of both coordinating with the outputs of others and of maximizing the time available for other activities.
- **Cost of Effectiveness.** It is he degree to which the use of the organizations resources 9 *e.g.*,human, monetary, technological and material) is maximized in the sense of getting the highest gain or reduction in loss from each unit or instance of use of a resource.
- **Need for supervision.** The degree to which a job performer can carry out a job function without either having to request supervisory assistance or requiring supervisory intervention to prevent an adverse outcome.
- **Interpersonal impact.** The degree to which a performance promotes feeling of self-esteem, goodwill and cooperation among co-workers and subordinates.

These criteria relate to past performance and behavior of an employee. There is also the need for assessing, as was pointed out earlier, the potential of an employee for future performance, particularly when the employee is tipped for assuming greater responsibilities.

Timing of Evaluation

How often should an employee be assessed ? The general trend is to evaluate once in three months, or six months, or once in a year. According to a survey conducted in 1997 by Arthur Anderson, 70 percent of the organizations conduct performance appraisal once a year. Newly hired employees are rated more frequently that the older ones. Frequent assessment is better than phased evaluation. Feedback in the latter is delayed and the advantages of timely remedial measures by the employee are lost. Frequent evaluation gives constant feedback to the rate, thus enabling him or her to improve performance if there is any deficiency. The performance of trainees and probationers should be evaluated at the end of respective programs.

Approaches to Performance Appraisals

Creamer and Janosik note that performance appraisal is not about a single event, such as completing a standard review form, but rather a process that is ongoing. Appraisal activities, as an ongoing process, should connect the process to organizational functioning and have as their focus staff improvement, not simply salary adjustment and/or disciplinary action. Davis

(2001) proposed a model of performance appraisal for use in student affairs that includes three phases : Getting started/renewal, Achievement, and Evaluation. The model includes detailed suggestions for conducting an appraisal interview.

Creamer and Janosik outline several approaches to performance appraisal, including behavior based approaches, results-focused approaches, and appraisals of team performance.

Behavior-Based Approaches

These approaches tend to use specific performance factors to evaluate staff. Measures of performance can be either quantitative or qualitative.

One approach is the conventional rating scale. These scales use words or phrases to describe the degree to which certain behaviors or characteristics are displayed. Categories for behaviorally anchored scales can be created from job descriptions. If there are no appropriate behaviors or characteristics within job descriptions, supervisors should work with staff to determine what behaviors and characteristics would be most useful in an appraisal setting.

Another way of approaching this type of appraisal is the behaviorally anchored scale. In this approach, broad categories of practice are identified, ideally through collaborations between supervisors and staff. Specific job behaviors are then linked to the categories. Measures of staff member behavior are rated on a scale in relation to specific behavior items, such as "understands department functions."

Henderson (1980) notes that job-dimensions usually yield similar broad categories; such as planning, setting priorities and responsiveness to supervision. Categories such as these may be useful in framing evaluation criteria in this approach to appraisal.

Another means of approaching behaviour-based appraisal is the behavioural frequency scale. Here, desired behaviors are described and the staff member is evaluated on how often those behaviors occur.

The weighted checklist is another way of approaching behavior-based appraisal. This method provides a list of performance related statements that are weighted. Staff members are judged on a scale indicating the degree to which the statement accurately describes performance.

A final approach to behavior-based appraisal is the forced-choice method. Here, a list of performance related statements about job performance are evaluated on how well they discriminate among staff and how important they are to unit or institutional performance. Discrimination and desirability statements are placed on a grid in clusters that differ on discrimination but are closely related in desirability. Discrimination and desirability are multiplied to yield a total scale score.

Results-Focused Approaches

Creamer and Janosik note that there are both advantages and disadvantages to results-based performance appraisal approaches. On the positive side, they produce short and long-term results in the context of original performance and organizational objectives, are generally perceived as fair, tend to generate high levels of commitment to the organization, and they encourage a high level of participation and are thus defensible. On the negative side, they can be overly results oriented - especially in educational organizations, and they may be inflexible.

If supervisors determine that the advantages outweigh disadvantages, results-focused approaches may be incorporated. There are two general techniques of enacting results-focused approaches : Management by Objectives (MBO) and Accountabilities and Measures (Grote, 1996).

Methods of Performance Appraisals

Numerous methods have been devised to measure the quantity and quality of employees' job performance. Each of the methods discussed could be effective for some purposes, for some organizations. None should be dismissed or accepted as appropriate except as they relate to the particular needs of the organization or of a particular type or employees. Broadly, all the approaches to appraisal can be classified into

- Past-oriented methods
- Future-oriented methods

Each group has several techniques are discussed in subsequent paragraphs.

Past-Oriented Methods

The major past-oriented methods are :

- Rating scales
- Checklists
- Forced choice method
- Forced distribution method
- Critical incident method
- Behaviorally anchored scales
- Field review method
- Performance tests and observations
- Annual confidential reports
- Essay method
- Cost accounting approach
- Comparative evaluation approach.

These methods are discussed below:

1. **Rating Scale**. Rating scales offer the advantages of adaptability, relatively easy use and low cost. Nearly every type of job can be evaluated with the rating scale, the only requirement being that the job-performance criteria should be changed. This way, a large number of employees can be evaluated in a short time, and the rater does not need any training to use the scale. There are some disadvantages in that the rater's biases are likely to influence evaluation, and the biases are particularly pronounced on subjective criteria such as cooperation, attitude and initiative, furthermore, numerical scoring gives an illusion of precision that is really unfounded.
2. **Checklist**. Here a checklist of behaviour descriptions is prearranged and each person is evaluated against such list. Rater merely record the list and a separate group can allocate weight ages for each list and finally arrive at total points or marks obtained.

   (*a*) *Advantages*

   (*i*) Checklist reduces subjectively because recording is done by some one else act as the rater. Rater, at the end put weight ages and adds marks.

   (*ii*) Comparison possible.

   (*b*) *Limitations*

   (*i*) Normally confined to staff of personnel department.

   (*ii*) Difficult for all jobs.

3. **Forced Choice Method.** This is a special type of checklist. Rater has to choose between two statements or more, all of which may be favorable or unfavorable. Appraisers job is to select that statement which is most appropriate to describe the employee. Sample statements for a salesman may be framed as follows :

   (*a*) Slow but steady

   (*b*) Avoid risks

   (*c*) Consult headquarters on important decisions

   (*d*) Meet the customer with confidence

   (*e*) Friendly and informal

   (*f*) Plain speaking.

   Here the rater does not know the desirable answer for a particular job. This is available in the 'key' kept confidential either in computer or files. The answers of rating are fed into the computer and marks obtained with the help of keys.

   - Advantage. Since appraiser does not know the "correct answer", the bias is minimized.
   - Limitations. Appraisers as well raters dislike this method, since they feel they are not taken into confidence by giving them the right answers.

4. **Forced Distribution Method.** One of the errors in rating is leniency- clustering a large number of employees around a high point on a rating scale on part of the raters. The forced distribution method seeks to overcome the problem by compelling the rater to distribute the rates on all points on the rating scale. This system is easy to understand and administer. The objective of this technique is to spread out ratings in the form of normal distribution which is open to criticism. Many times, this categorization is not found in work groups particularly when the size of the group is comparatively smaller. Forced distribution is more suitable for a large group.

5. **Critical Incidents Method.** The critical incidents method of employee assessment has generated a lot of interest these days. The approach focuses on certain critical behaviours of an employee that make all the difference between effective and non-effective performance of a job. The supervisors and when they occur record such incidents.

   In this method the supervisor is refrained to make or pass overall judgments and concentrate upon discussing facts as he sees them. The supervisor has to pay close attention to what an employee is doing. The method suffers from the defect that outstanding incident happens so frequently that individual's appraisal may not vary markedly between any two time periods. It has been observed most of the times the employees have neither positive nor negative incidents. If the critical event does not happen, it will be difficult to rate an employee. To overcome these problems Gerald Whitlock designed a specimen checklist which consists of a number of behaviour incidents which are considered to be the examples of uncommonly, ineffective or effective job behaviour. The usual method/ procedure in constructing the specimen checklist is to collect behaviour incidents from certain experts in this area. The number of such performance behaviours ranges from 80 -150 incidents equally divided between effective and ineffective behaviours. Few of the typical incidents re give at Figure 13.2.

Displayed unpleasant behaviour to a sales person.
Absented from work frequently.
Rejected inferior quality goods.
Developed new procedure to reduce paper work.
Developed a new process to reduce wastage.
Helped fellow employees to solve problems.
Etc. etc.

Fig. 13.2. *Check List for Critical Incidents.*

6. **Behaviourally Anchored Rating Scales (BARS)** :

Behaviourally anchored scales, sometimes called behavioural expectation scales, are rating scales whose scale points are determined by statements of effective and ineffective behaviours. They are said to be Behaviourally anchored in that the scales represent a range of descriptive statements of behaviour varying from the least to the most effective. BARS have the following features :

- Areas of performance to be evaluated are identified and defined by the people who will use the scales.
- The scales are anchored by descriptions of actual job behaviour that, supervisors agree, represent specific levels of performance. The result is a set of rating scales in which both dimensions and anchors are precisely defined.
- All dimensions of performance to be evaluated are based on observable behaviours and relevant to the job being evaluated since BARS are tailor-made for the job.
- Since the raters who will actually use the scales are actively involved in the development process, they are more likely to be committed to the final product.

The procedure for BARS is usually five stepped.

- **Generate Critical Incidents**. Persons with knowledge of the job to be appraised (job holders/supervisors) are asked to describe specific illustrations (critical incidents) of effective performance behaviour.
- **Develop Performance Dimensions**. These people then cluster the incidents into a smaller set (or say 5 or 10) of performance dimensions. Each cluster (dimension) is then defined.
- **Reallocate Incidents**. Any groups of people who also know the job then reallocate the original critical incidents. They are given the cluster's definitions, and critical incidents, and asked to redesign each incident to the dimension it best describes. Typically a critical incident is retained if some percentage (usually 50 to 80%) of this group assigns it to the same cluster as the previous group did.
- **Scale of Incidents.** This second group is generally asked to rate (7 or 9 point scales are typical) the behaviour described in the incident as to how effectively or ineffectively it represents performance on the approximate dimension
- **Develop Final Instrument**. Subsets of incidents (usually 6 or 7 per cluster) used as "behaviour anchors" for the performance dimensions.

BARS were developed to provide results that subordinates could use to improve performance. Superiors would feel comfortable to give feedback to the ratees. BARS help overcome rating errors. Unfortunately, this method too suffers from distortions inherent in most rating techniques. Though BARS technique is more time-consuming and expensive than other appraisal tools, yet it has got certain advantages, such as :

- **A more accurate gauge**, since person's expert in the technique does BARS, the results are sufficiently accurate.
- **Clear Standards**. The critical incidents along the scale help to clarify what is meant by "extremely good" performance, "average" performance and so forth.
- **Feedback.** The use of critical incidents may be more useful in providing feedback to the people being appraised.
- **Independent dimension**. Systematically clustering the critical incidents into 5 or 6 performance dimensions, helps in making the dimensions more independent of one another.
- **Rater–Independence**. The technique is not biased by the experience and evaluation of the rater.

7. Field Review Method.

This is an appraisal by someone outside the assessee's own department, usually someone from the corporate office or the HR Dept. The outsider reviews employee records and holds interviews with the ratee and his or her supervisor. The method is primarily used for making promotional decision at the managerial level. Field reviews are also useful when comparable information is needed form employees in different units or locations.

8. Performance Tests and Observations.

With a limited number of jobs, employee assessment may be based upon a test of knowledge or skills. The test may be of the paper-and-pencil variety or an actual demonstration of skills. The test must be reliable and validated to be useful. Even then, performance tests are apt to measure potential more than actual performance. In order for the test to the job related, observations should be made under circumstances likely to be encountered. Practically may suffer if costs of test development or administration are high.

9. Confidential Records.

Confidential records are maintained mostly in government departments, though its application in the industry is not ruled out.

10. Essay Method.

In the essay method, the rater must describe the employee within a number of broad categories, such as :

(*i*) the rater's overall impression of the employee's performance,

(*ii*) the profitability of the employee,

(*iii*) the jobs that the employee is now able or qualified to perform,

(*iv*) the strengths and weakness of the employee, and

(*v*) the training and the development assistance required by the employee. Although this method may be used independently, it is most frequently found in combination with others. It is extremely useful in filing information gaps about the employees that often occur in the better-structured checklist method.

11. **Cost Accounting Method/ Human Asset Accounting Method.**

    This method evaluates from the monetary returns the employee yields to his her org. A relationship is established between the cost included in keeping the employee and the benefit the org derives from him or her. Performance of the employee is then evaluated based on the established relationship between the cost and the benefit.

The current value of a firm's human organization can be appraised by developed procedures, by undertaking periodic measurements of "key casual" and "intervening enterprise" variables. They key causal variables include the structure of an organization's management policies, decisions, business leadership, strategies, skills and behaviour. The intervening variables reflect the internal state and health of an organization. They include loyalties, attitudes, motivations, and collective capacity for effective interaction, communication and decision-making. These two types of variable measurements must be made over several years to provide the needed data for the computation of the human asset accounting. These would be discussed in detail separately.

Future Oriented Tests

It is not enough if only the past performance is assessed ? It is important for organizations to assess how an employee can perform in the days to come. Focusing on employee potential or setting future performance goals can assess this. The commonly used techniques are MBO, psychological appraisals, and assessment centers.

1. **Management by Objective (MBO)**. Being discussed in detail subsequently.
2. **Assessment Center Method**. This concept is first started in German Army to evaluate the performance the soldiers'. The purpose of this method is to test candidates in a social situation using a number of assessors and a variety of procedures. The most important feature of the assessment center is job-related stimulations. This stimulation include the characteristics that managers feel are important for the job. On this basis the evaluators evaluate the employees.
3. **Psychological Appraisals.** Large organizations employ full-time industrial psychologists. When psychologists are used for evaluations, they assess and individual's future potential and not past performance. The appraisal normally consists of in-depth interviews, psychological tests, discussions with supervisors and a review of other evaluations. The psychologists the writes an evaluation of the employee's intellectual, emotional, motivational and other related characteristics that suggest individual potential and may predict future performance.

   The evaluation by the psychologist may be for a specific job opening for which the person is being considered, or it may be a global assessment of his or her future potential. From these evaluations, placement and development decisions may be made to shape the person's career. Because this approach is slow and costly, it is usually required for bright young members who, think, may have considerable potential within the org. Since the quality of the appraisal depends largely on the skills of the psychologists, some employees object to this type of evaluation, especially if cross-cultural differences exist.

4. **360 Degree Feedback (360 Degree Review).** 360 degree feedback is the most comprehensive and costly type of appraisal. It includes self ratings, peer review, and upward assessments; feedback is sought from everyone. It gives people a chance to know how they are seen by others; to see their skills and style; and may improve communications between people.

   360 degree feedback helps by bringing out every aspect of an employee's life. Cooperation with people outside their department, helpfulness towards customers and vendors, etc. may not be rewarded by other types of appraisal. This system also helps those who have conflicts with their manager.

   360 degree feedback generally has high employee involvement and credibility; may have the strongest impact on behavior and performance; and may greatly increase communication and shared goals. It provides people with a good all-around perspective.

   The Managing Individual Effectiveness (MIE) system at Bellcore is used for self-development. It gets feedback from peers, managers, subordinates, and the ratees themselves. According to a Bellcore representative, the results are better working relations; better communications; more information on management performance and style; increased effectiveness and productivity of individuals and the organization as a whole; knowledge of training needs; a better grasp of organizational priorities; and greater employee input in designing self-development plans.

   The Bellcore representative noted that, for success, expectations must be communicated clearly; employees must be involved early; resources must be dedicated to the process, including top management's time; confidentiality must be assured; and the organization, especially top management, must be committed to the program. This system requires a third party, such as a consultant, to begin the process, which may take months to start up.

   360 degree feedback may be given directly to the employees, who have the option of discussing them with their managers; or it may be given to the managers for use in a feedback meeting. Whichever method is chosen, training for the managers and ratees is necessary.

   Some off-the-shelf survey forms include job analysis techniques designed to form knowledge, skills and abilities based on interviews, focus groups, and questionnaires. These forms may help to kill two birds with one stone, by helping to create valid job descriptions and then providing feedback on performance. The knowledge, skills and abilities required by a job may be determined using traditional job-analysis techniques; competencies required by the job; strategic goals of the organization; development theory; or personality theory (*e.g.*, communication or leadership styles).

Other Methods used for performance appraisal are peer reviews, self appraisal and upward assessment that are used in various organizations.

PEER REVIEWS

A peer review program may be designed by a task force of three to six workers, to set the goals, benefits, and objectives of the program; design a criteria-based performance evaluation system; and conduct a pilot program (Training and Development, June 1992). During the pilot program, people may be encouraged to provide feedback on the system itself. Training and support should be available. Pilot programs are very important for any new system, because they let people iron out the bugs without letting the program lose credibility among other workers.

Peer reviews often have a high level of worker acceptance and involvement; they tend to be stable, task-relevant, and accurate. By helping peers to understand each others' work and by airing grievances in a non-threatening manner, peer reviews may also help people to get along better. For the organization, this means higher performance. For the people, this means a better place to work and less frustration; it may also help people to concentrate less on politics or working around people, and to spend more time on their work (or to put in less overtime).

Peer reviews may work best if all parties know that the reviews will not be used for setting pay, promotion possibilities, or disciplinary actions. However, a peer review system with the power to give promotions, raises, or disciplinary actions might be workable in some businesses, if the employees think it's a good idea.

In the peer ranking approach, the manager is typically asked to assess the overall performance of an employee by ranking them in relation to other employees. Some attempted to deal with the inherent subjectivity of this method by using a forced-ranking method, which meant distributing ratings so they conformed to a normal distribution curve. But as T. Peters (1987) points out, this means creating a statistical imperative to evaluate a pre-determined portion of employees as losers.

Self-Reviews

Self-reviews are based on the idea that employees are most familiar with their work, and that their involvement is essential. Employees rate themselves on a number of criteria, usually with a formal survey form, and suggest improvements. They help to clarify their own goals, and expose areas of weakness so they may be worked on. The manager may be left out of the process, although an exchange of views between the worker and manager may help their relationship, and boost the employee's own understanding.

Herbert H. Meyer (Academy of Management Executive, 1991) said that self-review changes the role of the manager to counselor, rather than judge—a role from which the manager can do more to support people. He wrote that self-review "...enhances the subordinate's dignity and self respect." Involving the employee as an equal in the review process is more likely (according to Meyer) to increase commitment to action plans, making the entire process both more satisfying and more productive.

Self-reviews tend to have low halo error and result in little paperwork for managers. However, people may not see their own deficiencies as others do, so self-review should be used alongside other methods.

Upward Assessments

Upward assessments are used in a large number of organizations, running from Honda and Chrysler to Motorola and NASA. These programs tend to be somewhat shocking to managers at first, but, if designed well, they can result in strong improvements. The rated managers become the program's biggest fans. Amoco's Bill Clover described this as the "SARAH reaction : Shock, Anger, Rejection, Acceptance, Help" (Training, March 1993).

Most managers do not realize that what they say sometimes does not match up to what they do. Upward assessments can help managers to keep their words and actions consistent, while showing areas where managers can improve their performance. This can greatly increase their credibility.

The process is more important than the survey form; it can't be successful unless both raters and managers "open up." Managers must be helped to accept and deal with the results of the assessment. Outside consultants may have experience, needed skills, and an "objective outsider" image, so people can open up to them without fear of reprisal. If cost is a major issue, it may be possible to hire an intern from a local doctoral program in organizational or I/O psychology.

Upward assessments may only be run with managers who have three or more direct reports. Someone other than the manager and ratees must assemble the completed survey forms into a report for the manager; some survey publishers do this.

Many consultants recommend using upward assessments at least every two years. This helps managers to check their progress and refreshes the findings of the past survey in their minds; however, it doesn't make the cost unbearable. After the first assessment, the program may be run in-house.

USE OF APPRAISAL DATA

The final step in evaluation process is the use of appraisal data. The data and information generated through performance evaluation must be used by the HR dept.

In one way or the other, data and information outputs of performance-appraisal programme can critically influence these coveted employer-employee reward opportunities. Specifically, the data and information will be useful in the following areas in HRM :

- Remuneration administration
- Validation of selection programmes
- Employee training and development programmes
- Promotion, transfer and lay-off decisions
- Grievance and discipline programmes
- HR planning.

PERFORMANCE APPRAISAL STEPS

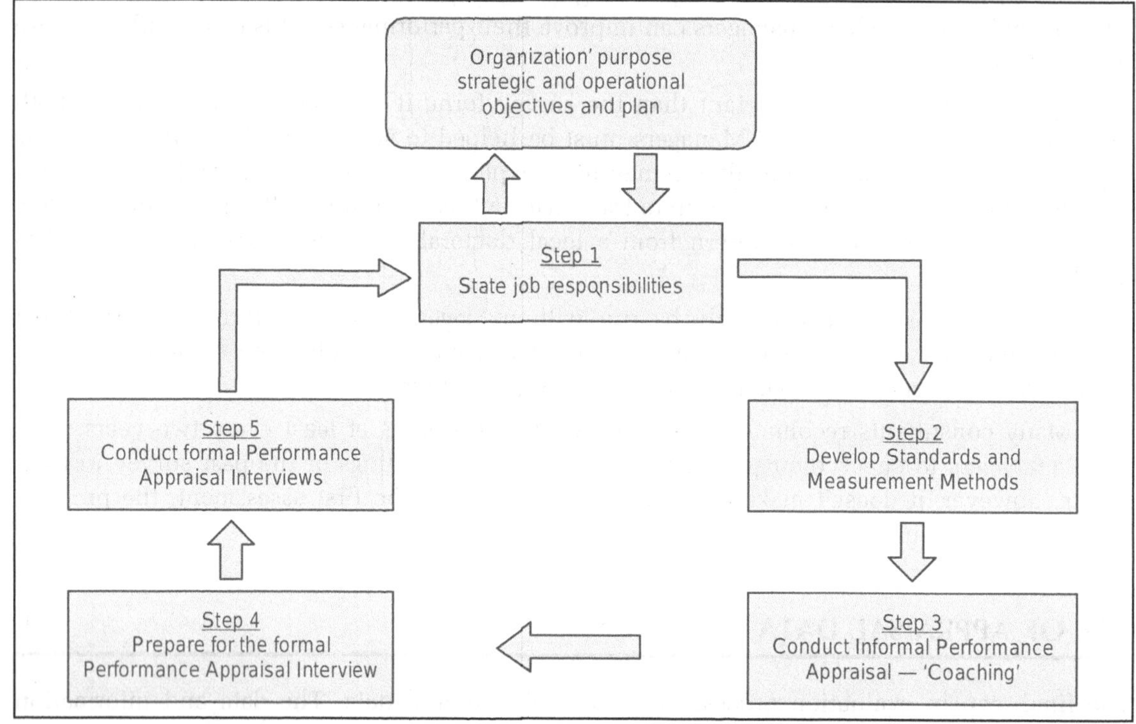

Fig. 13.3. *Performance Appraisal Steps.*

Comprehensive and effective participation within performance appraisal process consists of :

Step 1. State Job Responsibilities.

Step 2. Develop standards and measurement methods.

Step 3. Conduct Informal Performance Appraisal.

Step 4. Prepare for formal performance appraisal interview.

Step 5. Conduct Formal Performance Appraisal Interviews.

The performance appraisal of employee stems from the strategic objectives, and plans of the company. It is the vision that lays the foundations of knowledge, skills and abilities required by the employees of the company at present and in future.

Step 1 : State Job Responsibilities. The performance of an employee is primarily dependent on the fact that the employee should have clear idea of the performance related expectations. The appraisal has a major role in explaining the employer's expectations to the employee in terms of work output, which can become the basis for assessing his or her performance.

Step 2 : Develop standards and measurement methods. Clear and specific standards of performance are major elements of a valid and reliable performance appraisal system. The key is to develop standards that measure the essential job duties and responsibilities utilizing a balance of process, outcome, and individual and group based performance standards. The development of reliable, valid, fair, and useful performance standards is enhanced by employee participation, as workers possess the requisite unique and essential information necessary for developing realistic standards.

Step 3 : Conduct Informal Performance Appraisal. Informal interviews and constant consultations, coaching and helping in overcoming problems assist both the assessor and the employee in problem solving and reducing last minute conflicts. It also assists in improving and achieving standards so established.

Step 4 : Prepare for formal Performance Appraisal Interview. The assessor must prepare for an appraisal interview and must have facts and figures to substantiate what he tells the ratee.

Step 5 : Conduct Formal Performance Appraisal Interviews. Employee participation in an appraisal interview is associated with variety of desirable appraisal related outcomes–related outcomes, including appraisal system fairness, appraisal satisfaction, supervisory support, satisfaction with supervisors, appraisal system acceptance, and greater employee acceptance of negative feedback.

PERFORMANCE MANAGEMENT

'Performance management' aims at establishing a high performance culture in which individuals and teams take responsibility for the continuous improvement of business process and for their own skills and contributions provided within the framework provided by the effective leadership.

Specifically, performance management is about aligning individual objectives to organizational objectives and ensuring that individuals uphold corporate core values. It provides for expectations to be defined at agreed in terms of role responsibilities and accountabilities (expected to do), skills (expected to have) and behaviours (expected to be). The aim of the 'performance management' is to develop the capacity of people to meet or exceed the expectations and to achieve their full potential to the benefit of themselves and the organization. Performance management is concerned with ensuring that the support and guidance to develop people is readily available.

(*a*) Empowering, motivating and rewarding employees to do their best.

(*b*) Aligning everyone's individual goals to the goals of the organization *i.e.,* focusing employee's task on the right things and doing them right.

(*c*) Proactively managing and resourcing performance against agreed accountabilities and objectives.

(*d*) The process the behaviours by which managers manage performance of their employees to deliver a high achieving organization.

(*e*) Maximizing the potential of individuals and teams to benefit themselves and the organization, focusing on achievement of their objectives.

Performance management is a planned process of which primary elements are agreement, measurement, feedback, positive reinforcement and dialogue. It is concerned with measuring outputs in the shape of delivered performance compared with expectations expressed as objectives. Performance management focuses on targets, standards and performance measures and indicators. It is based on the agreement of role requirements, objectives and performance improvement and personal development plans. It provides the setting for ongoing dialogues about performance that involves the joint and continuing review of achievements against objectives, requirements and plans.

Performance management is concerned with inputs and values. The inputs are the knowledge skills and behaviour required to produce expected results. Developmental needs are identified by defining these requirements and assessing the extent to which the expected levels of performance have been achieved through the expected use of knowledge and skills and through appropriate behaviour that upholds core values.

Performance management is a continuous and flexible process, which involves managers and those whom they manage acting as partners within a framework that sets out how they can best work together to achieve the required results. It is based on the principle of management by contract and agreement rather than management by command. It relies on consensus and cooperation rather than control and coercion.

Performance management focuses on future performance planning and improvement rather than on retrospective performance appraisal. It functions as a continuous and evolutionary process, in which performance improves over time. It provides for regular and frequent dialogues between managers and individuals about performance and developmental needs. It is mainly concerned with individual's performance but it can also be applied to teams. The emphasis is on development, although performance management is an important part of the reward system through the provision of feedback and recognition and the identification of opportunities for growth. It may be associated with performance or contribution-related pay, but its developmental aspects are much more important.

There are five issues that need to be considered to obtain a full understanding of performance management :

(*a*) the meaning of performance;

(*b*) the significance of values;

(*c*) the meaning of alignment;

(*d*) managing expectations;

(*e*) the significance of discretionary behaviour.

The Meaning of Performance

Performance is often defined simply in output terms- the achievement of quantified objectives. Performance is not only the matter of what people achieve but also of how people achieve it. *The Oxford English Dictionary* confirms this by including the phrase 'carrying out' in its definition of performance; 'The accomplishment, execution, carrying out, working out of anything ordered or undertaken.' High performance results from appropriate behaviour, especially discretionary behaviour, and the effective use of the required knowledge, skills and competencies. Performance management must examine how results are attained because this provides the information necessary to consider what needs to be done to improve those results.

The concept of performance has been expressed by Brumbrach (1988) as follows :

"Performance means both behaviours and results. Behaviours emanate from the performer and transform performance from abstraction to action. Not just the instruments for results,, behaviours are also outcomes in their own right – the product of mental and physical effort applied to tasks- and can be judged apart from results."

This definition of performance leads to the conclusion that when managing performance both inputs (behaviour) and outputs (results) need to be considered. It is not a question of simply considering the achievement of targets, as used to happen in 'management of objectives' schemes. Competency factors need to be included in the process. This is the so called 'mixed model' of performance management, which covers the achievement of expected levels of competence as well as objective setting and review.

Performance Management and Values

Performance is about upholding values of the organization—'living the values'. This is an aspect of behaviour but it focuses on what people do to realize core values such as concern for quality, concern for people, concern for equal opportunity and operating ethically. It means converting espoused values into values in use : ensuring that the rhetoric becomes reality.

The Meaning of Alignment

One of the most fundamental purposes of performance management is to align individual and organizational objectives. This means that everything people do at work leads to outcomes that further the achievement of organizational goals. This purpose was well expressed by Fletcher (1993), who wrote :

"The real concept of performance management is associated with an approach to creating a shared vision of the purpose and aims of the organization, helping each employee understand and recognize their part in contributing to them, and in so doing, manage and enhance the performance of both individuals and the organization."

Alignment can be attained by a cascading process so that objectives flow down from the top and at each level team or individual objectives are fined in the light of higher levels goals. But it should also be a bottom-up process, individuals and teams being given the opportunity to formulate their own goals within the framework provided by the defined overall purpose, strategy and values of the organization. Objectives should be agreed and not set, and this agreement should be reached through open dialogue that take place between managers and individuals throughout the year. In other words, this needs to be seen as partnership in which responsibility is shared and mutual expectations are defined.

Managing Expectations

Performance management is essentially about the management of expectations. It creates a shared understanding of what is required to improve performance and how this will be achieved by clarifying and agreeing what people are expected to do and how they are expected to behave. It uses these agreements as the basis for measurement and review, and preparation of plans for performance improvement and development.

Performance Management and Discretionary Behaviour

Performance management is concerned with the encouragement of productive discretionary behaviour. As defined by Purcell and his team at Bath University, School of management (2003) :

'Discretionary behaviour refers to the choices that people make about how they carryout their work and the amount of effort, care, innovation and productive behaviour they display.'

Purcell and his team, while researching the relationship between HR practices and business performance, noted that 'the experience of success seen in performance outcomes helps reinforce positive attitudes.'

GUIDING PRINCIPLES OF PERFORMANCE MANAGEMENT

Egan (1995) proposes the following guiding principles for performance management :

'Most employees want direction, freedom to get their work done, and encouragement not control. The performance management system should be a control system only by exception. The solution is to make it a collaborative development system, in two ways. First, the entire performance management process- coaching, counseling, feedback, tracking, recognition, and so forth – should encourage development. Ideally, team members grow and develop through these interactions. Second, when managers and team members ask what they need to be able to do to do bigger and better things, they move to strategic development.

PERFORMANCE MANAGEMENT AND PERFORMANCE APPRAISAL

It is sometimes assumed that performance appraisal is the same thing as performance management. But there are significant differences. Performance appraisal can be defined as the formal assessment and rating of individuals by their managers at, usually, an annual review meeting. In contrast performance management is a continuous and much wider, more comprehensive and more natural process of management and clarify mutual expectations, emphasize the support role of managers who are expected to act as coaches rather than judges, and focuses on the future.

Table 13.1. Comparison of Performance Appraisal with Performance Management

Performance Appraisal	*Performance Management*
Top-down assessment.	Joint process through dialogue.
Annual Appraisal meeting	Continuous review with one or more formal reviews.
Use of ratings	Ratings less common
Monolithic system	Flexible process
Focus on quantified objectives	Focus on values and behaviours as well as objectives.
Often linked to pay	Less likely to be a direct link to pay.
Bureaucratic – complex paper work	Documentation kept to minimum.
Owned by HR department	Owned by Line mangers.

The research conducted by the CIPD in 2003 (Armstrong and Baron, 2004) elicited the following views from practitioners about performance management :

- We expect line managers to recognize performance management as a useful contribution to the management of their teams rather than chore.
- Managing performance is about coaching, guiding, motivating and rewarding colleagues to help unleash potential and improve organizational performance. Where it works well it is built on excellent leadership and high quality coaching relationships between managers and teams.

- Performance management is designed to ensure that what we do is guided by our values and is relevant to the purposes of the organization.

The research conducted

The research conducted by CIPD in 1997 (Armstrong and Baron, 1998) obtained the following additional views from practitioners about performance management :

- A management tool which helps managers to manage.
- Driven by corporate purpose and value.
- To obtain solutions to their work.
- Only interested in things you can do something about and get a visible improvement.
- Focus on changing behaviour rather than paperwork.
- It is about how we manage people- it is not a system.
- Performance management is what managers do naturally—it is a natural process of management.
- Based on accepted principles but operates flexibly.
- Focus on development not pay.

PERFORMANCE MANAGEMENT PROCESS

Performance management should be regarded as a flexible process, not as a system'. The use of the tem system implies rigid, standardized and bureaucratic approach that is inconsistent with the concept of performance management as a flexible and evolutionary, albeit coherent, process that is applied by managers working with their teams in accordance with the circumstances in which they operate. As such, it involves managers and those whom they manage acting as partners, but within a framework that sets out how they can best work together.

Performance Management Cycle

Performance Management can be described as a continuous self renewing cycle.

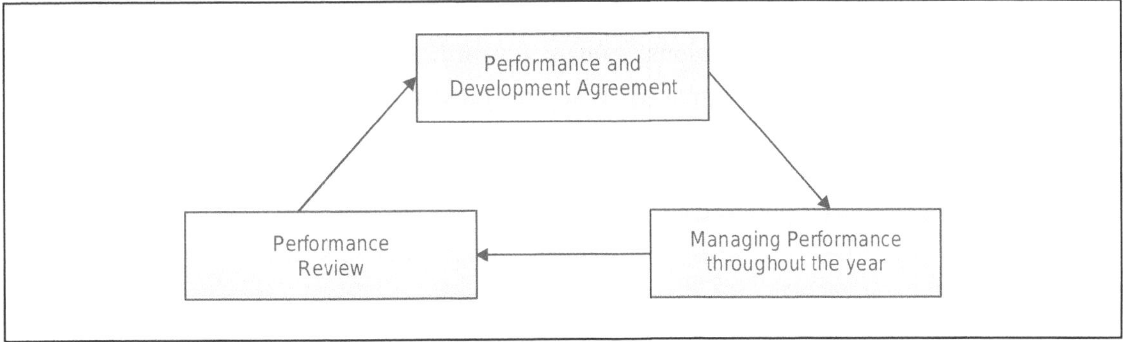

Fig. 13.4. *The Performance Management Cycle.*

Performance Agreements

Performance Agreements form the basis for development, assessment and feedback in the performance management process. They define expectations in the form of a role profile that sets out role requirements in terms of key results areas and the competencies required for effective performance. The role profile provides the basis for agreeing objectives and methods of measuring performance and assessing level of competency method. The performance agreement incorporates any performance improvement plans that may be necessary, and a personal development plan. It describes what individuals are expected to do but indicates what support will they receive from their managers.

Performance management emerge from the analysis of role requirements and the performance review. An assessment of past performance leads to an analysis of future requirements. The two processes can take place at the same meeting.

Defining Role Requirements. The foundation for performance management is a role profile that defines the role in terms of the key results expected, what role holders need to know and be able to do (competencies), and how they are expected to behave in terms of behavioural competencies and upholding organizations core values. Role profiles need to be updated every time a formal agreement is developed.

Objectives. Objectives describe something that has to be accomplished. Objective setting that results in an agreement on what the role holder has to achieve is an important part of the performance management processes of defining and managing expectations, and forms the point of reference for performance reviews. Objectives can be classified as :

- *On going role or work objectives* – all roles have built-in objectives that may be expressed as key result areas in a role profile.
- *Targets* – these define the quantifiable results to be attained as measured in such terms as output, throughput, income, sales, levels of service delivery, cost reduction and reduction of reject rates.
- *Tasks/ projects* – objectives can be set for the completion of tasks or projects by a specified date or to achieve an interim result.
- *Behaviour* – behavioural expectations are often set out generally in competency frameworks but they may also be defined individually under the frame-work headings.

Many organizations use the "SMART" mnemonic to summarize the criteria for objectives :

'S' – *Specific* - clear, unambiguous, straight forward, understandable and challenging.

'M' – *Measurable* – quantity, quality, time and money.

'A' – *Achievable* – challenging but within the reach of a component and committed person.

'R' – *Relevant* – relevant to the objectives of the organization so hat the goal of the individual is aligned to corporate goals.

'T' – *Time framed* – to be completed within an agreed time scale.

Measuring Performance in Achieving Objectives

Measurement is an important concept in performance management. It is the basis for providing and generating feedback, it identifies where things are going well to provide the foundations for building further success, and it indicates where things are not going so well, so that corrective action can be taken.

Measuring performance is relatively easy for those who are responsible for achieving quantified targets, for example sales. But this difficulty is alleviated if a distinction is made between the two forms of results—outputs and outcomes.

An output is a result that can be measured quantifiably, while an outcome is a visible effect that is the result of effort but cannot necessarily be measured in quantified terms.

There are components in all jobs that are difficult to measure quantifiably as outputs. But all jobs produce outcomes even if they are not quantified. It is therefore often necessary to measure performance by reference to what outcomes have been attained in comparison with what outcomes were expected, and the outcomes may be expressed in qualitative terms as a standard or level of competency to be attained.

Use of Performance Measure

The CIPD survey of performance management in 2003 (Armstrong and Baron, 2004) revealed that in order of importance, the following performance measures were used by the respondents :

- Achievement of objectives.
- Competence
- Quality
- Contribution to team.
- Customer care.
- Working relationships.
- Productivity.
- Flexibility.
- Skills/learning targets.
- Aligning personal objectives with organizational goals.
- Business awareness
- Financial awareness.

Tools of Performance Management

Major tools used by performance management are discussed in succeeding paragraphs.

Performance and Development Reviews

Many organisations without performance management systems operate 'appraisals' in which an individual's manager regularly (usually annually) records performance, potential and development needs in a top-down process. It can be argued that the perceived defects and the line manager's disregard for the performance appraisal led to the development of more rounded concepts of performance management. Nevertheless, organisations with performance management systems need to provide those involved with the opportunity to reflect on past performance as a basis for making development and improvement plans, and the performance and development review meeting provides this chance. The meeting must be constructive, and various techniques can be used to conduct the sort of open, free-flowing and honest meeting needed, with the reviewe doing most of the talking.

Learning and Development

Employee development is the main route followed by most organisations to improve organisational performance, which in turn requires an understanding of the processes and techniques of organisational, team and individual learning. Performance reviews can be regarded as learning events, in which individuals can be encouraged to think about how and in which ways they want to develop. This can lead to the drawing up of a personal development plan (PDP) setting out the actions they propose to take to develop themselves. To keep development separate from performance and salary discussions, development reviews may be held at other times.

Increasing emphasis on talent management also means that many organisations are re-defining performance management to align it to the need to identify, nurture and retain talent. Development programmes are reflecting the needs of succession plans and seeking to foster leadership skills. However, too much of an emphasis on talent management may be damaging to overall development needs and every effort needs to be made to ensure that development is inclusive, accessible and focused on developing organisational capability.

Coaching

Coaching is an important tool in learning and development. Coaching is developing a person's skills and knowledge so that their job performance improves, leading to the achievement of organisational objectives. Coaching is increasingly recognised as a significant responsibility of line managers, and can play an important part in a personal development plan. They will take place during the review meetings, but also and more importantly should be carried out throughout the year. For some managers coaching comes naturally, but for many they may not and training may be needed to improve their skills.

COMPETENCY MAPPING AND PERFORMANCE MAPPING

Hay-Mcber Company founder David McClelland, a Harvard University psychologist in the late 1960's, pioneered competency methodology. His research helped to identify performance aspects not attributable to a worker's intelligence or degree of knowledge and skill. McClelland's article appeared in *American Psychologist* in 1973, entitled "Testing for Competence Rather that for Intelligence."

Competency mapping is a process through which one assesses and determines one's strengths as an individual worker and in some cases, as part of an organization. It generally examines two areas : emotional intelligence or emotional quotient (EQ), and strengths of the individual in areas like team structure, leadership, and decision-making. Large organizations frequently employ some form of competency mapping to understand how to most effectively employ the competencies of strengths of workers. They may also use competency mapping to analyze the combination of strengths in different workers to produce the most effective teams and the highest quality work.

Definition

There are various definitions of competency but most of them refer to competence. Hogg, B. (1989) defined 'competencies are the characteristics of a manager that lead to the demonstrated of skills and abilities, which result in effective performance within an occupational area. Competency also embodies the capacity to transfer skills and abilities from one area to another."

Competency for a job can be defined *'as a set of human attributes that enable an employee to meet and exceed expectations of his internal as well as external customers and stakeholders.'*

Competency Mapping is a process of identifing key competencies for an organization and/ or a job and incorporating those competencies throughout the various processes (*i.e.*, job evaluation, training, recruitment) of the organization.

Competency Characteristics

Competencies are a signal from the organisation to the individual of the expected areas and levels of performance. They provide the individual with a map or indication of the behaviours that will be valued, recognised and in some organisations rewarded. Competencies can be understood to represent the language of performance in an organisation, articulating both the expected outcomes of an individual's efforts and the manner in which these activities are carried out. The various competencies required by employees are :

- Motives. The things a person consistently thinks about or wants and that which causes action. Motives 'drive, direct or select' behaviour to situation, and or information.
- Traits. Physical characteristics and consistent responses to situation, and or information.
- Self-concept. A person's attitude, attitudes and self image.
- Knowledge. Information a person has in specific content areas.
- Skill. The ability to perform a certain physical and mental task.

Knowledge and skill competencies tend to be visible and relatively 'on the surface' characteristics of people. Self-concept, trait, and motive competencies are more hidden, 'deeper' and central to personality. Knowledge and skill competencies are relatively easy to develop; training is the most effective way to secure these employees abilities. Core competencies are most difficult to assess and develop; it is most cost effective to select these characteristics.

Developing Competency Models

A competency model emerge's out of a well-designed job analysis. The job analysis should, at its starting point, carefully consider the work (tasks) that is done on the job. After cautiously describing the work, subject matter experts incumbent surveys, or other data-collection methods should be used to identify which Knowledge, Skills and Abilities (KSAs) are required to perform this work. These KSAs might very well be the competencies, or the KSAs might be clustered together to form slightly broader competencies. A final and very important step is to collect data from subject matter experts or incumbents in which they link the work and the competencies together. Many organizations that have had their competency models challenged in court have been able to successfully defend themselves with these sorts of data.

According to CIPD's 2007 Learning and Development survey, the most popular names found in employer competency frameworks are (in order) :

- Communication skills
- People management
- Team skills
- Customer service skills
- Results-orientation
- Problem-solving.

Competency frameworks can be developed in a number of ways. It is possible to draw on the competency lists produced in support of occupational standards and the framework of National Vocational Qualifications. Frameworks developed in this way are often linked with progression towards recognised qualifications. Competency lists are available on the web and these will come from a variety of sources. Many organisations develop their competency frameworks through an internal research programme, sometimes aided by advisers from an external consultancy. Methods of developing a framework range from importing an existing off-the-shelf package through to developing the entire thing from scratch. The best solution usually lies between these two extremes, namely internally generating a framework that builds in business relevance, but do this by adapting existing models that have already been widely used and have proved successful.

In a July 2007 *People Management* article Steve Whiddett and Sarah Hollyforde argued that; '*Many organisations develop a competency/ behaviour framework with a view to managing performance and progression more effectively. However, many managers and individuals find it hard to use the frameworks to help achieve their goals and, therefore, the goals of the organisation.*'

Formation of Competency Framework

Competency models are position models, which are at the heart of competency-based HR application. The bases of generating competency model are processes. If the flowcharts of the job are laid, determining the competencies is easier. If the competencies are not related to the specific process step, the model is not valid.

Sources of Competency Information.

1. **By Assumption**. Certain assumptions are assumed to be present in every employee.
2. **By Law of the Land**. Government and its associated regulatory agencies create requirements that apply to all workers.
3. **By Industry**. Individual industry has its own professional competency models and assessment approaches.
4. **By Organization**. The vision and mission statement f the organization reflect the overall philosophy of the organization.
5. **By Work Group**. Departments in many organizations especially large have their own vision and mission statements.
6. **By background information**. A special category of competency inputs for models comes with background knowledge of the company and industry in general.

The above inputs are generated from :

1. **Position Documentation**. Industry research, vendor information, customer feed back, certification and quality programmes all contribute towards position documentation.
2. **Process Documentation.** These are primarily the procedures manuals, flowcharts, time logs, job task analysis.
3. **Existing Documentation**. Job descriptions, union contracts, departmental planning documents, performance plans, and appraisal forms.
4. **Personal Development Process.** Training and development department is an excellent source of information on competencies.
5. **Interviews / Behavioural Event Interview/ Behavioural Description Interview**. Interview in all forms generate information for mapping competencies.

6. **Benchmarking**. Whether interviews or feedback, the important parameter in the development of the models is creating a benchmark of those employees who exceed and fall below performance standards.

Measure Competency Mapping Methods

There are five methods followed in most organizations.

1. Assessment Center.
2. Critical Incidents Technique
3. Interview Techniques
4. Questionnaires
5. Psychometric Test

Assessment Centres

Assessment center is a mechanism to identify the potential for growth. It is a procedure (not location) that uses a variety of techniques to evaluate employees for manpower purpose and decisions. An essential feature of the assessment centre as used by our organization is the use of situational test to observe specific job behavior. Since it is with reference to a job, elements related to the job are simulated through a variety of tests. The assessors observe the behavior and make independent evaluation of what they have observed, which results in identifying strengths and weaknesses of the attributes being studied.

Organization follows the elements as identified by the International Personnel Management Association (IPMA) for a process to be considered as assessment centre.

- A job analysis of relevant behavior to determine attributes, skills etc. for effective job performance and what should be evaluated by assessment center.
- Techniques used must be validated to assess the dimensions of skills and abilities.
- Multiple assessment techniques must be used.
- Assessment techniques must include job related simulation.
- Multiple assessors must be used for each assessed.
- Assessors must be thoroughly trained.
- Behavioral Observations by assessors must be classified into some meaningful and relevant categories of attributes, skills and abilities, etc.
- Systematic procedures must used to record observations.
- Assessors must prepare a report.

All information thus generated is integrated either by discussion or application of statistical techniques. Data thus generated can become extremely useful in identifying employees with potential for growth. Following are the some benefits of our assessment center.

- It helps in identifying early the supervisory / managerial potential and gives sufficient lead time for training before the person occupies the new position.
- It helps in identifying the training and development needs.
- Assessors who are generally senior manager in the organization find the training for assessors as a relevant experience to know their organization a little better.

The Assessment Center exercise provides an opportunity for the organization to review its HRM policies. Assessment center comprises a number of exercises or simulation which have been designed to replicate the task and demands of the jobs and to assess the strength and weakness and potential of the employees.

1. **Group Discussion**. In this candidates are brought together as a committee or Project team with one or a number of items to make a recommendation on. Candidates may be assigned a specific roles to play in the group or it may be structured in such a way that all the candidates have the same basic information. Group discussions allow them to exchange information and ideas and give them the experience of working in a team. In the work place, discussions enable management to draw on the ideas and expertise of staff, and to acknowledge the staff as valued members of a team. Some advantage of group discussion are :
   - Ideas can be generated
   - Ideas can be shared
   - Ideas can be tried out.
   - Ideas can be responded to by others.

   When the dynamics are right, groups provide a supportive and nurturing environment for academic and professional endevour. Group discussion skill has much professional application. Working in group is fun. A useful strategy for developing an effective group discussion is to identify task and maintenance roles that members can take up. Following roles, and dialogue that might accompany them in a group discussion have been identified.
   - Positive Task Roles
   - Positive Maintenance Role
2. **In Tray**. This type of exercise are normally undertaken by the candidates individually. The materials comprise of a bundle of correspondence and the candidate is placed in the role of somebody, generally, which assumed a new position or replaced their predecessor at short notice and has been asked to deal with their accumulated correspondence.
3. **Interview Simulation/Role Plays**. In these exercise candidates meet individually with a role player or resource person. Their brief is either to gather information to form a view and make a decision, or alternatively to engage in a discussion with the resource person to come to a resolution on an aspect or issue of dispute. Typically our HR team allow the candidate a 15-30 minutes time to prepare for such a meeting and will be given a short, general brief on the conduct of the meeting itself, consideration are also be given to preparatory notes.
4. **Case Studies/Analysis Exercises**. In this type of exercise the candidate is presented with the task of making about a decision about a particular business case. They are provided with a large amount of factual information which is generally ambiguous and, in some cases contradictory. Candidates generally work independently on such an exercise and their recommendation or decision is usually to be communicated in the form of brief written report and/or a presentation made to our assessors.

Critical Incident Technique

Despite numerous variations in procedures for gathering and analyzing critical incidents, researchers and practitioners agree that critical incidents techniques can be described as a set of procedures for systematically identifying the behavior that contribute success or failure of individual or organization in specific situation. First of all, a list of good and bad on the job behavior is prepared for each job. A few judges are asked to rate how good and how bad is good and bad behavior, respectively. Based on these rating a check-list of good and bad behavior is prepared.

The next task is to train our supervisor in taking notes on critical incidents or outstanding examples of success or failure of the subordinates in meeting the job requirements. The incidents are to be immediately noted down by the supervisor as he observes them. Very often the employee concerned is also involved in discussion with his supervisor before the incidents are recorded, particularly when an unfavorable incidents is being recorded, thus facilitating the employee to come out with his side of the story.

The objective of immediately recording the critical incidents is to improve the supervisor's ability as an observer and also to reduce the common tendency to rely on recall and hence attendant distortions in the incidents. Thus a balance sheet for each employee is generated which can be used at the end of the year to see how well the employee has performed. Besides being objective a definite objective of this technique is that it identifies areas where counseling may be useful.

Interview Techniques

Organization uses interview in some shape or form as a part of competency mapping. The interview consists of interaction between interviewer and applicant. Interview should be handled carefully to make it a powerful technique in achieving accurate information and getting access to material otherwise unavailable. Biasness and restriction or distortion of flow of information avoided to our best while interviewing.

Preparation should be made before the interview :

- Before the actual interview begins, the critical areas in which the questions will be asked first identified for judging ability and skills. It is advisable to write down these critical areas, define them with examples and form a scale to rate the responses. If there is more than one interviewer, some practice and mock interviews will help calibrate variation in individual's interviewer's rating.
- The second step taken is to scrutinize the information provided to identify skills, incidents and experiences in the career of the candidate, which may answer questions raised around the critical areas. This procedure will make interview less removed from reality and the applicant will be more comfortable because the discussion will focus on his experiences.
- An interview is a face-to-face situation. The applicant is "on guard" and careful to present the best face possible. At the same time he is tense, nervous and possibly frightened. Therefore during the interview tact and sensitivity can be very useful. The interviewer can get a better response if he creates a sense of ease and informality and hence uncover clues to interviewee's motivation, attitudes, feeling, temperament, etc., which are otherwise difficult to comprehend.

- The fundamental step taken is establishing rapport, putting the interviewee at ease conveying the impression that the interview is the conversation between two friends, and not a confrontation between employer and employee. One way to achieve this is by initially asking questions not directly related to job, that is, chatting casually about the weather, journey and so on.
- Once the interviewee is put at ease the interviewer starts asking questions or seeking information related to job. Here again it is extremely important to lead up to complex questions gradually.
- Showing surprise or disapproval of speech, clothes or answer to question can also inhibit the candidate. The interviewee is over-sensitive to such reactions. Hence, an effort to try and understand interview point of view and orientation can go a long way in getting to know the applicant.
- Leading questions should be avoided they give the impression that the interviewer is seeking certain kinds of answers. This may create a conflict in the interviewee, if he has strong view on the subject.
- The interviewers should be prepared with precise questions, and not take too much time in framing them.

Questionnaires

Questionnaires are written list of questions that users fill out and return. Assessors formulate questions about services based on the type of information they want to know. The questionnaire sources below provide more information on how we design questions. The techniques are used at various stages of development, depending on the questions that are asked in the questionnaires.

- **Common Metric Questionnaire** (CMQ). They examine some of the competencies to work performance and have five sections; Background, Contacts with people, Decision making, Physical and Mechanical Activities, and work setting.
- **Functional Job Analysis.** The most recent version of Functional job analysis uses seven scales to describe what workers do in jobs. These are : Things, Data, People, Worker instructions, Math, and Language. Each scale has several levels that are anchored with specific behavioral statements and illustrative tasks and are used to collect information.
- **Multipurpose Occupational System Analysis Inventory (MOSAIC)**. In this method each job analysis inventory collects data from the office of personnel management system through a variety of descriptors.- mainly Tasks and Competencies.
- **Occupational Analysis Inventory**. It contains 617 'work elements' designed to yield more specific job information while still capturing work requirements for virtually all occupations. Major categories of items are five folds; Information received, Mental Activities, Work Behavior, Work Goals and Work Context.
- **Position Analysis Questionnaires (PAQ)**. It a structured job analysis instrument mostly followed by our organization to measure job characteristics and relate them to human characteristics. It consists of 195 job elements which fall into the following five categories.
  - Information input (where and how the workers get information),
  - Mental Processes (reasoning and other processes that the workers use),
  - Work Output (Physical activities and tools used on the job),

- Relationship with other person and
- Job Context (the physical and social context of work)

- **Work Profile System (WPS).** It is designed to help employers accomplish human resources functions. The competency approach is designed to yield report targeted towards various human resources functions such as individual development planning, employee selection, and job description.

Competency mapping becomes essential for every organization to achieve excellence, gain competitive advantage, and renew then through proper restructuring. Today it is essential to leverage the human potential in respect of competency to understand both existing competencies and gaps if any.

THE SEVEN–S MODEL

McKinsey and Co has proposed the Seven-S Model for successful strategy implementation. McKinsey consultants found that neglecting anyone one seven key factors could make the effort change a slow painful, and even doomed process.

Structure. The McKinsey consultants point out that in today's complex and ever changing environment, a successful organization may make temporary structural changes to cope with specific strategic tasks without abandoning basic structural divisions throughout the organization.

Strategy. The Seven-S model emphasizes that, in practice, the development of strategy poses less of a problem that their execution.

Systems. This category consists of all formal and informal procedures that allow the organization to function.

Style. 'Style' refers to the pattern of substantive and symbolic actions undertaken by managers. It communicates priorities more clearly than words alone, and may profoundly influence performance.

Staff. Successful organization view people as valuable resources who should be carefully nurtured, developed, guarded and allocated. Top manager's devoute time and energy to planning the progress and participation of existing managers, and use job assignment policies to actively foster the development of new managers.

Skills. The term skills refer to the activities organization does best and for which they are known. (DuPont is known for Research). Strategic changes may require organization to add one or more new skills.

Superordinate Goals. This refers to guiding concepts, values, and aspirations and unites an organization in some common purpose. Superordinate goals are often captured in mission statement, but they can also be phrased as a simple slogan.

POTENTIAL APPRAISAL

Potential Appraisal is another powerful tool of employee development, whether managers realise it or not, they are accustomed to making potential assessments. Every time a manager recommends or fails to recommend an employee for a promotion, a potential assessment has, in fact, been made. The process of assessing the managerial potential of employees deals with the question of whether or not they have the ability to handle positions in the future which involve considerably more responsibility than what they have right now. As long as individuals are viewed as being able to handle increased or different responsibilities, they would be considered to have potential (either latent or visible). Potential appraisal may thus be defined as a process of determining an employee's strengths and weaknesses with a view to use this as a predictor of his future performance. This would help determine the promotabilty of an individual to a higher position and help chalk out his career plan. The fundamental difference between reviewing performance and assessing potential is in the criteria used. In reviewing performance, the criterion used is what goals the employee achieved and what skills he or she currently possesses that could be indicators of his or her ability to assume different or more advanced responsibilities. Managers cannot rely exclusively on past performance since a person's ability to adequately handle one level of responsibility does not necessarily mean that he or she can perform well in a position with a higher level or different responsibility. It is this that makes potential appraisal a very crucial and critical area. If an employee without requisite abilities is promoted to a higher position and does not perform as per expectations, then it becomes impossible to demote him. Thus, he is unable to perform at the higher level and becomes a 'passenger' in the system. It is rightfully assumed that every individual has potential, low or high. Many organizations have people whose potential being low; performance too is not up to the mark. Whilst the question in our minds hovers around how such people got into the system, the fact remains that they do not contribute to the organization's performance. A major problem that companies face is tackling the problem children. They can and have the ability to perform but do not perform and do not contribute to the organization's performance. This is mainly seen as an attitudinal problem. Further, these problem children bask in the glory of their potential but are unable to contribute to their own jobs. Dealing with workhorses too could be tricky. They can perform very well on routine tasks but have limited potential. Hence, their promotabilty is difficult and this creates frustrations for the employees. If promoted, they are unable to perform higher-level jobs and this too creates problems both for the individuals and the organisation. We easily conclude that 'stars' are ideal people to have in organisations. But retaining these stars could be difficult. They have high potential backed by high levels of performance and could be always on the lookout for greener pastures. Thus, as we see, potential appraisal is more intricate and complex vis-a-vis performance appraisal.

Because of the nature of the potential assessment activity, its timing and frequently is left to the manager's discretion. In assessing potential, managers are asked to make predictions about the future. These predictions concern many unknown factors, namely whether the individual can handle new responsibilities in a different managerial capacity, In addition, the potential assessment criteria is based mostly on an employee's process skills, which may be difficult to measure in a precise way. Thus, the timing and frequency of conducting potential assessment can be quite different from the more predictable timing of a performance review. For example, the potential assessment might occur when an employee has been on the job for one year, when an employee reaches certain 'mile-stones' (*i.e.*, every three years), or in preparation for major organizational shifts brought about by changes in the business such as reorganizations, expansion or rationalization. It is recommended that the potential assessment process take place at least over a six-month period, with a manager-employee meeting at both the beginning and end of the process. To begin the process, the manager and employee should meet to identify the process skills and the technical and administrative skills required for the employee's future responsibilities. The manager explains why these skills are necessary and explores with the employee how these skills might be learned and utilized on the current job. This includes nominating employees for some specific training programmes, both skill-based and knowledge-based. Some organisation may also organise such programmes on an in-house basis. Further on-the-job training could also be incorporated for the employees.

It is recommended that the manager observe the employee for at least three to six months to assess the extent to which the employee possesses and demonstrates the acquired skills. During the observation period, the manager should note specific behavioural examples of these skills and be prepared to discuss them with the employee at the concluding assessment meeting. The employee should also be prepared to discuss behavioural examples that demonstrate ability and need. At the assessment meeting, the manager and employee jointly review their observations. This discussion should include the identification of the employee's skill strengths and developmental needs. The manager then provides a written assessment in the form of 'summary statement'. Usually about one paragraph in length, the summary provides the employee with a brief, clear statement of where he or she stands regarding potential. An important concept to be conveyed during this meeting is that, while the employee may be assessed as having potential for a higher level or different position, no promises of a particular job can be made. Before the conclusion of this meeting, the pair should formulate a development plan (*i.e.*, decide on new development activities) that the employee can pursue in order to help realise his or her potential. Let us realise that there are no shortcuts to the successful implementation of potential appraisal. If potential appraisal is done in a systematic way it would contribute to having well designed career plan that would indicate the preferred growth path of an individual in an organisation. For example, a post-graduate diploma or degree holder in marketing management would aspire for career avenues in market research, sales management, advertising and such. An individual specialised in HRM could aspire for avenues in manpower planning, training, welfare, industrial relations and so on. Any professional organisation would make sincere efforts to match the individual career aspirations. This would obviously be a mutually beneficial activity for the individual and the organisation. Further, succession planning is the process where every individual manager is expected to develop a subordinate who would take over from him over a period of time. Many managers feel insecure about this process and avoid indulging in this development activity. What they fail to realise is that, if an individual has the potential and shows good performance, there is always room at the top, unless they themselves become un-promotable and stagnant. Succession planning too would succeed if and only if a good potential appraisal system exists and is in firm place. To conclude, if potential appraisal is not done in a planned manner, you may promote an undeserving employee. As a consequence, he does not succeed but would not accept a demotion back to his old slot. Thus, in a bid to develop a territory manager out of a super-salesman, and not doing it properly; you lose both in the process. But if implemented well, professional performance and potential appraisal could take the organisation on a fast development track and faster productivity through people.

Review Questions

1. What do you understand by Performance Appraisal ? Discuss its benefit to an industrial organization.
2. How can we integrate individual performance with Performance Management System of an organization ? Do we at all require performance appraisal systems ? Justify.
3. Traditional performance appraisal systems emphasizes on assessing the individual performance as an isolated factor. Briefly discuss the newer techniques of performance appraisal, critically reviewing the shortcomings of traditional system.

4. Discuss the effectiveness of MBO and BARS in performance appraisal. Develop KRA's for an HR manager of an organization and identify five important performance criteria for assessing the performance on a six point BARS.

PROJECT WORK

1. Critically review the performance appraisal system in India. Elaborate your answer visiting at least two organizations.
2. Develop a standard Performance Appraisal form for supervisors in an organization, selecting at least ten factors for review. Recommend your proposal development plan for such supervisors based on your review.

Case Study

MEGASOFT INDIA

MegaSoft is a MNC which has started its operations in India recently. It has its first branch at NOIDA, in National Capital Region, very close to Delhi. While starting their outfit their branch at NOIDA the company transferred some usiness accounts from New York to Noida. The objectives of starting the branch at Noida was to

(*a*) To activate NOIDA center.

(*b*) To recruit the best talents in IT and make use of their expertise for executing US job accounts at competitive compensation costs, to achieve price efficiency in their US market.

To start with the company recruited 100 software professionals, mostly from Infosys, TCS, Satyam, WIPRO, TCG group. After their induction the company immediately put them on job, based on mutually decided performance target. While deciding the performance target, the company, being new to India, adopted the US management culture, *i.e.*, kick-start with very ambitious target to earn variables, unparallel in Indian organization. The fixed compensation portion of the company was bench marked with the Cost to Company (CTC) of Indian software majors. The variables very kept very high; to earn the same, employees need to stretch. A performance target sheet for the employees covers following additional components, in addition to the quantitative target figures, in volume and value software development jobs.

- **Customer Focus**. Consistently meets the needs of internal and external customers.
- **Teamwork**. Collaborates within and across work groups, building and maintaining rapport and cooperation.
- **Respect for others**. Demonstrates respect for people from variety of ethnic, social and educational background.
- **Performance Initiative**. Continuously takes self motivated steps towards achieving organizational goals.
- **Application of Knowledge and Continuous Learning**. Effectively applies current knowledge and skills.
- **Innovation and Managing Change**. Readily adapts to change, demonstrates a willingness to learn, and seeks new challenge.
- **Performance Management and Development**. Uses the performance management programme effectively.
- Overall performance.

The managers based on 360 degree feed back measure all those performance areas. Being US MNC, customers feedback are from US clients, who do not have any direct contact with MegaSoft India employees, but often interact with them through videoconferencing to troubleshoot their software, which US companies purchased from MegaSoft, or to enquire about the BPO business issues. On several occasions, US clients alleged that employees of MegaSoft do not adhere to time schedule, they invariably appear late. Employees also do not bother about adequate homework before discussion on issues, brief on which the US clients send well in advance. Some US clients even threatened to withdraw their account with MegaSoft if the trend continued. In the performance review meetings the managers discussed these issues with the employees and employees gave the following responses :

US clients meeting through videoconferencing invariable takes place during midnight. They come to meeting after completing their strenuous target-bound tasks, for which they invariably have to stretch till 10p.m. almost daily. Even though MegaSoft do not have any system of attendance for the software developer, all developers make sure they come early in the morning and stay back, till they are able to complete their targeted job. Connectivity with US clients is often a major problem. At times MegaSoft India's employees cannot understand the American Accent and so also the problem with US clients to understand their accent. Clients expectations are skyrocketing. Even after signup, they change business process several times and always expect them to put those new aspects in the software, these results to redo, which means, wiping their earlier time investment for their jobs.

Assignment

MegaSoft is not prepared to change their performance criteria. You have been approached to suggest how the company can address this critical performance management issues.

Chapter 14

HUMAN RESOURCE AUDIT, HUMAN RESOURCE ACCOUNTING, MANAGEMENT BY OBJECTIVES AND BALANCED SCORE CARD

★ LEARNING OBJECTIVES ★

After reading this chapter, you will be able to understand :

- Human Resource Accounting, its scope, objectives and method of conduct.
- Understand the measurements of Human Resource Costs and Value.
- What is Human Resource Audit ?
- Objectives and Scope of Human Resource Audit.
- Uses and importance of Human Resource Audit.
- Process of Human Resource Audit.
- Methods of Human Resource Audit
- Management by Objectives
- Balanced Score Card

INTRODUCTION

As stated in previous Chapters men, material, finance and methods are the resources required for an organization. These resources are broadly classified as human (animate) and physical (inanimate) resources. The success of an organization depends on how best the scarce resources are utilized by humans. Therefore, the effective utilization of physical (inanimate) resources depends largely on the quality, caliber, skills and character of people, that is, the human resources working in it.

Since the early 1990's, one could easily observe that many companies in various industries are facing a shift towards information, expertise, skills, and technology because they are considered to be of great importance. Zuboff (198) calls it the Information Revolution and posits that this will transform the human society as dramatically as the *Industrial revolution* did. Today's time there are manifold titles such as the Information Economy, New Economy, and Knowledge-based economy.

'Human Resource Accounting' and 'Human Resource Audit' is the off shoot of various studies conducted in the areas of accounting and finance. Human Resource is an asset whose value gets appreciated over the period of time provided it is placed, applied and developed in the right direction. Organizations took few efforts to assign monetary value to human resources in its accounting practices. The traditional concept suggested that the expenditure on human resources is treated as 'charge against revenue' as it does not create any physical asset. At present there is a change and expenses incurred on any asset should be treated as capital expenditure as it yields benefits which can be derived for a long period of time and could be measured in monetary terms.

The modern search for a method provide Human Resource value information in external corporate reports has interested practicing Human Resource professionals since 1960's, when the R,G. Barry Corporation included Human Resource assets on a supplement to their balance sheet. Since that time there have been repeated efforts to include Human Resource value and other intangibles such as intellectual capital in corporate reports. The world over Human Resource budgets is getting attention and a trend is observed that in most countries the budget allocations to it are increasing. This has resulted in due;

(*a*) Realization of management and stakeholders that there exist a strong link between Human Resource and the strategic goals of the organization.

(*b*) There is an interest in developing Human resource as a profit centre especially in knowledge and service based sectors.

(*c*) There is a trend to outsource most of the Human resource functions like recruitment, selection etc.

(*d*) There is an increased interest in monitoring and managing human capital.

(*e*) More and more Human Resource Managers are today having formal education and have business or operations research background.

(*f*) Human Resource evaluation is more systematic and scientific; it is methodical and proactive.

(*g*) Return on Investment concept is now being extensively used as a tool for Human Resource evaluation.

The twelve approaches presented provide an array of useful tools to help the Human Resource Department develop a comprehensive strategy to shoe its contribution. Table 14.1 shows comparison of these approaches, as they are used to collect both qualitative and quantitative data from multitude of sources. The measurement focus is outlines, the relative cost is provided, and the relative value of information is presented.

Table 14.1. Comparison of Approaches to Measure the HR Contribution

Approach	*Measurement Focus*	*Relative Cost*	*Relative Value of Information*
1. HR Management by Objectives	Goal Setting for HR Performance Measure.	Low	Moderate
2. Surveys	Attitudes/perception	Moderate	Moderate
3. HR Case Studies	Qualitative Description and Data	Low	Low
4. HR Auditing	Efficiency and Existence of Practices	Low	Low
5. HR Key Factors	Program/Function Performance Measure	Moderate	Moderate
6. HR Cost Monitoring	Program/Function	Low	Low
7. HR Reputation	Attitudes/Perception	Moderate	Moderate
8. Competitive Benchmarking	Performance Measures/ Practices	High	High
9. Return on Investments	Benefits vs Costs	High	High
10. HR Effectiveness Index	Multiple Key Index	High	High
11. Human Capital/HR Accounting	Value of Skills/Capabilities/ Performance of Employees	High	Moderate
12. HR Profit Centers	Profit Contribution of Program Services	High	High

HUMAN RESOURCE ACCOUNTING

Human Resource Accounting is one of the latest concepts adopted by companies' world over. Human Resource Accounting is the off shoot of various research studies conducted in the areas of accounting and finance. Human Resource is an asset whose value gets appreciated over the period of time provided placed, applied and developed in the right direction. Human Resource Accounting aims at depicting the human resource potential in money terms while casting the organization's financial statements.

The traditional concept suggested that expenditure on human resource is treated as a 'charge against revenue' as it does not create any physical asset At present there is a change in this concept and the expenses incurred on any asset (as human resources) should be treated as capital expenditure as it yields benefits which can be derived for a long period of time and could be measured in monetary terms.

Concept

Accounting for Human Resource deals with measurement of costs; associated with recruiting, selecting, training, placing and developing employees of an organization. For the purpose of developing the concept of human asset/capital accounting we could use the term 'human asset' as the total value to an enterprise of its employees, plus the value, of any other asset owned by the company for exclusive benefit of its employees or to put it simply as equivalent to total value to an enterprise of its employees.

According to Klein and Prusak (1994) "we can define intellectual capital operationally as intellectual material that has been formalized, captured and leveraged to produce a higher valued asset."

The concept is based on the premise that human capital is owned by the employees and is rewarded by remuneration and employee benefits; in much the same way as loan capital is rewarded with interest. Alternatively employee remuneration and benefits are the equivalent of amortization or rent, which used to calculate human asset. The enterprise has control over but not ownership of human asset.

According to Meyer (1980, p. 148) there is no provision within generally accepted accounting principles for the disclosure of human assets *per se* unless they are acquired by purchase. Meyer 91980, p. 149) also makes the point that "the very concept (of human asset accounting) raises the question whether conventional financial statements' portrayal of economic resources may be ignoring the most vital resource an organization possesses." Accountants have however found ways to recognize the human asset.

Several classification systems have been proposed in order to organize the different components of intellectual capital into useful categories. Many agree with Sveiby (1997) who suggests that IC consists of three major elements :

- Human capital—which includes the know-how, capabilities, skills, and expertise of organization members
- Structural capital (or Organizational capital)—which includes the systems, networks, policies, culture, distribution channels, and other "organizational capabilities" developed to meet market requirements as well as intellectual property and
- Relational capital (or Customer capital)—which includes the connections of outsiders with the organization, such as customer loyalty, market share, rate of new customer acquisition etc.

Historical Development of Human Resource Accounting

The development of Human Resource Accounting (Figure 14.1) as a systematic and detailed academic activity began in early 1960's, however, traces could be found in Medieval European practices of calculating the cost of keeping prisoners versus the expected future returns from him. This however, was a rough measure with limited use. Falmholtz (1999) in his work divides the development of Human Resource Accounting into five stages :

(*a*) **Stage 1 (1960–66).** This marks the beginning of interest in Human Resource Accounting. The focus was primarily on deriving Human Resource Accounting concepts from other studies and fields like the economic theory of capital, psychological theories of leadership effectiveness, emerging concepts of human resource, as well as measurement of corporate goodwill.

(b) **Stage 2 (1966–71).** The focus during this period was primarily on development and validating different models of Human Resource Accounting. These models covered both costs and the monetary and non-monetary value of Human Resource. The aim was to develop some tools that would help the organization in assessing and managing their human resource/asset in a more realistic manner.

(c) **Stage 3 (1971–76).** This period was marked by widespread inters in the field of Human Resource Accounting leading to rapid growth in research in the area. The focus in most cases was on the issues of application of Human Resource Accounting in business organizations.

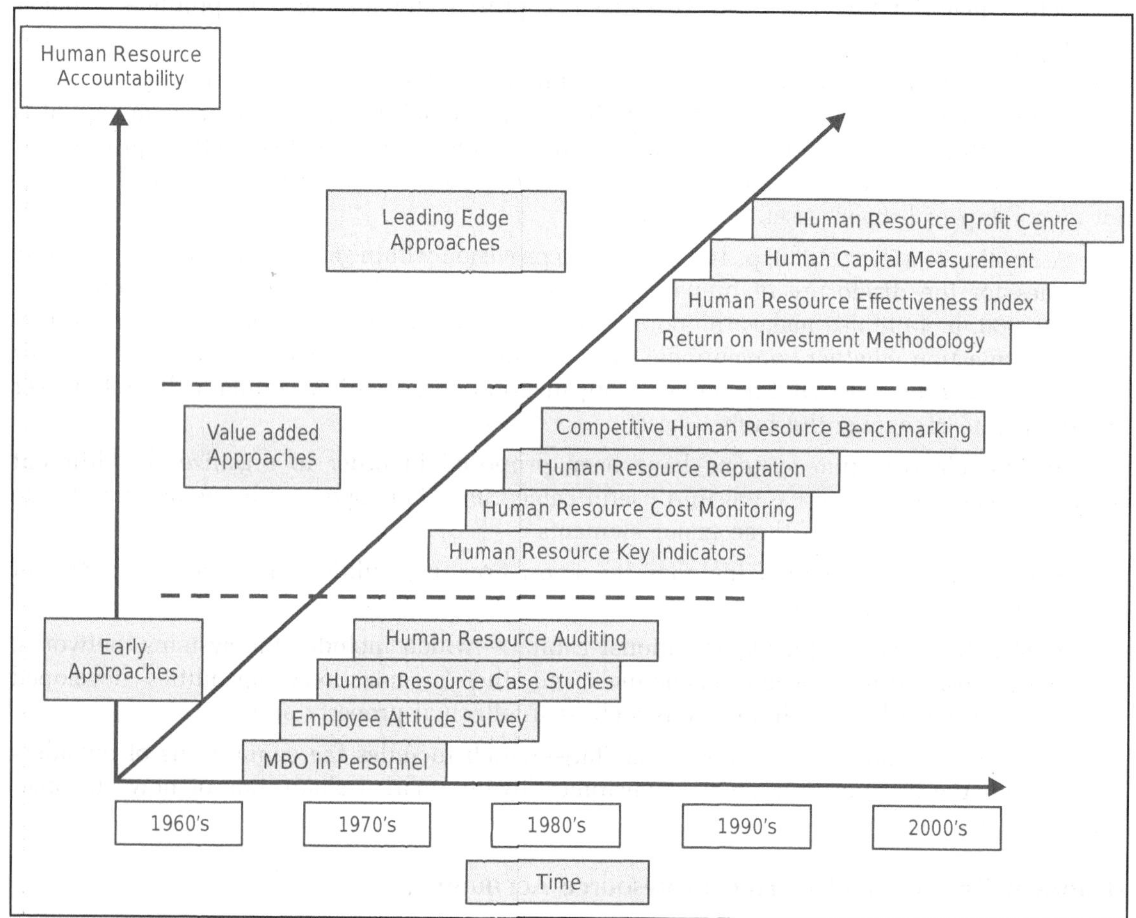

Fig. 14.1. *Human Resource Accountability Progress.*

(d) **Stage 4 (1976–80).** This was a period of decline in the area of Human Resource Accounting primarily because the complex issues that needed to be explored required much deeper empirical research than was needed for the earlier simple models.

(e) **Stage 5 (1980 onwards).** There was a sudden renewal of interest in the field of Human Resource Accounting partly because most of the developed economies has shifted from manufacturing to service economies and realized criticality of human asset for their organizations. Human assets were critical for the survival, growth and profits of an organization than the physical assets; the need was felt to have more accurate measure of Human Resource costs, investments and value. The important outcome of this interest was that by mid 90's the focus was on greater application of Human Resource Accounting to business management.

Today, human and intellectual capitals are perceived to be strategic resources and therefore, clear estimation of their value has gained significant importance. The increased pressure for corporate governance and corporate code of conduct demanding transparency in accounting have further supported the need for developing methods of measuring human value.

Definition

American Accounting Association has defined Human Resource Accounting *'as a process of identifying and measuring data about human resource and communicating this information to the interested parties.'* In simple terms, it is an extension of the accounting principles of matching costs and revenues and of organizing data to communicate relevant information in financial terms. Human Resource Accounting, thus, not only involves measurement of all costs/ investments associated with the recruitment, placement, training and development of employees, but also the quantification of economic value of people in an organization.

Flamholtz (1971) defines Human Resource Accounting as 'the measurement and reporting of the cost and value of people in an organization.'

Mr Woodruff Jr. Vice President, R.G. Batty Corporation defines it as follows :

'Human Resource Accounting is an attempt to identify and report investments made in human resources of an organization that are presently not accounted for in conventional accounting practice. Basically it is an information system that tells the management what changes over time are occurring to the human resources of the business.'

M.N. Baker defines Human Resources Accounting as follows :

'Human Resource Accounting is the term applied by the accountancy profession to quantify the cost and value of employees to their employing organization.'

Stephen Knauf has defined Human Resource Accounting as :

'The measurement of quantification of human organization inputs such as recruitment, training, experience and commitment.'

Thus, Human Resource Accounting may be defined as, 'a process of accounting which identifies, quantifies and measures human resources for the use of management to cope up with the changes in its quantum and quality so that equilibrium could be achieved in between the required resources and the provided human resources.'

Human Resource Accounting is the art of valuing, recording and presenting systematically the worth of human resources in the books of account of an organization. From the definition emerges the Human Resource Accounting brings out :

(*a*) Valuation of Human Resources.

(*b*) Recording the valuation in the books.

(*c*) Disclosure of the information in the financial statements the business.

Importance of Human Resource Accounting provides useful information to the management, financial analyst and employees as stated below :

- Human Resources Accounting helps the management in the employment, locating and utilization of human resources.

- It helps in deciding the transfers, promotion, training and retrenchment of human resources.
- It provides a basis for planning for physical assets vis-à-vis human resources.
- It assists in evaluating the expenditure incurred for imparting further education and training in employees in terms of benefits derived by the firm.
- It helps in determining the causes of high labour turnover.
- It provides valuable information to persons interested in making long term investment in the firm.
- It helps in improving the performance and the bargaining power. It makes each of them to understand his contribution towards the betterment of the firm vis-a-vis the expenditure incurred.

Benefits

In the field of managerial decision making, human resource accounting would help in making meaningful choices between various types of investments in Human Resource and other assets. It assists in evaluating the cost to company in

(*a*) Analyze the benefit of direct recruitment versus promotion.

(*b*) Analyze the benefit transfer and retention of an employee.

(*c*) Analyze the benefit between retention and retrenchment.

(*d*) Utility of cost reduction programmes.

(*e*) Impact of budgetary control on hum resource and organizational behaviour.

(*f*) Adds new dimension to budgetary control.

(*g*) Consideration of adequate return on investment.

(*h*) Decision on relocating factories.

Objectives

The aim of Human Resource Accounting is to depict the potential of Human Resource in monetary terms, while casting the organizations financial statements. The human resource accounting facilitates the effective and efficient management of human resource as it provides the manager with information needed to acquire, develop, allocate, conserve, utilize, evaluate and reward Human Resource. Human Resource Accounting helps in developing financial assessments for the people within the organization and monitoring of these assessments in the light of accounting policies of the companies. The purpose of Human Resource Accounting is to improve the quality of human resources decisions made both internally and externally concerning and organizations. Human Resource Accounting objectives could be :

(*a*) To assist management to take decisions on investment on human resource.

(*b*) To provide information on possible benefits and profits those are likely to accrue from human resource.

(*c*) To assess the efficiency of human resource.

Reniss Likert, (1971) has listed the objectives of Human Resource Accounting as :

(*a*) It furnishes the cost/value information for making management decisions about acquiring, allocating, developing, and maintaining human resources in order to attain cost-effectiveness.

(*b*) To allow management personnel; to monitor effectively the use of human resources.

(*c*) To provide a sound and effective basis of human asset control, that is, whether the asset is appreciated, depleted or conserved.

(*d*) It helps development of management principles by classifying the financial consequences of various practices.

Human Resource Accounting is a management tool which is designed to assist senior management in understanding the long term cost and benefit implications of the human resource decisions so that better decision can be taken. Lack of such an accounting prevents the management from taking decisions that may improve profits in the short run but may have serious long term repercussions.

Information Management in Human Resource Accounting

Human Resource Accounting depends heavily on the availability of accurate information. Human Resource Accounting is essentially a tool to facilitate better planning and decision making. The kind of data that need to be managed depends upon the end use that it is going to be used for by the organization.

Examples : If the purpose is control 'personnel costs', then a system of standard costs for personnel recruitment, selection and training has to developed; if the purpose is 'turnover costs', then a system to determine the actual costs of turnover and the need and efforts by management to retain manpower has to be developed; however, if the purpose is to determine 'accountability', then a system to evaluate managerial effectiveness is created.

Methods of Human Resource Accounting

The biggest challenge to Human Resource Accounting is that of assigning monetary values to different dimensions of Human Resource costs, investments and worth of employees. A number of valuations models have been developed to determine the present value. The two main approaches usually employed are :

(*a*) The 'Cost Approach' which involves methods used to determine the costs incurred by the company with regard to its employee.

(*b*) The 'Economic Value Approach' which includes methods based on the economic value of the human resources and their contribution to the company's gains. This approach looks at human resource as an asset and tries to identify the benefits flowing from the asset.

The Cost Approach

The 'Cost' can be stated to as 'sacrifice' made by an individual to acquire some anticipated benefit or service; in monetary terms it is the price, value or amount paid to obtain a service or good. All costs have two portions viz. the 'expense' and the 'asset portion'. The expense portion is that which provides for benefits during the current accounting year, whereas the asset portion is that which is expected to give rise to benefits in the future. Arriving at clear distinction however, remains a problem (Flamholtz, 1999). These two types of cost have given rise different methods of determining the cost. (Figure 14.2)

Historical or Actual Cost Method. In this method, the amount actually spent to recruit, train, familiarize and develop an employee is added as the opening value of cost of that employee.

It is the sacrifice made by an organization to acquire and develop a particular human resource. In this process only those outlays which have an expected value are taken. Under this method, the cost of acquisition *i.e.*, selection, hiring, training costs of employees are capitalised and written off over the expected useful life of the employees. In case, the personnel leave the company before the anticipated period of service, then the unamortised portion of costs remaining in the company's books is written off against the profit and loss account in that year. If the period of service exceeds the anticipated time, then amortisation of costs is rescheduled.

Opportunity Cost Method. Certain companies carry out evaluation of return of investment and compare it with other item. The companies carries out analysis q\and calculates the possible benefits that might have accrued if the amount spent on human resource was pent on something else. This method is usually applied to carry out internal assessment and is usually not for external reporting.

Replacement Cost Method. The replacement cost is the cost incurred to replace the existing employee. Under this method, the human resources are valued at their replacement cost *i.e.*, the monetary implications of replacing existing personnel. Replacement costs could be 'positional *i.e.*, replacing personnel from particular positions *i.e.*, replacing specific talent or ability of particular persons; or personal or the cost incurred to replace all the services expected to be rendered by the employee at the various positions that he might have occupied throughout his work life in the organization.

Competitive Bidding Method. This approach suggests competitive bidding for scarce employees in an organization *i.e.*, opportunity cost of employees linked to scarcity. The approach proposes the capitalizing of additional earning potential of each human resource within the company.

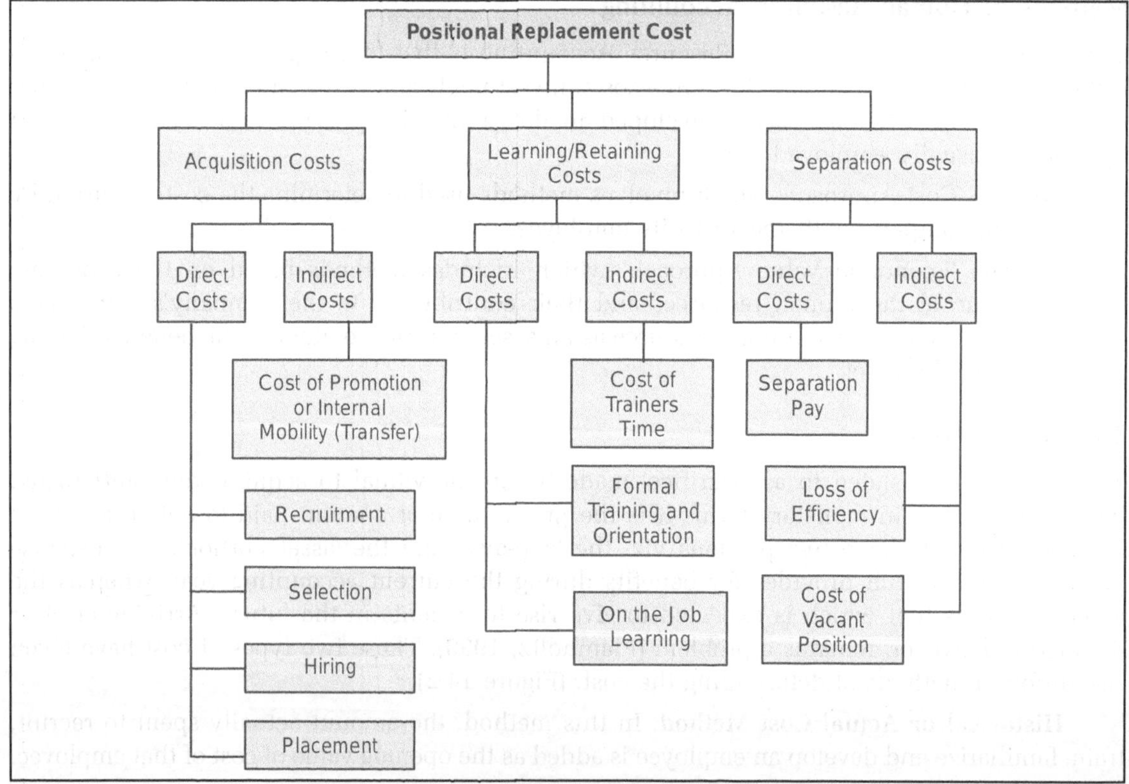

Fig. 14.2. *The Cost Approach.*

Standard Cost Method. Under this method, standard costs of recruiting, hiring, training, and developing per grade of employees are determined annually. The total standard cost for all personnel of the company is the value of human resources.

The Economic Value

The value of an object, in economic terms, is the present value of the services that it is expected to render in future. Similarly, the economic value of human resources is the present worth of the services that they are likely to render in future. Under this method, the net present value of incremental cash flows attributed to human resources is taken as the asset value. This may be the value of individuals, groups or the total human organization. The methods for calculating the economic value of individuals may be classified into monetary and non-monetary methods.

The Monetary Methods

Flamholtz's Model of Determinants of Individual Value to Formal Organizations

The value of an individual is the present worth of the services that he is likely to render to the organization in future. As an individual moves from one position to another within an organization, at the same level or at different levels, the profile of the services provided by him is likely to change. The present cumulative value of all the possible services that may be rendered by him during his/her association with the organization is the value of the individual. (Figure 14.3)

The value of an individual to an organization is uncertain. This value has two dimensions the first is the '**expected conditional value**', and the second '**expected realizable value**'.

The '**expected conditional value**' is the amount that the organization could potentially realize from the services of an individual during his/her productive service life in the organization. The expected conditional values are composed of three factors :

(*a*) Productivity or performance. The set of services that an individual is expected to provide in his/her present position.

(*b*) Transferability. Set of services that he or she is expected in different positions in the organization.

(*c*) Promotability. Set of services that are expected when the individual is able to assume higher level positions.

These three factors depend on great extent, on 'individual determinants' like motivation and energy level; and the 'organizational determinants' like opportunity to use these skills or roles and the reward system.

The '**expected realizable value**' is a function of the expected conditional value, and the probability that the individual will remain in the organization for the duration of his/ her productive service life. Since the individuals are not owned by the organization and are free to leave, ascertaining the probability of their turnover becomes important.

The interaction between the individual and organizational determinants mentioned above, leads to job satisfaction. The higher is the level of job satisfaction; the lower is the probability of employee turnover, resulting in higher than expected value.

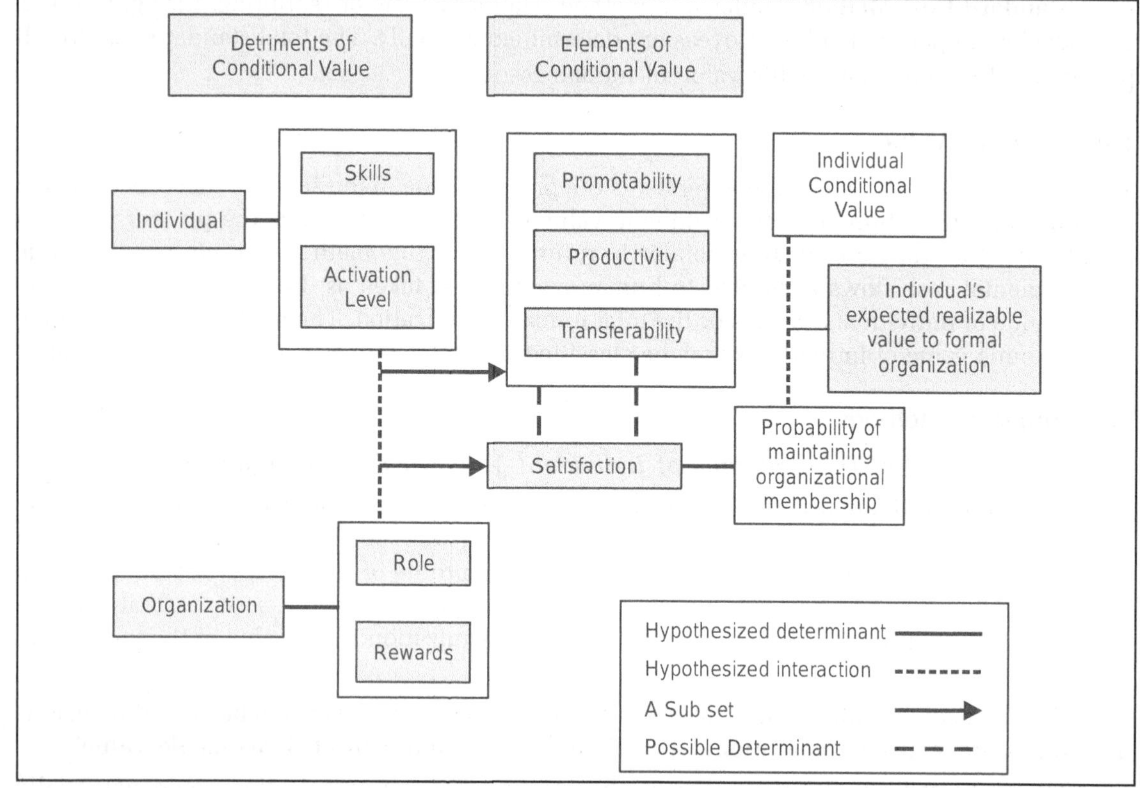

Fig. 14.3. *Flamholtz's Model.*

Flamholtz's Stochastic Rewards Valuation Model

This model was suggested by Flamholtz. It identifies the major variables that determine an individual's value to an organization, *i.e.,* his expected reliable value. The expected realizable vale of an individual is the present worth of future services expected to be provided during the period he is expected to remain in the organization. The movement or progress of people through organizational 'states' or roles is called a 'stochastic process'. The Stochastic Rewards Model is a direct way of measuring a person's expected conditional value and expected realizable value. It is based on the assumption that an individual generates value as he occupies and moves along organizational roles, and renders service to the organization. The model presupposes that an individual will move from one state to another state in the organization during a specified period of time. In this model, exit is also considered to be a state. Use of this model need generation of under mentioned information :

(*a*) The set of mutually exclusive states that an individual may occupy in the system during his/her career;

(*b*) The value of each state in the organization.

(*c*) Estimates the persons expected tenure in the organization.

(*d*) The probability that in future, the person will occupy each state for the specified time.

(*e*) The discount rate to be applied to the future cash flows.

The persons expected conditional value and expected realizable value would be equal id the person is certain to remain in the organization, in the predetermined set of states, throughout his expected service life. The model suggests five steps;

(*a*) Step 1-Forecasting the period an individual will remain in the ortganiuzation *i.e.*, his expected service life.

(*b*) Identifying the services states, *i.e.*, the roles that might occupy including, of course, the time at which he will leave organization; Estimating the value derived by the organization

The main drawback of this model is the extent of information required to make the necessary estimates of the values of the service states, the expected tenure, and the probability that the individual will occupy the state for the specified period of time. However, if this information can be made available, this model emerges as one of the most sophisticated models for determining the value of individuals.

The Lev and Schwartz Model

This model was developed by Brauch Lev and Aba Schwarts in 1971. They are of the opinion, that determination of the total of a firm's labour force is a straightforward extension of the measurement procedure of an individual value to the organization. Lev and Schwarts have divided the whole labour force into certain homogenous groups such as skilled, unskilled, technical staff, managerial staff etc. and in accordance with different classes and age groups are prepared for each group separately and the present value for the human capital is calculated. The aggregate present value of different groups represents the capitalized future earnings of the firm as a whole. They have advocated the use of cost of capital rate for the purpose of capitalizing the present value of the future earnings of the employees. According to them, the value of human capital represented by a person of age is the present value of his remaining future earnings from his employment. They have given the formula for calculating the value of an individual :

$$\boxed{E\left(V_y\right)} = \sum_{T=Y} P_y(t+1) \sum_{T} {}^{1(T)}\!\Big/_{(1+R)^{t-y}}$$

Where

$E(Vy)$ = expected value of a 'y' year old person's human capital.

T = the persons retirement age.

$Py\,(t)$ = the probability of person leaving the job/ organization.

$I\,(t)$ = expected earnings of the person in period I.

R = Discount rate.

Limitations of Lev and Schwartz Model

Like all Models this model also suffers from certain limitations :

(*a*) This model doesn't suggest how value of human resource should be recorded in Book of Accounts.

(*b*) This model takes wages and salary as a basis of value of human resource but value of human resource is not limited to the extent of cost incurred on them. It is different from traditional fixed assets. It has greater value than the cost incurred.

(*c*) The model ignores the possibility and probability that individual may leave an organization for reason other than death and retirement. The model's expected value of human capital is actually a measure of expected 'conditional value' of a person's human capital. The implicit condition is that the person will remain in organization until death of retirement.

(*d*) A person's value to organization is determined not only by the characteristics of the person himself but also by the organizational role in which the individual is utilized. An individual's knowledge and skill is valuable only if these are expected to serve as a means to given organizational ends.

MEASUREMENT OF GROUP VALUE

The Likerts and Bowers Model

Liker's and Bowers proposed a casual, intervening and end results variables, which determine the group's value to an organization. *Casual Variables* are those which can be controlled by the organization. These variables include managerial behaviour and organizational structure.

Intervening variables reflect organizational capabilities and involve group processes, peer leadership, organization climate, and the subordinates' satisfaction. Both the casual and intervening variables determine the end result variable of the organization. Figure 14.4 illustrate the elements used to measure human organizational casual and intervening variables.

The end result, dependent variables reflect the achievements of the organization or the total productive efficiency in terms of sales, costs, earnings, market performance etc. They are dependent on the casual and the intervening variables.

MANAGERIAL AND PEER LEADERSHIP	
Support Team Building	Friendly; pays attention to what you are saying; Listens to subordinates' problems; encourages subordinates to work as a team' encourages exchange of opinions and ideas
Goal Emphasis	Encourages best efforts; maintains high standards.
Help with work	Shows ways to do a better job; helps subordinates plan, organize and schedule; offers new ideas, and solutions
ORGANIZATIONAL CLIMATE	
Communication flow	Communication flow is amicable
Decision making practices	Subordinates know what is going on; superiors are receptive.
Concern for persons	Subordinates are involved in setting goals; decisions are made at levels of accurate information; persons affected by decisions are asked for their ideas; know-how of people of all levels is used.
Influence on department	The organization is interested in individual's welfare; tries to improve working conditions; organizes work activities sensibly.
Technological adequacy	From lower level supervisors, employees who have no subordinates
Motivation	Improved methods are quickly adopted; equipment and resources are well managed. Differences and disagreements are accepted and worked through; people in organization work hard for money, promotions, job satisfaction and to meet high money, promotion, job satisfaction and to meet high expectations from others and are encouraged to do so by policies, working conditions, and people.

GROUP PROCESS
Planning together, coordinating efforts
Making good decision's solving problems
Knowing jobs and how to do them well
Sharing information
Wanting to meet objectives
Having confidence and trust in other members
Ability to meet unusual work demands
SATISFACTION
With fellow workers; superiors; jobs; this organization compared with others; pay; progress in the organization up to now; chances for getting ahead in the future.
Source : Rensis Likert and David G. Bowers, "Improving the Accuracy of P/L Reports **Source** : Rensis Likert and David G. Bowers, (1973) "Improving the Accuracy of P/L Reports by Estimating the Change in Dollar Value of the Human Organization", *Michigan Business Review*, March.

Fig. 14.4. *Elements used to Measure Human Resource Organisation Causal and Intervening Variables.*

Hermanson's Unpurchased Goodwill Model

According to Hermanson, the unpurchased goodwill notion is based on the premise that 'the best available evidence of the present existence of un-owned resources is the fact that a given firm earned a higher than normal rate of income for the most recent year. Here Hermanson is proposing that supernormal earning are an indication of resources not shown on the balance sheet, such as human assets. Even though his method of valuing human resources is explicitly intended for use in a company's published financial statements rather than for internal consumption, this would necessarily involve forecasting future earnings and allocating any excess above normal expected earnings to human resources of the organization. However, the assumptions would be subject to the uncertainties involved in any forecast of future events.

This method suffers from several limitations : Firstly, since the methods limits recognition of human resources to the amount of earnings in excess of normal, the human resource base that is required to carry out normal operations is totally ignored. As a result, the value of human assets will be an underestimation. Secondly, the method only uses the actual earnings of the most recent year as the basis for calculating human assets, thereby, ignoring the forecasts of future earnings that are equally relevant for managerial decision making.

Human Organizational Dimensions Method

Based on the Likert-Bowers model of group's value to an organization, discussed earlier, this method is based on the relationship among causal, intervening and end-result variables. The causal variables influence the intervening variables, which, in turn, determine the organization's end result variables. Hence changes in the key dimensions of organisation can be used as dependable indicators for forecasting future changes in productivity and financial performance, monetary estimations of changes in human value of organisations. For computing a monetary estimate of the expected change in the value of human organization, the following steps are suggested :

- Measure the key dimensions of human organization, using a Likert scale at specified time periods. These are in non-monetary measurements.
- The scaled responses to questionnaire items called 'scores' are then standardized by statistical methods to take into account the degree of variability of the set of responses. This is done for responses in each time period.
- The difference between two standardized scores from one period to the next is then calculated. This difference (called delta) represents the change in an index of specified dimensions of the human organization.
- From present changes in dimensions of the human organization, the expected future change in end result variables is estimated. Specifically, for a given variable the delta is multiplied by coefficient or correlation between that variable and the end result variable. This provides an estimate in standard scores of the anticipated change in the end result variable attributable to a change in the human organisational dimension believed to cause that change.
- Lastly, the standard scores are converted into the measuring monetary units for the end result variables.

Methods for Valuation of Expense Centre Groups

Flamholtz proposes three methods for valuation of expense centre groups. In all these measures, the surrogate value is used for estimation. The three methods are :

1. Capitalization of Compensation
2. Replacement Cost Valuation, and
3. Original Cost Valuation

Capitalization

The capitalisation method involves capitalizing a person's salary and using it as a surrogate measure of human value. This value may be ascertained for groups as well as individuals. The value of the group is essentially the aggregate value of the individuals compromising the group.

Capitalization of compensation method is not considered an ideal method of group valuation because it ignores the possible effects of synergy. However, this method may be used to arrive at an approximation of a group's value to the firm.

Replacement Cost Valuation

The replacement cost of a group is defined as the sacrifice that would have to be incurred today to recruit, select, hire, train and develop a substitute group capable of providing a set of services equivalent to that of a group presently employed. This method involves considerable subjective estimates, which reduce its validity and replicability.

Original Cost Valuation

The original cost valuation method involves estimation of the original cost of recruiting, selecting, hiring, training, and developing a firm's existing human organization. The need for using original costs to value groups arises out of the necessity of estimating the cost of developing an effectively functioning team. Teamwork is essential for effective communication, decision-making, coordination and several other critical organisational processes. Yet, when the original costs are used to make an estimation of the value of the expense centre, the costs of generating this teamwork are largely ignored.

HUMAN RESOURCE AUDIT

The word 'audit' is derived from the Latin word 'audire', which means to hear. In the olden days, whenever the proprietors of a business concern suspected fraud, they appointed a person to check the accounts and to hear the explanations given by the persons responsible for keeping the accounts. The audit in those days was interested in ascertaining the facts from person maintaining the accounts whether he had properly accounted for all receipts and payments to his principal and to locate fraud and errors. However, the audit over a period of time has gone through a sea change and today it encompasses examination and evaluation of policies, procedures and practices in al phases of business to achieve the most effective administration of the organization.

Meaning and Objectives of Human Resource Audit

Of the four basic constituents of enterprise human capital is the one that really differentiate between companies. While everyone agrees to this, however, rarely do companies take a look at their personnel to satisfy themselves that indeed anyone, with whom the client or potential client interacts, fully represents the company in the best possible way. The solution is simple just as company carries out financial audit; it should also now carryout 'human resource' audit. It would imply assessing the entire workforce of the company.

The Human Resources Audit is a process of examining policies, procedures, documentation, systems, and practices with respect to an organization's Human Resources functions. The purpose of the audit is to reveal the strengths and weaknesses in the nonprofit's human resources system, and any issues needing resolution. The audit works best when the focus is on analyzing and improving the HR function in the organization. It can safely be stated that Human Resource Audit is the systematic assessment of an organization's Human Resource service excellence.

The audit itself is a diagnostic tool, not a prescriptive instrument. It will help you identify what you are missing or need to improve, but it can't tell you what you need to do to address these issues. It is most useful when an organization is ready to act on the findings, and to evolve its Human Resource function to a level where it's full potential to support the organization's mission and objectives can be realized.

A human resource audit evaluates the personnel activities used in an organization. The audit may include one division or entire company. It gives feedback about :

1. The function of operating managers.
2. The human resource specialists.
3. How well managers are meeting their human resource duties.

In short, the audit is an overall quality control check on human resource activities in a division or company and how those activities support the organization's strategy. Human Resource Audit encompasses (Figure 14.5) the :

(a) Audit of Corporate Strategy. Corporate Strategy concerns how the organization is going to gain competitive advantage.

(b) Audit of the Human Resource Function. Audit touches on Human Resource Information System, Staffing and Development, and Organization Control and Evaluation.

(c) Audit of Managerial Compliance. Reviews how well managers comply with human resource policies and procedures.

(d) Audit of Employee Satisfaction. To learn how well employee needs are met.

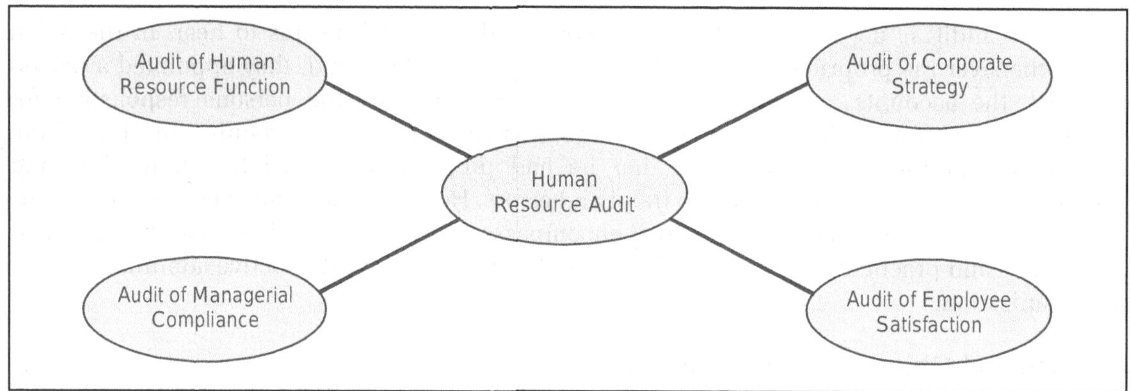

Fig. 14.5. *Constituents of Human Resource Audit.*

Definition

Human Resource Audit means the systematic verification of job analysis and design, recruitment and selection, orientation and placement, training and development, performance appraisal and job evaluation, employee and executive remuneration, motivation and morale, participative management, communication, welfare and social security, safety and health, industrial relations, trade unionism, and disputes and their resolution. Human Resource audit is very much useful to achieve the organizational goal and also is a vital tool which helps to assess the effectiveness of HR functions of an organization.

G. Seybord in his work 'Studies in Personnel Policies' says, "Human Resource Auditing refers to an examination and evaluation of policies, procedures and practices to determine the effectiveness of human resource management. It helps the personnel department to determine what should be one and what should not be done in future".

Extending the general meaning of auditing to the field of human resource management, Human Resource Auditing may be defined as *'the analysis and evaluation of personnel policies, procedures and practices to determine the effectiveness of personnel/ human resource management in an organization'*. In other words, human resource audit is a periodic review to measure the effectiveness of personnel management and to determine the steps required for more effective utilization of human resources.

Human Resource Audit can be defined as

"A process to review implementation of your institutions policies and procedures, ensure compliance with employment law, eliminate liabilities, implement best practices and educate your managers."

Benefits of a Human Resource Audit

Human Resource provides the various benefits to the organization. The Human Resource Audit enables the organization to identify the contribution of the personnel departments to the organization :

- Human resource audit enable organization to identify the human resource programmes which are most effective in achieving organizational objectives.
- It helps to find out the proper contribution of the HR department towards the organization.
- Development of the professional image of the HR department of the organization.
- Reduce the HR cost.
- Motivation of the HR personnel.
- Find out the problems and solve them smoothly.
- Provides timely legal requirement.
- Sound Performance Appraisal Systems.
- Systematic job analysis.
- Smooth adoption of the changing mindset.
  (*a*) Improves professional image of the personnel department as the audit identifies how well the human resource department is contributing to overall objectives of the organizations.
  (*b*) Encourages greater responsibility and professionalism among members of the personnel department. Human resource audit benchmarks human resource work to ensure continuous improvement.
  (*c*) Clarifies the personnel department's duties and responsibilities; promotes change and creativity.
  (*d*) Human resource audit helps in identifying critical personnel problems.

Objectives of Human Resource Audit

According to Gray, 'The primary objective of personnel audit is to know how the various units are functioning and how they have been able to meet the policies and guidelines which are agreed upon; and to assist the rest of the organization by identifying the gaps between objectives and results, for the end product of an evaluation should be to formulate plans for corrections of adjustments.'

The important objectives of human resource audit are :

(*a*) Review the organizational system of human resource practices.

(*b*) To analyze the factors involved in Human Resource Development and develop statements of findings with recommendations for correction, if any, on the :
- The extent of deviation from stated Human Resource Development policies.
- To what extent the objects are spelt out.
- To what extent the performance standards have been established.

(*c*) To seek information and answers to all such questions as; What happened ? Why it happened ? Etc.

(*d*) To evaluate the effectiveness of various personnel policies and practices.

(*e*) Evaluate units of the organization and their functioning.

(*f*) To identify existing human resource practices to meet the challenges of personnel and human resource management.

(*g*) Help organization by identifying the gap between objectives and results.

(*h*) To formulate plans for correcting deviations if any.

Elements

The Human Resource Audit focuses on the following elements of Human Resource management :

- Organizational Data.
- Strategic Human resource Management Overview.
- Staff Communication and Change Management.
- Human Resource Management Operational Delivery; and
- Human Resource performance measures.

Scope

The human resource audit process is the systematic assessment of an organization's human resource function and the process consists of auditing eight primary components (Figure 14.6) of human resource functions;

(*a*) Human resource information system;

(*b*) Attracting and Recruiting;

(*c*) Documentation;

(*d*) Training , development and career management;

(*e*) Compensation and benefits;

(*f*) Performance appraisal;

(*g*) Termination and internal mobility;

(*h*) Personnel policies and legal issues.

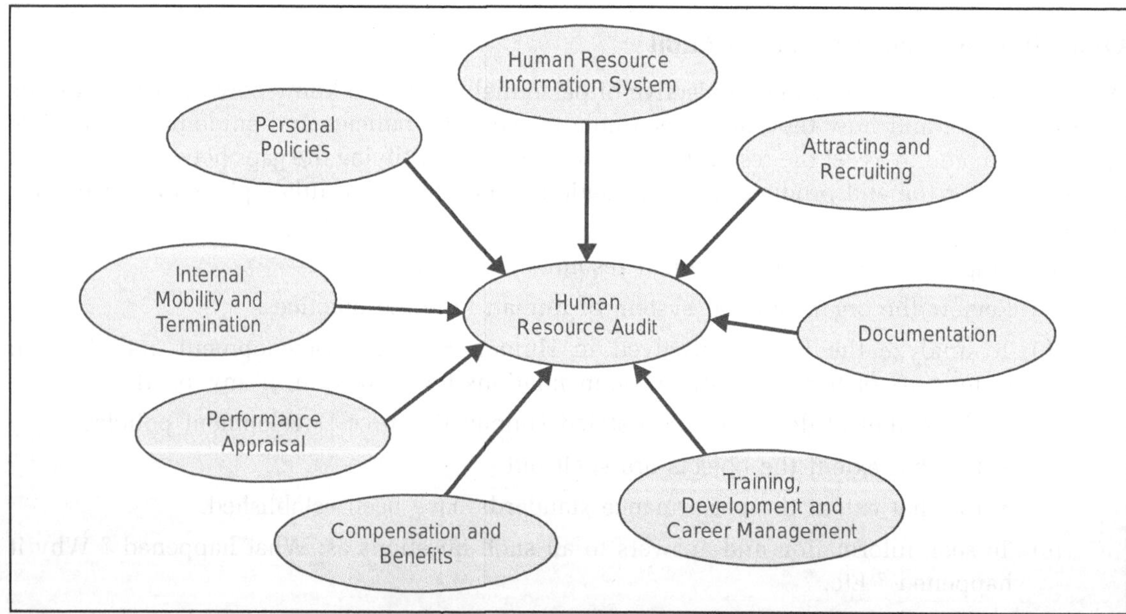

Fig. 14.6. *Comparison of Human Resource Audit.*

The areas like leadership, grievances, and performance appraisal and employee mobility have also been included in Human Resource Audit. Audit now encompasses all the areas like review and integration of corporate mission, goals, policies and objectives, manpower planning, career planning and development, and transfer policies, performance appraisal systems, training and development functions, recruitment and selection, etc.

Specifically the Human Resource Audit covers the under mentioned areas :

(*a*) **Audit of Human Resource Function.** This primarily involves carrying out audit of all Human Resource activities referred to in this book. The auditors are expected to determine the objective, identify the person responsible, review the performance, develop an action plan to correct deviations, follow up plan.

(*b*) **Audit of Managerial Compliance.** This involves audit of managerial compliance of personnel policies, procedures and legal provisions. How well are these complied with should be uncovered by the audit so that corrective action can be taken. Compliance with the legal provisions is particularly important as any violation makes the management guilty.

(*c*) **Audit of the Human Resource Climate.** The Human Resource Climate has an impact on employee productivity and efficiency. The quality of the Human Resource Climate in an organization is measured by examining turnover of employees, absenteeism, safety records and attitude surveys.

(*d*) **Audit of Corporate Strategy.** Corporate strategy helps the organization gain competitive advantage. By assessing the company's internal strengths and weaknesses and its external strengths and opportunities, the senior management devises ways of gaining advantage. The audit helps management to carryout analysis of internal strengths and weaknesses and devises strategy to exploit its strengths.

Importance of Human Resource Audit

Human Resource Audit has assumed importance in recent years due increased shift to services from manufacturing, knowledge based workforce, competitive environment and globalization. This has resulted in need for restructuring manpower and production strategies, management philosophies and practices etc resulting in regular conduct of Human Resource Audit. (Figure 14.7).

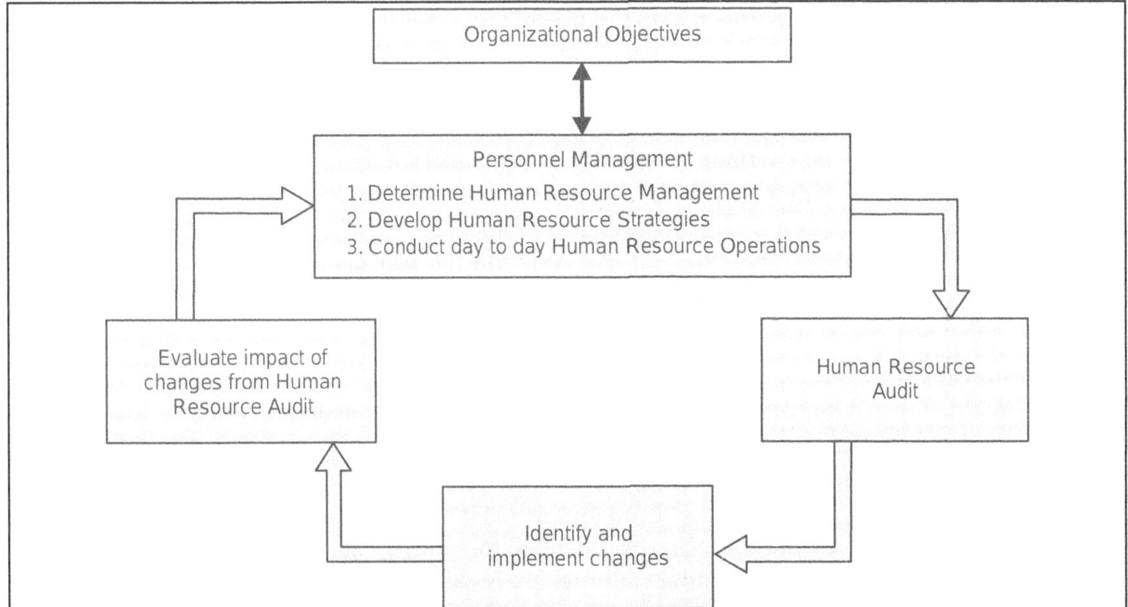

Fig. 14.7. *Human Resource Audit.*

The Human Resource Audit provides the management with inputs on two main issues :

(*a*) Assessing the quality of Human Resource Practices, policies and delivery.

(*b*) Reporting on extent of statutory Human resource compliance and remedial action required

(*c*) Assessing cost and benefits of Human Resource practices.

(*d*) Assessing Human Resource and line management relationships and ways these can be improved.

(*e*) Setting guidelines for establishing Human Resource performance standards.

(*f*) Identifying areas of change and specific recommendations to improve the same.

Role of Human Resource Auditor

The efficacy of the audit depends upon the person who has carried out the audit. The major roles of an auditor could be

(*a*) To ascertain the facts.

(*b*) To determine the effectiveness of a particular system prevalent in an organization by analyzing the current issues, such as :

- Why was the practice introduced ?
- What would be the result, if practice is discontinued ?
- What needs were intended to be fulfilled and have those been fulfilled or not ?
- What could be the best possible alternative for fulfilling such needs ?
- Are intended changes economically and operationally viable ?
- Are the intended changes sustainable from Trade Unions point of view ?
- Are the policies in consonance with government policy ?
- What should be the time frame to introduce change ?

Essential Steps in Human Resource Auditing

Though the process varies from organization to organization, generally it involves following steps :

(*a*) **Orientation.** The key staff members of the organization are to be made aware of the particular issues considered as significant. They should be oriented with plans and programmes of audit. The audit procedures must be clearly explained to them. This is required to make them understand the need of Human Resource Audit. It is recommended a meeting with a range of stakeholders, including Chief Executive Officer, Human Resource staff and line managers to held to agree the scope of the audit, expected deliverables and the consultative process.

(*b*) **Scanning.** The information available in the personnel records, manuals, appraisal forms, etc. are to be scrutinized thoroughly.

(*c*) **Survey.** It involves collection of information to determine issues, strengths and weaknesses, managerial philosophies and needs of the organization. This may be collected from the executives (Figure 14).

(*d*) **Interviews.** What question to be asked is to be decided ? This is based on the issues and the information collected from surveys. The audit efforts will be fruitful if clarity is obtained as to the key factors selected for audit. Clarity is obtained if accurate information is collected. Accurate information is collected through conducting information.

(*e*) **Synthesis.** The information gathered from the above step is synthesized to find out the present situation, priorities, and issues identified.

(*f*) **Analysis and Interpretation.** The data about human resource management is collected, synthesized, integrated and analyzed

(*g*) **Reporting and Feedback.** The results of analyses are documented and reported back for verification

(*h*) **Implementation.** No audit can be successful if the recommendations and findings are not taken cognizance of and acted upon.

Approaches to Human Resource Audit

There are five approaches and an auditor can use any of the approaches for purpose of audit.

(*a*) **Comparative Approach**. In the comparative approach the auditors identify another company as the model. The results of two or more organizations are compared with those of the model company.

(*b*) **External Audit**. The auditors often use standards set by an outside consultant as benchmark for comparison of own results. The company also at times gets their audit carried out by external auditors for getting un biased reports. This approach is called the external audit.

(*c*) **Statistical Approach**. Here the statistical tools are used to carryout analysis of the performances developed based on the organizations existing information.

(*d*) **Compliance Approach**. In this approach auditors review the past actions to determine if those activities comply with legal requirements and company policies and procedures.

(*e*) **Management by Objective**. It involves managers establishing objectives or specific goals for each individual and then performance measured against it.

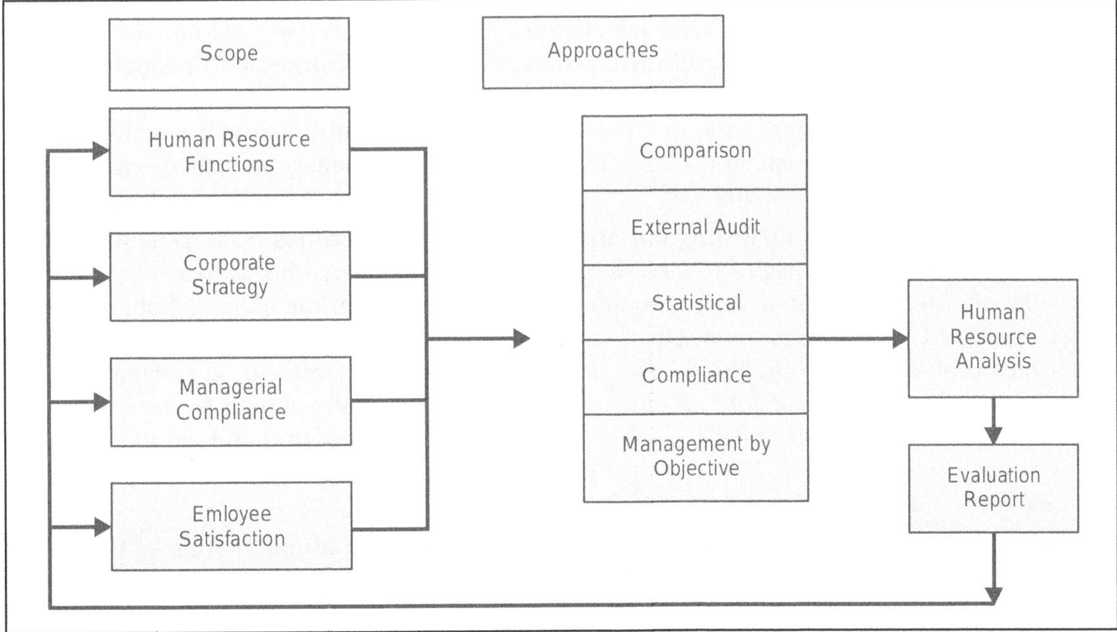

Fig. 14.8. *Human Resource Audit Process Cycle.*

Methods of Human Resource Audit

There are large techniques adopted by organization to carryout audit.

(*a*) **Interview**. Individual or Group

(*b*) **Workshops**. Workshops are usually interactive with large number of participants. The participants gather at a place to give feedback on Human resource functions and systems. The auditors usually divide the group into small sub groups and each sub group deals with a sub system of an organization. After analysis the sub group makes a presentation of the SWOT analysis and the auditors record the feed back.

(*c*) **Questionnaire**. Auditors can use questionnaires to obtain information from larger spectrum of targets. However, in this process the auditor should carryout a detailed study of the organization before creating a questionnaire, and. The auditor should map all the key

Procedure for Conducting Human Resource Audit

Human Resource Audit is carried out by the regular staff of the audit department or the personnel department. On occasions organizations also get audit carried out by external sources. Both sources of personnel audit should be followed in the organization as the external audit presents a true and fair view of the personnel policies and programmes as the auditor has no personnel interest in the conduct of the business.

When conducting any audit, it is important to have a plan of action which is broken down into a number of stages.

Stage 1. Pre-Audit Administration. In this stage the external and internal consultant opens discussions with management (and unions if appropriate) at the highest level to confirm their decision to conduct an audit and their commitment to follow appropriate courses of action which may eventually be recommended, contingent upon its results. The organizations higher level management is briefed on how the audit will proceed, with the auditor underlining the necessity for full company commitment to act upon it, and so to be seen to act upon it, by employees. The auditor will also begin to clarify the main areas of concern and subjects upon which the audit should focus, through open ended discussions with higher-level management. This ensures that senior management 'owns' the projects.

Step 2. Formulating and Testing the Audit Instruments. Questions need to be formulated and an audit questionnaire begins to take shape. Organizations might choose to accept a known, published off-the-shelf audit; to adapt an older audit used before in the organization; or to start from scratch and develop their own. Open ended group discussions with employees elsewhere in the organization help to provide further input concerning the areas to be covered and the form in which the question should be phrased. A pilot questionnaire should be tested amongst small sample of employees to check its applicability, misunderstandings and ambiguities. The entire project rests on the fact that the questionnaire is comprehensive, user friendly, succinct, unambiguous and relevant.

Stage 3. Audit Administration. The third stage involves the administration of the agreed audit questionnaire to those sections of the organization which have been targeted at earlier stages. The questionnaires are distributed and time limit laid on completion and an expected date of return clearly indicated.

QUESTIONNAIRE

A SURVEY ON PERFORMANCE APPRAISAL SYSTEM

(EXECUTIVE EMPLOYEES)

Dear respondent,

We are conducting a survey "to analyze the effectiveness of performance appraisal process in WIN-MEDICARE Pvt. Ltd".

In order to achieve the said objective we need some information which is to be used only for personal purpose. We assure you that the data provided to us will be treated as confidential.

Thanking you and expecting cooperation from your side.

(PREETI SHARMA)

STAFF PROFILE

NAME : ....

PLACE : ....

AGE : ....

DESIGNATION : ....

DEPARTMENT : ....

MONTHLY INCOME : ....

S.No.	Parameters	Yes	Partly	No
01	Whether you are aware about the existing performance appraisal system ?			
02	Whether the current system fulfills your expectation ?			
03	Do you think that in the existing system there is a transparency in evaluating the performance of the employees in executive category ?			
04	Whether you are satisfied with the current evaluating system ?			
05	Whether the parameters on which a executive is assessed in the existing system are sufficient to evaluate his performance ?			
06	Do you think that there is a need to change/replace the existing performance evaluating system ?			
07	Whether there is a need to add some more ingredients in the performance evaluating form for the executive category to make it more result oriented ?			
08	Whether the current system satisfied the expectation of the employees and link to their career growth ?			
09	Whether the current system in any way contributes to job rotation, skill up gradation related programmes/ issues of the employees in executive category ?			
10	Whether the current system motivates the employees for higher performance at the work place and help in increase the productivity ?			

Suggestions (If any) ....

Fig. 14.9. *Questionnaire for Survey.*

Stage 4. Audit Analysis and Interpretation. The completed questionnaires are processed by having codes allocated to answers, most of which are usually multiple choice responses, which are then used for statistical analysis. Results are initially printed in terms of percentages of respondents who indicate agreement or disagreement to individual items or as mean scores. Items subsumed under a particular heading may also be reported on as total or average scores for the category as a whole. The results then can be presented in tabular form and in graphs or charts. The use of multivariate statistics, such as factor analysis, multiple regression, or canonical correlation can reveal many interesting things about an organization. Just as finance section may use statistical models to tease out the underlying patterns and structures in their data, so too can advanced techniques be applied to human resource audit data to capture in a more dynamic fashion, relationships that exist between different categories of perceptions, and to yield predictive models to guide action programmes within an organization.

Step 5. Recommendation for Action. The final stage draws together a plan of action based on the problem areas identified by the audit. A programme of change may be recommended, comprising a number of stages or targets. Further audits may be necessary periodically to check the change targets have been reached.

QUALITY OF WORK FORCE AND ORGANIZATIONS PERFORMANCE

Work force refers to the employees in the organization in a collective form or a group. The quality of work force must be high, as it is the work force that achieves the organizational goals. If this work force experience a sense of frustration

Quality of Work Life

Rapid technological changes and their applications in business have resulted in employees developing a feeling of redundancy, social isolation and self estrangement. Such a feeling may result in lesser increase in productivity and inefficiency. This forced the academicians and practitioners to see the workplace problems with a different perspective, that is, social; perspective which revealed that productivity of employees were not only affected by the type of technology but also by the environment that prevailed at the work place.

Definition

Suttle has defined Quality of Work Life as *"the degree to which members of a work organization are able to satisfy important personal needs through their experiences in the organization."*

J Richard and J. Lloyd define Quality of Work Life as *"the degree to which members of a work organization are able to satisfy important personal needs through their experience in the organization."*

Quality of Work Life refers to organizational environment favouring or not favouring job climate. Improvement in Quality of Work Life specifically relates to improvement in organizational climate to improve efficiency and effectiveness through enhancement of human dignity and growth process through which the work force of the organization learn how to collaborate and work as a team for betterment to determine for themselves what actions, changes and improvements are desirable and workable.

Richard E. Walton has identified eight perquisites for good Quality of Work Life :

(*a*) Adequate and fair compensation.

(*b*) Safe and healthy working conditions.

(*c*) Opportunity to use and develop human capacities.

(*d*) Opportunity for career growth.

(*e*) Social integration in work force.

(*f*) Social relevance of work.

Purpose of Quality of Work Life

The main purpose or objective of Quality of Work Life programme is to integrate the socio psychological needs of people in the organization. There is a socio psychological impact due unique requirements of a particular technology, structure and processes of the organization and these needs to be addressed to get the best out of an employee.

Methods/Means to improve Quality of Work Life

As stated earlier the concept of Quality of Work Life is to create an environment where the worker is able to perform at its optimum efficiency and is happy to continue to work with the company.

Good Management Practices

Much has been said of about good people practices being a competitive advantage and a key focus area for most organizations in India today. So, it was time finally to honour companies that truly believe that their people are their most valuable asset and go beyond' what is expected to create a caring and an empowering workplace. To capture the spirit, The Economic Times and Great Places to Work Institute, India, recently presented the 'Best Workplaces Award 2008' in Mumbai.

The Top 10 Best workplaces for 2008 are :

1. RMSI Pvt Ltd.
2. Marriott Hotel, India.
3. Google India Pvt Ltd.
4. Aglient Technologies.
5. Classic Stripes Pvt Ltd.
6. American Express, India.
7. Cadbury India Ltd.
8. NTPC Ltd.
9. Godrej Consumer Products Ltd.
10. HILTI India Pvt Ltd.

The common sentiment at the event was encapsulated by executive president, Times Group, Bhaskar Das, "India has moved from an economy that had a cost advantage to one that has become the talent hunting ground for Fortune 500 companies. Therefore, in our times, it is not a luxury to have robust people management practices, it is key."

Prasenjit Bhattacharya, CEO, The Great Place to Work Institute, India, added that some of the learning's that have emerged from the survey and findings are that great places to work institutionalize some very basic aspects of work life that give immense value to their employees. These are :

They inspire success.

- Approachable management,
- Pride in corporate image.
- Transparency,
- Ethical practices.
- Focus on employee development.
- A caring environment
- Sharing power.
- Empowering employees.

Source : *Times Ascent* May 21, 2008. Page 1.

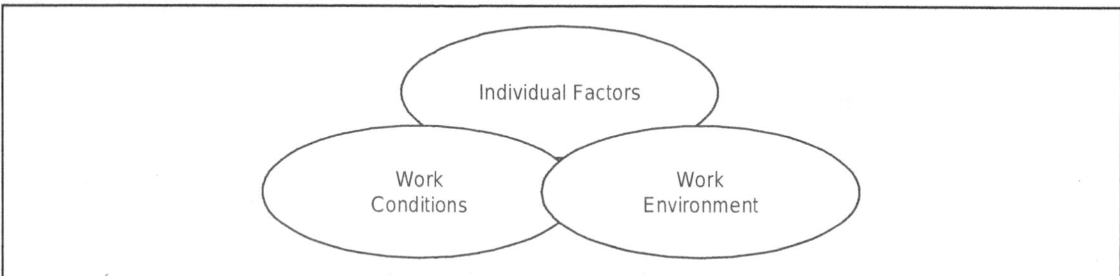

Fig. 14.10. *Factors Affecting Quality of Work Life.*

To improve Quality of Work Life management has to take steps :

(*a*) **Flexibility in Work Schedule**. The modern workers especially knowledge workers seek flexible work schedule, flexi working hours, staggered working hours—different time intervals for the beginning and end of working hours and compressed work-week—more working hours per day with lesser number of working days per week.

(*b*) **Autonomous Work Group**. The work today is performed in groups and hence, creation of autonomous work groups helps creating positive feeling among employees. The autonomous groups allow decision making, choice of method of accomplishment of task, work distribution and designing of work schedules.

(*c*) **Job Enrichment**. It involves designing the job in a manner it becomes interesting and challenging so that workers makes meaning out of that. The degree of job enrichment determines the Quality of Work Life.

(*d*) **Opportunity for Growth**. Individual seek growth and status. The work environment must provide him opportunity for personal growth and to develop his personality.

(*e*) **Stability**. Job security and stability are two factors which are high in priority for work force. Providing better wages and stability would help the work force to function better.

There are other factors such as participation (particularly in matters directly concerned with an individuals' working, has an important bearing on his satisfaction and performance), recognition, rewards, congenial relationships, adequacy of resources, welfare for family etc. all contribute to Quality of Work Life.

MANAGEMENT BY OBJECTIVES (MBO)

Management by objectives (MBO) is a systematic and organized approach that allows management to focus on achievable goals and to attain the best possible results from available resources. It aims to increase organizational performance by aligning goals and subordinate objectives throughout the organization

Management by Objectives (MBO) was first outlined by Peter Drucker in 1954 in his book 'The Practice of Management'. In the 90s, Peter Drucker himself decreased the significance of this organization management method, when he said : "It's just another tool. It is not the great cure for management inefficiency... Management by Objectives works if you know the objectives, 90% of the time you don't."

MBO emphasizes participation by all organization members. This can describe as process where by the supervisor and subordinate in an organization jointly identifies its common goal, define each individuals responsibilities and use these measures as guides for operating the unit and assessing the contribution of each of its members. Ideally, employees get strong input to identify their objectives, time lines for completion, etc. MBO includes ongoing tracking and feedback in the process to reach objectives.

Management by objective (MBO) is a systematic approach that allows management to focus on achievable goals and to attain the best possible results from available resources. This strategy for managing people, which focuses on managing teams based on their ability to complete individual and team goals, has been used in larger organizations since its inception. Small to midsize organizations, however, can also benefit from adopting this strategy, particularly if you also take on the S.M.A.R.T. (specific, measurable, achievable, realistic, and time-based.) method of implementation.

Management by Objectives philosophy can be stated as

(*a*) It is 'proactive' rather than reactive management.

(*b*) It is 'result oriented', emphasizing accomplishment.

(*c*) Focuses on change to improve 'individual and organizational effectiveness'.

Definition

Louis A Allen in his works states "Objectives are goals established to guide the efforts of the company and each of its components." Objectives are an end towards which the activities of an enterprise are directed.

George S. Odiorne, (1965) has, defined this concept as *"a system of management whereby the superior and subordinate jointly identify objectives, define individual major areas of responsibility in terms of results expected, and use these objectives and expected results as guides for operating the unit and assessing the contribution of each of its members."*

Examining a few key words will ensure better understanding of Odiorne's definition of Management by Objectives. First, he points out that MBO is a "system of management," an overall framework used to guide the organizational unit and outline its direction. Then he points out that "the superior and subordinate jointly identify objectives"; in other words, it is a participative management procedure that requires commitment and cooperation. Third, the definition deals with identifying the "results" that are expected; thus MBO concentrates on the output of the organization, evaluating people by assessing their contribution to this output.

Peter Drucker further states that in any organization there are multiple requirements to be met to ensure profitability and hence, "to manage business id the balance variety of needs and goals and there is need of multiple objectives." Peter Drucker went on to state that that the enterprise should set objectives in minimum eight areas viz. (1) Marketing; (2) Innovation; (3) Human Organization; (4) Financial Resources (5) Physical Resources (6) Productivity; (7) Social Responsibility and (8) Profit Requirements.

Managerial Focus

MBO managers focus on the result, not the activity. They delegate tasks by "negotiating a contract of goals" with their subordinates without dictating a detailed roadmap for implementation. Management by Objectives (MBO) is about setting objectives and then breaking these down into more specific goals or key results.

Principles of Management by Objective

The principle behind Management by Objectives (MBO) is to make sure that everybody within the organization has a clear understanding of the aims, or objectives, of that organization, as well as awareness of their own roles and responsibilities in achieving those aims. The complete MBO system is to get managers and empowered acting to implement and achieve their plans, which automatically achieve those of the organization.

Annual objectives lie at the very heart of the strategy implementation. They identify precisely what must be accomplished each year to achieve the organizations strategic goals. In the process, managers are provided with specific targets for the coming year's performance. Annual objectives clarify each person's/employee's roles in implementation of an organizations strategy. It is important that these objectives quantify performance so there can be little dispute over the results.

The principles of Management by Objectives are;

- Cascading of Organizational Goals and Objectives.
- Specific objectives for each member.
- Participative decision making.
- Explicit time period
- Performance evaluation and provide feedback.

Management by Objectives also introduced the 'SMART" method of checking the validity of the objectives, which should be 'SMART" The objective setting process is a difficult one for most individuals, particularly those who've never been asked to set objectives. The process seems daunting. However, it doesn't need to be. The process can be as simple as sitting down with the departmental objectives and asking the question, "How can I best help to meet these objectives ?" From the answer to this question results the core for setting the individual's objectives. For example, if the departmental objective is to improve the customer satisfaction score, the team can work on providing more self-service information to reduce the number of calls and call wait-time or offer tools to improve customer service levels by clarifying how to communicate with a customer.

- **Specific**. There are several key factors which should be present in the objectives that are set in order for them to be effective. They should be specific. In other words, they should describe specifically the result that is desired. Instead of "better customer service score," the objective should be "improve the customer service score by 12 points using the customer service survey."

- **Measurable.** The second example is much more specific and also addresses the second factor—measurable. In order to be able to use the objectives as a part of a review process it should be very clear whether the person met the objective or not.
- **Achievable.** The next important factor to setting objectives is that they be achievable. For instance, an objective which states "100 percent customer satisfaction" isn't realistically achievable. It's not possible to expect that everyone must be 100 percent satisfied with their service. A goal of "12 percent improvement in customer satisfaction" is better—but may still not be achievable if it's assigned to the database developer. They aren't likely to have enough influence over the customer interaction process to improve satisfaction by 12 percent.
- **Realistic.** This leads into the next factor—realistic. Realistic objectives are objectives that recognize factors which can not be controlled. Said another way, realistic goals are potentially challenging but not so challenging that the chance of success is small. They can be accomplished with the tools that the person has at their disposal.
- **Time-related.** The final factor for a good objective is that it is time-based. In other words, it's not simply, "improve customer service by 12 percent," it's "improve customer service by 12 percent within the next 12 months." This is the final anchor in making the objective real and tangible. This final factor is often implied in MBO setting. The implied date is the date of the next review, when the employee will be held accountable for the commitments that they've made through their objectives.

Elements of the Management by Objective System

Management by Objective systems varies enormously. Some are designed for use in a sub unit; others for the organization as a whole. Some emphasize corporate planning, others stress individual motivation.

Most effective MBO programme share the six elements (Carroll and Tosi, 1973, pp. 1–19) :

1. *Commitment to the Program.* At every organizational level, manager's commitment to achieving personal and organizational objectives and to the MBO process is required. Managers must constantly interact and meet those they supervise, first to set the objectives and then to review progress toward these objectives.
2. *Top Level Goal Setting.* Effective MBO programs usually start with the top managers, who determine the organizations strategy and set preliminary goals that resemble annual objectives in their content and terms. This procedure gives clearer picture to both the manager and the staff of what the top management hopes to accomplish and shows them how their work relates to achieving the organizational objectives.
3. *Individual Goals.* For an MBO program to be effective it is essential that each member and staff are have a clearly defined role and job responsibilities. The purpose of setting objectives at each level is to help employees understand clearly just what they are expected to accomplish and to help each individual to accomplish his or her targeted goals.

4. *Participation.* As a general rule the greater the participation of both managers and employees in setting the goals the greater are the chances that the goals will be achieved. One of the hallmarks of successful quality management programme is joint participation in setting goals.
5. *Autonomy in Implementation of Plans.* Once the objectives have been agreed upon, the individual enjoys wide discretion in choosing the means for achieving them, without being second-guessed by higher ranking manager.
6. *Performance Review.* Managers and employees periodically meet to review progress toward the objectives. During the review, they decide what problems exist and what they can each do to resolve them. If necessary, the objectives should be modified for the next review period.

Grote identifies the following core elements in MBO :

- Formation of trusting and open communication throughout the organization
- Mutual problem solving and negotiations in the establishment of objectives
- Creation of win-win relationships
- Organizational rewards and punishments based on job-related performance and achievement
- Minimal uses of political games, forces, and fear
- Development of a positive, proactive, and challenging organizational climate.

Management by Objective Process

To understand how MBO can be applied, it is necessary to look at the parts of the process. MBO can be divided into multiple steps in many combinations, but for the purpose of this article three steps will be discussed : organization objective setting, manager objective setting, and objective review.

Organization Objective Setting. This step requires the top managers of an organization to review the purpose for which the organization exists. In the military, this may require a review of the mission statement and a discussion of its meaning. This is an important requirement, for periodic review re-emphasizes the continuing need for the existence of the organization. With this mission in mind, the commander or supervisor and his staff must then set organizational objectives in areas where the unit will concentrate its efforts during the approaching objective-setting period. These objectives are (1) to provide direction to the entire organization and (2) to provide guidelines for subordinate-level managers to formulate their objectives. As a result of this organizational objective-setting step, Managers should realize that a mission statement is a goal that defines the continuing purpose of an organization. That mission statement, however, does not define specific methods of accomplishing the goal stated. MBO helps formulate these specific methods that are necessary to accomplish the mission.

Manager Objective Setting. Each individual manager in the organization must now determine the objectives for his shop or office. This procedure takes place in three general steps : identifying key result areas, writing objectives, and negotiating with the boss.

First, the manager must identify the key result areas of responsibility that are assigned to this unit. 4 In other words, just as the commander reviewed the whole organization in order to set organizational objectives, the manager reviews his part of the organization in order to set his objectives. It is important for the individual office or shop manager to identify the areas of his unit where most of the results are obtained. He will usually find that 20 percent of his area of responsibility will produce 80 percent of his results. It is important that he identify and zero in on these key result areas for MBO to be effective.

After a manager has identified his key areas of responsibility, he is ready to sit down and write his objectives. The main criteria that he should remember in writing objectives are that they should be specific, measurable, realistic, and results-oriented. They should be specific in that there can be no confusion about what is expected. They must be measurable for later accountability. They must be realistic but still challenging. The objectives should be results-oriented, concentrating on the output of the organization and not on its internal activities or procedures.

After the manager's objectives have been written, he enters the participative management phase of this technique. The subordinate manager sits down with his boss and they agree on the subordinate's objectives. This requires a realistic commitment on the part of both individuals. The agreement on the objective signifies the approval of the expected results (output) required of the subordinate. Progress toward these results can now be pursued by the subordinate until the requirement is reached or the goal is changed.

Objective Review

After the setting of objectives has been agreed upon by the officer or NCO manager and his boss, the stage is set for managing by these objectives. This managing process is the responsibility of the subordinate manager, and it is interrupted only by mutually arranged, formal review sessions with the commander. In other words, MBO requires that each individual have the freedom to perform a well-defined task without interference.

There are two types of objective reviews—intermediate and final.6 The purpose of the intermediate review is to determine progress and identify problems that stand in the way of accomplishing objectives. Most problems are not foreseeable at the time objectives are written; they appear only when action is taken to accomplish the objectives. The result of this intermediate session should be either to agree on a plan that resolves the blockage of objective accomplishment or to change the objectives.

The final review is to determine objective accomplishment. In this session the subordinate's objectives are reviewed for the entire period. In addition, the session concentrates on the renewal of the objective-setting cycle by establishing a basis from which to plan the objectives for the next period. The superior gains an additional benefit from this session since it provides him with inputs on which to evaluate the subordinate's performance.7 If the focus of the session is on the objectives and it does not break down into personal recrimination of the individual, then the review will be a true appraisal of performance, not personality.

Grote (1996) defines eight steps in the MBO Process :

- Formulate long-range goals and strategic plans.
- Develop overall organizational objectives.
- Establish derivative objectives for major operating units.
- Set realistic and challenging objectives and standards of performance for members of the organization.
- Formulate action plans for achieving the stated objectives.
- Implement the action plans and take corrective action when required to ensure the attainment of objectives.

- Periodically review performance against established goals and objectives.
- Appraise overall performance, reinforce behavior, and strengthen motivation. Begin the cycle again.

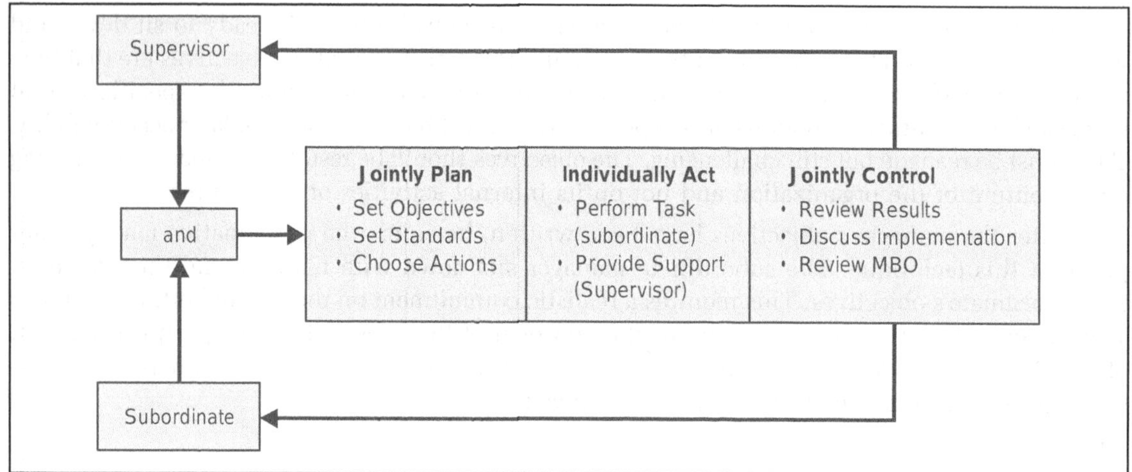

Fig. 14.11. *Management by Objectives Peter Drucker Model.*

Benefits of Management by Objective

The major benefits of Management by Objective are :

(*a*) Unity of Direction. The

(*b*) Means of Decentralization

(*c*) Stimulates motivation, provides greater satisfaction to employee.

(*d*) Basis of Control

(*e*) Better Communication.

(*f*) Coordination.

(*g*) Higher Productivity.

Where to Use MBO

The MBO style is appropriate for knowledge based enterprises when your staff is competent. It is appropriate in situations where you wish to build employees' management and self leadership skills and tap their creativity, tacit knowledge and initiative. Management by Objectives (MBO) is also used by chief executives of multinational corporations (MNCs) for their country managers abroad.

Advantages of Management by Objectives

The principle behind Management by Objectives (MBO) is to create empowered employees who have clarity of the roles and responsibilities expected from them, understand their objectives to be achieved and thus help in the achievement of organizational as well as personal goals. Some of the important features and advantages of MBO are :

- Clarity of goals—With MBO, came the concept of 'SMART" goals *i.e.,* goals that are :
  - o Specific
  - o Measurable
  - o Achievable
  - o Realistic, and
  - o Time bound.

  The goals thus set are clear, motivating and there is a linkage between organizational goals and performance targets of the employees.
- The focus is on future rather than on past. Goals and standards are set for the performance for the future with periodic reviews and feedback.
- Motivation—Involving employees in the whole process of goal setting and increasing employee empowerment increases employee job satisfaction and commitment.
- Better communication and Coordination—Frequent reviews and interactions between superiors and subordinates helps to maintain harmonious relationships within the enterprise and also solve many problems faced during the period.

Evaluation of Management by Objectives

In the review of literature on MBO Research, Carroll and Tosi (1973) focused on three key concepts—specific goal setting, feedback on performance, and participation—to determine whether the optimism was justified. They concluded that individuals who are successful in achieving their goals they have set tend to aim for increased performance. Employees who receive specific and timely feedback perform better and those who participate in goal setting show higher performance level. Carroll and Tosi (1973) concluded that the 'very process of participation leads to increased communication and understanding between managers and those they supervise.

BALANCED SCORE CARD

The balanced score card is a strategic planning and management system that is used extensively in business and industry, government, and nonprofit organizations worldwide to align business activities to the vision and strategy of the organization, improve internal and external communications, and monitor organization performance against strategic goals. It was originated by Drs. Robert Kaplan (Harvard Business School) and David Norton as a performance measurement framework that added strategic non-financial performance measures to traditional financial metrics to give managers and executives a more 'balanced' view of organizational performance. While the phrase balanced scorecard was coined in the early 1990s, the roots of the this type of approach are deep, and include the pioneering work of General Electric on performance measurement reporting in the 1950's and the work of French process engineers (who created the Tableau de Bord—literally, a "dashboard" of performance measures) in the early part of the 20th century.

The balanced scorecard has evolved from its early use as a simple performance measurement framework to a full strategic planning and management system. The "new" balanced scorecard transforms an organization's strategic plan from an attractive but passive document into the "marching orders" for the organization on a daily basis. It provides a framework that not only provides performance measurements, but helps planners identify what should be done and measured. It enables executives to truly execute their strategies.

A method of implementing a business strategy by translating it into a set of performance measures derived from strategic goals that allocate rewards to executives and managers based on their success at meeting or exceeding the performance measures. Balanced Score card enables the management to monitor and optimize business performance based on Key Performance indicators.

What is Balanced Score Card ?

The Balanced Score Card can be understood as a management system, which is structured according to the logic of the cybernetic management circle *i.e.,* "plan-do-check-act". Kaplan and Norton position the Balance Score Card as a tool for organizations to manage the demands of relevant stakeholders and to translate strategies into action ("from strategy to action"). Possible stake holders that are strategically relevant could be shareholders, customers or employees. Their demands are integrated into core management of companies within a "financial", "customer" or "learning" or "process" perspective. See Figure 14.10. Each perspective consists of relevant strategic goals, indicators and measures to achieve them. One should emphasis the fact that the concept remains open for integrating further relevant stakeholders and perspectives. Balanced Score card provides 'enablers' the focus on the achievement of strategic goals in the future (leading indicators) as well as results (lagging indicators) to depict he effectiveness and efficiency of measures in the past. Strategies can be usually interpreted as a set of hypothesis of 'causes and effects'. So within Balanced Score Card the relevant goals and corresponding indicators are linked to each other revealing this structure of casual relationships. Such relationships are relevant within each perspective and also between them. Objectives of the 'learning' perspective, serve as 'enablers' for the achievement of goals of the other 'over arching' perspective (*e.g.,* customers, finance).

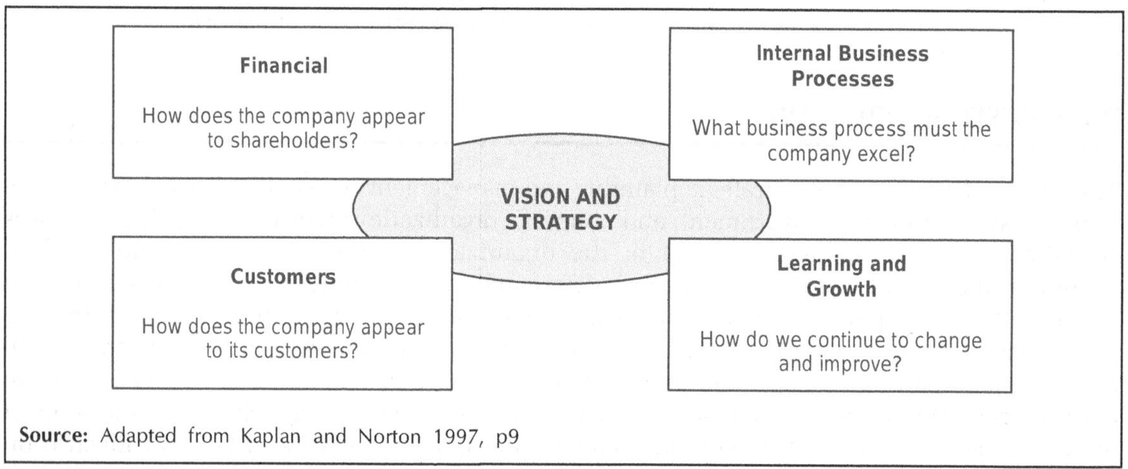

Fig. 14.12. *The Balanced Scorecard Approach.*

In the predominant 'financial perspective' objectives similar to traditional system of management and accounting are included to depict the financial performance of the company. In contrast to traditional management instruments, the Balanced Score Card concept stresses the importance of the 'value drivers' for future profitability. The 'customer perspective' aims at the identification of relevant customers and market segments that contribute to the financial goals. In the dimension of 'internal processes' firms should identify the structure efficiently, the internal value driving processes that are vital regarding the goals of customers and shareholders (*e.g.*, innovation, production, after sales etc. Kaplan and Norton, 1997, p. 89). Human Resource being an underlying strategic factor of success, Kaplan and Norton suggest a perspective for 'learning and development' that tries to depict all staff and organizational related aspects that are important regarding organizational reengineering processes (Weber and Schäffer 200, p 201).

Definition

Kaplan and Norton describe the innovation of the balanced scorecard as follows :

"The balanced scorecard retains traditional financial measures. But financial measures tell the story of past events, an adequate story for industrial age companies for which investments in long-term capabilities and customer relationships were not critical for success. These financial measures are inadequate, however, for guiding and evaluating the journey that information age companies must make to create future value through investment in customers, suppliers, employees, processes, technology, and innovation."

Benefits of Balanced Score Card

The major benefits of a balance score card are :

(*a*) Track performance and measure fulfillment of business goals.

(*b*) Obtain real-time overviews of Key Performance Indicators that will allow you to take immediate action.

(*c*) Evaluate overall business performance according to your strategic plan.

Stewart (1997) summarizes a number of methods for measuring Intellectual Capital. He divides his overview in measures that attempt to capture Intellectual Capital "as a whole" and those that focus on its components. Measures of the whole include :

- Market-to-book ratios—which simply compare the difference between published historical cost book value and the market value of the firm
- Tobin's Q—which relates the market value of the company to the replacement cost of its fixed assets and defines the difference as the value of Intellectual Capital and
- Calculated intangible value (CIV)—which computes the value of the intangible assets by a comparison between the company's performance and an average competitor that has similar tangible assets.

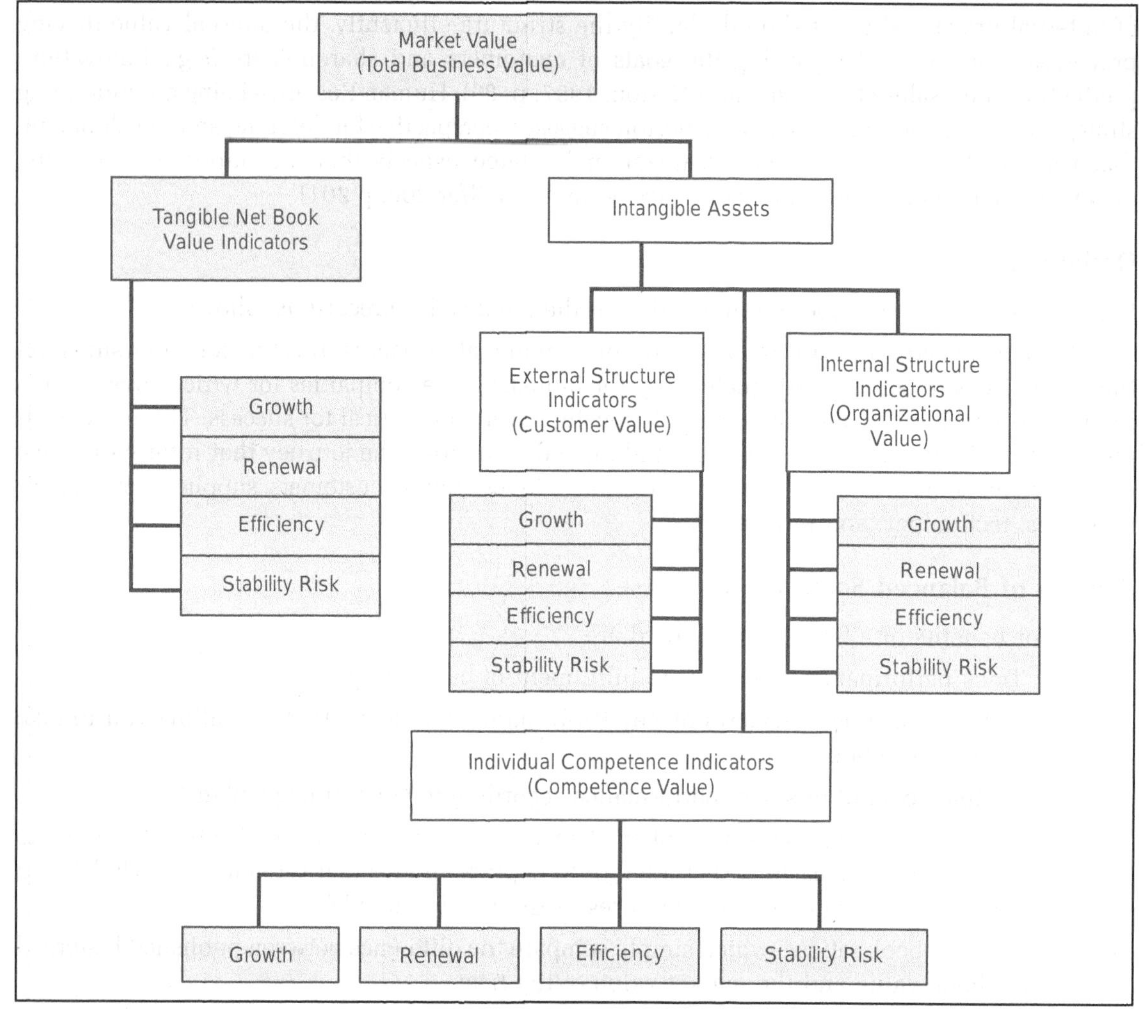

Fig. 14.13. *The Intangible Asset Monitor.*

RETURN ON INVESTMENTS

In the present economic and competitive situation it has become important for companies to know the return on their investment in order to attract investment and retain stake holder's interest in the company. The Return on Investments of Human Capital arguably offers the greatest long term value in an organization (Firz-enz, 2001). Jac Fitz-enz explains that in today's marketplace, every function must add value.

Building a comprehensive measurement and evaluation process is like putting pieces of puzzle in place over a period of time. The balanced scorecard process (Kaplan and Norton, 1996) or four levels of evaluation developed by Kirkpatrick (1975) offers the beginning point for such frame work.

The return on investment can be done by utilizing the concept of human resource problem solving, which sets investments in human resource development as the denominator and the return on investment as the numerator.

$$\text{Human Resource Return on Investment} = \frac{\text{Results (actual performance or expectations)}}{\text{Salary + Human resource development investment}}$$

The concept of Human Resource Return on Investment is expressed with the above equation. The denominator of the Human Resource Return on Investment is essentially the total amount of compensation for a targeted individual employee. The total compensation includes salary, a benefit package and investment in human resource development.

Return of Investment must satisfy three audiences; first, the HR staff members who use a process must have a simple approach. Second, an Return on Investment process must meet the unique requirements of the clients. The clients who request the HR interventions and approve projects need a process that will provide quantitative and qualitative results. They need a simple formula as used for other types of investments. Finally the process should withstand scrutiny and close examination. The process should produce consistent and accurate values and outcomes.

In preparing calculation, it is necessary to align the human resource training and development programs to be factored under investment category and then determine the proper range. Human resource development programs to be factored may include various types of on the job training (OJT) such as strategically shifting personnel and engaging in tasks with an educational significance. Since it is difficult to quantify these activities (to convert them into costs), these do not need to be included in the denominator.

Factors that Fortune 500 Companies are Measuring

Turnover costs

Employee replacement costs

Economic value of employee behaviors (absenteeism, smoking, etc)

Economic benefits of developing a superior selection test

Economic benefits of various training levels

Economic benefits of additional recruiting

Economic benefits of increasing job satisfaction, organizational commitment, or similar job attitudes

Economic benefits of high, medium, and low performance on a particular job

On the other hand, results must be added to the numerator. These are of two types of results : “results as a consequence” that have been realized as performance and ‘results as an expectation’ that represents the future prospects. If human resource development is considered as an investment for the future, it is appropriate to include expected results in the numerator (Company anticipates results from employees and invests according to the degree of this expectation.).

Criteria for Return of Investment Process

The process should meet the under mentioned criteria based on the inputs from HR Managers and Specialists.

(*a*) Simple. The process must be simple and avoid complex formulas, lengthy equations and complicated methodologies.

(*b*) Economical. Process should be economical, with the ability to be implemented easily.

(*c*) Credible. The assumptions, methodology, and outcomes must be credible.

(*d*) Theoretically Sound. The process should be theoretically sound and based on generally accepted practices.

(*e*) Account for Other Factors. The process must account for other factors that influence output variables.

Return of Investments Analysis

Return on Investment analysis is method of calculating the monetary benefits of human resource programs in relation to their costs. It is based on Kirkpatrick's (1994) framework for evaluating training programs with elaboration by Philips, and much of this discussion of Return on Investment is based on the work of Chmielewski and Philips, (2002).

There are five levels in evaluating human resource programme (Chmielewski and Philips, 2002 p.227).

1. *Reaction to Panned Action*. Measures employee satisfaction with the program and capture planned action.
2. *Learning*. Measure changes in employee knowledge, skills and attitude related to the program.
3. Job Application. Measures changes in on the job behaviour or job processes.
4. *Business Results*. Measure changes in business impact variables such as productivity.
5. *Return on Investment*. Compares program benefits to costs.

Level 1. Although reaction and satisfaction is important, a favourable input does not ensure that participants will implement the improvements or new process or that they will follow new guidelines or procedures.

Level 2. Learning, measurements focus on what participants learned during the HR program if there is a learning component. A learning check is helpful to ensure that participants absorb new skills and knowledge and that they know how to use it to make that HR program successful.

Level 3. Application and implementation, various follow up methods are used to determine if participants apply on the job what is needed to make the initiative successful. The frequency and use of skills are important measure at Level 3. This level also includes all the steps, actions, tasks, and processes involved in the implementation of the initiative.

Level 4. Focuses on the actual results achieved in the HR initiative, typical Level 4 measure include output, quality, cost, time and customer satisfaction.

Level 5. Compares the program's monetary benefits with the costs, although Return on Investments is expressed in several ways, it is usually presented as a percentage or benefit cost ratio. The evaluation cycle is not complete until the Level 5 evaluation; the final level of evaluation is conducted. Figure 14.14 shows the components to calculate HR initiatives.

I. Recruiting
   A. Inputs :
      Recruiting costs
      Advertising costs
      Resume management
      Branding
   B. Organizational Influencers/Impact Variables :
      Higher retention (lower attrition rates)
      Reduce turnover, etc.
   C. Return :
      Cost per hire per level
      Revenue per employee

II. Selection
   A. Inputs :
      Sourcing costs
      Hiring costs
      Person-job fit
      Time and productivity/Time of selectors
   B. Organizational Influencers/Impact Variables :
      Orientation process
      Assimilation
      Management
   C. Return :
      PBT (profit before taxes) per employee
      Productivity : individual, team, and organizational levels
      Productivity over time

III. Training
   A. Inputs :
      Needs assessments
      Cost of training and development per employee
      Cost of lost opportunities/work
      Cost of lost sales (for sales staff training)
      Project management costs
   B. Organizational Influencers/Impact Variables :
      Retention
      Technical competence
      Organizational commitment
   C. Return :
      PBT (profit before taxes per employee
      Productivity : individual, team, and organizational levels
      Productivity over time

IV. Performance Management
   A. Inputs :
      Hourly cost of implementation (employee hours)
      Cost of design
      Cost of performance management software
      Cost of training
      Cost to warehouse data
   B. Organizational Influencers/Impact Variables :
      Feedback to employees
      Employee-manager relationship
   C. Return :
      Productivity : individual, team, and organizational levels
      Revenue per employee

V. Coaching
   A. Inputs :
      Cost of assessments
      Cost to do coaching
      Time away from daily work
   B. Organizational Influencers/Impact Variables :
      Financial impact/benefit because of behavioral changes in the coaches
      Improved business performance, communication, and leadership skills
      Motivation, employee morale, employee commitment
   C. Return :
      Cost of turnover
      Employee productivity
      Satisfaction and commitment of direct and non-direct reports

VI. Succession Management
   A. Inputs :
      Cost to design program and software
      Cost of assessments
   B. Organizational Influencers/Impact Variables :
      Successful incumbent
      Meets financial projections
      Satisfies stakeholders
   C. Return :
      Prevented cost of lost time
      Employee productivity
      Cost to hire from outside vs. promote internally

Fig. 14.14. *Components to Calculate ROI HR Initiatives.*

Return on Investment Process Model

Figure 14.14 shows the steps that are necessary to calculate Return on Investment, beginning with the detailed description of the HR objectives and ending with reporting the results. Along the way, data is collected analysed to develop a credible evaluation of an HR project.

Evaluation Planning. The first two parts (Figure 14.14) of the Return on Investment process focuses on two critical planning issue. The first step is to develop appropriate objectives for the human resource initiative. These are often referred to as the ultimate objectives in a particular solution to a problem are implemented. With objectives having been determined the next step is to develop a detailed evaluation plan. This involves two documents; the first being the data collection plan which indicates the type of data collected, the method of data collection, data sources, the timing of collection and the various responsibilities. The second document is the return on investment analysis plan, which indicates how the HR program is isolated from other influences, how data are converted into monetary values, the appropriate cost categories, the expected tangible measures, and the anticipated target audience for communication.

Collecting Data. The data collected during the human resource programme measure reaction and satisfaction at Level 1 and learning at Level 2. Collecting data during the human resource program intervention ensures that necessary adjustments are made and the process is altered as necessary to keep the assignment on track. The satisfaction and learning data are critical for immediate feed back and necessary Human Resource intervention successful. The post program implementation data is compared with pre-program situations, control group difference and expectations. Data can be collected by using variety of methods. The important challenge in data collection is selecting the method or methods appropriate for the setting and the specific program, within the time and budget constraints.

Isolating the Effects of the Human Resource Program. In this step of the process, specific strategies are explored that determine the amount of performance improvement directly related to the program. The specific strategies in this program will pinpoint the amount of improvement directly related to the intervention. The result is increased accuracy and credibility of the Return on Investment calculation.

Converting Data into Monetary Value. To calculate the return on investment, business impact data are converted into monetary values and compared with intervention costs. This requires a value to be placed on each unit of data connected with the Human Resource program. It is essential to the process to divide data into hard and soft categories. Hard data are traditional measures of organizational performance—very objective, easy to measure, and easy to convert to monetary values. Hard data are common measures, have high credibility with management, and are available in every type of organization. The measure represents output, quality, cost, and time of work-related processes. The characteristics of hard data are :

- Objectively based
- Easy to measure and quantify
- Relatively easy to assign monetary values to
- Common measure of organizational performance
- Very credible with management.

HR interventions are designed to impact 'soft' variables; the category of soft data is also needed in evaluation. Soft data are sometimes subjective, may be difficult to measure, and are almost difficult to convert to monetary values. When compared to hard data, soft data are difficult to measure performance. Soft data can be grouped into several categories. Measures such as employee turnover, absenteeism, and grievances are considered soft data, not because they are difficult to measure but because it is difficult to accurately convert them to monetary values Figure 14.15. The characteristics of soft data are :

- Subjectively based in many cases.
- Difficult to measure and quantify, directly.
- Difficult to assign monetary values to
- Less credible as measure.
- Usually behaviorally oriented.

Work Habits
- Absenteeism
- Tardiness
- First Aid treatments
- Violation of safety rules
- Excessive Breaks

Customer Satisfaction
- Churn Rate
- Number of satisfied customer
- Customer satisfaction index
- Customer Loyalty
- Customer complaints

Work Climate
- Number of grievances
- Employee complaints
- Job satisfaction
- Employee Turnover
- Litigation

Development/Advancement
- Number of promotion
- Number of pay increases
- Requests for transfer
- Performance Appraisal Ratings
- Increase in Job Effectiveness

Job Attitudes
- Job Satisfaction
- Organizational Commitment
- Perception of Job Responsibility
- Employee Loyalty
- Increased Confidence

Initiative
- Implementation of new ideas
- Successful completion of projects
- Number of suggestions implemented
- Number of goals

Fig. 14.15. *Examples of Soft Data.*

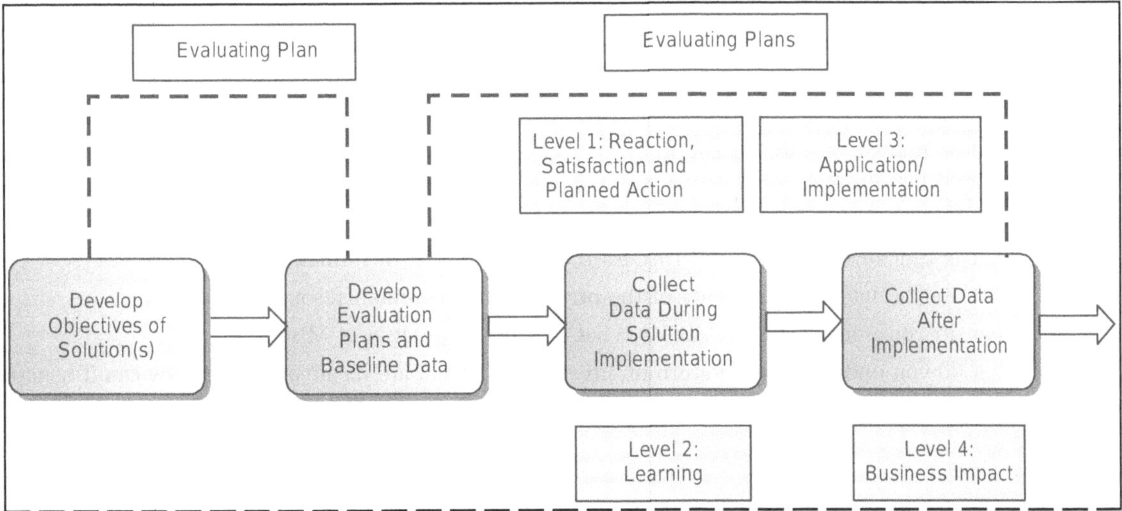

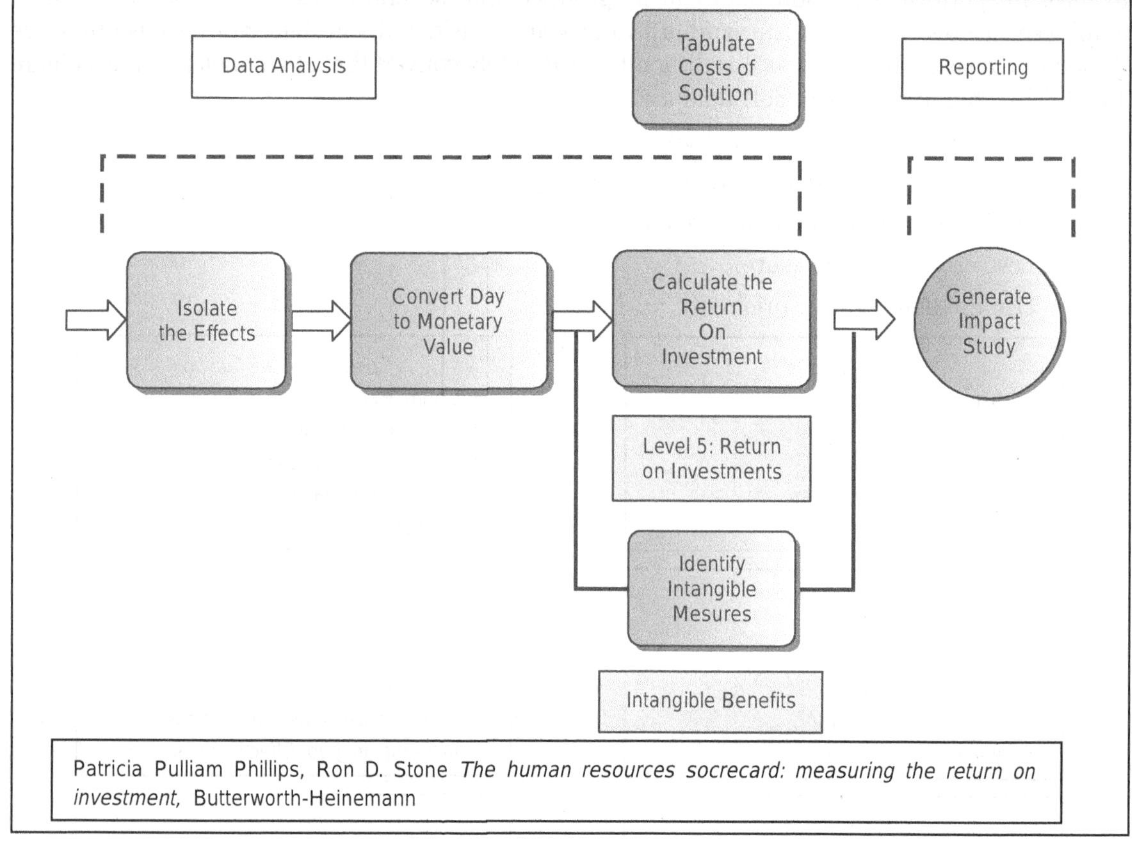

Fig. 14.16. *Return on Investment Methodology.*

Review Questions

1. Define 'Human Resource Accounting' and explain the objectives of Human Resource Accounting ?
2. Briefly explain the development of Human Resource Accounting ?
3. Explain briefly the various concepts of Human Resource Accounting, their advantages and limitations.
4. What is human resource accounting ? Discuss with reference to a few definitions of human resource accounting.
5. What do you understand by human resource audit ?
6. What is human resource cost ? Discuss the measurement of human resource cost.
7. What are the major components of the original cost of human resources ?
8. What do you understand by MBO ? What are the advantages of MBO ?
9. What do you understand by Return on Investment ? What are its advantages ? How can it benefit an organization ?

PROJECT WORK

Identify an organisation and make an attempt to work out the human resource costs of.

- Recruitment and selection
- Training for a period of one year.

Compare the cost figures worked out by you independently with the accounting figures maintained by the organisation. Analyze the differences and comment. Present it in the class.

Case Study

Bhushan Ltd. An engineering firm engaged in the manufacture of spares and components of critical nature needed by transporters and engineering industries had consistently an impressive track record as market leader. Mr. Raghavan an MBA from IIM, Ahmedabad with a Mechanical engineering background, had been in charge of the Mechanical Engineering Section since 1984. He was promoted as the Chief Executive of the Division in 1994. This was in recognition of his outstanding contribution to the development of new product lines, especially in the area of compressor-cum-vacuum pumps. Mr. Raghvan was also well known for his integrity, honesty, leadership and decisiveness. He was a brilliant engineer, and always worked hard to step ahead of his competitors in the field. He was virtually a think tank, and the management was proud of it.

During the last six months, he spent long hours redesigning the export model- compressor-cum-vacuum pump set. After his interactions with his foreign collaborators, he was convinced that with little more effort, the company would successfully design the model, thus saving the production costs as well as improving the efficiency by 16-20 percent. He depended entirely on Mr. Sankalp, a foreman of exceptional ability and tenacity. Moreover, Mr Sankalp was good at human relations and commanded respect from his immediate subordinates. Since the fabrication of the new model was in its infancy, everyone concerned felt it undesirable to let others know what was happening in this regard on the shop floor, and therefore it was clear to both foreman and the persons working under him, that the matter would not be brought to the notice of Mr. Rajat the new Works manager, a recent inductee. The men were on with their new jobs and were always delighted with any word of appreciation from their Chief Mr. Raghvan.

Mr. Rajat was young and energetic with a flair for mechanical engineering products. He had no knowledge of management, but always laid stress on proper supervisory activities. He knew his job well and always expected ot6hers to perform their duties as scheduled. .He could never tolerate indiscipline. One evening, before going home, Mr Rajat found some mechanist and helpers engaged in fabricating a spare part of the pump set as per order of Mr Raghvan. He was happy to find people so much involved in their work. However, his enthusiasm soon vanished when he discovered that what they were engaged in was not a normal part of their work. "Damn it." "What are you all up to ?" He shouted. The workers were perplexed; they did not know what to say. Mr Sankalp soon appeared and explained the ongoing projects and the benefits its success will bring to the company.

Mr. Rajat got very angry with the Mr. Sankalp and reprimanded him severely in the presence of all. Mr. Sankalp felt confused and hurt. Mr. Sankalp was also given a show cause notice demanding an explanation within 24 hours. Mr Sankalp wanted to report to Mr. Raghvan but he had left on a tour and would be back only after a month. Mr. Sankalp went to Mr. Rajat and handed over his resignation.

The news of Mr. Sankalp's resignation spread like a wild fire. Mr. Sanklp was known for his diligence and hard work. He had risen to be a supervisor from the level of ordinary helper by his devotion and hard work. His one weakness was that he was very sensitive and would never compromise on issues affecting his personality and dignity.

Questions

1. *Was Mr. Rajat right in accepting Mr. Sankalp's resignation ?*
2. *What do you think was the reason for Mr. Rajat to give show cause notice to Mr. Sankalp ?*
3. *How do you assess the action of Mr. Rajat ?*
4. *What are the remedial actions that you recommend to prevent such situations from repeating.*

❑❑❑

Chapter 15

INTERNAL MOBILITY

★ LEARNING OBJECTIVES ★

After reading this chapter, you will be able to understand :

- Internal Mobility Purpose
- Concept of Promotion
- Promotion Methods and Policy
- Demotion
- Concept of Transfer
- Need and Objective of Transfer
- Separation, its Types
- Succession Planning
- Obsolescence
- Plateaued Performers
- Work-Family Conflicts

INTRODUCTION

Internal mobility—the movement of employees from one position to another within a corporation—is an efficient and cost-effective method of talent deployment. Mobility and flexibility in the workforce is necessary to cope with ever changing workforce requirements of the organization. A successful internal mobility program begins with a company clarifying its purpose and the business goals it seeks to accomplish with an internal mobility initiative. Next, the corporation translates the business goals driving internal mobility into specific business policies. These business policies will in turn determine the organization of the staffing department delivering the service, how and when the initiative will apply, and the rules and procedures followed.

Both external and internal factors impact changes to be brought in the work force. The 'external factors' affecting workforce are technological changes; rise in demand and creation of new capacities creating demand of skilled and trained workforce; and availability of workforce.

The 'internal factors' that affect the workforce mobility are the retirement; employees leaving the organization; changes in organization structure leading to job redesign, job regrouping; changes in jurisdiction of department; etc. The changes in the workforce are brought about by promotion, transfer, lay off, and retirement. The mobility can take place between various departments or jobs (Figure 15.1).

Lateral transfers and vertical promotions are combined to form a career ladder by which an employee acquires different but related skills. Most firms (especially Governments) routinely transfer employees to different sections and departments.

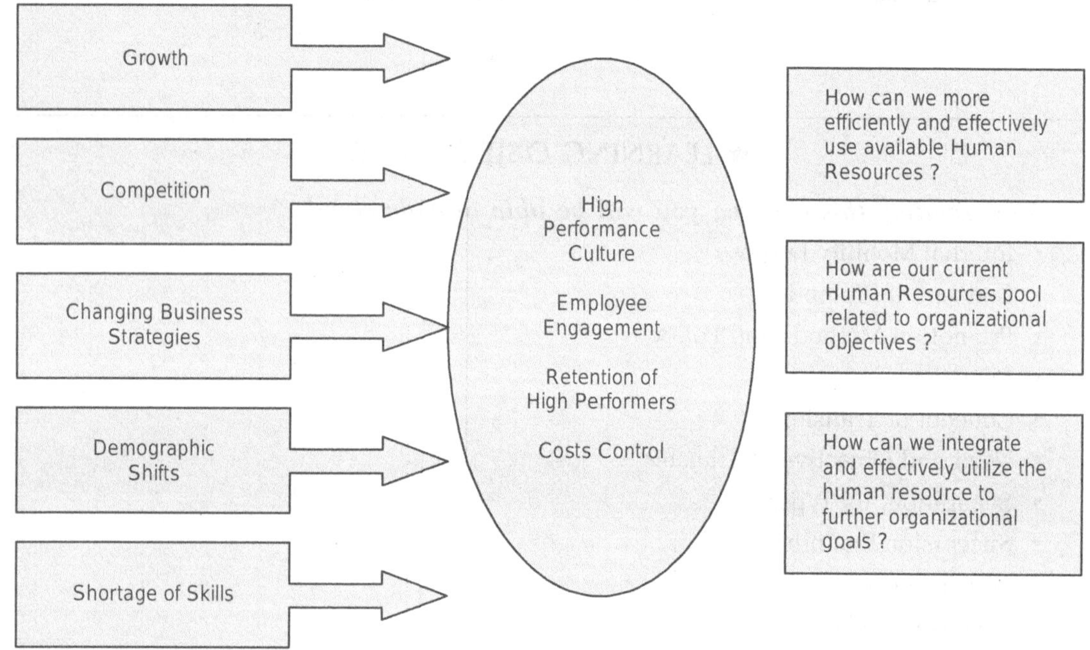

Fig. 15.1. *Factors Driving Internal Mobility.*

Goal

"The goal of 'Internal Mobility' is to create a highly responsive, high performance, sustainable, organization which meets its business targets today and in future."

PURPOSE OF JOB CHANGES

Job changes are primarily carried out to :

(*a*) **Improve Organizational Effectiveness**. Job changes are primarily carried out in an organization to improve its efficiency, by removing superfluous positions, redesigning jobs or regrouping them.

(*b*) **Maximize Employee Efficiency**. Job changes assist organization to deploy an employ based on his knowledge, skill, potential to utilize him in an optimum manner.

(*c*) **To Cope with Changes in Organizational Operations**. The objectives, utilization of technology and resources are adjusted to changing business environment. The employees are made to undergo a mobility to meet the challenges of business environment.

(*d*) **Disciplinary Action**. Job changes are utilized to discipline the employees of a company. Lay offs and demotions are used as tools to discipline an employee.

Internal Mobility could be affected by either by promoting, demoting, transferring an employee or separation.

PROMOTION

Promotions refer to upward movement of an employee from the present position to another one with increased pay, enhanced prestige and position and an enlarged span of control. Promotion also brings along with it enhanced responsibility. In India promotion has and will become contentious issue, due to aspects such as employment equity, affirmative actions to uplift the backward classes, and the concept of merit. Promotion decisions are traditionally based on aspects such as work performance history and 'meritorious work related grounds', the flattening organizational structures with limited promotional avenues are going to affect the employee behaviour and attitude and promotion decisions would lead to lot of debates and even unhappiness. Issues relating to promotion are negotiated between employers and Trade Unions.

In view of the above when promotions are affected following to be kept in mind :

(*a*) All employees should be provided with information regarding promotional opportunities.

(*b*) The criteria, qualification and standards that will apply in promotions must be clearly communicated to employees.

(*c*) Unsuccessful candidates should be provided with feedback regarding the reasons for their failure to be promoted.

(*d*) Employees from backward classes should be groomed for promotion.

(*e*) All employees should get equal opportunities, provided with a career path, training, experience and skills at each stage to be considered for promotion.

(*f*) Promotion decisions must be taken on specific criteria's such as competency, and taking into account the prior learning and relevant experience.

It is important that promotion decisions are not made on ad hoc basis. Proper policy guidelines should be formalized and all employees should be informed about it.

Concept

Promotion means giving higher position to an employee carrying higher status, more responsibility and salary. Employees given promotion when vacancies are available or when new posts are created. It is an upward movement of an employee in an organizational hierarchy. Promotion may be temporary or permanent based on organizational requirements.

'Upgradation' is also a methodology employed in many organizations. Upgradation implies moving into higher pay scales without additional span of control or responsibility. In upgradation there is no increase in status or position. Both 'promotion' and 'upgradation' is used to award an employee. Upgradation is tool employed by management to reward/motivate an employee as there are few positions/limited vacancies at higher levels.

Purpose of Promotions

Yoder *et. al.* (1958, p.58) in his work states that 'promotion provides incentives to initiative, enterprise, and ambition; minimizes discontent and unrest; attracts capable individuals; necessitates logical training for advancements and forms an effective reward for loyalty and cooperation, long service etc'. The purpose of promotions could be :

(*a*) Organizations promote an individual as an incentive for his performance as also enable him to meets his aspirations.

(*b*) Increase job satisfaction.

(*c*) Helps keep an efficient work force.

(*d*) Develops employee loyalty.

(*e*) Fill higher vacancies.

(*f*) Increase efficiency by utilizing the knowledge and skills of the employees.

(*g*) Acts as a challenge for the employees to improve proficiency to enable them to get promoted.

Criteria for Promotion

Promotions in an organization are made based on seniority (based on length of service), merit (based on ability of an individual) or a combination of both.

Seniority Based Promotion

Seniority implies the relative length of service in the same organization. Seniority has been suggested as the criteria for promotion on the plea that there is a positive correlation between length of service and experience which translates itself into better ability to give decisions. The system is also based on the social behaviour of people of giving respect to elders in the society.

Advantages of Seniority Based Promotion :

(*a*) It is simpler system as length of service can be easily determined and thereby judge seniority of an employee.

(*b*) It is transparent as each employee in an organization is fully aware of his position in the seniority list. Employee can himself place his seniority in an organization.

(*c*) It creates objective criteria and there is no scope of favouritism. It leads to sense of security in an employee.

(*d*) The system is usually supported by trade Unions and hence promotes better Industrial Relations.

Disadvantages of Seniority Based Promotion :

(*a*) The seniority based system has one major disadvantage that it does not help in employees learning. The employee after certain time just becomes a passenger and awaits his turn in promotion.

(*b*) In this system individual performance and worth is not recognized. It demotivates and acts as a damper on hard working employees.

(*c*) Efficiency suffers as each employee is promoted in his turn and there is no incentive to excel and perform better.

Seniority based promotion also acts as a damper as ambitious talented and hardworking employees do not come forward.

Data compiled by the Economic Times Intelligence Group indicating the number of years the Top Executives have spent with the companies. It would be appropriate to say some of the Top Executives never worked in any other company like B. Muthuraman of Tisco and M.S. Banga of Hindustan Lever.

Average Tenure of Top executives

Company	**Tenure**
Tisco	32
Mahendra & Mahendra	32
Hindustan Lever Limited	30
Siemens	29
ACC	29
BHEL	28
Asian Paints	26

Source : *The Economic Times, June 26, 2003.*

Fig. 15.2. *Period Spent with Concerns by Some Senior Employees.*

Merit as Basis of Promotion

Merit implies the abilities in terms of knowledge, skills and performance record of an employee.

Advantages of Merit System :

(*a*) It motivates competent employee to perform better.

(*b*) The company is able to attract talent from outside as ambitious persons are attracted to company.

(*c*) The merit based system assists in retaining talented and promising employees.

Disadvantages of Merit Based System :

(*a*) The judgment in organizations are usually subjective as it is very difficult to judge intangibles.

(*b*) Merit system is not appreciated by Trade Unions as their influence recedes.

(*c*) Merit indicates past achievement. It may not denote the future potential and past experience of an employee.

(*d*) Old employees feel insecure.

Seniority–cum–Merit

Both seniority and merit system suffer from certain limitations. None of them is by itself a complete criterion. Most of the organizations employ a combination of seniority and merit. A balance between both seniority and merit can be created by laying down a condition for promotion that an individual should have minimum length of service *e.g.*, five years or more before being considered for promotion. Organization may also give a relative weightage to seniority and merit or organizations could also lay down minimum qualifications and then promote an individual based on seniority.

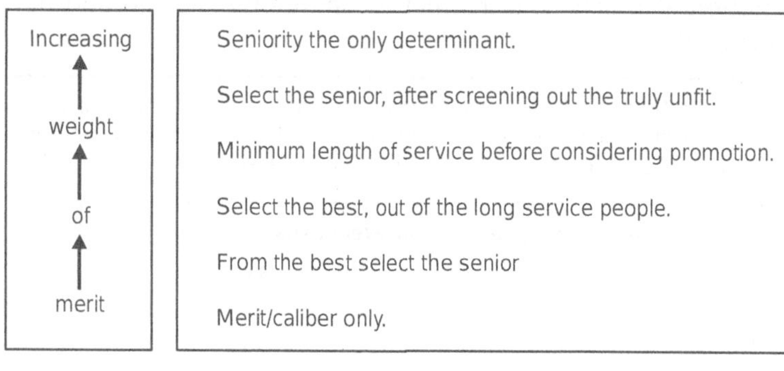

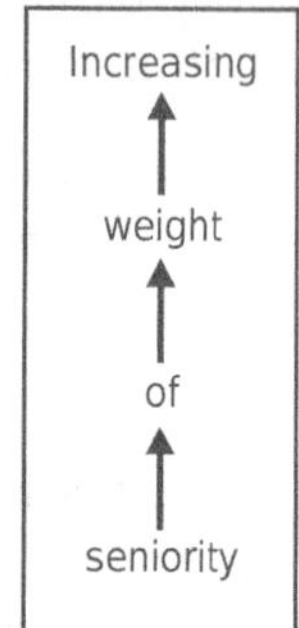

Fig. 15.3. *Merit-Seniority Spectrum for Promotion.*

Promotion Policy

The organization has to have a promotion policy regarding promotion of its employees. The company that has no recognized promotion policy is likely to have frustrated and restless employees. A good promotion policy should include :

(*a*) A uniform distribution of promotional opportunities throughout the company.

(*b*) The policy should be widely circulated and all employees should be aware of it. Multi chain promotion charts may be prepared for it. Dead end jobs should be labeled and the upward path should be well marked.

(*c*) The basis of promotion should be clearly specified. Weightage should be given to merit and seniority.

DEMOTION

Demotion refers to downward movement of an employee to a job on the organizational hierarchy. Demotion implies employee being assigned a job with lower pay and status. Demotion is serious an affects an employee emotionally.

Need for Demotion

Demotion may be caused due :

(*a*) **Adverse Business Conditions.** Most of the companies resort to layoffs or retrenchment due recession or other crisis. It is during these hard conditions the company/ organization may retrench junior employees and compel the employees with critical competencies and core employees are retained by offering lower pay until normalcy is restored.

(*b*) **Incompetence.** Some of the employees promoted may not be able to perform on the new assignments. In such situations the promoted employee is reverted back to his old assignment or demoted.

(*c*) **Technological Changes.** On account of changes in technology and work methods, some employees may be unable to handle or adjust in such a situation they may be relocated (transferred), retrenched or be demoted to a lower position.

(*d*) **Disciplinary Measures.** Demotions may be used as a tool of disciplinary action against erring employees. However, demotion should be used sparingly in exceptional situation.

Demotion Policy

The organization must have a clear and well articulated, widely publicized and communicated to all. The policy should include the under mentioned :

(*a*) The circumstances/conditions under which an employee can be demoted.

(*b*) The superior who is authorized to initiate demotion should be nominated.

(*c*) Before initiating demotion, actions should be taken to investigate the rule and regulation that has been violated.

(*d*) The application of demotion rule should be consistent and uniformly applied.

(*e*) Rules as to the seniority and position after demotion should be clearly enunciated. Guidelines for determining seniority of demoted employee and nature of demotion should be formulated.

(*f*) Demotion policy should be open rather than closed policy.

TRANSFER

Transfer is moving/reshuffling of employees from one unit of work place to another. It involves lateral mobility of employees from one position to another within an organization. Through transfer employees are relocated to jobs that are comparatively similar, equivalent in pay, responsibility and organizational level. Firms resort to transfer employees within two to three years period. Their argument is simple lateral transfers are necessary ingredients for skill formation and as a positive signal about the productivity of individual employee. Transfers may be voluntarily sought by employees or may be used as the sole prerogative of the managements. Transfers could be done on a mutual basis between two employees or as a sequence of transfers.

Definition

Edwin B Flippo defines :

"Transfer involves a change in job (along with it change in the place of the job) without change in position, pay or responsibility. Transfers are quite frequent."

Transfer can be defined as :

"Transfer is a change in job within the organization where the new job is substantially equal to the old in terms of pay, status and responsibilities. Transfer may be initiated by the organization or requested by an employee."

Types of Transfer

Transfers are classified based on the purpose for which it undertaken.

(*a*) *Production Transfer.* These transfers are undertaken to augment the manpower of the department where the production has to be increased or where the load has increased or from where the employees have left due retirement, discharge etc. Incase of restructuring and downsizing transfers prevents layoffs.

(*b*) *Shift Transfer.* As the name implies the employees are shifted from one shift to another.

(c) *Remedial Transfer.* These are resorted to remedy the wrong selection or placement of personnel. As a follow up employee is transferred to a more suitable job based on his abilities, knowledge and skills.

(d) *Versatile Transfer.* These are normally directed by management to provide opportunities and experience to employees. Such transfers are made to increase versatility of an employee by transferring them from one job to another and one department to another.

(e) *Replacement Transfers.* Replacement transfers are carried out in an organization as a policy based on an employee having worked at the assignment for a certain duration say three years. Replacement transfers are also carried out when a senior employee is transferred to take over from a junior employee.

Causes of Transfer

The transfers are usually carried out due :

(a) Variation in volume of work in different departments.

(b) Employee not able to perform at the position allocated.

(c) Matter of policy after an employee has served at the position for certain duration.

(d) On personal request of an employee due health or other grounds.

Benefits of Transfer

There are large numbers of benefits that accrue when transfers are done :

(a) Transfers are undertaken to enhance efficiency in the utilization of human resources through the redistribution of work force's size and strength according to changing needs.

(b) Transfer assists in replacing an employee caused due to displacement of an existing employee in a job.

(c) Transfer assists to meet the needs of an employee in terms of more convenient location, move to a job having better career prospects or work under a particular supervisor.

(d) Transfers are also carried out to keep promotion ladders open to individuals not having growth opportunities in their own departments.

(e) Transfers are undertaken to stall lay offs.

(f) Transfers are also undertaken to by management to utilize the crucial forms of competence with the employee.

(g) In organizations transfers are also undertaken as an development exercise so that an employee is exposed to various functions and becomes more versatile.

(h) Transfers are also undertaken as a disciplinary measure to diminish conflicts between colleagues.

(i) Transfers also help in reducing boredom and enhance morale.

Transfer Policy

Every organization should have a systematic, just and clear transfer policy which is transparent and communicated to all. The policy should avoid ad hoc and arbitrary approach to transfers. Every transfer involves a description and cost and hence, these should not be made frequently or without justified reason the interest of organization is paramount in all transfers.

A good transfer policy should include;

(*a*) Frequency of transfer and the minimum time period between transfers should be decided and should be publicized so that it is known to all.

(*b*) The authority which would handle transfers is to be decided upon. The best course is to have a separate officer usually of personnel department to handle all transfers.

(*c*) Criteria for transfer should be laid down.

(*d*) Policy for transfers on personal request should be clearly enunciated.

(*e*) Transfer should be clearly defined as permanent or temporary.

(*f*) The effect on pay and seniority on transfer should be clearly defined.

SEPARATIONS

Retirement, lay offs, resignations and dismissal separate the employees from their employers. Separations take place when the employee's service agreement with the organization comes to an end and employee leaves the organization. Separations are usually painful to both parties and should, therefore, be administered after careful deliberations.

Resignation

Resignations are voluntary separation initiated by the employee. An employee may resign on grounds of ill health, marriage, better opportunities etc. Sometimes an employee may be asked to resign from job as an alternative to termination of service due gross negligence, poor performance etc. Although some resignations may enable the company or an organization to rectify the mistakes but excessive turnover may prove costly to the organization. It is obligatory for the company to investigate each resignation as lot of investment has been done in recruitment, selection, and training of an employee and it is lost if an employee resigns leaves the establishment.

Lay Offs

The purpose of lay off is to reduce the financial burden on the organization in the event that human resources cannot be utilized profitably. Lay offs involve temporary removal of an employee from the payroll of the company or an organization with surplus skills.

Sec 2 (kkk) of the Industrial Disputes Act 1947, defines 'lay offs' as 'the failure, refusal or inability of an employer on account of shortage of coal, power or raw materials or accumulation of stocks, breakdown of machinery or by any other reason to give employment to a workman whose name appears on the muster rolls. Although lay offs are generally resorted to reduce financial burden but in fact it increases the financial burden on the company. As per Sec 25 (c) of the Industrial Disputes Act 1947 provides that whenever a workman (other than a 'budli' workman or a casual worker) whose name is borne on the muster rolls of an industrial establishment and who has completed not less than one year of continuous service under the employer, is laid off whether intermittently or continuously, he shall be paid by the employer for all days during which he is laid off (except for such weekly holidays as may intervene), compensation which shall be equal to fifty percent of the total of the basic wages and dearness allowance that would have been payable to him had he not been so laid off.

Lay offs involves cost to the organization and should be avoided.

RETIREMENT

Majority of the separations of employees from the organization are by way of retirement. Every organization should have clear-cut rules on retirement and it should help the employees to adjust after retirement. Retirement is an important event in his life and also has an important impact on the organization where he worked for a major portion of his life. It is in the interest of the organization that at the time of retirement of an employee that an interview is held.

Types of Retirement

Compulsory Retirement. Under this an employee must retire compulsorily after attaining a specific age. In India the Central and State Government employees are made to retire at attaining the age of 60 years. However, in private organizations employees can be given work for as they desire and an individual is able to perform.

Forced Retirement. Companies and even government employees are sometimes compelled to retire pre-maturely. This is primarily due some misconduct, as a part of disciplinary action etc. The employee under this could be forced to retire with or without benefits.

Premature Retirement. Premature retirement can be sought by an employee on his request or management may ask an individual to proceed on retirement due ill health, disability etc. In such conditions the individual usually receives full benefits of retirement.

Voluntary Retirement Scheme

Liberalization and opening up of Indian economy exposed Indian companies to competition, resulting in cost cutting by Indian companies to meet the challenges thrown. This resulted in many companies reducing the workforce by offering a 'golden handshake'. Voluntary Retirement Scheme which was very popularly referred to as 'golden handshake' was one very popular scheme to cut cost and remain competitive. Voluntary Retirement Scheme has been utilized by firms as a downsizing strategy to cut the size of wage bill by offering lucrative compensation to the employees opting out.

Voluntary Retirement Scheme involved separation of both managerial and non managerial cadre. The separation was carried out by mutual agreement between the organization and its employees. Though this was primarily designed to assist the service sector but it was extensively used by manufacturing sector to restructure their organizations to maker it more competitive and reduce costs. Among the manufacturing companies TISCO has been able to get better bargain than other companies.

SUCCESSION PLANNING

Succession planning is a process by which an organization ensures the continuity of leadership. It involves adaptation of specific procedures to ensure the identification, development and long term retention of talented individuals. Succession planning is important because the continued survival of the organization depends on the right people being in the right place at right times. Succession planning is systematic strategy to build capacity 'within the ranks,' allowing employees to be ready for new leadership roles as the need arises. Hence, Succession Planning is a critical element in talent management and, as such, a core strategic Human Resource initiative.

Definition

Succession Planning has been defined as *"a process to identify and develop people to replace current incumbents in key positions."* It has also been sates as *"a plan to fill key positions over time and is essential for the arrival and success of the organization."*

From definitions it can be deduced that Succession Planning is :

- Assured continuity of prepared leaders for key executive positions.
- A disciplined process of reviewing leadership talent.
- Increased opportunities for high potential workers. "The strategic, systematic and deliberate effort to develop competencies in potential leaders through proposed learning experiences such as targeted rotations and educational training in order to fill high level positions without favouritism."
- Increased talent pool of 'promotable' employees.
- Contribution to the organization's business plans.
- Assisting individuals to realize their own career plans within the organization.
- Developing strong leadership teams for strategic tasks.

The most important objective of succession planning is implementing a flexible, dynamic approach for developing strong leadership teams. This ensures that the organization has depth in its leadership capacity.

Framework of Succession Planning

The frame work of succession planning commences with management determining the strategic needs of the business. This is carried out by asking rigorously 'what business will need in the way of talent five (5) years hence ?' Thereafter an internal assessment of potential candidates is carried out objectively by carrying out 360 degree feedback to collect anonymous data from diverse stakeholders. Having then short listed the candidates who are likely to fill the vacancies they are put through rigorous steps of learning and development (Figure 15.4).

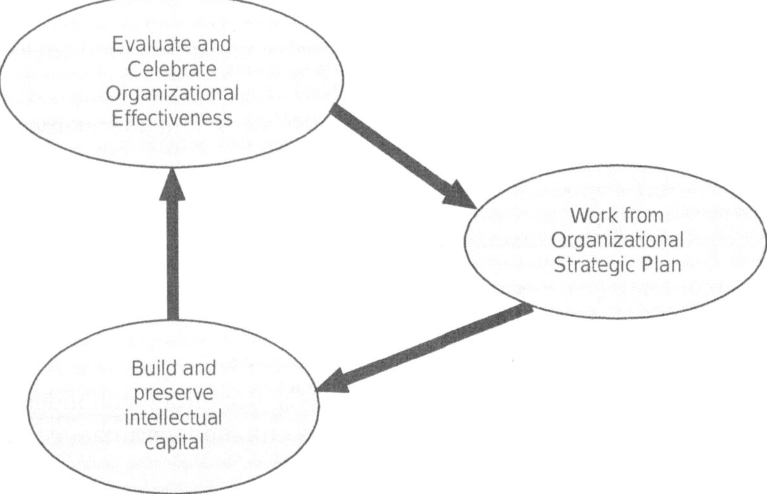

Fig. 15.4. *Succession Planning Framework.*

The main prerequisites for Succession Planning are :

(*a*) Commitment from the Top Management.

(*b*) Ownership

(*c*) Vision of what the organization will need.

(*d*) Snapshot of present conditions

(*e*) Openness to non traditional sources of talent.

(*f*) A well documented training and development program.

Elements of Succession Planning

Paula Singer has evolved a model of eight steps in Succession Planning :

(*a*) Determine the Organizations Strategic Direction.

(*b*) Identify 'critical' management and technical positions.

(*c*) Project Future Vacancies.

(*d*) Determine 'Executive Descriptors' for future leaders.

(*e*) Identify 'gaps' in staffing.

(*f*) Diagnose development needs

(*g*) Create a Deliberate Development Plan

(*h*) Review Progress and provide new assignments.

Succession Planning Mistakes

There are some mistakes made in succession planning.

(*a*) Lack of support from top management.

(*b*) Corporate politics—use of the corporate ladder to promote friends, allies, etc.

(*c*) The low visibility of many Succession Planning programs—to be successful, Succession Planning must enjoy the active support and direct participation of management employees at all levels.

(*d*) The rapid pace of organizational change creates considerable difficulty in predicting succession planning over a three year period.

(*e*) Succession Plans also fail due to much paper work and too many meetings.

OBSOLESCENCE

Obsolescence can be defined as "the degree to which an organizations professionals lack the up-to-date knowledge or skills necessary to maintain effective performance in either their current or future work." (Kaufman in Schreuder 2001 : 194)

Obsolescence simply means that an individual is becoming outmoded and out dated. Obsolescence occurs due to environment, organization climate, work change and the extent to which individuals 'keep up to date'.

Dealing with Obsolescence

Worker obsolescence is a result of a continuous process in which the balance between the employee and the job is upset, either by technological factors such as computerization or due organizational factors such as restructuring or even by acts on part of the employee. Once such balance is upset the attitude of an employee may change and results may be seen as frustration, hostility or resistance to change. Once the symptoms have been identified in the form of training courses, organizational changes or career counseling may follow to restore the balance between the worker and the job, until the cycle is repeated (Bracker and Pearson, 1986).

Organization Response

Organizations can take certain actions to prevent worker obsolescence and to reduce feelings of obsolescence. The actions include :

(*a*) Providing training and education;

(*b*) Encouraging continuous learning;

(*c*) Providing challenging initial work;

(*d*) Encouraging people to attend conferences and to subscribe to professional journals;

(*e*) Creating culture of growth and development.

CAREER PLATEAUING

Definition

Career Plateauing has been defined by **Leibowitz, Kaye** and **Farren** (1990, p. 28), *"the point in person's career when there is no longer any opportunity to progress in the organizational hierarchy."*

A distinction should be made between structural and content plateauing. Structural plateauing refers to a situation in which opportunities for promotion are restricted by the structure (pyramid) of the organization (Example is the Indian Defence Forces which has a very steep structural pyramid). Only few employees can make it to the top. Content plateauing occurs when an employee knows the job too well and no challenges are left. The challenge for managers is at least to address the problems of content plateauing, as it the easier one Leibowitz, *et. al.* (1990, p.28).

Kinds of Plateaued Performers

Leibowitz *et. al.* (1990, p.30) have identified four kinds of plateaued performers.

(*a*) **Productively Plateaued**. These employees experience job satisfaction because they feel that they have achieved their ambitions. They are loyal to the organization because they feel that the organization supports them in achieving their goals and recognizes their contribution.

(*b*) **Partially Plateaued**. Employees who are partially plateaued feel that the organization does not do much for them, but they usually have an interest that maintains their involvement in the job. These people are usually specialist to a certain field, but feel that their jobs lack excitement and that their organization does not support them enough in acquiring new skills.

(*c*) **Pleasantly Plateaued.** These employees do not aim at promotion, but prefer to remain where they are. They are unlikely to be innovative and usually stay with one organization.

(*d*) **Passively Plateaued.** Employees in this state feel that they have been in their jobs for too long and know them too well. They lack challenge and display no interest in additional training in their fields. However, these employees fell that they are helpless and cannot change their situations.

Dealing with Plateauing

Allen, Porter, Russel and Dobbins (1995 : 15-18 and Leibowitz *et. al.* (1990 : 32)) have listed out some actions to deal with employee plateauing :

(*a*) Change the structure of the organization;

(*b*) Pay for performance;

(*c*) Establish job rotation programmes to create lateral movement and broaden employee skills.

(*d*) Give candid feedback;

(*e*) Establish career plan and goals;

(*f*) Encourage career exploration;

(*g*) Encourage further education.

WORKING COUPLES AND WORK FAMILY CONFLICT

A working couple can be defined as 'any two people in an ongoing committed relationship, where both partners work, where they may or may not have children, and where decisions (family and work) are influenced by the working situation of each partner' (Guterman, 1991 : 169).

Working couples are more likely to experience work-family conflict than couples in which only one partner works.

Work family conflict has been defined by Greenhaus and Beutell (1985; 77) as 'a form of inter-role conflict in which the role pressures from the work and family domains are mutually incompatible in some respect.'

Types of Work Family Conflicts

Three types of work-family conflicts have been identified by Greenhaus and Beutell (1985).

(*a*) Time based conflict. These occur when time devoted to one role is so large and it cannot be devoted to another *i.e.*, time pressure in one role are so larger that it is impossible to satisfy the expectations of the other role.

(*b*) Strain based conflicts occur when performance in one role is adversely affected by the stress that is experienced in another. For example, a crisis in family may cause fatigue which in turn may result in poor work performance.

(*c*) Behaviour Based Conflict. This occurs when certain patterns of role behaviour are in conflict with expectations of behaviour in other roles.

Causes for Work Family Conflict

Conflict between work and family roles can for instance; be created by many factors as listed :

(*a*) Number of work hours;

(*b*) Lack of decision to work over time;

(*c*) Inflexible work schedule;

(*d*) Irregular starting time;

(*e*) Psychologically demanding work.

Dealing with Work Family Related Conflicts

Schreuder and Theron (2001 : 186) suggest, inter alia, the following actions.

(*a*) Greater sensitivity towards home life.

(*b*) Introduction to flexible benefits to assist employees with family needs such as childcare, education etc.

(*c*) Introduction of flexible work hours.

(*d*) Revision of relocation policies to make provision for the needs of the modern worker; and

(*e*) Introduction of alternate career paths.

Review Questions

1. What is meant by transfer ? Explain the role of transfer in placement of personnel.
2. Discuss transfer of employees. Compare transfer with promotion.
3. What is transfer ? Define transfer and enumerate types of transfer.
4. What do you understand by promotion ? Explain the basic features of promotion.
5. Discuss the benefits of promotion. Discuss the methods of promotion. Explain which method is better and why.
6. What do you understand by retirement ? Discuss various methods of retirement.
7. What is separation ? Explain the methods of separation.
8. What do you understand by succession planning ? How is it carried out in an organization ? Discuss.
9. The needs of society have compelled couples to work. Do you think that there is some tension if the couples work ? Recommend methods to limit the impact of work tension in families.

PROJECT WORK

Visit the nearest plant or company in your area. Study the internal mobility mechanism. Prepare a brief of the internal mobility process for discussion in class. You should be able to find out the advantages and disadvantages of the system studied and suggest recommendations.

Case Study

CASE STUDY : NAVIGATING THE HIGH SEAS : LLOYD'S REGISTER AND PEOPLECLICK HELP ANCHOR TALENT

In few industries is workforce globalisation felt more than with the international shipping and transport market. With growth in the industry reaching record highs and the need for skilled talent in great demand, Lloyd's Register Group was facing a complicated recruiting environment. Add to this the organisation's aggressive target to grow its very mobile employee base by over 40% in a five-year period, and the company recognised a need to improve its recruitment process rapidly.

The Challenge

The Lloyd's Register Group is an organisation that works to enhance safety and to approve assets and systems at sea, on land and in the air. The company has offices worldwide, in over 88 countries, and as the company prepared to grow substantially, it was clear that the current paper and email-based recruiting process would not facilitate the dynamic talent pools required for success.

With its diverse geographic nature, the recruitment function was logistically stretched. The team was struggling to ensure that all compliance and workflow challenges were met while at the same time applying their corporate standard across the board. Each local recruiter was very isolated from the overall process and was therefore limited in their ability to be effective. Additionally, the global Human Resources team for the Marine business was unable to provide the desired level of support to this disparate team, or any centralised management reporting.

Helping to lead the charge for a new system was Global Resourcing Manager, Barbara Richards. She worked with the business and the group IT function to identify the required elements for a recruitment management system that would support the level of growth Lloyd's Register required to achieve its growth objective.

Richards explained, "We required a speedy implementation in order for the organisation to be able to strategically compete and increase in the timeframe required."

The Solution

The team at Lloyd's Register selected the Peopleclick®Recruitment Management System to help make possible the company's recruitment goals. Several key criteria were used in the evaluation of potential solutions.

Speedy Implementation

Critical to Lloyd's Register's success in the industry was the ability to quickly scale up the business. In order to do so, it was essential that the organisation implement a system quickly and easily. Peopleclick's software-as-a-service architecture eliminated the need to install and update software at Lloyd's Register. A simple web browser provided all staff involved in the hiring process with access to the recruitment system.

The ease-of-use the Peopleclick system offered was equally important for adoption around the world. A familiar interface, similar to a standard email system offering drag-and-drop functionality, made the transition easy for team members regardless of location. This swift acceptance and comfort has made the implementation that much easier for Lloyd's Register.

Global Expertise

With the different equal employment regulations and compliance issues in each country, Lloyd's Register needed a partner with expertise in recruitment around the world. This was especially important to the organisation as it sought to grow a diverse talent base. It was equally important to Lloyd's Register that candidate data be protected and secure.

"By standardising on one system, we were able to easily enforce not only corporate standards, but those regulatory standards specific to each country," said Richards. "Peopleclick's easy-to-configure system allowed us to deploy one system but still customise workflows to meet the needs of our entire recruitment team."

Efficiency and Effectiveness

Paramount to the company's success was the replacement of their paper-based process with an automated and standardised solution. Peopleclick offered Lloyd's Register an easily-implemented solution which created a single repository for all candidate data. This immediately reduced the need for many of the arduous tasks the recruitment staff was forced to complete such as uploading candidate CVs and sending candidate information between recruiters via email.

Creation of a Strategic Talent Pool

Many of the top-tier candidates in the marine and shipping industries are incredibly mobile. Additionally, much of the highly-skilled talent in the industry is being constantly sought and recruited by competitors. Understanding this, Lloyd's Register knew that a pool of talent must be created and shared with its recruiters worldwide so candidate-rich areas could be identified and leveraged.

With the new recruitment management system, Lloyd's Register was able to create a global pool of talent. This pool consisted of new candidates in addition to current employees who may be seeking an opportunity to relocate or move up in the organisation. By assisting employees with internal mobility, the company could keep its retention rate high.

Corporate Brand

It was very important to Lloyd's Register to create a strong corporate presence in the marketplace, especially as demand for high-quality talent grew. Equally important was to create a dynamic and responsive candidate experience.

Lloyd's Register took advantage of Peopleclick's expertise to link their careers web site designed to offer insight into the company to a system which would enhance the candidate experience. Candidates can easily express interest in openings and track their own progress through the hiring process. The system automatically generates communications throughout the lifecycle to keep candidates appraised of their and develop an ongoing relationship. It was with this functionality that Lloyd's Register was able to significantly reduce the amount of time spent by recruiters responding to candidate's requests for status updates.

The Results

First implemented for Lloyd's Register offices in the United Kingdom, the company worked with Peopleclick to quickly roll out to China, the United States, Canada, Greece, the Netherlands, Norway, Sweden, Germany and the United Arab Emirates. As part of this process, the company launched a strong media campaign to promote the company to attract its much sought after talent.

"For some time we had wanted to create a global campaign to help showcase the company," Richards explained. "We were not able to do so until we had automated our recruitment process with Peopleclick because our old process could never have handled the volume that our campaigns produced."

After launching its pilot program in the UK, Lloyd's Register is well on its way to reaching its 40% overall growth goals. In its Marine division for example, in the first five months after implementation, the team was over half way to its goal for the growth in people for this budget year.

As Lloyd's Register continues to grow, the team is excited to put the new system to good use. "We will continue to grow our talent pool to best take advantage of our single, central database. This will allow our recruiters to identify candidates that may not otherwise have expressed interest in Lloyds and help promote us as a leading organisation in the marine industry," said Richards.

Questions

1. *Study the above case and find out the challenges as envisaged by the Lloyd's Register.*
2. *Do you agree with the company's decision to employ an external source to advice action to overcome challenges ?*
3. *How do you propose to go about improving the system ?*

Chapter 16

Application of Industrial Psychology and Morale

★ LEARNING OBJECTIVES ★

After reading this chapter, you will be able to understand :

- What is Industrial Psychology ?
- Fatigue
- What is Morale ?
- Importance of Morale
- Factors influencing Morale.
- Impact of Morale on Productivity
- Social Accountability

INTRODUCTION

Employee morale is the fundamental component of business operations—high morale coincides with job satisfaction, high work effort, creativity and initiative, a sense of pride in one's work, a commitment to one's organization, and the desire to put the achievement of group goals ahead of personal goals, thereby enhancing an organization's performance. Low morale, typically coincides to high absenteeism, labour turnover, unresolved grievances or strikes, impedes the achievement of the organization's desired outcomes. Widely recognized in the psychology, management and human relations literature as the primary factor governing worker effort and thus determining overall company performance (Howitt, 2002), morale is a group phenomenon. Organizations adopt varied techniques and methods to improve and sustain morale.

INDUSTRIAL PSYCHOLOGY

Background

Psychology deals with study of human behaviour. Industrial psychology primarily is the application of Principles of Psychology to the problems of man working in industry. Industrial Psychology originated in the first half of the twentieth century, applying basic psychological knowledge and principles to the personnel selection process during World War I. Subsequently, the use of generic psychological theory and research spread into industry, commerce, and the public sector, and extended beyond selection to leadership, motivation, attitudes and job satisfaction, learning and training and performance behaviour.

Industrial Psychology developed as a separate field of psychology after Dr. W.D. Scott spoke of possibilities of using psychological principles to the field of advertising. He published many papers on the application of principles of psychology to the fields of business and industry. However, the first major work on the application of principles of psychology in industry was published by Hugo Munsterberg titled *'The Psychology of Industrial Efficiency'* in 1913. He conducted research in real-world work situations and workplaces, with the goal of improving efficiency on the job. Industrial psychology grew as industry soon realized the importance of humans in its growth, productivity and achievement of organizational goals. George (1974) states that *"materials and machines are inert factors, but man with his ability to feel, to think, to conceive, and to plan is by far the most valuable and at the same time the most difficult element to inspire, control and motivate."*

The 21st Century poses interesting challenges to industrial psychology. The traditional accounting and management professions recognize that traditional corporate management systems must be enhanced to account for intangibles in knowledge based economy (Brookings Institute 2000). Large number of consulting firms are offering products designed to measure or demonstrate the relationship between human resource program and financial value.

Definition

Industrial Psychology is the study of people at work. It deals with behaviour, aptitude and reaction to various jobs and interaction. Thomas W. Harrell (1964) defines industrial psychology as :

"Industrial Psychology is the study of people at work in industry, and in business. It is the study of their aptitudes and their qualifications for jobs."

Industrial psychology could be defined as :

"The application of psychological principles and facts to the problems concerning human beings; working (or operating) in industrial, business, service and research organizations."

Scope

From the definitions it would be observed that the objective of Industrial Psychology was to apply the principles of psychology to get the best out of the human employed in the industry. To achieve this objective the Industrial Psychology must.

(*a*) Create an environment in which an individual *enjoys* his work.

(*b*) Assist in identifying the job best suited for an individual.

(*c*) Identify the reasons for stress and other industrial problems that arise and provide a base to mitigate the same.

(*d*) Carry out research in challenges likely to be faced by industrial workers and suggest ways to overcome the same.

Here the scope appears to emphasis more on research rather than administration. McCollom prepared a list of element identifying the scope of after interviewing many psychologists. His list included personal selection, personal development, and human engineering, productivity studies to ease fatigue, prevention of accidents, and labour relations. However, this scope also limits itself as it does not garner enough to assist in determining the future courses, hence, taking all factors together suggested scope is :

(*a*) *Consumer Behaviour.* Consumer psychology and marketing strategies, consumer research, cross culture studies, consumer typologies, social stratification, families, group communication, consumer decision making, selection and evaluation of alternatives. Store choice and purchase, post-purchase behaviour, market regulation.

(*b*) *Ergonomics.* Physical facilities for human to ease their work. Combining human and technology to optimize results and efficiency.

(*c*) *Human Resource Development/Management.* It includes analysing the training needs, evaluation, presentation of training and interpersonal and organizational management of human resource development. These have to be combined with individual and organization goals, personnel policies, purveyance and development.

(*d*) *Labour Laws and Relations.* Contract of employment, statutory conditions, dispute resolution etc. labour relation perspectives, parties involved in labour relations, etc.

(*e*) *Occupational Psychology.* Forming of concepts, cognitive development, problem solving, creativity, moral development, needs and motives, identity and self concepts, worth and wisdom, career models, career development , early, middle and late career issues and supporting systems of managing career.

(*f*) *Organizational Psychology.* Personality, working values, cultural diversity, working motives, management motivation, working design and organizational leadership. Group behaviour, team work, behaviour, organizational power and politics, organizational change and effectives.

Concepts of Industrial Psychology

The Industrial Psychology studies causation of behaviour. All activities of human beings whether simple or complex are not random, primarily covers seven areas personnel selection, training, performance appraisal, leadership, work motivation, work attitudes, and organizational issues. These can be broadly grouped into three areas viz. Individual, Relations in a Group and Environmental Conditions impacting efficiency.

(*a*) **Individual.** The Industrial Psychology treats each individual distinctly and states that there are major differences between two individuals. Here we ask how we can find the men whose mental qualities make them best fitted for the work which they have to do; secondly, under what psychological conditions we can secure the greatest and most satisfactory output of work from every man; and finally, how we can produce most completely the influences on human minds which are desired in the interest of business.

(*b*) **Relations in Group.** The fundamental nature of work and organizations is changing at an unprecedented rate. Corporations are "flattening out" by eliminating layers of management, increasing employee responsibilities, and restructuring themselves afterwards in previously unheard of configurations. Specialization has become the order of the day. The organizations are performing on group and team dynamics. One of the trends that will result from this approach is that fewer individuals are appointed on higher positions and team or group leaders are determined based on the objectives to be achieved. Employee empowerment is achieved by allowing employees and managers to work in a more group or team-oriented environment. Low-level employees are allowed a voice in how the product should be made and ways to improve it. This empowerment often extends to equipment, safety, policies, and self-management. Quality circles and self-managed work teams are just two of the more common names used to describe work groups that meet to discuss quality-related issues and implementation of continuous, work improvement programs. Other aspect here that challenges is the diversity of the work force in the globalized economy. The internal dynamics of behaviour has to be considered.

(*c*) **Environmental Conditions.** These are those factors that an organization creates for an employee to perform at his optimum. It includes both tangible like light, placing of equipment etc. (human engineering/ergonomics) and intangibles like relationships, management attitudes etc (Organizational Psychology).

Application of Industrial Psychology

Industrial psychology encompasses the entire gamut of Human Resource Management from induction till the man finally exits the organization. It is applied in the seven steps of Human Resource Management.

Selection and Placement of Personnel

Selection of an employee with proper skills and knowledge and placing him in a job suited for his skills is an important area of Human Resource Management. The psychologists have designed systematic tests to analyze personality, intelligence, aptitude, interest, dexterity etc. These tests assist the organization in identifying the correct person to fill in the vacancies in an organization. Like in selection, placement of employee is not simple. It has many psychological implications and hence, psychologists have evolved tests to assess the suitability to assess individual's behaviour with other employees, superiors, subordinates and in work environment to place an individual in job where an employee fits.

Training and Development

The psychologists assist organization to determine the future needs of the organization and in turn determine the requirements of skills and abilities. Industrial psychologists have evolved training programmes to help the existing workforce of existing as also to meet their future needs. The techniques in used industry have been discussed in detail in Chapter 8.

Wage Structure and Compensation

Job evaluation based on scientific techniques goes a long way in determining the wage structure and wage rate fixation. Industrial Psychologists help in job evaluation and in turn in designing a rational wage structure.

Performance Appraisal

The biggest help and assistance provided by psychologists in Human Resource Management is in the field of Performance Appraisal. The industrial psychology has replaced the traditional approach of performance appraisal by systematic and scientific techniques of evaluation. The results of performance appraisal are more reliable and can be effectively used for promotion, transfer, training and development etc (see Chapter 13).

Guidance and Counselling

Industrial; psychologists help in providing assistance to individual in selecting a job as per their knowledge, aptitude and skills. They also counsel the employee as he grows in his career path by counselling him on additional skills required, methods to acquire it etc.

Ergonomics/Human Engineering

Ergonomics or human engineering is a field in which Industrial Psychologists have contributed significantly. Human engineering is concerned to simplify work procedures and make it convenient for an individual to perform. The management based on data made available by Industrial Psychologist working on human engineering problem can redesign the tools; setup and other machines to optimize performance form the individual.

Morale and Motivation.

Industrial Psychologists also assist in determining morale by conducting various surveys and tests. Details are discussed subsequently in this chapter.

FATIGUE

Most of the efforts of Industrial Psychologist have been to reduce fatigue. Fatigue is commonly used to denote a decrease in the capacity or efficiency of a person to do the work because of previous work. In the words of Hareell, (1964), "Fatigue, or activity decrement, means a reduced capacity for further work as a consequence of previous activity where a person was trying almost as hard as he could." Broom states, "Fatigue is synonymous for tiredness. Nevertheless, fatigue does not arise solely from exhaustive physical and mental efforts on the job. Other factors being equal, fatigue will be greater with greater expenditure of effort, either physical or mental."

Fatigue connotes reduced capacity to work which arises because of expenditure of physical or mental effort on the work already done. The degree of fatigue is an aggregate of all different stresses of the day. Recuperation takes place mainly during night time sleep but free periods during the day and all kinds of pauses during work also make their contribution.

Strain and recuperation must balance over 24 hour cycle so that neither is carried over to the next day. If rest is unavoidably postponed until the following evening, this can only be done at the expense of well and efficiency.

Symptoms of Fatigue

Fatigue symptoms are both subjective and objective, the most important being :

1. Subjective feelings of weariness, somnolence, faintness and distaste of work.
2. Sluggish thinking resulting in percentage of rejects, rework, and spoiled work.
3. Reduced productivity.

4. Poor and slow perceptive, the rate of accidents, particularly during latter part of he day or week.
5. Unwillingness to work, labour turnover and absenteeism.
6. Decline in both physical and mental performance.

Measuring Fatigue

Ergonomics is interested only in quantitative measurement of fatigue in industry. What is the relationship between fatigue, work output and the level of stress ? The question asked in industry is simply whether the working conditions make excessive demands on the operatives or whether the stresses involved are physiologically acceptable. Measuring methods have a serious limitation in that till date there is no way of directly measuring the extent of the fatigue itself. All experimentation can merely measure certain manifestations or indicators of fatigue.

Currently there are six groups of methods used to measure fatigue.

1. Quality and quantity of work performed. Quantity of output can be expressed as numbers of items processed, time taken per item or conversely as number of operations performed per unit time.
2. Recording of subjective perception of fatigue.
3. Electroencephalography (EEG).
4. Measuring frequency of flicker fusion of eyes.
5. Psychomotor tests.
6. Mental tests.

More recently there has been the practice to study the combination of several indicators to make interpretations of the results more reliable. It is particularly important that subjective feelings of fatigue should be considered. A measurement of physical factors needs to be backed up by subjective perceptions before it can be correctly assessed as indicating a state of fatigue.

Measures to Reduce Fatigue

Managers and management can take many actions to reduce fatigue.

1. *Reduced work hours.* Studies have shown that 42 hours a week produces the best results. Short hours of work help in reducing absenteeism, accidents, sickness and negative feeling amongst workers.
2. *Rest Pauses. I*n work rest pauses are essentially required. It is always better to have scheduled rest periods. Rest periods should be so timed that it is given when the production starts falling.
3. *Work Study.* Efforts should be made to have studies carried out to reduce motions. The workers should also be given proper training. Training assist in reducing fatigue.
4. *Medical Facilities.*
5. *Improvement in Environments.*
6. *Employee counseling.* Employees who are depressed, sad or upset should be counseled. Efforts should be made to help employee to solve their problem.
7. *Job Enlargement and Job Rotation.* Job enlargement reduces monotony. Workers should be allowed freedom in setting their machines and in checking their output.

Music. Music at work place helps in reducing monotony. Production increases when music is played.

MORALE

Morale means many things to industry; a willingness to cooperate with company objectives, a sense of common purpose consistent with the firm's goals, enthusiasm for the job, happiness, toleration of unpleasantness, moral behaviour and mutual trust. Business people value morale because it reduces labour turnover, makes it easier to recruit good workers, and increase the productivity of the existing work force. The increase in productivity is not so much due hard work by employees, but because they do the right thing when not under supervision, do extra things without instructions, make suggestions for improvements, help each other and share information with each other and with the superiors.

What is Morale ?

What is Morale ? It has been stated in as "a positive and energetic attitude toward a goal" (Bateson and Mead, 1941); "the mental contribution to action" (Hocking, 1941); "the state of the spirits of an individual or group as shown in the willingness to perform assigned tasks" (Morris, 1981). Morale can also be described as a state of kind, mood or mental condition (Bennett, 1998). Morale is a by-product of motivation and group relationships in the organization. It is a mental process which once started permeates in the entire group creating a mood which results in the formation of a common attitude.

Morale may be defined in several ways. It may be thought of as an emotional attitude. Webster's Dictionary (1969) defines morale in the following ways :

- Moral principles, teachings, or conduct;
- The mental and emotional attitude of an individual to the function or tasks expected of him[/her] by his[/her] group and loyalty to it;
- A sense of common purpose with respect to a group;
- A state of individual psychological well-being based on factors such as a sense of purpose and confidence in the future .

Alexander H. Leighton has defined morale as;

"The capacity of a group of people to pull together persistently in pursuit of a common purpose."

Jack Halloran in, 'Applied Human Relations : An Organizational Approach', have defined as :

"Morale represents a composite of feelings attitudes and sentiments that contribute in general feelings of satisfaction."

Morale thus is a state of mind and spirit affecting willingness to work, which in turn affects organizational and individual objectives. Bewley (1999) summarizes that morale meant "emotional attitudes toward work, co-workers, and the organization. Good morale meant a sense of common purpose consistent with company goals and meant cooperativeness, happiness or tolerance of unpleasantness, and zest for the job." It shapes the organizational climate.

Morale is used to describe the 'organizational climate' prevailing. If the willingness, desire to work and contribute is high it is said the morale is 'high' and vice versa. Creating and maintaining high morale is a continuous process. We could state morale is essential in any effective organization. Loyalty, psychological well-being, purpose and confidence in the future—this definition embodies characteristics we strive for in our everyday lives, and therefore in our work. The word morale epitomizes what we pursue so fervently in our careers. We need it for ourselves, and strive to inspire and teach it in the organizations by which we are employed.

Approaches to Morale

Theoretical research has explored various methods to meet the challenge of good morale. Four important approaches can be distinguished to model individuals' underlying motivation to contribute to organization development, growth and productivity.

(*a*) **Altruism.** Pure Altruism as a type of pro-social preference means in the group context that an individual values an increase in the provision of the common good positively because he/she have individual or private preference for it, and/or additional resources are allocated to a relevant reference agent, *i.e.*, he/she wants others to benefit. Pure altruism however, appears to be counterfactual in most situations as a sole explanation for individuals contribution to group or organization. In pure altruism, contributions depend on the utility level achieved by fellow agents. Individuals contribute more to group when the utility level of the fellow agents is lower.

(*b*) **Social Norms.** These can be understood as socially shared beliefs about how one ought to behave *e.g.*, contributing to group or an organization. The prescribed behaviour is enforced by informal social sanctions. Social can be understood as a reaction by groups to overcome failures in an organizational good situation. The outcome of following a social norm is social approval or to be precise avoidance of disapproval. It should be clearly understood that the enforcement of norms is more important than specific content. Hence, 'reciprocal fairness' takes a key role as a norm enforcement device. Reciprocal fairness means that an individual responds to an action that is perceived to be kind in kind manner and to an action that is perceived as hostile or unfair in unfair or hostile manner. The perceived kindness, fairness or hostility of an action depends on the outcomes, intentions and procedural qualities associated with the action (Falk and Fischbacher, 2006).

(*c*) **Internalized Norms.** These norms differ from social norms by the nature of rewards and sanctions as a reaction to individual behaviour. If a norm is internalized, sanctions are internal and result in feelings of guilt, reduced self respect and other negative self-evaluations.

(*d*) **Intrinsic Motivation.** Intrinsic motivation in group dynamics implies that employee pursue an activity for the inherent satisfaction of the activity itself. In contrast, extrinsic motivation "refers to the performance of an activity in order to attain some separable outcome." The differences are subtle, in particular to internalized norm. With internalized norms, people feel an obligation or a commitment to contribute and non-performance results in negative feelings.. The two approaches converge to the extent the internalized norms are derived from the person's internalized values. It is not anticipated guilt or pride then that motivates cooperation but an intrinsic motivation to act according to one's value. The degree of internalization can be understood to determine the extent to which individuals perceive autonomy in their behaviour.

Morale thus is multidimensional in nature. It recognizes the influence of job situation on attitudes of individuals and also includes the role of human needs.

Good morale normally takes long time to build. It is fostered by frank but good relations between subordinates and superiors, by prospects for economic security and progress within the company, by recognition and reward of contributions to the company, by good explanations of the social contribution of the company's products and of a workers role in a production process. Collective activities improve morale.

Conditions for Good Morale

Good morale has three components; identification with the organization or internalization of its objectives, good moods, and trust and mutual affinity among members of the organization. A person may be judged to have internalized the objectives of the organization if they act so as to advance its interests without specific instructions and without any possibility of being monitored and rewarded. Identification is manifested by internalization of the organization's objectives as well as by efforts to demonstrate membership in it by expression of feelings of belonging. Moods are states of mind that affect the work habits and the pleasure or displeasure derived from work. Cooperation within an organization is fostered by network of trusting relationship of employees.

It is very difficult to disentangle the different motives and the kind of social interaction in concrete social dilemmas. Often individual behaviour is determined by several motives simultaneously or different people in the same context. Thus identification of preconditions for successful cooperation is the major challenge. It has been found that cooperation can be sustained id there is a large fraction of agents with the tendency to free-ride in a group. This is the case, if other agents in the group are motivated to voluntarily contribute and in addition to reciprocally punish free-riders at their own cost. Narrowly self interested agents are then provided incentives to contribute to common good. The composition of groups who have to sole a cooperation problem as well as their possibilities to punish fellow agents can thus become crucial (Gächter, 2006). A successful organization is more likely when :

(*a*) The resources users are able to design their own rules.

(*b*) The rules are enforced by local users.

(*c*) The sanctions applied are graduated.

(*d*) The better defined the rights to withdraw from the resources are;

(*e*) The more the collective action and monitoring reinforce each other.

These conditions make clear that morale alone does not suffice. Rather, it is necessary that such morale is embedded in an appropriate institutional setting including sanctions—but such sanctions are the most effective when they are voluntarily agreed by the users before the organization has been damaged.

Importance of Morale

Napoleon said, "Morale is too physical, three is to one." The statement is as applicable today as it was two centuries ago. Morale is vital as it reflects the organizational climate. Morale affects the attitudes of employees towards the organizations goals and objectives. The employee's attitude directly affects production. Morale must be maintained to :

(*a*) Studies conducted in 2002 by Business Research Laboratory, Hauppauge, New York, has shown a correlation between the length of time people intend to stay with their current employees is more dependent on 'soft' factors – like recognition given for work well done, pride in the employer – monetary award correlation. Morale helps in 'retention' of employees.

(*b*) Increased employee morale means a happier, more productive and high performing employee.

(*c*) There is a difference between what people do and how they do. High morale results in high interest in their jobs resulting in better quality of product and higher productivity.

(*d*) Morale results in creating a difference between meeting, or just meeting the productivity goals to exceeding goals.

(*e*) High morale results in cooperation amongst the employees and loyalty to the organization and its leadership.

(*f*) Morale is contagious, poor morale results in the abuse of leave accruals, accidents, illness, litigation, and workers compensation claims.

Measuring Employee Morale

Morale is intangible; it is the state of mind of employees. The managers must feel the pulse of its organization to assess morale. The methods employed to measure morale are discussed below.

Observation

The most common technique employed to measure morale is 'observation'. The managers and members of management try to observe day to day activities of employees. However, this method has its limitation as the managers are so busy in their day to day activities that they do not have time to observe employees. Theo Haimann in his work 'Professional Management—Theory and Practice' states, "The serious short comings of observation as a yardstick to measure current morale is that the activities and events indicate a change to a lowered morale which has already occurred. The manager, therefore, should be extremely keen in his observation in order to do as much as possible to prevent such change."

Attitude or Morale Survey

The management may conduct a survey to find out the state of morale. The opinion of employees may be known either by direct interview of use of questionnaire. In case of direct personal interview the manager attempts to find out about job, co-workers, supervision, work conditions, leadership and the organization from the employees. The details of interview are recorded for future reference. The process is time consuming, and the employees may not be forthright in their views due fear of repercussions. The questionnaire method involves use of questionnaire which is administered to a cross section or all the employees. This method is more appropriate due large coverage in short time and the anonymity of the responder can be maintained.

Morale Indicators

This is most popular method to determine the morale of an organization. There are factors that depict the attitude of an employee towards the organizations. The management must take cognizance and maintain a close watch on these factors. The major factors are (the first factor in explanation depicts high or good morale and the second depicts low or bad morale) is :

(*a*) **Reactions to rules/policies.** Strict adherence to rules vs. indifference or resistance.

(*b*) **Approach to introduction of new tools, processes or restructuring.** Excitement or willingness vs. resistance or apathy.

(*c*) **Longevity.** Long term out look of employee with organization vs. wanting to 'get out of the organization'.

(*d*) **Complaints.** Willingness to explore solutions vs. mainly looking for remediation.

(*e*) **Grievances.** Few vs. many.

(*f*) **Absences.** Few vs. Many (including unexplained).

(*g*) **Accidents.** Infrequent vs. Frequent.

(*h*) **Interaction amongst employees.** Respectful and cordial vs. disrespectful and fights/ brawls.

The factors enumerated above are sound indicators of any major variation in morale. Management must seek to identify the cause from the indicators and take remedial actions.

Gaining Information.

Although all the above methods are primarily to gain information from the employees, but all these may not meet the requirements of management as employees may not like to be identified especially if there is active trade union operating in the organization. Under such conditions the management can place suggestion boxes at suitable places in which employees can be asked to put in the suggestions or grievances. The organization can encourage quality circles and other sub groups to get information.

Methods to Improve Morale

Morale is intangible and is difficult to measure and determine, but it is the responsibility of the managers to get the best out of the employees and hence, he is responsible for ensuring that morale remains high. We have discussed above how to approach morale it being a group activity. Some of the methods that can be used to improve morale are discussed in succeeding paragraphs.

(*a*) **Communication.** Communication is the first and foremost to maintain high morale. Fostering communication and allowing employees to gain a sense of belonging and ownership of their work within the organization is another great way of improving morale. To do so, it is important for managers to set a good example. As stated by Bishop (1997), "a solution to the problem of meeting organizational needs...lies in a complete rethinking of traditional management practices. Managers need to abandon their role as controllers, decision-makers, and problem solvers, and hand over responsibility—and authority—to employees." In doing so, employees learn to gain a sense of autonomy in their work. They learn that their organization trusts and respects them, enough so to put faith their capacity to do well for the company. The management must communicate at all times its projects views and action being taken including its plans. Lack of information give rise to rumors and sense of insecurity amongst the employees, hence management must use all means to inform employees. Some of the important methods is the use of internet (e mails/ intranet), newsletters, memo; regularity in staff meetings, agency wide forums and information sessions. Management must ensure that it gives out the big picture. Also, having a common eating area (with good food that the employees are happy to eat) may foster open communication and cohesion among departments of the organization that may otherwise not be experienced.

(*b*) **Rewards and Recognition**. Recognizing employees can be much easier than many organizations often realize. According to Wardell (1999), when asked what three things managers could do to keep them working for the organization, employees responded "Say hello, thank you, and please." It is important for managers to remember that the people who work for them are their customers. They are the ones who will ultimately decide whether or not the organization will be effective and successful. Simple expressions of recognition and gratitude can make a major difference in whether or not employees perceive that they are valued by their organization. Another cost-free method of recognition that can be very effective is providing feedback to employees. It is important to let employees know where things stand both on a personal level within the organization as well as how they fit into the entire scheme of the organization as a whole. Some methods managers may utilize for doing this include holding one-on-one meetings with employees, holding joint staff meetings, sending group e-mails, taking employees on a company retreat, and creating a company newsletter. Workers love to hear how they are doing, and even if the feedback is not all positive, they will most often be open to initiating improvements, provided that good feedback is offered with the bad, and criticism is presented constructively. Other more formal methods of recognizing employees include peer recognition programs and focusing on the rewards that employee's value. Peer recognition programs give employees the power to reward each other and have proven to be very successful means of boosting morale. The success of peer recognition programs may be attributed to the employees' knowledge of who works hard and deserves recognition, coupled with the fact that workers usually value each other's influence more than their supervisor's pressure. These factors may lend more significance to reception of a reward.

(*c*) **Physical Conditions**. According to Jolivette (1998), lighting, temperature, and noise are three of the most crucial factors influencing morale. Subtle factors such as these can have a definite impact on how employees function. Although these are not problems as likely to be brought to the attention of managers, they should not be overlooked. When the lighting in the work environment is too much or too little, or noise is excessive, it can be difficult for workers to concentrate. Employees may overcome such distractions, but it can be taxing on the nerves and often leaves them with negative emotions—feelings of annoyance and exhaustion. Therefore it is best to take these factors into account and deal with them as best possible.

(*d*) **Setting Personal Example**. A very common method employed in Indian Defence Forces. The motto "Follow Me" is ingrained in every officer. Managers can achieve a lot by this. A manager can also set a good example by not being afraid to roll up his/her sleeves and join in when need arises. Here, a manager has the opportunity to demonstrate that he/she does not consider him/herself to be "above" his/her subordinates, that they are all a team and should function as one. The manager may also capitalize on such an opportunity as a way to get to know the employees and see what they do from a different perspective. Providing opportunity for learning and personal development is another major way organizations can demonstrate that they care about their employees and boost morale. According to Veninga (2000) forty per cent of American workers say they are bored with their jobs. They feel their talents are not being sufficiently utilized. There are several ways organizations can combat this.

(*e*) **Workers Participation**. The companies should promote industrial / internal democracy in the organization. Management should allow workers' participation in management. Whenever a change is introduced which affects workers they must be consulted and taken into confidence. Management should also encourage social group activities by the workers. This will help develop greater group cohesion which can be used by the management for building high morale.

Relation between Morale and Productivity

It is generally assumed that morale and productivity have a direct relationship with each other, *i.e.,* they are positively correlated. Researches in human behaviour contend that *high morale and high productivity go together.* It was contended that employees with high morale do not skip work, are the least tardy, show good team spirit and contribute their best to the attainment of the organizational objectives. Even today many CEO and supervisors feel that workers with high morale have high productivity.

Generally there is a positive correlation between high morale and productivity, but these are not absolutely related *i.e.,* increase of 10 percent in morale does not guarantee proportionate increase (*i.e.,* 10 percent) in productivity.

It has been observed that there are four possible combinations of morale and productivity.

(*a*) High morale and high productivity

(*b*) High Morale and low productivity

(*c*) Low morale and low productivity

(*d*) Low Morale and high productivity.

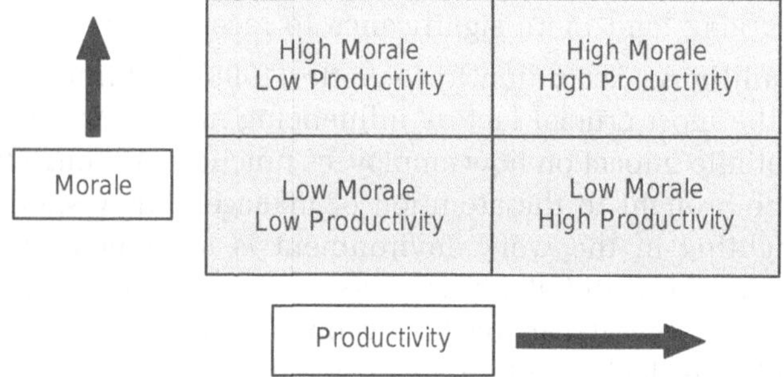

Fig. 16.1. *Relationship between Morale and Productivity.*

High productivity goes with high morale when the workers are highly motivated, the supervision is considerate of workers and the workers are highly trained. This is an ideal state and the organization makes the optimum use of the available human resources. A reverse of situation may be there in which low morale exist with low productivity.

High morale is associated with low productivity when the employees are merely happy and they are properly motivated to do work. Other reasons of low productivity may be inefficiency of supervision, faulty materials and old technology etc. Such situation cannot be sustained for long as will to work moulds workers attitude towards management and its policies, job and supervisors.

There may be occasions when low morale is associated with high productivity, but his cannot be sustained for long and the workers are likely to resent and the productivity may drop unless management looks into causes for low morale.

SA (Social Accountability) 8000

In 1997, the Council on Economic Priorities Accreditation Agency (CEPAA) was founded by the Council on Economic Priorities based in New York, in order to develop and manage a set of standards for 'social accountability', *i.e.,* a set of standards for treatment of employees that would be applied throughout a firm's worldwide operations (Figure 16.2). These set of standards have been named as SA (Social Accountability) 8000.

The SA 8000 certification process requires companies to meet uniform standards in areas like child labour, forced labour, working hours, health and safety, collective bargaining, disciplinary practices, compensation etc. The standards have been derived from International Labour Organization treaties, the Universal Deceleration of Human Rights, and the UN Conventions on Child Labour. The process was developed at the behest of International Labour Organization and monitoring is accomplished by independent auditing firms.

While the approach to setting standards for social/employment policy remains controversial, many firms are interested in ways such as this to guide them in their approaches to employee relations and working conditions around the world and to defuse the public and political charges of unfairness and exploitation in their overseas operations.

The Social Accountability 8000 Standard (SA 8000), along with other types of certification standards and corporate codes of conduct, represents a new form of voluntary "self-governance" of working conditions in the private sector, initiated and implemented by companies, labour unions, and non-governmental activists groups cooperating together. Advocates promote SA 8000 and similar codes as a necessary tool to improve workplace conditions, especially in nations that lack robust enforcement of regulatory standards.

Social Accountability 8000 Standards are based on international conventions of the International Labour Organization and related international human rights documents, including the Universal Declaration of Human Rights and UN Convention on the Rights of the Child. The standard also requires compliance with prevailing laws, regulations and other applicable requirements such as contractual agreements. SA 8000 is a consensus standard specifying minimum requirements in the following areas.

(*a*) **Child Labour**. The company must abide by laws governing minimum age, young workers, school attendance and safety during work.

(*b*) **Discrimination**. The company must not permit discrimination on basis of race, caste, national origin, religion, disability, gender, sexual orientation, union membership, or political affiliation.

(*c*) **Disciplinary Practices**. Corporal punishment, mental/ physical coercion, and verbal abuse are not permitted.

(*d*) **Working Hours**. The companies work schedule must be in accordance to the law of the land. Employees must not work more than sixty hours in a week; overtime (over 48 hours in a week) must be voluntary; and employees must be given at least one day off in seven .

(*e*) **Compensation**. Wages must be legal/ industry minimum and must cover basic needs.

(*f*) **Forced labour.** The company must not engage or support forced labour or hiring with bribes, or deposits required. It should allow employees to leave after a shift and permit them to quit.

(*g*) Freedom of Association and Right to Collective Bargain. The company respects the right of employees to form or join unions of their choice and to bargain collectively.

(*h*) Management System. The company must agree to : create a publicly available policy committed to compliance with applicable laws and other requirements. The company must maintain supporting documents and records.

Fig. 16.2. *Social Accountability 8000 Standard (SA 8000).*

Review Questions

1. What is meant by Industrial Psychology ? Discuss its features and scope.
2. Explain the importance of psychology to modern industrial enterprises with the help of suitable examples.
3. What are the basic principles of Industrial Psychology ?
4. Discuss the concept of Industrial Fatigue and distinguish between fatigue and monotony.

PROJECT

Case Study

CASE OF MISSING PLATES MUZAFFARNAGAR STEELS

One day Ramesh entered the floor of Muzaffarnagar Steels furious. He collected all the second shift employees and said, "if this was a joke than it is not one worth appreciating, and who ever has taken the plates should return them immediately and the matter would be closed or else the whole shift would be removed from pay roll." No one spoke. Finally one machinist, Harsh, offered to come early next day and make the plates a new on his own time. Sputtering, Ramesh left the shop floor. He could never find out what happened to the six plates.

Ramesh believed that the incident was an attempt by the night shift to extend its time with the company; since the night shift was working on a particular contract; if it was not replaced by new business, they were likely to be laid off. So far, no new contracts were forthcoming.

Harsh an employee remembered the meeting like this :

Ramesh had this meeting and said, "If this was a joke than it is not one worth appreciating, and who ever has taken the plates should return them immediately and the matter would be closed or else the whole shift would be removed from pay roll." He threatened them again with their jobs."

Most of the employees working in the shift claimed they never saw the plates; while some claimed these were not even manufactured at the first place. The night shift supervisor claimed that he had seen six pieces lying on an assembly table, but no one volunteered that he remembered making them.

Some speculated that one machinist, Rahim, was disgruntled enough to have been involved in the plate incident. The reason was that he supposedly had made them. Some speculated that this could have been the way for Rahim to get back at Ramesh for his layoff.

Mr. Dinesh, the union secretary, remembered that, Hardev's said he remembered he was there, but he didn't remember seeing the six plates. Basically it was Hardev's words against all others.

The foreman said the missing parts was a kind of slow down, a way for the employees to express their dissatisfaction with the way the nigh shift was being handled. He believed the parts were deliberately stolen or destroyed to make it look like the day shift has done it. He further reiterated that he has seen the six plates earlier.

It was also stated that these were not the only parts missing. Various employees noticed that large number of items have been misplaced. One of the employees stated that the company always had problems of things disappearing on night shifts. Some of the former night shifts lasted just about a year.

The workers morale went to low on the Ramesh declaration about removing the entire shift Ramesh was aware of this, aware of his threat and felt frustrated and angry. He returned home shaking his head and muttering about how ungrateful the employees seemed to be. He wondered what if anything he must do now to reduce apparent thefts, to build morale and to try and get the second shift on a positive and upbeat relationship.

❑❑❑

Chapter 17

KNOWLEDGE WORKER AND HUMAN RESOURCE MANAGEMENT

★ LEARNING OBJECTIVES ★

After reading this chapter, you will be able to understand :

- What is Knowledge Management ?
- Objectives of Knowledge Management.
- Explain employer concern of developing a Knowledge Management plan.
- Factors Knowledge Management.
- Methods of Knowledge Management
- Knowledge Workers and their characteristics.
- Managing Knowledge Worker–Organizational Perspectives.

INTRODUCTION

Knowledge Management is a newly emerging, interdisciplinary business model dealing with all aspects of knowledge within the context of the firm, including knowledge creation, codification, sharing, and how these activities promote learning and innovation. In practice, Knowledge Management encompasses both technological tools and organizational routines in overlapping parts. Intellectual material, knowledge, information, intellectual property, experience—that can be put to use to create wealth (Stewart, 1997) is at the heart of contemporary business model.

In practice, knowledge management often encompasses identifying and mapping intellectual assets within the organization, generating new knowledge for competitive advantage within the organization, making vast amounts of corporate information accessible, sharing of best practices, and technology that enables all of the above—including groupware and intranets.

The value of Knowledge Management relates directly to the effectiveness with which the managed knowledge enables the members of the organization to deal with today's situations and effectively envision and create their future. Without on-demand access to managed knowledge, every situation is addressed based on what the individual or group brings to the situation with them. With on-demand access to managed knowledge, every situation is addressed with the sum total of everything anyone in the organization has ever learned about a situation of a similar nature. Which approach would you perceive would make a more effective organization ?

History

An overarching theory of knowledge management has yet to emerge, perhaps because the practices associated with managing knowledge have their roots in a variety of disciplines and domains. Special thanks to Karl Wiig for supplying us with a pre-publication copy of "*Knowledge Management :Where Did It Come From and Where Will It Go?*" which appeared in *The Journal of Expert Systems with Applications*. This section draws heavily on that work but supplies only a small part of that value.

A number of management theorists have contributed to the evolution of knowledge management, among them such notables as Peter Drucker, Paul Strassmann, and Peter Senge in the United States. Drucker and Strassmann have stressed the growing importance of information and explicit knowledge as organizational resources, and Senge has focused on the "learning organization," a cultural dimension of managing knowledge. Chris Argyris, Christoper Bartlett, and Dorothy Leonard-Barton of Harvard Business School have examined various facets of managing knowledge. In fact, Leonard-Barton's well-known case study of Chaparral Steel, a company which has had an effective knowledge management strategy in place since the mid-1970s, inspired the research documented in her Wellsprings of Knowledge—Building and Sustaining Sources of Innovation (Harvard Business School Press, 1995).

Everett Rogers' work at Stanford in the diffusion of innovation and Thomas Allen's research at MIT in information and technology transfer, both of which date from the late 1970s, have also contributed to our understanding of how knowledge is produced, used, and diffused within organizations. By the mid-1980s, the importance of knowledge (and its expression in professional competence) as a competitive asset was apparent, even though classical economic theory ignores (the value of) knowledge as an asset and most organizations still lack strategies and methods for managing it.

Recognition of the growing importance of organizational knowledge was accompanied by concern over how to deal with exponential increases in the amount of available knowledge and increasingly complex products and processes. The computer technology that contributed so heavily to superabundance of information started to become part of the solution, in a variety of domains. Doug Engelbart's Augment (for "augmenting human intelligence"), which was introduced in 1978, was an early hypertext/groupware application capable of interfacing with other applications and systems. Rob Acksyn's and Don McCracken's Knowledge Management System (KMS), an open distributed hypermedia tool, is another notable example and one that predates the World Wide Web by a decade.

The 1980s also saw the development of systems for managing knowledge that relied on work done in artificial intelligence and expert systems, giving us such concepts as "knowledge acquisition," "knowledge engineering," "knowledge-base systems, and computer-based ontologies.

The phrase "knowledge management" entered the lexicon in earnest. To provide a technological base for managing knowledge, a consortium of U.S. companies started the Initiative for Managing Knowledge Assets in 1989. Knowledge management-related articles began appearing in journals like Sloan Management Review, Organizational Science, Harvard Business Review, and others, and the first books on organizational learning and knowledge management were published (for example, Senge's The Fifth Discipline and Sakaiya's The Knowledge Value Revolution).

By 1990, a number of management consulting firms had begun in-house knowledge management programs, and several well known U.S., European, and Japanese firms had instituted focused knowledge management programs. Knowledge management was introduced in the popular press in 1991, when Tom Stewart published "Brainpower" in Fortune magazine. Perhaps the most widely read work to date is Ikujiro Nonaka's and Hirotaka Takeuchi's *The Knowledge-Creating Company : How Japanese Companies Create the Dynamics of Innovation* (1995).

By the mid-1990s, knowledge management initiatives were flourishing, thanks in part to the Internet. The International Knowledge Management Network (IKMN), begun in Europe in 1989, went online in 1994 and was soon joined by the U.S.-based Knowledge Management Forum and other KM-related groups and publications. The number of knowledge management conferences and seminars is growing as organizations focus on managing and leveraging explicit and tacit knowledge resources to achieve competitive advantage. In 1994, the IKMN published the results of a knowledge management survey conducted among European firms, and the European Community began offering funding for KM-related projects through the ESPRIT program in 1995.

Knowledge management, which appears to offer an alternative to TQM and business process re-engineering initiatives, has become big business for such major international consulting firms as Ernst and Young, Arthur Andersen, and Booz-Allen & Hamilton. In addition, a number of professional organizations interested in such related areas as benchmarking, best practices, risk management, and change management are exploring the relationship of knowledge management to their areas of special expertise (for example, the APQC [American Productivity and Quality Council] and ASIS [American Society for Information Science]).

Definition

Knowledge management is concerned with organizing knowledge repositories (data bases etc.) so as to allow for easy retrieval and exchange of the information stored therein. Important concepts in knowledge management include domains, *i.e.*, fields of related concepts and terms, and ontology, *i.e.*, structures (typically hierarchies or networks) of interrelated terms for things, concepts, relationships, etc. in a given domain.

We define knowledge management as a business activity with two primary aspects :

1. Treating the knowledge component of business activities as an explicit concern of business reflected in strategy, policy and practice at all levels of the organization.
2. Making a direct connection between an organization's intellectual assets—both explicit [recorded] and tacit [personal know-how]—and positive business results.

There is a common thread among these and many other recent business strategies : A recognition that information and knowledge are corporate assets, and that businesses need strategies, policies and tools to manage those assets.

The need to manage knowledge seems obvious, and discussions of intellectual capital have proliferated, but few businesses have acted on that understanding. Where companies have take action—and a growing number are doing so—implementations of "knowledge management" may range from technology-driven methods of accessing, controlling, and delivering information to massive efforts to change corporate culture.

Opinions about the paths, methods, and even the objectives of knowledge management abound. Some efforts focus on enhancing creativity—creating new knowledge value—while other programs emphasize leveraging existing knowledge.

Components of Knowledge Management

Rudy Ruggles, leading Knowledge Management thinker/practitioners, has identified the following items as integral components of Knowledge Management :

1. Generating new knowledge.
2. Accessing valuable knowledge from outside sources.
3. Using accessible knowledge in decision making.
4. Embedding knowledge in processes, products, and/or services.
5. Representing knowledge in documents, databases, and software.
6. Facilitating knowledge growth through culture and incentives.
7. Transferring existing knowledge into other parts of the organization.
8. Measuring the value of knowledge assets and/or impact of knowledge management.

Need for Knowledge Management

Why do we need to manage knowledge ? Ann Macintosh of the Artificial Intelligence Applications Institute (University of Edinburgh) has written a "Position Paper on Knowledge Management Asset" that identifies some of the specific business factors, including :

- Marketplaces are increasingly competitive and the rate of innovation is rising.
- Reductions in staffing create a need to replace informal knowledge with formal methods.
- Competitive pressures reduce the size of the work force that holds valuable business knowledge.
- The amount of time available to experience and acquire knowledge has diminished.
- Early retirements and increasing mobility of the work force lead to loss of knowledge.
- There is a need to manage increasing complexity as small operating companies are transnational sourcing operations.
- Changes in strategic direction may result in the loss of knowledge in a specific area.

To these paraphrases of Ms. Macintosh's observations we would add :

- Most of our work is information based.
- Organizations compete on the basis of knowledge.
- Products and services are increasingly complex, endowing them with a significant information component.
- The need for life-long learning is an inescapable reality.

In brief, knowledge and information have become the medium in which business problems occur. As a result, managing knowledge represents the primary opportunity for achieving substantial savings, significant improvements in human performance, and competitive advantage.

It's not just a Fortune 500 business problem. Small companies need formal approaches to knowledge management even more, because they don't have the market leverage, inertia, and resources that big companies do. They have to be much more flexible, more responsive, and more "right" (make better decisions)—because even small mistakes can be fatal to them.

Categorization of Knowledge Management

The term "knowledge management" is now in widespread use, having appeared in the titles of many new books about knowledge management as a business strategy, as well as in articles in many business publications, including The Wall Street Journal. There are, of course, many ways to slice up the multi-faceted world of knowledge management. However, it's often useful to categorize them.

In a posting to the Knowledge Management Forum, Karl-Erik Sveiby identified two "tracks" of knowledge management :

1. *Management of Information.* To researchers in this track, according to Sveiby, "... knowledge = Objects that can be identified and handled in information systems."
2. *Management of People.* For researchers and practitioners in this field, knowledge consists of "... processes, a complex set of dynamic skills, know-how, etc., that is constantly changing."

Mechanistic Approaches to Knowledge Management

Mechanistic approaches to knowledge management are characterized by the application of technology and resources to do more of the same better. The main assumptions of the mechanistic approach include :

- Better accessibility to information is a key, including enhanced methods of access and reuse of documents (hypertext linking, databases, full-text search, etc.).
- Networking technology in general (especially intranets), and groupware in particular, will be key solutions.
- In general, technology and sheer volume of information will make it work.

Such approaches are relatively easy to implement for corporate "political" reasons, because the technologies and techniques—although sometimes advanced in particular areas—are familiar and easily understood, because enhanced access to corporate intellectual assets is vital. But it's simply not clear whether access itself will have a substantial impact on business performance, especially as mountains of new information are placed on line. Unless the knowledge management approach incorporates methods of leveraging cumulative experience, the net result may not be positive, and the impact of implementation may be no more measurable than in traditional paper models.

Cultural/Behavioristic Approaches to Knowledge Management

Cultural/Bbehavioristic approaches, with substantial roots in process re-engineering and change management, tend to view the "knowledge problem" as a management issue. Technology—though ultimately essential for managing explicit knowledge resources—is not the solution.

These approaches tend to focus more on innovation and creativity (the "learning organization") than on leveraging existing explicit resources or making working knowledge explicit.

Assumptions of cultural/behavioristic approaches often include :

- Organizational behaviors and culture need to be changed ... dramatically. In our information-intensive environments, organizations become dysfunctional relative to business objectives.
- Organizational behaviors and culture can be changed, but traditional technology and methods of attempting to solve the "knowledge problem" have reached their limits of effectiveness. A "holistic" view is required. Theories of behavior of large-scale systems are often invoked.
- It's the processes that matter, not the technology.
- Nothing happens or changes unless a manager makes it happen.

The cultural factors affecting organizational change have almost certainly been undervalued, and cultural/behavioristic implementations have shown some benefits. But the cause-effect relationship between cultural strategy and business benefits is not clear, because the "Hawthorne Effect" may come into play, and because we still can't make dependable predictions about systems as complex as knowledge-based business organizations. Positive results achieved by cultural/ behavioristic strategies may not be sustainable, measurable, cumulative, or replicable ... and employees thoroughly "Di-libertized" by yet another management strategy may roll their eyes. Time will tell.

Systematic Approaches to Knowledge Management

Systematic approaches to knowledge management retain the traditional faith in rational analysis of the knowledge problem : the problem can be solved, but new thinking of many kinds is required. Some basic assumptions :

- Its sustainable results that matter, not the processes or technology ... or your definition of "knowledge."
- A resource cannot be managed unless it is modeled, and many aspects of the organization's knowledge can be modeled as an explicit resource.
- Solutions can be found in a variety of disciplines and technologies, and traditional methods of analysis can be used to re-examine the nature of knowledge work and to solve the knowledge problem.
- Cultural issues are important, but they too must be evaluated systematically. Employees may or may not have to be "changed," but policies and work practices must certainly be changed, and technology can be applied successfully to business knowledge problems themselves.
- Knowledge management has an important management component, but it is not an activity or discipline that belongs exclusively to managers.

Types of Knowledge Management

Nickols' two kinds of knowledge parallel. Michael Polanyi's often-quoted distinction between explicit knowledge (sometimes referred to as formal knowledge), which can be articulated in language and transmitted among individuals, and tacit knowledge (also, informal knowledge), personal knowledge rooted in individual experience and involving personal belief, perspective, and values. (Polanyi, Michael. The Tacit Dimension. London : Routledge & Kegan Paul).

Tacit Knowledge

Tacit knowledge is generally described as :

- subconsciously understood or applied
- difficult to articulate
- developed from direct action and experience
- shared through conversation, story-telling etc.

Polanyi (1966) saying that it is personal, context-specific and therefore difficult to articulate. It may be compared to skill acquisition for example swimming. It may be possible to read the 'how-to' manual but such manuals do not embody the full reality of the experience in context. For instance swimming in a pool is very different from swimming in the sea.

According to Pan and Scarbrough (1999 p362) "Tacit knowledge is not available as a text. . . .It involves intangible factors embedded in personal beliefs, experiences, and values." Nonaka and Takeuchi (1995) refer to tacit knowledge as knowledge that comprises experience and work knowledge that resides only with the individual. Platts and Yeung (2000) considers tacit knowledge as "knowledge-in-action" which presumes that this is knowledge that has not be articulated as opposed to explicit knowledge that is readily accessible within the organisational domain. Blumentitt et al (1999) contend that information can be captured and stored in digital form whereas tacit knowledge repositories reside only in intelligent systems, that is within individuals.

Explicit Knowledge

Explicit knowledge is codified, and

- can be precisely and formally articulated.
- is easy to codify, document, transfer, share and communicate.

Its ready accessibility has lead to many ways of using it as a management tool. This is shown in the following quote (Radcliffe-Martin, Coakes and Sugden 2000) :

"Explicit knowledge is increasingly being emphasised in both practice and literature, as a management tool to be exploited for the manipulation of organisational knowledge. Groupware, intranets, list servers, knowledge repositories, database management and knowledge action networks allow the sharing of organisational knowledge (Scarbrough et al. 1999). Merali states that tools such as co-ordinated databases, groupware systems, intranets and internets are seen as the ultimate knowledge management systems for initiating and supporting discussion forums and communities of practice (1999). Managers hope that these tools will retain knowledge within the company when employees have left, and also that this will encourage learning and the flourishing of communities of interest across functional boundaries."

However, it is worth considering whether use of an intra-organisational intranet for example really manages knowledge or merely provides a means of disseminating information about the organisation in much the same way that a staff handbook used to do.

According to Pan and Scarbrough "Explicit is systematic and easily communicated in the form of hard data or codified procedures. It can be articulated in formal language including grammatical statements. This kind of knowledge can thus be transmitted across individuals formally and easily. Tacit knowledge is not available as a text and may conveniently be regarded as residing in the heads of those working in a particular organisational context. It involves intangible factors embedded in personal beliefs, experiences and values." (1999 p 362)

'While tacit knowledge can be possessed by itself, explicit knowledge must rely on being tacitly understood and applied, hence all knowledge is either tacit or rooted in tacit knowledge. A wholly explicit knowledge is unthinkable' according to Polanyi (1966).

Knowledge Management Process

In order to organize this site, a thesaurus—which has special meaning for information management—was created. It is comprised of KM terms that are grouped in categories. These categories imply the process of KM, which is circular (or spiral, depending on cultural references for growth) and unending. That is, participants in the KM process may enter it at any point, and traverse it repeatedly. Additionally, each category often presents decision-making opportunities, passive and active, and the categories help identify a knowledge domain. The categories are :

- Asset Utilization
- Knowledge Evaluation
- Knowledge Improvement
- Knowledge Accumulation
- Knowledge Generation
- Knowledge Sharing
- Knowledge Protection

KNOWLEDGE WORKERS AND HUMAN RESOURCE MANAGEMENT

The management of knowledge workers has been widely acknowledged. This has been primarily due to due the historic shift from a focus on physical and financial forms of capital as key production resources to one of human and intellectual capital (Martin and Moldoveanu, 2003). In contemporary environment wealth creation is less dependent on the control of resources but is more on the exercise of the specific knowledge or the organizational competencies (Blackler, 1995). To make knowledge-work productive will be the great management task of this century, just as to make manual work productive was the great management task of the last century.

Knowledge workers could perform much better if we only knew how to manage them, says Thomas Davenport. His suggestion : *Don't treat them the all same and measure them tactfully.*

It is the job of HRM to understand their needs and then act accordingly. A slight mistake in handling them could be very costly to the organization. Knowledge workers no doubt are an asset to any organization but this asset can further be enhanced through proper management. Knowledge workers can bring a positive change to the assets of the organization. All they need is proper handling.

"HRM and HRD *professionals therefore need to take account of the dynamics of the employment relationship or psychological contract in considering enabling intervention and strategy to ensure knowledge creation, transfer and retention."*

We have a choice here. We can get more productive with our knowledge work or we can lose our jobs. There are other parts of the world where people are very serious about being more productive, and are doing it for a lot less money than we charge. People should realize that unless they do knowledge work better, they're not going to be doing it at all..

HR Department can properly train these workers. Knowledge workers possess knowledge but this knowledge has to transfer within the organization at different levels. Training knowledge workers on how to utilize knowledge to get optimal results & then transferring knowledge through training & guidance from these who are knowledgeable in the brains of those who don't can be best achieved through human resource management interventions.

The knowledge workers should have an understanding of the overall business of their organization and how their work contexts fit within it. Such understanding is necessary for their active involvement in the organizational unlearning and relearning processes. They must be aware of what sort of change will affect their organization and how they will bring about that change. Only if they understand the implications of changes in their work contexts for the business enterprise, they can be influential in harmonize the organizational 'best practices' with the external reality of the business environment.

"...the objective is to achieve the synergy of data and information processing capacity of information technologies, and the creative and innovative capacity of their human members. Hence, the knowledge workers need to be facile in the applications of new technologies to their business contexts. Such understanding is necessary so that they can delegate 'programmable' tasks to technologies to concentrate their time and efforts on value-adding activities that demand creativity and innovation. More importantly, they should have the capability of judging if the organization's 'best practices' are aligned with the dynamics of the business environment. Such knowledge workers are the critical elements of the double loop learning and unlearning cycle that should be designed within the organizational business processes."

Definition

The knowledge worker is referred as such by the nature of work that he or she engages in. To be a knowledge worker is therefore not an occupational category but it is an act of producing knowledge- rich products and services. Juani Swart has defined knowledge worker as, *'employees who apply their valuable knowledge and skills (developed through experience) to complex, novel, and abstract problems in environments that provide rich collective knowledge and relational resources'* (2007:452).

An organization cannot logically claim to employ knowledge workers if they are not able to engage in knowledge work.

Characteristics of Knowledge Worker

Knowledge workers on the whole tend to work long hours with commitment related more to the nature of work rather than to the organization. Knowledge workers have strong sense of intrinsic motivation and are mostly interested in challenging work which requires considerable creativity and initiative (Alvesson, 2000). Knowledge workers also tend to identify with other like-minded professional more than the organization for which they work. Knowledge workers usually develop strong interpersonal networks that span organizational boundaries. Such workers tend to command high rewards, often because their know-what, know—how, and know—who is valuable and difficult to replace or imitate.(Barney, 1991). The core skills that they rely on to make their strong bargaining position includes problem solving; problem identification; and brokerage (Blackler 1995 : 1027). Social skills and client relationships are also important to the process of knowledge work (Starbusk 1992) given the social nature of knowledge production.

May et al. (2002), in their research on the job expectations in three countries found that for knowledge workers in US, Australia and Japan found pay was regarded as the first or second most important aspect of the job. This was followed by intrinsic nature of job in terms of variety, challenge and learning opportunities. One of the reasons why pay was so important as reward was that unlike other professions, knowledge workers had less hierarchy or appointment was tenure based; also the knowledge worker felt that his skills were priced on perceptual basis. Reed (1996) argues that knowledge workers do not rely on the intangible nature of their knowledge to create market niche for themselves.

One of the major factors that affect commitment, work effort, and job satisfaction of knowledge workers is the way they are organized and relate to management (May *et al.* 2002). Their status is based on the mastery of unique, inimitable and valuable skills. Knowledge workers are found not only inside the organization but across, drawing on their personal, professional and expertise networks. This has serious implications for the organizations, as these have limited control over the knowledge workers. The organizations thus follow non-standard forms of employment such as contracts for services and fixed term employment.

Managing Knowledge Workers—Organizational Perspective

There are number of critical and distinctive characteristics in organizations that facilitate knowledge production. These organizations operate under pressure where product and labour markets are unstable and technology is changing quickly. These organizations tend to develop innovative internal and external structures and forms in comparison to more traditional and bureaucratic organizations. Organizations can use some of the interventions listed to act as tools for proper management of knowledge workers and for enhancing their performance.

1. Job Design (team work)
2. Authority or Autonomy at work place
3. Loyalty towards the organization.
4. Training & Development
5. Motivation (Competitive compensation/ reward packages and other incentives)
6. Communication Channels
7. Monitoring and Evaluation
8. Work Life Balance.

Job Design (Team Work)

To design the job of knowledge workers is not an easy task for the management. Jobs are designed for predetermined pattern of work but in the case of knowledge workers they lack any such predetermined pattern of activities. Their activities and roles are like chameleon. They have to mould their roles with the requisite of the task at a given point of time. The management has to come up with a technique to design their jobs without any preset activities.

Knowledge workers are expected to work on multiple projects simultaneously. It is not uncommon to have several pending large projects with overlapping timelines and an assortment of smaller tasks that all need to get done. It is just not practical to assume that a knowledge worker can simply pick one thing, work exclusively on it until completed, and then move on to the next thing. This is especially true for managers that need to supervise the work of their staff while still getting their own work done.

Part of the challenge is that knowledge work can vary a great deal from one moment to the next. Some tasks like making a call or writing an email can be relatively simple and completed quickly. Other tasks like writing a proposal, preparing a client presentation, writing a software module, or doing research can be large and complex multi-step projects that require days or even weeks to complete.

Having to deal simultaneously with big projects and small tasks is a new challenge for knowledge workers.

"Best practice calls for emphasis on relationships, collaboration, and professionalism, and for deemphasis of formal performance measures."

Knowledge Workers jobs must be designed that reflect more of behavioral element rather then organizational element. Behavioral elements also known as the "core job dimensions" which brings in efficiency in a persons job as opposed to organizational element which aims at efficiency in a job. Their jobs should be based on the core job dimensions *i.e.,* skill variety, autonomy, task identity, task significance and feedback. Jobs should have more of these elements and less of organizational elements in order to make the work of knowledge workers more interesting.

William B. Werther, JR. Keith Davis, Human Resource and Personnel Management, (5th Edition, page 140-41.) writes that while managing Knowledge Workers *"—job designers draw heavily on behavioral research to provide a work environment that helps satisfy individuals."*

Increased Autonomy and Authority

Another challenge in the management of knowledge workers is that due to a non existent job description such as the work itself may not always be well defined. Knowledge workers have freedom of how to do their work. Knowledge workers have autonomy and discretion over how to perform work tasks; they are frequently given a desired outcome or result and asked to decide for themselves how to make it happen. Autonomy is important to maintain creativity in their work but total autonomy means total freedom. No one in the organization understands their work so no one has the authority to question them regarding their job.

Part of the job is to figure out what work needs to be done and how to go about doing it. Because of this, there is often no clear-cut way to declare when something is really done. When is the task of writing a marketing report or doing research for a project completed? How good, polished, or thorough does it need to be before it can be considered 'done'?

The real answer is that it depends on many factors : who is going to read it, why it's being prepared, how it is going to be used, etc. It takes judgement and experience to determine when you've reached the point of diminishing returns where additional work will not add enough value to justify the added cost and effort.

Of course, such creativity and inquiry-driven learning may be difficult to achieve within traditional command-and-control paradigm. As mentioned earlier, use of the information and control systems and compliance with predefined goals, objectives and best practices may not necessarily achieve organizational competence.

Knowledge workers have a lot of power, and they don't want things to be imposed on them. They don't like to be told what to do. This power of knowledge makes it difficult to bring knowledge workers under the control of management. They may put up with it for a while, but eventually they'll look for a job that gives them the autonomy they think they deserve.

Besides, managers can't easily enforce an order when work takes place in people's heads. You have to make it easy for knowledge workers to do what you want them to do. Given the need for autonomy in learning and decision making, such knowledge workers would also need to be comfortable with self-control and self-learning. In other words, they would need to act in an entrepreneurial mode that involves a higher degree of responsibility and authority as well as capability and intelligence for handling both."

Loyalty Towards the Organization

Another area for management consideration in managing knowledge workers is how to earn their loyalty for the origination. Loyalty translates itself in commitment at work. Commitment is the key to success. The best way to gain their loyalties is to have full trust in these workers which will in turn boost their morale and result in better performance.

"You have to make sure that your workers are indeed committed to their work before relying on that commitment in collaboration."

"Good research managers understand this implicitly : that relationships based on professionalism and mutual respect work far better than scales of accountability and incentive schemes in most knowledge-work settings."

Motivation

Motivation and commitment goes hand in hand. If knowledge workers are motivated only then they can give their best shot. In order to motivate knowledge workers they have to be given challenging tasks. They should be involved in the development of mission statement so that they feel a part of the organization.

"What motivates workers—especially knowledge workers - is what motivates volunteers. Volunteers, we know, have to get more satisfaction from their work than paid employees precisely because they do not get a pay check. They need, above all, challenge. They need to know the organization's mission and to believe in it. They need continuous training. They need to see results. Implicit in this is that employees have to be managed as associates, partners-and not in name only. The definition of a partnership is that all partners are equal."

Extensive Training and Development

The productivity of the knowledge worker is still abysmally low. It has probably not improved in the past 100 or even 200 years-for the simple reason that nobody has worked at improving the productivity. All our work on productivity has been on the productivity of the manual worker...The way one maximizes their performance is by capitalizing on their strengths and their knowledge rather than trying to force them into moulds. A good learning program for knowledge workers would combine classroom learning and learning at their workstations."

What most organizations do is hire smart people and leave them alone. A lot of effort goes into recruiting knowledge workers and assessing how capable they might be before they are being hired. But once they're hired they are left alone and nothing is done in objective terms to improve their performance. Even if they are performing satisfactorily there is still room for more. Process improvement has mostly been for other workers : transactional workers, manufacturing workers, and people in call centers. All the serious approaches to improving work have largely escaped knowledge work.

"We let knowledge workers get away with saying there's no process to their work, that every day is different. We don't measure much of anything about knowledge work."

People improve processes all the time; they just haven't done it with knowledge-work processes as much. It's an extrapolation of the same logic in other work, that processes can be improved. It is absolutely wrong to say that nothing can be done in case of improvement of process of knowledge workers.

Here is one number that indicates performance and productivity can be improved : IDC found that 1,000 knowledge workers can lose as much as $6 million a year just searching for nonexistent data, or repeating work that has already been done. Is it possible every knowledge worker is working to his or her potential ? It's possible, but unlikely. We can get a lot better at improving their performance.

Huge amount of money and time is spent on bringing in new technology to their company. Most organizations have no training or education on how to use these tools effectively in their work. For example the institute in which I am currently employed has a digital library, which is storehouse of information and knowledge. But unfortunately except for a few employees hardly anyone has the know-how to get to this information sea and utilize it to their benefit or the benefit of the Institute. There are several cases elsewhere.

Even when people are trained on knowledge-oriented applications, such as Excel, PowerPoint, CAD or CRM, the training focuses on how the software package works, not on how it fits into the context of the job. The vast majority of organizations that implemented CRM didn't really help their salespeople figure out how to use the system effectively to help them sell better. It's one of the reasons CRM has had the problems it has had. People were not comfortable using it with the customer around. And there weren't any good examples of how salespeople did their work, so a lot of CRM systems were not effective at all.

Monitoring and Evaluation

Monitoring and evaluation is the biggest challenge for the management in case of knowledge workers. Basically these workers do not like to be constantly monitored by their supervisors during their work or at their workplace. Similarly the work of knowledge workers is of novel and creative nature for which there are no set standards. Due to lack of benchmarks their performance cannot be measured through ordinary monitoring and evaluation machinery. Their work is highly cognitive that requires special system in order to prove whether they are positively contributing something to the organization or not. Their work is result oriented not process oriented.

The difficulties in observing knowledge work are more profound. Not only can't a supervisor observe effort directly in knowledge work, sometimes the supervisor can't understand what the worker is doing and may not be qualified to judge results.

Because knowledge work occurs in intellectual domains, it is also more difficult to see causality and to attribute results to particular worker actions. Results measures often don't faithfully capture the results you really care about. The productivity of knowledge work, in contrast, often has to do with how effort is allocated across multiple dimensions. By definition, knowledge work is more about how smart you work and less about how hard you work. Incentive schemes intended to extract more effort from knowledge workers often distort their effort allocations, forcing them to apply effort in the wrong places."

"The vice president of marketing may have come up the sales route and know a great deal about selling. But he knows little about market research, pricing, packaging, service, sales forecasting. The marketing vice president therefore cannot possibly tell the experts in the marketing department what they should be doing. In that sense, they are associates, not subordinates. The same is true for the hospital administrator or the hospital's medical director with respect to the trained knowledge workers in the clinical laboratory or in physical therapy."

Communication Channels

Knowledge work also requires more collaboration and communication with coworkers. The complexity and knowledge required to complete their tasks often makes it impossible for any one person to know or be able to accomplish everything single handedly that needs collaboration of teamwork.

While this collaboration is absolutely essential, it can also cause problems of its own if not managed properly since productive knowledge workers require large amounts of uninterrupted time to think and get into flow.

"—measuring performance is always difficult, and in knowledge work it is especially difficult. If you have no real chance of observing, understanding, or attributing the results of employee work, you become much more dependent on employees' willingness to openly communicate the meaning of their work. Fortunately, knowledge workers often have a commitment to the work itself that makes them inclined toward information sharing."

Knowledge sharing is crucial because it helps organizations promote best practices and reduce redundant learning efforts or 'reinventing the wheel' (Hansen, 2002; McDermott and O'Dell, 2001).

In knowledge-intensive industries, firms cannot compete if their employees guard their insights as personal secrets (Teece, 1998). To succeed in a knowledge economy, organizations need to develop systematic processes to create and leverage knowledge. However, the failure of firms in their effort to promote knowledge sharing has been documented in many cases because employees are reluctant to share their knowledge with others even when knowledge sharing is actively promoted (*e.g.*, Davenport, De Long, and Beers, 1998). A number of reasons have been given for these failures, such as the influence of organizational culture (Davenport, De Long, and Beers, 1998) or personal concerns of power and self-interest (Jarvenpaa and Staples, 2001). However, these arguments have not been empirically verified, and a coherent account of the factors hindering knowledge sharing is still lacking.

In this age, virtually all types of work have some aspects of knowledge work in one form or another. Even work that previously may have discouraged autonomy, discretion, and creative thinking is becoming more knowledge oriented as companies realize that they need help from all their employees if they want to remain competitive.

"Knowledge-intensive firms need to share knowledge held by employees if they are to gain the most from their intellectual capital and compete effectively in the marketplace."

Work Life Balance

The separation between personal and work life is getting more and more blurred, the two have mingled to the extent that it is difficult if not impossible to draw a line. The idea that you can compartmentalize your time into work and personal life just isn't practical anymore.

The job of knowledge workers is such that they have to be very active & work for long hours. Work pressure has disturbed their work life balance. Knowledge workers have to pay a heavy price by sacrificing their personal and family time in line of their duty. Their job is of demanding nature-demanding more and more time for accomplishing their tasks. In this era of competition no body want to be second to best. For best there is a price to pay. That price is paid by these knowledge workers.

Many of today dynamic organizations appear to be at the forefront of the trend towards workaholic cultures. These organizations are increasingly expecting people to work from 60 to 70 hours a week.

People are increasingly finding that work is squeezing out personal lives, and many are questioning this lifestyle. Balancing work life and personal life is likely to become one the most important upcoming issues for HRM.

Each affects and influences the other, which is why more and more people are realizing that managing their work and personal life as a whole not only makes sense, but is a better way to manage their time and increase their overall productivity.

One of the reasons why managing time at the tactical level has become more difficult in the last one hundred years is that the number of ways you can spend your time has increased dramatically, while the number of hours in a day remains the same.

Another aspect of knowledge work that traditional time management practices have not dealt with effectively is the rapid inflow of new work, ideas, and information that knowledge workers have to deal with.

There are a number of ways that others can communicate with you : email, telephone, fax, drop in visitors, meetings, memos, and regular mail. Each represents an opportunity for additional work to get added to your plate.

A question from a co-worker, an email from your boss, an action item from a meeting, a memo from marketing, not to mention your own ideas and insights that come up while doing your work.

All these different sources of input can easily overwhelm you if they are not managed properly. Since none of these communications carry an explicit 'there is some work in here for you' label, each has to be filtered and reviewed to determine if there is work involved and what that work actually is.

For many people, "the image of drowning in a sea of information, emails and paperwork is not too far from reality."

Review Questions

1. Briefly review the relevance of Knowledge Management in contemporary organizations.
2. What steps need to be initiated by the organization to integrate knowledge workers into the mainstream?
3. Explain the characteristics of knowledge workers.
4. What steps should be taken by an organization to manage a knowledge worker?

PROJECT WORK

Prepare a case study of two business leaders who have led the transformation of their organizations. Present the same in the class.

Case Study

Shri Sharma a first generation entrepreneur established a Modern Bank in 1986 as a private bank. The bank grew to become a 1000 crore business by 1992, and 5000 crore business. In 2000, the bank brought in Preeti Sharma a young MBA graduate as the Managing Director of the bank. Preeti focused her energy on building the brand of the bank among the middle class. During the period the bank recorded continuous business growth by 2006 the bank total business stood on 40, 000 crores.

Preeti emphasized the following :

- Recruiting top notch professional.
- Re-engineering the corporate brand of the bank
- Emphasized marketing and business development
- Adoption of technology for modernizing business operations

It was her belief that systems and procedures should take precedence over individuals in the bank, and after goals were set the executives should be given freedom to perform. A few hallmarks of her leadership and management approach were :

Emphasis on streamlining the systems and procedures.

Nurturing employees to strictly adhere to laid down norms/ systems.

Training of existing employees.

Continuous technology upgradation.

There was however difference between the promoter and Preeti which eventually led to her resignation. The bank soon started losing clients and its turnover dipped. The employees also put in papers to leave the company especially in the top and middle levels.

Questions

1. *Analyse the case from the learning inputs in the chapter.*
2. *Do a SWOT analysis in terms of the technology and performance management areas of the bank?*
3. *Suggest the steps for improving the knowledge management process in the bank.*
4. *Do you think that e-learning should take precedence over traditional training in the banks?*

Chapter **18**

INDUSTRIAL RELATIONS

★ LEARNING OBJECTIVES ★

After reading this chapter, you will be able to understand :

- Brief History of Labour Movement;
- Industrial Relations Theories
- Role of Government in Industrial Relations
- Industrial Disputes—Its cause, strikes, Gheraos, lockouts, picketing; Prohibition of strikes
- Measures to Improve Industrial Relations.

INTRODUCTION

Industrial relations has become one of the most delicate and complex problems of modern industrial society. Industrial progress is impossible without cooperation of labors and harmonious relationships. Therefore, it is in the interest of all to create and maintain good relations between employees (labor) and employers (management).

The labour—employer tussle can be traced back to time immemorial. The struggle primarily is on sharing the profit. Since states came into existence it has been an endeavour on part of state to manage labour relations. Labour-management relations policy formulation is one of the significant tasks of the national governments, and its successful formulation and implementation can influence the labour relations climate at the industry and enterprise levels.

Industrial Relations are concerned with systems, rules and procedures used by unions and employers to determine the reward for effort and other conditions of employment to protect the interest of the employed and their employers and to regulate the ways in which employers treat their employees.

It is a dynamic concept that depends upon the pattern of the society, economic system and political set-up of a country and changes with the changing economic and social order. It is an art of living together for the purposes of production, productive efficiency, human well-being and industrial progress. It comprises of a network of institutions, such as, trade unionism, collective bargaining, employers, the law, and the state which are bound together by a set of common values and aspirations. Knowledge of such institutions is important if we are to understand everyday industrial relations phenomena. It is a collective relationship which grows out of employment between employees and management in the day to day working of industry either individually or collectively through Trade Unions, and the part played by state in regulating the relations (Figure 18.1).

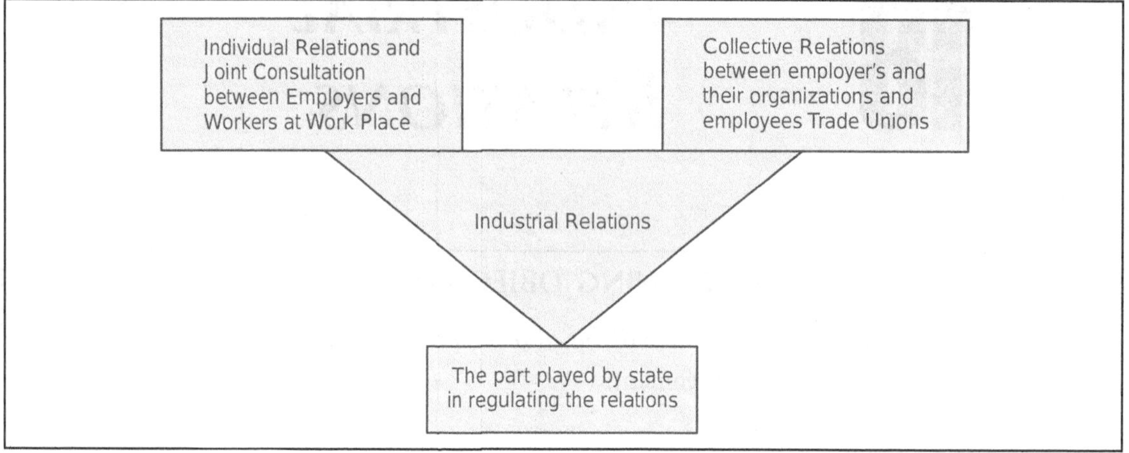

Fig. 18.1. *Industrial Relations.*

A sound industrial relations system is one in which relationships between management and employees (and their representatives) on the one hand, and between them and the State on the other, are more harmonious and cooperative than conflict and creates an environment conducive to economic efficiency and the motivation, productivity and development of the employee and generates employee loyalty and mutual trust. Industrial relations itself may again be described as being concerned with the rules, processes and mechanisms (and the results emanating there from) through which the relationship between employers and employees and their respective representatives, as well as between them on the one hand and the State and its agencies on the other, is regulated. Industrial relations seek to balance the economic efficiency of organizations with equity, justice and the development of the individual, to find ways of avoiding, minimizing and resolving disputes and conflict and to promote harmonious relations between and among the actors directly involved, and society as a whole. The rules, processes and mechanisms of an industrial relations system are found in sources such as laws (legislative, judicial, quasi-judicial), practices, customs, agreements and arrangements arrived at through a bipartite or tripartite process or through prescription by the State.

Industrial relations concerns with the relationship between the management and the employees of an industry. Industrial Relations in India stand highly regulated by the State. The Directive Principles of the State Policy place upon the Government the responsibility of :

"Securing legislation or economic organization, or any other way, to all workers, industrial or otherwise, work, living wages, conditions of work ensuring a decent standard of life, equal pay for equal work for both men and women, education, humane conditions of work, maternity relief, public assistance in case of unemployment, old age, sickness and disablement, full employment, leisure and cultural opportunities and participation of workers in the management of undertaking....."

With the liberalization of the economy industrial relations in India have changed over the last 10-15 years. There are different approaches to industrial relations, psychological, sociological, human relations, socio-ethical, Gandhian and systems approach.

LABOUR MOVEMENT

No discussion on industrial relations can be undertaken without having a glimpse of Labour movement. The labour movement is a broad term for the development of a collective organization of working people, to campaign in their own interest for better treatment from their employers and political governments, in particular through the implementation of specific laws governing labor relations. Labour unions and trade unions are common names for the specific collective organizations within societies, organized for the purpose of representing the interests of workers and the working class. Many elite-class individuals and political groups are also be active in and part of the labour movement.

In some countries including the United Kingdom and Australia the term is widely used to describe both a "political wing" and an "industrial wing". In Britain these are the Labour Party and Trades Union Congress (TUC) collectively. The Labour Party was created, as the Labour Representation Committee as a result of an 1899 resolution of the TUC.

At the time when Britishers came to India in sixteenth century, most people in the world did not have a boss. Nine out of ten people lived on farms and cultivated their own crops, slaughtered animals, tended gardens, and made their own clothes, candles, and soap. Most of the people who lived in towns and cities also did not have an employer. Many of the men were master craftsmen who made goods like shoes and furniture, from start to finish, in their own workshops. Sometimes a master craftsman hired skilled journeymen to work in his shop. But most of these journeymen only earned wages for a short time until they opened their own workshops. The majority of women also did not earn wages from an employer. Most women expected to and did become wives and mothers who worked at home raising children, boiling and ironing laundry, cleaning, marketing, and cooking.

The labour movement began during the industrial revolution, when agricultural jobs declined and employment moved to more industrial areas. The idea met with great resistance. In the 18th century and early 19th century, groups such as the Tolpuddle Martyrs of Tolpuddle, Dorset were punished and deported for forming unions, which was against the laws of the time.

The industrial revolution also brought thousands of women and children into the workforce for the first time. Businessmen in Europe and America built hundreds of textile mills that employed mainly women and some children. At first these factories employed the young, unmarried daughters of farmers; after the 1850s they began to hire immigrant women from countries such as Ireland, Canada etc. Many women also began to work for wages in their homes or in small shops called "slop-shops," sewing pre-cut cloth into finished clothing. In 1854, the New Haven Shirt Company in US employed almost 3,700 women who worked long hours for low wages sewing shirts in their homes. In the 1830s and 1840s, shoe manufacturers began to employ thousands of women who worked in their homes stitching the upper leathers of shoes.

The world-wide labor movement gained major impetus in the late nineteenth and early twentieth centuries from the Catholic Social Teaching tradition which began in 1891 with the publication of Pope Leo XIII's foundational document, Rerum Novarum, also known as "On the

Condition of the Working Classes," in which he advocated a series of reforms including limits on the length of the work day, a living wage, the elimination of child labor, the rights of labor to organize, and the duty of the state to regulate labor conditions. Following the release of the document, the labor movement which had previously floundered began to flourish in Europe and later in North America.

Throughout the world, action by the labour movement has led to reforms and workers' rights, such as the 2-day weekend, minimum wage, paid holidays, and the achievement of the eight-hour day for many workers. There have been many important labour activists in modern history who have caused changes that were revolutionary at the time and are now regarded as basic. For example, Mary Harris Jones, better known as Mother Jones, and the National Catholic Welfare Council were central in the campaign to end child labour in the United States during the early 20th century. An active and free labour movement is considered by many to be an important element in maintaining democracy and for economic development.

Labour Movement in India

Labour movement emerged in India in the middle of 1800 when Indian railway came into being along with its ancillary industries. Great Indian Railway Company and Great Indian Peninsular Railway Company (both were private enterprises) installed the first railways tracks in India in 1853 and in 1859 respectively. These developments were fuelled by the discovery of huge coal reserves in undivided Bengal in 1770. 1843 saw the birth of the first coal mines under the aegis of another private enterprise, The Bengal Coal Company. The first large scale mining operation started in Jharia. The British Tea Company, Assam Tea, started operating from 1839.

This has set the proper backdrop for the emergence of labour movement in India, particularly in undivided Bengal. The first ever Jute Mill in the sub-continent started operating in Bengal, at Rishra in 1854. The first ever cotton mill in India was established in Bauria, a suburb of the city of Calcutta (now renamed as Kolkata) in 1818. By 1880, India witnessed the growth of about 58 spinning and textile mills spanning all the major Presidencies (administrative division of British India) of our country. Tagore's ancestor, Prince Dwarkanath Tagore, not only founded the indigenous indigo company, but also purchased the Chinakuri coal mines in 1837 and founded The Bengal.

In 1833, Ram Mohan Ray, a representative of the landed gentry, had described the plight of the workers in the most thorough-going manner. The skilled workers in those days used to earn about 10–12 rupees a month, while unskilled ones would earn about 4 rupees a month. The consumer price index, in those days had a hike increase of about 75% compared to 1820. It may be mentioned that the wage of the jute workers remained stagnant during the period 1860 to 1892. During the period 1901 to 1911, the increase in the labour force in the construction sector was 18.2% and that of in the transport sector was 29.4%.

In the labour front, a real anarchy was the call of the day. There were no redressal forum, nor was there any process through which the workers could raise their legitimate demands democratically before the employers. Yet, the workers organized themselves and were trying to assert their rights. To "discipline" the budding labour movement, "Employers' and Workers' (Disputes) Act, 1860" was passed. Among other aspects, this Act conferred enormous power on the employer to coerce the workers. For example, according to this Act, an employer can institute fine or confine the worker to the factory premises lawfully for an indefinite period, should the workers refuse to "obey" the employer. In the same year, to tighten the coercive role of the state, the Britishers had instituted the Indian Penal Code, 1860, which is still in vogue in our country with only minor modifications. Finally, after a lot of blood-bath on the part of the workers and pressure from the civil society, Indian Factory Act, 1881, was passed, which banned the employment of a child below 7 years of age in a factory and fixed the working hour of workforce in the age group 7–12 at 9 hours.

Sashipada Banerjee took to the cause of betterment of Indian Labour; he started publishing "Bharat Sramajibi' (Indian Labourers) a journal exclusively devoted to the labourers in 1878 from Kolkata. This journal became a mouth piece of labour voice and started expressing the labour problems for the first time. He also founded the "BARANAGAR INSTITUTE" in 1880, to spread primary and hygiene education among the workers. He later founded a Savings Bank exclusively for the workers in Kolkata. A similar effort was initiated by Meghaji Narayain Lokhande in Bombay, (now renamed as Mumbai) in 1898; he also started a journal, named "Deenabandhu" (Friend of the Poor) in Marathi. Bhramho Samaj, in a parallel effort, founded the "Working Mens' Mission" to promote justice and spiritualism among the industrial workers.

Bengal can pride herself in attaining the landmark in the history of labour movement of India. Much ahead of their European brethren, Indian railway men joined a first ever strike in the month of April and May, 1862 demanding an 8-hours-a-day working pattern. The historic May Day in Chicago would take place around quarter of a century later. In the same year, the bullock-cart drivers went on a historic strike, which has shaken the fabric of the then Bengali society. The other provinces of India were not very far behind – Madras Presidency witnessed about 25 strikes and cease of work during the period 1882 to 1890. The Jute Mills of Bengal were run like a sweat-shop in those days, as it is run today. In the district of Howrah in Bengal, the Ghusuri Mill witnessed wildcat strikes twice in the years 1881 and 1890. In 1895 and in 1896, the Budge Budge Jute Mill in the suburbs of Kolkata witnessed the mightiest of the labour movements in the decade.

The strikes were limited to the firms and factories owned by the private owners, British or Indian alike. The labour movements struck fist against the British Rulers when in 1905. The workers in the Government Press joined a month-long strike. In the same year, the workers of the Burn Company in Howrah ceased work; the workers in the newly founded Tramways in Kolkata also followed suit. The Guards entrusted to oversee the smooth movements of the goods train of the East India Railways struck work to achieve yet another victory. In the same year, the British-owned Hoogly Jute Mill in Bengal witnessed a massive workers' movement and stalled the introduction of night-shift without adequate infrastructure provided by the company.

November 18, 1907 was a historic day in the annals of Indian Labour Movement, when the railway workmen in Asansol, in Bengal, started a cease work in support of their 43-point charter. The strike had spread rapidly in the whole country and no train could reach Kolkata for a few days. The Kolkata Port went idle and the Port workers absented themselves in solidarity with the striking railway workmen.

The first political strike by the Indian proletariat took place in July 13, 1908, when the workers of the Greeves and Cotton Mill in Bombay ceased work protesting against the trial of Indian nationalist Leader, Bal Gangadhar Tilak. In the same year, two workers' organizations were founded in Kolkata (Mohamedan Association and Indian Labour Union). As the workers of India and Bengal started organizing themselves, they were in a better position to offer resistance to the British imperialism and also attained a better bargaining edge to protect and extend their legitimate rights..

The labour at time was in dire conditions. According to a Royal Commission of Labour, instituted by the British in 1933, the working hours in all the cotton mills were 13 to 15 hours a day. The report of the Textile Factories Labour Committee mentioned in 1906 that the conditions inside the factories were "inhuman", the workers had to "put in hard labour" and after the shift was over, "they were so exhausted that a large number of them used to faint within the factory premises". The condition of the female workers was deplorable. Employing of child labour was rampant. The factory Labour Commission of 1908 noted that children in the age group 5-7 constituted a major workforce in most of the factories. 40% of the part-time workers were under-age children. In the jute mills, children in the age group 7-9 used to travel about 4 km in the early morning to reach the factory in time!

A large number of labour organizations came into being, notable among them being The Press Employees Association, Calcutta (1919), The Calcutta Tramways Employees Union (1919), Howrah Labour Union (1920), E.B. Railways Indian Employees Association (1920) and Bengal Mariners Union (1920). In 1919, the International Labour Organisation was founded as a part of the then League of Nations. In its first Conference, Mr. B P Wadia represented for India.

When Mahatma Gandhi joined the independence Movement, he changed the scenario of Industrial Relations in India. The workers closely participated in the struggle for independence and used methods such as 'satyagrah' (civil disobedience) with the support from leaders of the freedom movement. This in a way marked the beginning of the growing nexus between the fledgling trade union movement and political parties such as Indian National Congress, Communist Party of India etc.

In 1920, the All India Trade Union Congress (AITUC) was founded through a national convention which took place in Bombay during the period October 31 to November 2. The effect of such a historic event was evident almost immediately as the country saw a dramatic rise in the number of strikes. In 1921, only one year after the founding of the AITUC, as it is known today, the number of strikes rose to 376.

In November 1, 1925 the Workers' and Peasants Party was founded in Bengal. Soon many branches of this organization started spreading in other parts of India. Finally in December 1928, through an India-wide convention in Kolkata, the All India Workers and Peasant Party was born.

The textile barons of Bombay decided to reduce some of the allowances of the textile workers. To protest against such an act, 0.16 million workers ceased work from September 1925. The strike lasted for more than 11 days and the withdrawal of allowances was rolled back by the mill owners.

On April 9, 1936, about 20 thousand workers of Hukum Chand Jute Mill ceased work and they were successful in recovering the basic rights which were systematically curtailed over the years by the management. The historic Jute workers strike would go down as a milestone in workers' struggle because of its glorious role. 0.25 Million workers took part in the strike which began on February 26, 1937 and lasted 74 days long!

When the Second World War was in full swing, in 1940, 20 thousand workers of Calcutta Municipal Corporation organized a strike and partial success was achieved. During the period 1940-1943, Bengal witnessed a series of medium to large-scale workers' strike involving millions of workers in almost every firm and mill. The historic all-India Post and Telegraph workers' strike started from July 11, 1946. In support to these strikes, common people of India started lending their assistance. The city of Calcutta became absolutely paralyzed when a virtual general strike was called to extend support to the striking workers!

The trade union movement grew parallel to the freedom movement and by the time India had gained its independence, the trade union movement had graduated from infancy to the early adult stage. After 1947, there was a dramatic change that took place in the workers movement arena of our country. Various Central Trade Unions were founded, resulting in a division of the strength of the collective bargaining power of the workers. The rulers gave a clarion call to the workers to suspend their demands to build the country and sacrifice for the "Greater Common Good". Government of India embarked upon massive large scale industrialization. The large scale projects contributed to the strengthening of trade unions in India. A Macro development was taking place simultaneously with the growing influence of the socialist philosophy of the Soviet Union on the planners of Government of India. This resulted in laying emphasis on the rights of workers and the equitable distribution of wealth.

A major factor influencing the growth and evolution of trade union movement in India was the influence of the politicians. The blue collar workers were seen by these politicians as a means to developing the stature of union leaders in their respective parties, opening up avenues to corridors of power.

The socialist perspective of government have led it to enact number of legislative and legal support mechanisms for the rights of workers, and to guide their movement for self protection. The first major step was passing of The Industrial Disputer Act 1947 by parliament. Still 1947 witnessed about 1811 strikes, while 1950 witnessed only 814 strikes in the divided India.

The workers of the organized sector (government and semi-governmental offices) started a wildcat strike from the midnight of July 11, 1960. The police took recourse to terrible repression; several rounds of fire were targeted towards the striking workers, five workers became martyrs, 20 thousand workers were arrested. 2.5 million workers of the Central Government sector joined a strike in September 19, 1968.

The railway strike took place in May, 1974, under the leadership of Shri George Fernandes, it shook the entire political fabric of our country and ushered in a new tide of movements throughout the country.

Our country witnessed unprecedented upsurge in mass movements during the seventies. The Government of India declared an "Internal Emergency" from the mid-night of June 25 1975. It continued for about 18 months. The decade of eighties of the last century in this witnessed a new turning point as regards the workers' movement. The workers of different factories started revolting against the anti-Labour move perpetrated by the Central Trade Unions. As a result, the revolting workers started organizing themselves into new consolidations. This process of consolidation gave rise to two distinct trends :

- Spontaneous revolts, followed by clashes and violence, that ended sadly in the withdrawal of the movement, and
- Initiating organised, unified and protracted movement that culminated in a new form of struggle.

The first trend was embodied in the spontaneous revolt by the workers of Victoria Jute Mill in 1992 and the recent workers' uprising in the Tea Gardens in North Bengal, where a CITU leader was burnt to death by the angry workers. The second trend was heralded by the victorious workers of the Hindustan Levers. The movement of the Jute Worker of Kanoria Jute Mill in the 90s of the last century had taken the issues and just causes of the workers to the society at large. The growth of trade Unions and its membership is at Table 18.1

Table. 18.1. Growth of Trade Union and Membership

Year	*Number of Registered Trade Unions*	*Number of Unions submitting returns*	*Member of Unions Submitting returns*					*Average Member-ship per Union*
			Men		*Women*		*Total*	
			Number ('000)	*Percentage of total*	*Number ('000)*	*Percentage of total*	*Member-ship ('000)*	
1991	53535	8418	5507	90.3	593	9.7	6100	725
1992	55680	9165	5148	89.6	598	10.4	5746	627
1993	55784	6806	2636	84.1	498	15.9	3134	460
1994	56872	6277	3239	79.1	856	20.9	4095	652
1995	57952	8162	5675	86.8	863	13.2	6538	801
1996	58988	7242	4250	75.9	1351	24.1	5601	773
1997	60660	8872	6504	87.8	905	12.2	7409	835
1998	61992	7403	6104	84.2	1145	15.8	7249	979
1999	64817	8152	5190	81	1218	19	6407	786
2000	66056	7253	4510	83.2	910	16.8	5420	747
2001	66624	6531	4392	74.8	1481	25.2	5873	900
2002	68544	7812	5102	73.2	1871	26.8	6973	893

The present era of competition has made it imperative for organizations to define and sustain performance parameters at all levels (organization, group, and individual). In view of this it is imperative now that employees form part of the developmental process as partners. Another important factor is the booming information and communication industry. The knowledge workers have become the key factors for organizational growth and development. It is universally recognized that human are the greatest assets of the organization. This has led to paradigm shift in the mindset of employers as well as employees. The information and communication technology organizations are largely non-unionized. The dominant relationship between employer and employee is that of a partner and not servant master relationship. The policies and practices of information and communication technology organizations are based on four key features :

- Virtual reality in the organizations
- Flexible and adaptive work environments,
- Performance based and variable compensation structures and
- Democratic governance with provision for employer participation

The shifting focus of work has been aptly captured by Venkata Raman (2001) Table 18.2.

Table 18.2. How Focus has Shifted in Work

Aspect	*Traditional Agriculture*	*Early/Traditional Industry*	*Post Industrial Service/ High Technology*
Wealth	Land	Money	Mind/Information
Skill/Effort	Brawn/ Muscle	Machine-tending	Brain/mind, attitude, and ability matter, not just skill.
Management Philosophy	Unilateral	Pluralistic	Egalitarian
Management Style	Autocratic	Paternalistic	Collegial
Employment Context	Master Servant	Employer-employee	Partners
Relationship	One sided dependence	Interdependence	Mutuality and independence
Communication	Top down	Two way	Transparent
Motivation	Fear	Favour	Fairness
Performance Appraisal	Information. Confidential, boss	Formal one way	Formal, open, participative appraisals.
Control	Direction and control	Inducement	Consensus/commitment

Source : Venkata Raman, C.S. (2001), *Globalization and Labour Management Relations*, Sage Publications, New Delhi, p.303.

Why do Workers Organize?

There is volume of literature available on 'Why do workers organize?' Yet no definite reason that can be given as to why the workers unionize, large of theories have been proposed. One thing is very clear that workers organize/ unionize to get a better deal in terms of pay, allowances and other perks that affect them monetarily.

The urge to unionize often seems boiling down to one facet that collectively the workers can get a fair share of the pie and also provide them security.

DEFINITION, CONCEPT AND SCOPE

There is no unanimity on the meaning and scope of industrial relations since different terms, such as labour-management relations, employer-employee relations, union management relations, personnel relations, human relations, are in use and are used synonymously. The term 'Industrial Relations' comprises of two terms : 'Industry' and 'Relations'. "Industry" refers to "any productive activity in which an individual (or a group of individuals) is (are) engaged". By "relations" we mean "the relationships that exist within the industry between the employer and his workmen." In its stricter sense, the term "industrial relations" means relationship between management and workmen in a unit or an industry. In its wider connotation, it means the organisation and practice of multi-pronged relationships between workers and management, unions and workers, and the unions and managements in an industry.

The American Heritage® Dictionary of the English Language, Fourth Edition (Houghton Mifflin Company. Updated in 2003.) Published by Houghton Mifflin Company states *industrial relations as relations between the management of an industrial enterprise and its employees.*

According to Encycloaedia Britannica, "The subject of industrial relations includes relations and joint consultation between employers and workers at the place of work, collective relations between employers and their organizations and trade unions and part played by the state in regulating these relations."

Dale Yoder defines it as a *"Whole field of relationship that exists because of the necessary collaboration of men and women in the employment process of an industry."*

Tead and Metcalfe observed that "Industrial relations are the composite result of the attitudes and approaches of employers and employees towards each other with regard to planning, supervision, direction and coordination of the activities of an organization with a minimum of human efforts and frictions with an animating spirit of cooperation and with proper regard for the genuine well-being of all members of the organization."

Allan Flanders, defines *"the subject of industrial relations deals with certain regulated or institutionalized relationships in industry. Personal or in the language of sociology, "unstructured" relationships have their importance for management and workers, but they lie outside the scope of a system of industrial relations."*

Professor Clegg defines industrial relations in the broadest terms as *"encompassing the rules governing employment together with the ways in which the rules are made and changed and their interpretation and administration."*

To put it simply, industrial relations is that part of management which is concerned with the manpower of the enterprise. It is, thus, the relation created at different levels of the organization by the diverse, complex and composite needs, aspirations, attitudes and approaches among the participants. It is a highly complex and dynamic process of relationships involving not only employees and managements, but also their collective forums and the State. In an organization, these relationships may be personal and informal at one end, and may be highly institutional with legally prescribed structures and procedures, at the other end.

The four main parties who are actively associated with any industrial relations system are the workers, the managements, the organizations of workers and managements, and the State. Fundamentally, the term industrial relations refer to an organized relationship between two organized parties representing employers and employees regarding matters of collective interest. With the growth of professional management, the industrial relations scene is being represented by the representatives of both the employers and the employees. But the scope of industrial relations cannot merely be confined to common labour-management relations or employer-employee relations. It is a comprehensive and total concept embracing the sum total of relationships that exists at various levels of the organizational structure. More specifically, it connotes relations among workers themselves within the class of employees, relations among the managements within the managerial class, and relations between the two distinct classes of workers and management. It denotes all types of inter-group and intra-group relations within industry, both formal and informal. It consists of a complex network of relations that arise out of functional interdependence between workers and managements and between industrial organizations and society. Industrial relations are a social concept because it deals with social relationships in different walks of life. It is also a relative concept because it grows and flourishes or stagnates and decays in accordance with the economic, social and political conditions prevailing in a society and the laws made by the state to regulate them. The advances made in the field of science and technology also influence the state of industrial relations. There is greater divergence in industrial relations systems as a result of the divergent economic, social, political and cultural environments.

AREAS OF CONCERN OF INDUSTRIAL RELATIONS

From the definitions it can be summarized that the Industrial Relations primarily covers the under mentioned areas :

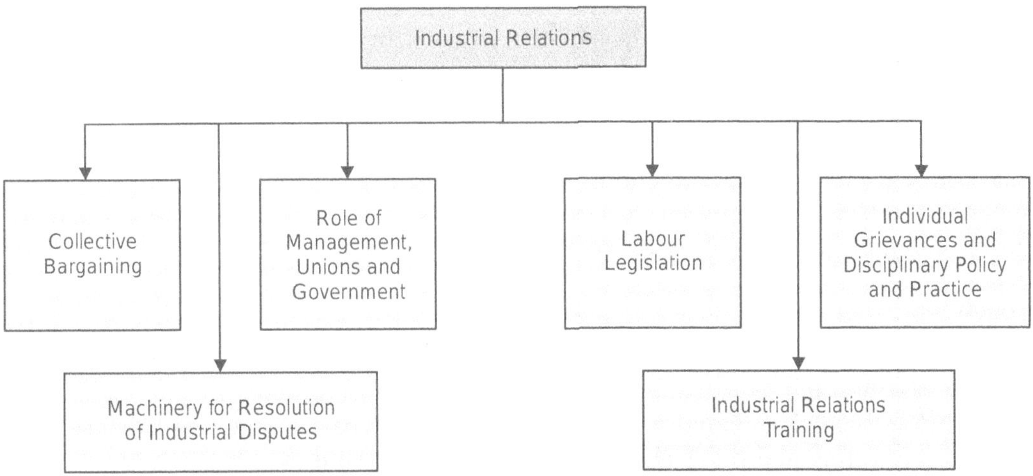

Fig. 18.2. *Areas of Concern of Industrial Relations.*

Objectives

Apart from the primary objective of bringing about sound and healthy relations between employers and employees, industrial relations aim :

1. To facilitate production and productivity;
2. To safeguard the rights and interests of both labour and management by enlisting their co-operation;
3. To achieve a sound, harmonious, and mutually beneficial labour management relations;
4. To avoid unhealthy atmosphere in the industry, especially work, stoppages, go slows, gheraos, strikes, lockouts; and
5. To establish and maintain industrial democracy.
6. To protect workers interest and improve their working conditions.
7. Establish industrial democracy based on labour partnership

The objectives of state in maintaining healthy industrial relations is to correct, an imbalanced, disordered, maladjusted social and economic order with a view to reshaping the complex socio-economic relationships and economic progress. It also controls and disciplines the parties concerned and adjusts their conflicting interests. In this process, it protects some and restrains others, depending upon the situation.

According to Kirkaldy, industrial relations in a country are intimately connected with the form of its political government; and the objectives of an industrial organization may vary from purely economic to purely political ends. He divides the objectives of industrial relations into four categories :

- Improvement in the economic conditions of workers in the existing state of industrial management and political government;
- Control exercised by the state over industrial undertakings with a view to regulating production and promoting harmonious industrial relations;
- Socialization or rationalization of industries by making the state itself a major employer; and
- Vesting of a proprietary interest of the workers in the industries in which they are employed.

The industrial relations objectives must follow the determination of business objectives which they should be intended to facilitate. In this context, the industrial relations policies and practices should not negate its intentions in other areas. For instance, if a company wishes to encourage voluntary retirement, its salaries, pensions, and working conditions should not encourage its employees to stay at all costs.

Approach

The problems posed in the field of industrial relations cannot be solved within the limits of a single discipline, and hence it is bound to be inter-disciplinary in approach. It is an interdisciplinary field that includes inputs from sociology, psychology, law, history, politics, economics, accounting and other elements of management studies.

Industrial relations, then, has a dual character, it is both an interdisciplinary field and a separate discipline in its own right (Adams 1988). It is much more of an art than it is a science. Industrial relations are largely an applied field concerned with practice and the training of practitioners rather than with theory and measurement. It is thus related to the basic social sciences as engineering is to the physical sciences or medicine is to the biological sciences.

Any problem in industrial relations has to be approached on a multi-disciplinary basis, drawing from the contributions of the above disciplines. The causes of an industrial dispute may be, by nature, economic, social, psychological or political or a combination of any of them. Labour economics provides an economic interpretation of the problems growing out of employer-employee relationship. Industrial sociology explains the social background of the workers, which is essential for the understanding of industrial relations. Industrial psychology clarifies certain concepts and provides empirical tools in areas such as recruitment, placement, training, fatigue and morale.

For instance, attitudes and morale surveys are powerful tools to discover causes of industrial strife and to evolve methods for their prevention. Labour laws and their interpretation by tribunals and courts contribute to the growth of industrial jurisprudence. Application of quantitative analysis and labour statistics throws light on the exact state of industrial relations during a particular period. Political aspects also assume importance in industrial relations, particularly in a developing economy dominated by centralized planning. In fact, the growth of industrial relations as a scientific discipline depends upon the extent to which it integrates the contribution of established disciplines in the social sciences.

There is no country where industrial relations are entirely a matter of tradition or custom nor is there a country where the employers, the workers or their organizations and the government do not at all interact to build up the country's industrial relations system. It has been a mixture of traditions, customs and a web of action, reaction and interaction between the parties. The industrial relations system may be conceived at different levels, such as national, regional, industrial and workplace. The concept of the system has been influential in establishing industrial relations as a discipline in its own right. The concepts of the system approach are operationally definable.

An industrial relations system may be defined as comprising the totality of power interactions of participants in a workplace, when these interactions involve industrial relations issues. It is viewed as an integral and non-separable part of the organizational structure and its dynamics. An industrial relations system includes all the individuals and institutions that interact at the workplace. Regardless of the level at which the system exists, an industrial relations system can be viewed as having three components :

(1) A set of individuals and institutions that interact;

(2) A context within which the interaction takes place; and

(3) An output that serves to govern the future relationship of the parties.

The components of industrial relations system are :

- **Participants**. The participants in the industrial relations sphere are composed of duly recognized representatives of the parties interacting in several roles within the system.
- **Issues**. The power interactions of the participants in a workplace create industrial relations issues. These issues and the consequences of power interactions find their expression in a web of rules governing the behaviour of the parties at a workplace.
- **Structure**. The structure consists of all forms of institutionalized behaviour in a system. The structure may include collective procedures, grievances, and settlement practices. Legal enactments relevant to power interactions may also be considered to be a part of the structure.
- **Boundaries**. In systems analysis, it is possible to find an issue which one participant is totally indifferent to resolving while, at the same time, the other participant is highly concerned about resolution of the same. These issues may serve to delimit systems boundaries.

At least there are three marked features of the systems approach. They are :

- **Inter-disciplinary**. Character : Some theorists regard the systems approach to be universally applicable to all human relationships, in small or large units. Its flexibility of application in the behavioural sciences has been aptly demonstrated.
- **Suitability to Work Organization and their Sub-systems**. The adaptability of the systems approach to organization is also a frequently discussed trait. This springs from the fact that organizations, and to some extent their sub-systems, are rational and purposeful.
- **Dynamic Aspects**. A systems approach is oriented towards the study of interactions and changing relations.

Based on various components and features of industrial relations, a number of writers have attempted to produce various functional approaches to industrial relations, which are discussed in subsequent paragraphs.

Dunlop's Approach

Among the contributions, the most outstanding has been that of Prof. John T. Dunlop of Harvard University. His systems treatment deserves special mention in view of its wider applicability. His book Industrial Relations Systems (1958) was a pioneering volume in which he presented an analytical framework of industrial relations. The stated purpose of this book is to present a general theory of industrial relations and "to provide tools of analysis to interpret and gain understanding of the widest possible range of industrial relations facts and practices."

Dunlop defines an industrial relations system in the following way :

An industrial relations system at any one time in its development is regarded as comprised of certain actors, certain contexts, an ideology, which binds the industrial relations system together, and a body of rules created to govern the actors at the workplace and work community. There are three sets of independent variables : the 'actors', the 'contexts' and the 'ideology' of the system.

Figure 1 : The Conceptualisation of an Industrial Relations System Figure 1 depicts the main elements of the system and the environmental features, or contexts to which Dunlop draws attention. The principal groups identifiable in the system and which constitutes the structure of an industrial relations system are as follows :

The Actors in a System : The actors are : (*a*) hierarchy of managers and their representatives in supervision, (*b*) a hierarchy of workers (non-managerial) and any spokesmen, and (*c*) specialized governmental agencies (and specialized private agencies created by the first two actors) concerned with workers, enterprises, and their relationships. These first two hierarchies are directly related to each other in that the managers have responsibilities at varying levels to issue instructions (manage), and the workers at each corresponding level have the duty to follow such instructions. The hierarchy of managers need have no relationship to the ownership of the capital assets of the workplace, the managers may be public or private or a mixture in varying proportions. The formal hierarchy of workers may be organized into several competing or complementary organizations, such as, works councils, unions, and parties. The specialized government agencies as actors may have functions in some industrial relations systems so broad and decisive as to override the hierarchies of managers and workers on almost all matters. In other industrial relations systems, the role of the specialized governmental agencies, at least for many purposes, may be minor or constricted.

The Contexts of a System : In an industrial relations system, the contexts or the determinants are of greater importance. The significant aspects of the environment in which the actors interact are the technological characteristics of the workplace and work community, the market or budgetary constraints that impinge on the actors, and the locus and distribution of power in the larger society.

The technological features of the workplace have a very far-reaching consequence for an industrial relations system influencing the form of management and employee organization, the problems posed for supervision, many of the features of the required labour force and the potentialities of public regulation. For instance, the mining industry has a different technological context as compared to the manufacturing industry. Their place of work, the methods of work, and the mode of living, have profound influence on evolving a particular pattern of industrial relations system. The mining communities have frequently been isolated from important urban areas and create special problems in human relations. Historically, this raises a range of questions concerning housing, community services and welfare activities which are frequently beyond the rules of workplace in many other sectors. Apart from the characteristics of the workplace, the development of technology also affects industrial relations by way of not only disturbing the existing employment patterns, but also by determining the size of the work force employed.

The market or budgetary constraints are a second feature of the environmental context, which is fundamental to an industrial relations system. These constraints often operate, in the first instance, directly upon the managerial hierarchy, but they necessarily condition all the actors in a particular system. The context may be a market for the output of the enterprise or a budgetary limitation or some combination of the two. The product market may vary in the degree and character of competition through the full spectrum from pure competition, monopolistic competition, to oligopoly and monopoly. These constraints are no less operative in socialist than in capitalist countries. The relevant market or budgetary constraints may be local, national, or international, depending on the industrial relations system.

The locus and distribution of power in the larger society, of which the particular industrial relations complex is a sub-system, is a third analytical feature of the environmental context. The relative distribution of power among the actors in the larger society tends to a degree to be reflected within the industrial relations system.

At this juncture, the concern is not with the distribution of power within the industrial relations system, but also outside the system. The function of one of the actors in the industrial relations system, the specialised governmental agencies, is likely to be particularly influenced by the distribution of power in the larger society.

The Ideology of an Industrial Relations System : The ideology is a philosophy or a systematised body of beliefs and sentiments held by the actors. An important element that completes the analytical system of industrial relations is the ideology or a set of ideas and beliefs commonly held by the actors that help to bind or to integrate the system together as an entity. Each industrial relations system contains its ideology or shared understandings. The ideology defines the role and place of each actor and the ideas, which each actor holds towards the place and function of the others in the system. Each of the actors in an industrial relations system may be said to have its own ideology. An industrial relations system requires that these ideologies be sufficiently compatible and consistent so as to permit a common set of ideas and an acceptable role for each actor.

The Establishment of Rules : The actors in a given context establish rules for the workplace and the work community, including those governing contracts among the actors in an industrial relations system. This network or web of rules consists of procedures for establishing rules, the substantive rules, and procedures for deciding their application to particular situations. The establishment of these procedures and rules is the centre of attention in an industrial relations system. Thus, the establishment and administration of these rules is the major concern or output of the industrial relations system. The actors who set the web of rules interact in the context of an industrial relations system taken as a whole. These rules are broadly grouped into three categories : (*i*) rules governing compensation in all its forms; (*ii*) the duties and performance expected from workers, including rules of discipline for failure to achieve these standards; and (*iii*) rules defining the rights and duties of workers. The rules change in response to change in the contexts and relative status of the actors.

The actors who set the rules may be workers and their unions representing one category; employers, managers and their associations constituting a second category; and government in the third category consisting of civil servants concerned with the administration of labour matters.

The Oxford Approach

According to this approach, the industrial relations system is a study of institutions of job regulations and the stress is on the substantive and procedural rules as in Dunlop's model. Flanders, the exponent of this approach, considers every business enterprise as a social system of production and distribution, which has a structured pattern of external—the former being an internal part of the industrial relations system such as code of work rules, wage structure, internal procedure of joint consultation, and grievance procedure. He views trade unions as an external organization and excludes collective agreements from the sphere of internal regulation. According to him, collective bargaining is central to the industrial relations system.

The "Oxford Approach" can be expressed in the form of an equation :

$$r = f\,(b) \text{ or } r = f\,(c)$$

where, r = the rules governing industrial relations

b = collective bargaining

c = conflict resolved through collective bargaining.

The "Oxford Approach" can be criticized on the ground that it is too narrow to provide a comprehensive framework for analyzing industrial relations problems. It overemphasis's the significance of the political process of collective bargaining and gives insufficient weight to the role of the deeper influences in the determination of rules. Institutional and power factors are viewed as of paramount importance, while variables such as technology, market, status of the parties, and ideology, are not given any prominence. This narrowness of approach constitutes a severe limitation.

The Industrial Sociology Approach

G. Margerison, an industrial sociologist, holds the view that the core of industrial relations is the nature and development of the conflict itself. Margerison argued that conflict is the basic concept that should form the basis of the study of industrial relations. The author criticised the prevalent approach to industrial relations, which was more concerned with studying the resolution of industrial conflict than its generation; with the consequences of industrial disputes than on their causes.

According to this school of thought, there are two major conceptual levels of industrial relations. One is the intra-plant level where situational factors, such as job content, work task and technology, and interaction factors produce three types of conflict – distributive, structural, and human relations. These conflicts are being resolved through collective bargaining, structural analysis of the socio-technical systems and man-management analysis respectively. The second level is outside the firm and, in the main, concerns with the conflict not resolved at the intra-organizational level. However, this approach rejects the special emphasis given to rule determination by the "systems and Oxford models". In its place, it suggests a method of inquiry, which attempts to develop sociological models of conflicts.

The Action Theory Approach

Like the systems model, the action theory approach takes the collective regulation of industrial labour as its focal point. The actors operate within a framework, which can at best be described as a coalition relationship. The actors, it is claimed, agree in principle to cooperate in the resolution of the conflict, their cooperation taking the form of bargaining. Thus, the action theory analysis of industrial relations focuses primarily on bargaining as a mechanism for the resolution of conflicts. Whereas the systems model of industrial relations constitutes a more or less comprehensive approach, it is hardly possible to speak of one uniform action theory concept.

The Marxist Approach

The class conflict analysis of industrial relations derives its impetus from Marxist social thinking and interpretation. Marxism is essentially a method of social enquiry into the power relationships of society and a way of interpreting social reality. The application of Marxian theory as it relates to industrial relations derives indirectly from later Marxist scholars rather than directly from the works of Marx himself.

Industrial relations, according to Marxists, are in the first instance, market-relations. To Marxists, industrial relations are essentially politicized and part of the class struggle. For Marxists industrial and employee relations can only be understood as part of a broader analysis of capitalist society in particular the social relations of production and the dynamics of capital accumulation. As Marx himself put it, "the mode of production in material life determines the general character of the social, political and spiritual process of life."

The Marxist approach is primarily oriented towards the historical development of the power relationship between capital and labour. It is also characterized by the struggle of these classes to consolidate and strengthen their respective positions with a view to exerting greater influence on each other. In this approach, industrial relations is equated with a power-struggle. The price payable for labour is determined by a confrontation between conflicting interests. The capitalist ownership of the enterprise endeavours to purchase labour at the lowest possible price in order to maximize their profits. The lower the price paid by the owner of the means of production for the labour he employs, the greater is his profit. The Marxist analysis of industrial relations, however, is not a comprehensive approach as it only takes into account the relations between capital and labour. It is rather, a general theory of society and of social change, which has implications for the analysis of industrial relations within what Marxists would describe as capitalist societies.

The Pluralist Approach

Pluralism is a major theory in labour-management relations, which has many powerful advocates. The focus is on the resolution of conflict rather than its generation, or, in the words of the pluralist, on 'the institutions of job regulation.' Kerr is one of the important exponents of pluralism. According to him, the social environment is an important factor in industrial conflicts. The isolated masses of workers are more strike-prone as compared to dispersed groups. When industrial jobs become more pleasant and employees' get more integrated into the wider society, strikes will become less frequent. Ross and Hartman's cross national comparison of strikes postulates the declining incidents of strikes as societies industrialize and develop appropriate institutional framework. They claim that there has been a decline in strike activity all over the world in spite of an increase in union membership. The theories on pluralism were evolved in the mid-sixties and early seventies when England witnessed a dramatic resurgence of industrial conflicts. However, the recent theories of pluralism emanate from British scholars, and in particular from Flanders and Fox. According to Flanders, conflict is inherent in the industrial system. He highlighted the need for a formal system of collective bargaining as a method of conflict resolution.

Fox distinguishes between two distinct aspects of relationship between workers and management. The first is the market relationship, which concerns with the terms and conditions on which labour is hired. This relationship is essentially economic in character and based on contracts executed between the parties. The second aspect relates to the management's dealing with labour, the nature of their interaction, negotiations between the union and management, distribution of power in the organization, and participation of the union in joint decision-making. The major critics of the pluralist approach are the Marxists according to whom exploitation and slavery will continue unabated in the institutional structure of pluralism. The only difference is that in such a social structure, the worker will be deemed to be a better-paid wage slave.

Weber's Social Action Approach

The social action approach of Weber has laid considerable importance to the question of control in the context of increasing rationalization and bureaucratization. Closely related to Weber's concern related to control in organizations was his concern with "power of control and dispersal". Thus a trade union in the Weber's scheme of things has both economic purposes as well as the goal of involvement in political and power struggles. Some of the major orientations in the Weberian approach have been to analyze the impact of techno-economic and politico-organizational changes on trade union structure and processes, to analyze the subjective interpretation of workers' approaches to trade unionism and finally to analyse the power of various components of the industrial relations environment – government, employers, trade unions and political parties. Thus the Weberian approach gives the theoretical and operational importance to "control" as well as to the power struggle to control work organizations – a power struggle in which all the actors in the industrial relations drama are caught up.

The Human Relations Approach

In the words of Keith Davies, human relations are "the integration of people into a work situation that motivates them to work together productively, cooperatively and with economic, psychological and social satisfactions." According to him, the goals of human relations are : (*a*) to get people to produce, (*b*) to cooperate through mutuality of interest, and (*c*) to gain satisfaction from their relationships. The human relations school founded by Elton Mayo and later propagated by Roethlisberger, Whitehead, W.F. Whyte, and Homans offers a coherent view of the nature of industrial conflict and harmony.

The human relations approach highlights certain policies and techniques to improve employee morale, efficiency and job satisfaction. It encourages the small work group to exercise considerable control over its environment and in the process helps to remove a major irritant in labour-management relations. But there was reaction against the excessive claims of this school of thought in the sixties. Some of its views were criticized by Marxists, pluralists, and others on the ground that it encouraged dependency and discouraged individual development, and ignored the importance of technology and culture in industry. Taking a balanced view, however, it must be admitted that the human relations school has thrown a lot of light on certain aspects such as communication, management development, acceptance of workplace as a social system, group dynamics, and participation in management.

The Gandhian Approach

Gandhiji can be called one of the greatest labour leaders of modern India. His approach to labour problems was completely new and refreshingly human. He held definite views regarding fixation and regulation of wages, organization and functions of trade unions, necessity and desirability of collective bargaining, use and abuse of strikes, labour indiscipline, workers participation in management, conditions of workand living, and duties of workers. The Ahmedabad Textile Labour Association, a unique and successful experiment in Gandhian trade unionism, implemented many of his ideas.

Gandhiji had immense faith in the goodness of man and he believed that many of the evils of the modern world have been brought about by wrong systems and not by wrong individuals. He insisted on recognizing each individual worker as a human being. He believed in non-violent communism, going so far as to say that "if communism comes without any violence, it would be welcome."

Gandhiji laid down certain conditions for a successful strike. These are : (*a*) the cause of the strike must be just and there should be no strike without a grievance; (*b*) there should be no violence; and (*c*) non-strikers or "blacklegs" should never be molested.

He was not against strikes but pleaded that they should be the last weapon in the armoury of industrial workers and hence should not be resorted to unless all peaceful and constitutional methods of negotiations, conciliation and arbitration are exhausted.

His concept of trusteeship is a significant contribution in the sphere of industrial relations. According to him, employers should not regard themselves as sole owners of mills and factories of which they may be the legal owners. They should regard themselves only as trustees, or co-owners. He also appealed to the workers to behave as trustees, not to regard the mill and machinery as belonging to the exploiting agents but to regard them as their own, protect them and put to the best use they can. In short, the theory of trusteeship is based on the view that all forms of property and human accomplishments are gifts of nature and as such, they belong not to any one individual but to society. Thus, the trusteeship system is totally different from other contemporary labour relations systems. It aimed at achieving economic equality and the material advancement of the "have-nots" in a capitalist society by non-violent means.

Gandhiji realized that relations between labour and management can either be a powerful stimulus to economic and social progress or an important factor in economic and social stagnation. According to him, industrial peace was an essential condition not only for the growth and development of the industry itself, but also in a great measure, for the improvement in the conditions of work and wages. At the same time, he not only endorsed the workers' right to adopt the method of collective bargaining but also actively supported it. He advocated voluntary arbitration and mutual settlement of disputes. He also pleaded for perfect understanding between capital and labour, mutual respect, recognition of equality, and strong labour organization as the essential factors for happy and constructive industrial relations. For him, means and ends are equally important.

Human Resource Management Approach

The term, human resource management (HRM) has become increasingly used in the literature of personnel/industrial relations. The term has been applied to a diverse range of management strategies and, indeed, sometimes used simply as a more modern, and therefore more acceptable, term for personnel or industrial relations management. Some of the components of HRM are : (*i*) human resource organisation; (*ii*) human resource planning; (*iii*) human resource systems; (*iv*) human resource development; (*v*) human resource relationships; (*vi*) human resource utilisation; (*vii*) human resource accounting; and (*viii*) human resource audit. This approach emphasises individualism and the direct relationship between management and its employees. Quite clearly, therefore, it questions the collective regulation basis of traditional industrial relations.

MODELS/THEORIES

The subject of industrial relations has undergone several changes because of vital contributions made by a number of disciplines. In developing theoretical models of industrial relations, it becomes necessary to appreciate the contributions made by various social scientists. Such models can be used for analyzing concrete situations and to build a systematic and comprehensive theory of industrial relations. The different perspectives and theories enable us to understand industrial relations institutions, structures, processes and behaviour of individuals. The practitioners of industrial relations consider theory as the opposite of practice. Nevertheless, any systematic practice implies some theory.

At its inception, the labour market was dominated by the classical economics view which espoused free and unregulated labour markets. This laissez-faire capitalism led to social injustices and inequities since labour did not have the power to bargain with employers on terms which even approached a degree of equality in bargaining strength. Industrial relations, therefore, initially came to espouse a degree of labour market regulation to correct this unequal bargaining power. Consequently industrial relations developed in the context of the theory that problems in labour relations emanate largely from market imperfections which operate against the interests of labour and cause imbalances in the power relationships of employers and employees. These imperfections were external to the enterprise. Additionally, the dominant position of the employer in what was formerly called the "master and servant" relationship prevented labour from enjoying rights. These causes for labour problems—external and internal to the enterprise - needed to be addressed through a range of initiatives, both by the State through protective labour laws, conciliation and dispute settlement machinery, by voluntary action on the part of employees to protect themselves and further their interests through trade unionism (but backed by State interventions to guarantee this right in the form of freedom of association), and by redressing the balance of power (through collective bargaining).

The focus on relations external to the enterprise—especially through national and industry level collective bargaining - was initially welcomed even by employers in several industrialized countries because it reduced competitive advantage based on labour costs. Besides, collective bargaining in particular transferred one of the most conflictual aspects of the employment relationship—wages—out of the workplace, and made it the responsibility of the respective representatives of employers and employees. Unions naturally welcomed it as it gave them an influential base outside the workplace. In developing countries, this concept sometimes had disastrous consequences because it facilitated the politicization of unions.

However, regulation of the external labour market did not necessarily address all the causes of labour problems. A more pluralistic view recognized that labour problems or issues do not relate only to conflict between employers and employees. They include many other forms of problems such as low productivity, absenteeism, high labour turnover, lack of job security, unsatisfactory or unsafe working conditions, non recognition of performance in standardized wage systems, and lack of motivation. Many of these problems cannot be addressed through measures directed purely at the external labour market, and require measures to be taken within the enterprise. Therefore another view, emanating from human resource management and increasingly important since the 1980s, is that labour problems arise not so much from factors external to the enterprise, as from unsatisfactory management of human resources within the enterprise. Corrective action should include the installation of human resource management policies and practices embodied in concepts such as recruitment and selection, leadership and motivation, employee development and retention, etc. The objective is to ensure a convergence of organizational and individual goals, and to balance individual and organizational needs. With the pressures on enterprises to adapt and change, it is not surprising that employers are pushing for greater concentration on issues at the enterprise level. In the final analysis the quality of an industrial relations system has to be judged by how it works in practice—and that means at the workplace level. This relative neglect provided the 'space' for the rise of human resource management.

In more recent times industrial relations has been influenced by other social sciences such as organizational psychology and behaviour. While labour problems are the result of imperfections in the employment relationship, industrial relations should be seen as the theories and methods which have been developed over time to address and correct these problems, in both the external and internal labour markets.

One of the major objectives of theorising industrial relations is to help the practitioners to understand what is taking place and causes for the same. Industrial relations theory might be useful to practitioners if it could help them in three respects :

- To understand the present industrial relations situation;
- Second, to forecast trends and to predict what will happen under specific given conditions; and
- Third, to help the practitioners to bring about certain desired changes and to avoid certain other changes in the present or in the future state of industrial relations.

One of the most difficult attempts in industrial relations is to build up a theory and to generalize on its activity, which is highly dynamic. A host of factors, both internal and external, and conflict generating as well as conflict resolving, influence the shape of industrial relations activity. The industrial relations system in an organization works in the context of pressures, tensions and conflicts, and is mainly related to power politics, economic, cultural and other differences. An inter-mix of such dynamic factors, and key institutional variables, is necessary in theorizing industrial relations.

Basically, there are two main stands in theorizing industrial relations. One group (externalists) lays emphasis on external factors like state of technology, methods of production, supply and demand in the product market and in the labour market, legal, political relationships, and so on. The environmental theorists have been primarily economists and to a smaller extent, lawyers, political scientists, and sociologists. They lay emphasis on the nexus between broad environmental changes and employer/employee relations. The in-plant theories of internalists have their origin in the "human relations school" propounded by Elton Mayo and others. These theorists stress on employee motivation, attitude and morale, styles of supervision, and forms of management leadership.

A.W.J. Craig presented the input-output model of industrial relations system in the late 1960s. In his model, the actors and the context are similar to those of Dunlop's model. The main components of Craig's model are :

(*a*) the inputs or the goals, and the values and power of the actors;

(*b*) mechanism for the conversion of inputs into outputs;

(*c*) the outputs of the system are the financial, psychological and social rewards for the workers. The output is in the form of the rules, which govern matters such as pay, working conditions, and hours of work.

The prominent contribution to the industrial relations literature is the 'systems' approach developed by John T. Dunlop who views industrial relations system as a sub-system of society.

Dunlop's Theory

One of the significant theories of industrial labor relations was put forth by John Dunlop in the 1950s. According to Dunlop industrial relations system consists of three agents—management organizations, workers and formal/informal ways they are organized and government agencies. These actors and their organizations are located within an environment—defined in terms of technology, labor and product markets, and the distribution of power in wider society as it impacts upon individuals and workplace. Within this environment, actors interact with each other, negotiate and use economic/political power in process of determining rules that constitute the output of the industrial relations system. He proposed that three parties—employers, labor unions, and government—are the key actors in a modern industrial relations system. He also argued that none of these institutions could act in an autonomous or independent fashion. Instead they were shaped, at least to some extent, by their market, technological and political contexts. Thus, it can be said that industrial relations is a social sub system subject to three environmental constraints—the markets, distribution of power in society and technology.

Dunlop's model identifies three key factors to be considered in conducting an analysis of the management-labor relationship :

- Environmental or external economic, technological, political, legal and social forces that impact employment relationships.
- Characteristics and interaction of the key actors in the employment relationship : labor, management, and government.
- Rules that are derived from these interactions that govern the employment relationship.

Dunlop emphasizes the core idea of systems by saying that the arrangements in the field of industrial relations may be regarded as a system in the sense that each of them more or less intimately affects each of the others so that they constitute a group of arrangements for dealing with certain matters and are collectively responsible for certain results".

In effect-Industrial relations is the system which produces the rules of the workplace. Such rules are the product of interaction between three key "actors"—workers/unions, employers and associated organizations and government.

The Dunlop's model gives great significance to external or environmental forces. In other words, management, labor, and the government possess a shared ideology that defines their roles within the relationship and provides stability to the system.

Role of Governments in Industrial Relations

During the past decades labour relations was viewed by governments as a means of preventing or minimizing conflict. In South and South East Asia this objective was achieved through dispute prevention and settlement mechanisms external to the enterprise (*e.g.*, conciliation, arbitration and labour courts). In India the objective was also achieved through restrictions or prohibitions on the freedom of action of employers in matters such as termination of employment, closures and even transfers of employees. On the other hand, several South East Asian countries resorted to measures to restrict trade union action and to control unions, as well as to avoid union multiplicity. While in South Asia the focus of industrial relations was on equity from the point of view of workers and unions, in South East Asia the emphasis was on economic efficiency and less on worker protection laws. Moreover, hierarchical management systems and respect for authority, which have mirrored the external social system, have been inconsistent with consultation, two-way communication, and even with the concept of negotiating the employment relationship. Japan, however, was an exception where, since the 1960s, workplace relations and flexibility facilitated by enterprise unionism dominated industrial relations in the larger enterprises. Australia and New Zealand continued to focus on centralized industrial relations, though the emphasis has radically changed in New Zealand during this decade, and is changing in Australia.

Major changes are taking place in Asia. Employers as well as some governments are viewing labour relations from a more strategic perspective *i.e.*, how labour relations can contribute to and promote workplace cooperation, flexibility, productivity and competitiveness. It is increasingly appreciated that how people are managed impact on an enterprise's productivity and quality of goods and services, labour costs, quality of the workforce and its motivation, and on the prevention of disputes as well as on aligning employee aspirations with enterprise objectives.

In India the directive principles of state policy are among the core guiding factors influencing the labour policy, supported by the various plan documents. Articles 39, 41, 42, 43 and 43 A pertain to labour industrial relations are governed.

International Factors

The establishment of a sound or harmonious industrial relations system is a central theme for governments, employers, workers and their representatives, in their endeavour to achieve economic and social development. Several changes on the international scene presently exert a major influence on how industrial relations need to be viewed.

- The internationalization of business, intense competition and rapid changes in technology, products and markets has increased the need for economies and enterprises to remain or become competitive. These trends have in turn necessitated a greater reliance than before on workers' skills, productivity and cooperation in achieving competitiveness.
- The new information technology, the limits of which are not known in terms of its potential to effect change, is exerting a tremendous impact on the structure of organizations, the nature of work and the way it is organized, and even on the location where work is performed. In societies of the future information and knowledge will be—as in fact they already are—crucial to competitiveness. Technology is already facilitating changes in organizational structures so as to create flatter organizations. This has resulted in less management by command and supervision, in more emphasis on cooperation, information-sharing and communication and in a more participative approach to managing people.
- Modern technology now makes it possible for aspects of work to be performed outside the enterprise, for example from overseas, and this trend is being given a further push by the influx of more females into employment and their preference in some cases, for part-time work.
- Many countries are undergoing a process of industrial restructuring which, in some cases, include privatization of public sector undertakings and technology upgrading. This process has resulted in several social consequences such as redundancy, all of

which have sometimes strained the relationships between employers and workers (and unions) and between the latter and the government.

- Another feature is the changes occurring in the workforces, to varying degrees, in both industrialized market economies and developing economies. Many countries have witnessed the emergence of workforces with higher levels of education and skills which need to be managed in a manner different from the way in which employees, especially blue collar employees, have hitherto been managed. This factor will assume more critical proportions in the future as a result of the increasing importance of the service sector and the growth of knowledge-intensive industries. The skills of an employee are, therefore, an issue on which the interests of employers and employees converge, and the "development" of the employee is now of mutual advantage to both employers and employees. Consequently, there is a greater need than before for a cooperative and participative system of industrial relations.
- The many emerging work arrangements do not fit into the traditional employment relationships. Increasing numbers of enterprises are differentiating between the core and peripheral workforce, which consists of those whose work, can be performed by persons outside the enterprise who specialize in it. The tendency is to contract and sub-contract with outsiders to perform their work. Even manufacturing companies are becoming essentially assembly firms, and many service organizations now act as brokers, "connecting the customer with a supplier with some intervening advice."
- Another category of employees consists of the increasing number of temporary and part-time employees in the rapidly expanding service industries, some of which experience peak periods (hotels, airlines, shops) requiring a flexible labour force. Thus, instead of one workforce, we are moving towards these various groups, each with different contractual arrangements and requiring to be managed differently. The indications are that at the beginning of the next century less than half the workforce in industrialized countries will be in full-time employment as we know it. These trends will not be confined to the highly industrialized countries, but will appear in the fast growing economies of Asia as costs rise, competitiveness increases, and more women participate in economic activity.
- The role of unions is changing, during the cold war, political considerations sometimes dominated or influenced union activities, attitudes and their role, especially in some of the developing countries. Unions are now gradually concentrating more on their traditional role in industrial relations, which is to improve the working conditions of their members and to protect their interests through negotiation.
- As a result of intense competition for goods and services and the recognition of the enterprise as an important engine of growth to an extent unknown in the past, the centre of gravity of industrial relations is now more than ever before the workplace, and managing human resources is now receiving the attention it should have been given much earlier.

INDUSTRIAL RELATIONS SYSTEM AT NATIONAL AND INDUSTRY LEVEL

Labour-management relations policy formulation is one of the significant tasks at the national level, and its successful formulation and implementation can influence the labour relations climate at the industry and enterprise levels. Such policy formulation, however, can be formulated not only at the national level through a tripartite process, but also at the industry level on a bipartite basis as between employers' and workers' organizations. Whether bipartite policy formulation becomes a part of national policy depends largely on the respective strengths of employers' and workers' organizations. In some of the industrialized market economies there is a greater likelihood than in developing countries of bipartite policy formulations being reflected in national policies due to the strength of the employers' and workers' organizations. In Sweden, for instance, in the past, the agreements between the union and the employers' organization tended to be translated into national policy instruments. The policies and methods of training of workers, for example, reflected what the two social partners had identified as appropriate for the industry. Or again, in Belgium the State recognizes the two social partners as the main formulators of social policy through collective bargaining; even the social security system is managed by the two social partners. The pervasive influence of bipartite arrangements is felt only where there is a 'balance of power' between the social partners. There is less likelihood of bi-partism impacting on national policy formulation in developing countries due to strong central governments in many cases, and their assumption of the role of identifying the direction of economic and social policies. The relative weakness of employers' and workers' organizations or of one of them, or the inability of such organizations to agree on the fundamentals of what the labour relations policy should be, often prevents bi-partism from influencing national policy formulation.

Freedom of Association

The fundamental premise of a sound industrial relations system is the recognition and existence of the freedom of association accorded to both employers and workers. This freedom should include recognition of organizations of workers and employers as autonomous, independent bodies, subject neither to their domination by each other or by the government. Observance by states of the basic principles of the ILO Convention relating to Freedom of Association and Protection of the Right to Organize No. 87 (1948) is often regarded as the yardstick by which a country's recognition of this freedom is measured.

In essence, the Convention postulates that workers and employers, without distinction whatsoever, have the right to establish and to join organizations of their own choosing with a view to defending their respective interests, subject to national legislation which determines the extent to which the guarantees in the Convention will apply to the armed forces and the police. Such organizations have the right to draw up their own constitutions and rules, to elect their representatives in full freedom, to organize their administration and activities and to formulate their programmes. Public authorities are required to refrain from any interference which would restrict this right or impede the lawful exercise of this right. The organizations are not liable to be dissolved or suspended by administrative authority. Organizations have the right to establish and to join federations and confederations which are entitled to the same rights and guarantees, and to affiliate with international organizations. The acquisition of legal personality by these organizations shall not be subject to restrictive conditions. In exercising the rights provided for in the Convention, employers and workers and their respective organizations are required to respect the law of the land, which should not impair the guarantees in the Convention both in respect of its content and its application.

Tripartism and Labour Policy Formulation

Tripartism is the process through which the foundation for a sound industrial relations system can be laid at the national level. Ideally, tripartism is the process whereby the government, the most representative workers' and employers' organizations as independent and equal partners, consult with each other on labour market and related issues which are within their spheres of competence, and jointly formulate and implement national policies on such issues. However, this ideal situation is seldom reflected in practice, especially in developing countries or in societies with fairly authoritarian governments which believe that the direction of economic and social development is largely their responsibility. A more realistic model where developing countries are concerned is one in which a government consults the most representative employers' and workers' organizations on labour market and related issues which are within their spheres of competence, and takes account of their views in national policy formulation and its implementation.

There are many examples of tripartite mechanisms at the national level, as well as informal applications of tripartism. In many countries there are minimum wage fixing bodies which reflect the participation of all three parties, often leading to a consensus on minimum wages, and sometimes on other minimum terms of employment. In some countries (as in Australia in recent years), agreements are reached at the national level among the three partners after a process of bargaining on important social policy issues. The principles agreed upon in the 1950s in Japan as a forerunner to its productivity movement did much towards assisting that country's productivity growth. In Japan, the Industry and Labour Conference has been a major form of cooperation at the national level, and consultative mechanisms (both tripartite and bipartite) exist at the industry level. In Singapore the National Productivity Board is a tripartite body, and is credited with much of the success in productivity improvement there. Tripartite participation in Singapore's National Wage Council has avoided a potential conflict on wages. The introduction of a flexible wage system in Singapore was made possible by a tripartite approach towards reaching a consensus on the issue in the late 1980s.

At the national level the mechanisms and procedures could be formal and institutionalized, or else informal and ad hoc. Where the labour administration system consults, on an ad hoc basis, workers' and employers' organizations on subjects falling within their purview, it represents a method of policy formulation on labour management relations. Sometimes these consultations may take place between the two social partners and other public authorities. For instance, a finance ministry may consult the social partners on an issue relating to wage policy.

National level policy formulation can take place through institutions which provide for periodic tripartite discussion and consultation. There are also examples of institutions with functions limited to a particular subject matter such as training, social security, minimum wages (for instance minimum wage fixing bodies) and safety and health. Such specialized bodies may even cover collective bargaining, as in the case of the Singapore National Wage Council created in 1972, which was empowered to issue annual guidelines to coordinate collective bargaining with overall economic policy so as to ensure that wages remain consistent with economic development.

The Role of the Law

Industrial relations systems are founded on a framework of labour law which exerts an influence on the nature of the industrial relations system. However, recourse to the law and its potential to influence the resulting industrial relations system may sometimes be over-emphasized. It is useful, therefore, to examine, from three points of view, the role of the law in influencing an industrial relations system—what its objectives should be and the areas it should cover, as well as what the law cannot achieve.

In any working situation people need to cooperate with each other if there is to be maximum gain to themselves, to management and to society as a whole. Cooperation, however, is not easily obtained as people working together have conflicting interests. Employees are primarily concerned with the security of their jobs and what they can earn, and the employer with what he can produce as cheaply as possible to obtain the maximum profit. When these conflicting interests have taken definite form and shape, the State has often stepped into protect some of these interests through legal control. Labour law has amply demonstrated the sociological theory that

"law is a social institution which seeks to balance conflicting interests and to satisfy as many claims as possible with the minimum of friction. Since the law must necessarily determine those interests which most urgently require protection over and above other interests, those of labour, where they lack self-reliance, have invariably formed a significant class of interests which the law protects. Hence, especially in some developing countries, the legal rules of an industrial relations system have been judged to some extent by the degree to which they further this end."

The three main functions of the law in an industrial relations system have been described as auxiliary, regulatory and restrictive.

The first function is the support it gives to the autonomous system of collective bargaining, its operation and observance of agreements. One major objective of labour law is to create the legal framework which is necessary for employers, workers and their organizations to function effectively and as autonomous groups in the industrial relations system. Hence the law should protect the freedom of association so that the two parties are accorded the protections and guarantees found in the International Labour Organization Convention on the Freedom of Association and Protection of the Right to Organize No. 87 (1948). Since one of the major purposes of such association is to enable workers and employers to protect and further their interests, the law should also provide the legal framework needed to promote collective bargaining. In this connection the International Labour Organization Convention on the Right to Organize and Collective Bargaining No. 98 (1949) would provide the necessary basis for such legislation.

The second function is one of providing a set of rules governing the terms and conditions of employment and supplementing those created by the parties themselves. The greater the coverage by collective bargaining, the less will be the regulatory function of the law. A second important function of labour law is to prescribe the minimum terms and conditions of employment which should be observed by employers in the course of conducting business. Therefore, the legal system often contains provisions stipulating the minimum conditions which must be observed in areas such as compensation for industrial accidents, social security, safety and health in enterprises, the minimum age of employment. Some countries may consider it appropriate to prescribe minimum wages. The basic rules to be followed in terminating employment may be another area of the employment relationship which would need to be covered by minimum standards. Methods for settling disputes, both individual and collective, through institutions such as labour courts, arbitration and conciliation systems, have not been an uncommon feature of State intervention through the law.

The third function prescribes what is permitted or forbidden in industrial conflict with a view to protecting the parties from each other, and the public from both of them. A third and more general role for the law in industrial relations is as an instrument of social change. The law does not always merely or solely reflect contemporary thinking in society and does not necessarily lag behind social and other values. It sometimes anticipates them and can, on occasion, be employed to fashion new ideas and to effect changes in behaviour. It is not always possible to leave crucial and complex social issues to be solved through purely voluntary action such as collective bargaining. Sometimes, especially in developing countries, the absence of strong and independent trade unions reduces the effectiveness and role of voluntary action, and necessitates greater regulation through legal prescription. In such situations desirable measures such as remedies for unfair dismissal, protection against acts of anti-union discrimination, the minimum conditions a contract of employment should conform to, safety requirements, etc., are prescribed by the law. But intervention on this ground should not lead to the introduction of rigidities in the labour market through overregulation.

Legal prescription should be viewed as merely laying down minimum terms and defining the permissible boundaries of action within which the two parties (employers and workers) must operate. Over regulation through law could have adverse consequences on building a sound industrial relations system through voluntary action, and on the competitiveness of enterprises. This has been perceived to be so in countries such as India and Sri Lanka, where employers have for some time canvassed for greater flexibility and less legislative control over industrial relations. A plethora of laws makes rapid adaptation to change difficult, and avoidance of laws can be a preoccupation of employers in such circumstances. Over regulation is sometimes based on the misconception that sound industrial relations can be achieved through the law. The creation of harmonious industrial relations needs to be achieved by other, non-legal means; the law cannot 'compel' parties to establish good relations. By way of analogy, in a different field of human relations, the law can prescribe the rules to be followed if people wish to marry. But the law cannot create a happy relationship or marriage. Similarly, harmonious industrial relations can be achieved not primarily through the law but through better human relations and human oriented practices at the enterprise level. Some countries, such as those in South Asia, which have a tradition of a plethora of labour laws, have tended to overlook the fact that if the energy expended by the State in enacting and enforcing a mass of labour laws had been spent in finding ways and means of encouraging mechanisms and systems geared to achieving sound labour relations, better results may have been achieved. In such countries parties tend to look to the law for the solution of what are essentially human relations problems, and creativity and innovation in industrial relations are consequently stifled. As a result, attention is focused more on dispute settlement rather than on dispute prevention, when emphasis on the latter is one way of building a sound industrial relations system.

Statute law is one of the specific means used by the State to condition industrial relations outcomes, and represents the most direct means of State intervention. Statutory regulation of minimum terms and conditions such as minimum wages, working conditions, safety and health, social security and protection become terms and conditions in contracts of employment which must conform to them; they cannot be 'bargained' away. Other statutory provisions may be of a more facilitating nature such as ones which establish the conditions and the environment for collective bargaining (*e.g.*, rights of association, unfair labour practices, and conciliation services); they are no less fundamental and important. Another–and more indirect–method through which the State influences industrial relations is the system of labour courts, tribunals or arbitration, which are a common feature in many countries. Through these institutions the State seeks to dispense equity in the employment relationship, and they may also protect collective interests as in the case of trade union rights. Such institutions have been considered necessary where the normal system of courts does not have the power or jurisdiction to apply equitable principles and to take into account the realities of the employment relationship, which results in a rather 'legalistic' view of labour relations. The pronouncements of these courts often constitute important limits to the freedom of action of the actors in industrial relations. Still another method of State intervention is through its 'administrative' role, for example, as conciliator or mediator.

Industrial Relations Policy

Prior to 1991, the industrial relations system in India sought to control conflicts and disputes through excessive labor legislations. These labor laws were protective in nature and covered a wide range of aspects of workplace industrial relations like laws on health and safety of labors, layoffs and retrenchment policies, industrial disputes and the like. The basic purpose of these laws was to protect labors. However, these protectionist policies created an atmosphere that led to increased inefficiency in firms, over employment and inability to introduce efficacy. With the coming of globalization, the 40 year old policy of protectionism proved inadequate for Indian industry to remain competitive as the lack of flexibility posed a serious threat to manufacturers because they had to compete in the international market.

With the advent of liberalization in1992, the industrial relations policy began to change. Now, the policy was tilted towards employers. Employers opted for workforce reduction, introduced policies of voluntary retirement schemes and flexibility in workplace also increased. Thus, globalization brought major changes in industrial relations policy in India. The changes can be summarized as follows :

- Collective bargaining in India has mostly been decentralized, but now in sectors where it was not so, are also facing pressures to follow decentralization.
- Some industries are cutting employment to a significant extent to cope with the domestic and foreign competition *e.g.,* pharmaceuticals. On the other hand, in other industries where the demand for employment is increasing are experiencing employment growths.
- In the expansionary economy there is a clear shortage of managers and skilled labor.
- The number of local and enterprise level unions has increased and there is a significant reduction in the influence of the unions.
- Under pressure some unions and federations are putting up a united front *e.g.,* banking.
- Another trend is that the employers have started to push for internal unions *i.e.,* no outside affiliation.
- HR policies and forms of work are emerging that include, especially in multi-national companies, multi-skills, variable compensation, job rotation etc. These new policies are difficult to implement in place of old practices as the institutional set up still needs to be changed.
- HRM is seen as a key component of business strategy.
- Training and skill development is also receiving attention in a number of industries, especially banking and information technology.

INDUSTRIAL DISPUTES

Causes of Industrial Disputes

The causes of industrial disputes can be broadly classified into two categories : economic and non-economic causes. The economic causes will include issues relating to compensation like wages, bonus, allowances, and conditions for work, working hours, leave and holidays without pay, unjust layoffs and retrenchments. The non economic factors will include victimization of workers, ill treatment by staff members, sympathetic strikes, political factors, indiscipline etc.

- **Wages and Allowances.** Since the cost of living index is increasing, workers generally bargain for higher wages to meet the rising cost of living index and to increase their standards of living. In 2002, 21.4% of disputes were caused by demand of higher wages and allowances. This percentage was 20.4% during 2003 and during 2004 increased up to 26.2%. In 2005, wages and allowances accounted for 21.8% of disputes.
- **Personnel and Retrenchment.** The personnel and retrenchment have also been an important factor which accounted for disputes. During the year 2002, disputes caused by personnel were 14.1% while those caused by retrenchment and layoffs were 2.2% and 0.4% respectively. In 2003, a similar trend could be seen, wherein 11.2% of the disputes were caused by personnel, while 2.4% and 0.6% of disputes were caused by retrenchment and layoffs. In year 2005, only 9.6% of the disputes were caused by personnel, and only 0.4% were caused by retrenchment.
- **Indiscipline and Violence.** From the given table, it is evident that the number of disputes caused by indiscipline has shown an increasing trend. In 2002, 29.9% of disputes were caused because of indiscipline, which rose up to 36.9% in 2003. Similarly in 2004 and 2005, 40.4% and 41.6% of disputes were caused due to indiscipline respectively. During the year 2003, indiscipline accounted for the highest percentage (36.9%) of the total time-loss of all disputes, followed by cause-groups wage and allowance and personnel with 20.4% and11.2% respectively. A similar trend was observed in 2004 where indiscipline accounted for 40.4% of disputes.
- **Bonus.** Bonus has always been an important factor in industrial disputes. 6.7% of the disputes were because of bonus in 2002 and 2003 as compared to 3.5% and 3.6% in 2004 and 2005 respectively.
- **Leave and Working Hours.** Leaves and working hours have not been so important causes of industrial disputes. During 2002, 0.5% of the disputes were because of leave and hours of work while this percentage increased to 1% in 2003. During 2004, only 0.4% of the disputes were because of leaves and working hours.
- **Miscellaneous.** The miscellaneous factors include
  - o Inter/Intra Union Rivalry
  - o Charter of Demands
  - o Work Load
  - o Standing orders/rules/service conditions/safety measures
  - o Non-implementation of agreements and awards etc.

Cause or Group	*Year*			
	2002	*2003*	*2004*	*2005*
Wages and Allowances	21.3	20.4	26.2	21.8
Personnel	14.1	11.2	13.2	9.6
Retrenchment	2.2	2.4	0.2	0.4
Lay off	0.4	0.6	-	0.2
Indiscipline	29.9	36.9	40.4	41.6
Violence	0.9	1	0.9	0.4
Leave and Hours of work/ shift	0.5	1	0.4	-
Bonus	6.7	6.7	3.5	3.6
Inter/Intra Union Rivalry	0.4	0.6	0.4	0.4
Non implementation of agreements and awards	3.1	1	1.1	0.9
Charter of Demands	10.5	8.8	5.7	7.1
Work load	0.5	0.4	0.7	1.1
Standing orders/rules/safety regulations	1.8	1	2.4	0.2

Fig. 18.3. *Percentage Distribution of Disputes by Causes.*

STRIKES

A strike is a very powerful weapon used by trade unions and other labor associations to get their demands accepted. It generally involves quitting of work by a group of workers for the purpose of bringing the pressure on their employer so that their demands get accepted. When workers collectively cease to work in a particular industry, they are said to be on strike.

According to Industrial Disputes Act 1947, a strike is "acessation of work by a body of persons employed in an industry acting in combination; or a concerted refusal of any number of persons who are or have been so employed to continue to work or to accept employment; or a refusal under a common understanding of any number of such persons to continue to work or to accept employment". This definition throws light on a few aspects of a strike. Firstly, a strike is a referred to as stoppage of work by a group of workers employed in a particular industry. Secondly, it also includes the refusal of a number of employees to continue work under their employer.

In a strike, a group of workers agree to stop working to protest against something they think is unfair where they work. Labors withhold their services in order to pressurize their employment or government to meet their demands. Demands made by strikers can range from asking for higher wages or better benefits to seeking changes in the workplace environment.

Strikes sometimes occur so that employers listen more carefully to the workers and address their problems.

Causes of Strikes

Strikes can occur because of the following reasons :

- Dissatisfaction with company policy
- Salary and incentive problems
- Increment not up to the mark
- Wrongful discharge or dismissal of workmen
- Withdrawal of any concession or privilege
- Hours of work and rest intervals
- Leaves with wages and holidays
- Bonus, profit sharing, Provident fund and gratuity
- Retrenchment of workmen and closure of establishment
- Dispute connected with minimum wages

Lockouts

A lockout is a work stoppage in which an employer prevents employees from working. It is declared by employers to put pressure on their workers. This is different from a strike, in which employees refuse to work. Thus, a lockout is employers' weapon while a strike is raised on part of employees. Acc to Industrial Disputes Act 1947, lockout means the temporary closing of a place of employment or the suspension of work or the refusal by an employer to continue to employ any number of persons employed by him.

A lockout may happen for several reasons. When only part of a trade union votes to strike, the purpose of a lockout is to put pressure on a union by reducing the number of members who are able to work. For example, if a group of the workers strike so that the work of the rest of the workers becomes impossible or less productive, the employer may declare a lockout until the workers end the strike. Another case in which an employer may impose a lockout is to avoid slowdowns or intermittent work-stoppages. Occupation of factories has been the traditional method of response to lockouts by the workers' movement.

Picketing

When workers are dissuaded from work by stationing certain men at the factory gates, such a step is known as picketing. If picketing does not involve any violence, it is perfectly legal. Pickets are workers who are on strike that stand at the entrance to their workplace. It is basically a method of drawing public attention towards the fact that there is a dispute between the management and employees.

The purpose of picketing is :

- to stop or persuade workers not to go to work
- to tell the public about the strike
- to persuade workers to take their union's side

Gherao

Gherao in Hindi means to surround. It denotes a collective action initiated by a group of workers under which members of the management are prohibited from leaving the industrial establishment premises by workers who block the exit gates by forming human barricades. The workers may gherao the members of the management by blocking their exits and forcing them to stay inside their cabins. The main object of gherao is to inflict physical and mental torture to the person being gheraoed and hence this weapon disturbs the industrial peace to a great extent.

Analysis of Strikes

In 1990, 1,825 strikes and lockouts were recorded. As a result, 24.1 million workdays were lost, from which 10.6 million were lost to strikes and 13.5 million to lockouts. More than 1.3 million workers were involved in these labor disputes. The number and seriousness of strikes and lockouts have varied from year to year. As can be seen from the below chart, there has been a steep decline in the number of strikes and lockouts. This continuous decline in strikes and lockouts indicates that the industrial relations in India are improving. There were 227 strikes in 2005, resulting in the loss of 10.81 million man-days, while the number of lockouts stood at 229 with a loss of 18.86 million man-days. In January-September 2006, there were only 154 strikes and 192 lockouts across the country, as compared to the statistics of 2005, which resulted in the time loss of 3.16 million man-days and 10.60 million man-days respectively.

Prohibition of Strikes and Lockouts

Employees are prohibited from striking according to the section 22 of Industrial Disputes Act 1947. Employees, who are working in a public utility service, cannot go on a strike without giving a notice of strike within the six weeks before striking. They can not go on strike either within fourteen days of providing the strike notice or before the expiry of the date of strike specified in any such notice. The same rule applies to the employers. Employers who are carrying on a public utility service can not lockout any of their employees without giving them a prior notice within six weeks before the lockout or within the fourteen days of giving such a notice. Moreover, the notice of strike or lockout is to be given in a prescribed manner showing the number of persons involved in the strike/lockout.

The notice of strike or lockout is not necessary when there is already a strike or lockout going on in the company. However, a notice should be issued on the day on which the lockout is declared just to intimate the appropriate authorities about the lockout. The employer is supposed to report the number of notices of strikes received by him to the appropriate Government or the authority prescribed by the government within the five days of receiving such notices.

Illegal Strikes and Lockouts

A strike or a lockout is illegal if it is declared in noncompliance with the section 22 (as defined above) of Industrial Disputes Act 1947, that is, if the notice period is not served or if the strike is held within the fourteen days of issuing the notice of strike. If a strike or lockout has already taken place and is being referred to a Board, the continuance of such a strike or lock out is not illegal provided it is in compliance with the provisions of act. Moreover, a lockout declared in consequence of an illegal strike or a strike declared in consequence of an illegal lockout shall not be deemed to be illegal.

Penalty for Illegal Strikes and Lockouts

A workman who is involved in an illegal strike can be penalized with imprisonment for a term extendable to a month or with a fine or fifty rupees or both. In similar way, an employer who initiates and continues a lockout is punishable with imprisonment extendable to a month or with a fine of one thousand rupees or both. According to Section 25 of Industrial Disputes Act 1947, no person should provide any sort of financial aid to any illegal strike or lockout. Any person who knowingly provides such a help in support of any illegal strike or lockout is punishable with imprisonment for a term which may extend to six months, or with fine which may extend to one thousand rupees, or with both.

Measures for Improving Industrial Relations

The following measures should be taken to achieve good industrial relations :

- **Strong and Stable Union.** A strong and stable union in each industrial enterprise is essential for good industrial relations. The employers can easily ignore a weak union on the plea that it hardly represents the workers. The agreement with such a union will hardly be honored by a large section of workforce. Therefore, there must be strong and stable unions in every enterprise to represent the majority of workers and negotiate with the management about the terms and conditions of service.
- **Mutual Trust.** Both management and labor should help in the development of an atmosphere of mutual cooperation, confidence and respect. Management should adopt a progressive outlook and should recognize the rights of workers. Similarly, labor unions should persuade their members to work for the common objectives of the organization. Both the management and the unions should have faith in collective bargaining and other peaceful methods of settling disputes.
- **Workers' Participation in Management.** The participation of workers in the management of the industrial unit should be encouraged by making effective use of works committees, joint consultation and other methods. This will improve communication between managers and workers, increase productivity and lead to greater effectiveness.
- **Mutual Accommodation.** The employers must recognize the right of collective bargaining of the trade unions. In any organization, there must be a great emphasis on mutual accommodation rather than conflict or uncompromising attitude. One must clearly understand that conflicting attitude does not lead to amicable labor relations; it may foster union militancy as the union reacts by engaging in pressure tactics. The approach must be of mutual "give and take rather than "take or leave." The management should be willing to co-operate rather than blackmail the workers.
- **Sincere Implementation of Agreements.** The management should sincerely implement the settlements reached with the trade unions. The agreements between the management and the unions should be enforced both in letter and spirit. If the agreements are not implemented then both the union and management stop trusting each other. An environment of uncertainty is created. To avoid this, efforts should be made at both ends to ensure the follow up of the agreements.
- **Sound Personnel Policies.** The following points should be noted regarding the personnel policies. The policies should be :
    - o Formulated in consultation with the workers and their representatives if they are to be implemented effectively.

- o Clearly stated so that there is no confusion in the mind of anybody.
- o Implementation of the policies should be uniform throughout the organization to ensure fair treatment to each worker.

- **Government's Role.** The Government should play an active role for promoting industrial peace. It should make law for the compulsory recognition of a representative union in each industrial unit. It should intervene to settle disputes if the management and the workers are unable to settle their disputes. This will restore industrial harmony.
- **Progressive Outlook.** There should be progressive outlook of the management of each industrial enterprise. It should be conscious of its obligations and responsibilities to the owners of the business, the employees, the consumers and the nation. The management must recognize the rights of workers to organize unions to protect their economic and social interests.

UNION LEGISLATIONS

Employment relations in India are governed by labour legislation passed as early as 1923 (Workmen, 1923). However, Industrial Disputes Act 1947 is the most important and most litigated of all labour legislation passed so far in India.

The Industrial Dispute Act 1947, is an Act to make provision for the investigation and settlement of industrial disputes and for certain other purposes. The law relating to industrial disputes in India is also known as the 'industrial law'. Industrial dispute are disputes, which are related to an industry.

Review Questions

1. Explain the concept of Industrial Relations. What is the significance of good industrial relations ?
2. What are the objectives of Industrial Relations? Discuss the weapons used by management and workers.
3. What are the causes of Industrial Disputes? Make suggestions for minimizing the effect of industrial dispute.
4. Discuss the Dunlop's approach to industrial relations.
5. One of the most difficult attempts in industrial relations is to build up a theory and to generalize on its activity that is highly dynamic. Discuss.
6. Analyse the strategic options that a management has for aligning Industrial Relations and Human Resource Practices.
7. Compare and contrast the domestic and international Industrial Relations.

PROJECT

1. Visit the industry located in your area and prepare a write up on emerging trends in Industrial Relations.
2. Study a manufacturing company and prepare a brief report on its Industrial Relations.

Case Study

VYSYA BANK

The Vysya Bank is a traditional bank with around 650 Branches across India. The majority of these branches are in the southern states of the country. The bank was established in 1930. The bank has gradually grown over a period of time. The Trade Union movement in the banks as old as the bank itself, the Trade Union has undergone change in its characteristics along with the trade union movement in the country. Traditionally the banking sector in the country has had very strong trade unions for officers as well as other staff.. Wage negotiations and pay settlements are based on collective bargaining at the industry and national level, with Indian Banks Association (IBA) on one side and the unions and associations of officers on the other. The national level agreement is a binding agreement. Any additional pay revision is made according to the bargaining capacity of the bank vis-à-vis the unions. The bank has four unions, two each for the officers and the other staff. The officers' association have been traditionally liberal with management while the other associations have been aggressive with the management and have protected the interests of the employees.

During the early 1980s, when the bank started computerization the officers and the workers opposed the move, they agreed to computerization only as a part of the guidelines of the national level agreement. However, the banking scene in India underwent change in early 1990s with large number of private sector banks coming into the field. The officers and the staff could sense the change and the competition they are likely to face. They agreed with the management that it was necessary to increase the levels of computerization in order to make bank competitive and provide better services to customers.

In early 1990 a MNC picked up a minority stake in the bank. By 2003 it was having significant holding in the bank. The new management brought new HR practices such as signing of MOU with the top management and also placed the various officers in these cadres on contract basis based on cost to company (CTC) approach. As far as the officers in lower cadre were concerned the bank adopted the cost to cost company in a phased manner and simultaneously rolled out a VRS policy for the workers in order to reduce their numbers over a period of time. The officers and employees association were initially non supportive but soon found that industry trends were similar, they had little choice.

Questions

1. *Analyze the case to determine the methods used to maintain health Industrial Relations?*
2. *Do you think the strategy adopted by the bank over a period of time was right?*
3. *Is the strategy followed by Bank after a substantial holding by an MNC correct? Suggest any changes you would like to recommend.*

❑❑❑

Chapter 19

TRADE UNIONS AND COLLECTIVE BARGAINING

★ LEARNING OBJECTIVES ★

After reading this chapter, you will be able to understand :

- Trade Unions
- Objectives, Importance
- Collective Bargaining
- Collective Bargaining Theories
- Collective Bargaining Definition, objectives
- Forms, Levels and Importance of Collective Bargaining

TRADE UNIONS

What is a Trade Union ?

The trade union is an association, either of employees or employers or of independent workers. It is a relatively permanent combination of workers and is not temporary or casual. It is an association of workers engaged in securing economic benefits for its members.

Trade unions are a major component of the modern industrial relation system. A trade union of workers is an organization formed by workers to protect their interests. *i.e.*, improve their working conditions etc. All trade unions have objectives or goals to achieve, which are contained in their constitution and each has its own strategy to reach those goals. Trade Unions are now considered a sub-system which seeks to serve the specific sub-groups interest and also considers itself a part of the organization, in terms of the latter's viability and contribution to the growth of the community of which it is a part.

Definition

According to Section 2(*b*) of the Trade Unions Act of 1926, "a trade union is any combination of persons, whether temporary or permanent, primarily for the purpose of regulating the relations between workers and employers, or between workers and workers and for imposing restrictive conditions on the conduct on the conduct of any trade or business, and includes the federation of two or more trade unions.

Sydney and Beatrice Web have defined Trade Union as a "Continuous association of wage earners for the purpose of maintaining or improving the conditions of their working lives."

G.D.H. Cole defines Trade Union as an association of workers in one or more occupations—an association carried on mainly for the purpose of protecting and advancing the member's economic interests in connection with their daily work.

Laster defines Trade Union as an association of employees designed primarily to maintain or improve the condition of employment of its members.

According to Cunnison, Trade Union is a monopolistic combination of wage earners who stand to the employers in a relation of dependence for the sale of their labour and even for the production, and that the general purpose of the association in view of that dependence is to strengthen their power to bargain with the employers.

Objectives of Trade Unions

Trade Union came into being for a variety of purposes. Individual workers found it more advantageous to band together and seek to establish their terms and conditions of employments. They realized that if they bargained as individuals, the employer would have a better leverage, for an individual would not matter as much as a group in terms of the running of the enterprise. A group's contribution is much larger than an individual's so are the effects of its withdrawal. An individual may not be able to organize and defend his interests as well as a group can. Therefore, workers saw the advantages of organizing themselves into groups to improve their terms and conditions of employment. Employers also found it advantageous to deal with a group or a representative of a group rather than go through the process of dealing with each individual over a length of time.

With the changed political, social and equational environment in terms of awareness of rights the right to organize, the right to bargain and settle terms and conditions of employment–labour or worker unions sprang up in order to protect and further worker in acquiring a foot hold in the labour movement also provided the impetus for the formation of labour unions.

Trade unions are formed to protect and promote the interests of their members. Their primary function is to protect the interests of workers against discrimination and unfair labor practices. Trade unions are formed to achieve the following objectives :

1. **Representation**. Trade unions represent individual workers when they have a problem at work. If an employee feels he is being unfairly treated, he can ask the union representative to help sort out the difficulty with the manager or employer. Unions also offer their members legal representation. Normally this is to help people get financial compensation for work-related injuries or to assist people who have to take their employer to court.
2. **Negotiation** is where union representatives, discuss with management, the issues which affect people working in an organization. There may be a difference of opinion between

management and union members. Trade unions negotiate with the employers to find out a solution to these differences. Pay, working hours, holidays and changes to working practices are the sorts of issues that are negotiated. In many workplaces there is a formal agreement between the union and the company which states that the union has the right to negotiate with the employer. In these organizations, unions are said to be recognized for collective bargaining purposes.

3. **Voice in decisions affecting workers**. The economic security of employees is determined not only by the level of wages and duration of their employment, but also by the management's personal policies which include selection of employees for lay offs, retrenchment, promotion and transfer. These policies directly affect workers. The evaluation criteria for such decisions may not be fair. So, the intervention of unions in such decision making is a way through which workers can have their say in the decision making to safeguard their interests.
4. **Member services.** During the last few years, trade unions have increased the range of services they offer their members. These include :
    - *Education and Training.* Most unions run training courses for their members on employment rights, health and safety and other issues. Some unions also help members who have left school with little education by offering courses on basic skills and courses leading to professional qualifications.
    - *Legal Assistance.* As well as offering legal advice on employment issues, some unions give help with personal matters, like housing, wills and debt.
    - *Financial Discounts.* People can get discounts on mortgages, insurance and loans from unions.
    - *Welfare benefits.* One of the earliest functions of trade unions was to look after members who hit hard times. Some of the older unions offer financial help to their members when they are sick or unemployed.

Characteristics of Trade Unions

The major characteristics of trade Unions are listed below :

- **Association of employees.** A trade union is essentially an association of employees belonging to a particular class of employment, profession, trade or industry. For example, there are unions for teachers, doctors, film, artistes, weavers, mine workers and so on.
- **Voluntary Association.** An employee joins the trade union out of his free will. A person cannot be compelled to join a union.
- **Permanent Body.** A trade union is usually a permanent body. Members may come and go but the trade union remains.
- **Common Interest**. The member of a trade union have certain matters of common interest—job security, better pay and working conditions and so on, which bring them together.
- **Collective Action**. Even when an individual employee has any grievance over certain management decisions, the matter is sorted out by the intervention of the trade union. Employees are able to initiate collective action to solve any problem concerning any particular employee or all the employees.

- **Rapport with the Management**. The trade union seeks to improve relations between the employees and employers. The officials of the trade union hold talks with The members of the management concerning the problems of the employees in order to find an amicable solution. It is thus possible for the employees to have better rapport with the management.

Importance of Trade Unions

The existence of a strong and recognized trade union is a pre-requisite to industrial peace. Decisions taken through the process of collective bargaining and negotiations between employer and unions are more influential. Trade unions play an important role and are helpful in effective communication between the workers and the management. They provide the advice and support to ensure that the differences of opinion do not turn into major conflicts. The central function of a trade union is to represent people at work. But they also have a wider role in protecting their interests. They also play an important educational role, organizing courses for their members on a wide range of matters. Seeking a healthy and safe working environment is also prominent feature of union activity. Trade unions help in accelerated pace of economic development in many ways as follows :

- by helping in the recruitment and selection of workers.
- by inculcating discipline among the workforce
- by enabling settlement of industrial disputes in a rational manner
- by helping social adjustments. Workers have to adjust themselves to the new working conditions, the new rules and policies. Workers coming from different backgrounds may become disorganized, unsatisfied and frustrated. Unions help them in such adjustment.

  Trade unions are a part of society and as such, have to take into consideration the national integration as well. Some important social responsibilities of trade unions include :

- promoting and maintaining national integration by reducing the number of industrial disputes
- incorporating a sense of corporate social responsibility in workers
- achieving industrial peace

Reasons for Joining Trade Unions

The important forces that make the employees join a union are as follows :

1. **Greater Bargaining Power**. The individual employee possesses very little bargaining power as compared to that of his employer. If he is not satisfied with the wage and other conditions of employment, he can leave the job. It is not practicable to continually resign from one job after another when he is dissatisfied. This imposes a great financial and emotional burden upon the worker. The better course for him is to join a union that can take concerted action against the employer. The threat or actuality of a strike by a union is a powerful tool that often causes the employer to accept the demands of the workers for better conditions of employment.
2. **Minimize Discrimination.** The decisions regarding pay, work, transfer, promotion, etc. are highly subjective in nature. The personal relationships existing between the

supervisor and each of his subordinates may influence the management. Thus, there are chances of favoritisms and discriminations. A trade union can compel the management to formulate personnel policies that press for equality of treatment to the workers. All the labor decisions of the management are under close scrutiny of the labor union. This has the effect of minimizing favoritism and discrimination.

3. **Sense of Security**. The employees may join the unions because of their belief that it is an effective way to secure adequate protection from various types of hazards and income insecurity such as accident, injury, illness, unemployment, etc. The trade union secure retirement benefits of the workers and compel the management to invest in welfare services for the benefit of the workers.
4. **Sense of Participation**. The employees can participate in management of matters affecting their interests only if they join trade unions. They can influence the decisions that are taken as a result of collective bargaining between the union and the management.
5. **Sense of Belongingness**. Many employees join a union because their co-workers are the members of the union. At times, an employee joins a union under group pressure; if he does not, he often has a very difficult time at work. On the other hand, those who are members of a union feel that they gain respect in the eyes of their fellow workers. They can also discuss their problem with the trade union leaders.
6. **Platform for Self Expression**. The desire for self-expression is a fundamental human drive for most people. All of us wish to share our feelings, ideas and opinions with others. Similarly the workers also want the management to listen to them. A trade union provides such a forum where the feelings, ideas and opinions of the workers could be discussed. It can also transmit the feelings, ideas, opinions and complaints of the workers to the management. The collective voice of the workers is heard by the management and give due consideration while taking policy decisions by the management.
7. **Betterment of Relationships**. Another reason for employees joining unions is that employees feel that unions can fulfill the important need for adequate machinery for proper maintenance of employer-employee relations. Unions help in betterment of industrial relations among management and workers by solving the problems peacefully.

Functions of Trade Unions

The ILO has maintained that unions "fulfill three important functions. The first is a democratic function : allowing all those who have work or want to work to have a say in their working life. The second is of course an economic function : helping to find the best possible balance in the production and the distribution of the fruits of growth. The third, which derives from the first two, is a social function : ensuring that all those who would like to work finds their place in society; these organizations can certainly help to eradicate poverty, as well as to combat the social exclusion of the most vulnerable, inner-city violence, social tensions and unrest, and indeed be a contributing factor to social stability." (ILO, World Labour Report 1997-98, supra, note 2, at 27).

Functions can be broadly classified into two categories :

(*i*) Militant functions,

(*ii*) Fraternal functions

Militant Functions

One set of activities performed by trade unions leads to the betterment of the position of their members in relation to their employment. The aim of such activities is to ensure adequate wages, secure better conditions of work and employment, get better treatment from employers, etc.; when the unions fail to accomplish these aims by the method of management in the form of go-slow tactics, strike, boycott, gherao, etc. Hence, these functions of the trade unions are known as militant or fighting functions. Thus, the militant functions of trade unions can be summed up as :

- To achieve higher wages and better working conditions
- To raise the status of workers as a part of industry
- To protect labors against victimization and injustice

Fraternal Functions

Another set of activities performed by trade unions aims at rendering help to its members in times of need, and improving their efficiency. Trade unions try to foster a spirit of cooperation and promote friendly industrial relations and diffuse education and culture among their members. They take up welfare measures for improving the morale of workers and generate self confidence among them. They also arrange for legal assistance to its members, if necessary. Besides, these, they undertake many welfare measures for their members, *e.g.,* school for the education of children, library, reading-rooms, in-door and out-door games, and other recreational facilities. Some trade unions even undertake publication of some magazine or journal. These activities, which may be called fraternal functions, depend on the availability of funds, which the unions raise by subscription from members and donations from outsiders, and also on their competent and enlightened leadership. Thus, the fraternal functions of trade unions can be summed up as :

- To take up welfare measures for improving the morale of workers
- To generate self confidence among workers
- To encourage sincerity and discipline among workers
- To provide opportunities for promotion and growth
- To protect women workers against discrimination

The functions of Trade Unions in various countries are enumerated in succeeding paragrphs.

Functions of Trade Unions in the USA

According to the first President of A.F.L. trade unions in the USA perform the following functions.

Protecting the wages of worker; increasing wages; reducing hours of work; securing just and human working conditions, improving the safety and sanitary conditions of the workshop; increasing the workers' share in the national income; introducing working rules and democratize labour management; freeing the labourer from tyrannies, petty or otherwise; achieving equality of opportunity for all workers; supporting legislation which aids workers and opposing harmful legislation; protecting and strengthening democratic institutions; aiding and promoting the cause of peace and freedom in the world; protecting the labour movement against corruption and racketeers; safeguarding the labour movement; encouraging workers to register and vote; encouraging the sale of union-made goods through the use of the union label; and participating in various community activities and in local government organizations, such as school boards and city councils.

Besides, they also take part in administration work; negotiation and administration of collective agreements; provision of educational and beneficial activities and participation in community, state and national affairs; provision of research facilities; get protective and social security legislations enacted by the state; provide life insurance and health benefit and pension programmes, recreational facilities, co-operatives, labour banks, credit unions, radio programmes and housing projects, etc. In the USA, trade unions been working as protective organizations, they have conferred immense benefits on society as a whole by strengthening democratic processes and seeking economic stability.

The methods which the trade unions deploy to achieve their goals include collective bargaining with the employers and influencing the state machinery through political activities to enact favourable labour laws. The strikes have been their major instrument.

Functions of Trade Unions in the UK

The British TUC Report Post-War Reconstruction distinguished three main sets of objectives namely :

(*i*) Maintaining and improving wages, hours and conditions of work, and also what wages can buy; and increasing the size of the real national income and the share of it which should accrue to the working people.

(*ii*) Providing and improving opportunities for the advancement of the workers to obtain "full employment" is an aim which trade unions have always pursued.

(*iii*) Extending the influence of the working class over the policy and purposes of industry and arranging for their participation in management.

Flandes and Cleggre have laid down the main objective of a trade union as under :

(*i*) Defining or improving the wages and conditions of work;

(*ii*) Raising the status of the worker as a citizen of industry and of society; and

(*iii*) Extending the area of social control of the nation's economic life and participating in that control;

Prof. Laski has said the trade unions to-day are pluralist in character and pragmatic in method; if they are not, they are unlikely to survive the demands made upon them by so swiftly changing an environment. The trade unions in Britain not only defend or improve the wages and conditions of labour but also raise the status of workers, both in industry and society. They extend the area of social control of the nation's economic life and participate in that control. John Price observes : 'In England, trade unions have provided cash benefits for themselves and have worked for the development of social services by the state, recognizing that the needs of the individual are, to a large extent, the responsibility of the whole community. Trade unions are helpful in creating such conditions of work and service and wage payment that, on the one hand, they avoid inequalities between the different sections of the community, and on the other hand, provide opportunities for the progressive raising of the standard of living of large numbers of people. They also provide for the development of the human personality in its manifold aspects by arranging for educational programmes.

Functions of Trade Unions in the Republic of China

In China, the functions of trade unions have been enumerated thus :

- To organize the workers to launch labour emulation drives, strengthen labour discipline and ensure the fulfillment of plans.

- To improve the material and cultural standards of workers' lives and to supervise the managements with a view to implement the various targets of the plan.
- To organize political, educational and technical studies as well as cultural and sports activities.
- To enroll members, collect funds and give reports about these activities.
- To educate the workers in the three R's vocational efficiency and current economic and political problems.
- To provide recreational facilities for the workers in the form of clubs and places of culture and by organizing dances, theatrical performances, music, concerts, cinema shows, games, sports, and facilities for physical education; circulating entertainment instruments and organizing libraries.
- To get equal pay for equal work.
- To guarantee material assistance to the workers in old age, and in case of illness or disability.
- To protect women and children from exploitation.
- To participate in various activities which are directed towards the improvement of living conditions.
- To enter into collective agreements with the management for mutually fulfilling the targets in respect of production, wages, labour norms, labour safety, welfare, social security, workers' participation in management, material obligations etc.

Functions of Trade Unions in India

As per the Indian Trade Union Act, 1926, the primary function of a trade union is to protect and promote the interests of the workers and the conditions of their employment. They can also have other objectives, which are not inconsistent with this primary purpose or opposed to any law. In India, trade unions generally undertake the following functions :

(*i*) To achieve higher wages and better working and living conditions for the members.

(*ii*) To acquire control over running of the industry by workers.

(*iii*) To minimize the helplessness of the individual workers by making them stand-up unitedly and increasing their resistance power through collective bargaining; protecting the members against victimization and injustice by employers.

(*iv*) To raise the status of the workers as partners in industry and citizens of society by demanding an increasing share for them in the management of industrial enterprises.

(*v*) To generate self-confidence among the workers.

(*vi*) To encourage sincerity and discipline among workers.

(*vii*) To take up welfare measures for improving the morale of the workers.

The National Commission on Labour has underscored certain basic functions to which trade unions have to pay greater attentions such as :

(*i*) To secure fair wages for workers.

(*ii*) To safeguard the security of tenure and improve conditions of service.

(*iii*) To enlarge opportunities for promotion and training.

(*iv*) To improve working and living conditions.

(*v*) To provide for educational, cultural and recreational facilities.

(*vi*) To cooperate and facilitate technological advancement by broadening the understanding.

(*vii*) To promote identity of interests of the workers with their industry.

(*viii*) To offer responsive cooperation in improving levels of production and productivity, discipline and high standards of quality.

(*ix*) To promote individual and collective welfare.

Besides these basic functions of trade unions, the Commission enjoined the following responsibilities upon the unions :

(*i*) Promotion of national integration.

(*ii*) Generally, influencing the socio-economic policies of the community through the active participation in their formulation at various levels.

(*iii*) Instilling in their members a sense of responsibility to industry and the community.

The First Five Year Plan while spelling out the role of trade unions emphasized that they should :

(*a*) Present plans to workers so as to create enthusiasm among them for the plans.

(*b*) Exercise the utmost restraint in regard to work stoppage.

(*c*) Formulate wage demands which are attuned to the requirements of economic development and are in keeping with considerations of social justice.

(*d*) Assume greater responsibility for the success of the productive effort.

STRUCTURE OF TRADE UNIONS IN INDIA

In India, the structure of trade union consists of three levels : plant/shop or local, the state and the centre. It is generally from the central level that the ideology of the important central federations of labour in India percolates down to the state and local levels. Every national or central federation of labour in India has state branches, state committees or state councils, from where its organization works down to the local level.

There are two types of organizations to which the trade unions in India are affiliated :

- National Federations, and
- The Federations of Unions

National Federations

The National Federations have all the trade unions in a given industry as their affiliated members. Every trade union, irrespective of the industry to which it belongs, can join a general national federation. Such federations are the apex of trade union policies a national character. The central union organizations are national federations of labour based on different political ideologies.

Because of their political leanings, the affiliated trade unions in the field of labour relations follow either a militant policy or a policy of cooperation with the employers and the government, or a policy of continuous strife and litigation.

The trade union leadership to these national organizations is generally provided by the politicians. Such leaders are found leading a dozen or more unions in a particular state. These unions may be in the petroleum industry, the transport industry, electricity supply undertakings or craft unions, such as the rickshaw pullers' union or taxi drivers' union. Some of the trade union leaders and Member's of Parliament and Members of Legislative Assemblies, cooperators of city corporations and members of important committees dealing with the labour policy of the country.

The national/central federations are empowered to decide the question of jurisdiction of the various local and national unions.

A majority of these federations allow their affiliates to bargain independently with their respective employers. The federations only act as coordinating authorities for different unions under their control. They also select delegates to represent workmen in international conferences organized by the International Labour Organisation or the International Confederation of Free Trade Unions. The all-India federation of trade unions has a regular structure. For example :

- The INTUC consists of a central organization, affiliated unions, industrial federation, regional branches and councils functioning under the direct control or supervision of the central organization, the assembly of delegates, the general council and the working committees. The INTUC functions through its affiliated unions, delegates, assembly, and general council (including office-bearers), the working committees of the general council and the Pradesh bodies.
- The UTUC consists of the general body ('delegates' assembly) general council, and the working committee of general council.
- The Hind Mazdoor Sabha (HMS) works through the general council, the working committee and affiliated organization.

Federations of Unions

These are combinations of various unions for the purpose of gaining strength and solidarity. They can resort to concerted action, when the need for such action arises, without losing their individuality. Such federations may be local, regional, state, national and international. There are a few organizations which are local in character, such as the Bharatiya Kamgar Sena, the Labour Progressive Federation, Chennai, the National Front of Indian Trade Unions and the Co-ordinating Committee of Free Trade Unions.

Many Unions are affiliated to one or the other type of the following central organizations of workers :

(1) The Indian National Trade Union Congress
(2) The All-India Trade Union Congress
(3) The Hind Mazdoor Sabha
(4) The United Trade Union Congress
(5) The Centre of India Trade Unions
(6) Bharatiya Mazdoor Sangh
(7) The National Front of India Trade Unions
(8) The United Trade Union Congress (LS)
(9) The National Federation of Independent Trade Unions

(10) The Trade Union Co-ordination Committee

(11) Indian Confederation of Labour

(12) Hind Mazdoor Kisan Panchayat

(13) National Labour Organization

Besides the affiliated unions and their federations, there are a large number of associations and federations which have not joined any one of the central workers'organizations. Some of these are :

(*i*) The All India Bank Employees' Association;

(*ii*) The All India Bank Employees' Federation;

(*iii*) The All India Insurance Employees' Association;

(*iv*) The All India Defence Employees' Federation;

(*v*) The All India Railway men's Federation;

(*vi*) The National Federation of Posts and Telegraphs Employees; etc.

At the international level, the World Federation of Trade Unions (W.F.T.U.) and the International Confederation of Free Trade Unions (I.C.F.T.U.) are two important organizations.

TRADE UNIONISM IN INDIA

The trade unionism in India developed quite slowly as compared to the western nations. Indian trade union movement can be divided into three phases.

The First Phase (1850 to 1900)

During this phase the inception of trade unions took place. During this period, the working and living conditions of the labor were poor and their working hours were long. Capitalists were only interested in their productivity and profitability. In addition, the wages were also low and general economic conditions were poor in industries. In order to regulate the working hours and other service conditions of the Indian textile laborers, the Indian Factories Act was enacted in 1881. As a result, employment of child labor was prohibited.

The growth of trade union movement was slow in this phase and later on the Indian Factory Act of 1881 was amended in 1891. Many strikes took place in the two decades following 1880 in all industrial cities. These strikes taught workers to understand the power of united action even though there was no union in real terms. Small associations like Bombay Mill-Hands Association came up by this time.

The Second Phase (1900 to 1946)

This phase was characterized by the development of organized trade unions and political movements of the working class. Between 1918 and 1923, many unions came into existence in the country. At Ahmedabad, under the guidance of Mahatma Gandhi, occupational unions like spinners' unions and weavers' unions were formed. A strike was launched by these unions under the leadership of Mahatma Gandhi who turned it into a satyagrah. These unions federated into industrial union known as Textile Labor Association in 1920. In 1920, the First National Trade union organization (The All India Trade Union Congress (AITUC)) was established. Many of the leaders of this organization were leaders of the national Movement. In 1926, Trade union law came up with the efforts of Mr. N N Joshi that became operative from 1927. During 1928, All India Trade Union Federation (AITUF) was formed.

The Third Phase (Post Independence)

The third phase began with the emergence of independent India (in 1947). The partition of country affected the trade union movement particularly Bengal and Punjab. By 1949, four central trade union organizations were functioning in the country :

- The All India Trade Union Congress,
- The Indian National Trade Union Congress,
- The Hindu Mazdoor Sangh, and
- The United Trade Union Congress

The working class movement was also politicized along the lines of political parties. For instance Indian National Trade Union Congress (INTUC) is the trade union arm of the Congress Party. The AITUC is the trade union arm of the Communist Party of India. Besides workers, white-collar employees, supervisors and managers are also organized by the trade unions, as for example in the Banking, Insurance and Petroleum industries.

Craft and General Union

A craft union is built around a certain specialized skill, which has necessitated a special type of training. Craft unions are open to Craft and General Union members of a certain trade/skill, like Air India's navigator's union. Alternatively, a general union is open to all members irrespective of their skills cutting across trades/skills and includes unskilled, semi and skilled workers. Developed Western Societies have the unions like the one just cited. In these places the industrial way of life has had a longer history.

Union Shop

When the union acts as supplier of labour, once an employee is employed then he has to join the union. Here the union makes employment conditional on union membership.

Check Off

The check-off system is a practice where the management collects an employee's union dues, as a wage deduction and gives a lump sum amount to the union. This is a facility that ensures totality of collection of union dues with no excuse for employees to a resist from paying for one reason or the other as it could happen in a voluntary system. Such a facility is provided only to a recognized union.

TRADE UNIONS IN INDIA

The Indian workforce consists of 430 million workers, growing 2% annually. The Indian labor markets consist of three sectors :

- The rural workers, who constitute about 60 per cent of the workforce.
- Organized sector, which employs 8 percent of workforce, and
- The urban informal sector (which includes the growing software industry and other services, not included in the formal sector) which constitutes the rest 32 per cent of the workforce.

At present there are twelve Central Trade Union Organizations in India :

- All India Trade Union Congress (AITUC)
- Bharatiya Mazdoor Sangh (BMS)
- Centre of Indian Trade Unions (CITU)
- Hind Mazdoor Kisan Panchayat (HMKP)
- Hind Mazdoor Sabha (HMS)
- Indian Federation of Free Trade Unions (IFFTU)
- Indian National Trade Union Congress (INTUC)
- National Front of Indian Trade Unions (NFITU)
- National Labor Organization (NLO)
- Trade Unions Co-ordination Centre (TUCC)
- United Trade Union Congress (UTUC) and
- United Trade Union Congress - Lenin Sarani (UTUC - LS)

UNION LEADERSHIP

One of the most crucial factors in this sphere is the leadership that is provided. The leadership provides the direction and goals for a particular union. The leader's task is to make the union effective, by improving the terms and conditions of employment of the worker and also by being concerned with the viability of the enterprise. The trade union organization based as it is, in many cases on individuals or the national federations and their ideologies, has not been able to evolve a professional cadre of leadership at the grass roots to the desired extent. In fact, quite often, a single union executive leader is responsible for running a large number of unions. "A survey of trade union leadership in Bombay in 1960 showed that one leader was president of 17 unions and secretary of two more. Another was an office bearer of 20 unions.* R.J.Mehta was President of the Free Trade Unions which control more than 14 unions.*

This brings us to a consideration of the next issue, *i.e.*, outside leadership vs. internal leadership. In fact, the Trade Union Act of 1926 makes a provision for this and allows for 10% of the leadership to be from outside the sphere of the organization.* An outside leader is one who is not a full time employee of the organization, whereas the internal leader is such a person. Many lawyers and politicians have been union leaders in the early part of their careers. The former President V.V.Giri was one such example, so were former Central Ministers like G.L.Nanda and Khadilkar. There are advantages and disadvantages either in terms of policy or in terms of implementation of administrative action, especially if he belongs to or has linkages with the ruling party. On the other hand his involvement with the plant level problems is much less as he is not on the shop floor to understand the intricate issues applicable to a particular plant. Not being an employee of the enterprise or an insider, he lacks the required depth of understanding of local issues and specifics. The outsider is a professional who has many units under his wing all of which demand his time, including the larger function of liaison. The insider would not only have greater knowledge of the enterprise specifies but also have more time for sustained work, being concerned as he is with just one enterprise. Also, external issues and ideologies are not unnecessarily inducted, which could happen when outside leaders are in control for whom ideology may be more important than getting the best deal under the circumstances.

The leadership role in a trade union has a variety of demands placed on it. Not only does it require a certain amount of technical knowledge of the nature of business of the particular organizations, but also a sympathetic understanding of the workers, their attitudes and their problems. A certain amount of commitment and empathy for a cause, even in uncertain conditions, is necessary. Till now the attraction for persons entering this occupation has been the possibility of a political career in the future. However, there have been some plant unions which have been run very professionally and have at the same time been concerned with the viability of the firm or the enterprise as well as the good of the workers. The erstwhile Simpson Workers Union under the stewardship of Gurumurthy was an example, and TLA is an example of an industry level federation.

TRADE UNION FINANCES

If an organization is to grow, survive and meet the needs of its rank and file members in terms of attaining their objectives etc. It needs money. For a variety of reasons, the finances of May trade unions have not been very bountiful. It must be noted that to every general statement, there are a number of exceptions and so is the case with some financially strong unions. Funds are needed for attracting and retaining competent staff for, however idealistic the cause, people do need to survive. It is only with competent staff that some of the objectives like research, comparative data generation, company studies, presenting demands and resolving workers problems can be achieved. Again, funds are necessary for political lobbying; for sending union representatives to the local bodies, state and central legislatures, if inertia sets in, an organization will wither away or the rank and file will shift to a more active and useful organization. Funds therefore are needed to pursue activities, which will in turn benefit the members who will then contribute, not only financially but also in terms of their services and sustain their membership. Activities resulting in something worthwhile will arouse the enthusiasm of the members and make them concerned for the allocation and proper utilization of scarce resources. The divisive nature of Indian trade unionism has also led to the dissipation of funds amongst a large number of organizations, with the result that there are many small unions without much financial backing and without much staff to do any substantial work. The generation of funds has been wholly inadequate. In some cases, subscriptions are not collected promptly or are paid by members only when they have a problem. In the former case, it is overlooked by the trade union management for fear of losing membership. On the other hand, there are according to some trader union executives, shrewd members who do not mind paying subscription to more than one union in order to protect their interest in times of need.

UNION FREE COMPANIES

There are companies without unions. Employees of such organizations realize the negative consequences of unionization and prefer to remain free from unions. They have misgivings of how effectively a union can improve unsatisfactory working conditions. Beyond perception of the ineffectiveness off the unions in the pursuit of personal goals, there are many other reasons why employees prefer to vote against unionization especially their belief that joining the union is an admission that others control their destiny.

Strategies and Tactics to Remain Union Free

Managers and management develop long term strategies and effective tactics to prevent unionization of their organizations. The major strategies used are :

(*a*) Effective supervision

(*b*) Open communication

(*c*) Effective personal research

(*d*) Healthy and safe working environment

(*e*) Effective employer and employee relations

(*f*) Effective remuneration.

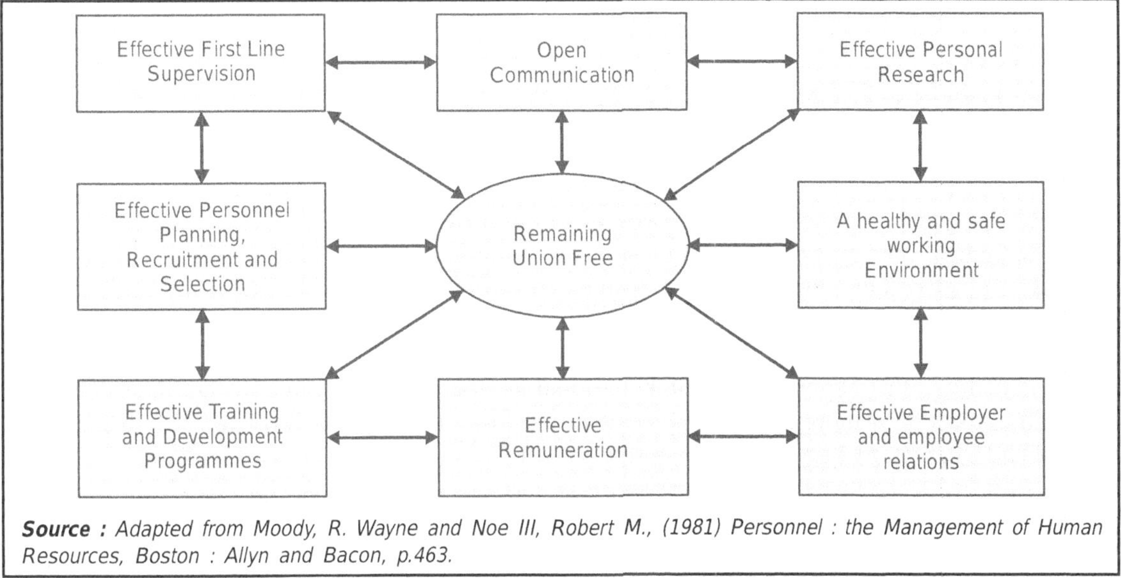

***Source :** Adapted from Moody, R. Wayne and Noe III, Robert M., (1981) Personnel : the Management of Human Resources, Boston : Allyn and Bacon, p.463.*

Fig. 19.1. *Strategies and Tactics for Remaining Union Free.*

Union Legislation

Trade Unions in India are governed by Trade Unions Act, 1926. The main objective of the Act is to provide for the registration of trade unions and to give registered trade unions a legal status.

In pursuit of the primary objective the Act contains 33 sections. The provision can be broadly divided into :

- Definitions (Sec 2).
- Registration of Trade Unions (Sec 4 and 5)
- Cancellation of registration (Sec 10)
- Appeals (Section 11)
- Change of name (Section-23)
- Amalgamation of trade unions (Section 24 to 26)
- Dissolution (Section 27)
- Annual returns (Section 28)

- Power to Make Regulations (Section 29 & 30)
- Penalties (Section 31)
- Who can file prosecutions (Section 32)
- Authorities under the act :
  - Registrar of Trade Unions (Section-3)
  - Labour Commissioner
  - Additional Registrar of Trade Unions
  - Additional Labour Commissioner (IR and E)
  - Deputy Registrar of Trade Unions
  - Joint Labour Commissioner (P)

COLLECTIVE BARGAINING

Introduction

Collective bargaining is the process of workers' organizations and employers' organizations (or individual employers) to negotiate on all areas relating to wages and terms of employment. For workers, collective bargaining helps to convey their voice to ensure decent pay and working conditions. It is also a means to gain a share in the benefits of economic progress. For employers, collective bargaining is a means to maintain social peace and prosperity, successful bargaining results in collective agreements. In various national labor and employment law contexts collective bargaining takes on a more specific legal meaning. In a broad sense, however, it is the coming together of workers to negotiate their employment.

A Collective agreement is a labour contract between an employer and one or more unions. Collective bargaining consists of the process of negotiations between representatives of a union and employers represented by management, in some countries by employer's organization in respect of the terms and conditions of employment of employees, such as wages, hours of work, working conditions and grievance-procedures, and about the rights and responsibilities of trade unions. The parties often refer to the result of the negotiation as a Collective Bargaining Agreement or as a Collective Employment Agreement.

In India and Sri Lanka, the overwhelming importance of the informal economy (with unions geared exclusively to the small formal sector), fragmented unions, weak industrial relations structures and conflictual employer-employee relations, all work against organisation and a climate of collective bargaining (Harris-White and Gooptu 2000). The concentration of unionisation on the formal sector explains the large difference in densities calculated in union members as a percentage of total employment, as well as union members as a percentage of paid employment in both India and Sri Lanka (see appendix). In India, because of their strength in the public sector and their close political links, unions have substantial influence over national policy-making (Kuruvilla et. al. 2002). In the British colonial tradition, unions tend to operate through political channels, with close connections between union organisations and political parties (Oberai, Sivananthiram and Ratnam 2001; Bhattacherjee 2002). However, as Kuruvilla et. al. (2002) argue, economic liberalisation has reduced this traditional political leverage in favour of the logic of competitiveness now shaping industrial relations.

Theories

At its inception, the labour market was dominated by the classical economics view which espoused free and unregulated labour markets. This laissez-faire capitalism led to social injustices and inequities since labour did not have the power to bargain with employers on terms which even approached a degree of equality in bargaining strength. Industrial relations, therefore, initially came to espouse a degree of labour market regulation to correct this unequal bargaining power. Consequently industrial relations developed in the context of the theory that problems in labour relations emanate largely from market imperfections which operate against the interests of labour and cause imbalances in the power relationships of employers and employees. These imperfections were external to the enterprise. Additionally, the dominant position of the employer in what was formerly called the "master and servant" relationship prevented labour from enjoying rights. These causes for labour problems—external and internal to the enterprise—needed to be addressed through a range of initiatives, both by the State through protective labour laws, conciliation and dispute settlement machinery, by voluntary action on the part of employees to protect themselves and further their interests through trade unionism (but backed by State interventions to guarantee this right in the form of freedom of association), and by redressing the balance of power (through collective bargaining).

Collective bargaining has been explained as a human right. The right to organize trade unions is identified as a human right in the Universal Declaration of Human Rights. The International Labour Organization's Declaration on Fundamental Principles and Rights at Work defines Collective Bargaining as a core fundamental right of workers.

Economic theories also provide many models which are able to explain collective bargaining : the first is the so-called Monopoly Union Model (Dunlop, 1944) according to which the monopoly union has the power to maximize the wage rate after that the firm has chosen the level of employment. This model seems to be unrealistic and is being abandoned by the recent literature. The second is the Right-to-manage model which was developed by the British school during the 1980s (Nickell); here the labour union and the firm bargain over the wage rate according to a typical Nash Bargaining Maximin can be written as

$$\Omega = U\beta\Pi 1 - \beta$$

where : U is the utility function of the labour union,

Π the profit of the firm and

β represents the bargaining power of the labour unions.

The third model is called the *Efficient Bargaining* (McDonald and Solow, 1981) where the union and the firm bargain over both wages and employment (or, more realistically, structured hours of work). The optimal solution requires that the marginal rate of substitution between wages and employment of one party is equal to its equivalent measure for the other (McDonald and Solow, 1981).

Definition

A sound industrial relations system is not capable of precise definition. Every industrial relations system has to take into account, and reflect, cultural factors. Systems cannot change culture, but only behaviour within a cultural environment. As such, one can only describe some of the elements which have generally come to be recognized as contributing to a sound industrial relations system. These elements would constitute a sort of 'checklist'. A relatively sound industrial relations system will exhibit some of these elements.

According to National Labour Relations Act of United States :

"For the purpose of [this act,] to bargain collectively is the performance of the mutual obligation of the employer and the representative of the employer and the representative of the employees to meet at reasonable times and confer in good faith with respect to wages, hours, and terms and conditions of employment or the negotiation of an agreement, or any question arising there under, and the execution of a written contract and incorporating any agreement reached if requested by either party, but such obligation does not compel either party to agree to a proposal or require the making of a concession."

Promotion of Collective Bargaining Convention, (1981) No. 154, its definition of collective bargaining is : "Article 2 [...] "collective bargaining" extends to all negotiations which take place between an employer, a group of employers or one or more employers' organisations, on the one hand, and one or more workers' organisations, on the other, for—(*a*) determining working conditions and terms of employment; [...]".

According to Dale Yoder, "Collective Bargaining is the term used to describe a situation in which the essential conditions of employment are determined by bargaining process undertaken by representatives of a group of workers on the one hand and of one or more employers on the other." In the words of Flippo, "Collective Bargaining is a process in which the representatives of a labour organization and the representatives of business organization meet and attempt to negotiate a contract or agreement, which specifies the nature of employee employer-union relationship."

Collective bargaining should involve determination of remuneration, not just other terms and/or conditions of employment. Remuneration includes "the ordinary, basic or minimum wage or salary and any additional emoluments whatsoever payable directly or indirectly, whether in cash or in kind, by the employer to the worker and arising out of the worker's employment". (Article 1, ILO Equal Remuneration for Men and Women Workers for Work of Equal Value Convention, 1951 (No. 100))

Objectives

A sound industrial relations system requires a labour management relations policy. There are many specific objectives of such a policy, all of which go to make up the policy at the national level. The following are some of the objectives, the emphasis varying from country to country depending on the priorities and stage of development of each of them at any given point of time :

- Employment and job security and increased employment opportunities.
- Raising living standards through improved terms and conditions of employment.
- Productivity improvement which enables employers to be more competitive and to increase their financial capacity to raise the living standards of the employees.
- Minimizing conflict, achieving harmonious relations, resolving conflicts through peaceful means and establishing stable social relationships.

In Western industrialized societies "harmony" and "harmonious relations" are not explicitly referred to either as an objective or as a means, though basically it represents an important objective in such societies. However, this concept is explicitly referred to in many Asian societies. Development has an economic and social dimension on the one hand and a cultural dimension on the other. The economic and social aspects involve guiding or influencing economic and social change in a desirable direction. This means not only economic development measured in terms of growth rates and per capita incomes, but also equity in terms of income distribution and employment opportunities, life expectancy, population growth rates, literacy, poverty alleviation, etc. As aptly stated by John Kenneth Galbraith: "It is one of the least advertised and for the very affluent the least attractive, of economic truths that a reasonably equitable distribution of income throughout the society is highly functional."

FORMS OF COLLECTIVE BARGAINING

There is a great deal of variation in the collective bargaining practices ranging from an informal oral agreement to very formal and detailed agreement.

Collective Bargaining usually takes one of the following forms :

- It may be a single plant bargaining, that is, bargaining may be between a single trade union. This type of collective bargaining prevails in the United States and India.
- It may be a multiple plant bargaining, that is, bargaining may be between a single factory or establishment having several plants and the workers employed in all these plants.
- It may be a multiple employer bargaining, that is, bargaining between all the trade unions of workers in the same industry through their federal organizations, and the employer's federation. This is possible both at the local and regional levels and is generally resorted to in the textile industry.

In India, collective bargaining has been classified under four categories. These are :

- Agreements which are negotiated by officers during the course of conciliation proceedings and are called settlements under the Industrial Disputes Act.
- Agreements which are concluded by the parties themselves without reference to a Board of Conciliation and are signed by them. Copies of such agreements, however, are sent to appropriate governments and to conciliation officers.
- Agreements which are negotiated by the parties on a voluntary basis when disputes are arbitrators for incorporation into the documents as parts of awards. These are known as consent awards.
- Agreements which are drawn up after direct negotiation between labour and management and are purely voluntary in character. These depend for their enforcement on moral force and on the goodwill and co-operation of the parties.

SUBJECTS FOR COLLECTIVE BARGAINING

The subject matter of collective bargaining covers a variety of issues affecting employment relationships between the workers and the management. According to Ghosh and Nath the issues covered in the collective bargaining are recognition of union or unions, wages and allowances, hours of work, leave and festival holidays, bonus and profit sharing schemes, seniority, rationalization and the issues relating to the fixation of workloads, and standard labour force, programmes of planning and development influencing workforce, issues relating to retrenchment and lay off, victimization for trade union activities, provident fund, gratuity and other retirement benefit schemes, incentive systems, housing and transport facilities, issues relating to discipline and shop rules, grievance procedure, working conditions and issues related to safety and accident prevention, occupational diseases and protective clothing, employee benefits such as canteens, rest rooms, medical and health services and creches, administration of welfare funds, cooperative thrift and credit societies and educational, recreational and training schemes. The Indian Institute of Personnel Management, Calcutta, gives the following as the subject matter of collective bargaining :

(*i*) Purpose of the agreement, its scope and the definition of important terms;

(*ii*) Rights and responsibilities of the management and of the trade union;

(*iii*) Wages, bonus, production norms, leave, retirement benefits and terms and conditions of service;

(*iv*) Grievance redressal procedure;

(*v*) Methods and machinery for the settlement of possible future disputes; and

(*vi*) Termination clause.

Activities in Collective Bargaining

A collective bargaining process generally consists of four types of activities—distributive bargaining, integrative bargaining, attitudinal restructuring and intra-organizational bargaining. Distributive bargaining : It involves haggling over the distribution of surplus. Under it, the economic issues like wages, salaries and bonus are discussed. In distributive bargaining, one party's gain is another party's loss. This is most commonly explained in terms of a pie. Disputants can work together to make the pie bigger, so there is enough for both of them to have as much as they want, or they can focus on cutting the pie up, trying to get as much as they can for themselves. In general, distributive bargaining tends to be more competitive. This type of bargaining is also known as conjunctive bargaining.

Integrative Bargaining

This involves negotiation of an issue on which both the parties may gain, or at least neither party loses. For example, representatives of employer and employee sides may bargain over the better training programme or a better job evaluation method. Here, both the parties are trying to make more of something. In general, it tends to be more cooperative than distributive bargaining. This type of bargaining is also known as cooperative bargaining.

Attitudinal Restructuring

This involves shaping and reshaping some attitudes like trust or distrust, friendliness or hostility between labor and management. When there is a backlog of bitterness between both the parties, attitudinal restructuring is required to maintain smooth and harmonious industrial relations. It develops a bargaining environment and creates trust and cooperation among the parties.

Intra-organizational Bargaining

It generally aims at resolving internal conflicts. This is a type of maneuvering to achieve consensus with the workers and management. Even within the union, there may be differences between groups. For example, skilled workers may feel that they are neglected or women workers may feel that their interests are not looked after properly. Within the management also, there may be differences. Trade unions maneuver to achieve consensus among the conflicting groups.

Characteristics of Collective Bargaining

The essential feature of collective bargaining :

- It is a group process, wherein one group, representing the employers, and the other, representing the employees, sit together to negotiate terms of employment.
- Negotiations form an important aspect of the process of collective bargaining *i.e.,* there is considerable scope for discussion, compromise or mutual give and take in collective bargaining.
- Collective bargaining is a formalized process by which employers and independent trade unions negotiate terms and conditions of employment and the ways in which certain employment related issues are to be regulated at national, organizational and workplace levels.
- Collective bargaining is a process in the sense that it consists of a number of steps. It begins with the presentation of the charter of demands and ends with reaching an agreement, which would serve as the basic law governing labor management relations over a period of time in an enterprise. Moreover, it is flexible process and not fixed or static. Mutual trust and understanding serve as the by-products of harmonious relations between the two parties.
- It is a bipartite process. This means there are always two parties involved in the process of collective bargaining. The negotiations generally take place between the employees and the management. It is a form of participation.
- Collective bargaining is a complementary process *i.e.,* each party needs something that the other party has; labor can increase productivity and management can pay better for their efforts.
- Collective bargaining tends to improve the relations between workers and the union on the one hand and the employer on the other.
- Collective Bargaining is continuous process. It enables industrial democracy to be effective. It uses cooperation and consensus for settling disputes rather than conflict and confrontation.
- Collective bargaining takes into account day to day changes, policies, potentialities, capacities and interests.
- It is a political activity frequently undertaken by professional negotiators.

Levels of Collective Bargaining

Collective bargaining operates at three levels :

- National level
- Sector or industry level
- Company/enterprise level

The third bargaining level involves the company and/or establishment. As a supplementary type of bargaining, it emphasizes the point that bargaining levels need not be mutually exclusive. Economy-wide (national) bargaining is a bipartite or tripartite form of negotiation between union confederations, central employer associations and government agencies. It aims at providing a floor for lower-level bargaining on the terms of employment, often taking into account macroeconomic goals. Sectoral bargaining aims at the standardization of the terms of employment in one industry.

Importance of Collective Bargaining

Collective bargaining includes not only negotiations between the employers and unions but also includes the process of resolving labor-management conflicts. Thus, collective bargaining is, essentially, a recognized way of creating a system of industrial jurisprudence. It acts as a method of introducing civil rights in the industry, that is, the management should be conducted by rules rather than arbitrary decision making. It establishes rules which define and restrict the traditional authority exercised by the management.

Importance to Employees

- Collective bargaining develops a sense of self respect and responsibility among the employees.
- It increases the strength of the workforce, thereby, increasing their bargaining capacity as a group.
- Collective bargaining increases the morale and productivity of employees.
- It restricts management's freedom for arbitrary action against the employees. Moreover, unilateral actions by the employer are also discouraged.
- Effective collective bargaining machinery strengthens the trade unions movement.
- The workers feel motivated as they can approach the management on various matters and bargain for higher benefits.
- It helps in securing a prompt and fair settlement of grievances. It provides a flexible means for the adjustment of wages and employment conditions to economic and technological changes in the industry, as a result of which the chances for conflicts are reduced.

Importance to Employers

- It becomes easier for the management to resolve issues at the bargaining level rather than taking up complaints of individual workers.
- Collective bargaining tends to promote a sense of job security among employees and thereby tends to reduce the cost of labor turnover to management.
- Collective bargaining opens up the channel of communication between the workers and the management and increases worker participation in decision making.
- Collective bargaining plays a vital role in settling and preventing industrial disputes.

Importance to Society

- Collective bargaining leads to industrial peace in the country.
- It results in establishment of a harmonious industrial climate which supports, which helps the pace of a nation's efforts towards economic and social development since the obstacles to such a development can be reduced considerably.
- The discrimination and exploitation of workers is constantly being checked.
- It provides a method or the regulation of the conditions of employment of those who are directly concerned about them.

Pre-conditions for Successful Collective Bargaining

A pluralistic outlook involves acceptance within a political system of pressure groups (*e.g.*, religious groups, unions, business associations, political parties and so on) with specific interests with which a government has dialogue, with a view to effecting compromises by making concessions. Pluralism implies a process of bargaining between these groups, or between one or more of them on the one hand and the government on the other. It therefore recognizes these groups as the checks and balances which guarantee democracy. It is natural that in labour relations in a pluralist society collective bargaining is recognized as a fundamental tool through which stability is maintained, while freedom of association is the sine qua non without which the interest groups in a society would be unable to function effectively. There can therefore be no meaningful collective bargaining without freedom of association accorded to both employers and workers.

The existence of freedom of association does not necessarily mean that there would automatically be recognition of unions for bargaining purposes. Especially in systems where there is a multiplicity of trade unions, there is a need for predetermined objective criteria operative within the industrial relations system to decide when and how a union should be recognized for collective bargaining purposes. The obvious way would be to recognize the most representative union, but the criteria used to decide it and by whom may differ. It is in some systems determined on the basis of the union needing to have not less than a particular percentage of the workers in the enterprise in its membership. This may be decided by a referendum in the workplace, or by an outside certifying authority (such as a labour department or an independent statutory body), or by reference to "check off". There may be a condition that once certified as the bargaining agent there cannot be a change of agent for a prescribed period (*e.g.*, one or two years) in order to ensure the stability of the process.

Especially in developing countries some of which have a multiplicity of unions, there is sometimes a problem of unions being unable to secure observance of agreements by their members. Where a labour law system provides for sanctions for breaches of agreements, the labour administration authorities may be reluctant to impose sanctions on workers. Where there is frequent non-observance of agreements or understandings reached through the collective bargaining process, the party not in default would lose faith in the process.

Support of the labour administration authorities is necessary for successful collective bargaining, and this implies that they will :

- Provide the necessary climate for it, *e.g.*, provide effective conciliation services in the event of a breakdown of the process, and provide the necessary legal framework for it to operate in where necessary;
- Not support a party in breach of agreements concluded in consequence of collective bargaining;
- As far as is practicable, secure observance of collective bargaining agreements;
- Provide for the settlement of disputes arising from collective bargaining if the parties themselves have not so provided.

It is an obvious condition for successful collective bargaining that both parties bargain in good faith. Otherwise the process is unlikely to yield positive and enduring results.

Representative and strong unions are necessary to ensure that there is equality in the bargaining positions of the parties and to ensure the observance of agreements. Where the employer is represented by an organization which is the other party to the process, such organization should be similarly effective.

Both the management and union should keep their managers and members respectively well informed as a lack of proper communication and information can lead to misunderstandings and even to strikes. Sometimes managers and supervisors who are ill-informed may inadvertently mislead the workers who work under them about the current state of negotiations, the management's objectives and so on. In fact, it is necessary to involve managers in deciding on objectives and solutions, and such participation is likely to ensure greater acceptance and therefore better implementation by them.

Advantages of Collective Bargaining

It is sometimes claimed that in non-industrialized countries settlement of wage issues through collective bargaining especially on a national or industry wise basis—can be an obstacle to a wage policy to promote specific economic objectives because wage rates are not necessarily fixed on criteria designed to promote specific economic and social objectives (other than as compensation for cost of living increases), and that they often tend to reflect the bargaining strength of the parties or the supply and demand conditions of labour. With some exceptions (such as Japan) wage increases through collective bargaining in Asia pay little attention to productivity, individual or group performance and to skills. However, collective bargaining has many advantages which have been claimed for it as a means of resolving differences between management and employees, though it has made little positive contribution to higher productivity and higher earnings by linking pay to performance and skills.

Collective bargaining has the advantage that it settles issues through dialogue and consensus rather than through conflict and confrontation. It differs from arbitration because the latter represents a solution based on a decision of a third party, while arrangements resulting from collective bargaining usually represent the choices or compromises of the parties themselves. Arbitration may invariably displease one party because it usually involves a win/lose situation, and sometimes it may even displease both parties.

Collective bargaining agreements often institutionalize settlement through dialogue. For instance, a collective agreement may provide for methods by which disputes between the parties will be settled. This has the distinct advantage that the parties know beforehand that if they are in disagreement there is an agreed method by which such disagreement may be resolved.

Collective bargaining is a form of participation. Both parties participate in deciding what proportion of the 'cake' is to be shared by the parties entitled to a share. At the end of an agreed term labour again insists on participating in deciding what share of the fruits of their labour should be apportioned to them. Collective bargaining is also a form of participation because it involves a sharing of rule making power between employers and unions, and this has eroded areas which in earlier times were regarded as management prerogatives *e.g.*, transfer, promotion, redundancy, discipline, modernization, production norms. However, in some countries such as Singapore and Malaysia, certain subjects such as promotion, transfer, recruitment, termination of employment on grounds of redundancy or reorganization, dismissal and reinstatement, and assignment of duties within the scope of the contract of employment, are regarded as management prerogatives and outside the scope of collective bargaining. But collective bargaining suffers from the drawback that it seldom deals with how to enlarge the "cake", as the way of increasing the share of each party without eroding competitiveness.

Collective bargaining agreements sometimes renounce or limit the settlement of disputes through trade union action or lock out. Therefore collective bargaining agreements can have the effect of guaranteeing industrial peace for the duration of the agreements, either generally or more usually on matters covered by the agreement.

Collective bargaining is an essential feature in the concept of social partnership towards which labour relations should strive. Social partnership in this context may be described as a partnership between organized employer institutions and organized labour institutions designed to maintain non-confrontational processes in the settlement of disputes which arise between employers and employees.

Collective bargaining has valuable by-products relevant to the relationship between the two parties. For instance, a long course of successful and bona fide dealings leads to the generation of trust. It contributes towards some measure of understanding by establishing a continuing relationship. Once the relationship of trust and understanding has been established, both parties are more likely to attack problems together rather than each other.

In societies where there is a multiplicity of unions and shifting union loyalties, collective bargaining and consequent agreements tend to stabilize union membership. For instance, where there is collective agreement employees are less likely than otherwise to change union affiliations frequently. This is also of value to employers who are faced with constant changes in union membership and consequent inter-union rivalries, resulting in more disputes in the workplace than otherwise.

Collective bargaining agreements which determine wage rates on a national or industry level, place business competition on a more equal footing as a result of some standardization of the costs of labour. This is probably a less important advantage today in the face of technological innovations and productivity drives.

Perhaps most important of all, collective bargaining usually has the effect of improving industrial relations. This improvement can be at different levels. The dialogue tends to improve relations at the workplace level between workers and the union on the one hand and the employer on the other. It also establishes a productive relationship between the union and the employers' organization where the latter is involved in the process.

As between the employer on the one hand and his employees and union on the other, collective bargaining improves relations for the following reasons or in the following ways :

- It requires a continuing dialogue which generally results in better understanding of each other's views.
- Where collective bargaining institutionalizes methods for the settlement of disputes, differences or disputes are less likely to result in trade union action.
- It could lead to cooperation even in areas not covered by collective bargaining arrangements.
- As between unions on the one hand and employers' organizations on the other, collective bargaining improves the industrial relations climate in the following ways :
- It acts as a means of exerting influence on the employer or the employee, as the case may be, where the unreasonable position of one party results in a deadlock. The employers' organization or the union, as the case may be, has an interest in exerting influence on its respective members; the maintenance of the relationship between the two parties is seen as important to issues well beyond the current dispute. Both parties know that the current dispute is only one of many situations which are likely to arise in the future, and that a good relationship needs to be maintained for the overall benefit of their respective members.

The entry of a union and employers' organization into a dispute facilitates conciliation or mediation. Sometimes one or both parties are able to divorce themselves from the main conflict or from their position as representatives of their members, and mediate with a view to narrowing the differences and finding compromise solutions.

Collective bargaining often leads employers' organizations and trade unions to establish links, and to look for and increase areas of common agreement. This in turn ensures to the benefit of their respective members.

As between unions and their members, collective bargaining tends to enhance the stability of union membership. Employees, who perceive that their union is able to secure collective bargaining agreements, or obtain concessions through collective bargaining, are less likely to frequently change their union affiliations.

Current Collective Bargaining Trends

In no country can it be said that collective bargaining has been entirely at the industry or enterprise level, since each system has a mix of both, even though not in equal measure. However, industrialized market economies have generally practiced bargaining at the industry level, except in the USA where there has been more bargaining at the plant or enterprise level. Industry level bargaining in the USA has mainly been in specific sectors such as coal, steel, trucking and construction.

During the last decade there has been a move towards more enterprise level bargaining in many countries due to numerous reasons. There has been a decline in union membership in several countries such as the USA, Britain, France, Netherlands and Australia. Increasing unemployment and difficult business conditions have made employers reluctant to commit to wage policies at the industry or national level. The emergence of governments in some industrialized countries more favorably disposed towards private enterprise has resulted in allowing market forces to operate, thus weakening negotiations at the national level. Many employers view centralized bargaining as facilitating a more equal distribution of incomes (which is one reason why many unions prefer centralized bargaining), but as depriving employers of the ability to use pay as an instrument for productivity improvement and to compensate for skills and performance. Strategic compensation systems are workable only if introduced at the enterprise level to match the goals sought to be achieved. In Sweden, which has been an extreme case of centralized bargaining, one of the strategies of the Swedish employers during the last ten years has been to decentralize collective bargaining. Germany, another country well-known for centralized bargaining, is displaying a tendency towards decentralized bargaining. The push by employers for flexibility in the context of increasing global competition has resulted in many flexibility issues such as new working time arrangements, a typical contracts and pay systems being needed to be dealt with largely at the enterprise level.

Compared with industrialized countries, collective bargaining in Asia has been minimal. There has been an increasing tendency towards bargaining on wages and terms and conditions, which has sometimes resulted in some form of arrangements among governments, employers and unions which lay down certain guidelines as in Singapore, and the Accords from 1983 onwards in Australia. Asia has had a mixture of industry and enterprise level bargaining, with the latter predominating. Apart from low unionization rates in several Asian countries which militate against industry level bargaining, increased competition and the need for flexibility does not make industry level bargaining popular in Asia. The Japanese have demonstrated how a combination of enterprise level bargaining and shop floor level mechanisms enable enterprises to adapt to rapidly changing business conditions and also to increase productivity.

In most countries, therefore, the tendency is to see the enterprise as the centre of gravity of industrial relations. It is likely that some of the main concerns of employers such as productivity, quality, performance, skills development, the need to be competitive and to make rapid changes to adapt to the global marketplace, will eventually result in less centralized collective bargaining.

Review Questions

1. Define Trade Unions. Why do workers organize into Unions?
2. Trace the Historical Evolution of Trade Union movement in India.
3. What are the aims and objectives of Trade Unions?
4. Explain the Structures and types of Trade Unions in India.
5. What are the functions of Trade Union?
6. Explain the Need and Scope of Trade Union.
7. Explain social responsibility of Trade Union.
8. Define Collective Bargaining. What do you think are the reasons why employees restore to collective bargaining?
9. Discuss the merits and demerits of collective bargaining. What are the future trends in Collective Bargaining ? Do you think collective bargaining has a future with knowledge workers?

PROJECT

Visit the nearest factory and see the Trade Union Office of the same. Find in detail the structure of Trade Union and its activities. Analyze the number of Unions in the factory and their leadership. Present in the class the merits of Trade Unions in a company.

Case Study

Role of Collective Bargaining in Corporate Change—Qantas Airways Limited

The world's airlines have undergone significant changes since the early 1980s. The major airlines in Australia have not been isolated from these transformations. Airline deregulation, exposure to the vagaries of international oil politics in the 1970s and again in 2000, the Gulf War, company mergers, full or part privatization of government owned airlines, increased international competition, strategic alliances within routes and between regions, two major recessions and the 1997-8 Asian currency crisis have contributed to pressures upon Australian airline companies to become more competitive. While dealing with these contexts, airlines have had to develop strategies to deal with both the longer cycles of the economy as well as seasonal market fluctuations.

The emphasis has been on cost cutting, especially reductions in labour costs through moderation of wage costs, increased productivity, and the introduction of flexibility through a motivated and more versatile workforce. Cutting labour costs in airlines both in Australia and overseas have involved measures such as reducing salary and wages bills through downsizing and eliminating expensive work practices. On some occasions and in some airlines in North America these measures have included wage reductions and wage freezes. At the same time, the imperative for airlines was to provide high quality service in order to maintain market share, improve revenues, and to maintain high safety standards in operations and maintenance.

Qantas Airways Limited has faced the full range of contextual pressures identified in the introduction. The Australian Government had purchased Qantas in 1947 and was the wholly government owned flag carrier on international routes. Trans Australian Airlines (TAA) was the government owned domestic carrier. From the late 1980s, Qantas experienced significant and complex change. TAA, which was renamed Australian Airlines, had endured continuous and significant change from 1985 at which time James Strong took over as CEO of the domestic operator. Australian Airlines was subsequently purchased by Qantas in 1993. Thus, when many Australian firms began to experience the market pressures of global competition in the late 1980s, Qantas was already an experienced player in a volatile international marketplace and in early 1990 had experienced the difficulties of merging two key operations.

The first aspect of government intervention was the deregulation of the airline industry. Airline deregulation was the least of Qantas's problems, although it affected its domestic operations after merger. The Australian Government deregulated the domestic airline industry in 1990 with a single stage termination of the two airline agreement after a two year period of notice. The objectives of transportation deregulation were to put in place new arrangements designed to promote increased competition and pricing flexibility which were designed to lead to greater economic efficiency in the industry and benefits to the consumer.

The second element of government policy was the decision to partly privatise Qantas. This was followed by the sale of 25 per cent of Qantas to British Airways in March 1993 and a $1.35 billion capital injection from the Government. Soon after, Qantas purchased the domestic carrier, Australian Airlines. Access to domestic routes gave Qantas the edge over Ansett on Australian routes through increased aircraft equipment capacity. Larger capacity Boeing 767 aircraft, already in Qantas's international fleet, were allocated to domestic routes improving on Australian Airline's market share and allowing for market growth. At the same time the company invested in improved cabin design and passenger seating.

Qantas management experienced persistent, internal difficulties in merging the dedicated domestic carrier and an international operator into a single airline. A second task Qantas management faced was overcoming an entrenched public service culture within Qantas and demonstrating to the unions and the staff that 'we need to run a business and costs are critical'. One manager from the private sector noted that:

One of the first things that I noticed when I came across was how slowly everybody walked. I just couldn't believe how they meandered along, and that just typified Qantas.

The appointment of James Strong in October 1993 to form an executive partnership with the new Chairman of the Board, Gary Pemberton, heralded a new era in the history of the airline and a new approach to strategic change. James Strong had been noted for his turnaround of Australian Airlines as Chief Executive Officer in the period of 1985-89. In appointing Strong, the Qantas Board held high expectations for him in the light of his experiences at Australian Airlines. However, they also recognised that Qantas was a much more complex affair to change than the former domestic carrier.

Not the least of Strong's problems was the creation of a unified organisational culture. The differences between the two workforces were quite marked :

When asked to the Qantas people who they worked for they said the Board or Mr Ward or the government and when asked to Australian Airlines people who they worked for the said "the customer".

For senior management, the challenge to create a new culture for the merged airline involved building up a new partnership between staff and management. This involved a need for 'the staff understanding that it is necessary to make a profit' by contributing to aprofitable company, reducing costs and building up a customer service focus. The strategy designed to improve Qantas's performance included in 1995–7 an extensive training programme, development of work teams, new classification structures, a share ownership scheme, changes in the management structure, and 'road shows' (where senior managers reported on the company and explained initiatives at meetings of employees), outsourcing, competitive tendering, and downsizing.

Strong's solution was to implement an integrated approach by appointing a group manager first in 1993, followed by a replacement in 1995, to manage organisational change. Both of these appointments reflected a perspective that strategic change needed to be closely managed from the top and facilitated by specialist change agents to drive the change. Politically, however, the industrial relations executives were in a powerful position to drive change through established industrial relations processes.

Before James Strong was appointed to head Qantas, the industrial relations structure reflected established bargaining relationships and a pre-deregulation approach to dealing with costs. One executive during the study described this period as one where Qantas bowed to the unions; costs were excessive; and a 10 per cent wage increase was granted without resolving many of the issues arising from the Qantas-Australian merger or obtaining flexibilities.

The period 1989 to 1993 was dominated by the industrial issues that arose out of downsizing during 1990, the 1991 enterprise agreement, and the 1992 merger with Australian Airlines. Despite the significance for industrial relations with the unions of these issues, no significant industrial disputes arose out of any of these three events as the company negotiated with the unions. Industrial agreements underwrote the workplace changes and from the company's perspective, the processes were driven by the HR section.

The General Manager Human Resources regarded employee training as pivotal in developing excellent customer service. However, there was a gap between the training and implementation because 'we didn't bother to change any of the procedures to empower them to actually do this.' During this period, the emphasis was upon competency based training programmes and accreditation within the context of the National Training Guarantee Act.

This executive's involvement with Qantas began with a consultancy project to ascertain staff attitudes to the merger with Australian Airlines and to determine why there were difficulties. The findings indicated that there were significant cultural differences in perspectives on working for the new Qantas organisation, as indicated above. Differences between the two cohorts were also expressed in responses to a "Have Your Say" programme which involved 35 focus groups of former Qantas and former Australian employees discussing the issues arising from the merger. Former Australian Airlines staff 'thought it (the programme) was the ant's pants because they are used to having their say about things', whereas 'it was anti-cultural to the old Qantas to allow people to talk like that'. When leadership programmes were introduced at the end of 1993 support was more forthcoming from ex-Australian managers than from those in the old Qantas. The problems identified by the former General Manager Human Resources in integrating training with what happens in the workplace as part of a strategic change process were addressed at this time :

We tried to make the point that people had to develop at work day by day and that really the focus was about 'at work', 'on the job' stuff—it wasn't about building a training empire away from work, because that's in effect the way the managers and supervisors all related.

Relationships with people, focus on quality service, feedback on performance and on-the-job development were held up as guiding principles around which the normal range of HR functions were to be promoted. The new management brought a view that staffs are the best people to consult when it comes to improving quality and restructuring the business. The challenge was to ensure that they were empowered to do this, although this 'empowerment' related only to managerial levels.

Notwithstanding the cycle of change affecting organisation of employee management in Qantas, collective bargaining with unions remained a central process in Qantas industrial relations. Labour cost reduction was a central plank of employee management in Qantas and Australian during the period. John Schaap, the Managing Director, prior to any public talk of purchase by Qantas, spoke of changes necessary in the airline to 'boost and improve productivity … [and] … work practice changes are the main platform from which we intend to achieve this productivity gain'.

Airline managers regard reduced labour costs as one of the significant and necessary features of survival in the deregulated airline industry. It is not the sole means of ensuring profitability and a competitive edge but is part of an overall corporate strategy, the pattern of which is to be found in the United States and Canada. There were a number of factors other than deregulation, which impacted on the airline workforce. Downsizing, the weakening of the industrial strength of the pilots' union, the same recessions which affected North America, the wage restraint written into the Accord, and the Gulf war were some of the contexts for industrial relations in the airlines. Thus, external pressures on labour costs arose in Australia from a number of sources which of themselves had little to do with airline deregulation.

Collective bargaining between management and the unions has been retained as a significant element in the Qantas change strategy notwithstanding a general failure to achieve productivity improvements in earlier enterprise agreements. Qantas undertook in the 1996 enterprise bargaining agreement (EBA) to maintain the existing industrial relationship, that is 'collective bargaining through Unions (and) that as a general position individual contracts will not be applied'. The EBA committed the parties to a recognition that 'good management practice carries with it the responsibility to effectively manage and implement change at the workplace'. The agreement thus bound unions and employees in a legal sense to the process of introducing change in Qantas. Two of the matters the Enterprise Bargaining Agreement III committed unions and management to were :

- (The recognition) that good management practice carries with it the responsibility to effectively manage and implement change at the workplace.
- That the existing industrial relationship will be maintained *i.e.*, collective bargaining through Unions and that as a general provision individual contracts will not be applied.

Attached to the EBA were individual agreements with the unions. These agreements committed the engineering and maintenance unions, other unions and Qantas 'to work together in an open and consultative way to improve company profitability, job security and to provide career path opportunities'. In the agreement with the Construction, Forestry, Mining and Energy Union, enhanced job security was linked to improved business performance in the Engineering and Maintenance Division. An agreement with the Transport Workers Union specifically addressed part-time employment with recognition that its introduction 'is intended to increase the efficiency of the port or department'. The National Union of Workers agreement contained a commitment to abide by the settlement of disputes provision in the award on the basis that 'the underlying philosophy of the enterprise agreement is to ensure that Qantas is a profitable and enduring business and (to) increase job security'.

Questions

1. *Analyze the case, and be prepare to present the same in the class.*
2. *Do you think the management had a clear perspective of importance of Collective bargaining?*
3. *What in your perspective were merits of Trade Unions Actions?*

Chapter **20**

EMPLOYEE DISCIPLINE AND GRIEVANCE PROCEDURE

★ **LEARNING OBJECTIVES** ★

After reading this chapter, you will be able to understand :

- What is discipline?
- Purpose and Nature of Discipline
- Kinds of Problems that Results in Indiscipline
- Approaches to Discipline
- Sources of Disciplinary Rules
- Grievances
- Grievance Procedures
- Employees health and Safety

INTRODUCTION

Discipline is the key to success. Discipline can be positively related to performance. It is the bridge between goals and accomplishments. Effective discipline should be aimed at the behaviour, and not at the employee personality. Theodore Roosevelt has said "With self-discipline almost everything is possible". Self discipline makes employee realize what is required at work. This is because the reason for discipline is to improve performance rather than punishing the employee.

Definition

W.R. Spriegel and **Edward Sohelge,** *"Discipline is the force that prompts an individual or groups to observe rules, regulations and procedures that are deemed necessary to the attainment of an objective."*

Micheal J. Jucious defines, *"Discipline used as a noun and preceded by the objective 'good' means that the workers winningly abide by company rules and executive order. To set right the indiscipline or improve its causes provided punishment provisions are known as discipline."*

Richard P. Calhoon, *"Discipline may be considered the force that prompts individual or groups to observe rules, regulations, standards, and procedures deemed necessary for an organization."* **Ordway Tead** defines it as *'Discipline is an orderly conduct of affairs by the members of an organization who adhere harmoniously in forwarding towards the end which the group has in view, and willingly recognize that, to do this, their wishes must be brought into reasonable unison with the requirements of the group in action.'*

Therefore discipline means securing consistent behaviour in accordance with accepted norms of behaviour. Discipline in an organization may be described as willing cooperation and observance of the rules and regulations of the organization by the management and the workers.

Nature of Discipline

Maintenance of Discipline is prerequisite to the maintenance of national health as it ensures maximum productivity and peace in the nation. Megginson in his work has stated that discipline in Industry involves three things viz. Self-discipline, Orderly Behaviour and Punishment.

Self-discipline implies that a person brings the discipline in himself with a determination to achieve the goals that he has set for himself in life. Orderly behaviour on the other hand refers to a condition that must exist for an orderly behaviour in the organization. Punishment is used to a remedial tool to prevent repletion of the mistake and for others to know the repercussions of a disorderly behaviour or deviation from accepted norms.

Purpose of Discipline

Purpose of discipline at work is to change behaviour. If an employee behaves in such a way that he or she shows that he or she has no intention of being bound by the contract of employment, then the employer can regard the contract as broken. The employer than has right to take disciplinary action. However, the employer/manager should ensure that there is no moral purpose behind disciplinary action, as it is not their responsibility or the right to impose their own moral code. It is the responsibility of the manager or employer to offer an opportunity for improvement and to help the employee to progress.

OBJECTIVES OF DISCIPLINE IN INDUSTRY

The objectives of discipline are to get (see Figure 20.1)

1. To get voluntary acceptance to rules, regulations and policies of the organization in members so that the objectives of the organization are achieved surely, certainly and economically.
2. To develop the feeling of adjustment so that they work according to situations.
3. To provide direction, right to leadership and getting cooperation.
4. To arouse the feeling of endurance and mutual cooperation among workers and management.
5. To instigate the feeling of respect for human being and human relations and create the atmosphere favourable to that.

6. To increase the morale and efficiency of the organization so that it can give maximum production on minimum cost.

1. To get voluntary acceptance.
2. To develop adjustments.
3. To provide direction.
4. To arouse endurance and cooperation
5. To instigate respect for humanity
6. To increase morale efficiency

Fig. 20.1. *Objectives of Discipline in Industry.*

PRINCIPLES OF DISCIPLINE

Some of the principles on which discipline should be based are listed below (Figure 20.2) :

1. **Code of Conduct**. The organization should lay down a proper code of conduct. The rules and regulations for the code of conduct should be prepared with the consent of both the parties. Notification of code of conduct that may result in discipline be widely distributed and notified. Actions that lead to misconduct can be listed and documented so the employees are aware of such actions. Effective discipline requires accurate, written record keeping and written notification to the employees. This will unable them to claim that they have not been notified, in advance, regarding the same. Thus less chance will be left for the employee to say that he "did not know" about the policy.
2. **Centralization of discipline.** On the basis of the code of conduct all employees should be equally treated. Breach of code of conduct should be punished impartially. Centralized means that the discipline decisions should be uniform throughout the organization. The greater the uniformity, higher will be the effectiveness of discipline procedure.
3. **Responsible Person**. Responsibility for disciplinary action should in the hands of a responsible person who may give order to the subordinates. Supervisors and managers need to be trained on when and how discipline should be used. It is necessary to provide training on counseling skills as these skills are used while dealing with problem employees. Moreover, discipline decisions taken by trained supervisors are considered fair by both employees and managers.
4. **Full Knowledge of Rules**. Workers should have full knowledge of the rules and administration. It should be clear as to which punishment is applicable on the violation of the rules. The employer should define the penalties and other actions like warnings, reprimands, discharge and dismissal well in advance. All these action plans must be communicated to the employees.
5. **Preventive Measures**. The management should exercise the preventive approach to maintaining discipline.
6. **Review Discipline Decisions/Appeal**. The person against whom the disciplinary action is taken should have the right to appeal to higher officials if he feels aggrieved. The

disciplinary decisions must be reviewed before being implemented. This will ensure uniformity and fairness of the system and will minimize the arbitrariness of the disciplinary system

7. **Natural Justice.** The principle of natural justice should be followed. The accused should have a fair chance of hearing and then only any action for indiscipline should be taken. The disciplinary decision should be fair enough for the employee. Both over-penalization and under-penalization are considered to be unfair for the problem employee. Moreover, an internal fairness is to be maintained, that is, two employees who have committed the same offense should be equally punished.
8. **Prompt Action.** 'Justice delayed is justice denied', the accused employee should get his decision promptly. There is no effective control on accusation punishment if decisions are delayed. The effective discipline should be immediate. The longer time lag between the misconduct offense and the disciplinary action will result in ineffectiveness of the discipline.
9. **Instrument of Progress**. Discipline system should be progressive in nature. Official disciplinary action is calculated as an instrument of progress of the organization. In a progressive discipline approach the severity of actions to modify behaviour increases with every step as the employee continues to show improper behaviour. The advantage of this approach is that employees can't take it for granted.
10. **Confidential Proceedings.** Disciplinary proceedings should be confidential and not in the presence of other persons. Otherwise he loses faith and respect of high officials.
11. **Impersonal Discipline.** Discipline should be handled impersonally. Managers should try to minimize the ill feelings arising out of the decisions by judging the offensive behaviour and not by judging the person. Managers should limit their emotional involvement in the disciplinary sessions.
12. **Discipline shall be Flexible and Consistent**. The manager administering discipline must consider the effect of actions taken by other managers and of other actions taken in the past. Consistent discipline helps to set limits and informs people about what they can and cannot do. Inconsistent discipline leads to confusion and uncertainty.

1. Code of Conduct
2. Centralization of Discipline.
3. Responsible person
4. Full Knowledge of Rules.
5. Preventive Measures
6. Review of Discipline Decisions/ Appeal
7. Natural Justice
8. Prompt Action.
9. Instrument of Progress
10. Confidential Proceedings
11. Impersonal Discipline
12. Discipline shall be flexible and consistent

Fig. 20.2. *Principles of Discipline.*

Symptoms of General Indiscipline

The symptoms of indiscipline in an organization are :

- Change in normal behaviour.
- Absenteeism.
- Increased grievances
- Lack of concern for performance.
- Go slow
- Disorderly behaviour.

Common Causes of Indiscipline

The common cause of indiscipline could be listed as

(*a*) **Unfair Management Practices**. Management sometimes indulges in unfair practices which results in indiscipline.

- Wage discrimination
- Non-compliance with promotional and transfer policies.
- Discrimination in allotment of work.
- Defective handling of grievances.
- Payment of low wages.
- Low quality of life being provided.

(*b*) **Absence of Effective Leadership**. Poor and ineffective leadership results in poor management in the areas of direction, guidance, etc.

(*c*) **Communication Barriers**. Lack of information in single most important cause of frustration and in turn.

KINDS OF PROBLEMS THAT RESULTS IN DISCIPLINARY ACTION IN INDUSTRY

There are usually four kinds of problems that are usually faced by the manager, which sometimes result in termination of employment.

(*a*) Inefficiency

(*b*) Sickness and unavoidable personal problems

(*c*) Cumulative discipline problems.

(*d*) Immediate discipline problems.

Inefficiency

Inefficiency is the incapacity of the subordinate to perform up to the required standard. This problem usually is for the immediate superior or supervisor to tackle before any disciplinary action can be initiated. Only when these have failed to improve the performance of the individual and the possibility of transferring the person to a more suitable job has been exhausted, should discipline procedure be instituted?

Sickness and Unavoidable Personal Problems

This is usually undertaken when the employee either is not finding job interesting and challenging, or is socially not being accepted in the work group, or is genuinely sick or has family problems. First step in such cases is to investigate the problem through sick visiting or counselling/interview. It is important to ask whether the employee whether he or she is likely to return to job. The disciplinary action to be initiated depends upon the length of the absence and the needs of the work.

Cumulative Discipline Problem

This is a peculiar case in which the employee is a habitual offender. The immediate supervisor should in this case counsel and interview the employee. Thereafter the disciplinary proceeding is set into motion. The process of disciplinary action would be as per the policy in vogue.

APPROACHES TO DISCIPLINE

Handling employee misconduct is a very critical task to be performed by the senior managers. Misconduct and other offensive behaviours often lead to decreased levels of productivity as they affect the individual performance of the employees. To manage discipline among employees, every company opts for a discipline policy which describes the approach it will follow to handle misconduct. Dale Yoder states, "Discipline is to regulate the human behaviour through reward and punishment." The statement stresses upon two aspects—positive and negative. Thus broadly defined, there are two approaches to discipline employees. They are :

- Positive Discipline Approach
- Negative Discipline Approach
- Progressive Discipline Approach

Positive Discipline Approach

It is an arrangement where a worker is motivated to work for himself and he is eager to obey and abide by the rules. It is mental action to influence the mind of the worker in such a way that he grows faith and esteem for the organization. Positive discipline has deep connection with the human relations aiming reaction.

Spriegel states, "Positive discipline does not re-establish the comprehension but brings it to use for the completion of a general objective. Positive discipline does not obstruct a person but makes him suitable to get more freedom without any extra formality. Positive discipline instigates effective co-operation. It depends on the proper acceptance by workers an efficient management and supervisors efficiency. It is a voluntary effort by workers and the management (Figure 20.3).

Positive discipline promotes cooperation and coordination with a minimum of formal organization. It reduces the need for strict supervision required to maintain standards and observe rules and regulations.

Negative Discipline

Negative Discipline describes a way to reduce undesirable behaviour, and increase desirable behaviour, by punishing the negative rather than rewarding the positive. Negative Discipline describes an action that is introduced after an undesirable behavior so that the behaviour will be not be repeated in the future. Negative Discipline is based on the premise that behaviour that is punished is behaviour that will be reduced (Figure 20.3)

	Positive Discipline	***Negative Discipline***
Concept	It is adherence to established norms and regulations, out of fear of punishment.	It is the creation of a Conducive climate in an organization so that employees willingly confirm to the established rules.
Conflict	Employees do not perceive the corporate goals as their own.	There is no conflict between Individual and organizational goals.
Supervision	Requires intense supervisory control to prevent employees from going off the track.	Employees exercise self control to meet organizational objections.

Fig. 20.3. *Difference between Positive and Negative Discipline Approach.*

Progressive Discipline

Progressive discipline is a process for dealing with job-related behaviour that does not meet expected and communicated performance standards. The primary purpose for progressive discipline is to assist the employee to understand that a performance problem or opportunity for improvement exists. The process features increasingly formal efforts to provide feedback to the employee so he or she can correct the problem. The goal of progressive discipline is to improve employee performance.

The process of progressive discipline is not intended as a punishment for an employee, but to assist the employee to overcome performance problems and satisfy job expectations. Progressive discipline is most successful when it assists an individual to become an effectively performing member of the organization.

Failing that, progressive discipline enables the organization with substantial documentation terminate the employment of employees who are ineffective and unwilling to improve.

Typical steps in a progressive discipline system may include these.

- Counsel the employee about performance and ascertain his or her understanding of requirements. Ascertain whether there are any issues contributing to the poor performance that are not immediately obvious to the supervisor. Solve these issues, if possible.
- Verbally reprimand the employee for poor performance.
- Provide a written verbal warning in the employee's file, in an effort to improve employee performance.
- Provide an escalating number of days in which the employee is suspended from work. Start with one day and escalate to five.

Code of Discipline in Industry

To maintain harmonious relations and promote industrial peace, a Code of Discipline has been laid down which applies to both public and private sector enterprises. It specifies various obligations for the management and the workers with the objective of promoting cooperation between their representatives.

The basic objectives of Code of Discipline are to :

- Maintain peace and order in industry.
- Promote constructive criticism at all levels of management and employment.
- Avoid work stoppage in industry.
- Secure the settlement of disputes and grievances by a mutually agreed procedure.
- Avoiding litigations.
- Facilitate a free growth of trade unions.
- Eliminate all forms of coercion, intimidation and violations of rules and regulations governing industrial relations.

The Code is based on the following principles :

- There should be no strike or lockout without prior notice.
- No unilateral action should be taken in connection with any industrial matter.
- Employees should follow go slow tactics.
- No deliberate damage should be caused to a plant or property.
- Acts of violations, intimidation and coercion should not be resorted.
- The existing machinery for the settlement of disputes should be utilized.
- Actions that disturb cordial relationships should be avoided.

To ensure better discipline in industry, management and unions agree on not indulging into various actions. These actions can be summarized as follows :

Management and Union(s) Agree

- that no unilateral action should be taken in connection with any industrial matter and that should be settled at appropriate level.
- that the existing machinery for settlement of disputes should be utilized with the utmost efficiency.
- that there should be no strike or lock out without prior notice.
- that neither party will have recourse to coercion, intimidation, victimization or go – slow tactics.
- that they will avoid litigation, sit-down and stay-in strikes and lock outs.
- that they will promote constructive co-operation between their representatives at all levels and as between workers themselves.
- that they will establish upon a mutually agreed grievance procedure which will ensure a speedy and full investigation leading to settlement.
- that they will abide by various stages in the grievance procedure and take no arbitrary action which would by-pass this procedure; and

Management Agrees

- not to increase workloads unless agreed upon or settled otherwise.
- not to support or encourage any unfair labor practice such as discrimination and victimization of any employee.
- to take prompt action for settlement of grievances and implementation of settlements, awards, decision and orders.

- to take appropriate disciplinary action against its officers and members in cases where enquiries reveal that they were responsible for precipitate action by workers leading to indiscipline.
- union agrees.
- not to engage in any form of physical duress.
- not to permit demonstrations which are not peaceful.
- that their members will not engage or cause other employees to engage in any union activity during working hours.
- to discourage unfair labor practices such as negligence of duty, damage to property and insubordination.
- to take prompt action to implement awards, agreements, settlements and decisions.

Factors Driving Code of Conduct

The code of discipline and conduct communicates to the employees, the expected behavior and the professional responsibilities. The significance of code of conduct is that each employee should behave and perform in a way that preserves the company values and commitments. The code expects employees to conduct business with integrity and honesty. Moreover, it expects the employer to be an equal opportunity employer.

The Code of Conduct policy of a company is determined on the basis of following factors :

1. **Honesty and integrity.** The organization expects the employees to observe honesty and integrity and such conduct should be fair and transparent. The employees should show truthfulness in actions throughout their tenure in the organization.
2. **Disclosure of information.** The employees should not disclose the company information to third parties and other outside organizations. However, the employers should reveal the various policies of the organization to their employees and make them aware about the code of conduct and other policies.
3. **Harassment.** The work environment should be free from all kinds of harassments, especially sexual harassments and verbal harassments. No physical harassments like hitting or pushing are acceptable on part of employees.
4. **Outside employment.** Employees should not indulge in to any kind of concurrent employment without the prior knowledge of employer.
5. **Conflict of interest.** An employee should not indulge into other professions or services or other interests which might conflict with the interest of the company. This means personal interests should not overshadow organizational interests.
6. **Confidentiality.** Employees should protect company's confidential information. The financial records and unpublished data should be kept within the organizations and should not be spread outside the organization.
7. **Equal opportunity employer.** This factor expects the employer to be an equal opportunity, that is, no discrimination should be done on the basis of caste, color, race, gender, religion or physical disabilities.
8. **Misusing company resources.** Employees should not misuse company resources, intellectual property, time and other facilities. They are provided to them for business purposes and thus, should be used in a cost effective way.

9. **Health and safety.** An employer should provide a safe and healthy work environment to its employees. Proper cleanliness and lightening should be provided. A health and safety committee can be set up by the employer consisting of representatives of workers as well.
10. **Payment and gifts.** The employees should neither accept nor offer any kind of illegal payments, donations, remuneration and gifts from outsiders.

SOURCES OF DISCIPLINARY RULES

There are large number of sources under which the rules and regulations governing the employees discipline can be formulated (Figure 20.4).

1. Legislation
2. Case laws
3. Collective Agreements
4. Arbitral Decisions
5. Works Committee
6. Unilateral Personnel Policies
7. Employment Contracts
8. Other Sources

Source : Mankidy, J., Murugavell, A., Gatchalian, J.C. and Gonzales, B.C. , *Disciplinary rules and procedures : India, Malaysia, Philippines* (Occasional paper / Labour Law and Labour Relations Programme)

Fig. 20.4. *Sources of Disciplinary Rules.*

Legislation

Historically governments have played dominant roles in bringing in regulations to maintain peace and harmony in Industry. There has been gradual emergence of body of principles governing disciplinary matters as a result of various decisions of the labour courts, industrial tribunals, civil courts, conferences, international laws and usages. In India the Industrial Employment (Standing Orders) Act 1946 stipulates the broad guidelines to be followed in dealing with employee misconduct. Besides this two other acts viz. the Industrial Disputes Act 1947 lays down certain provisions for the settlement of industrial disputes arising out of disciplinary matters and The Payment of Wages Act 1936 deals with the monetary aspects of penalties in disciplinary action.

The Standing Orders Act requires all industrial undertakings employing 100 or more person's to prepare draft Standing Orders, covering areas such as classification of workers, shift-working, holidays, disciplinary actions etc.

Case Laws

Case Laws play a dominant role in deciding disputes. Since the guidelines for disciplinary action provided in the legislation are not adequate, detailed procedure has been evolved out of case law. The principle of natural justice to be followed in departmental inquiries has come out of a case-law.

Collective Agreements

Collective bargaining gained momentum world over. Most of the collective agreements are at plant levels; however some of these especially in US and Europe are at national levels. Collective agreements may contain general statements, however, in all collective agreements there will be provisions stating that both management and employees have agreed to abide by the certified Standing Orders of the Company.

Arbitral

A dispute can be brought to arbitration at any stage after the imposition of punishment which includes discharge or dismissal. The arbitrator may look into various aspects including the inquiry proceedings, the workers previous record and prior disciplinary actions on the same or similar cases. Reference may be made to case laws or constitutional provisions but there are no clear cut guidelines provided anywhere which need to be strictly followed.

Works Committees

These committees are consultative bodies which aim at bringing about 'amity and good relations' by taking up issues related to working conditions. These committees have usually not played an dominant role in disciplinary cases but these do at time tend to resolve the issues.

Unilateral Personal Policies

On account of strong legal pressures as well as the predominance of trade union influence, it is rather difficult for employers to formulate disciplinary rules.

Employment Contract

Individual employment contracts do not specify disciplinary procedures although a provision to be bound by the existing rules and regulations is normally included. General reference such as "You as an employee will abide by all the rules and regulations of the company, which may also change from time to time" are common in most employment contracts.

Other Sources

Based on the recommendations of the ILO, tripartism in industrial relations was initiated in 1942 by setting up the Indian Labour Conference (ILC) consisting equal number of employee and government representatives. At its 16th Session in 1958, the Indian Labour Conference adopted a Code of Discipline to encourage voluntary maintenance of Industrial Relations in Industries. Although the Codes has been accepted by several unions and employers, however, the Ministry of Labour itself acknowledged that the Code has not had major influence in reducing the indiscipline and conflicts in the Industry.

GRIEVANCES IN INDUSTRY

Grievance means any type of dissatisfaction or discontentment's arising out of factors related to an employee's job which he thinks are unfair. A grievance arises when an employee feels that something has happened or is happening to him who he thinks is unfair, unjust or inequitable.

Definition

R.P. Calhoon, defined grievance as anything that aa thinks or feels is wrong generally accompanied by an actively disturbing feeling. It does not have to be justified."

M.J. Jucious defines it as, "Any discontent or dissatisfaction, whether expressed or not whether valid or not and arising out of anything connected with the company that an employee thinks, believes or even feels as unfair, unjust or inequitable."

Dale Beach has defined grievance as "Any dissatisfaction or feeling or injustice in connection with one's employment situation that is brought to the attention of management."

Keith Davis defines it as, *'Any real or imagined feeling of personal injustice which an employee has concerning his employment relationship.'*

Causes of Grievances

In an organization, a grievance may arise due to several factors such as :

- Violation of management's responsibility such as poor working conditions
- Violation of company's rules and regulations
- Violation of labor laws
- Violation of natural rules of justice such as unfair treatment in promotion, etc.
- Working conditions, and
- Personal factors

Grievance resulting from management policies include :

- Wage rates
- Leave policy
- Overtime
- Lack of career planning
- Role conflicts
- Lack of regard for collective agreement
- Disparity between skill of worker and job responsibility

Grievance resulting from working conditions include :

- Poor safety and bad physical conditions
- Unavailability of tools and proper machinery
- Negative approach to discipline
- Unrealistic targets

Grievance resulting from interpersonal factors include

- Poor relationships with team members
- Autocratic leadership style of superiors
- Poor relations with seniors.
- Conflicts with peers and colleagues

It is necessary to distinguish a complaint from grievance. A complaint is an indication of employee dissatisfaction that has not been submitted in written. On the other hand, a grievance is a complaint that has been put in writing and made formal.

Grievances are symptoms of conflicts in industry. Therefore, management should be concerned with both complaints and grievances, because both may be important indicators of potential problems within the workforce. Without a grievance procedure, management may be unable to respond to employee concerns since managers are unaware of them. Therefore, a formal grievance procedure is a valuable communication tool for the organization.

Grievance Procedure

Grievance procedure is a formal communication between an employee and the management designed for the settlement of a grievance. The grievance procedures differ from organization to organization.

1. Open door policy
2. Stepladder policy

Open Door Policy. Under this policy, the aggrieved employee is free to meet the top executives of the organization and get his grievances redressed. Such a policy works well only in small organizations. However, in bigger organizations, top management executives are usually busy with other concerned matters of the company. Moreover, it is believed that open door policy is suitable for executives; operational employees may feel shy to go to top management.

Stepladder Policy. Under this policy, the aggrieved employee has to follow a step by step procedure for getting his grievance redressed. In this procedure, whenever an employee is confronted with a grievance, he presents his problem to his immediate supervisor. If the employee is not satisfied with superior's decision, then he discusses his grievance with the departmental head. The departmental head discusses the problem with joint grievance committees to find a solution. However, if the committee also fails to redress the grievance, then it may be referred to chief executive. If the chief executive also fails to redress the grievance, then such a grievance is referred to voluntary arbitration where the award of arbitrator is binding on both the parties. See Figure 20.5.

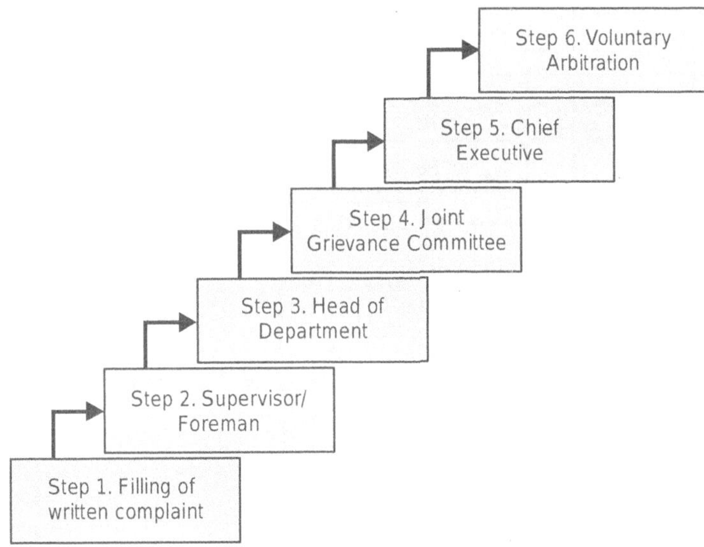

Fig. 20.5. *Stepladder Grievance.*

GRIEVANCE PROCEDURE IN INDIAN INDUSTRY

The 15th session of Indian Labour Conference held in 1957 emphasized the need of an established grievance procedure for the country which would be acceptable to unions as well as to management. In the 16th session of Indian Labor Conference, a model for grievance procedure was drawn up (Figure 20.6). This model helps in creation of grievance machinery. According to it, workers' representatives are to be elected for a department or their union is to nominate them. Management has to specify the persons in each department who are to be approached first and the departmental heads who are supposed to be approached in the second step. The Model Grievance Procedure specifies the details of all the steps that are to be followed while redressing grievances. These steps are :

Step 1. In the first step the grievance is to be submitted to departmental representative, who is a representative of management. He has to give his answer within 48 hours.

Step 2. If the departmental representative fails to provide a solution, the aggrieved employee can take his grievance to head of the department, who has to give his decision within 3 days.

Step 3. If the aggrieved employee is not satisfied with the decision of departmental head, he can take the grievance to Grievance Committee. The Grievance Committee makes its recommendations to the manager within 7 days in the form of a report. The final decision of the management on the report of Grievance Committee must be communicated to the aggrieved

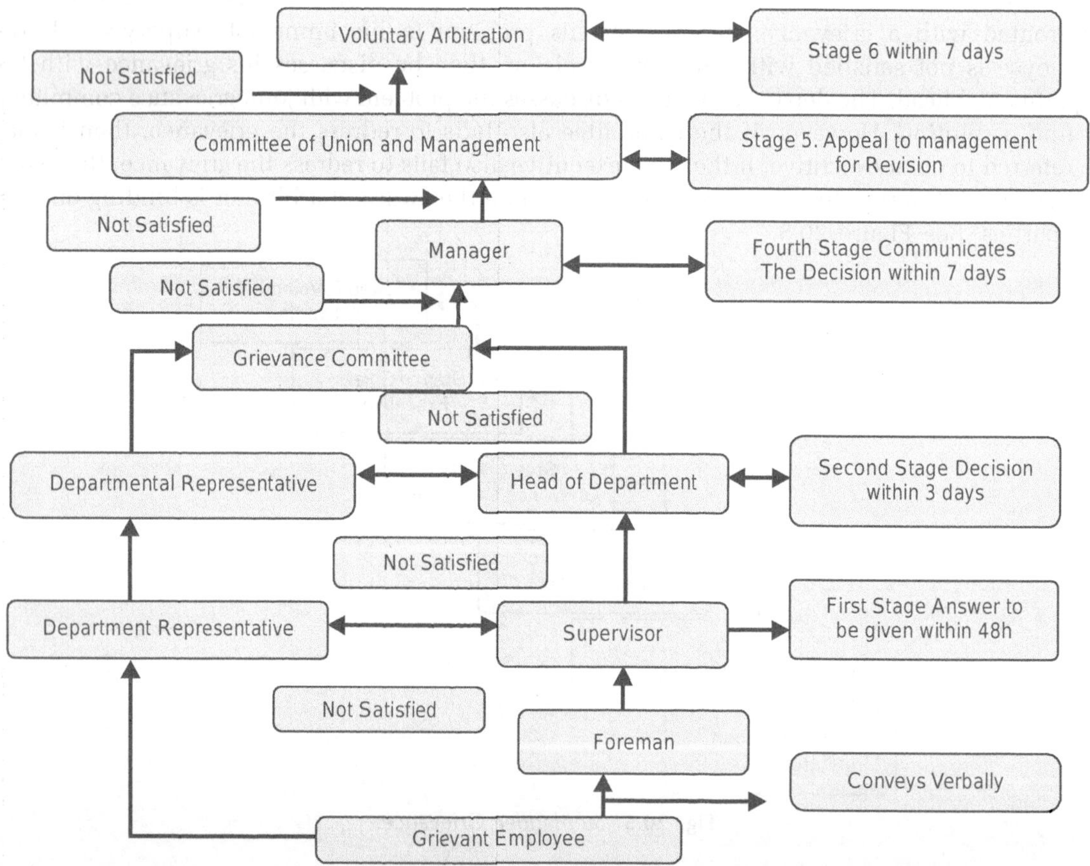

Fig. 20.6. *Grievance Procedure as Suggested by National Commission on Labour.*

employee within three days of the receipt of report. An appeal for revision of final decision can be made by the worker if he is not satisfied with it. The management must communicate its decision to the worker within 7 days.

EMPLOYEE HEALTH AND SAFETY

For smooth functioning of an organization, the employer has to ensure safety and security of his employees. Health and safety form an integral part of work environment. A work environment should enhance the well-being of employees and thus should be accident free.

The terms health, safety and security are closely related to each other. Health is the general state of well being. It not only includes physical well being, but also emotional and mental well being. Safety refers to the act of protecting the physical well-being of an employee. It will include the risk of accidents caused due to machinery, fire or diseases. Security refers to protecting facilities and equipments from unauthorized access and protecting employees while they are on work.

In organizations the responsibility of employee health and safety falls on the supervisors or HR manager. An HR manager can help in coordinating safety programs, making employees aware about the health and safety policy of the company, conduct formal safety training, etc. The supervisors and departmental heads are responsible for maintaining safe working conditions. Responsibilities of managers :

- Monitor health and safety of employees
- Coach employees to be safety conscious
- Investigate accidents
- Communicate about safety policy to employees
- Responsibilities of supervisors/departmental heads :
- Provide technical training regarding prevention of accidents
- Coordinate health and safety programs
- Train employees on handling facilities an equipments
- Develop safety reporting systems
- Maintaining safe working conditions
- Legislations governing Occupational Health and Safety in India
  - o The Factories Act 1948
  - o Mines Act 1952
  - o The Dock Workers Act (Safety, Health and Welfare) 1986.

Issues of Employees Health and Safety

Organizations frame many approaches to ensure health and safety of their employees. But not all of the approaches focus on contribution of both work design and employee behavior to safety. An organizational approach to safety is effective only when both the work design and employee behavior work in coordination towards it. Many organizational and individual issues emerge in management of employee health and safety. They can be summarized as follows :

1. **Physical Work Settings**. The physical settings of work affect the performance of employees to a great extent. Some of these factors include temperature, noise levels, and proper lighting affect job performance. Other work setting factors include size of work area, kinds of materials used, distance between work areas, cubicle arrangement, et al.
2. **Sick Building Syndrome**. It is a situation in which employees experience acute health problems and discomfort due to the time spent in a building (particularly their workplace). Some factors that lead to sick buildings include poor air quality, inadequate ventilation, improper cleanliness, rodents, stench of adhesives and glues, etc.
3. **Ergonomics**. The term comes from the Greek word 'ergon', which means "work," and 'omics' which means "management of." Ergonomics is the study of physiological, psychological, and engineering design aspects of a job, including such factors as fatigue, lighting, tools, equipment layout, and placement of controls. It is the interface between men and machines. Ergonomics is taken into consideration when designing the workstation for computer operators. Problems of back ache, eye strain and headache arise due to long working hours spent in front of computers.
4. **Engineering of Work Equipments and Materials**. Accidents can be prevented in a way by proper placements of dangerous machines. Moreover design of such machines and equipments also plays an important role in safety. Providing safety guards and covers on equipments, emergency stop buttons and other provisions help in reducing the accidents considerably.
5. **Cumulative Trauma and Repetitive Stress**. Cumulative trauma disorder occurs when same muscles are used repetitively to perform some task. This results in injuries of musculoskeletal and nervous system. Employees encounter high levels of mental and physical stress also.
6. **Accident Rates and Individuals**. An individual approach to safe environment helps in reducing the accident rates. This is generally because more problems are caused by careless employees than by machines or employer negligence. A positive attitude towards work environment and other practices promotes employee safety.

EMPLOYEE WELFARE

Comfort and improvement in employees work conditions (environment) and is provided over and above the wages. Welfare helps in keeping the morale and motivation of the employees high so as to retain the employees for longer duration. The welfare measures need not be in monetary terms only but in any kind/forms. Employee welfare includes monitoring of working conditions, creation of industrial harmony through infrastructure for health, industrial relations and insurance against disease, accident and unemployment for the workers and their families.

Labor welfare entails all those activities of employer which are directed towards providing the employees with certain facilities and services in addition to wages or salaries. Labor welfare has the following objectives :

- To provide better life and health to the workers
- To make the workers happy and satisfied

- To relieve workers from industrial fatigue and to improve intellectual, cultural and material conditions of living of the workers.
- The basic features of labour welfare measures are as follows :
- Labour welfare includes various facilities, services and amenities provided to workers for improving their health, efficiency, economic betterment and social status.
- Welfare measures are in addition to regular wages and other economic benefits available to workers due to legal provisions and collective bargaining.
- Labour welfare schemes are flexible and ever-changing. New welfare measures are added to the existing ones from time to time.
- Welfare measures may be introduced by the employers, government, employees or by any social or charitable agency.
- The purpose of labor welfare is to bring about the development of the whole personality of the workers to make a better workforce.

The very logic behind providing welfare schemes is to create efficient, healthy, loyal and satisfied labor force for the organization. The purpose of providing such facilities is to make their work life better and also to raise their standard of living. The important benefits of welfare measures can be summarized as follows :

- They provide better physical and mental health to workers and thus promote a healthy work environment
- Facilities like housing schemes, medical benefits, and education and recreation facilities for workers' families help in raising their standards of living. This makes workers to pay more attention towards work and thus increases their productivity.
- Employers get stable labor force by providing welfare facilities. Workers take active interest in their jobs and work with a feeling of involvement and participation.
- Employee welfare measures increase the productivity of organization and promote healthy industrial relations thereby maintaining industrial peace.
- The social evils prevalent among the labors such as substance abuse, etc are reduced to a greater extent by the welfare policies.

Labour Welfare Funds

Labour welfare refers to all the facilities provided to labor in order to improve their working conditions, provide social security and raise their standard of living. Majority of labour force in India is working in unorganized sector. In order to provide social security to such workers, Government has introduced Labour Welfare Fund to ensure assistance to unorganized labors. Five different welfare funds, which are governed by different legislations, are administered by Ministry of Labour. The purpose of these welfare funds is to provide housing, medical care, educational and recreational facilities to workers employed in beedi industry and non-coal mines and cine workers. The five legislations governing welfare funds are as follows :

1. **The Mica Mines Labour Welfare Fund Act, 1946.** Mica Mines Labor Welfare Fund Act, 1946, provides for levy and collection of cess on all mica exported as duty of Customs not exceeding 6.25% ad valorem. This is 4.5% ad valorem on export with effect from 1st November, 1990.
2. **The Limestone and Dolomite Mines Labour Welfare Fund Act, 1972.** The Limestone and Mines Labor Welfare Fund Act, 1972 provides for the levy and collection of cess

on Limestone and Dolomite as a duty of excise at such rate not exceeding one rupee per metric tone of limestone and dolomite. The rate of cess on Limestone and Dolomite is Re 1/- with effect from 27th December, 2000.

3. **The Iron Ore, Manganese Ore and Chrome Ore Mines Labour Welfare Fund Act, 1976.** The Iron Ore, Manganese Ore and Chrome Ore Mines Labor Welfare Cess Act, 1976 provides for levy and collection of cess on Iron Ore, Manganese Ore and Chrome Ore between 50p to Re. 1/-, Re. 1/- to ₹ 6/- and ₹ 3/- to ₹ 6/- respectively.
4. **Beedi Workers Welfare Cess Act, 1976.** Beedi Workers Welfare Cess Act, 1976 provides for levy of cess by way of excise duty on manufactured beedis from Re. 1/- to ₹ 5/- per thousand manufactured beedis. This is presently ₹ 2 per 1000 beedis with effect from 28th June, 2000.
5. **The Cine Workers' Welfare Fund Act, 1981.** The Cine Workers Welfare Cess Act, 1981 provides for duty of cess, at such rate not being less than one thousand rupees and not exceeding twenty thousand rupees, on every feature film submitted to the Chairman, Central Board of Film Certification. This is ₹ 20,000 per feature film of Hindi and English and for regional films it is ₹ 10,000 per film with effect from 20th April, 2000.

Employees Welfare Schemes

Organizations provide welfare facilities to their employees to keep their motivation levels high. The employee welfare schemes can be classified into two categories viz. statutory and non-statutory welfare schemes. The statutory schemes are those schemes that are compulsory to provide by an organization as compliance to the laws governing employee health and safety. These include provisions provided in industrial acts like Factories Act 1948, Dock Workers Act (safety, health and welfare) 1986, Mines Act 1962. The non statutory schemes differ from organization to organization and from industry to industry.

Statutory Welfare Schemes

The statutory welfare schemes include the following provisions :

- **Drinking water.** At all the working places safe hygienic drinking water should be provided.
- **Facilities for sitting.** In every organization, especially factories, suitable seating arrangements are to be provided.
- **First aid appliances.** First aid appliances are to be provided and should be readily assessable so that in case of any minor accident initial medication can be provided to the needed employee.
- **Latrines and urinals.** A sufficient number of latrines and urinals are to be provided in the office and factory premises and are also to be maintained in a neat and clean condition.
- **Canteen facilities.** Cafeteria or canteens are to be provided by the employer so as to provide hygienic and nutritious food to the employees.
- **Spittoons.** In every work place, such as ware houses, store places, in the dock area and office premises spittoons are to be provided in convenient places and same are to be maintained in a hygienic condition.

- **Lighting.** Proper and sufficient lights are to be provided for employees so that they can work safely during the night shifts.
- **Washing places.** Adequate washing places such as bathrooms, wash basins with tap and tap on the stand pipe are provided in the port area in the vicinity of the work places.
- **Changing rooms.** Adequate changing rooms are to be provided for workers to change their cloth in the factory area and office premises. Adequate lockers are also provided to the workers to keep their clothes and belongings.
- **Rest rooms.** Adequate numbers of restrooms are provided to the workers with provisions of water supply, wash basins, toilets, bathrooms, etc.

Non Statutory Schemes

Many non statutory welfare schemes may include the following schemes :

- **Personal Health Care (Regular medical check-ups).** Some of the companies provide the facility for extensive health check-up.
- **Flexitime.** The main objective of the flexitime policy is to provide opportunity to employees to work with flexible working schedules. Flexible work schedules are initiated by employees and approved by management to meet business commitments while supporting employee personal life needs.
- **Employee Assistance Programs.** Various assistant programs are arranged like external counseling service so that employees or members of their immediate family can get counseling on various matters.
- **Harassment Policy.** To protect an employee from harassments of any kind, guidelines are provided for proper action and also for protecting the aggrieved employee.
- **Maternity and Adoption Leave.** Employees can avail maternity or adoption leaves. Paternity leave policies have also been introduced by various companies.
- **Medi-claim Insurance Scheme.** This insurance scheme provides adequate insurance coverage of employees for expenses related to hospitalization due to illness, disease or injury or pregnancy.
- **Employee Referral Scheme.** In several companies employee referral scheme is implemented to encourage employees to refer friends and relatives for employment in the organization.

Review Questions

1. "To often discipline is thought of only in the negative sense, in reality, positive discipline is immeasurably more effective and plays a larger role in business management." Discuss the statement and indicate the principles to be borne in mind while taking disciplinary action.
2. 'Discipline is what leader makes.' Comment?
3. Explain the causes of Indiscipline in Industry. What is the Code of Discipline in India/Suggest improvements in it?
4. Define grievance and describe its causes. What is the need of Grievances procedure?

5. What do you understand by grievances? Discuss their various causes?
6. Explain the types and steps of grievance procedure.

PROJECT

Lately lot of concern is being exhibited in ensuring health of the employees ? Visit the nearest factory and find out the Government orders on employee welfare. See if these orders are being implemented in the industrial unit.

Case Study

A QUESTION OF INDUSTRIAL DISCIPLINE

In an industry as highly intensive as steel, the concern of management with the equipment and product is understandable. This concern has been translated into punitive measures against members of the work force who are deemed to have endangered either. More serious errors leads to suspension, while in small matters a fine will be deducted from a man's wages. A first hand is in charge of particular furnace and is directly responsible to the sample passer who has oversight for number of furnaces. The status of first hand has traditionally been very high in the steel plant. The Management imposed three days suspension on Ram, the first hand, it was said that he allowed an exceptionally high temperature on his furnace. This has caused considerable delay in the working of the furnace and was likely to have damaged the vessel. The union, however, protested to the management, both on the grounds of severity of the punishment and because it had been implemented before the union had time to discuss the matter with the management, as commonly concerned.

The management claimed that had the immersion temperature been taken at the right time, the situation would not have arisen, therefore Ram must be held responsible. The union contended that only way immersion temperature can be taken is by taking oxygen probe out of the furnace. The union also contended that Ram had done all that could be reasonably expected of him.

Labour relations disturbance between these categories of workers is very rare. This category of workers is accorded high status and authority based essentially on technical competence. There is indeed a considerable mystique surrounding the job of the first hand, which seems, mainly, to be based on the visual skills that were of paramount importance in the pre instrumentation days. Yet it was technical competence of Ram that was called in question. It is not surprising therefore, that the defence which Union Representatives employed was not just plea of mercy but was based on technical considerations.

Question

1. What are the major issues involved in the case?
2. Did the management take correct step in awarding punishment to Ram?
3. Why is the Union so perturbed in Ram being awarded punishment?
4. What remedial measures do you suggest to management so that such incidents are not repeated in future.

❑❑❑

Chapter 21

Work, Commitment, Engagement, Motivation, Job Satisfaction, Alienation and Stress

★ LEARNING OBJECTIVES ★

After reading this chapter, you will be able to understand :

- Work
- Nature of Work
- Theories of Work
- Work Ethics and Work Life Balance
- Organizational Commitment
- Concept of Organizational Commitment
- Classification of Organizational Commitment
- Motivation
- Motivation Theories
- Motivating Factors
- Importance of Motivation and Money as a Motivator
- Job Satisfaction, its importance and dimensions
- Contractual Areas relating to Job Satisfaction – The Knowledge, Psychological, Efficiency Reward, Ethical (Social Value) Contract and task Structure Contract
- Consequences of Job Satisfaction

WORK

Introduction

The future of work is strongly tied to the future of the employment relationship. Some of the more extreme predictions of change of employment patterns predict indeed the end of the traditional employment relationship or the employer age. In the millennium there has been anew breed of employees like the computer programmers, managerial consultants, independent contractors who hop from employer to employer, project to project, and manage their own careers. Here employment is being portrayed as tenuous and entailing fewer reciprocal obligations between firms and workers – with workers moving across organizations and building their own careers. There is also a strong lobby who view that change has been exaggerated, that the internal employment relationship remains at the core of the labour market and that, contrary to predictions, the degree of employment security and the extent of non standard employment contracts have been exaggerated (Taylor, 2003).

Nature of Work

Work is the exertion of effort and application of knowledge and skills to achieve a purpose. Most people work to earn a living to make money. But they also work because of other satisfaction it brings in, such as doing something worthwhile, a sense of achievement, prestige, recognition, the opportunity to use and develop abilities, the scope to exercise power and companionship. Within organization the nature of work is carried out by individuals and governed by employment relationship and the psychological contract.

The very nature of work what people do as members of organizations—rapidly changing ? Robert Reich, (1993) Former US Secretary of Labour, calls this the phenomenon of 'new work'.

"New work involves less rote repetition and more problem solving. Value is added by customizing and continuously improving a product or service to meet customer needs. New work is enhanced, not imperiled by technology. And it cannot be instantly duplicated overseas, because it depends on the one resource within the nation that remains durably here with us- our minds."

The employment relationship which has been in vogue for over three centuries is undergoing a fundamental change due changes in organizational structure. The employing organizations are becoming more permeable and resort to outsourcing their labour requirements the notion of employment relationship bounded by single employer becomes increasingly inappropriate and untenable. Decisions over whether or not to internalize or externalize employment areas are said to be made in relation to both strategic value and relative uniqueness of human assets. Decisions to externalize employment for non valuable and non unique employment posts are taken as synonymous with treating labour as commodity, subject to normal market disciplines. The employment relationship formed within sub contracting organization is assumed to be 'transactional' in nature.

An analysis published in *Fortune* (May 17, 1993) by Walter Kiechel III painted this picture of the workplace in the year 2000.

(*a*) The average company will become smaller, employing fewer people.

(*b*) The traditional hierarchical organizations will give way to a variety of organizational forms, the network of specialist foremost among them.

(*c*) Technicians, ranging from computer repairman to radiation therapists, will replace manufacturing operatives as the worker elite.

(*d*) The vertical division of labour will be replaced by a horizontal division.

(*e*) The paradigm of doing business will shift from making a product to providing a service.

(*f*) Work itself will be redefined : constant learning, more high order thinking, less nine to five mentalities.

THEORIES ABOUT WORK

Labour Process Theory

Labour Process Theory was originally formulated by Karl Marx. His thesis was that surplus is appropriated from labour by paying it less than the value it adds to the labour process. Capitalists therefore design the labour process to secure the extraction of surplus value. The human capacity to produce is subordinated to the exploitative demands of the capitalists, which is an alien power confronting the worker who becomes a 'crippled monstrosity by furthering his skills as if in a forcing house through the suppression of a whole world of productive drives and inclinations.'

Braverman (1974) stated that the application of modern management techniques, in combination with mechanization and automation, secures the real subordination of labour and de-skilling of work in the office as well as the shop-floor. He stated that the removal of al forms of control from the worker is 'the ideal towards which management tends,' and in pursuit of which it uses very productive innovation shaped by science. He saw this essentially the application of thoughts of Taylor.

This concept has its own critiques in Litter and Salaman (1982). They criticized the Baverman's theory as being too simplistic. They argued that there are numerous determinants in the control of labour process, and Baverman's version neglects the diverse and sophisticated character of management control as it responds only to technological advances but also to the changes in the degree and intensity of worker resistance and new product and labour market conditions.

Agency Theory Framework

First introduced in the literature of information economics to provide a theoretical model for the relationship between one party (principal) which delegates work to another party (agent). The agency theory received attention in the organizational control (Ouchi, 1979; Pennings and Woiceshyn, 1986; Thompson, 1967), presenting implications for compensation, risk, and information systems. Agency theory seeks to explain organizational behavior by focusing on the relationship between managers as agents of the firms and the stockholders as principals.

All employment relationships have some form of principal-agent relationship. It is sometimes described as the unending effort of the employer—the principal—to get the agent—the employee—to work. Thus, the idea is there are two actors in the employment relationship : principals and agents. The individuals within the organization are divided into two groups; the principals and the agents. Agency theory explains how to best organize relationships in which one party (the principal) determines the work, which another party (the agent) undertakes (Eisenhardt, 1985). The theory argues that under conditions of incomplete information and uncertainty, which characterize most business settings, two agency problems arise : *adverse selection* and *moral hazard*. Adverse selection is the condition under which the principal cannot ascertain if the agent accurately represents his ability to do the work for which he is being paid. Moral hazard is the condition under which the principal cannot be sure if the agent has put forth maximal effort (Eisenhardt, 1989).

The problems of adverse selection and moral hazard mean that fixed wage contracts are not always the optimal way to organize relationships between principals and agents (Jensen and Meckling, 1976). A fixed wage might create an incentive for the agent to shirk since his compensation will be the same regardless of the quality of his work or his effort level (Eisenhardt, 1985). When agents have incentive to shirk, it is often more efficient to replace fixed wages with compensation based on residual claimancy on the profits of the firm (Alchian and Demsetz, 1972). The provision of ownership rights reduces the incentive for agents' adverse selection and moral hazard since it makes their compensation dependent on their performance (Jensen, 1983).

The argument made above suggests that the provision of residual claims on the profits of a retail outlet provides a strong incentive for agents not to engage in moral hazard or adverse selection and so enhances the performance of a retail distribution system (Brickley and Dark, 1987). By turning individuals into residual claimants on the profits of retail outlets that they have purchased, franchising reduces the incentive to shirk (Alchian and Demsetz, 1972).

However, the argument that franchising provides a superior incentive to fixed wage employment (Williamson, 1991) assumes that the franchised outlets are run by owner-operators. If the franchised outlet is run by a passive owner who hires a manager to run the outlet, then the beneficial effects of franchising on adverse selection and moral hazard are lost. Passive ownership simply recreates the agency problems that franchising is designed to overcome (Bradach, forthcoming).

Moreover, passive ownership increases agency costs over those which exist when the owner hires outlet managers. In place of the cost of managing the agency relationship between the owner and the outlet manager, passive ownership imposes the cost of managing the agency relationship between the franchiser and the passive owner and the cost of managing the agency relationship between the passive owner and the outlet manager. Since the survival of new franchise systems depends on the franchisers' ability to economize on agency costs, those new franchise systems which allow passive ownership should be less likely to survive.

Exchange Theory

Exchange theory proposes that social behavior is the result of an exchange process. The purpose of this exchange is to maximize benefits and minimize costs. According to this theory, people weigh the potential benefits and risks of social relationships. When the risks outweigh the rewards, people will terminate or abandon that relationship.

Exchange Theory shows, human social; behaviour is shaped by the social relations in which it occurs. Social relations in turn are conditioned by the structures within which they are embedded. All relationships have give and take, although the balance of this exchange is not always equal. Exchange theory explains how we feel about a relationship with another person as depending on our perceptions of :

- The balance between what we put into the relationship and what we get out of it.
- The kind of relationship we deserve.
- The chances of having a better relationship with someone else.

In deciding what is fair, we develop a comparison level against which we compare the give/take ratio. This level will vary between relationships, with some being more giving and others where we get more from the relationship. They will also vary greatly in what is given and received. Thus, for example, exchanges at home may be very different, both in balance and content.

In organizational context it sets out to explain the rewards and costs incurred in the interaction between employers and employees. There are three concepts :

(*a*) **Rewards**. These are payoffs that satisfy needs emerging from interactions between individual and the organization.

(*b*) **Costs**. Includes fatigue, stress, anxiety punishments and the value of rewards that people have lost because of lack of opportunity.

(*c*) **Level of Comparison**. People evaluate the outcome of an interaction against the profit and this is satisfactory.

We also have a comparison level for the alternative relationships. With a high such comparison level, we might believe the world is full of lovely people just waiting to meet us. When this level is low, we may stay in a high-cost relationship simply because we believe we could not find any better elsewhere.

Work Ethics

Work ethics include not only how one feels about their job, career or vocation, but also how one does his/her job or responsibilities. This involves attitude, behavior, respect, communication, and interaction; how one gets along with others. Work ethics demonstrate many things about whom and how a person is. Work ethics involve such characteristics as honesty and accountability. Essentially, work ethics break down to what one does or would do in a particular situation. The begging question in a situation involves what is right and acceptable, and above board, versus what is wrong, underhanded, and under the table.

Work ethics are intrinsic; they come from within. A question may involve where they came from, if they come from within. Philosophically, this may lead to various perspectives; however, the truth about work ethics, and where they come from are answered from a Indian World view of "Karma". Work ethics come from God the creator. God made humans in His image, and His word proclaims these various work ethics — honesty, integrity, doing a job well, keeping things above board, and accountability factors.

Work Life Balance

The term 'work-life balance' describes a person's ability to effectively manage their paid work commitments with their career goals, personal, community and cultural responsibilities, interests and obligations. Work-life balance has also been described as :

"...a self defined, self determined state of well being that a person can reach, or can set as a goal, that allows them to manage effectively multiple responsibilities at work, at home, and in their community; it supports physical, emotional, family, and community health, and does so without grief, stress or negative impact."

"...people having some measure of control over when, where and how they work. It is achieved when an individual's right to a fulfilled life inside and outside paid work is accepted and respected as a norm, to the mutual benefit of the individual, business and society."

ORGANIZATIONAL COMMITMENT

Occupational Commitment has become an increasing concern of Managers. Due to recent changes in business situations, including uncertainties in the future, job rotation, organizational restructuring, employee resizing, job insecurity, perceptions and contingency work force growth Cappelli et.al., (1997) have suggested that employee commitment may be shifting from organization's to one's occupation. It is already an acknowledged fact that there are multiple notions of commitment and identity- to employer, union, work group, profession, etc.

In recent times, management has become increasingly interested in how to build and engender worker commitment to organizational goals as part of their quest for sustained quantitative advantage. Guest (1998) has argued that *'the concept of organizational commitment is at the heart of any analysis of Human Resource management.'*

Concept of Commitment and Engagement

The Oxford Dictionary states :

(*a*) Someone is committed when they are morally dedicated.

(*b*) Someone is engaged when they are employed busily.

Chiument (2004) gives meaning of engagement as :

"Engagement is a positive, two ways, relationship between an employee and their organization. Both parties are aware of their own and the others needs, and the way they support each other to fulfill those needs. Engaged employees and organizations will go the extra mile for each other because they see mutual benefit of investing in their relationships."

Guest (1987) suggested that Human Resource Management policies are designed to 'maximize organizational integration, employee commitment, flexibility and quality of work.'

Meaning of Organizational Commitment

Porter et. al. (1974) states, 'commitment refers to attachment and loyalty. It is the relative strength of the individual's identification with, and involvement in, a particular organization. It consists of three factors :

(*a*) A strong desire to remain member of the organization.

(*b*) A strong belief in acceptance of the values and goals of the organization.

(*c*) Readiness to exert considerable effort on behalf of the organization.

Definition

Commitment has been defined by Salanick (1977) as *'Commitment is a state of being in which individual becomes bound by his (sic) actions to beliefs that sustain his activities and his own involvement.'* Three features of behaviour are important in binding individuals to their acts :

(*a*) The visibility of acts.

(*b*) The extent to which outcomes are irrevocable;

(*c*) The degree to which the person undertakes the action voluntarily.

Commitment according to Salanick can be increased or harnessed 'to obtain support for organizational ends and interests,' through which ploys as participation in decision about actions.

Lee, Caswell and Allen (2000) defined occupational commitment as the *'Psychological link between an individual and his/her occupation that is based on an effective reaction to that occupation.'*

Individuals are viewed as psychologically attacking themselves. Thus an individual with higher organizational commitment will strongly identify with his occupation and his positive feeling towards it.

Classification of Organizational Commitment

Meyer and Allen (1991) realized one of the classification related to organizational commitment. They point out that organizational commitment has three elements as affective, continuance and normative.

(*a*) **Affective Commitment.** It refers to psychological attachment of an employee to the organization. It is the commitment in which employees feel the values, objectives and aims of their organizations as much as they assimilate. In this case, the employee strongly assimilates the values of the organization. The employee's stays with organization because they want to *i.e.*, the individual have emotional attachment with the organization. Affective commitment is considered as the best form in employees' commitment for their organization (Balay, (2000); Wasti, (2000); Cetin (2004)) . Riggo (2003) has stated that an Affective Commitment;

- Report higher levels of effort on the job.
- Individuals would be rated as having higher promotional potential.
- Having higher overall performance ratings.
- Show more 'extra role' or citizenship behaviour *e.g.*, helping other co-workers.
- Report less work related stress.
- Report higher levels of career and non-work satisfaction.

(*b*) **Continuance Commitment.** Is the commitment developed by employees' investments into their organization ? It refers to the cost associated with employee leaving the organization. Here the employee thinks they spend too much time and effort for their organizations and so it is a must for them to remain as employees in their organizations. In this the employee continues to stay because he has to for economic reasons or reasons of affect on status etc. Continuance commitment is the situation in which the employees stay in the organization while they take into consideration the cost they will pay if they leave the organization. In this context, affective commitment is affected by variables such as autonomy of work, certainty and significance of work, image of work, qualities the work requires, attitude, behaviour and approaches of the supervisor/ administrator and participation in management while continuance commitment is affected by variable such as age, working times, career satisfaction, will to quit job, education, marital status and other job opportunities.

(*c*) **Normative Commitment.** In this an employee perceives he has obligations to remain with the organization. Employees stay with the organization because they feel they should. Persons have a sense of obligations towards and organization.

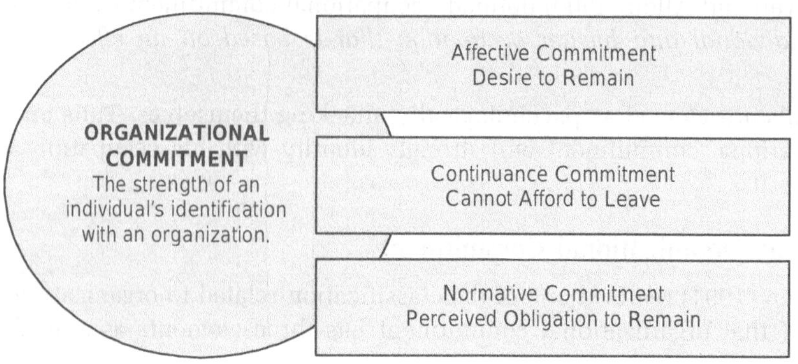

Source : *Nelson and Quick (2003).*

Fig. 21.1. *Classification of Organizational Commitment.*

It can be said that employees with high organizational commitment affect organizational performance in a positive ways, lessen the frequency of performing negative behaviour and improve quality of service. Individuals with organizational commitment are more compatible and productive and have higher levels of satisfaction, loyalty and responsibility. Organizational commitment not only increases the success in certain role, but also encourages the individuals to achieve many voluntary actions necessary for organizational life and high standard system success.

Motivation

Motivation has been derived from the word *'movere'*; meaning 'to move'. Motivation is the general term applying to the entire class of drives, desires, needs, wishes, and similar forces. Motivation is the cause of action (Mook, 1987). When we ask the question : "Why did he or she do that ?" we are inquiring about an individual's motivation. Motivation in organization involves acting to satisfy these drives, desires, and induce the subordinate to act in a desired manner.

Motivation is thought to have three primary functions : a directing function that to steers an individual's behaviour towards or away from specific goals, an activating function that energizes action in pursuit of goals and an organizing function that influences the combination of behavioural components into coherent, goal-oriented behavioural sequences (Green et al., 1984; Kandel et al., 1995). These can be stated as :

(*a*) What energizes human behaviour ?

(*b*) What directs of channels such behaviour ?

(*c*) How is the behaviour sustained or maintained ?

Rennis Likert in his work calls motivation as *'the core of management'*. Motivation is an effective instrument in the hands of management in inspiring the work force. Motivation helps employees to achieve higher performance and create a 'will of work'. Every manager performs a function of motivation for actuating the people to work for the accomplishment of the organizational goals.

Performance in an organization is considered as a function of ability and motivation, thus :

Job Performance = F(ability) (motivation)

Where *f* is the function.

Definition

Atkinson, J.W., in 'An Introduction to Motivation' has defined motivation as :

"The contemporary (immediate) influence on the direction, vigor and persistence of action."

Jones, M.R. in "Nebraska symposium on Motivation" :

"How behaviour gets started, is energized, is sustained, is directed, is stopped and what kind of subjective reaction is present in the organism while all this going on."

Vroom defines motivation as :

".....A process governing choice made by persons or lower organisms among alternative forms of voluntary activity."

Campbell et.al. define motivation as :

".... Motivation has to do with a set of independent/ dependent variable relationships that explain the direction, amplitude, and persistence of an individual's behaviour, holding constant the effects of aptitude, skill, and understanding of the task, and constraints operating in the environment."

To Pinder (1998) *"Work motivation is a set of energetic forces that originate both within as well as beyond an individual's being, to initiate work-related behavior, and to determine its form, direction, intensity, and duration."*

Motivation can be defined as a condition that is initiated by a physiological or psychological deficiency or need of an individual, which causes the individual to behave in a certain manner in order to achieve a particular goal or incentive.

From the above definitions it has been observed that there are some common denominators.

- What energizes human behaviour ? It points to *energetic forces within individuals* that drive them to behave in certain ways and to environmental forces that often trigger these drives.
- What directs or channels such behaviour ? There is the notion of goal orientation on the part of the individuals; their behaviour is directed *towards* something.
- How is this behaviour maintained or sustained ? It contains a *system orientation*, that is, it considers those forces in individuals and in their surrounding environments that feed either to reinforce the intensity of their drive, or the direction of their energy or dissuade them from following a particular course of action.

Many contemporary authors have also defined the concept of motivation. Motivation has been defined as : the psychological process that gives behavior purpose and direction (Kreitner, 1995); a predisposition to behave in a purposive manner to achieve specific, unmet needs (Buford, Bedeian, and Lindner, 1995); an internal drive to satisfy an unsatisfied need (Higgins, 1994); and the will to achieve (Bedeian, 1993). For our purposes, motivation is the inner force that drives individuals to accomplish personal and organizational goals.

MOTIVATION THEORIES

Psychological study of motivation searches for theories that describe the functions of motivation in natural systems such as humans and animals. Motivation theorists do not agree on a unified causal explanation of the behaviour of natural systems. Rather, causation has been attributed to such factors as the environment, physiology, the psyche or social forces with early researchers tending to focus on one or the other of these views. Understanding what motivated employees and how they were motivated was the focus of many researchers following the publication of the Hawthorne Study results (Terpstra, 1979). Five major approaches that have led to our understanding of motivation are Maslow's need-hierarchy theory, Herzberg's two- factor theory, Vroom's expectancy theory, Adams' equity theory, and Skinner's reinforcement theory.

In 1954, Maslow suggested that a person's needs could be diagramed as a five-level hierarchy (Ames and Ames, 1989). At the bottom are basic physiological needs (food, shelter, and clothing). Following is safety. For instance, employees need to be assured that the company cares about their safety. A more broad definition of safety goes beyond the physical aspect of it. It includes variables such as discrimination, favoritism, stereotyping, etc.). The next level of needs would be the social level. At this level the human need for love and a sense of belonging would be addressed when designing Teams, this level should be carefully considered. The fourth level is self-esteem. This need is met when respect among co-workers, management, team members and all different levels of the company structure exist. The last but not least important level of need is self-actualization. According to Maslow, this is the highest and most complex level. It relates to people's need to reach their full potential. One very common mistake in implementing motivational strategies is forgetting to meet the self-actualization level and concentrating too much on meeting only the basic levels of need. Financial rewards are necessary, but they often disregard the highest level in this hierarchy of needs (Figure 21.2).

While Maslow's need hierarchy enjoys great intuitive appeal, experimental evidence has provided only mixed support for his theory. In particular, the existence of a strict ordering of needs is not well supported. In response to this lack of evidence, Alderfer proposed a conceptually simpler framework know as ERG theory. Alderfer's theory proposes only three basic needs : existence, relatedness and growth. Existence needs correspond closely to Maslow's physiological and safety needs. Relatedness needs correspond to love needs. Growth needs correspond to Maslow's esteem and self-actualisation needs. Alderfer asserts that multiple needs may operate simultaneously and that there is no specific order in which needs are activated.

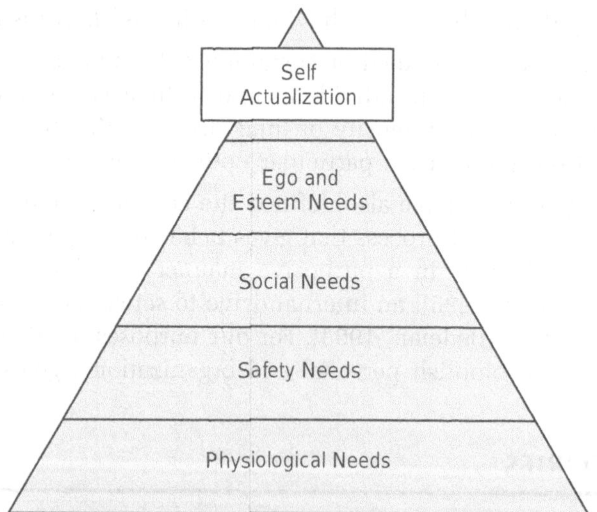

Fig. 21.2. *Maslow's-hierarchy of Needs Theory.*

Herzberg's work categorized motivation into two factors : motivators and hygiene (Herzberg, Mausner, and Snyderman, 1959). Motivator or intrinsic factors, such as achievement and recognition, produce job satisfaction. Hygiene or extrinsic factors, such as pay and job security, produce job dissatisfaction. The process of development of this theory consisted of interviews with more than 200 engineers and accountants. The interviewees were asked to recall incidents at work that they associated with experiencing high or low self-esteem. Results of these interviews indicated that positive feelings were often associated with achievement, recognition, etc., and negative feelings with the work environment such as company policies, relationships with co-workers and supervisors, job security, working conditions, etc. This theory proposes that adding achievement, recognition and variables of that kind to the work environment, increases motivation.

Vroom's theory is based on the belief that employee effort will lead to performance and performance will lead to rewards (Vroom, 1964). Rewards may be either positive or negative. The more positive the reward the more likely the employee will be highly motivated. Conversely, the more negative the reward the less likely the employee will be motivated.

Adams' theory states that employees strive for equity between themselves and other workers. Equity is achieved when the ratio of employee outcomes over inputs is equal to other employee outcomes over inputs (Adams, 1965).

Skinner's theory simply states those employees' behaviors that lead to positive outcomes will be repeated and behaviors that lead to negative outcomes will not be repeated (Skinner, 1953). Managers should positively reinforce employee behaviors that lead to positive outcomes. Managers should negatively reinforce employee behavior that leads to negative outcomes.

Concept of Motivation

The theories discussed give us some insight on how certain techniques need be applied. The need to recognize individual contributions is very much on the top of the list of motivational strategies. Why do people do what they do ? Three factors have been identified as playing a very important role in those decisions. They are (1) feelings, (2) values, and (3) needs. Need is the starting point of motivation.

- **Feelings.** Feelings or emotions can lead to positive or negative behavior. Generally, positive feelings lead to positive behaviors and negative ones tend to sabotage the work environment.
- **Values.** When talking about values we are referring to the importance we give to things. Values include honesty, fairness, loyalty, dignity, professionalism, etc., and their influence in an employee's priorities. Realistically, not all employees will share the same set of values, therefore it is a good idea to implement certain company values and encourage all employees to respect them.
- **Needs.** We talked more about the need hierarchy theory earlier in this report. Mainly, in order for a reinforce to be effective and for motivation to occur, the system has to fulfill not only the employees' basic needs but the more complex ones too.

Thereafter the need stimulates a person to act or drives him towards achieving a particular goal to fulfill that need.

Motivation thus can be seen as a chain reaction *i.e., felt needs* gives *rise to goals sought,* which cause tension, which gives rise to *actions*, the actions results in *achieving goal*, and in turn *satisfaction/getting some incentive* (Figure 21.3).

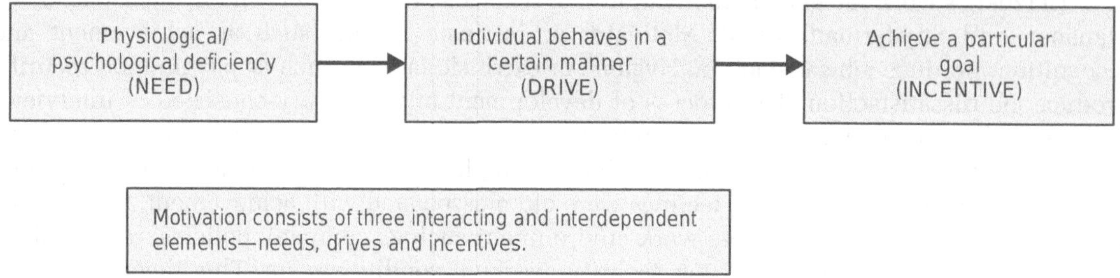

Fig. 21.3. *The Motivation Process.*

Types of Motivation

Motivation at work can take place in two ways :

(*a*) People can motivate themselves by seeking, finding and carrying out work (or being given work) that satisfies their needs or at least leads them to expect that their goals will be achieved.

(*b*) People can be motivated by management through such methods as pay, promotion, perks etc.

There are two types of motivation as originally identified by Hertzberg et.al. (1957).

Intrinsic Motivation

The self generated factors that influence people to behave in a particular way or to move in a particular direction. These factors include responsibility (feeling that the work is important and having control over one's resources), autonomy (freedom to act), scope to use and develop skills and abilities, interesting and challenging work and opportunities for advancement. Intrinsic motivation is fostered by commitment to the work itself; "there is no apparent reward except the activity itself" (Deci, 1975, p.23). Intrinsically motivated employees engage in activities to feel competent and self-determined in relation to the environment. Intrinsic motivation has advantages over extrinsic motivation in organizational activities that demand creativity and learning on the part of employees when organizational goals are unclear and when the exchange rests on highly incomplete contracts (Frey, 1997).

Extrinsic Motivation

What is done to or for people to motivate them ? These includes rewards, such as increased pay, praise promotion etc. Extrinsic Motivators can have immediate and powerful effect but will not necessarily last long. Extrinsic motivation occurs when employees are able to satisfy their needs indirectly through financial rewards and incentives for past performance. Extrinsic motivation results from incentives for behaving in a certain way based on the use of a price system. Extrinsic motivation can be used to coordinate resources by linking employees' monetary motive to the goal of the organization (Osterloh and Frey, 2000). The main characteristic of employees who are externally motivated towards knowledge sharing is that some external contingency, which is valued and expected to be obtainable, drives their involvement in knowledge sharing.

Osterloh and Frey (2000) point out that both kinds of motivation are crucial. They also note that there is a systematic dynamic relationship between the two types of motivation : intrinsic motivation and extrinsic motivation are not additive but rather interactive (Osterloh and Frey, 2000). Further, there might be a negative effect of introducing extrinsic rewards to people who are already intrinsically motivated (Frey, 1997). In that situation, extrinsic motivation is said to crowd out intrinsic motivation (Osterloh, Frost and Frey, 2002; Frey and Jegen 2001). The crowding out effect is especially significant when the monetary compensation is perceived as controlling and hence creates the feeling of being controlled from outside. Similarly, Janssen and Mendys-Kamphorst (2004) conclude that introducing financial incentives to agents to contribute to a socially desirable outcome tends to decrease the number of contributions.

MOTIVATING FACTORS

HRM Practices Affecting Extrinsic Motivation

To keep a person on the job, an organization needs to satisfy his/her needs. That could be achieved through the use of external reward systems that compensate subsidiary employees for the value of their job and their personal contribution to organizational performance. Well-developed compensation systems may include : (competitive) salary, bonuses, fringe benefits, paid-for education, etc. This system must be administered not unconditionally but rather selectively so the more effective an employee's performance, the more rewards the employee receives (Deci, 1975). Therefore, in order for the reward systems to motivate employees, an external control should be in place. The control is achieved through a performance appraisal system. An integrated part of most performance appraisal systems is the evaluation of past performance, identification of gaps between employees' past performance and management expectations, and the establishment of courses of action that aim to fulfill the identified gaps.

HRM Practices Affecting Intrinsic Motivation

Performance-based rewards are not enough to motivate employees to perform effectively on their job. Intrinsically motivated employees can derive satisfaction from doing an effective job per se : "they can become ego-involved with their jobs, emotionally committed to doing them well and take pride from evidence that they are effective in furthering the objectives of the company" (Vroom and Deci, 1970, p. 15). A number of studies on intrinsic motivation have shown that intrinsic motivation is more conducive to creative tasks in general and knowledge transfer in particular (Osterloh, Frost and Frey, 2002).

Management cannot administer intrinsic motivation directly. Instead, as the behavioral school of participative management (Theory Y) suggests, efforts should be made to structure jobs in a way that gives employees various opportunities to participate in decision making on important issues related to them. Furthermore, jobs should be designed to be challenging and interesting (Deci, 1975). What HRM practices could help organizations to achieve both ? Flexible working practices and job design could be beneficial for employees, allowing them to balance their work and other aspects of their lives. Horizontal and vertical transfers may help organizations to better allocate individual needs for growth and development. In addition to the learning experience and improved competencies, employees achieve a higher degree of self-actualization and involvement. In MNCs, international rotation helps to increase the level of integration and inter-unit trust (Edstrom and Galbraith, 1977), but at the same time exposes local employees to international challenges and demanding assignments. In sum, intrinsic motivation could be influenced by HRM practices with emphasis on self-actualization, self-control and self-regulation. The aim is to create conditions under which "effective performance can be a goal rather than a means to the attainment of some other goals" (Vroom and Deci, 1970, p. 16). By applying HRM practices in which the incentives are in the task or job itself, organizations would be able to give intrinsically motivated employees the freedom to determine how to do the job, where to search for needed competencies, etc.

HAMNER'S RULES FOR USING BEHAVIOUR MODIFICATION TECHNIQUES

1. **Rule1.** *Don't reward all individuals equally.* To be effective behaviour reinforcers, rewards should be based on performance. Rewarding everyone equally in effect reinforces poor or average performance and ignores high performance.
2. **Rule 2.** *Be aware that failures to respond can also modify behaviour.* Managers influence their subordinates by what they do not do as well as by what they do. For example, failing to praise deserving subordinate may cause that subordinate to perform poorly the next time.
3. **Rule 3.** *Be sure to tell individuals what they can do to get reinforcement.* Setting a performance standard lets individuals know what they should do to be rewarded : they can then adjust their work pattern accordingly.
4. **Rule 4.** *Be sure to tell individuals what they are doing wrong.* If a manager withholds rewards from a subordinate without indicating why the subordinate is not being rewarded, the subordinate may be confused about the behaviour the manager finds undesirable. They subordinates may feel that he or she is being manipulated.
5. **Rule 5.** *Don't punish in front of others.* Reprimanding a subordinate might sometimes be useful way of eliminating an undesirable behaviour. Public reprimand, however, humiliates the subordinates and may cause all the members of the work group to resent the manager.
6. **Rule 6.** *Be fair.* The consequences of behaviour should be appropriate. Subordinates should be given the rewards they deserve. Failure to reward subordinates properly or over-rewarding undeserving subordinates reduces the reinforcing effect of reward.

Source : Adapted from Hammer, W. Clay, "Reinforcement Theory and Contingency Management in Organizational Settings," in Henry L. Tosi and W. Clay Hammer, eds., *Organizational Behaviour and Management : A Contingency Approach,* rev. ed. 1977.

Motivational Factors

From above it can be summarized that some of the specific motivating factors that affect motivation. The motivational factors can be broadly divided into two groups :

Monetary Factors

(*a*) Salaries or wages. Salaries or wages is one of the most important motivational factors. Reasonable salaries must be paid on time. While fixing salaries the organization must consider such as :

- Cost of living
- Company ability to pay
- Capability of company to pay etc.

(*b*) Bonus. It refers to extra payment to employee over and above salary given as an incentive. The employees must be given adequate rate of bonus.

(*c*) Incentives.

(*d*) The organization may also provide additional incentives such as medical allowance, educational allowance, HRA , allowance, etc.

(e) Special individual incentives. The company may provide special individual incentives. Such incentives are to be given to deserving employees for giving valuable suggestions.

Non Monetary Factors

(a) **Status or Job Title**. By providing a higher status or designations the employee must be motivated. Employees prefer and proud of higher designations.

(b) **Appreciation and Recognition.** Employees must be appreciated for their services. The praise should not come from immediate superior but also from higher authorities.

(c) **Delegation of Authority**. Delegation of authority motivates a subordinate to perform the tasks with dedication and commitment. When authority is delegated, the subordinate knows that his superior has placed faith and trust in him.

(d) **Working Conditions**. Provision for better working conditions such as air-conditioned rooms, proper plant layout, proper sanitation, equipment, machines etc, motivates the employees.

(e) **Job Security**. Guarantee of job security or lack of fear dismissal, etc can also be a good way to motivate the employees. Employees who are kept temporarily for a long time may be frustrated and may leave the organization.

(f) **Job Enrichment**. Job enrichment involves more challenging tasks and responsibilities. For instance an executive who is involved in preparing and presenting reports of performance, may also asked to frame plans.

(g) **Workers Participation**. Inviting the employee to be a member of quality circle, or a committee, or some other form of employee participation can also motivate the work-force.

(h) **Cordial Relations**. Good and healthy relations must exist throughout the organization. This would definitely motivate the employees.

IMPORTANCE OF MOTIVATION

Motivation offers several importances to the organization and to the employees :

- Higher efficiency
- Reduce absenteeism.
- Reduces employee turn over.
- Improves a corporate image.
- Good relations.
- Improved morale.
- Reduced wastages and breakages.
- Reduced accidents.
- Facilitates initiative and innovation.

Money as a Motivator

It is normally believed that money acts as a motivator. In general the role of money as a motivator depends upon certain factors :

- Money fails to motivate people, when there is no direct relationship between reward and effort.
- Economic conditions of people influence the Importance of money. For poor person, the value of certain amount of money is quite high as compared to rich.
- Money is a significant motivator at lower level of employee's level however money may not be a significant factor for senior executives who have already fulfilled their lower level needs.
- Employees are concerned not only with the amount of money paid to them, but it should be fair and equitable as paid to that of the employees of same level or status.
- Social attitudes towards money and wealth also decide the motivation to earn more and more.

JOB SATISFACTION

Introduction

Job satisfaction is a complex and a multifaceted concept, which can mean different things to different people. Job satisfaction is usually linked with motivation, but the nature of relationship is not clear. Job satisfaction is more of an attitude and internal state. It could for example, be associated with a personal feeling of achievement, either

The heart of job satisfaction is in your attitude and expectations; it's more about how you approach your job than the actual duties you perform. Whether you work on the farm, a production line, in the corner office or on the basketball court, the secret is to understand the key ingredients of your unique recipe for job satisfaction.

Definition

Job satisfaction has been defined in several different ways and a definitive designation for the term is unlikely to materialise. A simple or general way to define it therefore is as an attitudinal variable :

'Job satisfaction is simply how people feel about their jobs and different aspects of their jobs. It is the extent to which people like (satisfaction) or dislike (dissatisfaction) their job (Spector, 1997).'

Locke (1976) defined Job Satisfaction as *'a pleasurable positive emotional state resulting from the appraisal of one's job or job experiences.'*

An alternative approach is that proposed by Sousa-Poza and Sousa-Poza, (2000) based on the assumption that there are basic and universal human needs, and that, if an individual's needs are fulfilled in their current situation, then that individual will be happy. This framework postulates that job satisfaction depends on the balance between work-role inputs—such as education, working time, effort—and work-role outputs—wages, fringe benefits, status, working conditions, intrinsic aspects of the job. If work-role outputs ('pleasures') increase relative to work-role inputs ('pains'), then job satisfaction will increase (Sousa-Poza and Sousa-Poza, 2000).

Other theorists (*e.g.*, Rose, 2001) have viewed job satisfaction as a bi-dimensional concept consisting of intrinsic and extrinsic satisfaction dimensions. Intrinsic sources of satisfaction depend on the individual characteristics of the person, such as the ability to use initiative, relations with supervisors, or the work that the person actually performs; these are symbolic or qualitative facets of the job. Extrinsic sources of satisfaction are situational and depend on the environment, such as pay, promotion, or job security; these are financial and other material rewards or advantages of a job. Both extrinsic and intrinsic job facets should be represented, as equally as possible, in a composite measure of overall job satisfaction.

This distinction, as described by Rose, relates to the double meaning of the word 'job' : the work tasks performed and the post occupied by the person performing those tasks.

Mumford has also defined Job Satisfaction as :

'The attainment of a good 'fit' between what the employee is seeking from his work- his job needs, exceptions and aspirations – and what he is required to do in his job – the organizational job requirements which mould his experience.'

Importance of Job Satisfaction

Clark (1998) summarizes the importance of job satisfaction for both employers and their workers :

"Job satisfaction is important in its own right as a part of social welfare, and this (simple) taxonomy [of a good job] allows a start to be made on such questions as 'In what respects are older workers' jobs better than those of younger workers ?' (and vice versa), 'Who has the good jobs ?' and 'Are good jobs being replaced by bad jobs ?'. In addition, measures of job quality seem to be useful predictors of future labour market behaviour. Workers' decisions about whether to work or not, what kind of job to accept or stay in, and how hard to work are all likely to depend in part upon the worker's subjective evaluation of their work, in other words on their job satisfaction."

Dimensions of Job Satisfaction

There is some doubt whether job satisfaction consists of a single dimension or a number of separate ones, this doubt has crept in because some workers may be satisfied with some aspects of their work and dissatisfied with others. There does, however, appear to be a positive correlation between satisfaction levels in different areas of work. This suggests a single overall factor of job satisfaction. However, it seems there is no one, general, comprehensive theory which explains job satisfaction.

Job Satisfaction is still considered by a number of critics to be, a complex concept and difficult to measure objectively. A wide range of variables relating to individual, social, cultural organizational and environmental factors affect the level of job satisfaction. The major factors that effect Job Satisfaction are :

- *Individual Factors* include personality, education, intelligence and abilities, age, marital status. Orientation to work.
- *Social Factors* include relationships with co-workers, group working and norms, opportunities for interaction, informal organization.
- *Cultural Factors* include underlying attitudes, beliefs and values.
- *Organizational Factors* include nature and size, formal structure, personnel policies and procedures, employee relations, nature of the work, technology and work organization, supervision and styles of leadership, management systems and working conditions.
- *Environmental Factors* include economic, social, technical and governmental influences.

These different factors affect job satisfaction of certain individuals in a given set of circumstances, but not necessarily in others. A strategic way of achieving job satisfaction is to establish a corporate culture that encourages communication and is directed towards quality work. It is particularly important for employees to see excellence rewarded, to not fear making mistakes, to work in an atmosphere of helpfulness, and to see a relationship between hard work and rewards. As the tool for such strategic changes, organizational culture can be altered by reshaping functions, such as the communications systems and by building teams and creating leaders. Managing change is the challenge for today's businesses and its success or failure will judge the viability of any firm in the years to come.

Contractual Areas Relating to Job Satisfaction

There are five different areas relating to job satisfaction :

(*a*) **The Knowledge Contract**. It is when the employees believe their skills are being adequately used and their knowledge is being developed to make them increasingly competent. It is recognized that different people have widely different expectations in this area, some want their skills developed while others are content with an 'easy life'.

(*b*) **The Psychological Contract**. It has been defined as '...the perceptions of the two parties, employee and employer, of what their mutual obligations are towards each other'. These obligations will often be informal and imprecise : they may be inferred from actions or from what has happened in the past, as well as from statements made by the employer, for example during the recruitment process or in performance appraisals. Some obligations may be seen as 'promises' and others as 'expectations'. The important thing is that they are believed by the employee to be part of the relationship with the employer. It is the psychological contract that effectively tells employees what they are required to do in order to meet their side of the bargain, and what they can expect from their job. It may not - indeed in general it will not - be strictly enforceable, though courts may be influenced by a view of the underlying relationship between employer and employee, for example in interpreting the common law duty to show mutual trust and confidence. A useful model of the psychological contract is offered by Professor David Guest of Kings College London (see Figure 21.4). In outline, the model suggests that :

- The extent to which employers adopt people management practices will influence the state of the psychological contract
- The contract is based on employees' sense of fairness and trust and their belief that the employer is honouring the 'deal' between them
- Where the psychological contract is positive, increased employee commitment and satisfaction will have a positive impact on business performance.

Inputs	***Contents***	***Outputs***
Employee Characteristics	fairness	Employee behaviour
Organizational Characteristics	Trust	Performance
Human Resource Practices	delivery	

Fig. 21.4. *A Model of Psychological Contract (Adapted from Guest et. al. 2002).*

(*c*) **The Efficiency/Rewards Contract.** This is composed of three areas. First, the effort-reward bargain, which is the amount the employer, is prepared to pay as opposed to the view of the employee about how much he is worth. While this probably an area of prime importance of management, it is not necessary a prime motivator for an employee. Second, work controls, which may be tighter loose but need to fit the employee's expectations. Third, the supervisory control, such as necessary back up facilities *e.g.*, information, materials, specialist knowledge etc.

(*d*) **The Ethical (Social Value) Contract.** It measure the values of the employee match those of the employer organization. In some organizations performance is everything, while others value other factors. Companies can be paternal or welfare oriented while others aim to achieve the characteristics of 'success'. The better the match of an organization's values with those of the employee, the higher the level of job satisfaction.

(*e*) **The Task Structure Contract.** This involves the degree to which the employee's tasks are regarded as being demanding and fulfilling. Particularly important are the number of skills required , the number and nature of targets, plus the feedback mechanism, the identity, distinctiveness and importance of tasks and the degree of autonomy and control over the tasks that employee has. According to Nguyen, Taylor and Bradley (2003), one of the variables that may be expected to influence job satisfaction is 'the degree of perceived autonomy that workers enjoy in the way they do their job'. The expected relationship is that more autonomy is associated with greater job satisfaction. Technology can affect the task-structure fir substantially and can reduce the fit by simplification and repetitiveness. However, it is also seen as a variable which can be improved dramatically by designing the technical system to meet the requirements of the task structure fit.

Causes of Job Satisfaction

Hodgetts (1991) has listed the organizational factors that can cause job satisfaction.

Pay and Pay Benefits. The importance of equitable reward in an organization cannot be overemphasized. Fair promotion policies and practices add to job satisfaction (Witt and Nye, 1992).The old adage "you get what you pay for" tends to be true when it comes to staff members. Across the population pay is quite minor predictor of happiness, but within organizations relative pay is important, especially how far workers think that they are being paid equitably, in comparison to others (Berkowitz *et al.*, 1987). If individuals believe they are not compensated well, they will be unhappy working for you.

Promotion. The level of satisfaction will depend upon the acceptability of the system in operation, be it system based on merit, or seniority, or whatever combination of the two.

Job. This would embrace :

(*a*) Skills Variety—the extent to which a job allows a worker to use a number of different skills and abilities in executing his or her duties (Glisson and Durick, 1988);

(*b*) Interest and challenge derived from the job, in particular moderate challenge (Katzell, Thompson andGuzzo, 1992);

(*c*) Lack of role ambiguity—how clearly the individual understands the job (Gilsson and Durick, 1988).

Leadership. There has been endorsement of people centered or participative leadership as a determinant of job satisfaction (Miller and Monge, 1986).

Work Group. It would appear that good intra-group working and supportive colleagues have value in not permitting job dissatisfaction to surface, rather than promoting job satisfaction. Social factors are important – worker feels satisfied if he belongs to a friendly and supportive working group, having a supervisor who uses the right skills, and belonging to an organization which is fairly small, has few levels in the hierarchy, and where there is participation in decision making.

Working Conditions. Where working conditions are good and comfortable, and safe, the setting appears to be appropriate for job satisfaction, though not necessarily high job satisfaction. Job satisfaction is partly innate (Arvey *et al.*, 1989). Extraverts have more job satisfaction, those high in neuroticism less, as with happiness in general. Also important is the 'fit' between person and job, both in terms of ability, and also challenge, sociability and values.

In addition to above other factors are :

(*a*) *Recognition.* Individuals at all levels of the organization want to be recognized for their achievements on the job. Their successes don't have to be monumental before they deserve recognition, but your praise should be sincere.

(*b*) *Responsibility.* Employees will be more motivated to do their jobs well if they have ownership of their work. This requires giving employees enough freedom and power to carry out their tasks so that they feel they *'own'* the results.

GENERATION GAPS

Difference in values held by different groups is often called *generation gaps*. The commentators describe the latest generation gaps a split over future prospects for fulfillment in the workplace (Rattan, S. (1993). "Why Busters hate Boomers" *Fortune*, October 4, pp 56-70). The implications for managers are significant, because the gap can represent a challenge to the longstanding idea that managers must be motivators and that employees need motivating pushes (or shoves from their managers. A recent *Fortune* report enumerated these differences.

There are three basic approaches to work : is it a job, a career, or a passion ? Depending on which type of work you are in right now, the things that give you satisfaction will vary.

- If you work at a JOB, the compensation aspects of the position will probably hold more appeal than anything else, and have the greatest impact on whether you stay or go.
- If you work at a CAREER, you are looking for promotions and career development opportunities. Your overall satisfaction is typically linked with your status, power, or position.
- If you work at a PASSION, the work itself is the factor that determines your satisfaction, regardless of money, prestige, or control.

Once you have identified the blend of status, power, or intrinsic enjoyment that need to be present in your work for you to feel satisfied, you then need to work on some of our seven 'ingredients' for a satisfying job. These ingredients are :

- Self-awareness
- Challenge
- Variety
- Positive attitude
- Knowing your options
- Balanced lifestyle

- A sense of purpose
- Self-Awareness

Consequences of Job Satisfaction

It is a commonplace view that if an organization does not create conditions for the minimum level of job satisfaction, there would be loss of productivity, employee turnover, absenteeism, and morale. However, the relationship between job satisfaction and performance at work may not be very clear. The old view that happy worker is a productive worker does not clarify the complex relationship between job satisfaction and productivity.

It may be important to distinguish between positive and negative aspects of job satisfaction. Herzberg et al. (1959) stated that (positive) satisfaction is due to good experiences, and that these are due to 'motivators'—achievement, recognition, the work itself, responsibility and advancement. Dissatisfaction is due to bad experiences caused by 'hygiene' factors - supervisors, fellow workers, company policy, working conditions, and personal life (Herzberg et. al., 1959). This was supported by critical incident studies in which workers were asked to describe occasions when they had felt exceptionally good or exceptionally bad.

Work Performance

The empirical evidence shows that link between job satisfaction and performance is weak (Iaffaldano and Muchinsky, 1985). However, Ostroff (1992) maintains that there is a link between job satisfaction and performance at organizational level. One explanation for the weak relationship between job satisfaction and performance at the individual level of analysis is that the research instruments used may not always be able to capture the many complex interactions at workplace. The content theories of motivation assume a direct relationship between job satisfaction and improved performance. The expectancy theories of motivation, however, recognize the complexity of work motivation and consider in detail the relationship between motivation, satisfaction and performance.

Vroom (1964) after twenty studies found no simple relationship, and only a low median correlation (0.14) between job satisfaction and job performance. Luthans suggests that, *"Although most people assume a positive relationship, the preponderance of research evidence indicates that there is no strong linkage between satisfaction and productivity."*

However, two factors does improve job satisfaction and performance viz. (*a*) job level and machine paced work (Petty, McGee and Cavender, 1984); (*b*) job level or position in hierarchy.

Argyle in his work *The Social Psychology of Work* suggested a probable relationship between

Employee Turnover

Employee turnover is of considerable concern for the management, because it disrupts normal operations, causes morale problems for those who stay behind

Analyses have been made of job satisfaction and labour turnover, and the correlation is typically –.20 to –.30 and rarely greater than –.40 (Mobley, 1982). Carsten and Spector (1987), in a meta-analysis of forty-seven studies, found an overall correlation of –.23 (but of –.51 under high unemployment, see below). Labour turnover correlates with different components of job satisfaction, but especially satisfaction with job content (Mobley et. al., 1979).

Absenteeism

Absenteeism is a major problem at work. There is a negative relationship between satisfaction and absenteeism thought the co-relationship is not high. Absenteeism is increased by job dissatisfaction, but is partly due to other demands viz. taking family to visit a place etc. Half of the absenteeism is due genuine sickness, and is greater in less skilled workers. There is a clearer correlation with voluntary or unexcused absence which is not due to sickness. The relationship is stronger for women, manual workers, workers in larger firms and younger workers (Metzner and Mann, 1953). These are the people who are absent more, so that there is a less skewed distribution; Smith (1977) states that outside factors can act to reduce the correlation between dissatisfaction and absenteeism.

Commitment to Organization

Commitment correlates with job satisfaction, and causation is in both directions. Organizational commitment is measuring job satisfaction.

Job Descriptive Index

The Job Descriptive Index is perhaps the most popular scale for measuring job satisfaction. It measure Smith's five facets of job viz. work, pay, promotions, co-workers and supervision. Table 21.1 provides the definitions of these items and sample items for measuring each one.

Table 21.1 Facets Measured by the Job Descriptive Index

Facet	*Description*
Work	Satisfaction with work and its attributes includes opportunities for creativity and task variety and ability to increase one's knowledge, responsibility, work volume, autonomy, and complexity. Satisfying work appears to be work that can be accomplished and is intrinsically challenging (routine work)
Pay	Satisfaction with work based on the perceived difference between actual pay and expected pay which in turn is based on perceived inputs and outputs of the job and the pay of other comparable employees. The personal financial situation of the employee, the economy, and the amount of pay an employee has received previously also influence satisfaction (income adequate for normal expenditure).
Promotions	Satisfaction with promotion is based on the employee's satisfaction with the company's promotion policy and the administration of that policy. It is thought to be a function of frequency of promotions, the importance of promotions, and the desirability of promotions (good opportunity for promotion).
Supervision	Satisfaction with supervision is based on an employee's satisfaction with his or her supervisor's knowledge and competence and the supervisor's warm, interpersonal orientation (hard to please).
People on the Job	Satisfaction with the people on the job, which is often called the coworker facet, refers to satisfaction with one's fellow employees or clients. Separate facets may be created using the same items to measure satisfaction with people such as staff and satisfaction with clients (helpfulness).
Job in General	Satisfaction with job in general reflects the employee's global long term evaluation of his or her job. It subsumes the evaluation of the above five facets and the interactions as well as the employee's evaluation of other long term situational and individual factors (better than most).
Adapted from W. K. Botzer , P.C. Smith, D.A. Kravitz, S.E. Lovell, K.B. Paul, B.A. Relly and C.E. Redy (1990) User's manual for Job Descriptive Index and the Job in General, (Bowling Green Off : Bowling Green State University) pp. 44-45.	

Job Diagnostic Survey

Hackman and Oldham (1980) developed a scale called the Job Diagnostic Survey to measure each one of the variables of their model. Survey measures employee satisfaction with job security, pay, co-workers, and supervision. In addition, items measure growth satisfaction and general satisfaction. See Table 21.2.

Table 21.2 Satisfaction Items from the Job Disgnostic Survey

Job Security@	The amount of Job Security I have How secure things look for me in the future of the organization
Pay@	The amount of pay and fringe benefits I receive. The degree to which I am fairly paid for what I contribute to the organization
Co-workers*	The people with whom I talk and with whom I work. The chances to get to know other people while on the job. The chance to help other people while at work.
Supervision*	The degree of respect and fair treatment I receive from my supervisor. The amount of support and guidance I receive from my supervisor. The overall quality of supervision I receive in my work.
General@	How satisfied I am with my job. The kind of work I do in this job. The frequency with which I think of quitting my job (reverse scoring). How satisfied most of my co-workers are with their jobs. The frequency with which my co-workers think of quitting their jobs.
Growth@	The amount of personal growth and development I get in doing my job. The feeling of worthwhile accomplishment I get from doing my job. The amount of independent thought and action I can exercise in my job. The amount of challenge in my job.

@ The response format for items in these facets is a seven point scale ranging from extremely dissatisfied to extremely satisfied.

* The response format for items in these facets is a seven point scale ranging from disagree strongly to agree strongly satisfied

Source : Hackman, J.R. and Oldham, G.R.(1980) *Work Design* © Addison-Wesley Publishing Co. Inc.

MINNESOTA SATISFACTION QUESTIONNAIRE

The Minnesota Satisfaction Questionnaire (MSQ) is designed to measure an employee's satisfaction with his or her job. Three forms are available : two long forms (1977 version and 1967 version) and a short form. The MSQ provides more specific information on the aspects of a job that an individual finds rewarding than do more general measures of job satisfaction. The MSQ is useful in exploring client vocational needs, in counseling follow-up studies, and in generating information about the reinforcers in jobs.

The MSQ is a paper-and-pencil inventory of the degree to which vocational needs and values are satisfied on a job. The MSQ can be administered to groups or to individuals, and is appropriate for use with individuals who can read at the fifth grade level or higher. All three forms are gender neutral. Instructions for the administration of the MSQ are given in the booklet. The MSQ Long Form requires 15 to 20 minutes to complete. The Short Form requires about 5 minutes. Unless the 15 to 20 minutes required for the Long Form is impractical, it is strongly recommended that the Long Form be used, as it provides much more information for the short additional administration time required.

Long-Form MSQ. Measures job satisfaction on 20 five-item scales :

Ability Utilization	Co-workers	Moral Values
Achievement	Creativity	Recognition
Activity	Independence	Responsibility
Advancement	Security	Supervision—HumanRelations
Authority	Social Service	Supervision—Technical
Company Policies	Social Status	Variety
Compensation		Working Conditions

Additionally, a 20-item General Satisfaction scale is also scored.

There are two versions of the long-form MSQ, a 1977 version and a 1967 version.

The 1977 version, which was originally copyrighted in 1963, uses the following five response choices :

Very Satisfied
Satisfied
"N" (Neither Satisfied nor Dissatisfied)
Dissatisfied
Very Dissatisfied

Normative data for the 21 MSQ scales for 25 representative occupations, plus employed disabled and employed non-disabled workers, are in the MSQ manual. A "ceiling effect" obtained with the rating scale used in the 1977 version tends to result in most scale score distributions being markedly negatively skewed—most responses alternate between "Satisfied" and "Very Satisfied."

The 1967 version adjusts for this ceiling effect by using the following five response categories :

Not Satisfied
Somewhat Satisfied
Satisfied
Very Satisfied
Extremely Satisfied

This revised rating scale resulted in distributions that tend to be more symmetrically distributed around the "satisfied" category, with larger item variance. Limited normative data are provided in the MSQ manual for the 1967 version. For this reason the 1967 version of the MSQ is best used where normative data are not required, such as prediction studies or within-organization comparisons where external norms are not necessary.

Short-Form MSQ. This form consists of 20 items from the long-form MSQ that best represent each of the 20 scales. Factor analysis of the 20 items resulted in two factors—Intrinsic and Extrinsic Satisfaction. Scores on these two factors plus a General Satisfaction score may be obtained. The short-form MSQ uses the same response categories used in the 1977 long form. Normative data for the three scales for six selected occupations are in the manual.

Review Questions

1. What is job satisfaction ? How can it be measured ?
2. How does job satisfaction influence work behaviour ?
3. Explain the factors influencing job satisfaction.
4. What are the determinants of job satisfaction ?
5. How does job satisfaction influence work behaviour ? Explain with reference to private sector in India.
6. What is motivation and why is it important ?
7. How is Maslow's hierarchy of needs related to motivation in organization ?
8. What is Herzberg's two factor approach to job satisfaction and dissatisfaction ? Why has this approach been criticized ?

Case Study 1

Pallavi Bhardwaj was a Senior Programme Officer in a medium size IT Company. She joined the company as a Junior Programme Officer and after four years he was promoted as Senior Programme Officer. Pallavi was hard working and sincere in her work and expected others to put in their best efforts. Both his superiors and subordinates generally appreciated her work behaviour. She was quite by nature and did not believe in loose talk.

Assistant manager Systems vacancy came up in the organization and Pallavi was confident that she would be promoted to the vacant position. However, one of his colleagues, who had joined the company later than she had, was promoted. Pallavi approached Senior Manager and HOD and expressed her concern that he had been discriminated and that he should have been promoted. Both of them told her that the management knew who was to be promoted and on what basis, and that he should not interfere in such matters. Since then Pallavi became extraordinarily quite and withdrawn.

Later one day, a team from consultancy firm came to the company and spent the day observing Pallavi and others at work. They came on the next two days also. During these days Pallavi felt a strained and tense atmosphere in the office. There was a feeling among the employees that something was brewing. In the following week rumours were afloat that company is on the blocs for sale to a MNC. Number of employees especially females approached Pallavi and wanted to know what was brewing up. Rumours led to apprehension of possible retrenchment. But Pallavi had little to say, and had heard nothing from her superiors.

Questions

1. What specific changes do you notice in Pallavi's behaviour and in what will the behaviour affect the performance of the company and why ?
2. As Pallavi's manager what steps would have taken if you noticed any change in her behaviour.

Case Study 2

FLEXIBLE WORK PRACTICES AT PREMJEET & CO

Introduction

Job-sharing was introduced by Premjeet and Co for the receptionist position almost five years ago. Shared by two people working part-time, the job-share arrangement was such a success that the firm has since negotiated a series of flexible work arrangements with a number of its staff.

Today, of the nine staff employed by the firm, only two work the standard hours of nine to five, five days a week.

The details below illustrates the staffing schedule for the nine staff at Premjeet and Co.

These work arrangements have been introduced in response to the needs of staff rather than as a matter of policy.

In the course of recruiting new staff, the firm found that people with the necessary qualifications and experience did not necessarily wish to work full time from nine to five, five days a week due to personal or family commitments. The firm sought a non-monetary solution to the problem of attracting and retaining staff by negotiating a series of flexible work arrangements with a majority of its staff.

Sita, job-shares the position of receptionist with Shikha. Working part-time was a choice she made after years of working in a full-time position, where she was working up to sixty hours a week, "I couldn't live without working and didn't want to work full-time again".

Neha who is responsible for monitoring company annual returns and maintaining the firm's database, made the decision to return to the workforce after her youngest child started school. Working between 9.30 a.m. and 3.30 p.m. twice a week means she can be at home in the afternoon. Her present working arrangement also enables her to maintain her interest in the sport of golf, playing twice a week.

Vradhi, an undergraduate accountant, is completing his University degree. The work arrangements negotiated with the firm enables him to start work later on Tuesdays and Thursdays and finish earlier on Mondays to attend classes.

Priyanka made the decision to return to the workforce as a practising chartered accountant. With two young children, working two days a week suits her needs.

Swati who is also completing her tertiary qualifications needed the practical experience but could only work one day a week. The firm offered to provide her with training and work experience with the opportunity for a full-time position on completion of her course.

According to Premjeet Kashyap, it's a choice of lifestyle to have a balance of work and leisure. A full time job does not necessarily suit some people. Their frustration and dissatisfaction in a full time job could translate into a decline in efficiency and productivity. Flexible work practices motivate staff to be more productive as they perform better when they are satisfied with their working arrangements.

"Also, I think you tend to retain staff longer by helping them balance their lifestyle and work. They are happier working under these arrangements and are more likely to stay longer."

Both management and staff agree that overall, work arrangements at Premjeet and Co. have worked extremely well.

Questions

1. How do you think have the flexible working hours benefited the company ?
2. What are the potential problems in such an arrangement ?
3. Does this system help in promoting excellence in the company.

How Does Your Practice Rate?

To evaluate your practice's performance in the area of job satisfaction and to identify where you might focus your efforts, complete the following self-assessment, which is structured around Frederick Herzberg's motivation-"hygiene" theory. As you answer each question, keep in mind the needs and concerns of your employees and colleagues.

	Yes	No
Name of the Employee		
Company and administrative policies		
Does the practice have a policy manual?	☐	☐
Are the policies easy to understand?	☐	☐
Do employees perceive the policies as fair?	☐	☐
Are all persons in the practice required to follow the policies?	☐	☐
Do employees have easy access to the policies?	☐	☐
Do employees have input into the policies?	☐	☐
Has the practice revisited or revised its policies recently?	☐	☐
Are your policies reasonable compared with those of similar practices?	☐	☐
Supervision		
Do the practice's supervisors possess leadership skills?	☐	☐
Do they treat individuals fairly?	☐	☐
Do employees feel that they can trust their supervisors?	☐	☐
Do the practice's supervisors use positive feedback with employees?	☐	☐
Does the practice have a consistent, timely and fair method for evaluating individual performance?	☐	☐
Salary		
Are your practice's salaries comparable to what other offices in your area are paying?	☐	☐
Are your practice's benefits comparable to what other offices in your area are offering?	☐	☐
Do your employees perceive that they are being paid fairly?	☐	☐
Do your employees perceive that their benefits are sufficient?	☐	☐
Does the practice have clear policies related to salaries, raises and bonuses?	☐	☐
Interpersonal relations		
Do individuals have opportunities to socialize with one another during the workday?	☐	☐
Do they have a sense of camaraderie and teamwork?	☐	☐
Does the practice deal with individuals who are disruptive?	☐	☐

Working conditions

Does your practice's equipment (everything from computers to scales) work properly? ☐ ☐

Is the facility clean and up to date? ☐ ☐

Are office conditions comfortable? ☐ ☐

Do individuals have adequate personal space? ☐ ☐

Work itself

Do employees perceive that their work is meaningful? ☐ ☐

Do you communicate to individuals that their work is important? ☐ ☐

Do you look for ways to streamline processes and make them more efficient? ☐ ☐

Achievement

Do individuals have clear, achievable goals and standards for their positions? ☐ ☐

Do individuals receive regular, timely feedback on how they are doing? ☐ ☐

Are individuals' talents being utilized? ☐ ☐

Are individuals adequately challenged in their jobs? ☐ ☐

Recognition

Do you recognize individuals for their major accomplishments on the job? ☐ ☐

Do you recognize individuals' small victories? ☐ ☐

Do you give employees recognition in a timely, meaningful way? ☐ ☐

Does the practice have a formal program (such as "employee of the month") for recognizing staff members' achievements on the job? ☐ ☐

Responsibility

Do individuals perceive that they have ownership of their work? ☐ ☐

Do you give them sufficient freedom and authority? ☐ ☐

Do you provide opportunities for added responsibility (not simply adding more tasks)? ☐ ☐

Advancement

Do you reward individuals for their loyalty? ☐ ☐

Do you reward individuals for their performance? ☐ ☐

Do you promote from within, when appropriate? ☐ ☐

Do you support continuing education and personal growth? ☐ ☐

If you answered "no" to any of the questions above, consider addressing those areas within your practice and seek input from your employees and colleagues.

❑❑❑

Chapter 22

HUMAN RESOURCE INFORMATION SYSTEM

★ LEARNING OBJECTIVES ★

After reading this chapter, you will be able to understand :

- What is Human Resource Information System ?
- Human Resource Information System, its scope, objectives and uses.
- Function of Human Resource Information System.
- Objectives and Scope of Human Resource Information System.
- Uses and importance of Human Resource Information System.
- Process of Human Resource Information System.

INTRODUCTION

A Human Resource Management System (HRMS), Human Resource Information System (HRIS), HR Technology or also called HR modules, refers to the systems and processes at the intersection between human resource management (HRM) and information technology. It merges Human Resource Management as a discipline and in particular its basic Human Resource activities and processes with the information technology field, whereas the programming of data processing systems evolved into standardised routines and packages of enterprise resource planning (ERP) software. On the whole, these ERP systems have their origin on software that integrates information from different applications into one universal database. The linkage of its financial and human resource modules through one database is the most important distinction to the individually and proprietary developed predecessors, which makes this software application both rigid and flexible.

Human Resource Information System provides management with strategic data not only in recruitment and retention strategies, but also in merging Human Resource Information System data into large-scale corporate strategy. The data collected from Human Resource Information

System provides management with decision-making tool. Through proper Human Resource management, firms are able to perform calculations that have effects on the business as a whole. Such calculations include health-care costs per employee, pay benefits as a percentage of operating expense, cost per hire, return on training, turnover rates and costs, time required to fill certain jobs, return on human capital invested, and human value added. It must be noted though, that, none of these calculations result in cost reduction in the HR function (Gerardine DeSanctis, 1986 : 15).

Human Resource Information System are seen to facilitate the provision of quality information to management for informed decision-making. Most notably, it supports the provision of executive reports and summaries for senior management and is crucial for learning organizations that see their human resource as providing a major competitive advantage. Human Resource Information System is therefore a medium that helps human resource professionals perform their job roles more effectively (Grallagher, 1986; Broderick and Boudreau, 1992).

Lawler and Mohrman (2001) in Hussain et al., (2007) established that the use of Human Resource Information System had consistently increased over the previous years, irrespective of, the degree of strategic partnership held by the Human Resource function. Definitely, Human Resource Information System usage had increased substantially even in firms where Human Resource had no strategic role. They cautioned, however, that Human Resource Information System usage and, in particular, fully integrated Human Resource Information System systems, did not necessarily ensure that HR would become a full strategic partner.

HRIS shape an integration between human resource management (HRM) and Information Technology. Even though these systems may rely on centralized hardware resources operationally, a small group of Information System specialists residing within the personnel department increasingly manage, support, and maintain them. Human Resource Information System support planning, administration, decision-making, and control., the system supports applications such as employee selection and placement, payroll, pension and benefits management, intake and training projections, career-path monitoring, equity monitoring, and productivity evaluation. These information systems increase administrative efficiency and produce reports capable of improving decision-making (Gerardine DeSanctis, 1986 : 15).

DEFINITION

A Human Resources Information System is a system that lets you keep track of all your employees and information about them. It is usually done in a database or, more often, in a series of inter-related databases.

Tannenbaum (1990) defines HRIS as a technology-based system used to acquire, store, manipulate, analyze, retrieve, and distribute pertinent information regarding an organization's human resources.

Kovach et al., (1999) defined HRIS as a systematic procedure for collecting, storing, maintaining, retrieving, and validating data needed by organization about its human resources, personnel activities, and organization unit characteristics. Furthermore, HRIS shape integration between human resource management (HRM) and Information Technology. It merges HRM as a discipline and in particular basic HR activities and processes with the information technology field (Gerardine DeSanctis, 1986 : 15).

As is the case with any complex organizational information system, an HRIS is not limited to the computer hardware and software applications that comprise the technical part of the system it also includes the people, policies, procedures, and data required to manage the HR function (Hendrickson, 2003).

COMPONENTS OF HUMAN RESOURCE INFORMATION SYSTEM

Kovach et al., (1999) presented the three major functional components in any HRIS by giving the model below :

The Input function enters personnel information into the Human Resource Information System. Data entry in the past had been one way, but today, scanning technology permits scanning and storage of actual image off an original document, including signatures and handwritten notes. The maintenance function updates and adds new data to the database after data have been entered into the information system. Moreover, the most visible function of a Human Resource Information System is the output generated. According to Kovach et al., (1999), to generate valuable output for computer users, the Human Resource Information System have to process that output, make the necessary calculations, and then format the presentation in a way that could be understood. However, the note of caution is that, while it is easy to think of Human Resource information systems in terms of the hardware and software packages used to implement them and to measure them by the number of workstations, applications or users who log onto the system, the most important elements of Human Resource Information System are not the computers, rather, the information. The bottom line of any comprehensive Human Resource Information System is to ensure information validity, reliability and utility first and the automation of the process second.

USERS OF HUMAN RESOURCE INFORMATION SYSTEM

HRIS meet the needs of a number of organizational stakeholders. Typically, the people in the firm who interact with the HRIS are segmented into three groups (Anderson, 1997) :

(1) HR professionals,

(2) Managers in functional areas (production, marketing, engineering etc.) and

(3) Employees.

HR professionals rely on the HRIS in fulfilling job functions (regulatory reporting and compliance, compensation analysis, payroll, pension, and profit sharing administration, skill inventory, benefits administration etc.). Thus, for the HR professional there is an increasing reliance on the HRIS to fulfill even the most elementary job tasks. As human capital plays a larger role in competitive advantage, functional managers expect the HRIS to provide functionality to meet the unit's goals and objectives. Moreover, managers rely on the HRIS's capabilities to provide superior data collection and analysis, especially for performance appraisal and performance management.

Additionally, it also includes skill testing, assessment and development, résumé processing, recruitment and retention, team and project management, and management development (Fein, 2001). Finally, the individual employees become end users of many HRIS applications. The increased complexity of employee benefit options and the corresponding need to monitor and modify category selections more frequently has increased the awareness of HRIS functionality among employees. Web-based access and self-service options have simplified the modification process and enhanced the usability of many benefit options and administration alternative for most employees.

FUNCTIONS OF HUMAN RESOURCE INFORMATION SYSTEM

Human Resource Information System's function can be broadly classified into two processes :

(*a*) Data Collection

(*b*) Data Management

The Guest's theory of HRM was based on four HR policy goals : strategic intentions, commitment, flexibility and quality. These policy goals, nevertheless, were related to HRM policies expected to produce desirable organizational outcomes. The four policy goals were described as :

- *Strategic intention :* ensuring that HRM is fully integrated into strategic planning by allowing coherent HRM policies, which enable line managers to use HRM practices as part of the day-to-day work
- *Commitment :* ensuring that employees feel bound to the organization and are committed to high performance through excellent behavior
- *Flexibility :* providing an adaptable organization structure and functional flexibility based on multiple skills.
- *Quality :* enabling a high quality of goods and services through high-quality flexible employees

For, Flint et al., (2005) the field of Human Resource Management (HRM) has in recent times been seen as moving away from a supportive - selecting, training, and retaining-(Porter, 1996) to a strategic role (Bartlett & Ghoshal, 2002). The latter explained that rather than being supportive, focusing on recruiting, training and taking care of benefits, HRM's role has become strategic building and using human capital to ensure competitive advantage. This is further explained using a diagrammatic presentation in Figure 2 to illustrate the strategic and supportive roles of HR, and HRM functions.

Functional HRIS must create an information system that enables an assimilation of policies and procedures used to manage the firm's human capital as well as the procedure necessary to operate the computer hardware and software applications (Hendrickson, 2003). While information technology affects Human Resource (HR) practices (Lengick- Hall et al., 2003) HRIS and HRIS administration comprise a distinct supporting function within HR. Some of the HRIS functions are given in succeeding paragraphs.

Integrating the Technologies of HR

Developments in Information Technology have dramatically affected traditional HR functions with nearly every HR function (example, compensation, staffing, and training) experiencing some sort of reengineering of its processes. However, this process of change has created significant challenges for HR professionals resulting in the transformation of traditional processes into on-line processes.

Increased Efficiency

Rapid computing technology has allowed more transactions to occur with fewer fixed resources. Typical examples are payroll, flexible benefits administration, and health benefits processing. Though technologies of early mainframes provided significant efficiencies in these areas, the difference is that the record processing efficiencies that were once only available to large firms are now readily available to any organization size (Ulrich, 2001).

Increased Effectiveness

Most often, as with processes, computer technology is designed to improve effectiveness either by in terms of the accuracy of information or by using the technology to simplify the process. This is especially the case where large data sets require reconciliation. However, onerous manual reconciliation processes may be executed faster, but also with near perfect accuracy using automated systems. For instance, pension and profit sharing applications, benefits administration, and employee activities are just to mention but a few. Using computer technology in these processes ensures accurate results and offer substantial simplification and timeliness over manual processing. Consequently, the vast majority of HR functions have had some degree of automation applied in order to gain both efficiency and effectiveness.

IT-Enabled Processes

While many of the application areas' gains are through increased effectiveness and efficiency over manual processing, some are only possible using contemporary technologies. Most notably, computer-based (web-based) training is a growing area of HR practice that was not available until computer software was created. Even computer based training was not as practical as it is today because it was geographically dispersed until the training was upgraded from computer-based to web-accessible training. However, by taking traditional computer-based training programs and making them accessible on the Internet, firms have created a powerful tool to upgrade and assess employee skill sets. Moreover, many other traditional HR functions have evolved Information Technology (IT) -dependent components with the advent of the Internet. Online recruitment centers, along with the ability to conduct virtual interviews, background checks, and personnel tests on-line have dramatically changed those processes, increasing the geographic reach of firms for potential employees.

OBJECTIVES OF HUMAN RESOURCE INFORMATION SYSTEM

An organization gains competitive advantage by using its employees effectively, drawing on their expertise and ingenuity to meet clearly defined objectives. Torrington et al., (2005 : 5) identified the role of the human resource functions with the key objectives. These four objectives are the corner stone of all HR activities. These include Staffing, Performance, Change-management and Administration. Staffing objective focuses on finding the appropriate pool of human resources needed to ensure fully and timely supply of work force (Ibid). It therefore involves designing organizational structures, identifying working conditions for different groups of employees followed by recruiting, selecting and developing the personnel required to fill the roles. Performance objective aims at ensuring workforce motivation and commitment for effective performance. Consequently, employees training and development remain important.

Typically, the better The Human Resource Information Systems (HRIS) provide overall :

- Management of all employee information.
- Reporting and analysis of employee information.
- Company-related documents such as employee handbooks, emergency evacuation procedures, and safety guidelines.
- Benefits administration including enrollment, status changes, and personal information updating.
- Complete integration with payroll and other company financial software and accounting systems.
- Applicant and resume management.

The HRIS that most effectively serves companies tracks :

- attendance and PTO use,
- pay raises and history,
- pay grades and positions held,
- performance development plans,
- training received,
- disciplinary action received,
- personal employee information, and occasionally,
- management and key employee succession plans,
- high potential employee identification, and
- applicant tracking, interviewing, and selection.

An effective HRIS provides information on just about anything the company needs to track and analyze about employees, former employees, and applicants. Your company will need to select a Human Resources Information System and customize it to meet your needs.

With an appropriate HRIS, Human Resources staff enables employees to do their own benefits updates and address changes, thus freeing HR staff for more strategic functions. Additionally, data necessary for employee management, knowledge development, career growth and development, and equal treatment is facilitated. Finally, managers can access the information they need to legally, ethically, and effectively support the success of their reporting employees.

In addition to focusing day to day working HRIS also toady meet the strategic human resource management and HR strategy. HRIS assists in a number of important themes associated with the notion of SHRM (Bratton and Gold 2003 : 37). These are :

- Re-engineering
- Leadership
- Workplace learning
- Trade unions

ADVANTAGES OF HUMAN RESOURCE INFORMATION SYSTEM

In today's corporate world human resources has come to play a very critical role in a business. Whether it concerns the hiring and firing of employees or whether it concerns employee motivation, the Human Resources department of any organization now enjoys a very central role in not only formulating company policies, but also in streamlining the business process.

To make a human resource department more effective and efficient new technologies are now being introduced on a regular basis so make things much simpler and more modernized. One of the latest human resource technologies is the introduction of a Human Resources Information System (HRIS); this integrated system is designed to help provide information used in HR decision making such as administration, payroll, recruiting, training, and performance analysis.

Human Resource Information System (HRIS) merges human resource management with information technology to not only simplify the decision making process, but also aid in complex negotiations that fall under the human resource umbrella. The basic advantage of a Human Resource Information System (HRIS) is to not only computerize employee records and databases but to maintain an up to date account of the decisions that have been made or that need to be made as part of a human resource management plan.

The four principal areas of HR that are affected by the Human Resource Information System (HRIS) include; payroll, time and labor management, employee benefits and HR management. These four basic HR functionalities are not only made less problematic, but they are ensured a smooth running, without any hitch. A Human Resources Information System (HRIS) thus permits a user to see online a chronological history of an employee from his /her position data, to personal details, payroll records, and benefits information.

The advantage of a Human Resource Information System (HRIS) in payroll is that it automates the entire payroll process by gathering and updating employee payroll data on a regular basis. It also gathers information such as employee attendance, calculating various deductions and taxes on salaries, generating automatic periodic paychecks and handling employee tax reports. With updated information this system makes the job of the human resource department very easy and simple as everything is available on a 24x7 basis, and all the information is just a click away.

In time and labor management a Human Resource Information System (HRIS) is advantageous because it lets human resource personnel apply new technologies to effectively gather and appraise employee time and work information. It lets an employee's information be easily tracked so that it can be assessed on a more scientific level whether an employee is performing to their full potential or not, and if there are any improvements that can be made to make an employee feel more secure.

Employee benefits are very crucial because they help to motivate an employee to work harder. By using a Human Resource Information System (HRIS) in employee benefits, the human resource department is able to keep better track of which benefits are being availed by which employee and how each employee is profiting from the benefits provided.

A Human Resource Information System (HRIS) also has advantages in HR management because it curtails time and cost consuming activities leading to a more efficient HR department. This system reduces the long HR paper trail that is often found in most HR divisions of companies and leads to more productive and conducive department on the whole.

COST AND BENEFIT OF HRIS

An HRIS system represents a large investment decision for companies of all sizes. Therefore, a convincing case to persuade decision makers about the HRIS benefits is necessary. The common benefits of HRIS frequently cited in studies included, improved accuracy, the provision of timely and quick access to information, and the saving of costs (Lederer, 1984; Wille and Hammond, 1981). Lederer (1984) discussed why the accuracy and timeliness of HRIS is very important in terms of operating, controlling, and planning activities in HR. In addition, Kovach et al., (2002) listed several administrative and strategic advantages to using HRIS. Similarly, Beckers and Bsat (2002) pointed out at least five reasons why companies should use HRIS. These are :

- Increase competitiveness by improving HR practices
- Produce a greater number and variety of HR operations
- Shift the focus of HR from the processing of transactions to strategic HRM
- Make employees part of HRIS, and
- Reengineer the entire HR function

In their 2002, HRIS survey, Watson Wyatt found that the top four metrics used in formal business cases supporting HRIS were improved productivity within HR organization, cost reductions, return on investment, and enhanced employee communications. However, companies realize many of these cost reductions and efficiency gains early in the implementation of an HRIS system, so they provide compelling evidence needing to get a project up and running. In fact, the payback period, or the time it takes to recoup the investment, may be as short as one to three years (Lego, 2001). HRIS contribute to cost reductions, quality/customer satisfaction, and innovation (Broderick and Boudreau, 1992). According to Sadri and Chatterjee (2003) computerized HRIS function enable, faster decision making, development, planning, and administration of HR because data is much easier to store, update, classify, and analyze. Moreover, while it may be possible to identify many of the relevant costs (e.g., software and hardware), it is more difficult to quantify the intangible benefits to be derived from an HRIS system. Beyond cost reductions and productivity improvements, HRIS potentially and fundamentally affect revenue channels. However, establishing direct and objective benefits measures is more difficult to achieve.

On the other hand, there are costs associated with HRIS implementation. Moreover, to capitalize on all HR possibilities, workers need to have personal computers and global Internet connections. Some companies facilitate this by providing employees computer discount programs to encourage home usage. In addition, there is inevitably transition costs associated with moving from traditional HR to an HRIS, including slowdowns, mistakes, and other consequences associated with changing legacy systems to integrated suites (Brown, 2002). Hardware costs for servers and software costs for application programs entail sizeable initial outlays and continuing costs over time as better technology becomes available. While many companies are adopting HRIS systems and extolling their benefits, others are reluctant in embarking on such an expensive and time-consuming change. Nevertheless, some firms are adopting less complex forms before attempting to transform their HR departments. However, for those who have already adopted HRIS, many are yet to realize its full benefits. A survey by Towers Perrin found that whiles 80 percent of respondents affirmed employee self-service ability to lower FIR costs, only 5 percent fully achieved this objective; another 35 percent had only partially achieved that objective, and only 3 percent was accelerating Human Resource's transformation to a strategic partner (Ibid).

DESIGNING A HUMAN RESOURCE INFORMATION SYSTEM

Human Resource Management System (HRMS) is the linking mechanism which connects all decision making centers in an organization. The development of Human Resource Information System into a mature, enterprise wide solution needs a well thought out process. Implementing HRMS with additional functionality, such as Financials, provides further advantage by enabling the use of an integrated database. Some key differentiators of good HRMS are :

- **Technology stack**—one database for all applications, to ensure data integrity;
- **Integration with the e-Business Suite**—including tight integration between such packages as Payroll, Financials, CRM, etc.;
- **Security and Hierarchies for Matrix Organizations**—a secure drag-and-drop program that graphically depicts versions of hierarchies/organizational charts and allows managers to see where an employee is aligned;
- **Single Sign-on**—the tight integration between Applications enabling users to switch between applications by selecting the appropriate role (*i.e.*, HR to Recruitment manager, to Accounts Payable);
- **Compensation Workbench**—a tool to manage and monitor compensation and guarantees for new hires and hires within the company; service overview.
- **Orphan Control**—provides alerts when a manager with assigned employees is moved, transferred, resigned or terminated, enabling employee re-assignment;
- **Ease of Input**—through templates that can be configured to simplify data entry for any number of personnel actions, alleviating the need to move between screens while performing data entry.

Developing successful information system solutions to business problems is a major challenge for business managers and professionals today. As mangers you would be required to propose and develop new and improved information systems for your companies. Most of the computer based information systems are conceived, designed and implemented using a systematic development process. Several major activities must be managed in a complete information development system. The process involves firstly *investigating* the need and then studying the economic and technical feasibility of a proposed application. *Analysis* of the system and whether it meets the business need of the organization, thereafter designing it. After the system has been designed then it is implemented. After the system has been established it is maintained and updated as per requirements.

MOST COMMON REASONS FOR HUMAN RESOURCE INFORMATION SYSTEM FAILURES

A number of reasons why human resource information systems fail in organizations are :

- There is lack of management commitment and resources, and inadequate numbers of personnel are made available for the project.
- A project team is not assigned for the duration of the project. It is important that the core project team stays with the project from the beginning to its implementation.

- As a result of political intrigue, conflict and hidden agendas, the project is set up for failure.
- Key personnel, *e.g.*, senior HR staff are not included in the project.

THE DEVELOPMENT, IMPLEMENTATION AND MAINTENANCE OF A HUMAN RESOURCE INFORMATION SYSTEM DATA BASE

The conversion from manual to Human Resource Information System is a significant task that requires careful planning. To be successful, it is imperative that the support from top management is obtained. It is also important the HR Department take full responsibility for the computerization effort, and not the data-processing department. Three main phases in this process is identified.These are :

1. Phase 1 Needs Analysis
2. Phase2 Design and Development
3. Phase3 Implementation and maintenance.

Review Questions

1. Explain the concept and function of Human Resource Information System in an industrial organization ?
2. Discus the various sub systems of a computerized Human Resource Information System ?
3. Define Human Resource Information System and explain its objective and functions.
4. Examine the applications of computerized Human Resource Information System in a modern organization.
5. How is Human Resource Information System beneficial to a big industrial undertaking ? Discuss.
6. "Human Resource Information System must be integrated with overall Management Information System of the organization." Elaborate with statement.
7. Explain the applications of Human Resource Information System in the management of human resource industry.

PROJECT WORK

Visit any one of the retail store or 'Big Bazar' in your area and study the Human Resource Management System. Present in your class the findings of your study.

Case Study

The Competitive Advantage of Information Technology

There is nothing like a punchy headline to get an article some attention. A recent piece in the Harvard Business Review (May 2003), shockingly labeled "IT Doesn't Matter," has garnered the magazine more than the buzz than at any time. The article is the talk of the day and every where you go it is cited. But without the title I doubt whether the article would have been noticed. Author Nicholas Carr's main point is that Information Technology is nothing more than the infrastructure of modern business, similar to railroads, electricity, or the internal combustion engineering advances that have become too commonplace for any company to wrangle a strategic advantage from them. Once innovative applications of information technology have now become merely a necessary cost. Thus Carr thinks today's main risk is not under using It but over spending on it.

Before we get to any further, let's have a reality check. First let's ask Mr. Hetal Maswani, the Executive Director of Reliance Retail, one of the premier business corporations in the world this question : "How important is information technology is to Reliance ?" Here's his answer "It is a business imperative. We're primarily a service oriented company, and the lifeblood for productivity is more about technology that it is about investing in plants and equipment. We tend to get a twenty percent return on technology investment."

Then let's ask the same question to Mr Neelam Dhawan, Managing Director HP India. Here's his answer, "Just about anything in business can be either sink-hole or a competitive advantage. Information technology is often a misunderstood field. You've got a lot of who don't know what they're doing and don't do it very well. For us, IT is huge advantage, just like for many other companies."

Finally, let's see what Andy Grove, former CEO and now Chairman of Intel Corporation, a direct question about IT, "Nicholas Carr's recent article in Harvard Business Review says, 'IT Doesn't Matter.' Is information technology so pervasive that it no longer offers companies a competitive advantage ?" Andy says, "In any field, you can find segments that are close to maturation and draw conclusion that the field is homogenous. Carr is saying commercial transaction processing in the United States and some parts of Europe has reached the top parts of the S Curve. But instead of talking about the segment, he put a provocative spin on it- that information technology doesn't matter – and suddenly the statement is grossly wrong. It couldn't be further from the truth. It's like saying I have an old three speed bike, and Lance Armstrong has a bike. So why should he have a competitive advantage ?"

Basically, Carr misunderstood what information technology is. He thinks it's merely a bunch of networks and computers. He notes, properly, that the price of those has plummeted and that companies bought way to much in recent years. He's also right that the hardware infrastructure of business is rapidly becoming commoditized and, even more, standardized. Computers and networks per se are just infrastructure. However, one of the article's most glaring flaws is complete disregard for the centrality of software and the fact that human knowledge or information can be mediated and managed by software.

Questions

1. Do you agree with the argument made by Nick Carr to support his position that IT no longer gives companies a competitive advantage ? Explain.
2. Do you agree with the argument made by the business leaders in this case in support of the competitive advantage that IT can provide to a business ? Why or Why not ?
3. What are the several ways that IT could provide a competitive advantage to a business ? Use some of the companies mentioned in this case as examples. Visit their websites to gather more information to help your answers.

Chapter 23

Leadership, Values and Corporate Social Responsibility

★ LEARNING OBJECTIVES ★

After reading this chapter, you will be able to understand :

- What is leadership?
- Leadership Styles.
- Ways of Conceptualizing Leadership and Approaches.
- Power and Organization Politics.
- Ethics and Values.
- Corporate Social Responsibility.

INTRODUCTION

There are as many definitions of leadership as the authors or research workers. In *Handbook of Leadership : A Survey of Theory and Research,* Stogdill (1974) noted that there are as many definitions of leadership as there are persons who have attempted to define the concept. Bennis and Nanus (1985) in their work *Leadership : Strategies for Taking Charge,* referred to leadership as most studied and least understood topic of any in social science. The term leadership has been taken from the vocabulary and without defining it precisely has been incorporated in the technical vocabulary of a scientific discipline. As a consequence it carries extraneous connotations that create ambiguity of meaning (Janda, 1960). Additional confusion especially in the defence forces has been caused by officers attending Long Defence Management Courses, and in general by researchers by the use of other terms as power, authority, management, controls etc to describe the same phenomenon. An observation by Bennis (1959) is as true today as it was when he made it many years ago :

Always, it seems, the concept of leadership eludes us or turns up in another form to taunt us again with its slipperiness and complexity. So, we have invented endless proliferation of terms to deal with it ..... and still the concept is not sufficiently defined.

WAYS OF CONCEPTUALIZATION LEADERSHIP

In *Handbook of Leadership : A Survey of Theory and Research*, Stogdill (1974) noted that there are as many definitions of leadership as there are persons who have attempted to define the concept. Bennis and Nanus (1985) in their work *Leadership : Strategies for Taking Charge*, referred to leadership as most studied and least understood topic of any in social science. Last five decades have seen as many as 65 different classification of leadership have been developed to define the dimension of leadership Flieshman et al., 1991.

Leadership is the **ability to influence** individuals or groups toward the achievement of goals.

Leadership, as a process, **shapes the goals** of a group or organization, **motivates behaviour** toward the achievement of those goals, and helps define group or organizational culture. It is primarily a process of influence.

We will define leadership as the process of directing and influencing the task related activities of group members. There are four important implications of this definition.

First, leadership involves other people- employees or followers. It also involves the willingness of employees/followers to accept directions from the leader. Group members help define the leader's status and make the leadership process possible. The leadership quality of a manager would be irrelevant if there is no group of followers.

Second, leadership involves unequal distribution of power between leader and the group members. Where does the power come from ? There are five bases of power of managers; reward power, coercive power, legitimate power, referent power and expert power. The greater the number of these power available to the manager, the greater his or her potential for effective leadership.

Third is the ability to influence the follower's behaviour in number of ways. Leaders have influenced soldier's in battlefield to make supreme sacrifice.

Fourth, is leader must have values. James McGregor Burns argues that leader who ignores the moral components f leadership may go down in history with bad reputation. Moral leadership concerns values and requires that followers be given enough knowledge of alternatives to make intelligent choices when it comes to respond to a leader's proposal to lead.

THE NINE DILEMMAS LEADERS FACE

Broad-based Leadership vs. High-visibility Leaders

Independence vs. Interdependence

Long-term vs. Short-term

Creativity vs. Discipline

Trust vs. Change

Bureaucracy Busting vs. Economies of Scale

People vs. Productivity

Leadership vs. Capability

Revenue Growth vs. Cost Containment

The Nine Dilemmas Leaders Face is based on The Nine Dilemmas Leaders Face, *Fortune Magazine* March 1996

Leadership Versus Management

Although some managers are able to influence followers to work toward the achievement of organizational goals, the conferring of formal authority upon a manager does not necessarily make that individual a leader. Yes, that individual has authority, but whether or not they are able to influence their subordinates may depend on more that just that authority.

Not all leaders are managers, and similarly, not all managers are leaders. Within a team environment, manager and leader are simply roles taken on by members of the team. Most teams require a manager to "manage" — coordinate, schedule, liaise, contact, organize, and procure — their affairs. The functions of this role may well be quite different from those of the leader (to motivate followers towards the achievement of team goals). Management roles need not presuppose any ability to influence. A leader, on the other hand, must have the ability to influence other team members.

FUNDAMENTAL DIFFERENCE BETWEEN A MANAGER AND A LEADER

A manager administers, but a leader innovates

A manager maintains, while a leader develops

A manager focuses on systems and structures, whereas a leader's focus is on people

A manager relies on control, but a leader inspires trust

A manager keeps an eye on the bottom line, while a leader has an eye on the horizon

A manager does things right, a leader does the right thing.

Researchers exploring leadership functions came to conclusion that to operate effectively groups needed someone to perform two major functions :

(*a*) Task Related Function–or problem solving function.

(*b*) Group maintenance or Social Function. This includes making sure individuals feel valued by the group, mediating disputes etc.

An individual who is able to perform both roles effectively would especially be an effective leader. However, an individual may have the skill, ability and temperament to play only some roles. This does not mean the group is doomed. Studies have revealed that most effective leader's are the one's who have some form of shared leadership, while the leader performs the task function, while another member performs the social function (Bales, 1951).

There is a difference between leadership and management. The leader and the men who follow him represent one of the oldest, most natural, and most effective of all human relationship. The manager and those he manages are a later product with neither so romantic, nor so inspiring a history. ***Leadership*** is of the ***spirit***, compounded of ***personality*** and ***vision*** – its practice is an art. *Management* is of the **mind**, ***more a matter of accurate calculation, statistics, methods, timetables, and routine*** – its practice is a science.'

Leadership Styles

There are two main functions of a leader viz. task related and group maintenance, hence, these tend to be expressed in two different styles. Managers have task orientation in that they closely supervise the employees to ensure the task is performed satisfactorily. Mangers with an employee orientation put more emphasis on motivating the employee rather then controlling them. They seek friendly, trusting and respectful relationships with employees, who are often allowed to participate in decisions that affect them.

Leadership style is the manner and approach of providing direction, implementing plans, and motivating people. Kurt Lewin (1939) led a group of researchers to identify different styles of leadership. This early study has been very influential and established three major leadership styles. The three major styles of leadership are (US Amy Handbook, 1973) :

- *Authoritarian or Autocratic.* This style is used when leaders tell their employees what they want done and how they want it accomplished, without getting the advice of their followers. Some of the appropriate conditions to use it is when you have all the information to solve the problem, you are short on time, and your employees are well motivated
- *Participative or democratic.* This style involves the leader including one or more employees in the decision making process (determining what to do and how to do it). However, the leader maintains the final decision making authority. Using this style is not a sign of weakness, rather it is a sign of strength that your employees will respect.
- *Delegative or Free Reign.* In this style, the leader allows the employees to make the decisions. However, the leader is still responsible for the decisions that are made. This is used when employees are able to analyze the situation and determine what needs to be done and how to do it. You cannot do everything! You must set priorities and delegate certain tasks. This is not a style to use so that you can blame others when things go wrong, rather this is a style to be used when you fully trust and confidence in the people below you. Do not be afraid to use it, however, use it wisely!
- *Paternalism has at times been equated with leadership styles.* Yet most definitions of leadership normally state or imply that one of the actions within leadership is that of influencing. For example, the Army uses the following definition :

  "Leadership is influencing people — by providing purpose, direction, and motivation — while operating to accomplish the mission and improving the organization."

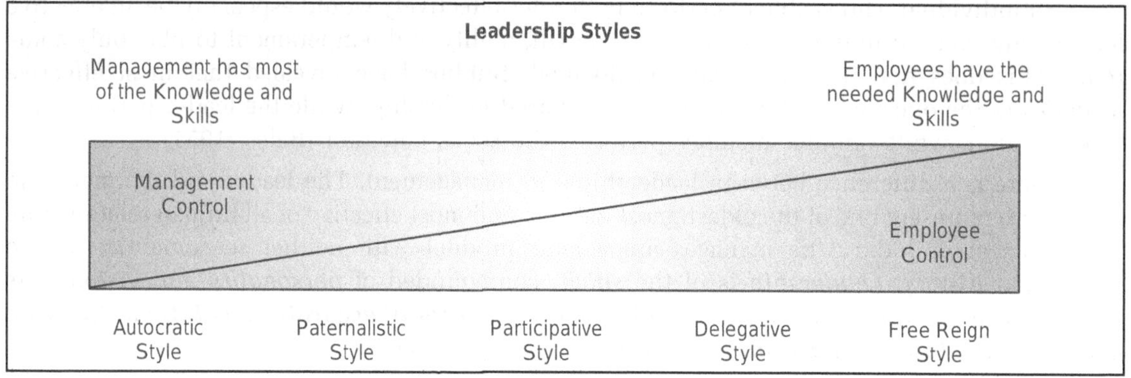

Fig. 23.1

APPROACHES TO LEADERSHIP

The subject of leadership is so vast and perceived to be so critical; it has generated a huge body of literature. Each researcher working in the field has tried to explain leadership from a different perspective. Broadly, there are four distinct approaches to leadership, viz. Traits theory, Behaviouristic theory, Contingency theory and Charismatic theories of leadership.

Traits Theory

Ask people what good leadership is, and it's quite likely you will get a response that suggests good leadership can somehow be defined in terms of traits or characteristics.

Similarly, if one were to ask people to design an experiment aimed at defining good leadership, it's likely the response will be an attempt to isolate the characteristics of leaders of organizations deemed to be successful (by whatever terms that success is measured).

This is exactly what the initial, formal research into leadership was all about. There was a sense among researchers that some critical leadership traits could be isolated. There was also a feeling that people with such traits could then be recruited, selected, and installed into leadership positions.

The problem with the trait approach lies in the fact that almost as many traits as studies undertaken were identified. After several years of such research, it became apparent that no such traits could be identified. Although some traits were identified in a considerable number of studies, the results were generally inconclusive.

Researchers were further confounded by questions about how to find commonality or generalizability from an examination of the traits of leaders as diverse as Stalin, Hitler, Martin Luther King Jr., John F. Kennedy, Churchill, Mother Theresa, Gandhi and Margaret Thatcher. Do these leaders have any trait in common ? Is this a list of traits all leaders must possess ?

- technical skill
- friendliness
- task motivation
- application to task
- group task supportiveness
- social skill

- emotional control
- administrative skill
- general charisma
- intelligence etc.

RM Stogdill, (1948) after thorough research concluded the 'person does not become leader by virtue of the possession of some combination of traits.' No traits are universal, also with traits action has to be taken. However, traits do matter and studies have revealed that there are some common traits which differentiate leaders from followers. The six traits which have been universally accepted are :

- *Drive.* Refers to constellation of traits and motives reflecting a high effort level
- *Leadership Motivation.* Leaders have strong desire to lead. They think a lot about influencing other, winning an argument or being greater authorityHarvard Psychologist David McClelland—two types of dominance :
  - o Personalized Power Motive—concerned with domination of others, results in dependent, submissive followers. Seeks power as an end itself.
  - o Socialized Power Motive—Uses power to achieve desired goals, or a vision. Develops networks, coalitions, gain cooperation from others, resolve conflicts in a constructive manner. Takes account of followers need and results in empowered, independent followers.
- *Honesty and Integrity.* Are virtues in individual ? Integrity is between and deed, refers to being truthful. Charles Cox and Cary Cooper British Psychologists said 'successful leaders preferred open style, where they truthfully informed workers of happenings.' Effective leaders are credible, with excellent reputations and high level of integrity.
- *Self Confidence and Emotional Stability.* Primarily it is remaining even tempered especially in adverse conditions and has faith in their ability to accomplish what they have set to do.
- *Cognitive ability.* It is the ability to gather and integrate enormous amount of information and decipher it. Thereafter be able to pick the correct and priority information for action.
- *Knowledge and Business.* The manager must have the necessary knowledge of the functions being performed by him. In addition he should have business acumen as all organizations are structured for profit. There is no organization or industry which can survive without profit.

Behaviouristic Theory

The results of the trait studies were inconclusive. Traits, among other things, were hard to measure. How, for example, do we measure traits such as honesty, integrity, loyalty, or diligence ? Another approach in the study of leadership had to be found.

To measure traits, researchers had to rely on constructs which lacked reliability and, given differing definitions, also lacked validity. After the problems with the trait approach became evident, researchers turned to an examination of leader behaviours. With behaviours, researchers could rely on empirical evidence. Behaviours, contrary to traits, could be observed. It was thus decided to examine the behaviours of successful (again, by whatever means success was measured) leaders.

The initial phases of the behavioural research seemed as frustrating as the trait approach — the number of behaviours identified was staggering. However, over time, it appeared that the key behaviours could be grouped or categorized. The most prominent studies were those undertaken by the University of Michigan and by Ohio State University.

Interestingly, both studies arrived at similar conclusions. Both studies concluded that leadership behaviours could be classified into two groups.

The University of Michigan studies (Rensis Likert) identified two styles of leader behaviour :

- Production centered behaviour : when a leader pays close attention to the work of sub-ordinates, explains work procedures, and is keenly interested in performance.
- Employee centered behaviour : when the leader is interested in developing a cohesive work group and in ensuring employees are satisfied with their jobs.

These two styles of leader behaviour were believed to lie at the ends of a single continuum. Likert found that employee-centered leader behaviour generally tended to be more effective.

Researchers at Ohio State leadership found results which suggested two basic leader behaviours or styles (Figure 23.1).

- Initiating structure behaviour : when the leader clearly defines the leader-subordinate, establishes formal lines of communication, and determines how tasks are to be performed.
- Consideration behaviour : the leader shows concern for sub-ordinates and attempts to establish a warm, friendly, and supportive climate.

Unlike the Michigan Studies, these two behaviours were not viewed as opposite ends of a continuum, but as independent variables. Thus the leader can exhibit varying degrees of both initiating structure and consideration at the same time.

Rather than concentrating on what leaders are, as the trait approach did, the behavioural approach forced looking at what leaders do. The main shortcomings of the behavioural approach were its focus on finding a dependable prescription for effective leadership.

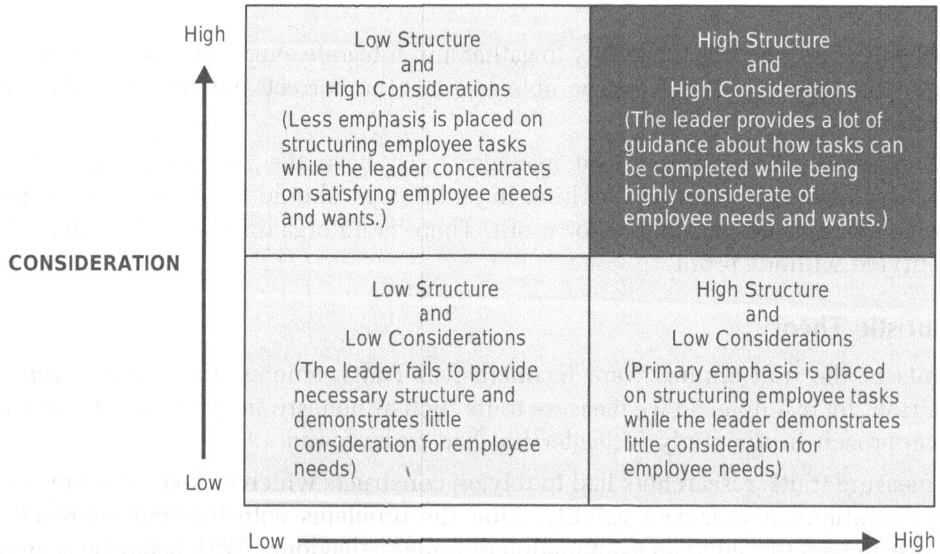

Fig. 23.2. *Leadership Style Studied at Ohio State University.*

The Managerial Grid

Blake and Mouton (1985) tried to show an individual's style of leadership on a 9x9 grid consisting of two separate dimensions, viz. concern for production and concern for people which are similar to the concept of employee-centered and production-centered styles of leadership as mentioned earlier. The grid has nine possible positions along each axis creating a total of eighty-one possible styles of leader behaviour. The managerial grid thus identifies the propensity of a leader to act in a particular way. The (9,1) style is known as task management which focuses wholly on production. Managers with this style are exceptionally competent with the technicalities of a particular job but are miserable failures in dealing with people. The (1,9) style in contrast emphasizes people to the exclusion of task performance and is known as country club style of management.

The ideal style of leadership, as envisioned by the theory of managerial grid is the (9,9) style or team management style where there is maximum concern for both people and production. The research evidence in favour of the view that managers perform best under (9,9) style is however scanty.

The basic criticisms against the behaviouristic theories are that :

- Lack of generalizations of the findings as they found to vary widely
- Ignoring the significant influence of the situational factors.

Contingency Theories

Managerial leadership has influenced organizational activities in many ways. These influences include motivating subordinates, budgeting scarce resources, and serving as a source of communication. Over the years researchers have emphasized the influences of leadership on the activities of subordinates. These emphasis by researchers led to theories about leadership. "The first and perhaps most popular, situational theory to be advanced was the 'Contingency Theory of Leadership Effectiveness' developed by Fred E. Fiedler" This theory explains that group performance is a result of interaction of two factors. These factors are known as leadership style and situational favorableness. These two factors will be discussed along with other aspects of Fiedler's theory. "In Fiedler's model, leadership effectiveness is the result of interaction between the style of the leader and the characteristics of the environment in which the leader works".

The first major factor in Fiedler's theory is known as the leadership style. This is the consistent system of interaction that takes place between a leader and work group. "According to Fiedler, an individual's leadership style depends upon his or her personality and is, thus, fixed". In order to classify leadership styles, Fiedlers has developed an index called the least-preferred coworker (LPC) scale.

The LPC scale asks a leader to think of all the persons with whom he or she has ever worked, and then to describe the one person with whom he or she worked the least well with. This person can be someone from the past or someone he or she is currently working with. From a scale of 1 through 8, leader are asked to describe this person on a series of bipolar scales such as those shown below :

Unfriendly 1 2 3 4 5 6 7 8 Friendly

Uncooperative 1 2 3 4 5 6 7 8 Cooperative

Hostile 1 2 3 4 5 6 7 8 Supportive

Guarded 1 2 3 4 5 6 7 8 Open

The responses to these scales (usually sixteen in total) are summed and averaged : a high LPC score suggests that the leader has a human relations orientation, while a low LPC score indicates a task orientation. Fiedler's logic is that individuals who rate their least preferred coworker in relatively favorable light on these scales derive satisfaction out of interpersonal relationship; those who rate the coworker in a relatively unfavorable light get satisfaction out of successful task performance". This method reveals an individual's emotional reaction to people with whom he or she cannot work. It is also stressed that is not always an accurate measurement.

"According to Fiedler, the effectiveness of a leader is determined by the degree of match between a dominant trait of the leader and the favorableness of the situation for the leader.... The dominant trait is a personality factor causing the leader to either relationship-oriented or task-orientated" . Leaders who describe their preferred coworker in favorable terms, with a high LPC, are purportedo derive major satisfaction from establishing close relationships with fellow workers. High LPC leaders are said to be relationship-orientated. These leaders see that good interpersonal relations as a requirement for task accomplishment.

Leaders who describe their least preferred coworker unfavorable terms, with a low LPC, are derived major satisfaction by successfully completing a task. These leaders are said to be task-orientated. They are more concerned with successful task accomplishment and worry about interpersonal relations later.

The second major factor in Fiedler's theory is known as situational favorableness or environmental variable. This basically is defined as the degree a situation enables a leader to exert influence over a group. Fiedler then extends his analysis by focusing on three key situational factors, which are leader-member, task structure and position power.

Each factor is defined in the following :

1. *Leader-member relations :* the degree to which the employees accept the leader.
2. *Task structure :* the degree to which the subordinate's jobs are described in detail.
3. *Position power :* the amount of formal authority the leader possesses by virtue of his or her position in the organization.

For leader-member relations, Fiedler maintains that the leader will has more influence if they maintain good relationships with group members who like, respect, and trust them, than if they do not. Fiedler explains that task structure is the second most important factor in determining structural favorableness. He contends that highly structured tasks, which specify how a job is to be done in detail provide a leader with more influences over group actions than do unstructured tasks. Finally, as for position power, leads who have the power to hire and fire, discipline and reward, have more power than those who do not. For example, the head of a department has more power than a file clerk.

By classifying a group according to three variables, it is possible to identify eight different group situations or leadership style. These eight different possible combinations were then classified as either task orientation or relationship orientated. The following information shows that task-orientated leadership was successful in five situations, and relationship-orientated in three.

FIEDLER'S CONTINGENCY THEORY OF LEADERSHIP

LEADER-MEMBER TASK POSITION POWER SUCCESSFUL LEADERSHIP

Relations Structure of Leader Style

Good — Structured — Strong — Task Orientation

Good — Structured — Weak — Task Orientation

Good — Unstructured — Strong — Task Orientation

Good — Unstructured — Weak — Consideration

Poor — Structured — Strong — Consideration

Poor — Structured — Weak — Consideration

Poor — Unstructured — Strong — Task Orientation

Poor — Unstructured — Weak — Task Orientation

"According to Fiedler, a task-orientated style of leadership is more effective than a considerate (relationship-orientated) style under extreme situations, that is, when the situations, is either very favourable (certain) or very unfavorable (uncertain)". Task-orientated leadership would be advisable in natural disaster, like a flood or fire. In and uncertain situation the leader-member relations are usually poor, the task is unstructured, and the position power is weak. The one who emerges as a leader to direct the group's activity usually does not know any of his or her subordinates personally. The task-orientated leader who gets things accomplished proves to be the most successful. If the leader is considerate (relationship-orientated), he or she may waste so much time in the disaster, which may lead things to get out of control and lives might get lost.

Blue-collar workers generally want to know exactly what they are supposed to do. Therefore, it is usually highly structured. The leader's position power is strong if management backs his or her decision. Finally, even though the leader may not be relationship-orientated, leader-member relations may be extremely strong if he or she is able to gain promotions and salary increases for subordinates. Under these situations is the task-orientated style of leadership is preferred over the (considerate) relationship-orientated style.

"The considerate style of leadership seems to be appropriate when the environmental or certain situation is moderately favorable or certain, for example, when (1) leader-member relations are good, (2) the task is unstructured, and (3) position power is weak". For example, research scientists do not like superiors to structure the task for them. They prefer to follow their own creative leads in order to solve problems. Now under a situation like this is when a considerate style of leadership is preferred over the task-orientated style.

Fiedler's theory has some very interesting implications for the management of leaders in organizations :

1. The favorableness of leadership situations should be assessed using the instruments developed by Fiedler (or, at the very least, by a subjective evaluation).
2. Candidates for leadership positions should be evaluated using the LPC scale.
3. If a leader is being sought for a particular leadership position, a leader with the appropriate LPC profile should be chosen (task-orientated for very favorable or very unfavorable situations and relationship-orientated for intermediate favorableness).

4. If a leadership situation is being chosen for a particular candidate, a situation (work team, department, etc.) should be chosen which matches his/her LPC profile (very favorable or unfavorable for task-orientated leaders and intermediate favorableness for relationship-orientated leader).

Several other implications can be derived from Fiedler's findings. First, it is not accurate to speak of effective and ineffective leaders. Fiedler goes on by suggesting that there are only leader who perform better in some situations, but not all situations. Second, almost anyone can be a leader by carefully selecting those situations that match his or her leadership style. Lastly, the effectiveness of a leader can be improved by designing the job to fit the manager. For instance, by increasing or decreasing a leader's position power, changing the structure of a task, or influencing leader-member relations, an organization can alter a situation to better fit a leader's style.

In conclusion, the Fiedler's Contingency Theory of Leadership, has been cautious of accepting all conclusions. Fiedler's work is not without problems or critics. Evidence suggests that other situational variables, like training and experience have an impact in a leader's effectiveness. There are also some uncertainties about Fiedler's measurement of different variables. For instance, there is some doubt whether the LPC is a true measure of leadership style. "Despite these and other criticisms, Fiedler's contingency theory represents an important addition to our understanding of effective leadership". Fred Fiedler's theory became an important discovery in the study of leadership. His theory made a major conrtibution to knowledge in the leadership area.

Heresy and Blanchard's Situational Model

The situational leadership model, developed by Paul Hersey and Kenneth Blanchard, suggests that the leader's behaviour should be adjusted according to the maturity level of the followers. The level of maturity or the readiness of the followers were assessed to the extent the followers have the ability and willingness to accomplish a specific task. Four possible categories of followers' maturity were identified :

R1 : Unable and Unwilling

R2 : Unable but Willing

R3 : Able but Unwilling

R4 : Able and Willing

The leader behaviour was determined by the same dimensions as used in the Ohio studies, viz. production orientation and people orientation. According to the situational mode, a leader should use a telling style (high concern for task and low concern for people) with the least matured group of followers who are neither able nor willing to perform (R1). A selling style of leadership (high concern for both task and relationship) is required for dealing with the followers with the next higher level of maturity that is those who are willing but unable to perform the task at the required level (R2). The able but unwilling followers are the next matured group and require a participating style from the leader, characterized by high concern for consideration and low emphasis on task orientation. Finally the most matured followers who are both able and willing require a delegating style of leadership. The leader working with this kind of followers must learn to restrain himself from showing too much concern for either task or relationship as the followers themselves do accept the responsibility for their performance. Though this theory is difficult to be tested empirically, it has its intuitive appeal and is widely used for training and development in organizations (Figure 23.3). In addition, the theory focuses attention on followers as a significant determinant of any leadership process.

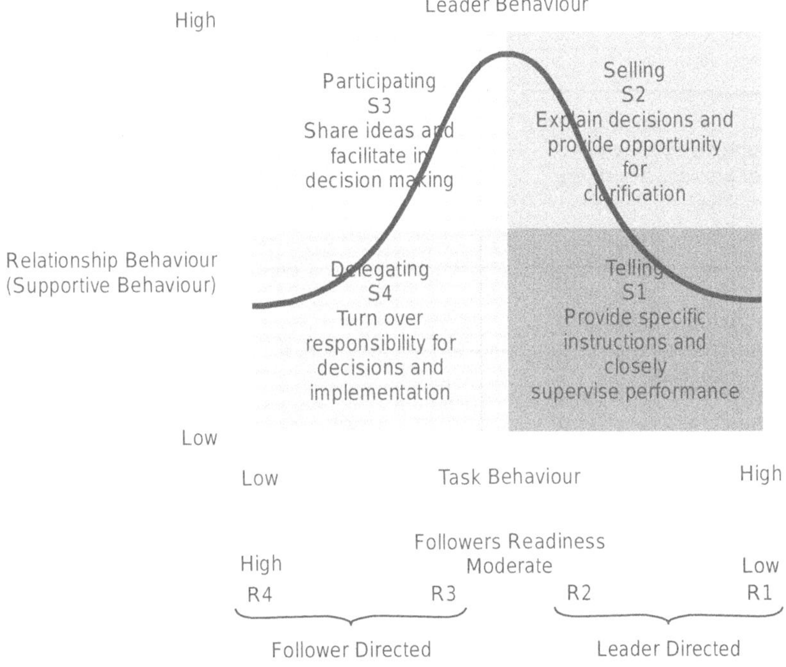

Fig. 23.3. *Hersey and Blanchard's Situational Leadership Theory.*

The Path Goal Theory

In the recent time, one of the most appreciated theories of leadership is the path-goal theory as offered by Robert House, which is based on the expectancy theory of motivation. According to this theory, the effectiveness of a leader depends on the following propositions :

- Leader behaviour is acceptable and satisfying to followers to the extent that they see it as an immediate source of satisfaction or as instrumental to future satisfaction
- Leader behaviour is motivational to the extent that :
  - o It makes the followers' needs satisfaction contingent or dependent on effective performance, and
  - o It complements the followers' environment by providing the coaching, guidance, support, and rewards necessary for realizing the linkage between the level of their performance and the attainment of the rewards available.

The leader selects from any of the four styles of behaviour which is most suitable for the followers at a given point of time. These are directive, supportive, participative, and the achievement-oriented according to the need and expectations of the followers. In other words, the path-goal theory assumes that leaders adapt their behaviour and style to fit the characteristics of the followers and the environment in which they work. Actual tests of the path-goal theory provide conflicting evidence and therefore it is premature to either fully accept or reject the theory at this point. Nevertheless the path-goal theory does have intuitive appeal and offers a number of constructive ideas for leaders who lead in a variety of followers in a variety of work environments (Figure 23.4).

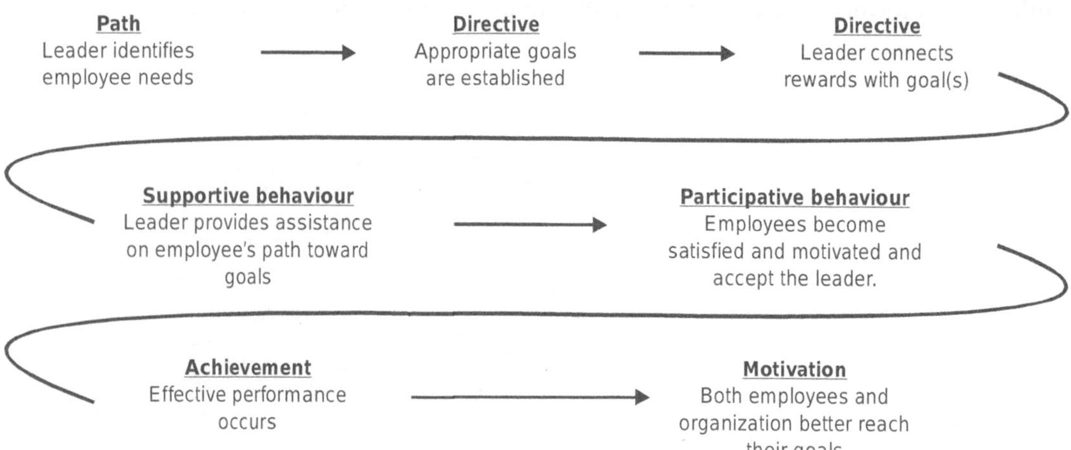

Fig. 23.4. *Path-goal Theory of Leadership.*

Transformational Leadership

James MacGregor Burns (1978) conceptualized leadership as either transactional or transformational. Transactional leaders are those who lead through social change. As Burns (1978) notes, politicians, for example, lead by "exchanging one thing for another : jobs for votes, or subsidies for campaign contributions." Transformational leaders on the other hand, are those who stimulate and inspire followers to both achieve extraordinary outcomes and, in the process, develop their own leadership capacity. Transformational leaders help followers grow and develop into leaders by responding to individual followers' needs by empowering them and by aligning the objectives and goals of their individual followers, the leader, the group, and the larger organization. It has been observed the transformational leadership can move followers to exceed expected performance, as well as to high levels to follower's satisfaction and commitment to the group and organization (Bass, 1985, 1988)

Transformational or charismatic leaders are those who could inspire their followers to transcend their own self-interests for the good of the organizations or for a greater objective. Thus leaders like Netaji Subhas Chandra Bose or Gandhiji could inspire their followers to submit their own personal goals of pursuing lucrative academic or professional careers and sacrifice everything for the sake of the freedom of their motherland from the British rules. By the force of their personal abilities they transform their followers by raising the sense of the importance and value of their tasks. Five leadership attributes have been identified as important in this context which are self-confidence, a vision, strong conviction in that vision, extraordinary or novel behaviour and ability to create an image of a change agent.

Bass (1985) extended charismatic leadership to a theory of transformational leadership where the leader is able to inspire and activate subordinates to "perform beyond expectations" and to achieve goals beyond those normally set. Bass' theory posits that the transformational leader achieves greater than expected performance through any one of three interrelated ways : (*a*) An increased level of awareness by subordinates about the importance of designated outcomes, (*b*) by getting individuals to transcend their own self-interest for the sake of the team, and (*c*) by altering the subordinates' need levels on Maslow's hierarchy or expanding the set of needs.

The transformational leader gains a greater commitment from subordinates and induces them to transcend personal self-interest for the betterment of the group or organization not only with charisma but also by serving as a coach, teacher, or mentor (Bass, 1985; Yukl, 1989). Thus, the transformational leader is able to activate higher-order needs of esteem and self-actualization among subordinates.

It is however important to note that the effect of cultural difference in the context of leadership must be considered in order to understand and identify the effective leadership behaviour. An extensive project has been undertaken jointly by GLOBE foundation and Wharton Business School to identify the impact of culture on leadership across the world, which concluded only recently. The study has identified lists of both positive and negative leader attributes which have been universally accepted across culture. The findings from the completed phases of the study however suggest the presence of a strong influence of cultural bias on the success and effectiveness of the leaders.

House's Theory of Charismatic Leadership

Charismatic leadership has become an important theoretical approach to explaining leader effectiveness since the concept was most fully described in a 1977 paper by Robert House. Prior to House's work, charismatic leadership theory was only loosely articulated and the research that was done tended to follow enthnographic, qualitative forms. Based in part on Weber's conception of personal power, charismatic leadership theory rests on the notion that a leader's influence on his or her followers is often beyond the legal and formal authority structure of a group or organization, and relies instead on the leader's personal charm, attractiveness, and persuasive communication. According to Weber, charismatic leaders are able to influence followers by articulating a compelling vision for the future, arousing commitment to organizational objectives, and inspiring commitment and a sense of self-efficacy among followers.

House (1977) defines charismatic leadership as referring to a leader who has charismatic effects on followers to an unusually high degree. These effects include devotion, trust, unquestioned obedience, loyalty commitment, identification, confidence in ability to achieve goals and radical changes in beliefs and values.

Charismatic leadership is stated to have three core components *i.e.*, 'envisioning, empathy, and empowerment.' A charismatic leader's envisioning behaviour influences followers' need for achievement, and the leader's empathic behaviour stimulates followers' need for affiliation. Followers' need for power is enhanced by a charismatic leader's empowerment practices. It is further suggested that the behaviours of a charismatic leader and the enhanced followers' needs promote clearer role perceptions, improved task performance, greater job satisfaction, stronger collective identity and group cohesiveness, more organizational citizenship behaviours, and stronger self-leadership among the followers.

Charismatic leadership theory asserts that exceptional leaders create a connection with followers, attend to their individual needs, and inspire followers to achieve beyond personal limits. By appealing to higher-order individual values and magnanimous ideals, charismatic leaders enhance the commitment of followers to an eloquent vision and arouse followers to develop new ways of thinking about problems. While tests of the theory have proposed a number of mechanisms by which charismatic effects are realized, a common set of behaviours generally characterize charismatic leadership. Charismatic leaders articulate a compelling often innovative vision the future, take personal risks, emphasize ideological aspects of the organization's mission, show sensitivity to followers' needs, and communicate in an emotional and enthusiastic manner. These leaders are personally attractive to stakeholders both internal and external to the organization, and are able to arouse emotion among followers and inspire commitment to organizational change.

POWER AND ORGANIZATIONAL POLITICS

During discussions of leadership, the question often arises : "Why or how are leaders able to get followers to follow ?" We have already discussed the notion that followers follow if they perceive the leader to be in a position to satisfy their needs. However, our discussion also included frequent reference to the concept of "power". We are now in a position to take a closer look at power.

Definitions of power abound. German sociologist, Max Weber defined power as "the probability that one actor within a social relationship will be in a position to carry out his own will despite resistance." Along similar lines, Emerson suggests that "The power of actor A over actor B is the amount of resistance on the part of B which can be potentially overcome by A." Power appears to involve one person changing the behaviour of one or more other individuals —particularly if that behaviour would not have taken place otherwise. Power refers to A's ability to influence B, not A's right to do so; no right is implied in the concept of power...

At this point it is useful to point out that power refers to A's ability to influence B, not A's right to do so; no right is implied in the concept of power. A related concept is authority. Authority does represent the right to expect or secure compliance; authority is backed by legitimacy.

For purposes of differentiating between power and authority, let us examine the relationship between the manager of a sawmill and her subordinates. Presumably, the manager has the authority—the right—to request that the sawyer cut lumber to certain specifications. On the other hand, the manager would not have the right to request that the sawyer wash her car. However, that sawyer may well accede to her request that he wash her car. Why ? It is possible that the sawyer responds to the power that the manager has over him—the ability to influence his behaviour.

Etizoni has made the classification of power as follows :

- Coercive Power. Involves forcing someone to comply with one's wishes. A prison would be an example of a coercive organization.
- Utilitarian Power. Is power based on a system of rewards or punishments ? Businesses, which use pay raises, promotions, or threats of dismissal, are essentially utilitarian organizations.
- Normative Power. Is power which rests on the beliefs of the members that the organization has a right to govern their behaviour. A religious order would be an example of a utilitarian organization.

Successful Leadership Versus Effective Leadership

Successful leadership has been defined as the ability to get others behave as the manager's intends them to. In this the job is done, and the mangers' needs may be satisfied, but the employee's needs are ignored. In effective leadership, the employees perform in accordance with the manager's intentions and at the same time, find their own needs satisfied. The positive feeling of the employees usually contribute to long term benefits such as loyalty, support, job satisfaction an important component of intrinsic motivation. Hence, success has to do with how the individual or group behaves, effectiveness describes the internal shape or predisposition of an individual or a group and thus is attitudinal in nature.

An individual interested in success tends to emphasize his position power and uses close supervision. On the other hand, if he intends to be effective, he will depend upon his personal power characterized by more general supervision. Position power can be delegated downward, but personal power cannot be delegated, but is generated upward from below through follower acceptance.

A manager can be successful but can be ineffective. On the other hand if the manager tends to be both successful; and effective, his or her influence tends to lead to a long run of productivity. It should however, be understood that a successful and effective frame work is a way of evaluating the response to a specific behavioural response and not to evaluating performance over period of time.

FIVE CHARACTERISTICS FOR EFFECTIVE LEADERSHIP

In the opening address to the Möbius conference Kim Clark, Dean of Harvard Business School, spoke about leadership with a small "l"—the sort of leadership that is needed in every organization to both serve and inspire our communities, businesses, and lives. "We live in really remarkable times," he said, stressing there remains "a lot of optimism amidst all this turbulence." Below, his advice on first-rate leadership.

1. Integrity. We need leaders with strong values grounded in a commitment to a life that is whole and consistent with the things they believe. They should take personal responsibility for their actions and be honest with others, and with themselves.
2. Energy. Leaders who energize and inspire other people make everyone around them better—not by administering, but by ministering.
3. Inspiration. Trust and confidence are vital, but it is a leader's responsibility to help create a vision of what is possible. They should inspire others to see the greatness that is within them.
4. Wisdom. Leaders need to be teachers. They must see beyond the horizon and understand the principles that underlie success. It is necessary to be a great communicator and teach in deed.
5. Courage. Leaders have to do hard things. They have to have standards and make tough decisions that might make them unpopular, and do the right thing though the wrong thing is easier. Courage is hard, but it can be developed.

Leadership Skills

Leadership theories and practices recognize the importance of skills how leaders behave and perform effectively. A list of suggested leadership skills in addition to one's given in box critical to success in the modern global integrated economy is given below.

1. *Cultural Flexibility.* In international assignments, skills refer to cultural awareness and sensitivity. Leaders today should be able recognize and value the diversity in their organizations.
2. *Communication Skills.* Effective leaders must be able to communicate, their views, vision directions in clear and lucid manner.
3. *Creativity.* Problem solving, innovation and creativity provide the competitive advantage in today's global market. With stakeholder expectations and environmental factors changing fast, ideas for adaptation and advantage are invaluable to organizations. Stakeholders are now multiplying in number, and the demands that they place on an

organization may range from keeping up with the needs of talented staff, and offering customers more choice and better service, to boosting the bottom line for shareholders. At the same time, companies are also being placed under greater pressure by numerous external changes in an increasingly competitive marketplace. One needs to think differently to survive in the globalized world. A good blend of creative people and engineers are essential to push growth. Profits and innovation go hand in hand. While innovation is 'doing' things differently, creativity is all about 'thinking' differently, says Mr. Premji founder of Wipro "Innovation is essentially the application of high creativity. It need not be restricted to just products; it applies to services, employee attitude and across all levels. Innovation is a fundamental mindset pursued seriously by an organization. It is imperative to imbibe the culture of innovation."

4. *Political Skills.* Politics is a normal part of leadership and organizational life, and political skill is one of the many factors that contribute to effective leadership, according to Gentry. The term "political skill" can be defined as the ability to effectively understand and influence others for personal and/or organizational benefit. Leaders need to know the relationships and cultural dynamics of the organization and understand how to respond to and affect their environment. Leaders who are unable to develop their political skill are at risk for career derailment. In other words, managers who are not politically astute run the risk of being demoted, fired or otherwise thrown off their intended career track. Leadership requires the demonstration of political skill. Political skill allows people to adapt and tailor their behaviour to the context and people involved. Managers, people in leadership, need to adjust to different environmental conditions, different individuals and different situations. Politically skilled people can diagnose a situation and adjust their behaviour accordingly.
5. *Community Building.* Community building as an approach is not new, but it has been practiced by a small minority. Community building is challenging all of us to look harder at this science of associations, the forms of community connections that we are building at the local level. As government, political party apparatus, and other local institutions lose influence, the community building movement has placed a heavier emphasis on increased resident involvement and institutional collaboration. Community building calls leaders to take a more active role as a new local planning and decision-making apparatus. Institutional and community collaboration is an important element in the evolution of community associations, and it tends to be emphasized by some of the prominent funder-driven community-building initiatives.[1] A strong partnership must have a compelling and clear purpose, based on self-interest, to sustain it through the difficult work of building and implementing initiatives.

ETHICS, VALUES FOR MANAGERS

For years conventional wisdom suggested that people do not leave companies, but rather they leave because of bad business management also known as bad managers. Poor business management practices are more related to the problem of poor business ethics or values than to the common symptoms such as poor delegation or poor communication.

Every organization, no matter size, should have a written business values statement of non-negotiable behaviours that will be demonstrated by everyone. Each employee from top down needs to consistently demonstrate the same values and ethics. Inconsistent values from managers can dramatically affect employee motivation and ultimately employee performance.

A recently released survey from Florida State University of 700 employees within numerous industries and employment levels provides an insight into the lack of ethics by many mangers.

- Failure to keep their (managers) word – 39%
- Insulting employees behind backs – 27%
- Blaming others for bosses mistakes – 23%

All of these behaviours demonstrate that these bosses lacked personal values and personal ethics. This lack of ethical behaviour may be attributed to top management because upper management has probably modeled the same behaviours. Finally, there are probably no core values adopted by the organization within the strategic plan. Even if there is a values statement, it is much more for show than for alignment of organizational performance.

Values are relatively permanent desires that seem to be good in them, like peace and goodwill. Ethics is the study of how our decision affects other people. It is also the study of people's rights and duties, the moral rules that people apply in making decisions, and the nature of the relationships among people.

Doctor Toner's definition of ethics, "the study of good and evil, of right and wrong, of duty and obligation in human conduct, and of reasoning and choice about them," reveals his contention that ethical behaviour support are the very core of profession.

Levels of Ethical Questions in Business

In business most ethical questions fall into one of the four categories, societal, stakeholder, internal policy or personal issues.

First, at the societal level, we ask questions about the basic questions in society *e.g.*, apartheid in South Africa, caste system in India etc. Another societal question can be stated as the role Government should play in business ? The second is the stakeholders – the suppliers, customers, shareholders and the rest. Here we ask question how company should deal with external groups affected by its decisions, as well as how stake holders should deal with the company. Third is the internal policy. Here we ask question about the nature of company's relations with its employees. Is the employment contract fair ? What are the mutual obligations ? Layoffs, benefits, work rules, motivation, and leadership are all ethical concerns here.

Fourth is personal, here is the question of inter-personal relationship, how persons should be treated. What obligations do we have for one and another ?

Responsibilities towards an Individual
Understand the team members as individuals - personality, skills, strengths, needs, aims and fears
Assist and support individuals - plans, problems, challenges, highs and lows
Identify and agree appropriate individual responsibilities and objectives
Give recognition and praise to individuals - acknowledge effort and good work
Where appropriate reward individuals with extra responsibility, advancement and status
Identify, develop and utilize each individual's capabilities and strengths
Train and develop individual team members
Develop individual freedom and authority

Debate what constitutes ethical practice goes back to Ramayana and beyond. It is impossible to enter debate here. What then constitutes ethics ?

Three approaches can base our work. First is the respect for other is a duty central to all behaviour and morality. This concept condemns any action performed in self interest and assumes morality to be a matter of exercise of reason. It is reasonable to say that people should be treated 'with respect and as ends in their own right, not solely as means to others ends' (Legge 1998, p.23). The Second is that ethical behaviour is the hallmark of any society especially Indian. Here the behaviour calls for values of justice, charity, generosity and its exercise brings mutual benefit to society and to all its members. Indian culture high light these attributes and these have been dealt in detail earlier. The third important constituent of ethics is that it ensures happiness and benefit to larger number in an organization or society. Legge (1998) defines this approach by reference to ethical being related to the consequence of the behaviour.

As recently as a decade ago, many companies viewed business ethics only in terms of administrative compliance with legal standards and adherence to internal rules and regulations. Today the situation is different. Attention to business ethics is on the rise across the world and many companies realize that in order to succeed, they must earn the respect and confidence of their customers. Like never before, corporations are being asked, encouraged and prodded to improve their business practices to emphasize legal and ethical behaviour. Companies, professional firms and individuals alike are being held increasingly accountable for their actions, as demand grows for higher standards of corporate social responsibility.

Ethics codes on their own have little meaning. Most companies have them, and many of them have been swiped from some other company. A quick survey of corporate values will tell you which ones guide most companies in the United States : honesty, integrity, trust, respect and then maybe commitment, or teamwork. No problem there. But do a little detective work with employee groups and they'll laugh you out of the room. (Toffler, 2003, pp.240-241). The same is true in India.

Some Principles for Good Business Ethics

Be Respectful : Treat others with the utmost of respect. Regardless of differences, positions, titles, ages, or other types of distinctions, always treat others with professional respect and courtesy.

Be Trustful : Recognize persons/ customers want to do business with a leader/company they can trust; when trust is at the core, it's easy to recognize. Trust defined, is assured reliance on the character, ability, strength, and truth.

Keep An Open Mind : For continuous improvement, the leader must be open to new ideas. Ask for opinions and feedback from both customers and team members and your company will continue to grow.

Meet Obligations : Regardless of the circumstances, do everything in your power to gain the trust of past customer's and clients, particularly if something have gone awry. Reclaim any lost business by honoring all commitments and obligations.

Have Clear Documents : Re-evaluate all print materials including small business advertising, brochures, and other business documents making sure they are clear, precise and professional. Most important, make sure they do not misrepresent or misinterpret.

Become Community Involved/ Civic Action Program : Remain involved in community-related issues and activities, thereby demonstrating that your business is a responsible community contributor. In defence forces civic action programs is your responsibility towards the community where you are deployed. In other words, stay involved.

Maintain Accounting Control : Take a hands-on approach to accounting and record keeping, not only as a means of gaining a better feel for the progress of your company, but as a resource for any "questionable" activities. Gaining control of accounting and record keeping allows you to end any dubious activities promptly.

VALUES

What are Values ?

Kluckhohn, C. *et. al.* (1951) defines value as 'a conception, explicit and implicit, distinctive of an individual or characteristics of a group, of the desirable which influences the selection from available modes, means and ends of action." In this definition the authors have emphasizes the affective (desirable), cognitive (conception), and cognitive (selection) elements as essential to the concept of value.

Values represent basic conviction that a specific mode of conduct or end state of evidence is personally or socially preferable to an opposite or converse mode of conduct or end state of existence (Rokeach, 1973). Once a value is internalized, it becomes a standard for guiding action or a criterion for selection of an action. Although values are internal to an individual, they are basically social products. They are generally acceptable to the society as a whole or a section of the society as preferred 'modes of conduct' or 'end states'.

SOCIETAL VALUES

The values are more to do with society and vary from country to country and region to region. However, for management purposes the values can be broadly classified as western and eastern. Values do not operate singly. Several values interact with each other and value systems or value orientations are formed. Most conceptual frameworks purpose such systems.

Kluckhohn-Strodtbeck Framework

Kluckhohn-Strodtbeck (1961) assumed that 'there is a limited number of common human problems for which all peoples at all times must find some solution..... While there is variability in solutions of all the problems, it is neither limitless nor random but is definitely variable within a range of possible solutions.... All alternatives of all solutions are present in all societies at all times but are differentially preferred'. By value orientation, Kluckhohn- Strodtbeck meant a patterned set of principles derived from peoples evaluative processes (cognitive, affective and directive) that give order and direction to people's actions and thoughts. Kluckhohn-Strodtbeck distinguishes value orientation from the psychologist's concept of value by emphasizing the importance of patterning and the basis on 'common human' problems. In addition, Kluckhohn-Strodtbeck refers to rank ordering of these value orientations in which the variations within each have characteristics patterns within each culture.

Based on these assumptions, Kluckhohn- Strodtbeck set out to define the general domain of universal human problems. They identified five fundamental problems faced by all people : human nature, relationship to nature, time orientation, activity orientation and relational orientation.

Rokeach Framework

Rokeach (1973) defines value as 'an enduring belief that a specific mode of conduct or end state of existence is personally or socially preferable to an opposite or converse mode of conduct or end-state existence' (p.5). For example, honesty is a preferable mode of conduct over dishonesty. Accomplishment is a preferable end-state of existence rather than failure.

Rokeach (1973) categorizes values as either terminal or instrumental. Terminal values are idealized or desirable end states of existence. Examples of terminal value include wisdom, comfortable life, or world at peace. Instrumental values are idealized or desirable modes of conduct that are instrumental to the attainment of terminal values. Instrumental values include cheerfulness, logic, responsibility, competence, and so forth. Rokeach (1973) proposed the existence of relatively small number of terminal values (about 18), and a somewhat larger number of instrumental values (about 60 to 70). Further he conceives both to be either socio-centric (society-centered, interpersonal) or self-centric (self-centered, interpersonal, concerned with personal competence).

Musser and Orke (1992) used this categorization to develop a typology of organizational moral systems. A terminal socio-centric and instrumental self centric competence value system was termed the value system of the 'effective crusader'; a terminal self centric and instrumental competence-oriented value system was called the 'Independent Maximizer'; and a terminal and instrumental self-centric moral value system was called that of the "honorable Egoist". Musser and Orke's data indicated that the Independent Maximizer type tended to have high score on Machiavellianism (deception, manipulation, deceit), while the Honorable Egoist type tend to have lowest score on Machiavellianism.

Musser and Orke indicate that people possessing the different value types behave quite differently. In a validation study, Musser and Orke developed matches between famous people and specific value types. They identified Mother Teresa and Mahatma Gandhi as Virtuous Advocates, Oliver North as an Effective Crusader, Donald Trump and Ivan Boesky as Independent Maximizers and Arsenio Hall as an Honorable Egoist. According to Musser and Orke, these are the behaviours associated with each value type.

- *Virtuous Advocates* are primarily concerned with helping the organization reach its goals rather than obtaining their own personal goals. They also tend to go about helping the organization achieve its goals in a manner that is sensitive to the needs and feelings of their associates. This other-centered, other-sensitive focus creates trust and helps associates risk more and be more innovative (Figure 23.4).
- *Independent Maximizers* are more concerned with seeking personal goals rather than those of the organization. They also strive to obtain these personal goals in an impersonal manner that often ignores the needs and feelings of their associates, which may lead to mistrust with team members. As a result, associates are less willing to take risks and eventually become stagnant.
- *Honorable Egoists* seek to achieve personal goals over those of the organization but attempt to do so in a manner that is sensitive to the feelings of their associates. However, team members may view these people with suspicion because of their primary focus on individual goals. Therefore, they are less likely to take risks and be more innovative.
- *Effective Crusaders* primarily seek to achieve organizational goals but they often go about doing this in a way that is insensitive to their associates. Therefore, team members often find themselves in a love-hate relationship with these leaders. They want to love them because they are trying to help the team meet its goals but their methods produce hurt and alienation.

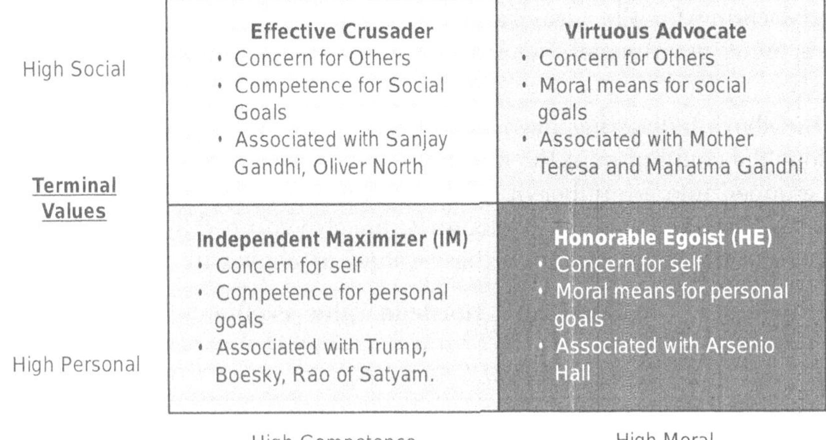

Fig. 23.5. *Musser and Orke Value System Matrix.*

According to Rokeach (1973) values serve the following functions :

(*a*) Predisposes us to favour one particular position over another.

(*b*) Lead individual to take a particular position on social issues.

(*c*) Guide our presentation of the self to others and help us to evaluate and judge or praise and blame others and us.

(*d*) Helps individuals to ascertain whether we are as moral and as competent as others are.

(*e*) Leads individuals to persuade and influence others by suggesting to us that beliefs, attitudes, values and actions of others need to be influenced or changed.

(*f*) Tells individuals how to rationalize in psychoanalytic sense, beliefs, attitudes and actions that would otherwise be personally and socially unacceptable.

Z

The Hofstede (1980) model identifies four dimensions, or indices, of culture. They were developed through a worldwide survey of employees in IBM. The indices measure four characteristics : individualism, uncertainty avoidance, power distance and masculinity. Scores on each range from 0 to 100. These scores should be interpreted as indicating a general sense of the values likely to be found in a particular culture. The index characteristics are described below.

- *Individualism (IDV).* The degree to which individual decision-making and action are accepted and encouraged by a society.
- *Uncertainty Avoidance (UAI).* The degree to which members of a society feel uncomfortable with uncertainty and ambiguity, which leads them to support beliefs promising certainty and to maintain institutions that protect uniformity.
- *Power Distance (PDI).* The degree to which members of a society accept that power in social institutions and organisations is distributed unequally.
- *Masculinity (MAS).* The degree to which traditional male values—assertiveness, performance, ambition, achievement and material success—are important to a society.

It may be contrasted with femininity, which stands for a preference in relationships, modesty, caring for the weak, and the quality of life. In a masculine society, even women prefer assertiveness (at least in men); in a feminine society, even men prefer modesty.

Each of the above indices has been described in terms of its extremes. Most countries are somewhere along the continuum in the moderately high or moderately low areas. In Table 23.1, countries are grouped into a number of cultural values : strong, high, medium-high, medium, low-medium, small, low and varied. The countries are also grouped by three geographic clusters. Take special note of the implications of these values as shown by the last column.

Table 23.1. Hofstede Value Profile

	Cultural Characteristics					*Illustrative Marketing Implications*
	Size (Million)	*Power Distance*	*Uncertainty Avoidance*	*Individualism*	*Masculimity*	
Cluster 1 Denmark, Sweden, Finland, Norway, Netherlands.	37	small	low	high	low	Relatively weak resistance to new product, strong consumer desire for novelty and variety. High consumer regard for 'environmental friendly' marketers and socially conscious firms.
Cluster 2 Belgium, France, Greece, Portugal, Spain, Turkey	182	medium	Strong	varied	Low-medium	Appeal to consumer's status and power position, reduce perceived risk in product purchase and use, emphasize product functionally.
Cluster 3 Austria, Germany, Switzerland, Italy, Great Britain Ireland	203	Small	Medium	Medium High	High	Preference for 'high performance' products; use 'successful achiever' theme in advertising: desire for novelty, variety and pleasure; fairly risk-averse market.

Examination of Table 23.1 should illustrate how country profiles might influence management practices. Some further examples based on Hofstede's findings are :

- New Zealand : individualistic, does not avoid uncertainty, believes in equality and traditional male values. This suggests that decentralisation will be practiced, with flat organization structure and individual decision-making.
- Japan : collectivist society, high on uncertainty avoidance but also on masculinity, relatively high on power distance. This suggests a system that seeks consensus, but is also competitive with clear distinctions in terms of power. Job security is stressed and jobs are allocated on the basis of sex.
- India : The Hofstede analysis for India shows a large power distance society and all other measures are relatively moderate. This would be indicative of the fact that India is in the midst of change. The traditional caste systems has been outlawed, however the large power distance score indicates that the attitudes still remain. This Power Distance score for India indicates a high level of inequality of power and wealth within the society. This condition is not necessarily subverted upon the population, but rather accepted by the population as a cultural norm.

Chakraborty Framework

Chakraborty is a strong advocate of Indian values and its society. He has suggested learning and understanding Indian values is possible by examining the traditional philosophical repertoire of knowledge. According to Chakraborty the values of Indians are anchored in the transcendental aspect of human existence. He has listed some of the values as core to Indian socio-cultural ethos as; respect for individuals, cooperation and trust, work as worship, containment of greed, ethical-moral boundaries, self discipline, and restraint, need to give, renunciation and detachment.

Values in Indian Society

Several studies have conducted on the values of Indian Society. According to Narendar (2007) Indian society can be characterized by the following components and dominant values.

(*a*) *Avoid Excesses*. Manu gives elaborate treatise on 'why' and 'what' a King should do to the exclusion of 'how'. It focuses on the virtue of gentle yet firm behaviour by the leader. In Manusmiriti, Manu writes that the King should be just, should punish the deserving, should be judicious and fair or else he would lose every thing. Manu further writes that the King must exert to control his senses; for he alone can keep his subjects under control if he has control himself. Excesses in life viz. kama, krodh does not help but if king considers each affair, in sharp and gentle manner he would be respected.

(*b*) Indian philosophy gives *predominance to individuals* 'main Braham hoon'; every Indian seeks 'moksha' from this cycle of birth and rebirth and strives inwardly to become complete or 'poorn' (complete).

(*c*) Every Indian leader took up the *path of righteousness*. Most of leaders in India shunned power did not chase material goods – Rig-Veda has enunciated the principle : 'Let man think well on wealth and strive to win it by the path of law (ritasya) and by worship. Indian generally believes in simple living and high thinking.

(*d*) The followers in India depict *high loyalty to their groups*, respecting harmony and thus expressing loyalty to individuals, so that harmony is not violated. Indians are *loyal to particular individuals* and would go out of the way to support him. Hence, there is a tendency to be near power center.

(*e*) Indians by and large believe in *'Karma'* and any failure or poor performance or result is shelved by stating that it is karma or destined to be so. The desire to change the status and restart or improve from that situation is not there and very large segment of population just live in dire strait.

(*f*) Security. The kutumb (family) system of the early parent-child relationship of dependence produces preferences for security rather than venturing out, for comfort rather than risk.

Organizational Values

Values-driven management can be defined by three characteristics which are exhibited by values-driven leaders : (1) they lead by example, (2) they consistently champion the values, and (3) their key decisions are values driven (Harmon 1996, p.272–273). According to Dolan and Garcia (2001, p.103) value-driven management is becoming an overall framework for the continual redesign of the corporate culture. Järvensivu (2007) defines value-driven management as a process where an organization first determines the core values to follow and then implements various practices to increase value congruence in the organization (2007, 3–4).

According to Collins and Porras (1997), core values are inherent and sacrosanct and so cannot be compromised either for convenience or for short-term economic growth. Four types of organizational values have been proposed (Woodcock and. Dave (1989), pp.10–15). :

(*a*) Power, elitism, and reward.

(*b*) Effectiveness, efficiency, and economy

(*c*) Fairness, teamwork and law and order.

(*d*) Defence, competitiveness and opportunism

Good firms posses a distinct and identifiable values that include both beliefs about superior quality of service, being the best and the importance of profit orientation and goal accomplishment. Table 23.2, list the common institutional value framework or organizational values and the range of attributes that depict it.

Table 23.2. Institutional Values Framework : Organizational Values

Organizational Values	*Range of Attributes*	
1. Economic	Profit Drives	Socially drives
2. Information as symbolic	Policy Focus	Communicative
3. Control/Power	Centralized	Distributed
4. Management Style	Participative	Autocratic
5. Locus of Decision Making	Decentralized	Centralized
6. Leadership Style	Informality	Formality
7. Communication Style	Open	Closed

8. Organizational Processes	Structured	Flexible
9. Task Coordination	Single way	Multiple alternatives
10. Impact on Work	Job Enrichment	Isolation
11. Focus of Work	Customer Focus	Internal Focus
12. Social Nature of Work	Participatory	Non-participatory
13. Team Behaviour	Cooperative	Competitive

Most of the values are easily identified within organizations. As value systems, clusters of similar value attributes often occur together within a focus organization, such as 'open communication, flexible process, participative management'. An attempt to produce generalized model negates the variety and range of values that might be incorporated. The strategic function of value should be to enhance the unique values systems that complement both strategy and organizational culture.

Harmon (1996) reviews on three common characteristics, which values-driven leaders exhibit whatever their industry, wherever they work : they lead by example, they consistently champion the values and their key decisions are values driven. Values-driven leaders define values in the context of where they work, they set standards, first for themselves and then for their team. They try to search opportunities to link values and performance. At first the effort is conscious, but over time it becomes an unconscious habit. (1996, 272–273)

Developing Values

Values can be developed in individuals and organizations by role modeling and open examination of the values practiced as against values espoused or desired. There is always a gap between exposed or desied and practiced values.

Value Clarification

Kirschenbaum (1977) has suggested 'value clarification' as an intervention for development of values in organization. Values change over time in response to changing life experiences. Recognizing these changes and understanding how they affect one's actions and behaviours is the goal of the 'values clarification' process. Values clarification will not tell you what your values should be; it simply provides the means to discover what your values are. Value clarification helps in identifying and prioritizing moral values. For the purpose of values clarification, Raths, Harmin and Simon identified seven criteria that must be met if a value is to be considered a full value. These criteria can be divided into three categories : choosing, prizing and acting (Figure 23.6).

Values Process Phases	Value Process Criteria
Choosing	1. Choosing Freely 2. Choosing from alternatives 3. Choosing after thought consideration of the consequences of each alternative.

Prizing	4. Cherishing – being happy with the choice. 5. Affirming the choice to others.
Acting	6. Doping something with the choice. 7. Acting repeatedly in same pattern of life.
Source : Adapted from rath, *I.E.*, Hermin, M., Simon, S.B. (1978). *Values and Teaching,* Columbus, Ohio : Merill Publishing Company.	

Fig. 23.6. *Three Stage Process.*

To be a full value, the value must be chosen freely from a list of alternatives, only after thoughtful consideration has been given to the consequences of each alternative. The value must be cherished and made known to other people. Raths *et. al.* attest that a value must meet all seven criteria outlined. The value must also be translated into behaviours that are consistent with the chosen value and integrated into the life style.

CORPORATE SOCIAL RESPONSIBILITY

In 1899, Andrew Carnegie, founder of the conglomerate U.S. Steel Corporation, published the book *The Gospel of Wealth*, which set forth the classic statement of *corporate social responsibility*. Carnegie's view was based on two principles : the charity principle and the stewardship principle. He saw business owners in a parent-like role to child like employees and customers who lacked the capacity to act in their own best interests.

Corporate social responsibility (CSR) and sustainable development is gaining increasing prominence in the global business culture, as many businesses attempt to accommodate the Corporate social responsibility agenda. The concept of corporate sustainable development is still the subject of controversy and therefore the indicators used to measure CSR continue to be the topic of debate. However, no matter what indicators are used, the notion of responsibility includes responsibility for people in the collective sense (such as communities) and also for individuals.

Research demonstrates CSR initiatives have a positive impact on employee morale, motivation, commitment, loyalty, training, recruitment and turnover. Benefits in these areas have been found to improve the bottom line of companies. Three surveys across Europe, the USA and a survey involving 25 countries found employees felt greater loyalty, satisfaction and motivation when their companies were socially responsible.

A recent survey of 257 CEOs by Korn/Ferry shows that 65 per cent of CEOs are taking responsibility for managing company reputation. Almost three-quarters of the CEOs regarded recruitment and retention as the main business objective of corporate reputation and almost the same percentage identified the hiring and retaining of key and talented people as one of the three top objectives of corporate and social responsibility initiatives. These HR concerns were regarded as more important than more commercial and business outcomes.

CSR demands that businesses manage the economic, social and environmental impacts of their operations to maximize the benefits and minimize the downsides. Key CSR issues include governance, environmental management, stakeholder engagement, labour standards, employee and community relations, social equity, responsible sourcing and human rights.

CSR is not about fulfilling duty to society; it should also bring competitive advantage. Through an effective CSR programme, companies can :

- Improve access to capital.
- Sharpen decision making and reduce risk.
- Enhance brand image.
- Uncover previously hidden commercial opportunities, including new markets.
- Reduce costs.
- Attract, retain and motivate employees.

Corporate social responsibility (CSR) means a commitment by a company to manage its roles in a society in a responsible and sustainable manner. Especially since the 1980's, CSR has become an increasingly important part of the business environment. Today there is a growing perception among enterprises that sustainable business success and shareholder value cannot be achieved solely through maximizing short-term profits, but instead through market-oriented yet responsible behaviour.

According to Milton Friedman, a business has no social responsibilities other than to maximize its profits. However, today there is a growing perception among enterprises that sustainable business success and shareholder value cannot be achieved solely through maximizing short-term profits, but instead through market-oriented yet responsible behaviour. This responsible behaviour of corporations can be called corporate social responsibility (CSR)" (EIC, 2005).

There are different approaches in explaining CSR. One of them is the classical theory stressing that the primary goal of company is to secure its shareholders' financial goals and to respond to their wishes relative to the corporation. Secondly, the social demanding theory of CSR means to promote and protect the general public's interests. On the other hand, the social activist theory holds that there exits a universal standard for determining responsible corporate conduct that is independent from the stockholders' interests (Brummer,1991).

DEFINITION

Corporate Social Responsibility can be defined as "what an organization does that affects the society in which it exists."

The corporate social responsibility has two basic principles. First, the Charity Principle required the more fortunate members of society to assist its less fortunate members, including the unemployed, the handicapped, the sick, and the elderly. These deprived people can be aided either directly on indirectly. Second, is the stewardship principle which requires businesses and fortunate individuals to view themselves as the stewards, or caretakers, of their property ? Rich hold their money 'in trust' for the rest of society and can use it for any purpose that society deems legitimate.

REASONS FOR CORPORATE SOCIAL RESPONSIBILITY

From the stakeholder approach, if companies are 'citizens' then they also have rights, duties and responsibilities to their stakeholders. CSR activities for company are important way to realize these duties and responsibilities, and offer several benefits to its stakeholders

CSR activities also provide businesses with the advantages of an improved image and reputation, an improved trust, a more prominent profile, a better market position, more business, increased employee motivation, increased attractiveness to potential recruits, cost savings and increased efficiency, and an improved company culture (Jenkins, 2001).

In our study, the companies indicate similar reasons. Overall, the community expectations, changing social values and public opinion are the basic causes of engaging in corporate social responsibility activities. The majority of companies (80%) see the CSR as a way for enhancing their public image and reputation. The building good relationship with the surrounding community and their employees is another motivation for the CSR programs.

TYPES OF CORPORATE SOCIAL RESPONSIBILITY ACTIVITIES

There are several CSR activities for both internal and external stakeholders. For example, loans, medical care, pension funds, maternity and safety programs are CSR activities for the internal stakeholders. The external CSR mainly consists of investment in community outreach, good employee relations, creation and maintenance of employment, environmental stewardship and financial performance etc. (Johansson and Larsson, 2000).

In the survey, the respondent companies were asked to list the types of their CSR activities. The sponsorships and student scholarships are the most popular CSR projects. 85 percent of them say that they support the sport and art activities.

Since the main motivation of CSR is to improve their public image for the companies, it isn't surprised that the most of CSR activities are the sponsorship projects. In Turkey (mainly in the city of Istanbul) the art festivals and organizations mostly are to be able to be realized by the sponsorship of private sector. Moreover, during the last years there has been a growing tendency among the Turkish companies to increase their sponsorship.

Secondly, there has been always a strong tradition of charity in the Turkish society, which contributes to a solid foundation of volunteerism. The most foundations and institutions provide funds for students. The results in our survey are consistent with that. The student scholarships are reported by the respondent companies as the most popular second CSR activity (65%).

Another important aspect of the charitable tradition is the strong relationship between companies and the NGOs. It is known that in Turkey there are many charitable organizations managing their activities by the donations of corporations. One of these organizations is the Private Sector Volunteers Association (OSGD) that was formed in 2002 to bring together concerned companies and professionals interested in CSR activities.

CORPORATE SOCIAL RESPONSIBILITY POLICY

Cooperation with stakeholders in determining of CSR policy is one way that companies can increase acceptance and receptiveness to their CSR practices, and helps facilitate their success (Zappala and Cronin, 2002).

The research suggests that the respondent companies view (in order of importance) the general public opinion, the Private Sector Volunteers Association (OSGD), NGOs and their employees as the key stakeholders to consult with regarding to the CSR.

The findings from the survey present that the companies consult with at least one stakeholder when deciding the projects on CSR. However, seeing CSR projects as a way to improve their public image and reputation, the companies largely (75%) identify the public opinion as the most important source in formulating their CSR policy. More importantly, 1 of 3 takes their employees' opinions in developing of the CSR policy, which means that they see their employees as a critical internal stakeholder.

Measuring Effectiveness

It may be concluded that the companies, measuring the effectiveness of CSR activities, place more importance on them. Evaluating CSR practices allow companies to assess the costs and benefits of any CSR programs, which is a critical indicator for expansion or modification of existing CSR practices. There are some evaluating methods. Mostly benchmarking, social auditing and self-reporting are used by companies. Another aspect of evaluating CSR activities is whether companies measure the effectiveness of CSR for the particular stakeholder groups (Zappala and Cronin, 2002).

In our research, the results suggest that 80% of the respondents indicate to have a formal policy for evaluating the effectiveness of CSR activities.

According to the data, the companies, assessing their CSR activities, utilize the methods of public image survey, customer satisfaction survey and return on investment (ROI). The results present that 63% of them mostly prefer the general public image survey. This is consistent with the overall results reported earlier. In another words, since the companies formulate their CSR activities for getting a good public image, they naturally evaluate the performance of their CSR activities by the public image surveys.

Secondly, customer satisfaction is a key success criterion when CSR activities are used as a marketing means especially. One-fourth of the respondents appraise their CSR activities by the customer satisfaction survey. As a result, the firms mostly consider that the impacts of CSR activities are more easily monitored by the external stakeholders such as community and customers.

HRM DIMENSIONS OF CORPORATE SOCIAL RESPONSIBILITY

Role of HRM

CSR is a strategic issue crossing departmental boundaries, and affecting the way in which company does business. However, human resource management department should be the primary responsible for managing CSR activities that offer also practically and theoretical new opportunities to HRM. Moreover, HR department has the potential to play a significant role in developing CSR activities in the organization. While CSR is expanding the role of HRM, it also supports the benefits of workplace practices. That contributes to organizational efficiency and success (Kramar, 2004)

Communicating with Employees

Another important aspect of an integrated stakeholder approach to CSR is whether the companies communicate their CSR activities to their stakeholders. This communication allows a company to gain additional benefits from their investment including improving their public image, increasing employee morale, and support from the community (Zappala and Cronin, 2002).

Especially, communicating with employees is a critical issue to improve the performance of CSR mission. That is why; almost all companies (97%) state to communicate their CSR policies and activities to their employees.

There are several mechanisms ways of communicating with employees, which are e-mail, company newsletters, regular staff meetings and posters. E-mail is the fastest way %r communication especially in large organizations. The findings of survey are consistent with that.

CSR Activities and HRM Functions

Successful CSR programs rely on enlightened people management practices. The HR department is responsible for many of the key systems and processes (*e.g.*, recruitment, training, performance appraisals) on which effective delivery depends. Getting the employment relationship right is a precondition for establishing effective relationships with external stakeholders. CSR does not change so much as broadens the HR agenda, and focuses on effective implementation (CIPD, 2002).

The CSR may increase attractiveness to current and prospective employees. For example, in 1995 the senior managers at Shell reported a tremendous loss of morale and a significant downturn in recruitment, when Shell suffered its difficulties in Nigeria and with Brent Spar. However, once Shell had made its commitment to CSR, through much greater transparency and engagement with external stakeholders, it found itself swamped with potential employees.

In addition to that, there are several studies confirming that CSR leads to an improved recruitment. A survey by Cone/Roper found that good corporate reputation come second only to career growth potential as the most important consideration for people when choosing a new employer—ahead of starting salary, fringe benefits, and social facilities (Pickering, 2005).

Today companies, having distinguished themselves as the frontrunners in CSR, have tried to translate the concept of CSR into a daily business reality using tools such as recruitment, selection etc (CSR Europe, 2002). According to a survey by the Points of Light Foundation (2003), 58 percent of U.S. companies use their employee volunteer programs for recruitment and retention purposes (BRS, 2005).

Secondly, the relationship between CSR and training function is a strategic issue, which is confirmed by 70% of the respondents in our survey. In particular, employees are more likely to respond if training programs incorporate policies, procedures, and systems used on the workplace how to meet the CSR objectives. The respondents do this mostly for the new employees. 85% of them train the new recruits on their CSR policy and projects during the orientation period. In this way, the new employees perceive the importance of CSR policy in the first stage.

HRM Practices

There is an extensive body of research demonstrating that CSR has positive effects on the human resource management practices such as improving trust and understanding, increasing employee motivation and loyalty, increasing efficiency, supporting company culture and communication effectiveness (Jenkins, 2001).

Today effective employee communication is delivering remarkable business results. The surveys show that employee communication is a strategic tool to improve corporate performance.

For example, a research by Watson Wyatt Worldwide found that a significant improvement in communication effectiveness is associated with a 29.5% increase in market value. Companies with the highest levels of effective communication experienced a 26% total return to shareholders from 1998 to 2002, compared to a 15% return experienced by firms that communicate least effectively (Watson Wyatt Worldwide, 2005). CSR activities particularly lead to a higher level of trust internally and externally among stakeholders. Fostering trust and credibility creates and maintains a positive workplace environment. This is very important since communication effectiveness require that the parties trust each other. This approach is confirmed by 60% of the companies in our survey. They say that the employees who engage in CSR activities have a better relationship with the company, and communicate more honestly with their bosses, co-workers and the customers. The respondents believe that the CSR programs can greatly accelerate trust-building and effective communication among the staff.

Secondly, corporate social responsibility programs encourage employee teamwork. Teamwork is the most effective way of quickly learning success stems, creating clear targets, communicating clearly, and trusting each other. Many CSR projects require volunteers to work cooperatively in teams to accomplish tasks. Such teams often involve a diverse mix of company and community representatives, spanning a variety of ages, races, cultures, and working styles. Companies mostly have harnessed the teamwork skills learned in volunteer activities to help everyone from line employees to senior executives work more collaboratively in their jobs.

Moreover, the studies indicate that CSR practices, such as employee volunteering, can create a shared sense of purpose and loyalty among employees, helping foster employee teamwork, and improve employee skills such as leadership (Zappala, 2004). According to our survey, the CSR activities are used by the companies as a strategic tool in encouraging cooperation and teamwork. They mostly (85%) stress the importance of CSR activities as a source of team inspiration. The respondents report that the employees who have similar interests come together in teams through the CSR Programs, which promotes cohesion among staff. It appears that the CSR programs are seen by the firms especially as an effective way to create a meaningful working environment.

On the other hand, employee motivation and satisfaction are core strategic objectives of any HR function. CSR activities can boost them in the workplace. The survey 2005 by KPMG shows that the companies suppose that employee motivation is a key driver in corporate social responsibility. The research includes a detailed analysis of the reports of the Global 250 companies, focused on why they are committed to corporate responsibility. The conclusion is that business drivers are diverse, both economic (75%) and ethical (50%). The top three are innovation and learning, employee motivation and risk management and reduction, with about 50% as motivating factors (KPMG; 2005; 5). There are similar results in our study as well. 85% of the companies believe that their CSR activities are extremely important to motivation employee. To the respondents, taking part in volunteer activities is a means for their staff to get to know each other, meet new people, do useful work together and put their own life in perspective, which is very crucial in increasing the motivation

Finally, in the study, the firms strongly emphasize the importance of building loyalty through the corporate social responsibility (65%). Indeed there are several studies showing the relationship between employees' loyalty and CSR activities. For example, according to the results from a survey among almost 25,000 people across 25 countries by Environics International, 80 percent of people who work for large companies state that they feel greater motivation and loyalty towards their jobs and companies the more socially responsible their employers become.

Moreover, a survey on European employees reports that almost 90 percent of the respondents express greater loyalty to employers who are socially

Another study of employees in the U.S. companies shows that a company's CSR activities have a positive effect on the average employees' satisfaction and loyalty. In particular, the employees involved in employer-sponsored community events are 30 percent more likely to want to continue working for their employer, and help it succeed (Cook, 2004). It seems that the Turkish companies have the correct strategy to strengthen the loyalty among their employees.

An Australian measurement process, the Reputex Social Responsibility Ratings provides a system to measure social responsibility performance and attempts to integrate the expectations of a variety of stakeholders. Two of its four criteria reflect the impact on people and have direct relevance to HR. Four categories of measurement are used : environmental impact; corporate governance; social impact and workplace practices.

The criteria used to measure workplace practices relate specifically to HR practices. The criteria include : employee involvement; fair and reasonable rewards and conditions; a positive commitment to diversity and work-life balance; industrial relations arrangements based on mutual respect; occupational health and safety arrangements; executive remuneration that is fair and reflect the concerns of internal stakeholders; independently verifiable performance measurement and evaluation systems and training and development policies. These criteria indicate that an organisation that is seen as socially responsible creates a culture that is perceived as open, fair and attractive to potential and existing employees.

Review Questions

1. Define various leadership styles.
2. Explain the various approaches to leadership.
3. Does leadership have any impact on organizational performance ?
4. Explain Ethics and its relevance.
5. Explain the relevance of values in today's context.
6. Do you think we should be adopting Indian ethos ? Substantiate your answer with some examples.
7. Discuss the various factors influencing the value system of an organization.
8. Analyze the relationship between CSR and business strategy.
9. Compare and contrast the international trends with Indian trends in CSR.

PROJECT WORK

1. Prepare an analytical report on three of the leading Indian corporate leaders.
2. Study the leadership styles in an organization of your choice and review it in the context of organizational performance.
3. Study TATA Steel efforts o CSR and present it in the class.

Case Study

"CSR : A Cornerstone of our Enduring Success"

At Indian Oil, corporate social responsibility (CSR) has been the cornerstone of success right from inception in the year 1964. The Corporation's objectives in this key performance area are enshrined in its Mission statement : "...to help enrich the quality of life of the community and preserve ecological balance and heritage through a strong environment conscience."

We at IndianOil have defined a set of core values for ourselves—Care, Innovation, Passion and Trust—to guide us in all we do. We take pride in being able to claim all our countrymen as our customers. That's why, we coined the phrase, "IndianOil – India Inspired", in our corporate campaigns. Public corporations like IndianOil are essentially organs of society deploying significant public resources. We, therefore, are aware of the need to work beyond financial considerations and put in that little extra to ensure that we are perceived not just as corporate behemoths that exist for profits, but as wholesome entities created for the good of the society and for improving the quality of life of the communities we serve.

As a constructive partner in the communities in which it operates, Indian Oil has been taking concrete action to realise its social responsibility objectives, thereby building value for its shareholders and customers. The Corporation respects human rights, values its employees, and invests in innovative technologies and solutions for sustainable energy flow and economic growth. In the past four decades, Indian Oil has supported innumerable social and community initiatives in India. Touching the lives of millions of people positively by supporting environmental and health-care projects and social, cultural and educational programmes.

Besides focussing primarily on the welfare of economically and socially deprived sections of society, Indian Oil also aims at developing techno-economically viable and environment-friendly productsandservices for the benefit of millions of its consumers, while at the same time ensuring the highest standards of safety and environment protection in its operations.

Sharing Profits

Every year, IndianOil sets aside a fixed portion of its profits for spreading smiles in millions of lives across the country through a comprehensive community welfare and development programme. About one-fourth of the community development funds are spent on the welfare of Scheduled Caste and Scheduled Tribe beneficiaries.

IndianOil has a concerted social responsibility programme to partner communities in health, family welfare, education, environment protection, providing potable water, sanitation, and empowerment of women and other marginalised groups. IndianOil has always been in the forefront in times of national emergencies. IndianOilPeople have time and again rallied to help victims of natural calamities, maintaining uninterrupted supply of petroleum products and contributing to relief and rehabilitation measures in cash and kind.

IndianOil's community-focussed initiatives include allotment of petrol/diesel station dealerships and LPG distributorships to beneficiaries from among Scheduled Castes, Scheduled Tribes, physically handicapped, ex-servicemen, war widows, etc. The Corporation has also unveiled kisan seva kendras as small-format retail outlets to reach quality products and services to people in the rural areas. IndianOil has also set up the IndianOil Foundation (IOF) as a non-profit trust to protect, preserve and promote national heritage monuments. The Corporation also supports a variety of endeavours in arts, culture, music and dance, apart from organising programmes on its own under the banners of IndianOil Art Exhibition, IndianOil Sangeet Sabha and IndianOil Kavi Sammelan.

As part of its environment-protection initiatives, IndianOil has invested close to Rs. 7,000 crore in state-of-the-art technologies at its refineries for production of green fuels meeting global standards. To further reduce dependence on precious petroleum products and secure the nation's energy security, the

Corporation is now in the process of commercializing various options in alternative fuels such as ethanol-blended petrol, biodiesel, and Hydrogen and Hydrogen-CNG mixture.

With safety, health and environment protection high on its corporate agenda, IndianOil is committed to conducting business with a strong environment conscience, so as to ensure sustainable development, safe work places and enrichment of the quality of life of its employees, customers and the community. IndianOil is also committed to the Global Compact Programme of the United Nations and endeavours to abide by the 10 principles of the programme, some of which are already part of the Corporation's Vision and Mission statements. It is the firm resolve of IndianOil people to move beyond business, touch every heart and fuel a billion dreams.

Questions

1. Critically examine the movement towards CSR in IndianOil.
2. Do you think success of CSR would be based on contextual factors ? If so explain in brief.
3. Briefly analyze the role of Indian Oil in enforcing CSR towards tribals.

Chapter **24**

STRESS AT WORK

★ LEARNING OBJECTIVES ★

After reading this chapter, you will be able to understand :

- What is stress ?
- Characteristics of stress.
- Causes and Levels of Stress
- Managing stress

INTRODUCTION

The nature of the workplace and of working conditions within the organizational environment is rapidly changing. Contemporary workplaces now entirely depend on human capital with an increased knowledge mind-set, a greater reliance on technology and a thirst for organizational efficiency and process optimizations (Dollard, 2003). With this modern cultural change arrives an increasing obligation for employees to perform at higher levels of intensity—while an escalating managerial directive forces them to improve both the quantitative and qualitative aspects of their role. Evidently, a by-product of this new organisational environment is a greater level of employee resistance stemming from an atmosphere fuelled by conflict, stress and often a misrepresented view of workplace justice. The majority of this conflict and stress is attributed to 'work design and the organisation and management of work, and an employee's social and environmental contexts, which have the potential for causing psychological, social and even physical harm'(Cox *et.al.* 2000)

Stress at work is a well known factor for low motivation and morale, decrease in performance, high turnover and sick-leave, accidents, low job satisfaction, low quality products and services, poor internal communication and conflicts etc. (Schabracq and Cooper, 2000; Murphy, 1995; McHugh, 1993). Moreover, Chusmir and Franks (1988) argued that all the aforementioned problems are related, directly or indirectly, to stress and they have an effect on overall organizational efficiency and effectiveness. The British Industrial Society Survey (2001) indicated that 91 per cent of the 492 human resource and personnel professionals questioned believed stress to be a problem in their organization. More specifically, 36 percent believed that it was a significant problem and 5 per cent indicated that it was a serious problem.

Armenakis and Bedeian (1999, p.307) considered stress as an obstacle to change planning and implementation and they argued that :

Receptivity, resistance, commitment, cynicism, stress, and related personal reactions are clearly relevant criterion variables to be considered in the framework of planning and implementing an organizational change.

WHAT IS STRESS ?

The common expression for stress is 'tension' One is said to be tense, when there is some anxiety, some fear of whether the desirable things may happen, whether something may go wrong, etc. It is a state of discomfort felt in the mind and experienced by the body. When there is tension, the body may become weak.

Hammond points out; there are actually three very distinct stress literatures.

(*a*) Literature which looks at social and psychological aspects.

(*b*) 'Ergonomics literature' – human factors – primarily laboratory based highly experimental in approach.

(*c*) Stress is also studied from the pscho-physiological and neuroscience perspective.

DEFINITION

In management literature, 'Stress' is defined as a response of the human body to a felt need. When one is hungry and there is an urge to eat food, the body is in a state of stress, which disappears when the need is fulfilled. This definition suggests that stress is a desirable condition, making one move towards fulfillment of needs. This is partly true. Stress occurs also when the need arises out of fear and the urge is to run and escape. This may sometimes, be not possible. In that case, there is no movement, the need remains unfulfilled and the stress condition does not disappear.

R.S.Schuler has defined stress as,

'A dynamic condition in which an individual is confronted with an opportunity, a demand, or a resource related to what the individual desires and for which the outcome is perceived to be both uncertain and important.'

Cox states that *'it is useful to think of stress as embedded in an ongoing process which involves individuals interacting with their environment, making appraisals of that interactions and attempting to cope with the problem that arise.'*

Edwards suggests stress is the result of a *'lack of fit between a person (in terms of their personality, aptitudes and abilities) and the environment, and a consequent inability to cope effectively with the various demands that it makes of him or her.'*

In the Maxwell Report, it was stated that definition of stress is 'the harmful physical and emotional responses that occur when the requirements of the job do not match the capabilities, resources, or needs the worker (Maxwell, 2004, p.39).'

CAUSES OF STRESS AT WORK

Stress is not caused by any external factor. It is created by oneself, by the way one thinks about the external factors. Yet there are situations, in which most people tend to get stressed. These are called stressors. In personal life, death of a close relative is a stressor. An important test in life, like a final examination; a transfer of residence; separation due to marriage, divorce or change of job; difficult financial demands; serious illness; likelihood of unpleasant secrets becoming revealed; are common stressors (see Figure 24.1). To welcome and entertain important visitors or having to deliver a speech for the first time, also cause considerable stress. Daniels et. al. (2003) states that there are nine sources of workplace stress.

1. Poorly designed/managed workload;
2. Poorly designed/managed work scheduling;
3. Poorly designed/managed physical environment;
4. Poorly designed/managed other sources of demand;
5. Lack of skill discretions;
6. Lack of decision authority or other forms of control;
7. Lack of support;
8. Poorly designed/managed procedures for eliminating conflict (*e.g.*, bullying/ harassment).
9. Individual differences.

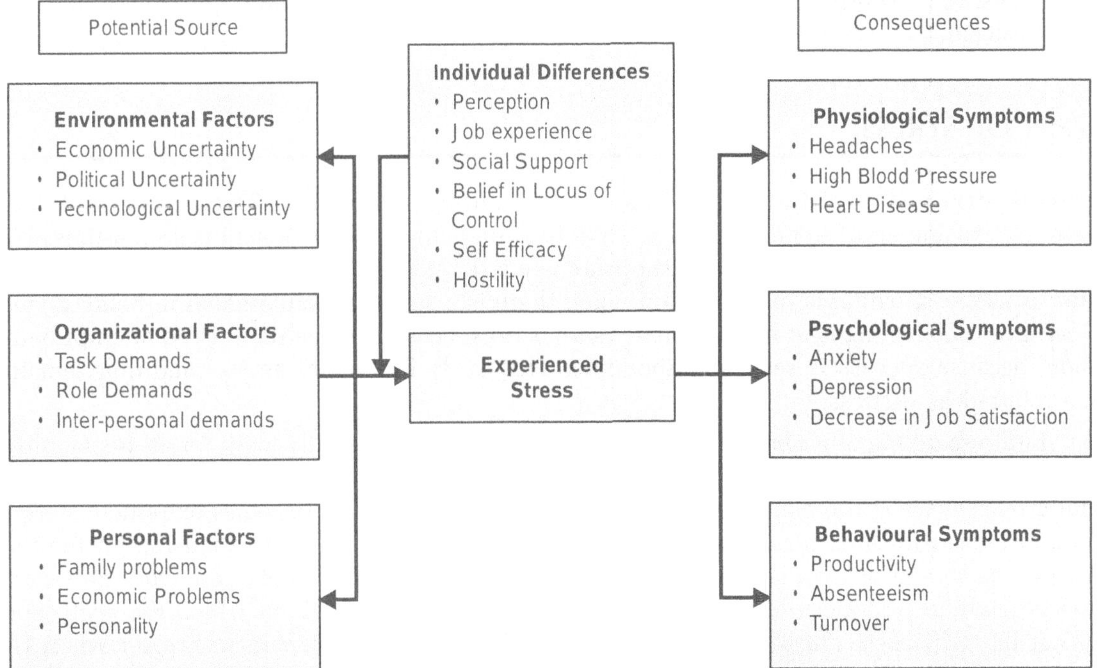

Fig. 24.1. *Model of Stress.*

Other Stressors

At work, the following may be stressors in addition to one given by Daniels et. al. (2003).

- Needs not met. These could be needs for power, for fulfillment, for use of knowledge
- Not being included by others as part of a group you want to belong to
- Not being recognized or valued for one's competence
- Feeling that one is not adequate for the task, particularly when compared to some one else
- Being denied what is due (rewards, work)
- Monotony or boredom
- Inequity in rewards, assignments
- Very little opportunity for growth
- Too little work, boredom
- Inadequate resources to do the assigned work, creating possibilities of failures
- Conflict in values at work, being required to do what one does not like to do
- Too many and conflicting demands at work from the role set
- Responsibilities not clear, ambiguity on what is expected
- Un-understanding, unpredictable, temperamental boss
- New unfamiliar work
- Being blamed

On close analysis, it will be found that all of the above situations are, in some way or other, causing perceptions of possible failure at work or non-recognition and consequent loss of self-esteem.

TYPES OF STRESS

Stress is identified as of two kinds. One is called EuStress, which is the condition in which there is drive and effort to fulfill the needs. Motivation is high. Achievement is seen as possible. The situation is challenging. Stress disappears when the need is fulfilled. There is success. The other is Distress, which is the condition when there is a sense of helplessness in being unable to achieve. The feeling is of frustration as there is no success, may be there is no attempt being made, because success is seen as impossible. This is dysfunctional stress condition remains also referred as distress.

EuStress on the other hand is necessary for the person to be fully alert, for all his faculties to come into play to face the situation. For example, a goalkeeper in football or hockey will be totally relaxed when the ball is at the other end of the ground, but becomes extremely alert as the ball moved towards him. His body stiffens, the eyes begin to bulge, focusing on the ball and the movement of the players, picking up the slightest of movements and every nerve and muscle ready to respond to those movements. That is EuStress, without which the goalkeeper cannot be at his best. So also, Eustress is experienced by the batsman in cricket when the bowler is on the run, and by the tennis player when the ball is about to be served at the other end.

Stress is Physical

When the goalkeeper or the batsman or the tennis player experiences Eustress, there are changes in the physical system. The muscles become tense, the eyes become sharper as compared to when one is under severe distress, the person sweats, the body becomes weak and loses strength.

Study of stress shows that the response is the same whether it is Eustress or Distress, except that the degree varies. The response is called the Fight or Flight response. When one senses danger, one is tempted to either stand and fight to ward off the danger or run away – Flight. The body conditions itself for either event, automatically, causing changes in the normal secretions of hormones and other chemicals, withdrawing from activities that are less important and diverting to activities that should have higher priority in that situation.. Food is less important. The muscles need more energy and therefore the blood carries substances to the muscles, diverting them from the stomach. More oxygen than normal is required. Therefore, the breathing becomes faster, the heart-beat rate increases, the blood vessels dilate to carry more oxygen. The liver releases more stored energy. The eyes and ears become more acutely sensitive to the sensations from outside.

The body is programmed to reverse these changes, and revert to normal, when the threat disappears. If however, one remains in a continuous state of stress, without becoming normal, the changed conditions tend to remain permanent, like a rubber band loses its elasticity when held extended for a long time. These abnormal conditions manifest as diseases and one suffers from high blood pressure, cardiac disorders, peptic ulcers, insomnia, constipation, fatigue, colitis, kidney problems, etc. Behaviourally, they lead to absenteeism, alcoholism, use of drugs, marital disharmony and so on, which are both organisationally and socially, undesirable

Stress is Psychological

Stress is experienced when one perceives a threat and the fight or flight response is called for. This perception is an interpretation that one makes within oneself, of the external factors. When one sees a dog on the street baring its teeth, one may either get frightened or remain calm. Both fright and calmness are psychological reactions. The choice is one's own and is not dictated by the dog. This choice is made, largely unconsciously, on the basis of one's beliefs about dogs in general, what one has heard about rabies being caused by dog bites, what one sees about the characteristics of the dog in question at that time, one's predilections towards animals, and so on.

When one becomes anxious in a situation, the situation does not create any anxiety. What one thinks about the situation creates the anxiety. If one is confident of tackling the situation, there is no anxiety. Therefore, the level of stress is caused by one's own perception of one's capability to cope with the situation. Thus, stress is a psychological response, depending upon one's level of fear, confidence, anxiety, anger, hurt, etc. The physical response is an automatic sequel to one's psychological condition. The physical changes depend on the extent of fear or confidence etc. Therefore, the management of stress essentially is in the control one has on one's emotions.

LEVELS OF STRESS

There are four basic levels of stress symptoms. The first is the normal initial response and is characterised by increased heart beat rates, increased blood pressure, dilation of pupils, sweat in palms and reduced activity in the stomach.

At the second level, there is more irritability, stuttering and stammering, difficulty in concentrating, restlessness, lack of appetite and tendency to increased smoking or drinking for those so habituated.

At the third level, there would be more headaches, stomach aches, diarrhoea, sweating, insomnia, depression etc. The fourth level would be characterised by ulcers, stroke, alcoholism, drug addiction, psychosis etc.

MANAGING STRESS

Stress cannot be avoided it should not be avoided. Without stress, there will be no attempt to try the difficult. One will give up much too easily. One will not succeed in doing even what one is easily capable of, because even the normal faculties will not come into play—like the goalkeeper, if he remained relaxed even at the last minute.

There are two aspects to take care of in managing stress. One is that one should not develop stress to the point that one becomes non-functional like Arjuna laying down his arms at the start of Battle of Kurukshetra. The second is to try to get back to normal as quickly as one can and not continue to be in a state of stress for too long.

The former is achieved essentially by an attitude that is developed by rational thoughts. The first is to realise that one's perceptions often distort the reality. The situation may not be as bad as it may seem to be. The second is to understand that a failure is not an unmitigated disaster. It is not possible to succeed all the time. It is not even necessary to succeed all the time. One failed effort does not mean that the person is no good. Nobody has succeeded without many losses. Even world champions sometimes lose a first round match to an unseeded player. Marconi and Thomas Alva Edison succeeded in their inventions after many attempts that failed. They saw failures as opportunities to learn.

The third is to recognise that worry and anxiety will not modify the situation, but will only disturb one's peace of mind and health. If one watches passengers at airports and railway stations, one will find how some of them remain quite relaxed and even sleeping while others are continuously making enquiries from officials about extent and causes of delays. Such constant enquiries only irritate, but do not expedite solutions. They add to stress of self and of others.

Another very valid concept is what is postulate in the Gita. You can only do. The results are not in your hands. The results, called failures or successes are in the future. One does not have control on the future. One can acquire some control on the present and that is what one does. Also the success or failure does not depend only on what one does. Many other factors impinge. Therefore, the Gita proposes, do your duty and do not worry about what the consequences or fruits may be. Only thoughts about the possible desirability of the fruits cause anxieties. Mother Teresa had expressed the same thought, when she is reported to have said to the industrialist Mr J.R.D.Tata, "Why are you worrying about poverty ? Your work is to open more industries, give more employment to people and leave the rest to God."

A situation that causes stress is a problem situation. The solution needs generating managerial options. People lose tempers and abuse officials as a result of stress. None of these solve the problems that may exist. Problem-solving needs calm, clear, analytical thinking. Clarity of thought and analysis improves with Eustress and deteriorates with DiStress. Managerial alternatives and options will be seen when one 'is concerned' with the matter, not when one is 'anxious'.

Awareness that nothing will be perfect and that anything that can go wrong will go wrong, helps to cope with the stress situations. People who demand of themselves Excellence always, are likely to develop high stress. Perfection is not necessary. It may also not be possible. Satisfying is often the only available option.

At work one must learn to delegate. Many people believe that they alone can do certain tasks. The golden rule is to make this statement invalid as quickly as possible. Stress is only one reason for doing so. The positive outcomes are many. As one rises in the hierarchy, it would be impossible to do all the jobs that have to be done. One needs to pass on to others. Time spent in making this happen, is good investment for the future.

Getting back to normal is relatively easy. One only has to get one's mind into a condition in which there is no stress. Any pleasant activity will make this possible. Hobbies help. The practice of Yoga is excellent to relax one's body and mind. Stress is relieved when one can share one's thoughts and feelings with someone else. Good tunes and ragas, like in bhajans and ghazals, have the capacity to soothe one's nerves, even if one is not listening.

As the Manager

As the boss, one can ensure that subordinates are not put to undue stress and also that they are helped to get out of stress situations as quickly as possible. The steps are

- Recognize the stress levels
- Show concern
- Encourage talking
- Listen
- Empathize
- Explain and show how work can be done or how he can come out of tension.
- Reassure
- Provide support
- Discuss and involve them in decisions
- Show respect to the individuals
- Avoid insult, denunciation, abuse, reprimand, particularly in public
- Avoid manipulation, coercion, blaming
- Avoid pressurizing too much
- Provide social support

All the above, render support and help to reduce anxieties. It is not suggested that the demands on people should be lowered. People like challenges. They must be given challenging assignments. That is the only way to growth. But if there is a sensing of extreme stress, it should be managed through reassurance, not by withdrawing the assignment.

Personality Types

Studies on Stress have identified that Type A personalities tend to get stressed much faster than Type B personalities. The characteristics of a Type A personality are an intense urge to achieve, impatience and restlessness, always on the move, hurrying, doing more than one task at a time. He keeps a heavy and tight schedule and dislikes waiting and relaxing. The Type B is exactly the opposite, takes things easy, finds time to relax, is not impatient and is not obsessed with winning all the time.

Instruments have been developed to identify the Type of any person. But no one is fully Type A or fully Type B. It is possible to move from one type to another. It is not as if Type B is the more desirable personality, because stress is not the only factor relevant for effectiveness. Achievement is equally important for effectiveness and there the Type A has a better chance to win.

Time Management

Inadequacy of resource is a common stressor. One needs resources to do a job and if the resource is not available, there could be stress. One important resource is Time. Many people find that they do not have enough time to do a job. Deadlines seem to be difficult to meet. This is true of individuals as well as of collectives. We read of committees asking for extension of time to do their jobs; of projects not being completed on time. Unfortunately, time is such a resource that nobody can give more or take away. Everybody has a definite amount of time available. Studies show that people are poor planners in terms of usage of time as a resource. Time is wasted in a number of ways. Therefore, if one learns ways to manage one's time better, there could be a better control on stress.

Time is wasted because of :

- non-productive work like searching for files, papers and references.
- available information being inadequate or incomplete
- meetings and lengthy reports
- indecisiveness, unable to make up one's mind
- correcting errors in instructions, assignments
- clarifying goals and roles
- too much routine, paperwork
- lack of prioritization

Once the cause is known, the remedy should be obvious. The best way to know the cause is to keep a detailed log of how one is using his time over a period of a week or so. Some of the remedies will be in the nature of readjustments of personal habits, like planning on priorities, avoiding drift in meetings, not insisting on perfectionism etc. Some remedies will be in the nature of reorganizing work systems in the office so that search and corrections are made minimal. Some will be in the nature of training others for better work practices, so that supervision can be less.

Indecisiveness has been mentioned as a time waster. This may happen because of lack of clarity on objectives or because of fatigue and the mind not being able to concentrate. Both are avoidable. Indecisiveness can also happen because of lack of knowledge on the subject. The time one takes to study a matter depends on one's skill. Experienced people run through a 100 page file, without reading every page, but picking up the important and relevant matter, while another may have to spend double the time reading every paper to determine its relevance. Thus, one way to manage time better is to improve one's skills at work.

STEPS TO BE FOLLOWED IN STRESS MANAGEMENT

Identifying unrelieved stress and being aware of its effect on our lives is not sufficient for reducing its harmful effects. Just as there are many sources of stress, there are many possibilities for its management. However, all require work toward change : changing the source of stress and/or changing your reaction to it. How do you proceed ?

First is effective management of change in the organizational environment will have an immediate impact on minimizing the level of conflict which occurs in the workplace. In turn, this will diametrically affect the amount of stress exhibited by employees during confrontational situations. Conflict has been directly attributed to organizational change – whether it be task, relationship or process conflict – since the majority of workplace disagreements start with change tension (Vakola, and Nikolaou, 2005, p. 39).

Secondly, is fair treatment, organizational research has indicated that employee's who believe they are being treated fairly and equitably within an organization will tend to have lower stress levels, be less resistant to change and engage in acts which are entirely beneficial to the organization–while those who feel the opposite will have higher stress levels, resist change entirely and engage in acts that are detrimental (Barling and Philips, 1993).

Thirdly, role of justice, undoubtedly, the management of fairness and justice in an organizational context is critical to an employee's decision–making process in determining his level of job satisfaction and willingness to continue.

Review Questions

1. What are the different roles of stresses ? Give examples of any two of them.
2. Critically examine the methods that can be used to limit stress at work place.
3. How do you think can manager help in reducing the stress at work place ?

PROJECT WORK

1. Interview an employee of your organization to find out his or her main stresses and how he or she can cope with them.

Case Study

EXEL CALL CENTRE

There is a growing concern that call centre jobs will be soon lost in India unless the costs and investments in human capital are managed better. There are approximate 15,000 call centers existing in India employing about 1 million people. Staff turnover varies according to location. In a survey 75 percent of employers in NCR reported turnover of approximately 40 percent, where as in Southern India the turnover is approximately 24 percent. For customer service representative average salary is around Rs 1,50 lakhs per annum.

The job of customer service advisor at Exel in NOIDA is two fold : selling and either answering bill enquiries, dealing with equipment/ service breakdowns, or querying repairs and selling. The customer's service advisor's are trained for only one of these jobs and remain doing these jobs for rest of their lives. Each customer service advisor works in a confined space of about 1.5m X 1.0m. In front of the customer's service advisors are the console which shows how many calls are waiting to be answered : up to ten calls may be waiting at one time and these are shown with flashing yellow lights. All information of the customer can be instantly called up on a computer screen using a key board, both of which are also in front of an operator.

Each customer's service advisor is given a one day training programme other than for language proficiency, before starting work. Strict performance standards are enforced that specify :

Each call should be closed (that is finished) within three minutes.

The language used to customer should be appropriate.

The conversation with the customer must not include any unnecessary social pleasantries.

Certain key words must be used to customers.

Calls are regularly monitored.

Nearly all customer's service advisor's work six day a week.

Turnover at Exel has been gradually increasing over the past two years. Absenteeism was running 20 percent in 2007–08 and it rose to 30 percent in 2008–09. Every member of the staff seems to be sick. The staff who returns from sick leave is interviewed by a member of HR department. The departments annual report on absenteeism shows that the most common complaints are migraines, stomach upsets, cold, 'flu and backache'. The conclusion is that high proportion of absence is not genuine, but that real reason is that staff wants a break from boring work. Do you agree with analysis ? What should be done to manage the absence problem ?

❑❑❑

GLOSSARY

- ***360 Survey.*** An employee feedback program whereby an employee is rated by surveys distributed to his or her co-workers, customers, and managers. HR departments may use this feedback to help develop an individual's skill or they may integrate it into performance management programs.

A

- ***Ability.*** Both the natural aptitudes and learned capabilities required to successfully complete the task.
- ***Access Discrimination.*** Involves hiring.
- ***Action learning.*** A variety of experiential learning activities in which employees are involved. These learning activities can involve a "real, complex and stressful problem". Usually in groups and teams with immediate relevance to the company.
- ***Action Research.*** A data based, problem oriented process that diagnoses the need for change, introduces the intervention, and then evaluates and stabilizes the desired change.
- ***Adaptive culture.*** An organizational culture in which the employees focus on the changing needs of customers and other stake holders and support initiatives to keep pace with these changes.
- ***Adding Value.*** To add value the *process* must achieve outcomes that significantly increase organization's capability to differentiate it from the other similar organizations and thereby increase it performance and enhance it growth and development. By doing so it must also ensure that cost that has been incurred is offset by the value generated.
- ***Adverse impact.*** The extent to which an assessment methodology produces different mean scores or success rates for different groups (social, ethnic, gender, religious). This is often expressed by the proportion of a standard deviation by which the minority group's mean score is different from the mean score of the majority group. Psychometric tests are usually seen as the major source of adverse impact in an assessment process. However, adverse impact has also been demonstrated in other assessment techniques such as the interview and assessment centers.
- ***Affirmative Action.*** Proactive policies aimed at increasing the employment opportunities of certain groups (typically, minority men and/or women of all racial groups).

- ***Agency theory*** requires designing compensation in a way that it serves the best mutual interest of share holders and the virtual owners, *i.e.*, the top executives of the organizations.
- ***Alienation.*** The Marxist concept that referred to the 'separation' of people from control over many material and social aspects of their lives. Based on the central accumulation of capital, alienation is seen as the basis of degraded conditions of life under capitalism.
- ***Alternative Dispute Resolution (ADR).*** A third party dispute resolution process that include mediation, typically followed by arbitration.
- ***Annual Objectives.*** Identify precisely what must be accomplished each year to achieve the organizations strategic goals.
- ***Appraisal.*** A central concept in the transactional view of stress. The concept focuses attention on the way someone understands the demands the environment is making of him or her. An individual appraises what is at stake and the resources—physical, intellectual, and emotional—he or she has to deal with the demand. Whilst an intuitively attractive approach to understanding stress, appraisal is a fuzzy construct which in practice has been difficult to define and measure.
- ***Appreciative Inquiry.*** An organizational change process that directs attention away from the groups own problems and focuses participants on the group's potential and positive elements.
- ***Apprenticeship.*** Method of on-the-job training in which an employee is trained under the guidance of highly skilled co-worker.
- ***Artificial Intelligence.*** Development of computational approaches to simulate intelligent human thought or behaviour.
- ***Assessment Centre.*** A popular assessment technique which comprises a range of assessment methodologies. The defining feature of an assessment centre is some simulation of the task. They are usually demanding events which can last from half a day to three or more days. The simulation of the job gives individuals a degree of insight into what is involved in the role. Assessment centres although widely used are also seen as problematic. They often have very poor construct validities—it is not clear what they are actually measuring and this reduces their ability to predict future job performance accurately.
- ***Artifacts.*** The observable symbols and signs of an organization's culture.
- ***Attitudes.*** Attitude is a mental position relative to a way of thinking or being. It is a cluster of beliefs, assessed feelings, and behavioural intention towards an object.
  - Positive attitude implies a way of thinking that is predominantly positive and optimistic.
  - Negative attitude is the opposite inclination, a negative attitude is predominantly pessimistic.
- ***Attribution Process.*** The perceptual process of deciding whether an observed behaviour or event is caused largely by internal or external factors.
- ***Attrition.*** It is the ratio of number of employees leaving an organization to the total number of employees on the pay roll of an organization.
- ***Authority*** can be defined as the right to make decisions, to direct the work of others, and to give orders.

- ***Authoritarian Management.*** Management style characterized by high concern of production and efficiency but low concern for employees, opposite of country club management, also referred to as task management.
- ***Auto-generation of Skills.*** The suggestion that new skills can be spontaneously generated, in particular industrial sectors, by the progressive and expanding nature of technology. It is particularly applied in the IT and computing occupations where, since their inception, there seems to be no slackening in the Process of new specialization and skills being created.
- ***Autonomy.*** The amount of control an individual has over his or her working life. Autonomy can relate to performance goals (the outputs of a role) and performance methodologies (the way in which goals are achieved). Increased autonomy is normally associated with higher levels of job satisfaction. However, too much autonomy can involve a high level of role ambiguity and role uncertainty which can be potent sources of stress for many individuals. [Back to top].

B

- ***Background Screening/Pre-employment Screening.*** Testing to ensure that employers are hiring qualified and honest employees and that a prospective employee is capable of performing the functions required by the job. The screening can involve criminal background checks, verification of past addresses, age or year of birth, corporate affiliations, bankruptcies, liens, drug screening, skills assessment and behavioral assessments.
- ***BCG Matrix.*** An approach to corporate level strategy advocated by the Boston Consulting Group, also known as the portfolio framework.
- ***Balanced Score Card.*** A reward system that pays incentive or bonuses for improved results on a composite of financial customer, internal process and employee factor.
- ***Basic Assumption Group***—the psychodynamic approach to understanding group functioning suggests that, alongside the functional reasons for the group's existence, group members may also be operating on some basic 'unconscious' assumptions about what the group is there for. This approach to understanding group functioning provides a useful reminder of the potential complexity of group processes and group functioning and the limits of simplistic approaches to groups.
- ***Behaviour Modification***—the attempt to change behavioural responses by adjusting the environmental consequences of responses. Behaviour modification is fairly commonplace in therapeutic settings, for example to increase the social interaction of a patient. It is less common in work settings where behavioural responses such as greeting customers are targeted. Its advocates claim it has impressive success rates. Its critics claim it is highly manipulative and undermines human dignity.
- ***Behavioural Theories of Management***—an approach that studied the actual minute-by-minute behaviour of managers. It discovered little evidence for the kinds of optimal rational behaviour suggested by conventional theories.
- ***Benchmarking*** is the practice of comparing any item or product with other competing organizations similar item or product to offer competitive choice to customer. In compensation it is comparison with other organizations of the packages offered.

- ***Bicultural Audit.*** A diagnosis of cultural relations between companies prior to merger and a determination of the extent to which cultural clashes are likely to occur.
- ***'Big Five' Personality Dimension.*** The five abstract dimensions representing most personality traits : conscientiousness, agreeableness, neuroticism, openness to experience and extroversion (CANOE).
- ***Bio-data.*** Bio-data is based on a simple psychological truism that the best predictor of future performance is past performance. In practice, bio-data involves the combination of biographical information, normally statistically weighted so as to produce a score which can be used as a predictor of job-relevant criteria such as tenure, sales, and success in training. The technique tends to be underutilized in the UK but is very popular in the USA with test publishers producing generic bio-data questionnaires.
- ***Bounded Rationality*** :
  - An influential concept developed by the Chicago School of the 1950s and 1960s; it challenged rationalist perspectives and suggested that the rationality of actual economic and firm behaviour was always partial, or 'bounded' by human limitations.
  - It also implies processing limited and imperfect information and satisfying rather than maximizing when choosing among alternatives.
- ***Bite–sized Learning.*** It refers to 'light touch' or modular work place learning where subject matter is divided into short chunks in order to achieve speed, reduce cost and time and increase ease of learning as also enhance motivation level of participants or learners. This approach to learning was popularized by the Learning and Skills Council in its Bite sized Learning Campaign.
- ***Blue Collar Workers***. Employees working in manufacturing industry at floor level involving manual work.
- ***Brainstorming.*** A freewheeling, face to face meeting where team members aren't allowed to criticize but are encouraged to speak freely, generate as many ideas possible, and build on the ideas of the others.
- ***Bureaucracy.*** Weber's focus on a particular type of organization that he felt was increasingly dominant in modern society. Bureaucracy is the embodiment of formal rationality and processes of subtle control.
- ***Bureaucratic personality.*** Merton's notion that modern bureaucratic processes produce forms of depersonalization and dehumanization. This is represented in a narrow and one-dimensional kind of individual.
- ***Burnout***—an extreme emotional state characterized by emotional exhaustion, a diminished sense of personal accomplishment, and cynicism. Originally identified in social workers, the concept is now applied more generally. One problem with burnout research is establishing whether it is a cause or effect of other responses such as job satisfaction and work performance.

C

- ***Care Principle.*** The moral principle stating that we should benefit those with whom we have special relationship.

- ***Career*:** 'The total sequence of employment related positions, roles, activities and experiences encountered by and individual' (Jackson 2000).
- ***Casual Variables*** are those which can be controlled by the organization. These variables include managerial behaviour and organizational structure.
- ***Centrality.*** The degree and nature of interdependence between the power holder and others.
- ***Centralization.*** The degree to which formal decision authority is held by a small group of people, typically those at the top of the organizational hierarchy.
- ***Ceremonies.*** Planned and usually dramatic displays of organizational culture, conducted specifically for the benefit of audience.
- ***Chain of Command.*** The plan that specifies who reports to whom in an organization; such reporting lines are prominent features of any organizational chart.
- ***Change Agent.*** The individual leading or guiding the process of change in an organizational situation.
- ***Channelise*** is the process of directing the inputs for obtaining the desired results.
- ***Change Management***—the leadership and direction of the process of organizational transformation especially with regard to human aspects and overcoming resistance to change.
- ***Charismatic Leadership***—a term originally found in the New Testament describing one of the gifts of the Holy Spirit. And rather like religious leaders who are able to excite followers with a vision of the Promised Land. It is used in the leadership literature to describe those leaders who can make followers feel they are 'on a mission'. Charisma seems to have its psychological basis in the ability of some individuals, wittingly or unwittingly, to encourage others to project positively onto them. This means they may well be ascribed abilities and qualities which they do not actually possess. In Freudian terms it engenders a psychological confusion about who they are and means we may be encouraged to transfer our feelings about those who took care of us earlier on in our life. Charisma therefore encourages regression such that we become somewhat dependent on charismatic leaders (for example, to make difficult decisions on our behalf). Charisma is therefore better seen as the outcome of a process projection rather than as a trait.
- ***Charter*:** A groups clear and achievable set of objectives.
- ***Classical Conditioning***—the learning which results from the association of stimuli with reflex responses. For example, punitive authority figures experienced early on in life may reflexively elicit feelings of anxiety which become 'conditioned', creating patterns of emotional responses which carry on into adult life. Classical conditioning is used in clinical settings to help patients 'unlearn' anxieties such as phobias. In the workplace it can help individuals understand some emotional responses and the behaviours which these generate. However, as a framework for understanding higher forms of learning it is limited.
- ***Classical Theory***—the first recognized school of organization theory, based on F. W. Taylor's Scientific Management, and extending to studies of work and administrative systems. Emphasizes on a 'formal' approach to organizations.
- ***Coalitions***—one of the central tactics of power whereby two or more interest groups informally join forces in order to increase their joint power in relation to another group or groups.

- ***Coaching*** (work coaching) is a method used by managers and supervisors to provide positive or constructive feedback to employees to help them continue excellent performance or identify ways to improve performance.
- ***Coercive Power.*** The negative side of reward power, based on the influencer's ability to punish the influencee.
- ***Cognitive***—concerned with the psychological processes of perception, memory, thinking and learning (Coffield et al 2004).
- ***Coherent Approach*** is an approach that holistically considers all factors affecting a particular decision.
- ***Collective Bargaining.*** One or more unions meeting with representatives from an organization to negotiate labor contracts.
- ***Collaborative Management.*** Management through power sharing and subordinate participation : the opposite of hierarchical imposition of authority.
- ***Collective Mobility Project.*** A distinctive claim on professional status that is actively pursued by a particular occupational group over time, and which utilizes a range of strategies embracing the whole occupation.
- ***Collective Strategy.*** Occurs when people at different organizations collaborate to determine how organizations with common concerns will approach certain issues.
- ***Competency***—an underlying characteristic of an individual which is causally related to effective or superior performance. Competency models have become extremely popular. They are seen as providing a common language for organizations to define the requirements of a role and assess individuals against. The notion of competency frameworks has attracted a good deal of criticism. They can represent little more than wish lists. As they are essentially descriptive they have little explanatory value. Some critics have claimed they also represent an insidious way in which modern economies seek to extend control over individuals.
- ***Competencies.*** The set of character features, knowledge and skills, attitudes, motives and traits that comprise the profile of a job holder and enable him or her to perform effectively in his or her role (Harrison 2005).
- ***Competency Building.*** It is the process of building the skills and other capabilities of an employee to improve their productivity and performance.
- ***Competency Mapping.*** Process of identifying the competencies.
- ***Conflict.*** The process in which one party perceives that its interest are being opposed or negatively affected by another person.
- ***Consideration***—one of the two factors identified statistically by the Ohio State University researchers. Consideration is a statistical factor which emerges from correlations between questions emphasizing the importance of good relationships with subordinates. Leaders who score highly tend to be supportive, encouraging, and attempt to arbitrate in order to maintain effective relationships. ***Constructs*** : Constructs is a set of dimensions used by individuals to differentiate between people, things, and events. Individuals appear to possess a stable preference for using particular constructs to differentiate between the individuals they are interacting with. Constructs in skill terms therefore provide the 'action-relevant categories' that people collect information with.

- ***Contingency Theory***—the next major school of thought after classical theory to focus on the issue of organization structure, suggested that appropriate structures are 'contingent' on a variety of contextual factors, like size, technology, and environment.
- ***Coping Styles***—the concept of coping styles attempts to capture the variety of ways in which individuals try to cope with the demands of the environment. A common distinction is between 'problem'- and 'emotion'-focused strategies. There are many competing frameworks for describing and understanding coping styles. One important question is whether they genuinely capture the diversity of the stress experience.
- ***Cost Benefit Analysis of Training*** helps an organization to measure the cost benefit of training, keeping in view long term perspective. Thus this analysis makes an incremental (short-term) approach redundant.
- ***Critical Management Studies***—a new school of thought that applies critical theory to organizations. Stresses the divisions within the management body and the insecurities of much management work.
- ***Culture*** is made up of the values, beliefs, underlying assumptions, attitudes, and behaviors shared by a group of people. Culture is the behavior that results when a group arrives at a set of - generally unspoken and unwritten - rules for working together. An organization's culture is made up of all of the life experiences each employee brings to the organization.

D

- ***Decision-making***—not a focus on the optimal definition of individual decisions, but rather a focus on everyday managerial interaction.
- ***Decision-making Theories***—a cluster of theories of organization, from mainly American writers in the 1980s, that each developed a distinctive aspect of why managerial decision-making was only partly rational.
- ***Demand*** refers to the number and characteristics (*e.g.*, skills, capabilities, abilities, pay levels, experience etc.) of people needed for a particular job at a given point of time and at a particular place.
- ***Departments*** are the entities organizations form to organize people, reporting relationships, and work in a way that best supports the accomplishment of the organization's goals. Departments are usually organized by functions such as human resources, marketing, administration, and sales. But, a department can be organized in any way that makes sense for the customer.
- ***Dependency***—the view (derived from systems theories) that the possession of organizational power can be explained by the extent to which organizations are dependent on particular groups or individuals to cope with key areas of uncertainty.
- ***Depersonalization***—the tendency to see 'out-group' members as more similar than they actually are. Depersonalization means that in-group members tend to treat out-group member's not as unique differentiated individuals but as members of a social group assumed to possess particular characteristics.

- ***Deregulated***—One which is not subject to any direct government restrictions, constraints or regulations.
- ***Deskilling.*** Braverman's thesis that skill represents the central asset possessed by workers, and those modern capitalist systems of work design, like Taylorism, degrade or deskill work, as a means of controlling and cheapening it.
- ***Dialogic Learning.*** A style of learning that involves interacting with others in a ways which produce a growing understanding of the culture of the organization, and how the organization typically achieves its goals (Mezirow 1985).
- ***Diffusion***—the process by which management knowledge and ideas are disseminated or spread. It involves mediating groups, such as consultants and gurus that act as agents of dissemination.
- ***Disciplinary Power.*** Foucault's notion that in modern societies power and control were not some imposed structure, but was dispersed in all social relations. Power is sustained by 'disciplines' such as regimes of professional expertise and technologies of surveillance.

  Progressive discipline is a process for dealing with job-related behavior that does not meet expected and communicated performance standards.
- ***Double Loop Learning.*** A concept to describe the style of learning that involves questioning why certain problems occur in the first place and identifying and tackling root causes instead of only surface symptoms (Argyris 1977).
- ***Downsizing*** means to reduce the number of employees in an organization. Downsizing or lay-offs reduce the size of a work force. Used sparingly, and with planning, downsizing can be an organizational lifesaver, but when layoffs are used repeatedly without a thoughtful strategy, downsizing can destroy an organization's effectiveness. Also known as : reduction in force.
- ***Dramatization***. A necessary sense-making device in organizations. The 'theatrical' quality of much organizational life, whereby events are brought together so that coherent messages and meanings can be delivered.
- ***Dress Code***. A work dress code is a set of standards that companies develop to help provide their employees with guidance about what is appropriate to wear to work. Work dress codes range from formal to business casual to casual. The formality of the workplace dress code is normally determined by the amount of interaction employees have with customers. Learn more about work dress codes.

E

- ***Educate.*** To bring up from childhood so as to form habits, manners, mental and physical aptitudes (Onions 1973).

  To give intellectual, moral and social instruction, especially as a formal and prolonged process (Pearsall and Trumble 1996).
- ***Effective Leadership.*** Although intelligence, initiative and self assurance are associated with high managerial performance, the single most important factor may be manager's supervisory ability.

- ***Emergent Strategies*** are unplanned responses to unforeseen circumstances by non-executive employees within the organization.
- ***Employee Involvement***—a recent movement of work improvement, dating from the 1990s, which emphasizes a wide range of methods including communications and changes in work culture, as well as work redesign. Employee involvement is creating an environment in which people have an impact on decisions and actions that affect their jobs. Employee involvement is not the goal nor is it a tool, as practiced in many organizations. Rather, employee involvement is a management and leadership philosophy about how people are most enabled to contribute. Find out more about employee involvement. You can create a work environment and supervisory interactions which encourage the people you employ to develop and practice self-discipline. When people practice self-discipline, they control their own behaviour.
- ***Employee Specification.*** Employee specification is a statement of minimum required employee qualifications, viz. physical, educational, work etc., which represent the possession of minimum acceptable human qualities by the prospective employee necessary to perform a job.
- ***Empowerment***—the process of displacing decision making downwards to the workforce, or lower levels of management, to enable them to use their skills more effectively and flexibly. The emphasis is often on better engagement with customers.
- ***Equal Value Work***—work that is deemed to be of the same value (in terms of factors like skill and responsibility) as other though different work, so that different jobs can nevertheless be rewarded equally.
- ***Equity Theory***—this view of motivation focuses on the comparison processes people utilize to assess whether their rewards equate with their inputs. It encourages the consideration of what social comparisons are operating. Equity theory suggests that individuals strive towards equity, where inputs and outputs are deemed to be fair. Equity theory also explores how individuals react to conditions of over- and underpayment.
- ***Explicit Knowledge***—knowledge that has been articulated and codified.

F

- ***Faces of Power***—the influential approach developed by Lukes, that theories of power divide into three major perspectives (or 'faces') : behavioural, decision-making, and radical theories.
- ***Factor Analysis***—a statistical technique reducing large data sets to the smallest number of 'factors' required to 'explaining' the pattern of relationships in the data. It has fierce advocates and vehement critics. The former see it as neutral and scientific. The latter argue that it generates statistical abstractions, which have little explanatory value and are not necessarily psychologically meaningful. ***Fashion perspective*** : the view that changes in management knowledge can be compared with changes in popular taste. In particular, management ideas often display a fashion life cycle of growth and decline.
- ***Five-factor Model***—a popular factor analytically derived model of personality. Five-factor theorists argue that much of the variation we can observe in each other's personalities can to a large extent be 'explained' by using just five factors : extraversion,

neuroticism, agreeableness, conformity, and openness to experience. However, critics of this approach argue that it represents a gross oversimplification of the complexities of personality.

- ***Flexible Firm***—a type of organization design in which overall flexibility comes from having a core of high-skill employees (functional flexibility) and a periphery of less secure workers that can be expanded or contracted (numerical flexibility).
- ***Flexible Specialization***—the term coined by Sabel to indicate idealized models of high-skill innovative production which have been linked with the German industrial system.
- ***Flextime*** is a system whereby employees contract to work a specific number of hours a week but are free to vary the hours of within certain limits. The employees assume responsibility for completing a specific job.

  360 degree feedback is a method and a tool that provides each employee the opportunity to receive performance feedback from his or her supervisor and four to eight peers, reporting staff members, co-workers and customers.
- ***Fordism***—the dominant method of production for much of the last century. Identified with mass production and assembly-line technology, Fordism is characterized by large-scale semi-skilled workforces, standardized production, and work control via Taylorism.
- ***Function***—The body of activity that has to be provided to the organization, and the personnel most directly responsible for that provision.

G

- ***G***—the idea that intelligence is one thing G has been one of the most enduring ideas in psychology. The general ability factor, identified initially with factor analysis, suggests that if someone is good at one kind of test (*e.g.*, verbal reasoning), the chances are that they will be good at any another kind (*e.g.*, spatial reasoning). Critics of G see the emphasis on one general factor as obscuring important differences in our individual ability structures.
- ***Gendering Process***—a perspective that sees gender segregation as continually sustained and negotiated by specific groups of actors (rather than as an imposed structure of discrimination).
- ***General Adaptation Syndrome***—adapting to external stressors seems to involve a set of similar reactions. The discovery of the general adaptation syndrome established stress as a distinct area of research. However, seeing stress as essentially a response is criticized for being too narrow and excluding a number of other important facets of stress such as the impact of an individual's 'appraisal' of a stressor.
- ***Goal Programming.*** It is a mathematical problem in which constraints of linear programming problems are treated as goals in the objective function. Effort is made to come as close as possible to the achievements of the goals in order of priority set by the decision makers.
- ***Goal-setting.*** The motivational impact of being involved in setting performance goals for the work role an individual occupies. Like knowledge of results, although goal-setting appears to have positive motivational properties it can be organizationally difficult

to implement as it involves managers being willing to share some power with subordinates. Often goals are set (such as share price) over which an individual worker in reality has no control.

- ***Group Technologies***—the set of job redesign techniques based around group working, rather than the individual, isolated worker.
- ***Groupthink***—the distortion of reality testing and suspension of critical thinking which can occur in highly cohesive teams. Groupthink has been used to explain disasters such as Chernobyl and massive errors of political judgment such as the 'Bay of Pigs' invasion of Cuba sponsored by the United States.

H

- ***Hierarchy of Needs***—the suggestion that more or less all of us are motivated by the same set of needs and that, as we mature psychologically and to the extent that our circumstances allow, we all progress up a hierarchy of needs by first fulfilling 'lower-order' needs such as physiological and safety needs to the point where our behaviour is increasingly motivated by 'higher-order' psychological needs, such as the need to 'self-actualize' fulfil our potential as human beings. Though an extremely influential idea and often taught as if it were true, there is actually very little strong empirical evidence for the existence of such a hierarchy.
- ***Holism***—the view that social phenomena are integrated into single wholes (such as a common culture). Holism opposes the mechanistic view that analyses events by breaking them down into constituent parts. It suggests that the essence of the whole is present in all parts and hence often places importance on mundane events, which are seen as microcosms of the whole.
- ***Holistic View.*** Looking at a system, situation, organization, collection of activities as a whole that is greater than the mere sum of its parts.
- ***Homogeneity***—the extent to which group members share similar characteristics such as similar attitudes, values, and personalities. Homogeneity can enhance the cohesiveness of the group the perception of a shared identity. But too much homogeneity is presumed not to be a good thing for effective team functioning as it may lead to little challenge of a consensus. Homogeneity is the opposite of heterogeneity the extent to which group members differ in their characteristics. Research supports the idea that a moderate degree of heterogeneity supports effective team functioning.
- ***Human Capital.*** The knowledge, skills, competencies and attributes embodied in individuals that facilitate the creation of personal, social and economic well being (OECD 2001, p. 18)
- ***Human Resource.*** A human resource is a person or employee who staffs and operates a function within your organization. Read the definition of a Human Resource.
- ***Human Resource Development*** is the framework for helping employees develop their personal and organizational skills, knowledge, and abilities. Human Resource Development includes such opportunities as employee training, employee career development, performance management and development, coaching, succession planning, key employee identification, and organization development.

- ***Human Resource Management*** is the function within an organization that focuses on recruitment, management, and the direction of the people in the organization. Human Resources management is also performed by line managers.
- ***Human Resource Information System (HRIS)*** is a software or online solution for the data entry, data tracking, and data information needs of the Human Resources function within a business. Normally packaged as a data base, hundreds of companies sell some form of HRIS and every HRIS has different capabilities.
- ***Human Resource Personnel.*** Personnel's performing human resource functions, such as handling employee benefits or recruiting, interviewing, and hiring new personnel in accordance with policies and requirements that have been established. Today's human resources workers juggle these tasks and, increasingly, consult top executives regarding strategic planning.

I

- ***Impression Management***—this assumes that, contrary to static trait-based explanations of human behaviour, social life is much more dynamic and creative. From this perspective individuals are seen as being constantly involved in 'impression management' attempting to define themselves and the encounter they are involved in. Individuals are concerned with the effectiveness of their own impression management activities and those they are interacting with. This perspective has been criticized for underestimating the extent to which roles and behaviour in them are predetermined, for example by the distribution of power. ***Informal careers*** : careers that exist outside the (formal) career structure of organizations and professions, typically the sorts of careers that women have, and often occurring in secondary occupations and sectors.
- ***Initiating Structure.*** Is one of the two factors identified by the Ohio State University researchers in their factor analytic study of leadership behaviours. Initiating structure is a statistically arrived at dimension emerging from correlations between responses to questions describing the need to define and complete activities. The Ohio researchers have been criticized for not developing a theoretical account of what their dimensions might reflect in personality or motivational terms.
- ***Insidious Power***—an extension of Weber's original emphasis on indirect forms of control. Insidious forms of power are not obvious or oppressive. They are based on forms of self-control and unnoticed rules. Compare with Foucault's notion of 'disciplinary power'.
- ***Intervening Variables*** reflect organizational capabilities and involve group processes, peer leadership, organization climate, and the subordinates' satisfaction.
- ***Interview.*** Interview is a powerful factor in the employee selection process in most organizations. While the job interview may not deserve all the attention that the job interview receives, it is still a powerful force in hiring. Other background checking and work history references provide much less personalized and more factual information.
- ***Screening Interview***. Screening interviews qualify a candidate before he meets with a hiring authority for possible selection. Screening interviews are used to qualify a candidate before he or she meets with a hiring authority for possible selection. Screening interviews are usually quick, efficient and low cost strategies that result in a short list

of qualified candidates. These interviews save time and money by eliminating unqualified candidates via phone or email.

- ***Hiring Interviews*** allow the employer to assess the fit of the candidate. The candidate also interviews the employer for job suitability. Most of these interviews take place in an office setting one-on-one or in a small group.
- ***Institutional Perspective***—the view that new knowledge is often taken up in organizations under pressure from wider 'institutional' forces, such as the state or competitive forces. This produces 'isomorphism' whereby many organizations end up adopting the same ideas.
- ***Intelligence***—many competing definitions exist for one of the most controversial concepts in psychology. The most influential in the assessment of intelligence in workplace settings is 'the innate ability to perceive relationships and identify co-relationships'. The assumption is that much of the variation in intelligence can be explained by one general ability factor (G).
- ***Intelligence Quotient (IQ)***—currently IQ is calculated by estimating where, under the normal distribution curve, someone's performance on an IQ test places him or her. The curve is standardized such that the mean score is 100 and the standard deviation around the mean is 15. An average IQ is therefore between 85 and 115. The scale will go from 55 to 145 (three standard deviations below and above the mean).

J

- ***Japanization***—the process whereby, in countries outside Japan, local industries adopt Japanese management and production methods, or what are regarded as Japanese methods (cf. 'the Japanization of British industry').
- ***Job.*** Hackman defined - A job is a group of positions that are similar as to kind and level of work.
- ***Job Analysis.*** A job analysis is the process used to collect information about the duties, responsibilities, necessary skills, outcomes, and work environment of a particular job. You need as much data as possible to put together a job description, which is the frequent outcome of the job analysis. US Department of Labour defined job analysis as 'the process of determining, by observation and study, and reporting pertinent information relating to the nature of specific job. It is the determination of the tasks which comprise the job and of the skills, knowledge, abilities and responsibilities required of the worker of a successful performance and which differentiate one job from all others.'
- ***Job Classification.*** A job classification is grouping of jobs on some specified basis such as kind of work or pay.
- ***Job Characteristics Model.*** A popular model of motivation and job satisfaction which has stood the test of time. It combines measurement of objective characteristics of work and psychological states in an attempt to explain and predict the 'motivational potential' of a job. The model has provided some of the core constructs used in job satisfaction research. However, the model is criticized for not including some important elements of job roles such as the management practices which impact on them.

- ***Job Descriptions*** are written statements that describe the duties, responsibilities, most important contributions and outcomes needed from a position, required qualifications of candidates, and the reporting relationship of a particular job. Robert N Ford (HBR) states—Job description is an organized, factual statement of the duties and responsibilities of a specific job.
- ***Job Enrichment***—the provision of genuine and meaningful humanization of work (as opposed to low-level improvements). Based on the introduction of more varied, autonomous, and complete work tasks.
- ***Job Offer***. A job offer letter is a document that confirms the details of an offer of employment. The job offer letter includes details such as job description, reporting relationship, salary, bonus potential, benefits, and more. The job offer letter generally confirms the terms
- ***Job Satisfaction***—the feelings or 'affective response' someone experiences in a job role. Some researchers argue that it is possible to capture the level of job satisfaction with one question. Others suggest we can have strong negative feelings about one aspect of our job (*e.g.*, pay) but feel positive about other facets of it (*e.g.*, colleagues). In addition, researchers have developed sophisticated models of the key components of our 'affective response' to work which map the nature and intensity of feelings. Job satisfaction has been treated as both a cause and effect of other organizational variables such as 'burnout' and 'work performance'.
- ***Job Simplification.*** The breaking up of the work that needs to be performed in an organization into the smallest identifiable tasks.
- ***Job Specialization.*** The assignment of workers to perform small, simple tasks.
- ***Job Specification.*** A Job specification is 'a statement of the minimum acceptable human qualities necessary to perform a job properly.
- ***Just-in-time Production***—the major production system to have succeeded the traditional assembly line. JIT is based on principles of total quality, continuous improvement, and unit batch sizes, typically linked with Japanese systems of work organization.

K

- ***Knowledge.*** Knowledge can be viewed as a type of commodity – something 'out there' that can be searched out and acquired, assessed, codified and distributed across the organization. In this sense, it is an intangible asset that can have unique competitive value for an organization. Yet knowledge can be viewed as a process, emerging from within the individual but intimately shaped by relations with others. In this sense knowledge is dynamic, changing as the individual's understanding and interpretation of the world around him or her changes. (Harrison 2005, p. xix)
- ***Knowledge Economy.*** Knowledge Economy is a way of describing a world in which 'knowledge' has become the key to wealth. In this, the application of knowledge adds more value than the traditional factors of capital, raw materials and labour. And the 'knowledge worker' assumes a unique status.
- ***Knowledge Management.*** A term often used to describe the capture and storage of information, usually by electronic means, although in its broader sense it refers to

'using the ideas and experience of employees, customers an suppliers to improve the organization's performance. It has come into regular use for three reasons :

1. The use of knowledge as a competitive weapon;
2. The increasing awareness of how easy it is to lose knowledge;
3. New technology's facilitation of knowledge sharing (Skapinker 2002)

- ***Knowledge Productivity.*** A term coined by Professor Joseph Kessels (1996) to refer to an organization's ability to generate, disseminate and apply knowledge to products, processes and services. Knowledge productivity should therefore enable an organization to continuously develop adapt and improve and regularly innovate.
- ***Knowledge of Results.*** This concept refers to the motivational impact of feedback of the outcomes of performance. Although knowledge of results has a well-established motivational effect, in reality in workplace settings, information is often only provided if performance falls below a threshold. Providing knowledge of results can also run counter to the culture of an organization if, for example, historically information on the performance of contracts was restricted to a small group of senior managers.
- ***Key Skills.*** The six 'key skills' identified in the UK governments educational strategy are those of

  1. Communication
  2. Use of Information Technology
  3. Working with others
  4. Improving own learning and performance
  5. Problem solving
  6. Working with numbers – mathematical skills

  In addition to above there is one more skill that is a must for Indian that is language skills.
- ***Knowledge Work***—new forms of employment that revolve around the dominant role of science and technology in modern economies, and the significance of information technologies. This work is said to be distinctively 'analytic' and to involve problem-solving and abstract reasoning. Knowledge work is performed by knowledge workers, seen as an emerging dominant group in economic and political terms.

L

- ***Labour Process.*** Marx's focus on the dynamics of the employment relationship. In capitalist societies, where labour is bought and sold, this is seen as a site of conflict. There are great pressures for employers to intensify their control, and for workers to resist.
- ***Leadership.*** leadership is evidenced by effective attempts to influence others. Theories of leadership attempt to explain why some individuals are more effective than others at influencing. Theories have focused on differences in behaviour, style, and personal attributes.
- ***Leadership Functions.*** The group maintenance and task related activities that must be performed by the leader, or someone else, for a group to perform effectively.

- ***Leadership Style***—the characteristic approach to leadership demonstrated by a leader or the various patterns of behaviour favoured by leaders during the process of directing and influencing workers. One influential framework developed by the University of Michigan differentiates between democratic and autocratic leadership styles. Democratic leadership styles reduce the power differential between leaders and subordinates. Democratic leaders are more willing to share power and encourage participation in decision-making.
- ***Learning***—learning can be defined as the cognitive and physical activity giving rise to a relatively permanent change in knowledge, skill, or attitude. A distinction is often made between declarative learning, which increases knowledge of facts, and procedural learning, which improves knowledge of procedures. Most workplace learning involves a mixture of both. Theories of learning attempt to explain how learning occurs in individuals. The importance of learning to modern economies is evidenced in terms such as the 'learning organization', 'knowledge workers', and 'lifelong learning'. ***Learning*** - A qualitative change in a person's way of seeing, experiencing , understanding and conceptualizing something in the real world (Marton and Ramsden 1988).
- ***Learning Organization.*** Peter Senge defined the learning organization. He said they were "organizations where people continually expand their capacity to create the results they truly desire, where new and expansive patterns of thinking are nurtured, where collective aspiration is set free, and where people are continually learning how to learn together."
- ***Learning Strategies***—while there is not much solid evidence for 'learning styles', the idea that there are relatively enduring differences in the way individuals prefer to learn, there is reasonably strong evidence for the idea of learning strategies. These are more fluid differences in the way individuals learn. They divide into cognitive and behavioural strategies. The former essentially involves trying to organize the material mentally, for example by attempting to see connections in the material; the latter involves more practical activities such as getting others to check understanding. Choosing the correct learning strategy seems to have an important effect on the impact of training.
- ***Line Function***. The Human Resource manger performs the line function in his department by exerting the line authority. Human Resource manger does not usually exercise the line authority outside his department but exerts an *implied authority*.
- ***Line Managers*** are authorized to direct the work of subordinates–line managers are always someone's superior. It is the line manager who is directly responsible for meting the targets and accomplishes the organizational goals and objectives

M

- ***McDonaldization***. Ritzer's thesis that extends Weber's ideas on bureaucratic rationality. The debasement of social relations that is symbolized in the fast-food restaurant is spreading to all areas of culture and economic life.
- ***Male Power***—the active role that men play in differentiating their work from women, the basis of the gendering process.

- ***Managing Human Resources.*** Managing human resources refers to the functions that a manager performs relative to the organization's employees. Managing human resources includes, but is not limited to these functions. Learn more about managing human resources.
- ***Management by Objectives.*** Management by objectives (MBO) is a systematic and organized approach that allows management to focus on achievable goals and to attain the best possible results from available resources. It aims to increase organizational performance by aligning goals and subordinate objectives throughout the organization. Ideally, employees get strong input to identify their objectives, time lines for completion, etc. MBO includes ongoing tracking and feedback in the process to reach objectives.
- ***Managerial Rationality***—the view that behaviour is controllable and predictable, and that it is directed towards achieving formal organizational goals.
- ***Market Segmentation***—the idea that real labour markets are never 'perfect' markets in the sense that all workers compete equally. Labour markets are divided into relatively self-contained segments such as primary and secondary markets, internal and external markets, and men's versus women's work.
- ***Micro Credit.*** It is the extension of small loans (micro loans) to the unemployed, to poor entpreneurs and to others living in poverty who are not considered *bankable.*
- ***Mission*** or Purpose is a precise description of what an organization does. It should describe the business the organization is in. It is a definition of "why" the organization exists currently.
- ***Mission Statement***—an organization's description of itself, the declaration of values, goals, and aspirations that authoritative groups agree upon as being the central account of the organization's unique sense of direction.
- ***Motivation***—the extent to which an individual is engaged by the work role he or she occupies. Theories of motivation suggest that motivated behaviour occurs either because work fulfils psychological needs or because of more rational decision-making processes where there appears to be a clear connection between effort and performance and value outcomes.

N

- ***Negativity.*** Negativity is the feeling and expressing of unhappiness, anger, frustration, or upset to other employees in your workplace; it is often accompanied by resistance. According to Gary S. Topchik, author of Managing Workplace Negativity, negativity is often the result of a loss of confidence, control, or community. Knowing what people are negative about is the first step in solving the problem.
- ***Networking.*** It is building a web of interpersonal relationships for mutually beneficial purposes such as business referrals, customer acquisition, complementary product offerings, and sharing information. Networking means establishing, maintaining and utilizing contacts made for purposes beyond the reason for the initial contact.
- ***New Service Work***—white-collar work that has emerged from the lengthy process of 'industrializing' the office, often characterized by pervasive use of information technologies, and an emphasis on customer-related skills. The call centre is the classic example.

- ***New Technology***—a term coined around the mid-1970s to describe technical systems based on information technology and the microprocessor. New technology has a massive and still expanding range of applications in most industrial and commercial operations.
- ***Non-verbal Communication***—the impact of gestures, gaze, expressions, and other symbols capable of substituting for words and conveying information. Social skill involves decoding sources of non-verbal communication, particularly gaze. In assessing the validity of another individual's impression management activities we are constantly checking for a correspondence between information conveyed by verbal and non-verbal channels of communication.
- ***Norm***—a rule which governs or constrains the behaviour of group members. Norms in the workplace can relate directly to performance by dictating acceptable levels of quality and quantity. Norms also exist to determine attitudes towards timekeeping, absenteeism, and standards of personal appearance. Norms are powerful determinants of behaviour. They can work to support the interests of senior management or can operate to undermine them.
- ***Norming***—one framework for understanding the development of groups suggests that one important stage groups go through is the development of norms about the way in which tasks will be tackled and members will relate to one another.

O

- ***Occupation***. An occupation 'is a group of jobs that are similar as to kind of work and are found throughout an industry or the entire country' Dale S. Beach.
- ***Occupational Control***—an umbrella term that includes all the aspects of an occupation's market situation, such as influence over status and material rewards, control of entry to the occupation and accreditation, the way the work is performed, routine definitions of good practice, and so on.
- ***Operant Conditioning***—the arrangement of environmental contingencies *i.e.,* what follows a response to strengthen or weaken the connection between a stimulus and a response. This framework for understanding how we learn has been extremely influential from the 1950s onwards. Its impact can be seen now-a-days in 'programmed instruction', where there is a very tight specification of stimulus and response and a clear connection between responses and reward. It is also visible in the 'competence revolution' which specifies job demands in clear behavioural terms. Critics argue that it fails to take any account of the 'black box' what is happening in someone's mind when they are learning.
- ***Orientation.*** It the process for welcoming a new employee into your organization. New employee orientation, often spearheaded by a meeting with the Human Resources department, generally contains information about safety, the work environment, the new job description, benefits and eligibility, company culture, company history, and anything else relevant to working in the new company.
- ***Organization.*** Involves all the elements of organizational design; not only the formal structures of organizational charts but also the systems, processes and people dimensions that are essential to making these work' (CIPD 2003)

- ***Organizing.*** Dynamic process needed if organizational design is to be effectively implemented and regularly renewed. The skills involved in how to organize and regularly re-organize are as important as knowing what organizational design to choose (Whittington and Mayer 2002).
- ***Organizational Context.*** The internal and external organizational circumstances that shape and help to explain the organizational situation being examined. Often organizational context is summarized by reference to culture and structure, but they themselves emerge from the interplay of more fundamental factors. Research indicates that three of the most powerful are :

  1. Top Management's Vision and Values;
  2. Line Managements Style and Actions at all organizational levels;
  3. HR strategies and practices (Harrison 2005).
- ***Organizational Culture***—the set of beliefs, values, and norms, together with symbols like dramatized events and personalities, that represents the unique character of an organization, and provides the context for action in it and by it.
- ***Organizational Design***—the application of principles discovered by theories of organization structure to planning the relations between departments, the grouping of tasks, and the flow of work in organizations. ***Open Door Policies***. Modern theories that reflect the variety of managerial choice also imply a wide range of different designs. An open door policy means, literally, that every manager's door is open to every employee. The purpose of an open door policy is to encourage open communication, feedback, and discussion about any matter of importance to an employee.
- ***Outsourcing*** is paying a second party to perform one or more of your internal processes or functions. Business process outsourcing of certain functions is an increasingly popular way to improve basic services while allowing HR professionals time to play a more strategic role in their organizations.

P

- ***Paid Time Off***. Definition of the paid time off of an employee involves making payment of salary for the period/duration of vacation, sick days, and personal days.
- ***Paradigm Shift.*** A permanent change in the established pattern of thinking by organizational members about their work organization; a radical shift in the way they understand their world.
- ***Performance Management System***. A system devised/ employed to improve the performance of the employees in an organization.
- ***Personal File Access Policy.*** All employees, former employees, and representatives of employees may view certain documents from their personnel file with advance notice to Human Resources staff. Documents that relate to the employee's qualifications for hire may be viewed. Documents that may not be reviewed are also described.
- ***Personal Front***—one of the main outcomes of our impression management activities is the construction of a 'personal front'—the attempt to define oneself as a particular kind of individual. In organizations there may be a restricted range of officially sanctioned

fronts individuals can operate from behind. A distinction is often made between acquisitive fronts which enhance one's standing and protective fronts which enable individuals to deal with any perceived deficiencies. The concept 'persona' has virtually the same meaning.

- ***Personality***—defined as the relatively enduring combination of traits which makes an individual unique and at the same time produces consistencies in his or her thought and behaviour. Critics of the concept argue that our behaviour is not sufficiently consistent across situations to infer the existence of stable underlying entities such as traits.
- ***Position***—is group of similar tasks and responsibilities assigned to one individual. The term is used in this narrow technical sense to facilitate more precise discussion of the job analysis technique.
- ***Post-Fordism; neo-Fordism***—new systems of work that succeed the Fordist system and arise out of the so-called crisis of Fordism. Post-Fordism refers to any succeeding system, while neo-Fordism implies that the new system is not truly innovative but only a refinement or modification of basic Fordist principles.
- ***Power Resources***—the scheme of categories or types of power developed by French and Raven. This suggests there are five distinct bases or resources that organizational power-holders rely on : reward power, coercive power, legitimate power, referent power, and expert power.
- ***Professionalism—***the process by which given occupations become professions, in the sense of attaining professional status. The emphasis here is on the strategies occupations adopt (*e.g.*, competing with rival professional groups or developing powerful professional associations) rather than whether they possess the traits or features that correspond with some model of a profession.
- ***Promotion.*** The advancement of an employee from one position to another position that has a higher salary range maximum is called a promotion.
- ***Psychodynamic Theory***—psychodynamic theory assumes that much of our behaviour stems from 'the unconscious' which houses our basic instinctual needs (essentially sex and aggression), reconciling the satisfaction of these with the requirements of reality sets up conflicts. The 'defence mechanisms' we develop to manage these conflicts become an important part of our behaviour. Critics of this tradition argue that it is essentially unscientific. It utilizes unobservable phenomena and generates hypotheses that are difficult to falsify.
- ***Psychometric Tests***—formed from the Greek words for mental and measurement, psychometric tests attempt to quantify some psychological attribute or attributes of an individual. The technical quality of psychometric tests varies enormously. The standard psychometric technical requirements are reliability and validity. But in addition to whatever technical merits tests possess, test usage has attracted other criticisms.

  Insensitive test administration, a lack of understanding of the 'status of the evidence' (*e.g.*, assuming personality tests provide straightforward insights into personality), and using the wrong tests for a role have all served to undermine the potential value of psychometric tests to individuals and organizations.

Q

- ***Quality*** is a measure of excellence; quality defines desirable characteristics of a product, a process, or a service.

R

- ***Rationalization.*** Weber's concept of the increasing spread and dominance of hard, market-based criteria in all areas of social and economic life.
- ***Recruiters*** are employed by a company for the purpose of finding and qualifying new employees for the organization. Third party recruiters are subcontracted to by a company for the same purpose. Several different types of third party recruiters exist, but the main difference between them lies in how they are compensated, up front or by a company-paid percentage of the hired person's first year pay.
- ***Recognition*** is providing attention or favorable notice to another person. Recognition can be written, verbal, or monetary. In the workplace, the second purpose for employee recognition is to communicate and reinforce the behaviours and actions you'd like to see the employee do more often.
- ***Reflexivity***—the ability of a team to reflect critically on the way it tackles tasks or members relate to one another. This may involve some quite uncomfortable and socially difficult challenges amongst team members. Reflexivity may be encouraged by changes in group membership or interventions by outsiders. One argument is that reflexivity is a basic ingredient for successful complex decision-making groups.
- ***Reliability***—reliability represents the accuracy of an assessment methodology and is normally expressed as a correlation coefficient ranging from 1 to 0. For example, it could represent the extent to which interviewers' ratings of candidates are correlated. For a psychometric test, it can be estimated by calculating the extent to which questions all seem to be measuring the same thing or by identifying whether the rankings of individuals' scores in a group remain similar if they are tested on another occasion.
- ***Rhetoric***—intrinsic persuasiveness contained in particular messages and communications. Particular themes and narratives of fashionable management knowledge can have a powerful rhetorical impact.
- ***Roles***—the set of external expectations about a role incumbent's behaviour. These can be explicit as defined in a job description or can be implicit and acquired through observation and internalization. Although roles are essentially seen as external to individuals they can exert a powerful influence on behaviour and may through internalization, impact on an individual's attitudes, values, and even personality.
- ***Rules***—many social psychologists argue that behaviour in social situations is rule governed. Social effectiveness, from this perspective, is determined by the extent to which individuals understand and follow the rules. Most of the rules we follow are so well learned we are no longer conscious of them and only become aware of them when someone breaks them.

S

- ***Self-actualization***—the idea of a hierarchy of needs suggests that the desire to fulfill one's potential is the final cause of motivated behaviour. Few people become self-actualizing according to this view of motivation. Those who do, generally in their fifties, are seen as possessing a similar set of ideals, values, and attitudes. Once motivated by this need, individuals experience a spiraling need for challenge in their work which means they are always seeking to develop their capacities and realize their potential. In practice it has been difficult to define and measure self-actualization with any rigour.
- ***Self-stereotyping***. Is the tendency to see members of the in group as more similar than they actually are. This leads to in-group bias—the tendency to treat in-group members more favourably than out-group members.
- ***Semiconductor***—a material that, in terms of its physical properties, is between a conductor and an insulator. The commonest semi-conducting material, silicon, was used in the transistor, the world's first electronic switch, and is still the basis of modern microprocessors and information technology.
- ***Severance Pay*** is money that an employer might want to provide for an employee who is leaving their employ. Normal circumstances that might warrant severance pay include layoffs, job elimination, and mutual agreement to part ways for whatever reason. Severance pay usually amounts to a week or two of pay for each year of service to the company. In some instances, a severance package might include extended benefits and outplacement assistance.
- ***Sex Typing*** (of jobs)—the existence of stereotyped attitudes towards men's or women's abilities so that they are seen as fitted for or unsuited for particular forms of work, the basis of divisions between men's and women's work.
- ***Situations***—many social psychologists argue that it is the features of social situations which have more impact on behaviour than traits. They argue that our behaviour is too variable across situations to infer the existence of the stable underlying entities called traits. For these psychologists situations are to be understood as discrete entities each with it's own set of roles, rules, goals, and relevant concepts. This perspective understates the presence of stabilities—individuals behaving similarly across dissimilar situations—and the utility of trait measures as predictors of behaviour.
- ***Situational Leadership***—this view of leadership emphasizes the interaction between the leadership style of an individual and the features of the environment he or she is operating in. Situational leadership theories differ in whether they view leadership style as relatively fixed or as something which can be fairly readily adjusted by the leader to 'fit' the situation. If leadership style is seen as fixed then it follows that leaders are more effective in some environments than others. Increasing effectiveness would mean changing the environment rather than changing leadership style.
- ***Skills***—seen as 'natural units' of behaviour, the hallmark of skilled performance is smooth progression towards a goal. Understanding how individuals acquire skills involves more emphasis on the 'cognitive' aspects of learning. This focuses attention on the changes occurring in the 'mental models' people construct of the environments they are interacting with. For example, the differences between the way skilled and unskilled individuals categorize the information they are having to process can provide important insights into how skill development can be facilitated.

- ***Skilled Incompetence.*** Term coined by Chris Argyris (1996) to describe the way in which once successful organizations rest on their laurels for too long, causing strategies and behavioural patterns to become increasingly inappropriate in the face of new challenges. The learning that once enabled them to become highly competent has become outdated and is now the biggest barrier to their survival.
- ***Socialization.*** Is a process by which an individual comes to appreciate the values, abilities, expected behaviours, and social knowledge essential for assuming an organizational role and for participating as an organization member.
- ***Social Identity Theory***—a theory of group formation which stresses the psychological basis of group formation. The need for self-esteem is seen as the basis for our identification with groups and therefore our need to see the groups we belong to as positively distinctive. Social identity theory contrasts with accounts of group formation which stress the functional basis for the existence of groups and inter-group conflict. In the workplace there is normally a mix of both functional and psychological reasons for conflict between groups.
- ***Social Learning Theory***. the idea that some forms of social learning are so important they produce changes which are sufficiently enduring to be considered a stable part of our personality is an important one in the psychology of individual differences. Critics would argue that social learning theory tends to underplay the importance of genetic and biological differences.
- ***Social Skills.*** a commonplace assumption nowadays, but the idea that social interaction and social life more generally could be viewed as involving a set of skills which were similar to workplace skills was initially controversial. Like all skills, the hallmark of social skill is smooth progression toward a goal. As with other workplace skills they have a cognitive and behavioural component. These involve constructing effective 'models' of the environment (essentially other people) and developing sets of behavioural routines. Courses enhancing social skills (communicating, listening, self-assertion, negotiation, and counselling) are now central features of workplace development.
- ***Socio-Technical Systems.*** an approach to work redesign advanced by the Tavistock Institute for Human Relations, based on seeing work as a system of social relations between workers, as well as a technical system of formal design.
- ***Staff Managers*** advise and assist the line managers in accomplishing the goals and objectives. Human Resource Managers in most organizations operate as staff and assist the line managers in functions like recruiting, hiring, retaining, compensating etc.
- ***Stories***—a particularly coherent aspect of organizational symbolism. Stories dramatize specific organizational events; they assemble a cast of characters and a plot, and frequently have a functional purpose, such as controlling uncertainty, or enabling complex decisions to be taken.
- ***Strain***—the outcome of an inability to deal effectively with stressors. Strain is therefore evident in a range of physical and psychological signs and symptoms. The physical evidence of strain is thought to include hypertension, gastric disorders, coronary heart disease, skin disorders, and a range of psychosomatic illnesses. Psychologically strain can result in depression, sleep loss, suspiciousness, and 'burnout'.
- ***Strategy***. A route has been chosen for a period of time and from range of options in order to achieve organizational and business goals.

- ***Strategic Choice***—or managerial choice. The view that, because of the power that organizations dispose of, in practice managers are often not constrained by contextual factors (like technology or environment) but exercise great discretion. Strategic choice is an implied criticism of contingency theory.
- ***Strategic Capability***. Strategic capability provides the vision, the rich and sustained learning and knowledge development, the integrity of purpose and the continuous direction and scope to the activities of the firm that are needed to secure long term survival. It is based on profound understanding of the competitive environment, of the resource base, capacity and potential of the organization, of the strategy process and of the values that engender commitment from stake holders to corporate goals' (Harrison and Miller 1999).
- ***Strategic Control*** is the process of assessing progress towards strategic goals and taking corrective action as needed.
- ***Strategic Human Resource Management*** can be stated to mean 'formulating and executing human resource systems, methods, tools and techniques that produce the competencies and behaviour in an employee that an organization requires or may require in a future to achieve the strategic objectives.'
- ***Stress***—the result of an interaction between the environment and an individual whereby the individual appraises the demands of the situation and does not have the resources—physical or intellectual—to deal effectively with these demands.
- ***Stress Management***—interventions designed to reduce the impact of stressors in the workplace. These can have an individual focus, aimed at increasing an individual's ability to cope with stressors. Stress-management program can also have an organizational focus and attempt to remove the stressors in a role. For example, improving communication may reduce uncertainty. Programs with an organizational focus are relatively rare.
- ***Stressor***—an external demand the environment makes on the individual. Stressors in the workplace can include those embedded in our social relationships : a bullying supervisor, for example. They can also be present in the roles we occupy or because of factors such as noise, dust, or heat in the physical settings we work in.
- ***Subjectivity*** (in the labour process)—an approach that focuses on the active strategies that all organizational members develop in their work, and through which they construct aspects of social identity, often connected with 'positive resistance' or workers resisting in support of the broader interests of being effective in their jobs.
- ***Succession Planning*** is a process whereby an organization ensures that employees are recruited and developed to fill each key role within the company. Succession planning ensures you can fill key roles from within your organization.
- ***Supply*** in human resource refers to both the numbers and characteristics of people available for those particular jobs
- ***System***—a perspective that views organizations (or any social body) as consisting of an interdependent group of units (or subsystems) that pursues some goal or purpose, and exists within an environment with which it interacts.
- ***System of Professions***—the set of relationships between clusters of professional groups that often resolves itself into rivalry and conflict, as groups compete for 'jurisdiction' or control over a specified area of work.

T

- ***Tacit Knowledge.*** Knowledge that has been embedded deep in the individual or the collective subconscious, expressing itself in habitual or intuitive ways of doing things that are exercised without conscious thoughts or efforts (Nonaka 1991).
- ***Tacit versus explicit knowledge***—the two basic knowledge types. Knowledge, on the one hand, can be informal, intangible, and experience based; or, on the other hand, it can be formalized and codified.
- ***Task***—is an action or related group of action designed to produce a definite outcome or result.
- ***Taylorism***—the regime of work control developed by F. W. Taylor. Taylorism, or Scientific Management, was the first major industrial system to systematically rationalize and control the work process, by separating skills from the shop floor and fragmenting jobs.
- ***Team roles***—one extremely influential view of work teams is that individuals try to carve out for themselves distinctive team roles such as the 'plant'—the ideas person. The basic idea is that the effectiveness of a team is determined by the spread of roles it has available. Although not particularly well supported academically, the notion of team roles has nonetheless become extremely popular and thus a common framework for people in the workplace to understand the way in which teams function.
- ***Technological determinism***—the view that the effects of any new technology on work and employment are simply defined (*i.e.*, determined in a fixed way) by the inherent capabilities and functions of the technology itself. This is invariably criticized for ignoring factors in the context of work and the role of human agents.
- ***Telecommuting*** is a more recent trend in which employees can work from their choice of location and communicate through the use of computers, express mails, fax, telephones etc.
- ***Theories.***Constructs that are products.
- ***Total Institution***—a concept developed by Erving Goffman to indicate an organization that completely confines and encompasses the lives of inmates, ordering all daily routines, and thereby forcibly changing behaviour and self.
- ***Total Quality Management (TQM)*** usually involves the introduction of continuous monitoring. It refers to initiatives designed to improve the quality of products and services to meet customer's requirements.
- ***Tournament Theory.*** In the is compensation is the prize in a series of tournaments or contests among middle and top level managers, who aspire to become CEO's.
- ***Toyotaism***—the system of production identified with the Japanese auto giant Toyota, and especially with its plant in Toyota City. Essentially identical with JIT, but the focus on a single manufacturer is intended to stress that the kind of integrated production and supply chain that is the JIT ideal in fact occurs in very few places.
- ***Train***. To instruct and discipline in or for some particular art, profession, occupation or practice; to exercise practice, drills (Onions 1973).

  To teach a specified skill especially by practice (Pearsall and Trumble 1996).

- ***Training.*** Training involves an organized attempt to assist learning through instruction, observation, or practice. Training goals normally reflect the demands of a job role although 'management development' tends to have somewhat less specific goals. There is a great deal of research interest in what affects the extent to which training transfers into workplace behaviour. The impact of training on the success of an economy is an issue much disputed by economists. But the success of economies which invest heavily in training suggests there is some link between the level of training and the success of an economy.
- ***Training Benchmark*** helps an organization to measure the efficacy of their career development activities. It requires making use of various training evaluation models and benchmark metrics to understand the relative significance of training programmes.
- ***Training Cycle*** is a systematic goal oriented approach that produces results not only for the learner but also for the organization.
- ***Transactional Leadership Style***—this leadership style emphasizes the 'bread and butter' aspects of leadership : planning, organizing, coordinating, and timetabling. The leader enters into a transaction with subordinates : compliance is exchanged for reward. This leadership style is differentiated from the transformational leadership style which is supposed to involve the alignment of subordinates around a vision. However, in organizations both styles of leadership are important. The distinction may also be more apparent than real (see transformational leadership).
- ***Transformational leadership***—this view of leadership tries to restore the idea of leaders possessing special gifts and abilities. The transformational leader is the leader who is able to energize, align, and excite followers by providing a compelling vision of the future. Some have argued the identification of the transformational leadership style is the result of research methodology, which encourages people to fantasize about socially distant leaders.
- ***Two-factor Theory***—the idea that job satisfaction and job dissatisfaction are caused by two separate sets of factors. Job satisfaction is essentially the result of 'motivators' (satisfying higher-order psychological needs such as that for self-actualization). Job dissatisfaction is caused by the absence of 'hygiene factors' such as pay and working conditions which reflect the need to avoid pain. Whilst an extremely influential theory, many doubts have been raised about the independence of these factors and the original research methodology.
- ***Type-A and Type-B Personalities***—one contributor to coronary heart disease (CHD) is thought to be the presence of a stress-prone personality—the type A. This represents a cluster of traits which give rise to a hard-driving, work-involved, competitive style and a strong sense of urgency. Type Bs in contrast does not have the same sense of urgency or competitiveness. Although the general link between type As and CHD appears well established the precise mechanisms causing the elevated risks are unclear.

V

- ***Validity***. Validity represents the relevance of an assessment methodology. Although the concept is normally encountered in the context of psychometric tests it can be applied to evaluate any assessment methodology. There are a number of quite different facets to the notion of validity, ranging from the acceptability of a process to individuals (face validity) through to the ability of the method to predict outcomes (criterion validity).

- ***Values*** are traits or qualities that are considered worthwhile; they represent an individual's highest priorities and deeply held driving forces. Values include qualities such as integrity, resourcefulness, achievement, and honesty.
- ***Value Statements*** are grounded in values and define how people want to behave with each other in the organization. They are statements about how the organization will value customers, suppliers, and the internal community. Value statements describe actions which are the living enactment of the fundamental values held by most individuals within the organization.
- ***Variable Pay Plan.*** Profit sharing is an example of a variable pay plan. Profit sharing is taking a percentage of a company's annual profits and then dividing the pool of money generated across all employees using a formula for distribution. Profit sharing payments are only made if the company has been profitable for the time period specified. Find out more about profit sharing. Variable pay is used generally to recognize and reward employee contribution toward company productivity, profitability, team work, safety, quality, or some other metric deemed important. Variable pay changes depending upon the circumstances.
- ***VIE Theory***—whilst some theories of motivation assume the existence of psychological 'needs' which motivate behaviour, VIE theory stresses the more rational cognitive processes involved. This focuses attention on the extent to which individuals can perceive means–end connections between their efforts and valued rewards. Doubts have been raised about the extent to which individuals do undertake the complex calculations involved in projecting their behaviour into the future.
- ***Vision***. Vision is general statement of its intended direction that evokes emotional feelings in organizational members. (James Higgins and Julian Vincze 1993, p. 5). It is a statement of what the organization wants to become. It should resonate with all members of the organization and help them feel proud, excited, and part of something much bigger than themselves. A vision should stretch the organization's capabilities and image of itself. It gives shape and direction to the organization's future.

W

- ***Workers' Resistance***—the process of struggle against the control imposed by the labour process. The importance of considering 'resistance' lay in the fact that Braverman's influential theory appears to ignore it.
- ***Work Sharing*** is designed to give flexibility to those people who for some reason cannot work a full day. Work modules are two hour work units, the scheduling of which can be moved about to increase diversity and reduce opportunities for workers to become bored.
- ***Work Orientation***—represents a kind of 'super attitude' towards work that constitutes a broad disposition towards certain kinds of employment. The most researched is the instrumental orientation. Work orientations are regarded as 'externally' generated from employees' background, rather than from their experiences within work.

- ***Work Segregation***—distortions in the distribution of jobs whereby men or women tend to be pushed into certain kinds of occupations, so that these become highly feminized or masculinized.

Z

- ***Zero-base Budgeting*** does not use the previous year's budget or expenses in setting a new budget, since the company's circumstances and finances may have changed. When building a budget from a zero base, every expense must be justified.
- ***Zone of Indifference (Area of Acceptance).*** According to Barnard and Simon, respectively, inclinations conditioning individuals to accept orders that fall within a familiar range of responsibility and activity.

❑❑❑

Bibliography

Adair, J. (2003). *Learning from Great leaders- Inspiring Leadership,* London (UK): Thorogood Publishing

Albretch, T.E., and Bach, B.W. (1997). *Communication in complex organizations: A Relational approach.* Orlando: Harcourt Brace.

Albrechtsen, H., A.M. Pejtersen, and B. Cleal (2002). Empirical Work Analysis of collaborative film indexing. In H. Bruce et. al. (eds.), *Emerging Framework and Methods: Proceedings of the Fourth International Conference on Conceptions of Library and information Science.* Greenwood Village, CO.: Libraries Unlimited, pp. 85–108.

Allen, N.J. and J.P. Meyer, (1990). 'The Measurement and Antecedents of Affective, Continuance and Normative Commitment to the Organization', *Journal of Occupational Psychology,* 63 (1), pp. 1–18.

Allen, T.D., Poteet, M.L., Russel, J.E.A., and Dobbins, G.H., (1995). *Influence of Learning and Development Factors on Perception of Plateauing.* Paper Presented at the Tenth Annual Meeting of the Society for Industrial and Organizational Psychology, Orlando.

American Accounting Association Committee of Accounting for Human Resources, (1973) 'Report of the Committee on Human Resources Accounting,'*The Accounting Review Supplement to* Vol. XLVIII.

Alred, G., garvey, B. and Smith, R (1998) *Mentoring Pocketbook.* Alresford: Management Pocketbooks.

Allen, B.J. (2005). Social Constructionism. In S May and D.K. Mumby (Eds.), *Engaging organizational theory and research.* New Delhi: Sage, pp. 35–53.

Andrews, K.A. (1971), *The Concept of Corporate Strategy,* New York: Dow-Jones Irwin.

Advisory, Conciliation and Arbitration Service. (2003) *Job evaluation: an introduction.* London: ACAS. Available at: http://www.acas.org.uk/index.aspx?articleid=682

Armstrong, M. (2003). *Handbook of Strategic Human resource Management,* New Delhi: Crest Publishing House.

Armstrong, Michael *A Handbook of Personnel Management Practice,* 3rd ed. Kogan Page.

Armstrong, M. and Baron, A. (2004) *Managing performance: Performance management in Action.* London: Chartered Institute of Personal Development

Arnold, J. (1997). *Managing Careers in 21st Century.* London: Paul Chapman Publishing Company.

Arvey, R.D. and Murphy, K.R. (1998), 'Performance Evaluation in Work Settings', *Annual Review of Psychology,* 49.

Avedon, L. (1995). *Older workers in transition. ERIC Digest.* Columbus: ERIC Clearing House on Adult, Career and Vocational Education (ED 400474)

Bacon, N. (2003), 'Human Resource management and Industrial Relations'. In P. Ackersand A. Wilkinson (eds.), *Understanding Work and Employment: Industrial Relations in Transition.* London: Oxford University Press.

Bakke, E.W. (1948). *From Tactics to Strategy in Industrial Relations,* New Haven: Labour Management Centre, Yale University.

Bakke, E.W. (1958). *The Human Resources Function.* New Haven: Labour Management Centre, Yale University.

Balay, R., (2000). *Organizational Commitment of administrators and Teachers,* Nobel Yayin Dagitim.

Bales, Robert F. (1951). *Interaction Process Analysis,* Reading, Mass.: Addison-Wesley.

Ban, Carolyn and Riccucci, Norma (eds) *Public Personnel Management: Current Concerns, Future Challenges.* New York, NY: Longman, pp. 21–34.

Bandura, A.(1977). Self-efficacy: Toward a unifying theory of behavioural change. *Psychological Review,84*(2), pp. 191–215.

Bandura, A.(1982). Self-efficacy mechanism in human agency. *American Psychologist, 37*(2), pp. 122–147.

Bannister, D., and Fransella, F. (1986). *Inquiring man: The Psychology of personal constructs,* 3rd ed. London.

Barling, J. and Phillips, M., *Interactional, formal and distributive justice in the workplace: An exploratory study.* Journal of Psychology, 1993, Vol 127, Pg. 649–657.

Baron, J. and Kerps, D. (1999), *Strategic Human Resources,* John Wiley and Sons, Inc.

Baruch, Y. (1996) Organizational career planning and management techniques and activities in use in high-tech organizations. *Career Development International,* 1 (1) 40–49.

Baruch, Y. and Peiperl, M. A. (1997). High flyers: glorious past, gloomy present, any future? *Career Development International,* 2 (7) 354–358.

Baruch, Y. (2004). *Managing Careers.* London: Prentice Hall.

Barney, J. (1991), "Firm resources and sustained competitive advantage", *Journal of Management,* Vol. 17 No.1, pp.99–120

Baron, J.N. and Kreps, D.M. (1999). *Strategic Human Resources: Frameworks for general Managers.* New York: John Wiley and Sons.

Bass, B. M. (1985). *Leadership and performance beyond expectation.* New York: Free Press.

Bass, B. M. (1990). From transactional to transformational leadership: Learning to share the vision. *Organizational Dynamics,* (Winter): 19–31.

Bass, B. M. and Steidlmeier, P. (1998). *Ethics, Character and Authentic Transformational Leadership,* at: http://cls.binghamton.edu/BassSteid.html

Bauer, T.N., Morrison, E.W., and Callister, R.R. (1998). Organizational Socialization: A Review and Directions for Future Research. In G.R. Ferris (Ed.) *Research in personnel and human resource management 16,* Stamford, CT: JAI press, pp. 149–214.

Baverman, H. (1974), *'Labour and Monopoly Capital'*, New York: Monthly Review Press.

Beach, Dale S., (1980). *Personnel- The Management of people at Work,* Fourth Edition, New York: Macmillan

Beardwell, I; L. Holden and T. Claydon (2004), *Human Resource management; A Contemporary Approach,* 4th ed., Harlow: Prentice Hall.

Beatty, Richard and Schneider, Graig Eric, (1975). *A case of Positive Reinforcement,* Business Horizons, April, 1975.

Becker, B.E. and Gerhart, S (1996) The Impact of Human Resource Management on organizational performance: progress and prospects, *Academy of Management Journal,* **39** (4), pp. 779–801

Becker, B.E., M.A. Huselid and D. Ulrich (2001), *The HR Scorecard. Linking people, strategy and performance,* Harvard Business School Press.

Beckhard, R., (1969) *Organizational Development Strategies and Model,* Reading, Mass: Addison Wesley.

Beckhard, R. and Harris, (1987). *Organizational Transitions: Managing Complex Change.* (2nd ed.) Reading, MA: AddisonWesley.

Beckhard, R. and Pritchard, W. (1992). *Changing the Essence.* San Francisco: Jossey Bass.

Beer, M., and Spector, B. (1984). 'Human Resource Management: The Integration of Industrial Relations and Organizational Development.' In K. Rowland and G. Ferris (eds.), *Research in Personnel and Human Resources Management,* vol. ii. Greenwhich Conn.: Jai Press.

Beer, M., B. Spector, P.R. Lawrence, D. Quinn Mills and R.E. Walton (1984), *Managing Human Assets,* New York: The Free Press.

Bennis, W.G. (1959). Leadership Theory and Administrative Behaviour: The Problem of Authority, *Administrative Science Quarterly,*4, p. 259

Bennis, W. (1989) *On Becoming a Leader.* Reading, MA: Addison Wesley.

Bennis, W., Benne, K, and Chin, R., Eds. (1985). *The Planning of Change.* 4th Ed., New York: Holt, Rinehart, and Winston, 98105.

Bennis, W. and Nanus, B. (1985). *Leaders.* New York: Harper and Row.

Bentley, T. (1990), *The Business Training,* 2nd edition, New Jersey: McGraw Hill Book Company.

Berger, P.L., and Luckmann, T. (1966). *The social construction of reality: A tratise in the sociology of knowledge.* New York: Doubleday.

Bernardin, J.H., *Human Resource Management: An Experimental Approach,* New Delh; Tata McGRaw Hill.

Betz, N. E. (2001). Career self-efficacy. In F. T. L. Leong and A. Barak (Eds.), *Contemporary models in vocational psychology* (pp. 55–77). Mahwah, NJ: Erlbaum.

Bhaskar-Shrinivas, P., Shaffer, M. and Luk, D. (2005) Input-based and time based

Black, J. S., Gregersen, H. B. and Mendenhall, M. E. (1992). *Global Assignments.* San Francisco: Jossey-Bass.

Blake, Robert R. and Mouton, Jone S (1969) *Building a Dynamic Organization through Grid Organization Development,* Reading, Mass: Addison Wesley.

Blake, Robert R. and Mouton, Jone S. (1978) *The New Managerial Grid,* Houston: Gulf Publishing.

Blanchard, P.N. and Thacker, J.W. (1998), *Effective Training: Systems, Strategies and Practices,* New Jersey: Prentice hall.

Blyton, P. and Turnbull, P. (2004), *The Dynamics of Employee Relations.* London: Palgrave Macmillan

Bolt, J. (1993), "Achieving the CEO's agenda: education for executives", *Management Review,* No.May, pp.44–9.

Bontis, N. (1996) There's a price on your head : managing intellectual capital strategically, *Business Quarterly,*Summer, pp. 4–47.

Bontis, N (1998) Intellectual Capital: an exploratory study that develops measures and models, *Management Decision,* 36(2), pp. 63–76.

Bontis, N., Dragonetti, N.C., Jaconsen, K. and Roos, G. (1999). 'The Knowledge toolbox: a review of the tools available to measure and manage intangible resources,' *European Management Journal,* **17** (4), pp. 391–402.

Bordin, E.S. (1990). Psychodynamic Model of career Choice and satisfaction. In D. Brown and L. Brooks (Eds.), *Career choice and development* (2nd ed.) (pp. 102–144)). San Francisco: Jossey Bass.

Bordin, E.S (1994). Intrinsic motivation and the active self: Convergence from psycho-dynamic perspective. In M. Savickas and R. Lent, *Convergence in career development theories: imp[lications for science and practice* (pp. 53–61). Palo Alto: Consulting Psychologist Press.

Boulter, N., Dalziel, M. and Hils, J. (2004). *People and Competencies – A Handbook,* New Delhi: Crest Publishing House.

Boxall, P (1996). 'The Strategic Human Resource Management Debate and the Resource Based View of the Firm', *Human Resource Management Journal,* 6/3: pp. 59–75

Boxall, P. and Purcell, J. (2003) *Strategy and Human Resource Management.* Basingstoke: Palgrave Macmillan.

Brager, G. and Holloway, S. (1992). "Assessing the Prospects for Organizational Change: The Uses of Force Field Analysis." *Administration in Social Work.* 16(3/4), 1528.

Braverman, H. (1974) *labour and Monopoly Capital,* New York: Monthly Review Press.

Bretz, R.D.; G.T. Milkovich; W. Read (1992), 'The Current State of Performance Appraisal Research and practice: Concerns, Directions and Implications', *Journal of Management* (18).

Bridges, W. (1998). *Creating You and Co.* Brearley Publishing

British Institute of Management, (1951), *Job Evaluation: A Practical Guide,* London.

Brookings Institute (2000). Understanding intangible sources of Value: Human capital sub group report (on line). http://www.brook.edu/es/research/projects/intangibles/doc/sub_hcap.htm.

Brown, B.L. (1998). *Career Mobility. A choice of necessity?* Columbus: ERIC Clearing House on Adult, Career and Vocational Education (ED 414436).

Brown, D. and Brooks, L. (1991). *Career Counseling Techniques.* Boston: Allyn and Bacon.

Brown, S. and Sessions, J.G. (2003). Attitudes, Expectations and Sharing. *Labour,* **17**, 543 – 69.

Bruce, H., et. al. (eds.), *Emerging Framework and Methods: Proceedings of the Fourth International Conference on Conceptions of Library and information Science.* Greenwood Village, CO.: Libraries Unlimited

Brumbrach, G.B. (1988) Some Ideas, issues, and predictions about performance management, *Public Personnel Management,* Winter, pp. 387–402.

Brummer, J. James, (!1991) *Corporate Responsibility and Legitimacy: An Interdisciplinary Analysis,* New York: Greenwood Press

Bryson, John M. (1996). *Strategic Planning for Public and Non Profit Organizations.* San Francisco, CA: Jossey Bass.

Burack, Eelmer H., and Smith, Robert D. (1977). *Personnel Management- A Human Resource Systems Approach,* Minnesota: West Publishing

Bureau of Labour Statistics, *Glossary of Currently Used Wage Terms,* Bulletin 983, US Government Printing Press

Burton, R.M. and Obel, B. (2004), *Strategic Organization Diagnosis and Design: The Dynamics of Fit.* Boston: Kulwer Academic Publishers.

Butler, J.E., G.R. Ferris and N.K. Napier (1991). *Strategy and Human Resources Management,* Cincinnati, OH: South Western Publishing Co.

Cairo, Peter C. (1983). "Counselling in Industry", *Personnel Psychology,* Spring p.1–18

Caldwell, R (2001) Champions, Adapters, consultants and synergists; the new change agents in HRM, *Human Resource Management Journal,* 11 (3), pp. 39–52.

Caldwell, R (2004) Rhetoric, facts and self fulfilling prophesies: exploring practitioners' perceptions of progress in implementing HRM, *Industrial Relations Journal,* 35(3), pp. 196–215.

Campbell, Andrew. *"Tailored, Not Benchmarked."* Harvard Business Review, March 1999.

Campbell, J.P., Dunnette, M.D., lawer, III, E.E., and Weiæk, K.E., (1970), *Managerial Behaviou, Performance, and Effectiveness,* new York: McGraw–Hill

Campbell, R.E. and Hefferman, J.M. (1983). Adult vocational behaviour. In W.B. Walsh and S.H. Osipow (Eds.), *handbook of Vocational Psychology: Vol. I. Foundations* (pp. 223–260). New Jersey: Lawrence Erlbaum Associates.

Cappelli, P and Crocker-Hefter, A. (1996) 'Distinctive Human Resources are firms' core competencies', *Organizational Dynamics,* Winter, pp. 7–22.

Cappelli, P. and H. Singh (1992), Integrating strategic human resource and strategic management. In D. Lewin, O.S. Mitchell and P. Sherer (eds.), *Research Frontiers in industrial relations and human resources,* (pp. 165–192), Madison, WI: Industrial Relations Research Association.

Cappelli, L., Bassi, H., Katz, D., Knoke, P., Osterman, P., and Useem, M. (1997). *Change at Work,* New York: Oxford University Press.

Carrell, M.R., and Kuzmitts, F.E., (1982), *Personnel: management of Human Resources,* Merill: Colombus, Ohio.

Carroll, Stephen J., Jr., and Tosi, Henry L. Jr., (1973) *Management by Objectives: Application and Research,* New York: Macmillan

Casico, W.F. (1989), *Managing Human Resources,* McGraw-Hill, New York.

Casico, W.F. (1991). *Applied Psychology in Personnel management,* 4th Edition., Englewood, Cliffs., NJ: Prentice- Hall.

Casico, W.F., and Bailey, E., (1995). 'International Human Resource management: The state of Research and practice', in In Shenkar, O., (E.d.), *Global Prospectives of Human Resources Management,* Englewood Cliffs, NJ: Prentice Hall, pp 15–36.

Cecil, R.D. and Rothwell, W.J. (2007). *Next Generation Management Development: The Complete Guide and Resource,* San Francisco, CA: Pfeiffer.

Cetin, M.O. (2004). *Organizational Culture and Organizational Commitment* Nobel Yayin Dagitim,

Chakraborty, S.K. (1991). *Management by Values.* Oxford: Oxford Publishing Company.

Chartered Institute of Personnel and Development (2002), *Developing Managers for Business Performance,* London: Chartered Institute of Personnel and Development

Chartered Institute of Personnel and Development (2002 a) *Code of Conduct for Equal Opportunities,* London: Chartered Institute of Personnel and Development

Chartered Institute of Personnel and Development (2003), *Employee Absence,* London: Chartered Institute of Personnel and Development

Chartered Institute of Personnel and Development. (2003 a) Managing employee careers: issues, trends and prospects. Survey report. London: Chartered Institute of Personnel and Development.

Chartered Institute of Personnel and Development. (2004) *Coaching and buying coaching services. Guide.* London: Chartered Institute of Personnel and Development.

Chartered Institute of Personnel and Development (2004a) *How to develop reward strategy,* London: Chartered Institute of Personnel and Development

Chartered Institute of Personnel and Development (2005), *Training and Learning.* Change Agenda. London: Chartered Institute of Personnel and Development.

Chartered Institute of Personnel and Development. (2005) *UK global comparisons leadership forecast 2005–2006: best practices for tomorrow's global leaders. Survey report.* London: Chartered Institute of Personnel and Development. Available at: http://www.cipd.co.uk/surveys

Chartered Institute of Personnel and Development (2007). *Learning and Development: Annual Survey Report* 2007. London: Chartered Institute of Personnel and Development.

Chartered Institute of Personnel and Development. (2007) Reward Management: Annual Survey Report 2007. London: CIPD. Available at: http://www.cipd.co.uk/surveys

Chartrand, J.M. (1996). Linking theory with practice. A Socio-cognitive interactional model for career counselling. In M.L. Savickas and W.B. Walsh (EDs.), *handbook of career counseling. Theory and practice* (pp. 121–134). Palo Alto: Davies – Black Publishing.

Chhabra, T.N., Ahuja, K.K. and Jain, S.P. (1977). *Managing People at Work,* Delhi: Dhanpat Rai and Sons.

Cherrington, David J. (1995). *The Management of Human Resources,* Englewood Cliffs, NJ: Prentice- Hall

Clutterbuck, D. (2004). *The HR Guide to Organizational Change – Managing Work- Life balance,* Chartered Institute for Personnel and Development , UK.

Chaudron, D. (1992). "How OD can help TQM." *OD Practitioner.* 24(1), 1418.

Chaudron, D. (1993, June). *Organization Development Does not Equal Total Quality Management.* Presentation to the San Diego Organization Development Network.

Chartered Institute of Personnel and Development (2002). *Corporate Social Responsibility and HRM's Role*, London

Clutterback, D. (2004) *Everyone needs a mentor: fostering talent in your organization.* 4th ed. London: Chartered Institute of Personnel and Development

Clutterback, D. and Megginson, D. (1999). *Mentoring Executives and Directors.* Oxford: Butterworth Heinemann.

Cohen, S. and Brand, R. (1993). *Total Quality Management in Government.* San Francisco: Jossey Bass, Inc.

Collins, J.C. and J.I. Porras (1997), *Built to Last,* New York: Harper.

Cook, Trevor, (May 2004) *Communicating with Employees,* A Jackson Wells Morris White Paper, www. trevorcook.typead.com

Cooper-Thomas, H.D., and Anderson, N. (2006). "Organizational socialization: A New theoretical model and recommendations for future research and HRM practices on organizations. *Journal of Management Psychology, 21*(5), pp 234–279

Cox, T, Griffiths, A, Barlowe, C, Randall, R., Thomson, L, and Rial-Gonzalez, E. (2000) *Organisational interventions for work stress: A risk management approach* , Sheffield,.

Crites, J.O. (1969). *Vocational Psychology. The study of vocational behaviour and development.* New York: McGraw-Hill.

Crites, J. O. (1973). *Theory and research handbook for the Career Maturity Inventory.* Monterey, CA: CTB/McGraw-Hill.

Crites, J.O. (1981). *Career Counseling. Models. Methods and materials.*New York: McGraw-Hill Book Company.

Cully, M., O'Reilly, A., Millward, N., Forth, J., Woodland, S., Dix, G. and Bryson, A. (1998). The 1998 workplace employee relations survey: first findings (online) *www.dti.gov.uk/ emar/.*

Cunningham, I., Dawes, G. and Bennett, B. (2004). *The handbook of work based learning.* Aldershot: Gower.

Davenport, T.O. (1999). *Human Capital,* San Francisco, CA: Josey Bass,

Davis, Keith, (1981), *Human Behaviour at Work.* New Delhi: Tata McGraw Hill, New Delhi.

Debra L. Nelson, et. al., (2003). *Organizational Behaviour,* Thomson.

Deci, E.L. (1972). Intrinsic motivation, extrinsic reinforcement, and inequity. *Journal of Personality and Social Psychology,* 22 (1), 113–120.

Deci, E. (1975). *Intrinsic Motivation.* New York and London: Plenum Press

Decker, P. and Naten B. (1985), *Behaviour Modeling Training: Principles and Application,* New York: Prager.

DeCenzo, David A., and Stephen P. Robbins, (1989). *Personnel/ Human Resource Management,* Third Edition, New Delhi: Prentice-Hall of India.

Deming, W.E. (1982). *Quality, Productivity and Competitive Position,,* Cambridge, MA.: Massachusetts Institute of Technology Press.

Derr, C.B. (1986). *Managing the New careerist.* San Francisco, CA: Jossey- Bass.

Dickmann, M. (1997). *The IPD guide on International management development.* London: IPD.

Dickmann, M., and Harris, H. (2005). Developing career capital for global careers: the role of international assignments. *Journal of World Business,* Vol. 40, No. 4, November, pp39–40.

Dollard, M. F, (2003) *Introduction: Costs, theoretical approaches, research designs* In M. F. Dollard, A. H. Winefield, and H. R. Winefield (Eds), *Occupational stress in the service professions*, London Taylor and Francis, 2003, Pg 1–43.

Drucker, Peter F. (1954) The Practice of Management, New York: Harper and Row

Drummond, K.E. (1989), *Human Resource Management for the Hospitality Industry,* New York: Van Nostrand Reinhold.

Dessler, Gary. (2004). *Human Resource Management.* 10th ed. Englewood Cliffs, NJ: Pearson/ Prentice-

Dunette, M. (1976), *Aptitudes, Abilities and Skills,* Chicago: Randy Macnally

Dyer, L. and Holder, G. Strategic Human Resource Management and Planning. In: yer, L. (ed) (1998) *Human Resource Management: Evolving roles and Responsibilities*. Washington DC: Bureau of National Affairs.

Edvinson, L. and M. Malone (1997), *Intellectual capital: the proven way to establish your company's true value by finding its hidden brainpower,* London: Piatkun Publ.

Egan, Gerard. (1993). *Adding Value: A Systematic Guide to Business-Driven Management and Leadership.* San Francisco: Jossey-Bass.

EIC, EIC Network Promotes Corporate Social Responsibility, 10 May 2005, Euro Info Centre, www.eic.ie

Eisenhardt, K. M. (1985). Control: Organizational and economic approaches. *Management Science,* 31(2), 134–149.

Eisenhardt, K. M. (1988). Agency and institutional explanations of compensation in retail sales. *Academy of Management Journal*, 31(3), 488–511

Evans, P., Puck, V. and Barsoux, J.L. (2002) *The global chnallenge: frameworks for international human resource management,* Boston, MA: McGraw-Hill.

Ezell, M., Menefee, D., and Patti, R. (1989). "Managerial Leadership and Service Quality: Toward a Model of Social Work Administration," *Administration in Social Work.* 13(3/4), 7398.

Falk, Armin and Urs Fischbacher (206). A Theory of Reciprocity, *Games and Economic Behaviour* 54(2): 293–315.

Farnham, D. (1921). *America vs. Europe in Industry,* New York: Ronald Press.

Ferris, G.R. (ed.) *Research in personnel and human resource management,* greenwich, CT: JAI Press.

Fisher, Cynthia D., Shoenfeldt, Lyle F., and Shaw, James B., (2002). *Human Resource Management,* Boston: Houghton Mifflin Co.

Flamholtz, Eric G. (1971). 'A Model for Human Resource Valuation: A Stochastic Process with Service Rewards.' *The Accounting Review* (April).

Flamholtz, Eric G. (1999). *Human Resource Accounting: Advances in Concepts, Methods and Applications,* Third Edition, Kulwer Academic Publishers.

Fleishman, E.W. and Quaintance, M.K.. (1984), *Taxonomies of Human Performance: The description of human tasks,* Orlando, FL.: Academic Press Inc.

Fletcher, C. (1993). *Appraisal: routes to improved performance,* London: Institute of Personnel Management.

Flippo, Edwin B., (1984). *Personnel Management,* Sixth edition, New York: McGraw-Hill.

Fombrun, C.J., Tichy, N.M., and Devanna, M.A. (1984) *Strategic Human Resource Management,* New York: Wiley

Fournies, F. (1999). *Why Employees Don't Do What They're Supposed to Do and What to Do About It',* New York: McGraw-Hill.

Freeman, R.B. and M.M. Kleiner. (2005). The Last American Shoe Manufactures: Decreasing

Productivity and Increasing Profits in the Shift to Continuous Flow Production. *Industrial Relations,* **44**, 307–330.

Frey, B. (1997). On the relationship between extrinsic and intrinsic work motivation. *International Journal of Industrial Organizations,* 15 (4), 427–439.

Frey, B. and Jegen, R. (2001). Motivation crowding theory. *Journal of Economic Surveys,* 15 (1), 589–611.

Friedman A, and Phillips, M. (2004) Continuing Professional Development: developing a vision. *Journal of Education and Work;* 17 (3), pp 362–375

Gächter, Simon (206). *Conditional Cooperation: Behavioural Regularities from the Lab and the Field and Their Policy Implications.* Mimeo: University of Nottingham.

George, C.S. (1974), *Management for Industry and Business,* New Delhi: Prentice Hall

Gerhart, B., C.O. Trevor and M.E. Graham (1996), 'New directions in compensation research: Synergies, risk, and survival. In G.R. Ferris (ed.) *Research in personnel and human resource management,* (vol. 14, pp. 143–203), Greenwich, CT: JAI Press

Gilbert, G. (1992). "Quality Improvement in a Defense Organization," *Public Productivity and Management Review.* 16(1), 6575.

GMAC Global Relocation Services/ Windham International (2000). *Global relocation trends: 2000 survey report.* New York: GMAC Global Relocation Services/ Windham International.

Goldstein, Leonard, Timothy Nolan, and J. William Pfeiffer. (1993). *Applied Strategic Planning.* New York: McGraw Hill.

Goldsmith, M. and Lyons, L. (2006). *Coaching for Leadership: The Practice of leadership coaching from the world's greatest coaches.* 2nd ed. San Francisco: Pfeiffer.

Gormely, William T., and David L. Weimer (1999) *Organizational Report Cards.* Cambridge, MA: Harvard University.

Grant, R.M., (1991) The resource-based theory of competitive advantage: implications for strategy formulation, *California Management Review,* 33(3), pp. 114–35.

Gratton, L. and Hailey, V.H. (1999). 'The rhetoric and reality of new careers,' in *Strategic Human Resource Management,* eds L. Gratton, V.H. Hailey, P. Stiles, and C Truss, Oxford: Oxford University Press.

Gratton, L; V.H. Hailey, P. Stiles and C. Truss (1999). *Strategic Human Resource Management,* Oxford: Oxford University Press.

Greenhaus, J.H., and Beutell, N.J. (1985). Sources of Conflict between work and family roles. *Academy of Management Review,*10, 77.

Gruindy, T., and Brown, L. (2003). *Value-based Human Resource Strategy – developing Your Consultancy Role*, UK: ELSEVIER Butterworth Heinemann.

Guest, D. (1998), 'Beyond HRM: Commitment and Contract Culture', In Sp[arrow, P. and Marchington, M (eds), *Human Resource Management: the New Agenda*, London: Pitman.

Guest, D.E. and Conway, N. (2002) *Pressure at Work and Psychological Contract*, London: CIPD.

Gunz, H. P., Jalland, R. M. and Evans, M. G. (1997). New strategy, wrong managers? What you need to know about career streams. *Academy of Management Executive*, 12 (2) pp 21–37.

Guterman, M. (1991). Working Couples: Findings a balance between family and career. In *New Dimensions in Career Planning and the Workplace*, ed. J.M. Kummerow, Palo Alto, California: Davies Black Publishing, p. 167–193.

Gutteridge, T. G., Leibowitz, Z. B. and Shore, J. E. (1993). *Organizational Career Development*, San Francisco: Jossey-Bass.

Hall, D. T. (1986). *Career Development in Organizations*, San Francisco; Jossey-Bass.

Hall, P. J. and Mirvis, P. H. (1995). Careers as lifelong learning in Howard, A. (Ed) *The changing nature of work*, San Francisco: Jossey Bass.

Hall. Gueutal, Hal G., and Dianna L. Stone, (eds.) (2005). *The Brave New World of eHR: Human Resources Management in the Digital Age*. San Francisco: Jossey-Bass.

Hammonds, Keith H. (2003) *How Google Grows... and Grows....and Grow'* Fast Company, April.

Harrell, T.W. (1964). *Industrial Psychology*, London: Oxford and IBH.

Harris, H. (1997) *Women in International management: an examination of the role of home country selection processes in influencing the number of women in international management positions*. Carnfield: Carnfield University.

Harris, H. and Brewster, C. (1999) An integrative framework for pre-departure preparation. In Harris, H. and Brewster, C., *International HRM*. London: Routledge.

Harris, H. and Brewster, C. and Sparrow, P. (2003). *International Human Resource Management*. London: Chartered Institute of Personnel and Development.

Harris, H. and Dickman, M. (2005) *International Management Development*. A Guide. London: Chartered Institute of personnel Development.

Henderson, R.I. (1982). *Compensation management: Rewarding Performance* (3rd ed.) Reston, Va.: Reston Publishing Co. Inc.

Herriot, P. and Pemberton, C. (1995). *New Deals*, Chichester: John Wiley.

Herriot, P. and Pemberton, C. (1996). Contracting Careers. *Human Relations*, 49 (6) 757–790.

Herzberg, Fredrick, (1966). *Work and the Nature of Man*, new York: The World Publishing Co.

Heywood, J.S. and Wei, X. (2006). Performance Pay and Job Satisfaction. *Journal of Industrial Relations*, **48**, 523–40.

Hirano, R. (1969). 'Personnel Management in Foreign Corporations'. In R. Ballon (ed.), *The Japanese Employee*. Tokyo: Sophia University.

Hirsh, W. and Carter, Alison (2002). *New Directions in Management Development*. Brighton: Institute of Employment Studies.

Hofsted, G. (1980). *Culture's consequences: international differences in work related values.* London: Sage Publications.

Hofsted, G (1993) Cultural Constraints in management theories. *Academy of management Executive.* Vol. 7, No. 1. pp 81–94.

Hofsted, G. (2001) *Culture's consequences.* 2nd ed. Thousand Oaks, CA: Sage.

Hofsted, G. (2004) *Cultures and organizations: software of the mind.* Rev. ed Maidenhead: McGraw Hill.

Holbeche, L. (1999, *Aligning human resources and business strategy,* Amsterdam: Elseview.

Honey, P. (2006) Line managers need all the help they can get, especially when they don't realize it. *Organizationx and People.* Vol. 13, No. 4, November, pp 2–8.

House, R., Javidan, M. and hanges, P. (2002) Understanding Cultures and implicit leadership theories across the globe: an introduction to project GLOBE. *Journal of World Business,* Vol. 37, No. 1, Spring. Pp. 3–10.

Howitt, P. (2002), "Looking inside the labour market: A review article", *Journal of Economic Literature,* Vol. XL No. March, p. 125–138.

Hussey, D. (1996), *Business-driven Human Resource Management,* Chichester: Wiley.

Hutchinson, S., Kinnie, N. and Purcell, J. (1998). *Getting fit, staying fit: developing lean and responsive organizations.* London: Institute of Personnel and Development.

Hyde, A. (1992). "The Proverbs of Total Quality Management: Recharting the Path to Quality Improvement in the Public Sector," *Public Productivity and Management Review.* 16(1), 2537.

IDS (2002) *Human Resource Management System,* London: IDS.

IDS (2004) Searching for magic bullet, *HR study 783,* October pp. 2–6.

International Labour Organization (1951). *Payment By Result,* New Delhi: Oxford and India Book House.

International Labour Organization (1960), *Job Evaluation, Studies and Reports,* New Series No. 56,.Geneva, Jackson, C., Arnold, J., Nicholson, N., and Watts, A. G. (1998). *Managing Careers in 2000 and Beyond,* Brighton, Institute of Employment Studies.

Jacoby, S (1985). *Employing Bureaucracy: Managers, Unions, and the Transformation of Work in American Industry, 1900–1945.* New York: Columbia University Press.

- (1991). 'Pacific Ties: Industrial Relations and Employment Systems in Japan and the United States since 1900.' In Lienchtenstein and H. Harris (eds.) *Industrial Democracy in America: The Ambiguous Promise.* New York: Cambridge University Press.
- (1997). *Modern Manors: Welfare Capitalism since the New Deal.* Princeton: Princeton University Press.
- (2003). 'A century of Human resource Management'. In B. Kaufman, R. Beaumont and R. Helgott (eds.), *Industrial Relations to Human Resource and Beyond: The Evolving Process of Employee Relations Management.* Armonk, NY: M.E. Sharpe.

Janda, K.F. (1960). Towards the explication of the4 concept of leadership in terms of Concept of Power. *Human Relations, 13,* pp. 345–363.

Janssen, M. and Mendys-Kamphorst, E. (2004). The price of a price: On the crowding out and in of social norms. *Journal of Economic Behavior and Organization,* 55, 377–395.

Jarvis, J. (2004) Coaching and buying coaching services. A guide. London: CIPD. (Available at: http://www.cipd.co.uk/guides

Jenkins, Heledd, (2001) *Corporate Social Responsibility Engaging SMEs in the Debate: Initial Research Findings,* Cardiff: BRASS The ESRC Centre.

Johansson, Ellen and Larsson, Paullina (2000). *Pole Position with Corporate Social Responsibility: Case of SKF in Malaysia*, Goteborg: Goteborg University International Business Master Thesis.

Jones, C. and Lichtenstein, B.M.B. (2000) The 'architecture' of careers: how career competencies reveal firm dominant logic in professional services. In Peiper, M., Arthur, M. and Geoffee, R. (eds). *Careers Frontiers,* Oxford: Oxford University Press, pp. 153–176.

Jones, P.H. (2000). *Embedded Values in Innovation Practice: Toward a Theory of Power and Participation in Organizations.'* Ann Arbor. MI: Dissertation Abstracts International.

Jones, P.H. (2002, June). Embedded Values in Process and Practice: Interactions between disciplinary Practices and formal Innovation Processes. In *Proceedings of the 11th International Forum on Design Management Research*, Boston, Massachusetts.

Jones, P.H. (2002). When successful products prevent strategic innovation. *Design Management Journal,* 13 (2), 30–37.

Jyothi, P., *Training of Trainer: Material composed for training programme,* Hyderabad: Institute for Public Enterprises.

Kanter, R. (1983). *The Change Masters*. New York: Simon and Schuster.

Kaplan, R. and Norton, D. (1996) *The balanced scorecard: translating strategy into action.* Boston, MA: Harvard Business School Press.

Kaplan, R. and Norton, D. (2004), "Measuring the Strategic Readiness of Intangible Assets," *Harvard Business Review,* February.

Kaufman, B. (2000). 'Personnel/ Human Resource Management: Its Roots as Applied Economics.' In R. Backhouse and J. Biddle (eds.) *Toward a History of Applied Economics.* Durnham, NC: Duke University Press.

- (2004) *The Global Evolution of Industrial Relations: Events, Ideas and the IIRA.* Geneva: International Labour Organization.

Kearns, P (2005 a) *Evaluating the ROI from Learning,* London: CIPD

Kearns, P (2005 b) *Human Capital Management,* Sutton, Surrey: Reed Business Information.

Keasrly, G., (1984). *Training and Technology,* New York: Adison-Wesley.

Kelly, G.A. (1955) *The psychology of personal constructs,* New York: Norton (2 volumes).

Kiechel III, Walter (1993). 'How we will work in the year 2000', *Fortune,* May 17, 1993, p. 39.

King, D. (1968). *Training within the Organization*, Cox and Wyman Ltd.

Klein, K.J. and Kozlowski, W.J. (eds.), *Multilevel theory, research and methods in organizations,* San Francisco: Josey- Bass.

Kluckhohn, C. et. al (1951). 'Values and value Orientation in the theory of action', In T. Pearsons andE.A.,Shils (eds), *Towards the General Theory of Action',* Cambridge, MA.:Harvard University Press.

Kluckhohn, F. and F.L. Strodtbeck (1961). *Variations in Value Orientation.* Evanston, IL.: Rowe Peterson.

KPMG, (2005) KPMG International Survey of Corporate Responsibility Reporting; Amsterdam.

Kirschbaum, Howard (1977). *Advanced value Clarification,* San Diego, CA: Pfeiffer and Co.

Laird, Dugan (1985). *Approaches to Training And Development* (2nd ed.). Reading, MA: Addison-Wesley.

Lawler, E.E., S.A. Mohran and G.E. Ledford (1995), *Creating High Performance Organizations,* San Francisco: Josey- Bass.

Levy, P.E..; J.R. Williams (2004), 'The Social Context of performance Appraisal: A Review and Framework for the Future'. *Journal of Management,* (30).

Lee, Katheribne (March 2000) *The future of Training Programs,* www.hr.com

Leap, Terry l and Michael D. Crino, (1990). *Personnel/ Human Resource Management,* New York: Macmillan.

Ledvinka, James (1995). 'Human Resource Planning' in Jack Rabin, Thomas Vocino, W. Bartley Hildreth and Gerald Millers, eds., *Handbook of Public Personnel Administration,* New York, NY: Marcel Dekker, pp. 217–240.

Legge, K. (2005), *Human resource management: Rhetoric and realities.* (Anniversary Edition), Hounds mills, Basingstoke: Macmillan Business.

Leibowitz, Z.B., Kaye, B.L.. and Farren, C. (1990). Career Gridlock, *Training and Development Journal,* April, p. 29–35.

Lewis, C.P. (1997), *Building a Shared Vision: A Leaders Guide to Aligning the Organization,* Portland: Productivity Press.

Lichtenstein, N. andf Harris, H. (1993). *Industrial Democracy in America: The Ambiguous Promise.*New York: Oxford University Press.

Likert, R. (1971). 'Human organizational Measurements: Key to Financial Success', *Michigan Business Review,* May 1971, pp. 1–5.

Livingston, J. Sterling, (1988), 'Pygmalion in Management', *Harvard Business Review,* (September-October 1988), pp 121–130.

London, M. and Stumpf, S. A. (1982). *Managing Careers,* Reading, MA: Addison-Wesley.

Mabey, C. and Iles, P.A. Career development practices in the UK: a participant perspective. In Mabey, C. and Iles, P.A. (1994) *Managing Learning.* London: Thomson/Open University

Manski, Charles F. (2000). Economic Analysis of Social Interactions. *Journal of Economic Perspectives* 14(3): 115–36.

Marchand, D.A., Kiettinger, W.J. and Rollis, J.D. *Information Orientation – The Link in Business Performance,* Oxford, UK: Oxford University Press.

Martin, L. (1993). "Total Quality Management: The New Managerial Wave." *Administration in Social Work.* 17(2), 115.

Mathis, Robert L, and Jackson, J H. (1982) *Personnel – Contemporary Perspectives and Applications,* West Publishing, New York

Maxwell, C, (2004) *Occupational Health and Safety Review (The Maxwell Report).*

Mayo, A. (2001) *The Human Value of the Enterprise: Vaulting people as assets,* London: Nicholas Brealey

Mendenhall, M., Punnett, B.J. and Ricks, D.A. (1995) *Global management.* Cambridge, MA: Blackwell.

Meyer, J.P. and Allen, N.J. (1991). 'A Three Component of Conceptualization of organizational Commitment' *Human Resource Management Review,* I(1), 61–98.

Milakovich, M. (1991). "Total Quality Management in the Public Sector," *National Productivity Review.* 10, 195213.

Milakovich, G.T. and Newman, J.M. , *Compensation,* New Delhi: TATA McGraw.

Mintzberg, Henry (1994) *The Rise and Fall of Strategic Planning.* New York, NY: Free Press.

Mondy, R. Wayne, and Noe, Robert M. (1996). *Human Resource Management.* Upper Saddle River, NJ: Prentice-Hall.

Morrisey, G.I. (1970) Management by Objectives and Results, Reading, Massachusetts: Addison-Wesley.

Mumford, A. and Gold, J. (2004) *Management Development: Strategies for Action.* 4th ed. London: Chartered Institute of Personnel Development.

Murphy, K.R. and Cleveland, J.N. (1995) *Understanding Performance Appraisal,* Thousand Oaks: Sage.

Myers, Kenneth H. (1996) *Total Contingency Planning for Disasters.* New York: John Wiley and Sons.

Nalbantian, R., Guzzo, R.A., Kieffer, D. and Doherty, J. (2004) *Play to your strengths,* New York: McGraw-Hill.

Nanus, B. (1992). *Visionary Leadership.* San Francisco: Jossey Bass.

Napier, Rod, et al. (1998). *High Impact Tools and Activities for Strategic Planning.* New York: McGraw-Hill.

Nedd, A., Ferris, G.R., and Rowland, K.M., (Eds). (1990) *Research in personnel and human resources management: International human resource management,* Suppl. 1, Greenwich, CT

Newman, D. and Hodgets, R. (1998), *Human Resource Management,* Ne w Jersey: Prentice Hall.

Nutt, Paul C., and Robert W. Backoff (1992). *Strategic Management of Public and Third Sector Organizations.* San Francisco, CA: Jossey Bass.

Nadler, Leonard, and Wiggs, Garland D. (1986). *Managing Human Resource Development.* San Francisco: Jossey-Bass.

Odiorne, George S. (1965) *Management by Objectives,* New York: Pitman

Organization Resource Counselors (2000) *Worldwide Survey of international assignments policies and practices.* London and New York: Organization Resource Counselors.

Organization Resource Counselors (2004) *Worldwide Survey of international assignments policies and practices.* London and New York: Organization Resource Counselors.

Osborne, D. and Gaebler, T. (1992). *Reinventing Government.* Reading, MA: Addison Wesley.

Osterloh, M. and Frey, B. (2000). Motivation, knowledge transfer, and organizational forms. *Organization Science,* 11 (5), 538–550.

Osterloh, M., Frost, J. and Frey, B. (2002). The dynamics of motivation in new organizational forms. *International Journal of the Economics of Business,* 9 (1), 61–78.

Ostroff, C. and Bowen, B.E. (2000), Moving HR to a higher level, in Klein, K.J. and Kozlowski, W.J. (eds.), *Multilevel theory, research and methods in organizations,* San Francisco: Josey- Bass.

Paauwe, J. (2004), *HRM and performance. Achieving long term viability,* Oxford: University Press.

Pareek, Udai , and T.V. Rao (1995), *"Designing and Managing Human Resource System",* Oxford

New Delhi: IBH.

Pepper, A., *Managing Training and Development Function,* Aldershot: Gower Publishing,

Packard, T. (1989). Participation in decision making, Performance, and job satisfaction in a social work bureaucracy. *Administration in Social Work.* 13(1), 5973.

Packard. T. and Reid, R. (1990). "OD in a Fire Department: Lessons in Using Parallel Structures and Institutionalization," *Consultation.* 9, 167184.

Patching, K. (1998), *Management and Organisation Development,* London: Macmillan.

Perry, James L., and Debra J. Mesch (1997) 'Strategic Human Resource Management,' in Carolyn Ban and Norma Riccucci (eds) *Public Personnel Management: Current Concerns, Future Challenges.* New York, NY: Longman, pp. 21–34.

Peiper, M., Arthur, M. and Geoffee, R. (eds). (2000). *Careers Frontiers,* Oxford: Oxford University Press,Pejtersen, A.M. (1985). Implications of users' value perception for the design of a bibliographic retrieval system. In Agrawal, J.C. and P. Zunde (eds.), *Empircal Foundations of Information and Software Science,* New York: Plenum, pp. 23–37.

Pejtersen, A.M

Pfeffer, J. (1994), *Competitive advantage through people: Unleashing the power of the work force,* Boston: Harvard Business School Press.

Philips, J. (1997), *Handbook of Training Evaluation and Measurement Methods,* Texas: Houston Gulf.

Pickering, Alan, Socially Responsible Investment and International Development, May 2001, Just

Pensions, www.uksif.org

Pigors, Paul and C.A. Myers (1987). *Personnel Administration,* Tokyo: McGraw Hill Kagakusha

Pigors, Paul and Pigors, F. (1987), *The Case Method, in Training and Development Handbook,* London: McGraw Hill.

Porter, M.E. (1980), *Competitive Strategy,* The Free Press: New York.

Porter, L.W., Steers, R., Mowday, R., and Boulian, P. (1974) "Organizational Commitment, Job Satisfaction, and Turn Over amongst Psychiatric Technicians", *Journal of Applied Psychology,* 59, pp. 603–609.

Prabhaksr rao, D. (1993), 'Human Assets Accounting: An Evaluation of the Indian Practices,' *ASCI Journal of Management,* Vol. 22.

PricewaterhouseCoopers (2000) *International Assignments: European policy and practice: key trends 1999/2000.* London: PricewaterhouseCoopers

Pruger, R. and Miller, L. (1991). "Efficiency," *Administration in Social Work.* 15(1/2), 42.

Purcell, J., Kinnie, K., Hutchinsin, Rayton, B.,and Swart, J., (2003), *People and Performance: How People Managementimpacts on Organizational Performance,* London: CIPD.

Purcell, J., Kinnie, K., Hutchinsin, Rayton, B.,and Swart, J., and Rayton, B. (2005), *Vision and Values: Organizational culture and values as a source of competitive advantage* London: CIPD.

Purcell, J., Kinnie, N. and Hutchinson, S. (2003) *Understanding the people and performance link: Unlocking the black box*. London: Chartered Institute of Personnel and Development.

Putnam, R. (1996) Who killed civic America? *Prospect,* March, pp. 66–72.

Quinn, R.E. (1984), 'Applying the competing values approach to leadership: Towards an integrative model', in J.G. Hunt, R. Stewart, C. Schriesheim, and D. Hosking (Eds.), *Mangers and leaders: An International Perspective,* New York: Pergamon. Quinn, R.E. (1988), *Beyond rational Management: Mastering the paradoxes and competing Demands of High Performance,*San Francisco: Josey- Bass.

Rabin, Jack., Thomas Vocino, W. Bartley Hildreth and Gerald Millers, eds., *Handbook of Public Personnel Administration,* New York, NY: Marcel Dekker.

Randall L Schuler, et. al., (1989)***Effective Personnel Management,*** Third Edition, New York: West Publishing,

Rao, T.V. (2004). *Performance Management and Appraisal Systems – HR Tools for Global Competitiveness,* London: Sage Publications.

Rao, V.S.P. (2001). *Human Resource Management and Text and Cases,* New Delhi: Excel Books.

Rapp, C. and Poertner, J. (1992). *Social Administration: A Client Centered Approach*. New York: Longman Rasmussen, J. (1986). *Information Processing and Human- Machine Interaction: An Approach to Cognitive Engineering,* New York: North- Holland.

Reich, Robert, (1993). ' "New WorK" is the way for Labour' *Philadelphia Inquirer,* September 6, 1993.

Robey, D. (1991). *Designing Organizations* 3rd ed., Homewood, IL: Irwin, p. 42.

Rogers, Carl (1961) *On Becoming a Person: A Therapist's View of Psychotherapy*, Houghton Mifflin,

Rokeach, Milton (1973). *The Nature of Human Values.* New York: Free Press.

Roos, J., Roos, G., and Dragonetti, N.C. (1997) *Intellectual capital: navigating in the new business landscape.* London: Macmillan.

Rose, M., (2001), *Disparate Measures in the Workplace.... Quantifying overall job satisfaction,* Paper presented at the 2001 BHPS Research Conference, Colchester, available at http://www.iser.essex.ac.uk/bhps/2001/docs/pdf/papers/rose.pdf

Rose, M., (2003) 'Good deal, bad deal? Job Satisfaction in Occupations', *Work Employment and Society*, Vol. 17, No. 3, pp. 503–530.

Rousseau, D. M. (1995). *Psychological Contracts in Organizations: Understanding written and un written agreements.* New bury Park: Sage.

Rousseau, D.M., and Schalk, R. (Eds.) 2000. *Psychological Contracts in employment: Cross-national perspectives.* Thousand Oaks, CA.: Sage Publications.

Salanick, G.R. (1977). "Commitment and Control of Organizational Behaviour and Belief", in Staw, B.M., and Salanick, G.R., *'New Directions in Organizational Behaviour',* Chicago: St Clair Press.

Savickas, M. and Lent, R. (1994). *Convergence in Career Development Theories,* Pal Alto, Californai: Consulting Psychologists Press, Inc.

Scarborough, H., Swan, J. and Preston, J. (1999). *Knowledge Management: A Literature Review,* London: Institute of Personnel and Development.

Scarborough, H, and Elias, J (2002) *Evaluating Human Capital,* London: CIPD

Scarborough, H and Carter, C (2000) *Investigating Knowledge Management,* London: CIPD.

Schein, E. (1978) *Career dynamics: matching individual and organizational needs.* Welwyn: Pearson Higher Education.

Schein, E. (1985). *Organizational Culture and Leadership: A Dynamic View,* San Francisco, CA: Jossey Bass.

Schein, E.H. (1992). *Organizational Culture and Leadership.* San Francisco, CA: Jossey Bass.

Schein, E.H. (1996). "The Three Culture Management: The Key to Organizational Learning." *Sloan Management Review* 38, 1 pp. 9–30.

Schein, E.H. (1999). *The Corporate Culture Survival Guide: Sense and Nonsense about Culture Change.* San Francisco, CA: Jossey Bass.

Schein and Edgar (February 1990). Organizational Culture. *American Psychologist,* 45.

Schein, V.E., Mueller, R. and Lituchy, Y. (1996) .Think manger-think male: a global phenomenon? *Journal of Organizational Behaviour.* Vol. 17, No. 1. pp 33–41.

Schippmann, J.S. (1999). *Strategic Job Modeling: Working at the Core of Integrated Human Resources,* Mahwah, NJ.,: Lawrence Erlbaum Associates.

Schreuder, A.M.G., and Theron, A.L., (2001). *Careers: An Organizational Perspective.* Kenwyn: Juta and Co Ltd.

Schuler, R.S. (1998), *Managing Human Resources,* Cincinnati, OH: South-Western.

Schuler, R.S. and Jackson, S.E. (eds.) (1999), *Strategic Human Resource Management,* Oxford: Blackwell.

Schuller, T (2000) Social and Human capital; the search for appropriate techno-methodology, *Policy Studies,* 21 (1), pp. 25–35.

Senge, P.M. (1997). *The Fifth Dimension. The Art and Practice of the Learning Organization.* Century Business.

Senge, P. (1990). *The Fifth Discipline.* New York: Doubleday Currency Shenkar, O., (E.d.), (1995). *Global Prospectives of Human Resources Management,* Englewood Cliffs, NJ: Prentice Hall, pp 15–36.

Shaffer, L. F., and Shoben, J. E. (1956). *The psychology of adjustment: A dynamic and experimental approach to personality and mental hygiene* (2nd ed.). Boston: Houghton Mifflin.

Sibson, R.E. (1967). *Wages and Salaries*(Revised Ed.). New York: American Management Association.

Singh, Col (Dr) Narendar, (2008). Leadership in 21st Century. New Delhi: Manas publications

Skinner, B.F. (1974). *About Behaviorism.* New York: Alfred A. Knoph.

Sousa-Poza, A and Sousa-Poza, A.A., (2000). 'Well-being at work: across-national analysis of the levels and determinants of job satisfaction', *Journal of Socio-Economics,* Vol. 29, No. 6, pp. 517–538.

Sparrow, P., Harris, H. and Brewster, C. (2004) *Globalizing human resource management.* London: Routledge.

Spector, P.E., (1997) *Job Satisfaction: Application, Assessment, Causes and Consequences,* London: Sage

Steiner, George Albert. (1997) *Strategic Planning: What Every Manager Must Know*. New York: Free Press.

Stitt-Gohdes, W. (1997) *Career Development*. Columbus, Ohio: ERIC Clearing House on Adult, Career and Vocational Education.

Stogdill, RM, 'Handbook of Leadership: A Survey of the Literature', *Journal of Psychology*, 1948, 25, pp. 35–71

Stone, Thomas S.(1989), *Understanding Personnel Management*, CBS College Publishing.

Storey, J. (2003) When companies become networks. In: Gooderham, P. and Nordhuag, O. (eds). *International management: cross-boundary challenges*. Oxford: Blackwell.

Storey, J. (ed.) (1989), *New perspective of Human Resource Management*, London: Routledge.

Subramanian, K.N. (1979), *Wages in India*, New Delhi: Tata McGraw-Hill.

Sugarman, B. (1988). "The WellManaged Human Service Organization: Criteria for a Management Audit," *Administration in Social Work*. 12(2), 1727.

Super, D. E (1949). *Appraising vocational fitness by means of psychological tests*. New York: Harper and Brothers.

Super, D. E., and Crites, J. O. (1962*). Appraising vocational fitness by means of psychological tests* (2nd ed.). New York: Harper and Row

Super, D. E., Crites, J.O., Hummel, R., Moser, H., Overstreet, P. and Warnath, C. (1957). Vocational development: A framework for research. New York: Teachers College Press, Columbia ·University.

Sveiby, K.e. (1997) The new organizational wealth: managing and measuring knowledge-based assets. San Francosco, CA: Berrett-Koehler Publishers.

Syrett, M. and Lammiman, J. (2003). Boardroom Education. Oxford: Capstone

Swart, Juani (2007) 'HRM and Knowledge Workers'. In Boxall, Peter F, Purcell, John and Wright, Patrick M. The Oxford handbook of Human Resource Management, London: Oxford University Press

Swiss, J. (1992). "Adapting TQM to Government," Public Administration Review. 52, 356362. Tamkin, P., Hirsh, W. and Tyers, C. (2003) Chore to champions: The making of better people managers. Brighton: Institute of Employment Studies.

Taylor, R. (2003) "generation next', People Management, September 11.

Tichey, N. (1983). Managing Strategic Change. New York: John Wiley and Sons.

Trompenaars, F. (1993) Riding the waves of culture: understanding cultural diversity in business. London: Economist Books.

Thogersen, John (2006). Norms for Environmentally Responsible Beghaviour: An extended Taxonomy and a Preliminary Assessment. Mimeo: Aarhus School of Business, Aarhus, Denmark.

Thomson, A., Storey, J., Mabey, C., Gray, C., Farmer, E. and Thomson, R. (1997). *A Portrait of Management Development*, London Institute of Management.

Thomson, A., Storey, J., Mabey, C., Gray, C., Farmer, F. and Thomson, R. (1998). *Management Development : the views of the membership of the Association of MBAs*. London : Association of MBAs.

Thomson, A., Mabey, C., Storey, J. and Gray, C., and Iles, P. A. (2000). *Management Development in Theory and Practice* Oxford: Blackwells (in publication).

Thomson, A., Mabey, C., and Storey, J. (1998). The determinants of managerial development: choice or circumstance? *International Studies of Management and Organization,* 28, 1, Spring 91–113.

Tinarelli, S. (2000) *Employers' Guide to the Employment Equity Act,* Pretoria: Van Schack.

Tung, R.L. (1998) American expatriates abroad: from neophytes to cosmopolitans. *Journal of World Business.* Vol. 33, No. 2. pp 125–144.

Ulrich, D. and D. Lake (1990), *Organizational capability: Competing from the inside out.* New York: John Wiley and Sons.

Ulrich, D. and Huselid, M.A. (2001). *The UK Scorecard: Linking People, Strategy and Performance,* Harvard: Harvard Business School Press

Vakola, Maria and Nikolaou, Ioannis, Attitudes Towards Organizational Change: What is the Role of Employees' Stress and Commitment?, *Employee Relations,* 2005, Vol. 27, p 160–174.

Van Maanen, J., and Schein, E.H. (1979). Toward a theory of organizational socialization. In *Research in Organizational Behaviour I,* pp. 209–264.

Vicenete, K.J. (1999). *Cognitive Work Analysis: Toward Safe, Productive and healthy Computer-based Work,* Mahwah, NJ.,: Lawrence Erlbaum Associates

Von Glinow, M.A. and Chung, B.J. (1990). 'Comparative human resource management practices in the United States, japan, Korea and The Peoples Republic of China', In Nedd, A., Ferris, G.R., and Rowland, K.M., (Eds). *Research in personnel and human resources management: International human resource management,* Suppl. 1, Greenwich, CT, pp. 153–171.

Vroom, V. and Deci, E. (eds) (1970) *Management and motivation.* Penguin Books, London.

Vroom, V. and Yetton, P. (1973). *Leadership and Decision Making.* Pittsburgh: University of Pittsburgh Press.

Wanous, J.P. (1992). *Organizational Entry: Recruitment, selection, orientation and socialization of newcomers (2nd ed.).* Reading, MA: Addison-Wesley Publishing.

Wasti, A.S. (2000). *Leadership and Applied of Human Resource,* Turk Psikologlar Dernegi Yayinlari.

Watson Wyatt Worldwide, Connecting Organizational Communication to Financial Performance: 2003/2004 Communication ROI Study, July 25, 2005, Watson Wyatt Worldwide, www.watsonwyatt.com

Wellin, M. (2007) *Managing Psychological Contract: Using the personal deal to increase business performance.* Aldershot: Gower.

Wendell, French, (1974). *The Personnel management Process,* Boston: Houghton Mifflin Co.

Werther, William B. and Keith Davis, *Human Resource and Personnel Management,* Fourth Edition, New York: McGraw-Hill, (1993), p. 176.

Werther, William.B., and Keith Davis, Human Resource Management and Personnel Management, 5th Edition, McGraw-hill, 1996.

Whittington, R. and Molley, E., (2005) *HR's role in organizing: shaping change.* Research Report. London: Chartered Institute of Personnel and Development.

Whyte, W.F. (1957, March- April). Economic incentive and Human Relations (pp. 73–80). *Harvard Business Review* in Belcher, D.W. (1974). *Compensation Administration,* Englewood Cliffs, N.J.: Prentice Hall.

Woodcock, M. and F. Dave (1989). *Clarifying Organizational Values,* Englewood Cliffs, NJ: Prentice Hall.

Woods, R. (1995), *Human Resource Management,* Michigan: AHMA.

Xenikou, Athena and Adrian Furnham (1996). A Correlational and Factor Analytical Study of Four Questionnaire Measures of organizational Culture. *Human Relations,* 49.

Yukl, G.A. (1994) *Leadership in Organization.* 3rd ed. Englewood Cliffs, NJ: Prentice Hall.

Zappala, Gianni and Cronin, Caitlin, *"The Employee Dimensions of Corporate Community Involvement in Australia: Trends and Prospects"*, Paper Presented at the 6th ANZTSR Conference; 27–29 November, 2002 Auckland, New Zealand, 1–24.

Zappala, Gianni, "Corporate Citizenship and Human Resource Management", Honorary Research Associate Working Paper, Sydney, 2004, 1–16

INDEX

A

B

C

D

E

J

K

L

M

N

O

P

Q

R

S

T

U

V

W

❑❑❑